STUDIES IN
GENESIS

STUDIES IN
GENESIS

by
Robert S. Candlish

KREGEL PUBLICATIONS
Grand Rapids, Michigan 49501

STUDIES IN GENESIS Published in 1979 by Kregel Publications,
a division of Kregel, Inc. All rights reserved.

Library of Congress Cataloging in Publication Data

Candlish, Robert Smith, 1806-1873.
    Studies In Genesis.

    First published under title: Contributions towards the exposition
of the Book of Genesis.

    Reprint of new ed., carefully rev., published in 1868 by A. and
C. Black, Edinburgh, under title: The Book of Genesis expounded
in a series of discourses.
      1. Bible, O.T. Genesis—Sermons. 2. Sermons, English —
Scotland. I. Title.
BS1235.C32 1979   222'.11'06   79-14084
ISBN 0-8254-2315-5

Printed in the United States of America

CONTENTS

FOREWORD

It is not difficult to see why Charles Haddon Spurgeon described this as "*The* commentary upon Genesis". In his own preface, Robert Candlish modestly offers the work "merely as a contribution *towards* the exposition of the Book of Genesis, not by any means entitled to the character of a *full and exhaustive* exposition." Yet this is the secret of this unique study. Freed from the onerous ties of giving detailed, exegetical comment on each and every verse, the noted author concentrated on the great doctrinal and biographical features of Genesis to produce a commentary of quite outstanding importance to preachers and teachers.

Robert Candlish was both Principal of New College and Minister of Free St. George's Church, Edinburgh, at the time of its publication in 1868, so the mind of a leading evangelical scholar and the pastoral faculties of a renowned preacher are perfectly blended here.

Surely there can be no treatment of the Garden of Eden and the Fall more richly suggestive to preachers than this one. Again — freed from the precise duties of the conventional commentator, Dr. Candlish wrote not to elucidate the meaning of the text but rather to bring out the spiritual meaning and application. His is all message rather than technical information.

All the major events of Genesis are expounded to bring out the Doctrine of Grace. Here, in every chapter, is the essence of a score of searching, spiritual sermons, either to lift up God's people or to cut to the heart the unsaved. There are thoughts and observations numerous enough and profound enough to do credit to a prince of the Puritan era — but expressed with a simplicity and economy of language seldom mastered by those worthies.

Here, as Spurgeon insisted, is the very best of commentaries on Genesis, yet, it is written in so warm and flowing a style as to be suitable for reading for sheer spiritual pleasure (with the exception of the opening chapters on creation, which are more philosophical in character).

Nearly ten years before penning this foreword, I preached a long series of evangelistic sermons from the Book of Genesis. It was Candlish who was at that time my greatest source of help outside of the Bible, and my uninhibited enthusiasm for his work arises from that practical experience. There is certainly no twentieth-century evangelical work which yields so much help in the applicatory and suggestive front.

The present publishers are to be most warmly commended for undertaking the reissue and repopularizing of this highly significant classic which will again refresh and inspire many of the Lord's messengers.

Spurgeon's Metropolitan Tabernacle   PETER M. MASTERS, LITT. D.
London, England 1979

1

CREATION VIEWED AS MATTER OF FAITH

Through faith we understand that the worlds were framed by the word of God ; so that things which are seen were not made of things which do appear. Hebrews 11:3

THE view taken in this Lecture I hold to be important, not only in its practical and spiritual bearings, on which I chiefly dwell, but also in relation to some of the scientific questions which have been supposed to be here involved. It lifts, as I think, the divine record out of and above these human entanglements, and presents it, apart from all discoveries of successive ages, in the broad and general aspect which it was designed from the first and all along to wear, as unfolding the Creator's mind in the orderly subordination of the several parts of his creation to one another, with special reference to his intended dealings with the race of man. On this account I ask attention to what otherwise might appear to some to be an irrelevant metaphysical conceit.

It is proposed, then, to inquire what is implied in our really believing, as a matter of revelation, the fact of the creation. This may seem a very needless inquiry, in reference to a fact so easily understood. " In the beginning God created the heaven and the earth." " The worlds were framed by the word of God." Can any thing be easier than to comprehend and believe this great truth thus clearly revealed? Who can be at a loss to know what is meant by believing it? It is remarkable, however, that in speaking of that faith whose power he celebrates as the most influential of all our principles of action, the apostle gives, as his first instance of it, our belief of this fact of the creation. " Through faith,"—that particular energetic faith, which so vividly realises its absent object, unseen and remote, as to invest it with all the force of a present and sensible impression,— through this precise faith, " which is the substance of things hoped for, the evidence of things not seen," " we understand that the worlds were framed by the word of God ; so that things which are seen were not made of things which do appear."

Now, this faith is peculiar in several respects, and its peculiarity is as much to be observed in the belief of the fact of creation, as in the belief of the fact of redemption,—including, as such belief does, a reliance on the promises connected with that fact and ratified and sealed by it, springing out of a reliance on the person promising. It is especially peculiar in respect of its source, or of the evidence on which it rests. The truths which it receives, it receives on the evidence of testimony, as truths revealed, declared, and attested, by the infallible word of the living God.

This is a point of great importance, as it affects both the kind of assent which we give to these truths, and the kind and degree of influence which they exert over us. There is the widest possible difference between our believing certain truths as the result of reasoning or discovery, and our believing them on the direct assertion of a credible witness whom we see and hear,—especially if the witness be the very individual to whom the truths relate, and indeed himself their author. The truths themselves may be identically the same ; but how essentially different is the state of the mind in accepting them ; and how different the impression made by them on the mind when accepted.

I. The difference may be illustrated by a simple and familiar example. In the deeply interesting and beautiful work of Paley on Natural Theology—for so it may still be characterised, in spite of lapse of time and change of taste—the author, in stating the argument for the being of a God, derived from the proofs of intelligence and design in nature, makes admirable use of an imaginary case respecting a watch. He supposes that, being previously unacquainted with such a work of art, you stumble upon it for the first time, as if by accident, in a desert. You proceed to exercise your powers of judgment and inference in regard to it. You hold it in your hand, and after exhausting your first emotions of wonder and admiration, you begin to examine its structure, to raise questions in your own mind, and to form conjectures. How did it come there, and how were its parts so curiously put together? You at once conclude that it did not grow there, and that it could not be fashioned by chance. You are not satisfied to be told that it has lain there for a long period,—from time immemorial,—for ever ; that it has always been going on as it is going on now ; that there is nothing really surprising in its movements and its mechanism ; that it is just its nature to be what it is, and to do what it does. You utterly reject all such explanations as frivolous and absurd. You feel assured that the watch had a maker ; and your busy and inquisitive spirit immediately sets itself restlessly to work, to form some conception as to what sort of person the maker of it must have been. You gather much of his character from the obvious character of his handiwork ; you search in that handiwork for traces of his mind and his heart ; you speculate concerning his plans and purposes ; your fancy represents him to your eye ; you think you understand all about him ; you find the exercise of reasoning and discovery delightful, and you rejoice in the new views which it unfolds.

But now suppose that, while you are thus engaged, with the watch in your hand and your whole soul wrapt in meditative contemplation on the subject of its formation, a living person suddenly appears before you, and at once abruptly announces himself, and says, It was I who made this watch—it was I who put it there. Is not your position instantly and completely changed? At first, perhaps, you are almost vexed and disappointed that the thread of your musing thoughts should be thus broken, and your airy speculations interrupted, and you should be told all at once on the instant, what you would have liked to find out for yourself,—that the riddle should be so summarily solved, and a plain tale substituted for many curious guesses. But you are soon reconciled to the change, and better pleased to have it so. The actual presence of the individual gives a new interest—the interest of a more vivid and intense reality—to the whole subject of your previous thoughts. Nor does this new impression depend merely upon the greater amount of information communicated ; for the individual now before you may explicitly tell you no more than, in his absence, the watch itself had virtually told you already. Neither does it arise altogether from the greater certainty and assurance of the revelation which he makes to you ; for in truth your own inferences, in so plain an instance of design, may be as infallible as any testimony could be. But there is something in the direct and immediate communication of the real person, speaking to you face to face, and with his living voice, which affects you very differently from a process of reasoning, however clear and unquestionable its results may be.

Your position, in fact, is now precisely reversed. Instead of questioning the watch concerning its maker, you now question the maker concerning his watch. You hear, not what the mechanism has to say of the mechanic, but what the mechanic has to say of the mechanism. You receive, perhaps, the same truths as before, but with a freshness and a force unknown before. They come to you,—not circuitously and at second hand, but straight from the very being most deeply concerned in them. They come home to you without any of that dim and vague impersonality—that abstract and ideal remoteness—which usually characterises the conclusions of long argument and reasoning. They are now invested with that sense of reality, and those sensations and sentiments of personal concern, which the known face and voice of a living man inspire.

II. Now, let us apply these remarks to the matter in hand. We are all of us familiar with this idea, that in contemplating the works of creation, we should ascend from nature to nature's God. Everywhere we discern undoubted proofs of the unbounded wisdom, power, and goodness of the great Author of all things. Everywhere we meet with traces of just and benevolent design, which should suggest to us the thought of the Almighty Creator, and of his righteousness, truth, and love. It is most pleasing and useful to cultivate such a habit as this ; much of natural religion depends upon it, and holy Scripture fully recognises its propriety. " The heavens declare the glory of God : the firmament showeth his handiwork." " All thy works praise thee, Lord God Almighty." " Lift up your eyes on high, and behold—Who hath created these things ? " " O Lord, how manifold are thy works ! in wisdom hast thou made them all : the earth is full of thy riches."

It is apparent, however, even in these and similar passages, that created things are mentioned, not as arguments, but rather as illustrations ; not as suggesting the idea of God, the Creator, but as unfolding and expanding that idea, otherwise obtained.

And this is still more manifest in that passage of the Epistle to the Romans which particularly appeals to the fact of creation as evidence of the Creator's glory,—evidence sufficient to condemn the ungodly : " For the invisible things of him from the creation of the world are clearly seen, being understood by the things that are made, even his eternal power and Godhead ; so that they are without excuse : because that, when they knew God, they glorified him not as God, neither were thankful ; but became vain in their imaginations, and their foolish heart was darkened " (i. 20, 21). Here it is expressly said, that from the things that are made might be understood the invisible things of God, even his eternal power and Godhead ; so that atheists, idolaters, and worshippers of the creature, are without excuse. But why are they without excuse ? Not because they failed to discover God, in this way, from his works, but because, when they knew God otherwise, they did not glorify him, as these very works might have continually taught them to do ;—not because they did not in this way acquire, but because they did not like in this way to retain, the knowledge of God.

For the fact of the creation is regarded in the Bible as a fact revealed ; and, as such, it is commended to our faith. Thus the scriptural method on this subject is exactly the reverse of what is called the natural. It is not to ascend from nature up to nature's God, but to descend, if we may so speak, from God to God's nature, or his works of nature ; not to hear the creation speaking of the Creator, but to hear the Creator speaking of the creation. We have not in the Bible an examination and enumeration of the wonders to be observed among the works of nature, and an argument founded upon these that there must be a God, and that he must be of a certain character, and must have had certain views in making what he has made. God himself appears, and tells us authoritatively who he is, and what he has done, and why he did it.

Thus " through faith we understand that the worlds were made by the word of God ; so that things which are seen were not made of things which do appear." We understand and believe this, not as a deduction of reasoning, but as a matter of fact, declared and revealed to us. For this is that act of the mind which, in a religious sense, is called faith. It involves in its very nature an exercise of trust or confidence in a living person,—of acquiescence in his word,—of reliance on his truth, on himself. It implies the committing of ourselves to him,—the casting of ourselves on him,—as faithful in what he tells, and in what he promises. We believe on his testimony. We believe what he says, and because he says it. In thus simply receiving a fact declared by another, and that other fully credible and trustworthy, the mind is in a very different attitude and posture from that which it assumes when it reasons out the fact, as it were, by its own resources. There is far more of dependence and submission in the one case than in the other,—a more cordial and implicit recognition of a Being higher than we are,—a more unreserved surrender of ourselves. The one, in truth, is the act of a man, the other of a child. Now, in the kingdom of God—his kingdom of nature as well as his kingdom of grace,—we must be as little children. When I draw inferences for myself concerning the Author of creation,—when I reason out from his works the fact of his existence, and the chief attributes of his character, —I am conscious of a certain feeling of superiority. The Deity becomes almost, in a certain sense, my creature,—the product of my own elaborated process of thought. I am occupied more with my own reasonings than with the transcendent excellences of Him of whom I reason. The whole is very much an exercise of intellect, attended, certainly, with those emotions of beauty and sublimity which the exercise of the intellect on matters of taste calls forth ;—but with scarcely anything more of the real apprehension of an unseen Being, in my conclusions respecting the author of nature, than in my premises respecting nature itself. The God whom I discover is like the dead abstract truth to which a train of demonstration leads. I myself alone have a distinct personality ;—all else is little more than the working of my brain on its own imaginations.

But now, God speaks, and I am dumb. He opens his mouth, and I hold my peace. I bid my busy, speculative soul be quiet. I am still, and know that it is God. I now at once recognise a real and living Person, beyond and above myself. I take my station humbly, submissively at his feet. I learn of him. And what he tells me now, in the way of direct personal communication from himself to me, has a weight and vivid reality infinitely surpassing all that any mere deductions from the closest reasoning could ever have. Now in very truth my "faith" does become "the substance of things hoped for, the evidence of things not seen." Now at last I am brought into real personal contact with the Invisible One. And he speaks as one having authority. He whom now I personally know and see tells me of the things which he has made; and so tells me of them, that now they start forth before my eyes in a new light. The idea of their being not only his workmanship, but of his explaining them to me as his workmanship, assumes a distinctness—a prominence and power—which cannot fail to exercise a strong influence and exert a sovereign command over me, as a communication directly from him to me.

Such is that faith respecting the creation which alone can be of a really influential character. Thus only can we truly and personally know God as the Creator.

III. But it may be asked, Are we, then, not to use our reason on this subject at all? That cannot be; for the apostle himself enjoins us, however in respect of meekness we are to be like children, still in understanding to be men. Certainly we do well to search out and collect together all those features in creation which reflect the glory of the Creator. Nay, we may begin in this way to know God. It is true, indeed, that God has never, in point of fact, left himself to be thus discovered. He has always revealed himself, as he did at first, not circuitously by his works, but summarily and directly by his word. We may suppose, however, that you are suffered to grope your way through creation to the Creator. In that case you proceed, in the manner already described, to deduce or infer from the manifold plain proofs of design in nature, the idea of an intelligent author, and to draw conclusions from what you see of his works, respecting his character, purposes, and plans. Still, even in this method of discovering God, if your faith is to be of an influential kind at all, you must proceed, when you have made the discovery, exactly to reverse the process by which you made it. Having arrived at the conception of a Creator, you must now go back again to the creation, taking the Creator himself along with you, as one with whom you have become personally acquainted, and hearing what he has to say concerning his own works. He may say no more than what you had previously discovered ; still, what he does say, you now receive, not as discovered by you, but as said by him. You leave the post of discovery and the chair of reasoning, and take the lowly stool of the disciple. And then, and not before, even on the principles of natural religion, do you fully understand what is the real import and the momentous bearing of the fact,—that a Being, infinitely wise and powerful, and having evidently a certain character, as holy, just, and good,—that such a Being made you,—and that he is himself telling you that he made you,—and all the things that are around you ; " so that things which are seen were not made of things which do appear ;" the visible did not come from the visible ; it was not self-made. God tells you that.

Much more will this be felt, if we become personally acquainted with God otherwise than through the medium of his works. And so, in fact, we do.

Even apart from revelation,—on natural principles,—the first notion of a God is suggested in another way. It is suggested far more promptly and directly than it can be by a circuitous process of reasoning respecting the proofs of intelligence in creation. It is conscience within, not nature without, which first points to and proves a Deity. It is the Lawgiver, and not the Creator, that man first recognises,—the Governor, the righteous Judge. The moral sense involves the notion of a moral Ruler, independently altogether of the argument from creation. And the true position and purpose of that argument is, not to infer from his works of creation an unknown God, as Creator, but to prove that the God already known as the moral Ruler is the Creator of all things,—or rather to show what, as the moral Ruler, he has to tell us in regard to the things which he has created. The truth is, when we go to the works and creatures of God, we go, not to discover him, but as having already discovered and known him. We must, therefore, go in the spirit of implicit and submissive faith, not to question them concerning him, but to hear and observe what he has to say to us concerning them, or to say to us, in them, concerning himself.

But still further, we go now to the record of creation, not only recognising God through the evidence of his works and the intimations of the conscience or moral sense, but acquainted with him through the testimony of his own word. In that word, he reveals himself, first as the Lawgiver, and then as the Saviour. The first word he spoke to man in paradise was the law, the second was the glorious Gospel; he made himself known first as the Sovereign, and then as the Redeemer. Now, therefore, it is in the character of the God thus known that he speaks to us concerning the creation of all things; and our faith as to creation now consists,—not in our believing that all things were and must have been made by a God,— but in our believing that they were made by this God; and believing it on the ground of his own infallible assurance, given personally by himself to us. This God we are to see in all things. We are to hear his voice saying to us, in reference to every object,—I created it; I made it, such as you see it, and for the purpose for which you must perceive it to be manifestly intended; and I am now telling you that I did so.

Thus, by faith, we are to recognise, instead of a dim remote abstraction, a real living being; personally present with us, and speaking to us of his works, as well as in them and by them. We are to exercise a personal reliance on him, as thus present and thus speaking to us—a reliance on his faithfulness, in what he says to us concerning his character and doings in creation. Then assuredly our faith will make more vividly and tangibly intelligible the great fact that he made each thing and all things, and will give to that fact more of a real hold over us, and far more of intense practical power, than, with our ordinary vague views of the subject, we can at all beforehand conceive. Nor will it hamper or hinder the freest possible inquiry, on the side of natural science, if only it confines itself to its legitimate function of ascertaining facts before it theorises. For the facts it ascertains may modify, and have modified, the interpretation put on what God has told us in his word. And he meant it to be so. He did not intend revelation to supersede inquiry, and anticipate its results. Of course, his revelation must be consistent with the results of our inquiry,—as it has always hitherto, in the long run, been found to be. But it was inevitable that our understanding of his revelation should be open to progressive readjustment, as regards the development of scientific knowledge, while the revelation itself, as the Creator's explanation of his creation for all mankind, remains ever the same.

IV. Thus, then, in a spiritual view, and for spiritual purposes, the truth concerning God as the Creator must be received, not as a discovery of our own reason, following a train of thought, but as a direct communication from a real person, even from the living and present God. This is not a merely theoretical and artificial distinction. It is practically most important. Consider the subject of creation simply in the light of an argument of natural philosophy, and all is vague and dim abstraction. It may be close and cogent as a demonstration in mathematics, but it is as cold and unreal ; or, if there be emotion at all, it is but the emotion of a fine taste, and a sensibility for the grand or the lovely in nature and thought. But consider the momentous fact in the light of a direct message from the Creator himself to you,—regard him as standing near to you, and himself telling you, personally and face to face, all that he did on that wondrous creation-week,—are you not differently impressed and affected?

1. More particularly,—see first of all, what weight this single idea, once truly and vividly realised, must add to all the other communications which he makes to us on other subjects. Does he speak to us concerning other matters, intimately touching our present and future weal? Does he tell us of our condition in respect of him, and of his purposes in respect of us? Does he enforce the majesty of his law? Does he press the overtures of his Gospel? Does he threaten, or warn, or exhort, or encourage, or command, or entreat, or tenderly expostulate, or straitly and authoritatively charge? Oh! how in every such case is his appeal enhanced with tenfold intensity in its solemnity, its pathos, and its power, if we regard him as in the very same breath expressly telling us,—I who now speak to you so earnestly and so affectionately, I created all things,—I created you. To the sinner, whom he is seeking out in his lost estate, whom he is reproving as a holy lawgiver, and condemning as a righteous judge, and yet pitying with all a father's unquenchable compassion, how awful and yet how moving is the consideration, that he who is speaking to him as a counsellor and a friend, is speaking to him also as the Creator! And while he bids the sinner, in accents the most gracious, turn and live, he says to him still always,—It is thy Maker, and the Maker of all things, who bids thee, at thy peril, turn. And is there any one of you who are his saints and servants disquieted and cast down? Is there not comfort in the thought, that thy Maker is thy husband and thy redeemer? Is there not especial comfort in his telling thee so himself? Is there any thing in all the earth to make thee afraid? Dost thou not hear him saying to thee,—I, thy Saviour, thy God made thee, made it, made all things? It is my creature, as thou art, and it cannot hurt thee, if I am with thee.

On this principle we may, to a large extent, explain the importance which believers attach to the glorious fact, that he who saves them has revealed himself to them, and is revealing himself, as the Creator. All must have remarked, in reading the devotional parts of the Bible, such as the book of Psalms, how constantly the psalmist comforts and strengthens himself, and animates himself in the face of his enemies, by this consideration,—-that his help comes from the Lord, who made the heavens and the earth,—that his God made the heavens. He made all things; the very things, therefore, that are most hostile and perilous, his God made. This is his security. The God whom he knows as his own, made all things, and is reminding him, whenever any thing alarms or threatens him, that he made it. And if now, my Christian brother, the God who made all things, evil as well as good,—sickness, pain, poverty, distress,—is your Saviour; if he is ever seen by you, and his voice is heard telling you, even of that which presently afflicts you, that he made it as he made you,—how complete is your confidence.

When God appeared to Job, in such a way that Job himself exclaimed, "I have heard of thee by the hearing of the ear, but now mine eye seeth thee;" it was mainly, if not exclusively, as the Creator that he revealed himself. Coming forth to finish the discussion between Job and his friends, the Lord enlarges and expatiates on all his wondrous works,—on the power and the majesty of his creation. On this topic he dwells, speaking to Job personally concerning it, conversing with him face to face as a friend. And the full recognition of God as doing so, is enough both to humble and comfort the patriarch,—to remove every cloud,—to abase him in dust and ashes,—and to exalt him again in all the confidence of prayer.

2. Again, secondly,—on the other hand, observe what weight this idea, if fully realised, must have, if we ever regard the Lord himself as personally present, and saying to us, in special reference to each of the things which he has made,—I created it, and I am now reminding you, and testifying to you, that it was I who made it. What sacredness will this thought

stamp on every object in nature,—if only by the power of the Spirit, and through the belief of the truth, we are made really and personally acquainted with the living God; if we know him thus as the Lawgiver, the Saviour, the Judge.

We go forth amid the glories and the beauties of this earth and these heavens, which he has so marvellously framed. We are not left merely to trace the dead and empty footsteps which mark that he once was there. He is there still, telling us even now that his hand framed all that we see; and telling us why he did so. Thus, and thus only, do we walk with God, amid all that is grand and lovely in the scenes of creation; not by rising, in our sentimental dream of piety, to the notion of a remote Creator, dimly seen in his works, but by taking the Creator along with us, whenever we enter into these scenes, and seeing his works in him. It is true, there is a tongue in every breeze of summer, a voice in every song of the bird, a silent eloquence in every green field and quiet grove, which tell of God as the great maker of them all; but after all, they tell of him as a God afar off, and still they speak of him as secondary, merely, and supplementary to themselves,—as if he were inferred from them, and not they from him. But, in our habit of mind, let this order be just reversed. Let us conceive of God as telling us concerning them as his works. While they reveal and interpret him, let him reveal and interpret them. And whenever we meet with any thing that pleases our eye, and affects our heart, let us consider God himself, our God and our Father, as informing us respecting that very thing: I made it,—I made it what it is,—I made it what it is for you.

And if this vivid impression of reality, in our recognition of God as the Creator, would be salutary in our communing with nature's works, much more would it be so in our use of nature's manifold gifts and bounties. " Every creature of God is good, and nothing to be refused, if it be received with thanksgiving; for it is sanctified by the word of God and prayer" (1 Tim. iv. 4, 5). Still it is to be received and used as the creature of God, and as solemnly declared and attested to be so, by God himself, in the very moment of our using it. If we fully realised this consideration ; if, on the instant when we were about to use, as we have been wont, any of the creatures of God provided for our accommodation, God himself were to appear personally present before us, and were to say, Son,—Daughter,—I created this thing which you are about to use,—this cup of wine which you are about to drink, this piece of money that you are about to spend, this brother or sister with whom you are now conversing,—and I testify this to you, at this particular moment,—I, your Lord and your God,—I created them,—such as they are,—for those ends which they are plainly designed to serve ;—would we go on to make the very same use of the creature that we intended to make ? Or would not our hand be arrested, and our mouth shut, and our spirit made to stand in awe, so that we would not sin ?

Let none imagine that this is an ideal and fanciful state of feeling. It is really nothing more than the true exercise of that faith by which " we understand that the worlds were made by the word of God ; so that things which are seen were not made of things which do appear ; " and it is the preparation for the scene which John saw in vision, when, being in the Spirit, he beheld, and lo ! a throne was set in heaven, and one sat on the throne, and round about the throne the emblems of redeeming love appeared, with the representatives of the redeemed Church giving glory to him that sat on the throne, worshipping him that liveth for ever and ever, casting their crowns before the throne, and saying, " Thou art worthy, O Lord, to receive glory, and honour, and power ; for thou hast created all things, and for thy pleasure they are and were created " (Rev. iv.)

My plan does not require me to enter at any length, if indeed at all, into the vexed questions which have clustered around the Mosaic cosmogony ; questions as to the relations of science and revelation which I own myself incompetent to discuss. I have tried in this Lecture to indicate the point of view from which, as it seems to me, the narrative in the first two chapters of Genesis ought to be regarded. It is God's own account of the origin of the present mundane system, given by inspiration, for all times and for all men. And it is his account, specially adapted by himself to the end, not of gratifying speculative curiosity, but of promoting godly edification. Therefore, there is purposely excluded from it whatever might identify it with any particular stage of advancement and enlightenment among mankind. It is this very exclusion, indeed, which gives to it a breadth and universality fitting it equally for all systems, as well as for all ages. Then again, as on the one hand it is not the design of God to tell us here all that we might wish to have learned from him respecting this earth's long past history, or even respecting the adjustment of its present order,—so, on the other hand, it is his design to present this last topic to us chiefly in its bearing on the great scheme of providence, including probation and redemption, which his revealed word is meant to unfold. He tells the story of our birth only partially. And in telling it, he casts it in the mould that best adapts it to that progressive development of his moral government which his inspired Scriptures are about to trace.

Hence, amid dark obscurity hanging over many things, the salient prominence given to the Word as the Light of the world, its light of life,—to the Spirit moving in the ancient chaos,—to the satisfaction of the Eternal at each step in the creative work,—to the succession of six days and the rest of the seventh.

And hence also, as regards man, the twofold account of his origin,—that in the first chapter bringing out his high and heavenly relation to the Supreme, whose image he wears, and that in the second chapter describing rather his more earthly relations, and the functions of his animal nature. For these two accounts, so far from being inconsistent with one another, are in reality the complements of one another. Both of them are essential to a complete divinely-drawn portrait of man as at first he stood forth among the creatures ; spiritually allied to God, in one view, yet in another view, the offspring as well as the lord of earth. Both therefore appropriately culminate,— the one in the Sabbatic Institute, the pledge and means of man's divine life,—and the other in that ordinance of marriage, peculiar to him alone, in which his social earthly life finds all its pure and holy joy.

These particulars will come up again for consideration. I notice them now because I would like my first paper to be studied as having an important bearing on the subjects to which they relate.

2

THE CREATION OF THE WORLD AND MAN VIEWED
ON ITS HEAVENLY SIDE

Genesis 1:1-2:3

This divine record of creation, remarkable for the most perfect simplicity, has been sadly complicated and embarrassed
by the human theories and speculations with which it has unhappily become entangled. To clear the way, therefore, at
the outset, to get rid of many perplexities, and leave the
narrative unencumbered for pious and practical uses, let its
limited design be fairly understood, and let certain explanations be frankly made.

I. In the first place, the object of this inspired cosmogony,
or account of the world's origin, is not scientific but religious.
Hence it was to be expected that, while nothing contained in
it could ever be found really and in the long run to contradict
science, the gradual progress of discovery might give occasion
for apparent temporary contradictions. The current interpretation of the Divine record, in such matters, will naturally,
and indeed, must necessarily, accommodate itself to the actual
state of scientific knowledge and opinion at the time ; so that,
when science takes a step in advance, revelation may seem to
be left behind. The remedy here is to be found in the exercise of caution, forbearance, and suspense, on the part both of
the student of Scripture and of the student of science ; and, so
far as Scripture is concerned, it is often safer and better to
dismiss or to qualify old interpretations, than instantly to adopt

new ones. Let the student of science push his inquiries still further, without too hastily assuming, in the meantime, that the result to which he has been brought demands a departure from the plain sense of Scripture ; and let the student of Scripture give himself to the exposition of the narrative in its moral and spiritual application, without prematurely committing himself, or it, to the particular details or principles of any scientific school.

II. Then again, in the second place, let it be observed that the essential facts in this Divine record are,—the recent date assigned to the existence of man on the earth, the previous preparation of the earth for his habitation, the gradual nature of the work, and the distinction and succession of days during its progress. These are not, and cannot be, impugned by any scientific discoveries. What history of ages previous to that era this globe may have engraved in its rocky bosom, revealed or to be revealed by the explosive force of its central fires, Scripture does not say. What countless generations of living organisms teemed in the chaotic waters, or brooded over the dark abyss, it is not within the scope of the inspiring Spirit to tell. There is room and space for whole volumes of such matter, before the Holy Ghost takes up the record. Nor is it necessary to suppose that all continuity of the animal life which had sprung into being, in or out of the waters, was broken at the time when the earth was finally fashioned for man's abode. It is enough that then, for the first time, the animals of sea, and air, and land, with which man was to be conversant, were created for his use,—the fish, the fowls, the beasts, which were to minister to his enjoyment and to own his dominion.

III. And finally, in the third place, let it be borne in mind that the sacred narrative of the creation is evidently, in its highest character, moral, spiritual, and prophetical. The original relation of man, as a responsible being, to his Maker, is directly taught ; his restoration from moral chaos to spiritual beauty is figuratively represented ; and as a prophecy, it has

an extent of meaning which will be fully unfolded only when
"the times of the restitution of all things" (Acts iii. 21) have
arrived.   Until then, we must be contented with a partial and
inadequate view of this, as of other parts of the sacred volume;
for "the sure word of prophecy," though a light "whereunto
we do well to take heed," is still but "as a light shining in a
dark place, until the day dawn and the day-star arise in our
hearts" (2 Peter i. 19).   The exact literal sense of much that is
now obscure or doubtful, as well as the bearing and importance
of what may seem insignificant or irrelevant, will then clearly
appear.   The creation of this world anew, after its final baptism
of fire, will be the best comment on the history of its creation
at first, after the chaos of water.   The manner as well as the
design of the earth's formation of old out of the water, will be
understood at last, when it emerges once more from the wreck
and ruin of the conflagration which yet awaits it,—"a new
earth, with new heavens, wherein righteousness is to dwell"
(2 Pet. iii. 13).

Our present concern, therefore, is with the moral and
spiritual aspect of this sacred narrative.   Our business is with
man,—with the position originally assigned to him, by creation,
in the primeval kingdom of nature, and the place to which he
is restored, by redemption, in the remedial kingdom of grace.
Of his abode in the renewed kingdom of glory, it is but the
shadowy outline which we can in the meantime trace ; but, so
far as it goes, it is interesting and suggestive.

Thus, then, let us view the scene which the opening section
of Genesis presents to us.

There is a plain distinction between the first verse and the
subsequent part of this passage.   The first verse speaks of
creation, strictly so called, and of the creation of all things,—
the formation of the substance, or matter, of the heavens and
the earth, out of nothing ;—"In the beginning God created
the heavens and the earth."   The rest of the passage speaks

of creation in the less exact sense of the term; describing the changes wrought on matter previously existing; and it confines itself, apparently, to one part of the universe—our solar system, and especially to this one planet—our earth, concerning which, chiefly, God sees fit to inform us.

The first verse, then, contains a very general announcement; in respect of time, without date,—in respect of space, without limits. The expression, " in the beginning," fixes no period; and the expression, "the heavens and the earth," admits of no restriction. For, though heaven denotes sometimes the atmosphere, or the visible starry expanse above, and, at other times, the dwelling-place of God and of the blessed; yet, when heaven and earth are joined, as in this text, all things are evidently intended (Ps. cxxxi. 2, etc.) And the announcement here is, that at an era indefinitely remote, the whole matter of the universe was called into being. It is not eternal,—it had a beginning. God has not merely, in the long course of ages, wrought wonderful changes on matter previously existing. Originally, and at the first, he made the matter itself.

At the period referred to in the second verse, the materials for the fair structure of this world which we inhabit are in being. But they are lying waste. Three things are wanted to render the earth such as God can approve—order, life, and light. The earth is " without form "—a shapeless mass. It is " void,"—empty, or destitute of life. It has " darkness " all around its deep chaotic " waters." One good sign only appears. There is a movement on the surface, but deep-searching. " The Spirit of God moved on the face of the waters."

We have here the first indication in the Bible of a plurality of Persons in the unity of the Godhead; and, in the chapter throughout we trace the same great and glorious doctrine of the ever-blessed Trinity, pervading the entire narrative. This truth, indeed, is not so much directly stated in the Scriptures as it is all along assumed; and we might reasonably expect it to be so. God is not, in the written word, introduced for the first time to men. He speaks, and is spoken of, as one previously known, because previously revealed. And, if the doctrine of the Trinity be true, he must have been known, more or less explicitly, as Father, Son, and Holy Ghost. An express and formal declaration, then, of this mystery of his being, was not needed, nor was it to be expected. The most natural and convincing proof of it, in these circumstances, is to trace it, as from the very first taken for granted and recognised, in all that is said of the divine proceedings. Now, in this passage, we find precisely such intimations of it as might have been anticipated. Not to speak of the form of the word " God," which, in the original, is a plural noun joined to a singular verb, we have the remarkable phrase (ver 26), " Let us make ;" and, in the very outset, we have mention made of God ;—of his WORD, " God said ;"—and of his Spirit, " the Spirit of God moved." So, also, it is said, in the Psalms (xxxiii. vi.), " By the word of the Lord were the heavens made, and all the hosts of them by the breath," or Spirit, " of his mouth."

The gradual process by which the earth is brought into a right state may be traced according to the division of days. But there is another principle of division, very simple and beautiful, suggested by the repeated expression, " God saw that it was good." That expression may be regarded as marking the successive steps or stages of the divine work, at which the Creator pauses, that he may dwell on each finished portion, as at last he dwells on the finished whole, with a holy and benevolent complacency. The phrase occurs seven times (ver. 4, 10, 12, 18, 21, 25, 31). It does not divide the work exactly as the days divide it. On the second day it does not occur at all ; and on the third and sixth days it occurs twice. The work is divided among the days, so that each day has something definite to be done,—something complete in itself. 1. Light,—2. Air (the elastic firmament or sky),—3. Earth (dry land as separated from the sea),—4. the Luminaries in heaven as means of light and measures of time,—5. Fish and Fowl,—6. Beasts, and MAN himself,—these are the works of the successive days. The relation, however, of the several parts to the whole, is better seen by noting the points at which the divine expression of satisfaction is inserted : " God saw that it was good."

The main design of the whole work is to supply the wants or defects of the chaotic earth. These were three :—the want of order, of life, and of light. Light is first provided ; then order is given that the earth may be fitted for the habitation of living creatures ; and finally, living creatures are placed in it.

Now, the series of operations by which this threefold object is accomplished, is exactly marked by the intervals at which it is said, " God saw that it was good." Thus, I. On the introduction of LIGHT, which is a simple act, the Creator's joy is expressed emphatically, but only once (ver. 4). II. The ORDERING of the world, however, is a more complicated and elaborate process. In the first place, there must be the adjustment of the waters ; that is, on the one hand the separation of the cloudy vapour constituting the material heavens above, from the waters on the earth's surface below, by the air, or elastic atmosphere, being interposed ; and on the other hand, the separation on the earth's surface of the dry land from the sea. Secondly, there must be the arrangement of the dry land itself, which is to be clothed with all manner of vegetation, and stored with all sorts of reproductive trees and plants. And thirdly, there must be the establishment of the right relation which the heavens and the heavenly bodies are to have to the earth as the instruments of its light, and the rulers of its seasons. Accordingly, at each of these three stages of this part of the work,—the reducing of the shapeless mass of earth to ORDER,—the language of divine approbation is employed (ver. 10, 12, 18). III. The formation of LIFE also, or of the living beings for whose use the world is made,—admits of a similar sub-division. First, the fishes and the fowls are produced; secondly, the terrestrial beasts; and thirdly, man himself. And still, as the glorious work rises higher and higher, there is at each step the pause of divine congratulation; as, in the end and over all, there is the full contentment of Infinite Wisdom; "rejoicing in the habitable parts of the earth, his delights being with the sons of men" (ver. 21, 25, 31, and Prov. viii. 31).

The following scheme will show this division clearly:

God saw that it was good on the production of—

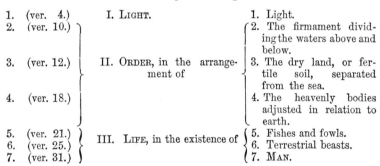

1. (ver. 4.)   I. LIGHT.   1. Light.
2. (ver. 10.)
3. (ver. 12.)   II. ORDER, in the arrangement of
4. (ver. 18.)

2. The firmament dividing the waters above and below.
3. The dry land, or fertile soil, separated from the sea.
4. The heavenly bodies adjusted in relation to earth.

5. (ver. 21.)
6. (ver. 25.)   III. LIFE, in the existence of
7. (ver. 31.)

5. Fishes and fowls.
6. Terrestrial beasts.
7. MAN.

I. The first step in this glorious process, is the breaking in of LIGHT on the gloom in which the earth was shrouded (ver. 3-5). In this step the ETERNAL WORD comes forth from the bosom of Deity. He "whose goings forth have been from of old, from everlasting" (Micah v. 2),—"the Word who was in the beginning with God and was God" (John i. 1-3),—he is that word which went out from God, when "GOD SAID, Let there be light." For this is not the utterance of a dead sentence, but the coming forth of the living WORD. In the Word was life, and this life in the Word,—this LIVING WORD,—was the "light." Immediately, without the intervention of those luminaries in which afterwards light was stored and centered, the LIVING WORD himself going forth was light,—the natural light of the earth then : as afterwards, again coming forth, he became to men the light of their salvation.

In this light God delighted as good ; for the light is none other than that very Eternal Wisdom who says ;—" The LORD possessed me in the beginning of his way, before his works of old, and I was daily,"—from day to day, as the marvellous work of these six days went on,—" I was daily his delight, rejoicing always before him " (Prov. viii. 22, 30). Such was the mutual ineffable complacency of the Godhead, when the Word went forth in the creation, as the light, and when all things began to be made by him (John i. 3, 4). And in this first going forth of the Eternal Word, the distinction of light and darkness, of day and night, for the new earth, began (Ps. civ. 2). This was the first day—the first alternation of evening and morning ;—not perhaps the first revolution of this globe on its axis, but its first revolution, after its chaotic darkness, under the beams of that divine light, which, shining on earth's surface as it passed beneath the glorious brightness, chased, from point to point, the ancient gloom away.

II. To light succeeds ORDER. Form, or shape, or due arrangement, is given to the natural economy of this lower world, and that by three successive processes.

1. In the first place, the waters are arranged (ver. 6-10). The earth is girt round with a firmament, or gaseous atmosphere ; at once pressing down, by its weight, the waters on the surface, and supporting, by its elasticity, the floating clouds and vapours above ; and so forming the visible heaven, or the azure sky (Ps. civ. 3). This is the work of the second day. Then, a bed is made for the waters, which before covered the earth, but which now, subsiding into the place prepared for them, lay bare a surface of dry land (Ps. civ. 6-13). This is done on the third day. And thus, by a twofold process, the

waters are reduced to order. In the language of Job, " He girdeth up the waters in his thick clouds ; and the cloud is not rent under them : he holdeth back the face of his throne, and spreadeth his cloud upon it." This surely must allude to the separating of the waters above the firmament from the waters under the firmament. And as to these last, the description proceeds, " He hath compassed the waters with bounds, until the day and night come to an end " (Job xxvi. 8-10). So, also, in another place, the Lord, challenging vain man to answer him, asks, " Who shut up the sea with doors, when it brake forth as if it had issued out of the womb ; when I made the cloud the garment thereof, and thick darkness a swaddling band for it ? " Here we have plainly the firmament dividing the waters. And I " brake up for it," for the sea that once covered the earth, " my decreed place, and set bars and doors, and said, Hitherto shalt thou come, but no farther ; and here shall thy proud waves be stayed." Here we have with equal plainness the gathering together of the waters and the appearing of the dry land (Job xxxviii. 8-11). The same twofold process in disposing of the waters is indicated by the psalmist ; —" O give thanks therefore to him, that by his wisdom made the heavens, for his mercy endureth for ever ; to him that stretched out the earth above the waters, for his mercy endureth for ever " (Ps. cxxxvi. 5, 6) ;—and by the Apostle Peter ;—" By the word of the Lord, the heavens were of old, and the earth, standing out of the water and in the water " (2 Pet. iii. 5).

2. Secondly, the dry land is next itself prepared (ver. 11-13). The green and fertile earth, rising out of the waters, is stored with all the seeds and elements of prodigal vegetation (Ps. civ. 14-18). This also is on the third day.

3. In the third place, on the fourth day, the heavenly bodies, in their relation to this earth, are formed or adjusted. The light, hitherto supplied by the immediate presence of the WORD, which had gone forth on the first day—the very Glory

of the Lord, which long afterwards shone in the wilderness, in the temple, and on the Mount of Transfiguration, and which may yet again illumine the world—the light, thus originally provided without created instrumentality, by the LIVING WORD himself, now that the chaotic mists are cleared away from the earth's surface, is to be henceforward dispensed through the natural agency of second causes. A subordinate fountain and storehouse of light is found for the earth. The light is now concentrated in the sun, as its source, and in the moon and stars, which reflect the sun's beams ; and these luminaries, by their fixed order, are made to rule and regulate all movements here below (Ps. civ. 19-23). They are appointed "for signs,"—not for tokens of divination (Isa. xliv. 25 ; Jer. x. 2),—but for marks and indications of the changes that go on in the natural world ;—and " for seasons,"—for the distinction of day and night, of summer and winter, seed-time and harvest (Jer. xxxi. 35). Again, therefore, let us " give thanks to him that made great lights, for his mercy endureth for ever ; the sun to rule by day, for his mercy endureth for ever; the moon and stars to rule by night, for his mercy endureth for ever " (Ps. cxxxvi. 7-9).

Thus, all things are ready for living beings to be formed —those living beings which belong to the social economy of which MAN is head.

III. Accordingly, LIFE—life in abundance—is now produced. For the Eternal Word, or Wisdom (Prov. viii. 22-31), in the whole of this work of creation, in which he was intimately present with the Father, rejoiced especially in the earth as habitable ; and above all, " his delights were with the sons of men." In the first place, in the waters, and from the waters, he causes fishes and fowls to spring :—fishes to move in the bosom of the sea, and fowls to float in the liquid air and fly abroad in the open firmament of heaven. This he does on the fifth day (ver. 20-23). Secondly, on the sixth, he causeth all beasts to be produced from the earth (ver. 24,

25). And, in the third place, on the sixth day also, he creates MAN (ver. 26, 27).

These three orders or classes of living beings are severally pronounced good. But man is specially blessed (ver. 26, 27). There is deliberation in heaven respecting his creation : " Let us make man." He is created after a high model—" after our likeness." He is invested with dominion over the creatures : "Let them have dominion over the fish of the sea, and over the fowl of the air, and over all the earth, and over every creeping thing that creepeth upon the earth." He is formed for holy matrimony, for dwelling in families : "male and female "—one male and one female—" created he them."

Thus, in four particulars, is man exalted above the other animals. In the first place, the counsels of the Godhead have respect to man. To his creation, as well as to his redemption, the Father, the Son, and the Holy Ghost consent. Then, secondly, the image of God is reflected in him,—in his capacity of intelligence, his uprightness of condition, and his immaculate purity of character,—in his knowledge, righteousness, and holiness (Eph. iv. 24 ; Col. iii. 10). A third distinction is, that the other animals are subjected to him,—not to his tyranny as now, but to his mild and holy rule ;—as they shall be when sinners are consumed out of the earth, and the wicked are no more (Ps. civ. 35 ; viii. 6-8 ; Rom. viii. 20-22). While his fourth and final privilege is, that marriage, and all its attendant blessings of society, are ordained for him. This the prophet Malachi testifies, when, sternly rebuking his countrymen for the prevailing sin of adultery and the light use of divorce, he appeals against the man who shall " deal treacherously with the wife of his youth,"—" his companion and the wife of his covenant,"—to the original design and purpose of God in creation. "Did not he make one ?"— a single pair,—" yet had he the residue of the spirit,"—the excellency or abundance of the breath of life. "Wherefore, then, did he make one ?"—limiting himself to the creation of a single pair?—"That he might seek a goodly seed,"—or in other words, that holy matrimony,—based upon the creation of the one male and the one female, and the destination of them to be "one flesh,"—might purify and bless the social state of man (Mal. ii. 14-16).

Such was the primitive constitution of life in this world. Man stood forth, godlike and social, having under him, as in God's stead, all the creatures; and for his life, and for theirs, that food was appointed which the earth was to bring forth (ver. 29, 30). The two previous stages in the creation are subservient to this last. Light and order are means, in order to life, which is the end. Life—animal, intellectual, moral, spiritual, social, divine—life is the crown and consummation of all. The Creator beholds it, and is satisfied, and rests.

"Thus the heavens and the earth were finished, and all the host of them. And on the seventh day God ended his work which he had made; and he rested on the seventh day from all his work which he had made. And God blessed the seventh day, and sanctified it; because that in it he had rested from all his work which God created and made" (Gen. ii. 1-3).

The rest of God is not physical repose after weariness or fatigue, nor is it absolute inactivity. During all the period of his rest, from that first day of rest downwards until now, he worketh still (John v. 17); and he must continually work for the continual preservation of his creatures (Ps. civ. 28, 29). But he pauses from his work of creation,—from the creation of new kinds and orders of beings; though he still carries on his work of providence. He rests from all his work which he has made. He rests and is "refreshed" (Exod. xxxi. 17). And his original day of rest is blessed and sanctified.

Into the rest of God, with all its blessedness and sanctity, man at first might enter; and hence the seventh day, as the day which was the beginning of the rest of God, became the

"Sabbath made for man" (Exod. xx. 11 ; Mark ii. 27). To the people of God still, in every age, there is a promise left, that they shall again enter into his rest. And the promise is still subsisting. For the rest of Canaan was not that rest, but only its type and shadow. So the Apostle Paul argues, building his argument on that solemn denunciation in the ninety-fifth Psalm ;—"I sware in my wrath, They shall not enter into my rest." "For if Joshua had given them rest, then would he not afterward have spoken of another day. There remaineth therefore a rest to the people of God " (Heb. iv. 8, 9). And as the rest still remaineth for the people of God, so also the day of rest, which is its type and earnest ;— the blessed and holy Sabbath.

Such is the unanswerable reasoning, as it would seem, of the inspired apostle, founded upon the Lord's appeal to the Israelites, when he exhorts them to hear his voice. " Harden not your heart," is the voice of God, their Maker, " as your fathers did, who provoked me in the wilderness, and to whom I sware in my wrath that they should not enter into my rest." Harden not your hearts, lest you also come short of that rest. But were not they who were thus addressed already in possession of that rest into which God sware that their fathers should not enter ? Certainly they were, if that rest was the rest of Canaan which Joshua gave them ; in which case God "would not have spoken of another day " (Heb. iv. 8). But he does speak of " another day," when he says, even to those who were dwelling in the rest which Joshua gave them, " To-day, if ye will hear my voice, harden not your hearts, lest to you, as to your fathers, I swear in my wrath that ye shall not enter into my rest." This God would not have said, if Joshua had really given them that rest with reference to which he " sware in his wrath." It was a rest, therefore, different from that which Joshua gave that the Lord had in view, when he sware to the fathers in the wilderness that they should not enter into his rest ; and their exclusion from the rest which Joshua gave, was but a presage of their exclusion from a rest infinitely more precious. This was a rest from which even they who did actually enter into the rest that Joshua gave, might yet be for ever debarred. In a word, it was his own rest. " My rest," says the Lord.

Now this rest has been long prepared. For " the works were finished from the foundation of the world ; and he spake in a certain place of the seventh day on this wise, and God did rest on the seventh day from all his works " (Heb. iv. 3, 4). Of this original rest it is, and not of any image of it afterwards appointed, that God speaks when he says, " If they shall enter into my rest." No rest hitherto given on earth,— either by Joshua to the Old Testament Church, or by Jesus to the New,—is or can be the rest of God, into which his people, if they come not short through unbelief, are to enter. That rest remaineth for them, after they have ceased from their works, as God did from his (Heb. iv. 10). And the type or pledge of it remaineth also ;—perpetual and unchange- able, as the promise of the rest itself ;—the type and pledge of it, instituted from the beginning, in the hallowed rest of the weekly Sabbath.

Through the help of this Sabbatic Institution, if only we obtain a spiritual and sympathising insight into its significancy, we may enter into the rest of God by faith, and in the spirit, even now, as we realise the blessed complacency of the Creator, rejoicing in his works.

Pause, therefore, O my soul ! at every stage of the won- drous process here described, and especially at its close ; and behold how good it is ! See how all was fitted for thee ; and what a being art thou, so fearfully and wonderfully made (Ps. cxxxix. 14) ; thyself a little world ; and for thy sake this great world made ! How marvellous are God's works ! How precious also are thy thoughts unto me, O God ! Let me see, as God saw, everything which he has made. Behold, it is very good. And blessed and joyful is the rest which succeeds.

Man, however, who was the crown, has become the curse of this earth. The work of God has been destroyed; and he must create anew. And it is, first of all, man himself that he must remodel and reform. The chaos now is not in matter but in mind,—not in the substance of this earth, but in the soul of man. In that world now there is darkness, disorder, death. But "in the WORD is life."

And, in the first place, "the life is the light of men." He shines into the darkened understanding, and all is light—"For God, who commanded the light to shine out of darkness, hath shined in our hearts, to give the light of the knowledge of the glory of God in the face of Jesus Christ" (2 Cor. iv. 6). The glory of God, the true and living God, is seen in the Living Incarnate Word, the man Christ Jesus, the light of life, the author of salvation. "I have heard of thee with the hearing of the ear, but now mine eyes seeth thee" (Job xlii. 5,—seeth thee in Christ, the Holy One, the Just, the Saviour.

Again, secondly, by the same Living Word, the disorder of the soul is remedied. Christ, the Sun of Righteousness,—God in Christ,—becomes the centre of attraction. Away from that centre, all the powers of the soul move and mingle irregularly. Restore the balance, by making God supreme, and all again is adjusted rightly; things above and things below are separated; the inconstant waves of passion retire, and leave the solid ground of principle; and the glory of heaven rules and blesses the whole man.

Finally, in the third place, the end of all this is life,—the life of the soul,—its life with Christ in God (Eph. ii. 1 ; Col. iii. 3). Now the life of the soul is love,—for the soul lives in being loved, and in loving; and God is revealed to the darkened soul, and restored to his supremacy in the disordered soul, in order that the dead soul may be quickened, so as to feel and return his love.

Such is the new creation of the soul, after the image of

God, in respect of knowledge or light, righteousness or order, and holiness or life, which is love. And this new creation being finished, a new rest follows; a rest of God; a rest in God; a rest with God;—as now a reconciled Father and all-satisfying portion. Into this rest let my weary spirit enter. It is mine in Christ, in whom, believing, I am created anew. " Return unto thy rest, O my soul, for the Lord hath dealt bountifully with thee " (Ps. cxvi. 7).

But after all this, and beyond it all, there still " remaineth a rest for the people of God." For we cherish the sure hope, that when this work of new creation in the souls of the redeemed shall be ended, the face of the earth itself shall be again renewed for their habitation; and the Lord shall again rest, and rejoice in all that he has made, blessing and hallowing a new and better Sabbath in our regenerated world (Ps. civ. 30).

Meanwhile, the primitive institution of the Sabbath,—as the sign of that rest into which spiritually and by faith we enter now, as well as the foretaste of the rest which remaineth for us in the world to come,—is surely a delightful truth; and its observance cannot but be a precious privilege. This world, with all that it contains, was made for man. Man himself was made for God, for entering into God's rest. And that he might all the better do so, the Sabbath was made for him. " God blessed the Sabbath-day and hallowed it." The blessing is not recalled, the consecration is not repealed. There remaineth a rest unto the people of God,—and a day of rest. Let us not fall short of the rest hereafter. Let us not despise the day of rest now.

3

THE CREATION OF MAN
VIEWED AS ON THE SIDE OF EARTH; AND HIS
EARTHLY ORIGIN AND RELATIONS

Genesis 2:4-25

THIS is a separate and independent account of the origin of man; quite distinct, and meant to be distinct, from the former. The two, when fairly viewed, are not at all inconsistent with one another: they are rather supplementary to one another. In the first, man comes forth in his high spiritual or heavenly nature, as allied to God and capable of intercourse with God; in the second he appears as "of the earth, earthy" (1 Cor. xv. 47);* having an earthly origin and earthly relations. He is godlike, in respect of the divine proposal and decree,—"Let us make man in our image, after our likeness." But he is also "a living soul;" an animal like his co-occupiers of the earth; with animal propensities and animal connections. And it is that aspect of his nature and condition which this chapter brings out, to balance the higher ideal suggested by the narrative that precedes it.

This may partly explain a puzzle which was once more troublesome than it is likely to be now. For it is to be observed, that throughout this last account, God is called by a name not used in the preceding section; the name "LORD," or "Jehovah," being joined to the name "God." The reason may be this. The single name "God," denoting power or might, is more suitable while the process of creation, by God's

* See "Life in a Risen Saviour," where I have expounded this passage.

mighty power, is described, as it were, on the side of his
sovereign creative fiat, "Let it be," "Let us make." Now,
however, in reviewing the work as complete, and entering into
its providential phase, the additional idea involved in the
name "Jehovah"—that of self-existence and unchangeable
majesty, with special reference to his providence—becomes
appropriate. All things are made by him as the Almighty
God. They subsist by him as being also the everlasting
Jehovah, "the same yesterday, to-day, and for ever." "I am
Jehovah, I change not; therefore ye sons of Jacob are not
consumed" (Mal. iii. 6).

A similar distinction is intimated in the Lord's first introduction of himself to Moses (Exod. vi. 3) ; "I appeared unto
Abraham, unto Isaac, and unto Jacob, by the name of God
Almighty, but by my name Jehovah was I not known to them."
In his dealings with Abraham, Isaac, and Jacob, God chiefly
manifested himself as the Almighty Creator. In what he did,
and in what he promised, he asserted his prerogative of omnipotence. In his dealings, again, with the Israelites in Egypt,
when he returned after a long interval to visit them,—it
chiefly concerned them to know him as the ever-living and
unchanging God of Providence. The dispensation which he
originates as the Almighty God, he sustains and carries forward as the unchangeable Jehovah. And hence, accordingly,
the Lord Jesus would have revealed himself to the devout
Jews of his time as bearing this very character, and this very
name ; with special reference to their great father Abraham,
and his immortal hope : "He desired to see my day, and he
saw it and was glad. For before Abraham was, I AM"
(John viii. 58).

In this chapter, the state of things on the earth at its first
creation is briefly described. "These are the generations,"—
or, as we would say, the following is the account of the
original condition,—" of the heavens and of the earth when

they were created, in the day that the LORD God made the earth and the heavens" (ver. 4). Such is the usual beginning of a new section in the narrative,—the title or heading of a new chapter. Whenever the inspired compiler or historian opens a fresh fountain in the stream of his annals, he employs the formula of genealogical succession or derivation : " These are the generations."

In the present instance, this formula introduces a description of the world, both natural and moral, as it stood completely adjusted, on the day of the finished creation.

I. The economy of the kingdom of inanimate nature, or of the vegetable world, was fitted at once to maintain the sovereignty of God, and to provide for the welfare of man, viewing man as a compound being, having both body and soul. " The LORD God made every plant of the field before it was in the earth, and every herb of the field before it grew : for the LORD God had not caused it to rain upon the earth, and there was not a man to till the ground. But there went up a mist from the earth, and watered the whole face of the ground. And the LORD God formed man of the dust of the ground, and breathed into his nostrils the breath of life ; and man became a living soul " (ver. 5-7).

Three things, it is here implied, are ordinarily necessary to the growth of plants and herbs :—soil, climate, and culture. The vital energy of the earth itself, in which all various seeds are lodged, is the first element (ver. 5). The influence of rain and dew from heaven comes next (ver. 6). And lastly, there must be superadded the labour of the hand of man (ver. 7 compared with ver. 5).

This is the law of nature, or rather of nature's God. Originally, only the first of these powers could be in action ; and, therefore, it is probable that, at the first, God created the plants and herbs, or caused them to spring up, in full maturity, so as to fit the new, or renewed, earth for the immediate use of the animals, and also to prepare its soil for the subsequent

operation of heaven's genial moisture, and man's faithful husbandry. Afterwards, the mist or vapour from the earth
supplied the watery sky. And finally, the forming hand and
inspiring Spirit of God brought forth man,—a corporeal and
spiritual being,—having bodily powers and mental intelligence,—having life, both animal and rational. He was thus
fitted to till the ground ; and the employment was fitted for
him. The energies of his bodily frame were exercised by
labour ; while his spirit was exercised by the intelligence and
the faith which the particular kind of labour assigned to him
required. He was placed in his true position. He was conscious at once of mastery over the earth which he was to till—
and of dependence on the heaven from whence he was to
expect the influence that alone could bless his toil. He had
to work and to wait. It was a wholesome discipline ; it was
a becoming attitude then. It is so still. Our business now
is to realise that very position in the kingdom of grace, which
man at first held in the kingdom of nature. It is the position
of working and waiting. " Be patient, therefore, brethren,
unto the coming of the Lord. Behold the husbandman waiteth
for the precious fruit of the earth, and hath long patience for
it, until he receive the early and latter rain. Be ye also
patient. Stablish your hearts, for the coming of the Lord
draweth nigh " (James v. 7).

II. The moral world also,—the spiritual kingdom, was
rightly adjusted. 1. Man, as a sentient being, was placed in
an earthly paradise (ver. 8-15). 2. As a rational and religious
being, he was subjected to a divine law (ver. 16, 17). 3. As
a social, or companionable being, he was furnished with human
fellowship (ver. 18-25).

1. In the first place, provision was made for his wellbeing,
as a sentient creature. He was placed in the garden of Eden ;
and Eden was well stocked with all trees of beauty and of
usefulness, and well watered with rivers,—rich in golden sands,
and in most costly precious stones. " And a river went out

of Eden to water the garden ; and from thence it was parted, and became into four heads. The name of the first is Pison : that is it which compasseth the whole land of Havilah, where there is gold ; and the gold of that land is good : there is bdellium and the onyx stone. And the name of the second river is Gihon : the same is it that compasseth the whole land of Ethiopia. And the name of the third river is Hiddekel : that is it which goeth toward the east of Assyria. And the fourth river is Euphrates " (ver. 10-14).

Many have laboured to ascertain the site of Eden ; and so various and doubtful have been the opinions formed, that some have regarded the countries and rivers here named as no longer existing ; the deluge, as is supposed, having swept away all the ancient landmarks. But although several of the marks given by the sacred historian may have been obliterated and lost, through convulsions of nature and the hand of man, his description is so circumstantial that it must be intended to point out, even since the flood, the place where Eden was. It is probable that they who lived before us, and for whom Moses wrote, might recognise the spot ; and it is not impossible, that they who come after us may be able to recognise it better than we can do now. It may have been the design of the Holy Ghost to employ his servant Moses,—writing by Divine inspiration, not for himself but for the faithful in after-ages,—to leave on record a map by which, when the proper time comes, the exact locality of paradise may be again identified.

Meanwhile, in a vague and general way, the most learned and laborious researches seem to fix down the site of Eden to some part of the region which the Euphrates and its kindred streams water, as they fall into the Persian Gulf (Gen. xxv. 18 ; Dan. x. 4). The Ethiopia, or Cush, spoken of in the thirteenth verse, is not the region in Africa known under that name, but a territory in Asia, embracing the country of the Midianites and part of Arabia (Numb. xii. 1 ; Exod. ii. 21). Hence it is not impossible, nor by any means unlikely, that in the latter days the place where Eden was,—bordering on the limits of the promised land as the original grant to Abraham extended it eastward (Gen. xv.),—may be destined yet to come again into note, as sharing the final fortunes of that land, whatever these may be (Ps. lxxii. 8). And for this end, perhaps, it has pleased God to give this geography of it beforehand, by which it may be known when the history of this earth is to be wound up.

In this garden, then, man was placed, not for idleness; his animal and sentient constitution does not fit him for being happy in idleness; but for an easy charge and for pleasant labour; to dress and keep a garden, spontaneously fruitful in trees pleasant to the sight, and good for food;—"And the Lord God took the man, and put him into the garden of Eden to dress it and to keep it" (ver. 15). Thus, in the lowest view of his nature, as an animal being or "living soul," man was so situated, that his tastes and talents,—his powers and suscepti- bilities,—were exercised and satisfied to the very utmost measure of perfection in the creature.

2. In respect also, secondly, of the highest as well as the lowest part of his frame, man found in paradise his right place,—the place of free and accountable subjection to his Maker. He was made to feel his dependence, and to recognise his responsibility. He was under law. "And out of the ground made the Lord God to grow every tree that is pleasant to the sight, and good for food; the tree of life also in the midst of the garden, and the tree of knowledge of good and evil. And the Lord God commanded the man, saying, Of every tree of the garden thou mayest freely eat: but of the tree of the knowledge of good and evil, thou shalt not eat of it: for in the day that thou eatest thereof, thou shalt surely die" (ver. 9, 16, 17).

There was a covenant; and there were the sacraments of a covenant,—the signs and seals of it. These were two; the tree of life, and the tree of the knowledge of good and evil.

Every covenant between God and man has two parts—a promise, and a requirement or condition. And hence every covenant may have two sacraments,—the one, chiefly a sign and seal of the thing promised ; the other, chiefly a sign and seal of the thing required. In that first transaction, the tree of life was the sacrament, or the sign and seal, of the thing promised and guaranteed by God to man in paradise,—which was life. The other tree was the sacrament, or the sign and seal, of the thing required,—which was perfect obedience, to be tested and proved by abstinence from a single specified act of disobedience.

Thus, also, in regard to the new covenant,—the covenant of grace and salvation made with Christ, and with his people in him,—there are two parts, a promise and a requirement. The promise is the restoration and support of life ; and the requirement is union with Christ by faith, or the personal application and appropriation of the righteousness wrought out, and the redemption purchased, by him. There are, accordingly, two sacraments, alike under the Levitical and under the Christian form of that covenant. The sacrament of the Passover, or of the Lord's Supper, is mainly the sign and seal of the thing promised,—a new life, and the sustaining of it, by feeding upon the Lamb that was slain to procure it. The sacrament of Circumcision, or of Baptism, on the other hand, is the sign and seal of the thing required,—the cutting off of the corruption, or the washing away of the guilt of the flesh. This is really effected through faith in him who has taken away sin by the sacrifice of himself. With him, in his death and in his rising again, the believer is now identified. And of this identification, Circumcision or Baptism is the symbolic pledge.

According to this analogy, man had in paradise an outward and sensible pledge and token, both of the blessing promised, and of the terms on which it was promised.

The tree of life evidently typified and represented that eternal life which was the portion of man at first, and which has become in Christ Jesus his portion again. It is found, accordingly, both in the paradise which was lost, and in the paradise which is regained. For "saith the Spirit to the churches, To him that overcometh will I give to eat of the tree of life which is in the midst of the garden" (Rev. ii. 7). The garden becomes at last a city, for the multitude of the redeemed to dwell in; and "in the midst of the street of it is the tree of life," and "blessed are they who have right to it" (Rev. xxii. 2, 14). By the use of this tree of life in paradise, man was reminded continually of his dependence. He had no life in himself. He received life at every instant anew from him in whom alone is life. And of this continual reception of life, his continual participation of the tree of life was a standing symbol.

Again, by the other sacramental tree, man is reminded of what is his part in the covenant, or of the terms on which he holds the favour of his God which is his life. The fatal tree is to him, even before his fall, in a certain sense the tree of the knowledge of good and evil. It is a standing memorial of the reality of the distinction. It suggests the possibility of evil, —of disobedience,—which otherwise, in the absence of all lust, might not occur. And so it is a test and token of his sub-mission to his Maker's will. Hence the fitness of this expedient, as a trial of man's obedience. If he was to be tried at all, it could scarcely, in paradise, be otherwise than by means of a positive precept. And the more insignificant the matter of that precept was, the better was it fitted for being a trial;— the less was the temptation beforehand; and the greater, con-sequently, the sin. Such a tree, then, might well serve the purpose intended. It might seal and ratify man's compliance with the will of God, and his enjoyment of the life of God. Or, on the other hand, it might occasion his sin and his death.*

* See Lectures (the Cunningham Lectures) on the Fatherhood of God; appendix iv.

Thus man, in paradise, could not live without God. He could not but recognise God as placing him in the garden, giving him work to do, and all the trees of the garden to enjoy. He could not fail to recognise God also, as dispensing life to him continually and requiring from him continually a perfect obedience. Such is the true original position of man in respect of his Maker; a position of grateful and cheerful dependence. In this position he has the fullest scope for delighting in God, admiring his works, enjoying his gifts, and partaking of his life. And yet he can never fail to recognise, in its utmost extent, the sovereignty of God; having the sign of the Divine authority and his own subjection ever in his eye and within his grasp.

It was a high position. But he who is least in the kingdom of God, is in a higher and better. The believer in Jesus has the sign and seal, not of his own fallible obedience, but of the perfect and perfected obedience of the Righteous One;— which is a surer title, and can never fail. And he is nourished for immortality, not by the tree of life springing from earth, but by the bread of life that came down from heaven.

3. Lastly, in the third place, man in paradise was a social, as well as a sentient and religious being: and in respect of this part also of his nature, God provided for him. Among the lower animals, man could claim subjects, to whom, in token of his authority, he gave names (ver. 19, 20). But he could recognise no fellow; "there was not found an help meet for him" (ver. 20). He needed an equal. And one was found for him;—"The Lord God said, It is not good that the man should be alone; I will make him an help meet for him" (ver. 18); not a servant, not an inferior, but a companion—another self—whom he must love and cherish as his own body (Eph. v. 28). Out of his very ribs, accordingly, a spouse was formed for him; and Adam welcomed her as part and parcel of himself;—"This is now bone of my bone, and flesh of my flesh: she shall be called Woman, because she was taken out of Man"

(ver. 23). Hence arose an intercourse, pure and blessed, with out sin and without shame (ver. 24, 25). Blameless and fearless, the two walked together in the sight of him who made them for one another, and made both of them for himself.

Such were the first parents of our race, in their state of probation ; happy in their outward circumstances—in their relation to God—and in their union with one another. Thus, in the most favourable circumstances, the experiment was tried, of the ability of man, in his best estate, to live, and to retain life, on the terms of a covenant of works. Even in his state of innocency, the law could not save him, in that " it was weak through the flesh,"—through his liability to sin (Rom. viii. 3). And if it would not do for man then, how much less will it do for us now ? How true must it be, that a mere legal enactment—the mere peremptory enforcement of a law—instead of insuring compliance, will provoke and stimulate opposition in our nature ? Let us thank God through Jesus Christ our Lord, that in him in whom there is to us now no condemnation, we are placed at once, if we believe, on a better footing, in this respect, than Adam himself ever held. The second Adam, substituting his own righteousness for ours, —and the free grace of God instead of any prescribed or stipulated condition on our part,—enables us in a new spirit and with a new heart, upright and sincere, to serve God, without fear, in holiness and righteousness before him, all the days of our life.

It is true that, although thus far delivered,—set free from the sentence of condemnation and blessed with the first fruits of the Spirit,—we are constrained to sympathise with the groans of creation, which has been made subject to vanity, for man's sake. The painful sweat of the brow and the sad cry of famine among the weary children of labour,—hard, precarious, ill-requited labour,—too frequently present a far different picture from the scene of peace and plenty which the young and fresh world displayed ; and even at the best, they who are most at ease have weariness of spirit as their portion here below. Where are the rich plains and golden streams of paradise ? Where its simple innocence, and the tree in whose fruit was life ever fresh and new ? Would the beasts and the fowls now flock at man's call around him, to rejoice in his presence and await his pleasure ? The few who can now be brought to dwell at home with him, serve but to show how happy this intercourse might have been ; and even these few fare but miserably at his hands ; while the greater number fly at his approach, or scowl in defiance against him. And how is the social economy deranged and out of joint ! The very love of husband and wife itself is dishonoured. Even into holy marriage, and its kindred ties of family and of brotherhood, the taint or suspicion of sin's poison is insinuated. Every where corruption is felt, or feared ; and all have learned to be ashamed.

But it shall not be always thus. A new world is to arise. " The earth shall yield her increase," and " God's blessing" shall be added, when " he shall judge the people righteously, and govern the nations upon earth" (Ps. lxvii. 4, 6). The creatures shall again rejoice under man's dominion, when he who was " made a little lower than the angels, and then crowned with glory and honour," receives " praise out of the mouth of babes and sucklings,"—the little children of whom his kingdom is composed,—and "stills the enemy and the avenger" (Ps. viii ; Heb. ii.) And then also, they who are accounted worthy to receive that world, and the resurrection from the dead, shall neither marry nor be given in marriage, neither shall they any more be liable to death, for they shall be as the angels of God (Luke xx. 35, 36).

Then shall be realised what some impious dreamers would affect to aim at now ; and plenty, peace, and purity shall reign. Then may those laws and institutions be safely dispensed with or disparaged, which at present restrain the lawless passions that otherwise would make this earth a hell. But wo to all who would prematurely touch these safeguards, whether with the rude hand of violence, or the more refined and subtle influence of a factitious sanctity and a spurious kind of purity,—such as, at the best, is but an unequal warfare with the impure. Wo to those who remove landmarks, or encourage insubordination, or despise holy marriage, whether for the licence of unbridled lust, or in vain idolatry of the virgin state.

The present ordinance of God on this earth enjoins labour, with its attendant right of property,—dominion, with its distinction and gradation of orders,—and matrimony, with its train of blessed charities. These are the very bulwarks of the social fabric. And however much all of them are now affected by the character of vanity to which the whole creation is subjected, they are the only alleviations of its groans. They are the remnants of a better order of things ; and, through the grace and blessed hope of the Gospel, they become the pledges to the redeemed, of a happier industry, a more peaceful reign, and a purer fellowship, when Christ shall have subdued all things to himself, and the universal song shall be : " O LORD our Lord, how excellent is thy name in all the earth ! " (Ps. viii.).

4

DEVOTIONAL AND PROPHETIC
VIEW OF THE CREATION, BEING AN APPENDIX TO
THE TWO PRECEDING PAPERS

Psalm 104

T HIS psalm is, as I understand it, a meditation on the work of creation, and on the earth as it came from its Maker's hands, and as it may once again appear, when he renews its face. It may be used without violence as a devotional accompaniment to the historical record in the beginning of Genesis. It may fill our hearts and mouths with praise, as we dwell on the wondrous details of that first manifestation of the glory of God ; while it carries forward our glowing hopes to still more illustrious manifestations of the same glory yet to come.

When and by whom it was composed, is altogether uncertain. Some have argued, from the entire absence of any allusion to Jewish rites, or to events in Jewish history, that it must be a patriarchal song of praise, indited before Israel came out of Egypt, and received the law in the wilderness. Others again—so contradictory and conjectural is the judgment of interpreters,—and these, too, men of unrivalled learning and sagacity, have recognised in this psalm, and particularly in its opening description, so unequivocal a series of allusions to the Tabernacle service, the priestly costume, and the Shechinah glory in the holy place, as to fix its date, beyond question, under the dispensation of Sinai.

The explanation, probably, is, that God's discovery of himself in the redemption from Egypt, and his discovery of himself in the creation of the world, are not so different as might be supposed. He who discovers himself in both instances is the same,—the

Eternal Word,—the Son,—whose dwelling is in the bosom of the Father, and whose office it is to declare the Father (John i. 18). And his manner of discovering himself, and declaring the Father, is not apt to change. When he comes forth from the Father, on whatever occasion, and for whatever work, he appears as " the brightness of the Father's glory." Hence, we may expect a close analogy,—or rather an exact identity,—among all the manifestations of the Godhead, in the person of the only begotten of the Father. First of all, at the creation of the world ; next, at the gate of paradise, after the fall ; afterwards, in fellowship with Abraham and the patriarchs ; and then again, and anew, in the Jewish economy and worship ;—subsequently, also, in the days of his flesh, when, even as he dwelt in a lowly tabernacle of humanity among men, his glory was beheld on the Mount of Transfiguration ;—then, in his ascension to heaven, and his appearances to the martyr Stephen and the persecuting Saul ;—once more, in his second advent, when he is to come in his own glory, and the glory of his Father, and of the holy angels ;—and, finally, in his eternal sojourn on earth, when the tabernacle of God is to be with man, and the Lord is to be with his people for ever ;—on all these occasions it is the same blessed Jehovah who comes forth, and in the same state and style.

In the very first utterance of praise with which this psalm opens, the devout worshipper hails his triumphant King,—" Bless the Lord, O my soul. O Lord, my God, thou art very great ; thou art clothed with honour and majesty" (ver. 1). Have we not here the believer welcoming his expected Lord ? The loyal subject bursts forth into admiring strains of joy, as he beholds his Sovereign and Saviour, long hidden, but now at last revealed in his glory. Especially, if we connect this psalm with that which precedes it,—as the singular coincidence of the one in its close, and the other in its commencement, " Bless the Lord, O my soul," would lead us to do,—we cannot fail to recognise the real scene of this magnificent ode as laid in the latter days upon the earth.

That psalm—the hundred and third—most pathetically describes the dispensation of grace under which we are now placed. In it the believer gratefully recounts all the Lord's benefits of which he is already made a partaker—the pardon of sin—the healing of his nature's disease—his redemption from wrath—his possession of the Lord's crowning favour and love—his contented satisfaction with the portion allotted to him—and the renewal of his youth day by day (Ps. ciii. 3-5). Further, he expresses his confidence in the Lord's providential government of the world (ver. 6-14). He appeals to the experience of God's rule over Israel (ver. 7); and he specially describes the nature of the Divine administration, and the principles which regulate the present dealings of God with the children of men;—these principles being substantially two,—that of long-suffering patience toward all (ver. 8, 9), and that of special and distinguishing grace towards his people (ver. 10). This grace, in its source and manner, is as far above their desert, or even their comprehension, as the heaven is above the earth (ver. 11). In its result or effect it fully and freely justifies the sinner,—making as complete a separation between him and his guilt, as there is between the rising and the setting sun (ver. 12). And moreover, in its continual exercise, it goes forth in movements of tenderest sympathy and concern, as the grace of one who is touched with the feeling of man's infirmity (ver. 13, 14). Such grace, thus tender and sympathising, is peculiarly needed; since, even in his best estate, man is altogether vanity (ver. 15, 16). Even the believer, calling upon his soul to bless the Lord for the inestimable present benefits of grace and salvation, groans under his subjection to vanity and death (Rom. viii. 23). But he comforts himself; first, with the general assurance, that the Lord is faithful and true,—that he is the same yesterday, to-day, and for ever (ver. 17, 18); and then, more particularly, with the anticipation of the Lord's future and glorious kingdom (ver. 19).

Here is the salvation by hope, of which Paul speaks (Rom. viii. 24). The believer, out of the very depths of his depression,—groaning within himself by reason of vanity,—sees the coming glory. " The Lord hath prepared his throne in the heavens." Shall we say that, being already prepared in the heavens, that throne is soon to be revealed as coming down to this earth ? It is the throne of God and of the Lamb. For it is of the Lamb that it is said, that his " kingdom ruleth over all" (ver. 19 ; see also Rev. xvii. 14, and xxii. 3).

And what means the sudden and abrupt strain of triumph with

which the psalm concludes ? (ver. 20-22). Why are the angels summoned—the hosts of the Lord—and his ministers that do his pleasure ? What is this solemn and sublime occasion, on which all his works, in all places of his dominion, are so loudly, and as it were, impatiently called to bless him ? Whence this hallelujah, this emphatic benediction of thine, O soul ! but now lost in the complaint that we are all dust ?—" Bless the Lord, O my soul ! " What is the event on account of which thou hast summoned the whole creation of God to join with thee, in so exultingly praising and blessing the Lord ?

Shall we say that it is the renewed earth—the new heavens and the new earth—the earth fresh once more from the Creator's hand ; —as on the day when first the morning stars sang together, and all the sons of God shouted aloud for joy, " and the Lord saw all that he had made, and behold it was very good ? "

Let the hundred and fourth psalm be the reply. Observe how, in its opening doxology, it takes up the dying strain of its predecessor,—seizes the very note which closed the preceding song,— and ere its echo has melted away in silence, strikes, on the same key, a new and kindred anthem of praise ! " Bless the Lord, O my soul ! "—so ends the one psalm. Yes,—" Bless the Lord, O my soul ! "—so begins the other. It is plainly a continuation,—a renewal,—a resuming of the same theme. It is the believer welcoming his Lord ; the rapt and meditative saint, in prophetic imagination, as if already risen, meeting the returning Saviour. And with what wonder and adoring rapture is he filled ! " O Lord, my God, thou art very great ; thou art clothed with honour and majesty ! " He sees the Lord as he is. He beholds the King in his glory. " O Lord, how great art thou ! "

Such being the opening of this psalm, its whole scheme and structure is in accordance with its commencement. It is a manifestation of the glory of God in creation ;—first, in that original creation of this earth for which the Eternal Word came forth from the bosom of the Father ;—and subsequently again, in that new creation with a view to which we look for his coming forth yet once more. Hence the description turns upon that first work of creating power, as the type and shadow of the other. It represents the earth, hitherto without form, void of being, and shrouded in thick darkness,—changed into the garden of the Lord, by the introduction successively of light and order, as subservient to life.

I. LIGHT breaks in on the thick gloom of the chaotic waters. And here, as in Genesis, it is the glorious Creator himself who is the LIGHT. "Thou coverest thyself with light as with a garment" (ver. 2). "God said,"—his WORD went forth ;—not a dead utterance, but his WORD ;—and in the WORD " was life, and the life was the light of men." Hence, when " God said, let there be light,"— when his living Word, whose life is light, went forth,—"there was light."

It is, therefore, at the first, the Light of life that dispels the darkness,—consisting, not in rays emanating from material luminaries, which as yet pierced not the dim vapour that enveloped the earth,— but in the presence of the Creator himself. It is such light as is to shine in that day of which Isaiah speaks, when he describes the earth reeling to and fro like a drunkard, and being removed like a cottage, and the Lord punishing the host of the high ones,—and thereafter adds :—" The moon shall be confounded, and the sun ashamed, because the Lord of Hosts shall reign in mount Zion, and in Jerusalem, and before his ancients gloriously" (Isa. xxiv. 23 ; see also Isa. xvi. 19 ; and Rev. xxi. 23). Thus, when the Word goes forth in creation, there is light ;—" Thou coverest thyself with light as with a garment."

II. By the same direct and immediate agency of the creating Word, ORDER, as well as LIGHT, is introduced. He is himself the ORDER, as he is the LIGHT, of the world. His very presence implies a right arrangement and adjustment of the elements of nature, hitherto blended and confounded in one watery mass of vapour.

1. This watery chaos must be reduced to order. There must be a separation between the upper material heaven and this lower earth ; and on the earth itself, between the sea and the dry land. " The heaven, even the heavens, are the Lord's, but the earth hath he given to the children of men" (Ps. cxv. 16). Hence, at his presence, the heavens must be set in order, as it were, for himself, and the earth for the habitation of man.

The Lord appears in royal state, with a retinue of attendant angels and ministering spirits innumerable ; and he and his train must have fit accommodation. A palace, a temple, or at least a tabernacle, must be prepared for him. For this end, the azure sky, with its many-coloured drapery of clouds, is formed above the firmament, hanging upon the expansive air, by which the vapours above are divided from the denser waters below. The " heavens,"—the visible arching canopy over our heads,—God " stretcheth out like a curtain,"—making, as it were, his dwelling there ; as afterwards he dwelt in the bright pillar of cloud, and in the curtained tent in the wilderness (ver. 2). He has his " chambers" there, with their " beams laid in the waters,"—the waters above the firmament,—the cloudy vapours which seem to hide his glory, as in the recess of the holy place, within the vail (ver. 3). Nor does he want the means and instruments of motion when he would arise, he and the ark of his strength. He has " a chariot" in the drifting and swift-driving " clouds ;" and the fleet " winds " are his winged coursers, on which he " walketh" and flieth all abroad (ver. 3). His attendants also are provided for and accommodated in his train. " His angels " are in the " spirits," or breezes as they blow. " His ministering servants" are in the lightning's winged " fire " (ver. 4).

Thus the Lord, covering himself with light as with a garment, uses the upper firmament or heaven, with all its constituent parts, as his own. He retains it in his own hands, and all its elements he reserves under his own immediate control : " fire and hail, snow and vapour, stormy wind, fulfilling his word " (Ps. cxlviii. 8). These are not given to man to be controlled or managed by him : the Lord and his angels are ever in the midst of them.

Hence the solemn awe with which a devout spirit may well contemplate the sublime expanse above. He need not be ashamed to tremble when the fierce war of the elemental storm is raging. He sees and feels a present God, and he may think of the day when, in some way even such as this, the Lord shall come with innumerable spirits, to judge, to consume, and yet again to renew the earth.

The heaven above being thus prepared as God's throne, the earth is ordered as his footstool : its " foundations" are " laid, that it should not be removed for ever" (ver. 5). And it is fashioned as a dwelling-place for his creatures (ver. 6-13). The waters under the heaven are gathered into one place, and the dry land appears. " The deep," which covered " the earth as a garment," and whose " waters stood above the mountains," hastens, at God's " voice of thunder," to its appointed " place " (ver. 6, 7). Then is seen the graceful alternation of hill and dale,—the lofty mountain and the deep-drawn secluded valley (ver. 8, *marginal reading*) ; and the sea occupies its proper bed, its " bounded " channels, leaving the earth free from its " returning " tide (ver. 9).

This also is the Lord's doing. It is he alone who can limit ocean's wide flow, and keep its proud waves in check. In vain shall the conqueror of an earthly kingdom, at the bidding of his crowd of flatterers, presume to arrest its swelling flood. It is the arm of God alone that controls it. And to prove that it is so,—to mock the scoffers who reckon on the stability of nature, and say all things continue as they were from the beginning of the creation,—to show that by his word alone the earth is kept standing out of the water and in the water,—the world is suddenly, by the Lord's visitation for sin, overflowed with water until it perishes ; as, for the same cause, it is once again to be destroyed by the fire,—unto which, by the same word, it is kept in store and reserved (2 Pet. iii. 7).

But not only is the dry land separated from the waters of the sea,—these waters are now themselves made subservient to its further preparation for the habitation of life. Not now rushing over it in an overflowing flood, but distilling gently in " springs," and rivulets, and streams, amidst the " valleys and hills " (ver. 10), and descending softly, in refreshing dews and fertilising showers, from the vapoury " chambers " of the heavens (ver. 13) ; they fit the earth for the abode of the " beasts of the field, and the wild asses " of the desert, and the winged songsters that make all the air melodious (ver. 11, 12) ; so that being now ready to be given to man, " the earth is satisfied with the fruit of the Lord's works " (ver. 13). Thus the first stage in the introduction of order is completed.

2. The dry land, however, though now separated from the waters which once overflowed it, and refreshed by the streams amid the hills and the rain from heaven, needs yet a further process of arrangement. Vegetation must be imparted to it (Gen. i. 11, 12).

Accordingly, " grass and herb, for food " (ver. 14)—" wine, oil, and bread " (ver. 15)—" trees of the Lord, full of sap,"—" cedars of Lebanon, where the birds may nestle,"—" fir-trees for the stork ;" —and even in the " high hills " and the bare and rugged " rocks," some coarse and scanty produce which may suffice for the adventurous " goat " and the timid " cony ;"—all the seeds of vegetable nature, whether in the luxuriance of Carmel's plain and Lebanon's forest, or in the desolation of the rugged and dreary wilderness,— all are stored in the bounteous bosom of mother earth, and all for her children's nourishment. Such is the second part of this process of adjustment.

3. One other arrangement remains to be made. The light which burst all abroad, wide-spread and unconfined, on the first coming forth of the living and creating WORD,—while, as yet, no rays from any luminary in the upper sphere could penetrate the darkness of the chaotic waters,—is now stored up in the heavenly bodies, and ordinarily the earth is to be indebted to them for this blessing (Gen. i. 14-18). This method of illumination is turned to account for the distinction of seasons on the earth,—and especially, for perpetuating the grateful vicissitude of day and night, already instituted by God himself, that the period of toil might sweetly alternate with the welcome season of balmy sleep (ver. 19-23). And here, by a marvellous economy, provision would seem to be made, even for the violence with which, by reason of sin, earth for a time is filled. For while the " roaring " and ravenous " beasts " find night their congenial time for roaming, and shun the cheerful light of the sun ;—" man," on the contrary, " goeth forth unto his work, and to his labour, until the evening."

Thus the entire ordering of the heavens and the earth is finished ; and the devout soul comes to a solemn pause of wonder, admiration, gratitude, and joy,—" O Lord, how manifold are thy works ! in wisdom hast thou made them all ; the earth is full of thy riches " (ver. 24). The earth thus illuminated and arranged, having received light and order, is full of God's riches,—richly furnished for the dwelling-place of man and of beast. Nay, the very sea itself, although it might seem to have been cast off by the emerging earth as but a worn-out covering and burdensome encumbrance, which had been serviceable in the dark and cold night of chaos, but of which, as the cheering beams of heavenly light broke in, it was glad to get rid—even " this great and wide sea," so far from being thrown aside, at least in the meanwhile,—for is there not a time coming when " there shall be no more sea ?" (Rev. xxi. 1)—is found to teem with manifold wonders of creating wisdom. " The earth is full of thy riches. So is this great and wide sea." Countless myriads of living creatures, forming part of man's system or economy, harbour in its depths, and swarm amid its shallows (ver. 25). Its surface is sub-servient to the use of man, as it wafts on its wide bosom the busy agents of commerce, the eager votaries of science, discovery and adventure, the ministers of philanthropy, the messengers of salvation, heralds to all nations of the tidings of great joy ;—thus uniting distant lands in one holy brotherhood, and equalising God's benefits over all the earth—" There go the ships " (ver. 26). While in its vast unfathomed caves, far out of the reach of man, whom he might destroy, sports that monster, whatever it may be, which GOD hath formed, and God alone can control—meet type of the great enemy whom God at last is so signally and terribly to punish—" There is that leviathan whom thou hast made to play therein " (ver. 26. See Job xli. and Isaiah xxvii. 1).

III. The light and the order introduced into the earth are sub-servient to the life with which it is to be stored. The fishes, accord-ingly, the fowls, and the beasts of the field,—all the animals with which man is conversant, and over which he has dominion,—with MAN himself, laborious man, the lord of all, have passed in review before the devout soul in this psalm. The whole glorious work of creation is at an end.

The Sabbatic rest of God succeeds (ver. 27, 28). He rests from creating ; he rests that he may bless the creatures which he hath made. " These all," the creatures made by thee, now " wait upon thee." They are still dependent upon thee. The Creator has not withdrawn from the world which he hath formed into the mysterious seclusion of absolute repose, leaving it as a machine to go on of itself. " My Father," says the blessed Jesus, " worketh hitherto," even during his Sabbath of rest, " and I work." There is rest, inasmuch as he ceases from creating. There is continual work still, inasmuch as he never ceases to watch over, and preserve, and bless his creatures. His Sabbath, so far from precluding, as the Jews imagined, even the doing of good, may consist in that very labour. The Lord rejoices in the rest of a holy complacency over the works of his hands. But he continually works in caring for their well-being. Such also,—analogous and corresponding to the Sabbath of the Creator,—is the Sabbath of the creature. It consists in fellowship with the rest of holy complacency into which the Creator entered ; and in caring, as he does, and working, if need be, for the saving of life, and the doing of good (Mark iii. 4 ; John v. 17).

And now, what a scene is here presented to the eye of the worshipper in this psalm ! God is present before him in his glory, in the glory in which he came forth to this world, when light began to be—the glory in which he reposed, when he saw everything that he had made, and behold it was very good. What a bright and glowing picture,—God dwelling with his creatures,—all of them waiting upon him, " gathering " his manifold " gifts," and " filled with the good " that flows from his " open hand ! " (ver. 27, 28).

But, alas, a change comes over the landscape. There is a blight in this seemingly serene atmosphere—a curse on this smiling earth. " The creation is made subject to vanity. It groaneth and travaileth together in pain." There is sin, and death by sin, and a character of weary and bitter vanity is stamped on all things here below (ver. 29. See Rom. viii. 20).

Thus, too often, as one may have felt it, when the eye is filled with the glory of some gorgeous scene of autumnal riches, spread out in the plain beneath our feet ; and the ear is charmed with the exuberant melody of a thousand blended voices in the surrounding groves, and in the sky, high over head ; when all the air, on every side, breathes a balmy peace, and no sights anywhere appear save only sights of rural innocence and beauty, of quiet life and love ; when the soul is wrapt in a silent ecstasy of unspeakable joy—ah, may not the memory suddenly come over us of some recent and kindred deathbed, or some desolate abode of famine, or some careworn face of woe ! How, in a moment, is the spell broken—the charm dissolved—the glory and the loveliness all melted away ! Yes, surely the earth is cursed for man's sake (Gen. iii. 18) ; the whole creation is made subject to vanity. And " as for man, his days are as grass : as a flower of the field, so he flourisheth. For the wind passeth over it, and it is gone, and the place thereof shall know it no more" (Ps. ciii. 15, 16). Sin has wrought sad havoc and ruin. It has caused the Lord " to hide his face ;" and trouble and decay, vanity and vexation of spirit, change and death and the dreary grave, await all the dwellers on the earth. " Even they who have received the first fruits of the Spirit do still groan within themselves" (Rom. viii. 23).

But they " wait for the manifestation of the sons of God" (Rom. viii. 19). They "wait for the adoption, to wit, the redemption of the body" (Rom. viii. 23). And the subjection of the creature to vanity, is " in hope" (Rom. viii. 18, 19) ; "because the creature itself also shall be delivered from the bondage of corruption into the glorious liberty of the sons of God."

At present the sons of God are hidden : they are his hidden ones. High as is their rank and marvellous the love of which they are the objects, sealed as they are with the Holy Spirit, the first-fruits of their inheritance, the world knoweth them not, even as it knew Him not (1 John iii. 1). "Their life is now hid with Christ in God ; but when he who is their life shall appear, they also shall appear with him in glory" (Col. iii. 4). It is for this manifestation, this public appearance, this open acknowledgment of the sons of God, that the earnest expectation of the creature waiteth ; and into their glorious liberty the creature itself also shall be delivered.

Is not this that new creation of this lower world, which is to fit it for being the home of the Lord's redeemed ? The present groans of creation are the pangs of its coming regeneration. It is to come forth again from the hand of the Great Creator, fashioned gloriously anew ;—even as the sons of God, for whose manifestation it waiteth, and into whose liberty it is to be delivered, are to have " their vile bodies fashioned like unto His glorious body, according to the working whereby he is able even to subdue all things unto himself " (Phil. iii. 21). In the words of the psalm (ver. 30), " He sendeth forth his Spirit,"—the Spirit which moved on the waters of old,—and there

is again a new " creation." He " reneweth the face of the earth."
Once more it is such as he can pronounce to be very good ; for it is
the new earth "wherein dwelleth righteousness." " The glory of the
Lord shall endure for ever ; the Lord shall rejoice in his works "
(ver. 31).

Such is the certainty of this renewal of the earth. It is bound
up with the Lord's glory enduring for ever, and with his rejoicing in
his works. As surely as his glory must endure for ever, and he must
rejoice in his works, so surely must he send forth his Spirit, and
renew the face of the earth.

Nor is the manner of this renewal concealed from us. The earth
is shaken, the hills are set on fire, at the sight and touch of the Lord
coming in judgment (ver. 32). There is a repetition of the scene
with which the original creation opened ; but with an incalculable
increase of glory, the glory of redeeming grace and love being superadded to the glory of creating power. " The Son of man cometh in
the clouds,"—" making the clouds his chariot,"—"in his own glory,"
the glory that is peculiar to him, as the only begotten of the Father,
God manifest in the flesh, the Lamb slain for his people, the King
and Head of his redeemed : in this glory, which is his own, he cometh,
as well as " in the glory of his Father, and of the holy angels" (Luke
ix. 26). At his appearance, "the earth trembleth, and the mountains
smoke." There is a dissolution of the elements of nature. The great
globe itself is convulsed and burnt up with fire. But the issue is
glorious and blessed. It is such as to call forth a new and more
rapturous song of praise (ver. 33, 34) ; as the believing soul, rejoicing
in the resurrection of the body and the renewal of the face of the
earth, finds at last an abode of purity and peace, where before it
experienced so much of the weariness and vanity of the flesh, and
groaned, being burdened. " I will sing unto the Lord as long as I
live : I will sing praise to my God while I have my being. My
meditation of him shall be sweet : I will be glad in the Lord."
Then the meek shall inherit the earth (Ps. xxxvii. 9, 11), when
" sinners are consumed out of it, and the wicked are in it no more"
(ver. 35). Now, while it is subject to vanity and filled with violence, the meek have often no refuge from their groanings but the
grave, where " the wicked cease from troubling and the weary are

at rest." But it shall not be always thus. This earth is too precious in God's sight to be wholly given over as reprobate. It is precious as the work of his hands, in which at first he rejoiced. And it is precious also as the scene of his Son's obedience, sufferings, and death, in which he delighteth still more. There is a place prepared for the devil and his angels, into which the ungodly shall be cast. But "the earth is the Lord's," and "the King of glory shall at last enter in" to possess it (Ps. xxiv.).

"The earth is the Lord's, and the fulness thereof; the world, and they that dwell therein" (Ps. xxiv. 1). He hath "given it" indeed "to the sons of men" (Ps. cxv. 16), and grievously have they abused the gift. But it is the Lord's still. He made it. He "founded it upon the seas, and established it upon the floods" (Ps. xxiv. 2). It is his, and he means to claim it as his. It sympathised in darkness with the agony of his cross; and by the earthquake and the opening of the graves, acknowledged his victory. Resuming it therefore out of the hands of those who have destroyed it, redeeming it and purifying it anew, he will himself "establish the mountain of his house in the top of the mountains, and exalt it above the hills" (Isa. ii. 2). "His tabernacle is to be with men" (Rev. xxi. 3).

"Who," then, "shall ascend into the hill of the Lord? and who shall stand in his holy place?" (Ps. xxiv. 3). A pertinent and pointed question. It is the one question, above all others, which, in these circumstances, is worthy of an answer. And what can the answer be? If the earth is the Lord's, and if his hill and his holy place are to be there, who can enter in or abide but those that are his—that are his fully, honestly, unreservedly? Uprightness, sincerity, truth in the inward parts, is the test or qualification. There must be single-eyed honesty in dealing with men, and in seeking the face of the God of Jacob (Ps. xxiv. 4-6). He alone can enter in "whose heart is fixed, who desires one thing of the Lord and seeks after it," with singleness of eye and unity of aim, "even that he may dwell in the house of the Lord all the days of his life, to behold the beauty of the Lord, and to inquire in his temple" (Ps. xxvii. 4). This is he who, being justified freely by the grace of God, receiving a perfect righteousness and rejoicing in a perfect reconciliation—moved by the Spirit to lay aside all guile, and to enter directly and immediately into the favour and the service of God,—walks as one whose heart is right with God, and consequently, as to man, is in its right place. He is an Israelite indeed. He is one of the "meek," the "merciful," the "pure in heart," who are blessed, because they are to "inherit the earth, to obtain mercy, and to see God" (Matt. v. 5-8).

With such a train, the Lord is to claim the earth as his own. When all is ready, when the face of the earth is renewed, and sinners are consumed out of it, there is a shout heard as of a rushing multitude drawing near—the shout of those who have come with the Lord or met him in the air (1 Thess. iv. 16, 17). The earth is formally summoned to open "her gates, even her everlasting doors." There is an illustrious conqueror waiting to be admitted. He enters with his company of risen and changed saints (1 Cor. xv. 51). He is "the King of Glory !"—He who spoils principalities and powers, who subdues all things to himself, who wrests from death his sting, and from the grave his victory. He takes possession accordingly, as the King of Glory, of his ransomed and recovered earth. And the humble believer, who has shared the bitterness of his cross, rejoices in his crown. Exulting in the regeneration of this earth, and its consecration anew as the Lord's, he exclaims, in an ecstasy of uncontrollable joy, " Bless thou the Lord, O my soul ! Praise ye the Lord" (Ps. civ. 35).

5

THE FIRST TEMPTATION—
ITS SUBTLETY AS IMPEACHING THE GOODNESS, JUSTICE, AND HOLINESS OF GOD

Genesis 3:1-5

But I fear lest by any means, as the serpent beguiled Eve through his
subtlety, so your minds should be corrupted from the simplicity that
is in Christ.   2 Corinthians 11:3

THE agent in the temptation is undoubtedly not a mere
serpent, but an evil spirit under the form of a serpent.   He
possesses and abuses the powers of reason and speech.   The
serpent was probably by nature more subtle than any beast of
the field; and on that account this form may have been
selected by the tempter.   But that there was here present one
more subtle still, is plainly to be inferred, from the repeated
allusions to this history in other parts of the Bible.   Thus
Job speaks of the "crooked serpent" being made by God's
hand (chap. xxvi. 13).   Isaiah foretells the punishment of
"leviathan, the piercing serpent—even leviathan, that crooked
serpent" (chap. xxvii. 1).   And in the Revelation, we read of
"the great dragon being cast out, that old serpent, called the
devil and Satan, which deceiveth the whole world;" and
again, of "the dragon, that old serpent which is the devil and
Satan, being bound a thousand years" (Rev. xii. 9, and xx. 2).
All these expressions plainly indicate, that the great spiritual
adversary of our race;—the Devil, or the calumniator, traducer,
and libeller; Satan or the enemy; takes one of his titles at

least from the sad transaction in which, under the form of a serpent, he had so memorable a share.

Various questions are here raised. Had the serpent originally the same reptile and grovelling form which he has now? Or is that form the just result and punishment of his instrumentality in this work of the Devil? How did he communicate with Eve, so as to suggest thoughts to her mind? Why does Moses give no direct notice of the real nature of this transaction, so as explicitly to reveal the actual character of the tempter?

The same remark applies here which I made in regard to the doctrine of the Trinity. The written word was not the commencement of a revelation concerning God and the spiritual world. It was addressed to men who had already heard of these things. We should expect, therefore, that whatever information the Scriptures give on the great primary facts of religion,—such as the existence of God, and of spirits good and evil,—would be given rather indirectly, in the way of taking them for granted, than directly, in the way of positive announcement. That it is so, may be regarded as strong internal evidence of the divine authority of this book ; while as to the doctrines themselves, it is the most satisfactory of all kinds of proof to find them thus all along, and all throughout, incidentally and undesignedly assumed ; rather than formally, as if for the first time, revealed and taught.

In the present case, the historian relates the scene of the temptation just as it might pass before the senses ; leaving us to gather from it, as if we had ourselves been eye-witnesses, its true nature, meaning, and consequences. That the transaction, however, was real, cannot be doubted by any who consider fairly what Christ says of the author of it,—" he was a murderer from the beginning, and abode not in the truth " (John viii. 44) ; and how Paul speaks of his victims, as " beguiled by the serpent, through his subtlety " (2 Cor. xi. 3).

The art of this temptation is very much the same as that

which still prevails over men in whom there is " an evil heart of unbelief in departing from the living God " (Heb. iii. 12). It is by arguments of unbelief that the wily fiend solicits to sin.

I. Thus, first, he insinuates doubts regarding the equity and goodness of God :—" Yea, hath God said, Ye shall not eat of every tree of the garden ?" (ver. 1). Can it be ? Has he really subjected you to so unreasonable a restraint ? And the insinuation takes effect. Suspicion begins to rankle in the woman's breast. In her very manner of citing the terms of the covenant, she shows that she is dwelling more on the single restriction, than on all the munificence of the general grant. In the Lord's first announcement of it, the main stress is laid upon the grant. It is expressed with a studied prodigality of emphasis ; " of every tree of the garden thou mayest freely eat." And the single limitation is but slightly, though solemnly, noted ; " but of the tree of the knowledge of good and evil, thou shalt not eat of it." The woman, however, drinking in the miserable poison of suspicion which the serpent has instilled, reverses this mode of speaking. How disparagingly does she notice the fulness and freeness of the gift ;—" we may eat of the fruit of the trees of the garden !" That is all the acknowledgment she makes ; and there is no cordiality in it. It is not " every tree," nor, " we may freely eat ;" but, " we may eat of the fruit of the trees ;" —as if the permission were grudgingly given ;—and as if it were altogether a matter of course, and even less almost than her right. On the other hand, she dwells upon the prohibition, amplifying it and magnifying it as an intolerable hardship ;—" but of the fruit of the tree which is in the midst of the garden, God hath said, Ye shall not eat of it, neither shall ye touch it " (ii. 16, 17 ; iii. 2, 3).

Is not this the very spirit of Jonah, to whom it was nothing that Nineveh was given him as the reward of his

faithful preaching, if the gourd that refreshed him was removed? Is it not the temper of Haman, who, amid all the
riches and splendour of court favour, cried out in bitterness of
soul;—"All this availeth me nothing, so long as I see Mordecai the Jew sitting at the king's gate?"

II. Then, again, secondly, the tempter suggests doubts
about the righteousness and truth of God as lawgiver and
judge: "Ye shall not surely die." For this he finds the
woman already more than half prepared. She very faintly
and inadequately quotes the threat. She cites God as saying,
not "in the day that thou eatest thereof, thou shalt surely
die," but far more vaguely,—"lest ye die" (ii. 17; iii. 3).
The same feeling of lust after the forbidden thing which made
her exaggerate the severity of the prohibition, tempted her to
extenuate the danger of transgression. Of this tendency,
Satan knows how to avail himself. You are right in your
half-formed surmises; you may venture to take the risk;
there cannot really be much sin and danger in so harmless an
act; "ye shall not surely die" (ver. 4).

III. For, thirdly, he has a plausible reason to justify
doubt and unbelief on that point. It cannot be that ye shall
be so harshly dealt with, "for God doth know that in the day
ye eat thereof, then your eyes shall be opened, and ye shall be
as gods, knowing good and evil" (ver. 5).

There is great difficulty in conceiving the exact meaning
of this assurance of the tempter, or the precise expectation
or desire it was fitted to excite in the minds of our first
parents. It may be observed, however, that the temptation
throughout is well adapted to the two parts of the constitution
of man, the will and the understanding. Satan proposes to
the will more freedom, and to the understanding more knowledge, than God saw fit at first to grant. Has God imposed a
restraint upon your will, or your freedom of choice?—that is
his first suggestion. He cannot surely mean to make the increase of your knowledge fatal;—that is his last.

But what increase of knowledge was the eating of the tree to give?

In reply, let us ask, what did our first parents previously know upon this subject of good and evil? In the first place, they knew good,—both the doing of good, and the receiving of good,—both obedience, and as the fruit of it, happiness. Again, secondly,—they knew the possibility of evil, by the prohibition of an act and the intimation of a penalty. But, thirdly,—evil itself they did not know, having no personal experience of either the doing or the suffering of it. This additional knowledge Satan promises ; and he argues that it cannot possibly destroy them, since it is analogous and similar to that of the living God himself.

Nor is it Satan alone who represents the matter in this light, else it might be set down as one of his lies. The Lord God (ver. 22) speaks in the same way ; "the man is become as one of us, to know good and evil." Some, indeed, regard these words as spoken in severe irony or sarcasm ; others consider them as stating, not what man actually became, but what he sought to become. In their plain meaning, however, they convey a far more serious and awful impression. Man, when he would be wise, intruded into the province of Deity. He aspired and attained to a kind of knowledge proper and safe to Deity alone ; it could not be merely the knowledge of the distinction between good and evil. That knowledge is the property of all moral intelligence, and man possessed it from the first. The mere presence of the tree, apart from the eating of it, gave knowledge, to that extent, of good and evil. Man thus knew the nature of good, and the possibility of evil. He sought to know more,—to know evil, not as a possibility merely, but as a reality,—not negatively, but positively,—not by symbol, but in fact,—by personal acquaintance and experience, by free and voluntary choice.

But how, in respect of this knowledge, should he be as

God? The utmost caution is needed here, but a thought may be hazarded. The Deity, in respect of his omnipresence and omniscience, being present everywhere and knowing everything, is intimately and personally cognizant of evil. Wheresoever evil is, there God is. He knows the evil—knows it by real and actual presence in the evil—is acquainted with it, more truly than the very doer of it, or the sufferer of it. And it is the prerogative and perfection of God to be thus ever present where evil is, intimately, personally, intelligently present,—thus to know it, and yet to be holy and to be blessed ; to know evil only to hate it. His uncreated infinite nature is not affected. He knows good and evil, and he lives evermore,—for he is the Holy One ; of purer eyes than to behold iniquity. Man, a created and imperfect being, would believe that he, too, might safely and with impunity know evil, as the Creator must needs know it, by intimate personal acquaintance with it ; that he might know evil without loving it, or at least without loving it too much ; without loving it, in the end, more than the Creator himself, knowing it as he does, must be willing to allow as excusable, and perhaps inevitable. Here lies the subtlety of this argument,—" Ye shall be as gods, knowing good and evil," as God does ; for you will contrive to persuade yourselves that he knows good and evil, just as you will do. You will be as God,—by making him out to be such an one as yourselves. So Satan, himself better informed, persuades man to believe ; that his holiness is as inviolable as his Maker's, or, which is the same thing, that his Maker's is as flexible as his ; that the acquaintance with evil which uncreated perfection alone can stand, created imperfection may with impunity covet.

This, then, was the order of the temptation : first, the goodness of God must be disbelieved ; secondly, his justice ; and lastly, his holiness. It begins with a rebellion of the will, or the heart, against the moral attributes of God, as the

Governor of his creatures. It ends in blindness of the understanding, or the mind, as to his essential perfections as the
infinite and eternal Creator. God ceases to be recognised as
good, and just, and holy. Man, at the suggestion of Satan,
would himself be as good, as just, as holy as God.

1. He sets up his own goodness against that of God.
Instead, of feeling, as the psalmist did, when he said, "Thou
art my Lord, my goodness extendeth not to thee" (Ps. xvi. 2),
or as the Lord Jesus intimates that a creature should feel
even if he had fulfilled all righteousness,—accounting himself
"an unprofitable servant, who had done only that which was
his duty to do" (Luke xvii. 10); instead of this,—instead of
thus magnifying the goodness of the Lord,—man begins to
presume upon his own. He suspects the Divine love; and
so far from being willing to receive his Maker's bounty as a
free and unmerited gift,—he claims it as a right, questions its
liberality, and resents any restriction upon it as a wrong.

2. In justice, also, he would cope with the Almighty; he
would be more righteous than God. He presumes to sit in
judgment on the sentence which the Judge of all the earth
denounces against transgression,—to arraign its equity, and
dispute its truth; and, instead of standing in awe at the
remembrance of what the Lord actually has said, in which
case he would not have sinned, he reckons on what, as he
thinks, ought to be the Lord's rule in dealing with him, and
so practically condemns him that is most just (Job xxxiv. 17).

3. Finally, he will not see why God should be more perfect, more pure, and more holy than himself; why it should
be more dangerous for him than for his Maker to touch what
is unholy, to know what is evil; why he should not be as
God; or, at all events, why God should not be as himself.
For if he cannot rise to the holiness of God, he will bring
down that holiness to his own level; confident that amid all
his acquaintance with the mystery of iniquity, he may contrive to retain at least as much holiness as the Creator, know-

ing it himself, can fairly require or expect in his frail and imperfect creature.

What infatuation is here! What guilt triple-dyed! What ungrateful pride! What presumption and profanity!—pride, in man's overweening estimate of his own worth, presumption in his daring defiance of God's righteous judgments, profanity in measuring himself by Jehovah, or Jehovah by himself, as if the high and holy God were such an one as he!

Such is the art of the first temptation. Such also is the art of Satan's temptation still.

He begins by insinuating distrust of the Lord's liberal and bountiful loving kindness, so that the soul frets and chafes under the wholesome restraints of duty, and, insensible to the free grant of all other trees, takes it amiss that one should be withheld. The badge of dependence, however slight in itself, irritates and provokes. The feeling of obligation is irksome. Man does not like to be reminded of the Lord's right over his own gifts; he longs to have and use them on another footing, as belonging wholly to himself, without restriction, and without control.

In such a mood of mind, Satan easily persuades his victim to call in question the reasonableness and the reality of God's righteous sentence of wrath: "Ye shall not surely die,"—*ye* who are so high in God's favour and, on the whole, so exemplary; one offence, or two, will not be reckoned against *you*. "Ye shall not *surely* die;"—there may, there must, be some way of escape at last. "Ye shall not surely *die*:" at the worst, some milder visitation will be held sufficient; it may be necessary, for propriety's sake and for the vindication of God's consistency, that some slight token of his displeasure should be inflicted upon you; but it would be strange and harsh severity were his terrible threatening to be executed to the letter,—were you, for such an offence, to be utterly destroyed.

To this sophistry, Satan the rather wins consent, because

he has another lie still in reserve. The offence itself cannot be so very heinous in God's sight as might be inferred from his strong denunciation of it, nor can he be so very holy as not at least to have some indulgence for it. He who knows so much evil, and knows it so intimately, cannot be so utterly intolerant of it, as in no circumstances, and to no extent, ever to look on sin, or suffer iniquity to dwell before him. He must be somewhat more like his creatures than this would imply,—more nearly such an one as they are,—having more sympathy with them, or, at all events, more allowance to make for them. He knows evil, so as at least to seem to connive at it. And if they know it, so as to go a little further, and consent to it, the difference cannot be so very material as to require that they should be held altogether without excuse.

Such unutterable blasphemy men, half unconsciously, take in from the calumnies which Satan scruples not to vent against the most high God. Thus, with his lies, perverting the whole character of God,—divesting it of all that is attractive in goodness, terrible in righteousness, and venerable and awful in the majesty of holiness ; and infusing into men's hearts, rankling suspicion, reckless defiance, and unshrinking familiarity with evil under the very eye of purity itself, as if that eye were nearly as indifferent to it as their own,—the devil leads captive those who listen to his wiles, promising them liberty : and persuading them that they may be, not merely subjects and children of God, but " as gods" themselves. And with these arts he continues to deceive them ; and as the god of this world, he blinds their unbelieving minds, until the light of the knowledge of the glory of God, in the face of Jesus Christ, shines into their hearts (2 Cor. iv. 6).

Then, indeed, the truth flashes on the startled conscience. I see God now, not as Satan would represent him, but as he really is. I see him in Christ. Behold how he loves sinners, when he gives his only begotten Son to the death for them, and with him also freely gives them all things. See how he judges and condemns the guilty, laying their guilt on the head of his Son, and exacting of him the penalty. Mark his infinite abhorrence of sin,—his absolute separation from all evil,—in the hiding of his face from his Holy One when he was made sin for us. Is this the God of whom I have entertained hard thoughts, as if he were austere and arbitrary,—with whose authority, at the same time, I have taken liberties, as if he never could execute his threatenings,—and to whom, above all, I have dared secretly to ascribe a degree of tolerance and complacency in looking upon evil, such as one like myself might feel? I awake as from a dream. How have I been deluded! I excused myself, by reflecting on him and on his law,—as if that law might turn out to be less pure, less strict, and less reasonable, than it professes to be. But "the law is holy, and the commandment holy, and just, and good." And what am I? A miserable sinner, without apology or excuse—I am undone. "Woe is unto me, for I have seen the King, the Lord of Hosts." "O wretched man that I am! who shall deliver me from the body of this death?"

"But I thank God, through Jesus Christ our Lord," in whom, at last, taught by the Spirit, and misled no longer by the Devil, I see and feel the free love, the strict justice, and the perfect holiness of my God,—reconciling me to himself in righteousness, and causing me, as I enter into the mind of Christ on the cross, to know evil, as Christ then did ; and with him, to die unto sin, that I may live unto God (Rom. vii. 12-25 ; Is. vi. 5-7).

This is "the simplicity that is in Christ," of which the apostle speaks (2 Cor. xi. 3), when he expresses his fear, lest the minds even of those espoused to Christ should be corrupted from that simplicity, "as the serpent beguiled Eve through his subtlety." It is the simplicity of faith, as opposed to the subtlety of unbelief : the simplicity of a little child, as opposed to the subtlety of a proud understanding and a perverse heart. And unquestionably there is continual need of godly jealousy for there is a strong bias or tendency, in the soul of every man, against simplicity, and in favour of subtlety. The Gospel itself is often felt to be too simple—too direct and straightforward ; it must be made more elaborate, more complicated and refined. The plan of reconciliation which God proposes is too plain, and comes too immediately to the point. Men would rather deal more circuitously with God, and have more ado made about their return to him, and a costlier and more cumbrous apparatus of means and conditions introduced. The simple truth and love of God, they pervert into a system of formal, or painful, self-righteousness. The doctrine of grace is no longer freely and unequivocally proclaimed, without embarrassment and without reserve. Awkward expedients are adopted to engraft on it precisely such notions and practices as might be suitable were God really such, after all, as Satan represents him to be,—a hard master,—and yet a weak and lenient judge. His grace is no longer free ; and the result is, that soon a system of penances and pardons is made to tamper with his righteousness ; and his holiness itself is found to admit of indulgence and compromise. But let us abide by the simplicity that is in Christ,—the simplicity which owns a sovereign authority in God's law, and a sovereign freeness in his salvation ; while, at the same time, it recognises the perfection of holiness in his nature, and rejoices, accordingly, in the "renewing of the Holy Ghost," as perfecting holiness in ours. Let us, thus saved by the free grace and sanctified by the free Spirit of God, stand fast in the holy liberty with which Christ has made us free ; not being entangled again with the yoke of bondage, nor suffering our minds to be corrupted from the simplicity that is in Christ, by such subtlety as that through which the serpent succeeded in beguiling Eve.

6

THE FRUIT OF THE FIRST SIN—THE REMEDIAL
SENTENCE

Genesis 3:6-21

He that committeth sin is of the devil ; for the devil sinneth from the
beginning. For this purpose the Son of God was manifested, that he
might destroy the works of the devil. 1 John 3:8

THE lust of the flesh, the lust of the eye, and the pride
of life, make up, in the estimate of the apostle John
(1 Epistle ii. 16), " all that is in the world,—which is not
of the Father, but of the world." These three carnal principles, the tempter successfully called into action, in the case of
our mother Eve. The lust of the flesh he excited by the
representation that " the tree was good for food," and that the
use of it should not have been withheld. The lust of the eye
was beguiled by the " pleasant look " of the tree,—under
which no danger or death could be supposed to lurk. The
pride of life appeared in the ambition which aspired to an
equality in knowledge or wisdom with God, and the self-confidence which presumed on the holiness of the creature being
as able to stand the contact and contamination of known evil,
as that of the Eternal Creator himself. " When the woman
saw that the tree was good for food, and that it was pleasant
to the eyes, and a tree to be desired to make one wise, she
took of the fruit thereof, and did eat, and gave also unto her
husband with her ; and he did eat " (ver. 6).

There is a question raised here, regarding the difference

between the woman's temptation and sin, and the man's. It is an idle question. The only scriptural ground for making any distinction is supposed to be found in the saying of the apostle, "Adam was not deceived, but the woman being deceived was in the transgression" (1 Tim. ii. 14). But the meaning there seems to be merely that the man was not the first to be deceived and transgress—that the woman took the lead in this guilty act,—not that their guilt ultimately was diverse. The impression naturally made by reading the narrative is, that Eve, in giving the fruit to Adam, repeated substantially the serpent's arguments, or at least used similar arguments herself, and that not till both had eaten were their eyes simultaneously opened. Certainly, in Scripture, Adam is represented as the party responsible for himself and his posterity (Rom. v. 12-21 ; 1 Cor. xv. 22-45). Hence, it has been supposed, not improbably, that it was with her husband's full knowledge and concurrence that Eve ate the fruit,—that they consulted together before eating, and sinned and fell together. Certainly they suffered together ; and together they obtained mercy.

The immediate effects of their act of disobedience were a sense of shame,—"the eyes of them both were opened, and they knew that they were naked" (ver. 7) ; and a dread of judgment,—"Adam and his wife hid themselves," through fear, as Adam afterwards admits—"I was afraid" (ver. 8, 10).

This was the fulfilment of the threatening—"Thou shalt surely die,—dying, thou shalt die." There was present death felt, and future death feared. Literally, therefore, on the very day of their eating they died. Their own hearts condemned them,—hence their shame ;—God they knew to be greater than their hearts,—hence their fear. Both their shame and their fear had respect undoubtedly to their bodies. They were ashamed of their bodily nakedness—they were afraid of bodily death. But the real cause of shame was not in their bodily

members, but in the guilt of their souls; and the real cause
of fear was not their liability, as creatures of the dust, to dissolution, but their liability, as immortal and spiritual beings,
to a far more awful doom. Their shame, therefore, and their
fear, prove that they really died; that having sinned, they in
that very day came under the guilt and the curse of sin,—the
guilt of sin, causing shame,—the curse of sin, causing fear.
Such is their instant knowledge of evil.

But this is not all. Shame and fear cause them to shrink
from God, and to hate his appearance—for now, "the carnal
mind is enmity against God" (Rom. viii. 7). They feel that
they have something to be concealed; and as they contrive to
cover their bodily nakedness from one another, so they would
fain hide their moral guilt from their Maker. They fly from
him whom they were wont to welcome—they seek a dark
lurking-place among the trees of the garden. There, however,
his hand finds them—they must meet their God;—" And the
Lord God called unto Adam, and said unto him, Where art
thou?" (ver. 9).

As shame and fear drive them away from God, so, when
they are brought into his presence, the same feelings still prevail, and prompt the last desperate expedient of deceit or
guile, marking the extent of their subjection to bondage,—the
bondage of corruption. They do not deny, but they palliate,
their sin. Ungenerously and ungratefully, as well as impiously,
Adam seems to charge, as the cause of his fault, God's best
gift to him: " The woman gave me of the tree." Nay, in an
indirect manner, he would even accuse God himself: " The
woman whom thou gavest me, she gave me of the tree." It
was thou who gavest me this woman, who has occasioned my
fall. Thus man, when tempted, is ready to say that he is
tempted of God (ver. 12; James i. 13). Eve, again, has her
apology also. She would cast the blame on the serpent:
" The serpent beguiled me, and I did eat " (ver. 13).

But both are without any real or valid excuse. Their sin

was wilful, committed against light and love ; in the face, too, of a warning from the God of truth, such as might have prepared them for Satan's lies. The attempt to extenuate their sin only proves how helplessly they are debased by it, as the slaves of a hard master, who, having them now at a disadvantage, through their forfeiture of the free favour of God, presses unrelentingly upon them, and compels them to be as false and unscrupulous as himself.

Shame, therefore, fear, and falsehood, are the bitter fruits of sin. Guilt is felt ; death is dreaded ; guile is practised. The consciousness of crime begets terror ; for "the wicked flee when no one pursueth." The sinner, no longer erect, bold, and true, before the open face of his God,—having that in him and about him which will not bear the light or stand in the judgment,—would bury himself out of view in obscure by-paths, and under a thick cloud of forest leaves.

How vain the attempt ; but how natural, when sin has darkened the mind ! We fancy that God sees us not, when it is only we that see not him ; we seek a shade or screen which may intercept our view of God, and feel as if it really intercepted also God's view of us ; and thus we are as self-confident in our ignorance or forgetfulness of God, as if it were he that was ignorant or forgetful of us. We resort to the trees of some garden,—the affairs or amusements of the world, the forms and ceremonies of religion, or its wordy technicalities, or its fervours and passions, or its busy activities ; nay, even the very means of grace themselves,—whatever, in short, may serve to fill a certain space, and bulk to a certain size, as a barrier between God and the heart that shrinks from too direct an approach to him. And we soothe ourselves with the notion that this hedge behind which we are sheltered serves the same purpose on God's side as on ours ; that he will not come nearer—with any narrower inspection or closer appeal—to us, than we are disposed to come to him. Then, when God does find us out,—when he calls us forth from our concealment,—when, breaking in upon our refuges of lies, our well-contrived retreats of worldly indifference or spiritual delusion, he summons us at once to meet him, personally, face to face ; when he convinces us of sin ; how apt are we to evade his charge and to excuse ourselves. To what miserable shifts and apologies have we recourse,—casting the blame on one another,—on God's kind bounty,—or on the tempter's urgency of solicitation ; when all the time we are conscious that the committing of the transgression was our own free choice,—that we did evil because we loved the doing of it.

How degrading is the bondage of sin ! How entirely does it destroy all honesty and honour, as well as purity and peace! The sinner, once yielding to the tempter, is at his mercy. And having lost his hold of the truth of God, he is but too glad, for his relief from despair, to believe and to plead the lies of the devil.

God, however, has a better way. He has thoughts of love towards the guilty parents of our race. For the sentence which he goes on to pronounce, when he has called them before him, is not such as they might have expected. It is not retributive, but remedial, and in all its parts it is fitted exactly to meet their case.

I. In the first place, their complaint against the serpent is instantly attended to. He is judged and condemned :—" And the Lord God said unto the serpent, Because thou hast done this, thou art cursed above all cattle, and above every beast of the field ; upon thy belly shalt thou go, and dust shalt thou eat all the days of thy life : and I will put enmity between thee and the woman, and between thy seed and her seed ; it shall bruise thy head, and thou shalt bruise his heel " (ver. 14, 15).

Though the language here employed is applicable literally to the serpent, as a mere beast of the field, doomed to a gro-velling life, and destined, from its venomous rancour, to be ever the object of man's more powerful resentment,—the sentence must have been intended and understood in another sense also. Thus, licking or eating the dust, is uniformly made a sign of the defeat and degradation or submission of the adversaries of God and of his people. It is said of Christ that "his enemies shall lick the dust,"—and of the nations that they "shall lick the dust like a serpent," for fear of him (Ps. lxxii. 9 ; Micah vii. 17). Of his church also it is said, that "kings and their queens, once her oppressors, shall lick the dust of her feet " (Is. xlix. 23). And of the great enemy himself, with reference to the period of his final overthrow, it is said that " dust shall be the serpent's meat " (Is. lxv. 25). Then, again, Satan is represented as about to be bruised under the feet of Christ's believing people, and that shortly, by the God of peace (Rom. xvi. 20). And the whole description of his desperate struggle in the last dispensation (Rev. xii. 7-17), is evidently a comment on the brief announcement in this passage of Genesis. The shout of triumph is heard in heaven:— " For the accuser of our brethren is cast down, which accused them before our God day and night. And they overcame him by the blood of the Lamb, and by the word of their testimony." But not without a bruising of the church's heel, is this final bruising of Satan's head accomplished. For it is added, "Woe to the inhabiters of the earth and of the sea ! for the devil is come down unto you, having great wrath, because he knoweth that he hath but a short time." There is a fierce persecution instigated by Satan, before his time is out. The victory, however, is not doubtful ; already his ruin is anticipated in the courts of the sanctuary above.

Thus, the sentence pronounced upon the serpent, as the instrument of the temptation, reaches its real author. Satan, flushed with victory, is to be discomfited by the very race over which he has triumphed. And their success over him, it is particularly intimated, is to be the result, not of artful and insidious guile, but of open warfare. The contest may be long, and he may gain partial conquests; but in the end the issue is sure.

How far the phrase, "the seed of the woman," as here used, should be limited to the Messiah personally, is not very clear. The prophet Micah probably refers to this first prediction. Foretelling that "out of Bethlehem-Ephratah he is to come forth, who is to be ruler in Israel, and whose goings forth have been from of old, from everlasting," he adds, that deliverance is not to be "until the time that she which travaileth hath brought forth;"—intimating that it is of "the seed of the woman" he has been speaking (Micah v. 2, 3). And the apostle's argument would seem to apply here: "He saith, not seeds, as if there were many, but one seed, which is Christ" (Gal. iii. 16). Undoubtedly it is Christ who is principally pointed out; though, at the same time, as the seed of the serpent may have a wider signification, denoting all of his party among men (Matt. iii. 7; John viii. 41); so, also, the seed of the woman may be held to mean all who take part with the Lord, and are one with him in his holy war. At all events, this condemnation of their tempter opened a door of hope to our race; his defeat could scarcely fail to imply their deliverance.

But, it may be asked, what means this indirect mode of conveying such an assurance of mercy? Why does God speak to the serpent, and not to our first parents themselves? May it not be partly to intimate that the main and chief end of God, in the dispensation of grace, is his own glory? "I do not this for your sakes," else I would address myself to you; "but for mine holy name's sake, which ye have profaned" (Ezek. xxxvi. 22, 23). It is not because they have deserved any thing at his hands, nor is it merely out of compassion to them, that he interferes. But it concerns his honour that the adversary should not triumph; for his own name's sake he must needs be glorified in the overthrow of the great enemy, who has apparently frustrated the chief end of his creation of the world. And does not this view render the assurance of mercy to our race even more strong and emphatic than if it were immediately given to themselves? It humbles our first parents, and us in them; and yet it encourages them and us. They blamed the serpent, and now the serpent is judged. They even charged God foolishly; as if it were his fault that the devil had beguiled them; and now they see that so far from God being, in any sense, accessory to their temptation, his glory is thereby so assailed that it can be vindicated only in the instant condemnation, and final destruction, of the tempter who has prevailed over them.

All this, however, will be better understood when it is seen, in the end of time, what is the purpose of God in first exposing our nature to trial at Satan's hand, and then making that very nature the instrument of Satan's more terrible ruin. Meantime it is plain that it is in part, at least, for the settlement of God's controversy with Satan, that our race and our world are spared; the fall and recovery of mankind being made subservient to the completion of God's purpose of wrath against a previous host of rebels, whose malignity was thus to be more fully brought out, that in their utter and eternal misery, God's righteous severity might be more signally glorified.

II. Having disposed of the serpent, the sentence proceeds, secondly, to deal with his victims more directly, and announces to both the woman and the man a period of prolonged existence on the earth. Their fear is, in so far, postponed. The woman is still to bear children,—the man is still to find food.

This prolonged existence is to be to Adam and his partner, as well as to their posterity, nothing more, in the meantime, than a dispensation of long-suffering. It is to be of the nature of a respite granted to criminals under sentence of death. But such a respite, in the case of sentenced felons, does not imply their exemption, during the interval of postponed retribution, from all tokens of their condemned state. On the contrary, they are all the time under prison discipline. And even though, in many instances, the respite may ultimately end in a free pardon, there are hardships inseparable from their intermediate position, and fitted to prepare them the better for their final deliverance. Hence the sentence, suspending generally the doom of death, has some drawbacks connected with it. 1. The woman is to live, and to be the mother of living children, being called Eve on that very account (ver. 20) ;—but she is to bring forth children in sorrow (ver. 16). 2. She is to be subject to her husband ; for such is the import of the phrase, " Unto him shall be thy desire, and he shall rule over thee " (ver. 16) ; it denotes the dependence of affection or of helplessness on the one hand, and the assertion of authority and power on the other. 3. The man, also, is to bear the punishment of sin (ver. 18) ; the earth, indeed, is not to refuse its return of food to his labour ; but that labour is to be with sweat of face and anxiety of heart, not light and joyous as it was before. And, 4. both he and his are to lie under the doom of vanity and mortality ; " for dust he is, and unto dust he must return " (ver. 17). This universal liability to death,—the constant memento and memorial of guilt,— planting a thorn in every pleasure and making love itself a source of pain, is the standing and too unquestionable evidence of the real nature of the sentence which spared mankind on the earth. It is a sentence suspending judgment, indeed, but still plainly indicating both the bitterness of sin, and the reality of wrath to come.

But let us thank God that the dispensation of free grace, to which the dispensation of long-suffering patience is subordinate and subservient,—for the sake of which, in fact, it is appointed,—makes special provision for alleviating these elements of suffering in man's present state. In the gospel there are promises of good, corresponding to the several conditions of severity under which the tenure of a prolonged season of mercy is granted; and by these promises, in the case of believers, the inevitable ills of life are soothed.

Thus, in the first place, over against the pain and sorrow of conception to which the woman is doomed, is to be set the promise, that, "although she was first in the transgression, nevertheless continuing in faith, and charity, and holiness, with sobriety, she shall be saved in child-bearing" (1 Tim. ii. 15). Again, secondly, to meet her case, as made subject to the man, she is invested with a new right to his full and reciprocal affection; husbands being adjured to love their wives even as Christ loves the church, which he has redeemed with his own blood (Eph. v. 25-33); the real explanation this, as I may observe in passing, of the marvellous influence of the gospel of Christ in restoring woman to her true place in society, and investing her, as wife and mother, with her best patent of nobility. Further, thirdly, although the earth is cursed for man's sake, and in all labour now there must be sweat and sorrow,—there is an assurance to believers, that if they cast their care on the Lord, he will care for them ; and if they seek first the kingdom of God and his righteousness, all those things" about which men are wont to be anxious, "shall be freely added unto them" (Matt. vi. 33). And finally, in the fourth place, the doom of mortality to which believers are still subjected, is relieved by the prospect of rest in their departure from this life, and of a glorious resurrection beyond the grave ; for " precious in the sight of the Lord is the death of his saints" (Ps. cxvi. 15); and it is their privilege to utter the undaunted challenge,—" O death, where is thy sting? O grave, where is thy victory? The sting of death is sin ; and the strength of sin is the law. But thanks be to God, which giveth us the victory through our Lord Jesus Christ " (1 Cor. xv. 55-57).

III. And now, Satan being put aside, who, as the father of lies, prompted guile,—and death being postponed, so as to give hope instead of fear,—the sentence goes on to provide for the removal of the shame which sin had caused :—" Unto Adam also and to his wife did the Lord God make coats of skins, and clothed them " (ver. 21). The animals whose skins were made into clothing could not be slain for food, for animal food was not yet allowed to man. In all likelihood they were slain in sacrifice. If so, it must have been by God's appointment. The covering of the nakedness of our first parents with the skins of these animals, represented the way in which sin is covered, by the imputed worthiness of the great Sacrifice,—the righteousness of the Lamb slain for its remission.

Thus the sentence is complete, as a remedial provision for the disorder introduced by the fall. Its last and crowning blessing depends upon the other two, and necessarily fits into them, and follows from them. Hence I have the greater confidence in drawing from a very brief, and apparently almost incidental intimation, a large spiritual inference. The fact of the Lord God clothing our first parents with coats of skin is shortly enough stated ; but the argument which it suggests for the divine appointment of animal sacrifices is strong and cogent.

The very fact that the Lord God himself " made," or ordained, this particular kind of clothing, is significant. It would scarcely have been necessary that he should thus interfere, had it been merely a contrivance for decency or comfort that was needed. In that matter, Adam and his wife might have been left to their own resources. When God concerns himself with the materials of their dress, something higher and holier must be intended. Does he care for the difference between a covering of fig-leaves and coats of skins ? No. But the skins have a spiritual meaning, arising out of the sacrificial use of the beasts to which they belonged. And as the clothing of skins is thus appointed by God, so also must be the sacrificial use of the victims furnishing the skins.

But besides this inference from the verse itself, its connection with the whole following history—in which the practice of animal sacrifices is manifestly taken for granted as having the sanction of God—suggests irresistibly the idea that the divine origin of the rite is here implied. And it is implied in the very manner in which we might expect it to be so,—in a writing addressed to men familiar with the subject. No Israelite living under the dispensation of Moses, when reading the account of God's clothing our first parents with skins, and afterwards accepting Abel's offering of a lamb, could have a moment's hesitation in concluding that, from the beginning, the sacrificial institute formed an essential part of the service which God required of fallen man.

It is interesting to observe the correspondence between the temptation to this first sin,—the result of it,—and the remedial sentence pronounced. This may be exhibited in a tabular form :

Temptations to Sin.	*Results of Sin.*	*Remedies (in the inverse order from the preceding).*
1. The pride of merit (1-3).	1. The shame of guilt (7).	1. Satan's condemnation, restoring to man the liberty of TRUTH (14, 15).
2. The presumption of security (4).	2. The fear of death (10).	2. God's dispensation of long-suffering, restoring HOPE (16-20).
3. The ambition of an equality with God (5).	3. The guile of bondage to Satan (12, 13).	3. God's provision of an atoning sacrifice and justifying righteousness, restoring CONFIDENCE OF FAITH (21).

The first element in the temptation was a sense of merit, disposing man to claim the divine bounty, as if it were his right, and to consider himself unfairly treated if any restriction were imposed upon it. Corresponding to this, the first consequence of the sin was a sense of shame—a feeling of nakedness. When he was tempted to sin, he disparaged the goodness of God and exaggerated his own ; when he had actually sinned, he shrank from God and was ashamed of himself.

The second element in the temptation was a sense of security,—giving him unwarrantable confidence in braving the Divine justice. And as the analogous counterpart, the second effect of the sin was a sense of danger,—causing him even to flee when none was pursuing.

The third element in the temptation was a sense of liberty ; defying control and asserting independence ; aspiring to the freedom of the Godhead. The third effect of the sin was the fitting sequel of that—a sense of bondage. Man knew evil, but not so as to retain superiority over it. He became the slave of the evil one. His tempter became his tyrant, exercised dominion over him, and constrained him to meet the accusations of his conscience and his God, by having recourse to the miserable shifts of servile cowardice and guile.

For these three melancholy fruits of sin the sentence provides appropriate remedies ; but they are applied in the reverse order. The last is first met. By victory gained over the evil power, his victims are delivered from his degrading thraldom, and are at liberty to appear again undisguisedly before the Holy One,—to lay aside all guile, and submit themselves unreservedly to God. Thereupon God, dealing with them himself, apart from all the claims and contrivances of Satan,—taking the whole matter of the sinner's standing before him into his own hands, and exercising his high and sovereign prerogative, —grants a respite from death. And in the third place, to complete his purpose of love, he provides for the covering of sin's nakedness and shame, and for the sinner's acceptance in his sight ; clothing him with a perfect righteousness, the righteousness of a full and finished work of vicarious obedience and expiatory blood.

Thus is the sinner rescued from Satan's wiles, and made free to meet his God, once more, without fear and without shame. And thus also is man,—redeemed man,—advanced ultimately to a higher point in the scale of intelligent and moral being, than unfallen man could ever have reached ; in as much as victory over evil transcends mere exemption from it. He has known evil, as well as good ; and through his very knowledge of the evil, he now knows the good all the more. The seed of the woman prevails,—not by withdrawing from the power of evil, or consenting to any compromise with it,— but by conquering it, through experience of its malignity, and endurance of its worst and last infliction. The seed of the serpent does his utmost ; but the seed of the woman passes through the fiery trial unhurt,—save only that his heel is bruised. This is all the mischief that the adversary can do,— even when allowed his fullest scope,—and he does it at the expense of his own head. For now the seed of the woman,— the serpent's seed being thus thoroughly baffled,—obtains a new grant of life on a new footing before God, and is invested with a new covering,—so that the shame of his nakedness may appear no more.

Behold here, O my soul, the travail of his soul, who is pre-eminently the Seed of the woman. He put himself in thy place, and encountered thine adversary. Satan, the prince of this world, came to him—to tempt—to try—to accuse and subdue him. But he had nothing in him (John xiv. 30, 31). He might indeed bruise his heel, but he could not touch a hair of his head. He met more than his match in the seed of the very woman whom he had beguiled. Jesus, in his utmost trial, when he knew evil as none but he—the HOLY ONE— could know it, in its stinging guilt and heavy curse, still triumphed over its power. And this same Seed of the woman has also won, by his laborious obedience, a new life for himself and his people. By the one sacrifice of himself, offered once for all to the Father, he has brought in an everlasting right- eousness, and perfected for ever all them that are sanctified.

Thus, to Jesus, the Seed of the woman, thou owest, O my guilty and enslaved soul, God's true liberty instead of Satan's lying bondage—prolonged life instead of instant death—and

instead of the shame of thine own nakedness the white
raiment of the worthiness of the Lamb that was slain.   Only
be thou united to Jesus as thy Saviour,—be one with him, as
the Seed of the woman,—and thou art partaker with him in
his victory—his life—his beauty.   Here indeed, in this
present world, thy salvation may not be complete.   In the
protracted struggle with Satan thou mayest receive many a
wound.   In thy labour there may be toil and sweat.   The
sense of thine infirmity, for thou art a child of the dust, may
cause thee sorrow ; and the sense of thy nakedness, for thou
art prone to sin, may cause thee shame.   Still be thou in
Christ ; abiding in him as the Seed of the woman and thy
Saviour ; and thou shalt have confidence and good hope
through grace.   Satan may wound thee, but only in thy heel.
His own head is bruised ; and he has no power over thee,—
no power to keep thee under condemnation,—no power to
keep thee under bondage,—no power to prevail against thee,
either as the accuser or as the oppressor.   Then, though thou
hast toil and travail, thou hast life too,—life in him who liveth
and was dead, and is alive for evermore.   Thou art among the
really living, of whom Eve is now become the mother.   And
finally, though the shame of thy nakedness often troubles thee,
thou hast always a covering provided for thee.   Thou art
arrayed in white robes, washed and made white in the blood
of the Lamb (Rev. viii. 13, 14).

7

THE FIRST FORM OF THE NEW DISPENSATION—THE CONTEST BEGUN BETWEEN GRACE AND NATURE

Genesis 3:22-4:15

PART FIRST

By faith, Abel offered unto God a more excellent sacrifice than Cain, by which he obtained witness that he was righteous, God testifying of his gifts ; and by it he, being dead, yet speaketh. Hebrews 11:14

THOUGH excluded from the garden of Eden, man is not sent to any great distance from it, and is not separated from all connection with it. He is indeed expelled ; and a reason is assigned for his expulsion of a very solemn and mysterious nature—" The Lord God said, Behold the man is become as one of us to know good and evil : and now, lest he put forth his hand, and take also of the tree of life, and eat, and live for ever ; therefore the Lord God sent him forth from the garden of Eden, to till the ground from whence he was taken " (chap. iii. 22, 23). The transaction is represented according to human usage. There is, as it were, deliberation in the heavenly court before the decree goes forth ; and the ground of it is stated, not ironically, as some suppose ; for the Lord, on this occasion, is full of pity ; but in gravest seriousness. By violating the condition of obedience, of which the one tree was the sacramental symbol, man has lost all title to the privilege of life, which the other tree sacramentally signified and sealed. His act of disobedience—with the knowledge of evil and subjection to evil which it entailed on him—deprived him of the power of tasting the pure delights of the life of which that tree was the pledge and means. Not till sin is expiated, and death swallowed up in victory, is man again admitted to the tree of life, and he is then entitled and enabled to enjoy it upon even a higher footing than he did originally—not as ignorant of evil, but as now really Godlike, knowing it in Christ, and in Christ triumphing over it. But mark the grace of God ; and how, in wrath, he remembers mercy. He does not break off man's connection with the blessed garden altogether. Even paradise lost is made to appear, in the eyes of those who worshipped in faith before its gates, as already virtually paradise regained.

I. For it is most probable that the stated place of worship, under the new order of things, was the immediate neighbourhood of the garden : " So he drove out the man : and he placed at the east of the garden of Eden cherubims and a flaming sword which turned every way, to keep the way of the tree of life " (chap. iii. 24).

These cherubims are very generally regarded as angels, appointed to keep back all who might presumptuously dare to approach the now forbidden gates. There is no more entrance for sinful man by the old path of a direct personal obedience. He must enter now, if at all, by the new and living way of the Saviour's righteousness. The Law, with its ministers of flaming fire, drives men away. It is the Gospel which sets angels at all the doors to bid men welcome once more (Rev. xxi. 12).

It may be doubted, however, if this name " cherub," or " cherubim," ever denotes angels. This is the first mention of cherubim in the Bible ; and in mentioning them, the sacred writer speaks of them as familiar and well known to those whom he addresses. He gives no description or explanation of them—he simply says, " God placed cherubims " (or more literally, the cherubim) " at the east of the garden." Such language would surely be understood as denoting the same kind of cherubim with which the Israelites were already acquainted. Now these are described in the book of Exodus (Exod. xxv. 18). They were gorgeous golden figures, bending over the mercy-seat, and having the glory of God resting upon them, and the voice of God going forth from between them. The same figures were placed afterwards in the holy place of the temple (1 Kings vi. 23) ; and it is most likely that Solomon increased their number to four, adding two new ones to the two formerly in use in the tabernacle. Cherubim were ‚mbroidered on the curtains of the tabernacle (Exod. xxvi. 1), and on the great veil which divided the holy place and the most holy (Exod. xxvi. 31). They were also engraved on the walls of the temple (1 Kings vi. 29-35) ; where, as if to identify them with the cherubim placed near the pleasant trees of the garden, they are described as interspersed with palms and flowers. Thus we find that cherubim formed an essential part of the furniture or apparatus of the holy place, where the Lord was understood to manifest himself in the character in which he is worshipped by sacrifice. It is one of the attributes of the Lord's throne, or his seat, or his chariot, that the cherubim are with him. Whether he is represented as at rest, or as in motion, the glorious symbol of his presence, in flaming fire, is associated with these accompaniments (Numb. vii. 89 ; Ps. lxxx. 1, and xcix. 1 ; xviii. 10).

But the fullest view of the cherubim is given in the visions of Ezekiel, where we have a description of their outward appearance. They were compound figures, each having the face of a man, a lion, an ox, and an eagle, with a human body in the upper part, but with wings, and with somewhat of the form of the other animals beneath (Ezek. i. 4, and x. 2). The pictures of the cherubim, indeed, are obscure ; in the main, however, they agree in representing them as emblematic figures of animals. Man is prominently their head ; but he appears with the peculiar prerogatives of other animals allied to his own. And in all the visions of Ezekiel, as well as in the other passages already referred to, we recognise them as forming part of the train or attendance of Jehovah, in his resting, as well as in his movements from place to place.

Finally, these same cherubim, or living creatures—called, rather unhappily, in our version, "the four beasts,"—appear in the Apocalyptic vision of John (Rev. iv. 6, etc.), as taking a conspicuous share in the worship of the heavenly sanctuary.

Thus we trace the cherubim, from their first appearance in the garden of Eden to their manifestation in the glorious pattern which John saw of the Redeemer's triumphal court and throne. And if we now reverse this process, and retrace them from the last to the first book of the Bible, we may form a probable opinion respecting their symbolical meaning. In the Revelation (v. 6-14, and vii. 11), they are expressly distinguished from angels, and represented as, along with the twenty-four elders, assenting to the strains which the angels raise. In answer to the angelic hymn, "Worthy is the Lamb that was slain," and in glad accord with the doxology of universal nature, "Blessing and honour, and glory and power, be unto Him that sitteth on the throne, and unto the Lamb, for ever and ever,"—the four beasts, with the worshipping elders, are heard saying, "Amen." Again (xiv. 3), along with the twenty-four elders, they are seen presiding over the vast multitude of the followers of the Lamb, "on the mount Sion," in the singing of the new song which none could learn but they who were redeemed from the earth. They are not, therefore, angelic, but human symbols, in some way associated with the church or redeemed creation ; and they are significant of its glorious power and beauty, as presented before the throne of God and of the Lamb. The very same character may be ascribed to the living creatures of Ezekiel's visions, and to the cherubim, wherever they are mentioned in the Old Testament. They typify and shadow the complete church, gathered out of all times and nations, and from the four corners of the world, waiting in attendance on her Lord and Saviour, in his redeeming glory.

Thus in the holy place of the tabernacle and of the temple,

the mercy-seat sprinkled with atoning blood—the cherubim bending over and looking upon it—the glory of the Lord, the bright Shechinah light resting in the midst—fitly express, in symbol, the redemption, the redeemed, and the Redeemer. It is a symbolical representation of believers, having their steadfast eyes fixed on the propitiation, whereby God is brought once more to dwell among them. It is Jehovah meeting, in infinite complacency, with the church which atoning blood has bought and cleansed. And thus always, when faith beholds God as the God of salvation, he appears in state with the same retinue. Angels, indeed, are in waiting; but it is upon or over the cherubim that he rides forth—it is between the cherubim that he dwells. The church ever contemplates him as her own, and sees him rejoicing over her in love.

The cherubim placed at the east of paradise after it was lost, surely bore the same import. In connection with the flaming sword, they marked the place in which the Lord manifested himself, and towards which he was to be worshipped. That fiery emblem might represent the terror of the divine justice—if we are not rather to identify it with the brightness of the Shechinah-glory which afterwards shone in the bush, in the temple, and on the way to Damascus. The cherubic figures, on the other hand, betokened the grace of the church's redemption. These together kept the way of the tree of life.

The worshippers, as they stood, awed, yet hopeful, around the gate of paradise, felt their exclusion from the blessedness within. But they saw a human figure mysteriously fashioned there—they saw a pledge of the restitution. That there was, in the primitive worship, a holy place, where the presence of the Lord was manifested, is plain from the language used in respect to the bringing of offerings—"they brought them unto the Lord"—to some set or appointed spot (chap. iv. 3, 4); and also from what is said of the exile of Cain—"he went out from the presence of the Lord"—from the place where the Lord revealed himself by symbol and by oracle to those who

worshipped at his altar (chap. iv. 16). And it would seem
that this primitive holy place was substantially identical with
the shrine of the Levitical ritual, and with the heavenly scene
which Ezekiel and John saw. It was within the garden, or at
its very entrance, and it was distinguished by a visible display
of the glory of God, in a bright shining light, or sword of
flame—on the one hand driving away in just displeasure a
guilty and rebellious race ; but on the other hand shining with
a benignant smile upon the typical emblems or representations
of a world and a people redeemed.

Thus, near the seat of original innocence—which now was
by expressive symbols presented to his view in a new and still
attractive light, as the seat of the glory of redemption—Adam
and his seed were to worship and serve God.

A seed accordingly was given to him. Two sons were
born, probably at one birth, since it is not said of Eve that
she conceived again and bare Abel (which is the usual scriptural
form in intimating a second birth), but simply that she bore
him after Cain. "And Adam knew Eve his wife ; and she
conceived, and bare Cain, and said, I have gotten a man from
the Lord. And she again bare his brother Abel " (chap. iv. 1, 2).
That a difference was from the very first put between the two
by Eve, and it may be presumed by her husband also, is plain
from the remarkable language which she applies to the first-
born, "I have gotten a man from the LORD ;" and, indeed,
from the very names given to the two brothers respectively.
Cain signifies acquisition or gain; Abel, vanity or loss.
Whence this difference thus early put by their parents between
the two sons, born at the same time, and in precisely the same
circumstances? Already, it would seem, it was understood
that the race was to be divided into two great sections, of
which the one only was to be reckoned as truly and spiritually
the seed of the woman,—while the other bore the character,
and fell under the doom, of the seed of the serpent. Possibly
Eve regarded her first-born as the very individual who was

to be the Saviour, and understood at the same time that this Saviour was to be a divine person. So some at least interpret her words,—"I have gotten a man," or the man, "the LORD," the very Jehovah—him who is God as well as man. More probably, however, taking the words as they stand, "I have gotten a man from the LORD," we are to consider her as simply recognising his birthright, and so welcoming him as peculiarly the heir of the promise. At all events, it is plain that in her judgment Cain was chosen rather than his brother. But the election of grace is otherwise, as the sequel too clearly proves.

Thus, in the very beginning of the dispensation of grace, the sovereignty of God is manifested, according to the principle,—"Jacob have I loved, and Esau have I hated" (Mal. i. 2, 3; Rom. ix. 11-13). And thus, too, it is seen that God "judgeth not as man judgeth," and that no privileges of the flesh will avail in his sight. Cain is the first-born,—the heir. His parents receive him as a prize; while his brother is in comparison but lightly esteemed. How blind is the wisdom, how false the confidence of man! Cain, whose birth was so welcome, is the lost one. He whose very name was "Vanity," becomes the first inheritor of the blessedness of the redeemed.

Their different occupations have been supposed to mark a difference of rank and station. "Abel was a keeper of sheep, but Cain was a tiller of the ground" (ver. 2). Cain, as the first-born, follows his father's calling, being lord of the soil; Abel, as in some degree subordinate, tends the cattle. The division of labour, as well as the difference of ranks, being thus early introduced, may be regarded as not only suitable to the condition of man, but agreeable to the appointment of God. It is his will that men should differ in their tastes, talents, and pursuits; and that in different spheres they should serve one another. But all such differences are of no account in the kingdom of his grace and glory.

II. The brothers, representatives of the two great classes

into which, in a religious view, the family of man is divided,
manifest their difference in this respect, not in the object, nor
in the time, but in the spirit, of their worship. "And in
process of time it came to pass, that Cain brought of the fruit
of the ground an offering unto the Lord. And Abel, he also
brought of the firstlings of his flock, and of the fat thereof"
(ver. 3, 4).

They worship the same God, and under the same revelation
of his power and glory. Their seasons of worship also are the
same; for it is agreed on all hands that the expression, "in
process of time," or "at the end of days," denotes some stated
season, most probably the weekly Sabbath. Again, their
manner of service was to a large extent the same. They presented offerings to God; and these offerings, being of two
kinds, corresponded very remarkably to the two kinds of
offerings ordained under the Levitical dispensation—those
which were properly expiatory, and those which were mainly
expressive of duty, gratitude, and devotion.

Hence it would seem that the service of God, even thus
early, had in it all the elements which we afterwards find in
the Mosaic ritual,—a holy place, where the symbols of the
divine glory and of human redemption appeared;—stated times
or seasons of devotion; in particular, the weekly Sabbath;—
and an appointed manner of worship, consisting of offerings of
different kinds. The religion of fallen man has always been
the same.

Especially it has been the same in the way of fallen man's
approach to his offended God; which has always been through
blood, and the same blood,—the blood of "the Lamb slain
from the foundation of the world" (Rev. xiii. 8). With this
blood of THE LAMB, the blood of Abel's sacrifice is expressly
associated by the apostle, when he speaks of "the blood of
sprinkling that speaketh better things than that of Abel"
(Heb. xii. 24). In that sublime passage, Paul is reminding
believers of their peculiar privileges, as living under the

economy of the gospel; and, among the rest, he mentions "the blood of sprinkling,"—the blood of Jesus,—"which speaketh better things,"—which more effectually purges the conscience and gives peace,—than the blood of mere animal sacrifices could do. For "the blood of Abel" there referred to is not the blood of his slain body crying for vengeance;—it would not be to the purpose of the apostle's argument to compare or contrast Christ's blood with Abel's, in that sense of it. It is the blood which Abel shed when he offered his sacrifice that is intended,—the blood of such sacrifices as he presented, and all the faithful continued to present, until Christ died. Such blood could speak of pardon and reconciliation only symbolically and typically. The blood of Christ speaks of the real blessing really purchased and bestowed.*

Still Abel did well to present the blood of his lamb,—not as in itself the ground of his acceptance,—but as the token of his reliance for acceptance on the better sacrifice which his lamb prefigured. He worshipped in faith,—recognising and realising his own fallen state, and beholding both the glory of the righteous Judge, requiring satisfaction for sin, and the glory of the gracious Father, reconciling the sinner to himself. Through this faith alone could he acceptably present an offering to God,—whether it was such a burnt-offering as he did present, or such a meat-offering of thankfulness and peace as Cain chose to bring. To present either, in any other spirit, must be sin. To trust in the mere animal sacrifice,—the mere bodily service,—would have been superstition. To reject that sacrifice, in its spiritual and typical meaning, and to appear before God, with whatever gifts, without atoning blood, as Cain did,—was infidelity.

III. The two brothers, then, worshipped God according to the same ritual; but not with the same acceptance. How the

---

* See exposition of the passage in my Lectures on the Fatherhood of God. Appendix 2.

Lord signified his complacency in the one, and his rejection of the other, does not appear. It may have been by sending fire from heaven to consume Abel's offering; as in this way he acknowledged acceptable offerings, on different occasions, in after times (Lev. ix. 24; Judges vi. 21; 1 Kings xviii. 38). Why the Lord put such a distinction between them is a more important point, and more easily ascertained. It is unequivocally explained by the Apostle Paul (Heb. xi. 4). Abel's sacrifice was more excellent than Cain's, because he offered it by faith. Therefore his person was accepted as righteous,— and his gift as well pleasing to the Lord.

This agrees with the history, in which it is not said that God had respect to Abel's sacrifice, and then to himself; but, first, he had respect to Abel, and then to his offering. So it must ever be. The acceptance of the person must precede the acceptance of the service; and the acceptance of the person is by faith. The sacrifice of Abel had no more efficacy, in itself, than the offering of Cain, to recommend him to the favour of God. He was not accepted on account of his offering; nor was Cain rejected on account of his. But Abel believed; and through his faith he received a justifying righteousness in the sight of God, even God's own righteousness in which he believed,—the finished and accepted righteousness of "the Seed of the woman," who is no other than the Son of God himself (Rom. i. 17, and iii. 21). And the sacrifice which he offered as the expression of his faith, and of his appropriation of the righteousness which is by faith, became, on that account, a sacrifice of a sweet-smelling savour (Gen. viii. 21; Exod. xxix. 18). Cain, on the other hand, presented an offering which also, in its own place, and had it been presented in faith, would have been accepted by God. Had he first been reconciled to God, through the justifying righteousness and atoning blood of the promised Seed of the woman,—and had he then, in token of that reconciliation, and in the exercise of faith in that righteousness, offered the appointed typical sacrifice of expiation,—" he would have obtained witness that he was righteous " (Heb. ix. 4), that he was accepted as right eous, and that his heart, submitting to God's righteousness, was now right with God. And thereafter, in the character of one righteous,—justified, reconciled, and renewed, he might have come with his sacrifice of praise and thanksgiving, presenting the first-fruits of his substance, in grateful pledge of his willing dedication of himself, and all that he had, to God. Such offerings of a material substance God himself ordained under the law, to be typical and emblematic of the new obedience which his people must willingly render, after having made a covenant with him by sacrifice of another kind (Ps. l. 5-15). And similar offerings, but of a more spiritual and moral nature, he still requires, under the dispensation of the gospel, when he calls upon believers " to present their bodies a living sacrifice to him " (Rom. xii. 1), " to offer the sacrifice of praise continu- ally, that is, the fruit of their lips, giving thanks to his name," and " to do good and to communicate, since with such sacrifices he is well pleased " (Heb. xiii. 15, 16).

Such might have been the meaning, and such the accept- ance of Cain's offering, had he first himself " obtained witness that he was righteous," in terms of the righteousness of God appropriated by faith. Then, " God would have testified of his gifts." But Cain went about to establish a righteousness of his own. He brought his offering as one entitled, in his own name, to present it,—as one seeking, by means of it, to conciliate or satisfy his God. His was not the guileless sim- plicity and uprightness of a sinner receiving a free pardon, and, in consequence, rendering a free service,—forgiven much, and therefore loving much. It was the cold and calculating homage of contented self-confidence, paying, more or less con- scientiously, its due to God, with heart unbroken by any true sense of sin, and spirit unsubdued by any melting sight of the riches of redeeming love. Hence, " unto Cain and to his offering, the Lord had not respect " (ver. 5).

PART SECOND —UNBELIEF WORKING BY WRATH, MALICE,
AND ENVY

Genesis 4:5-15

Not as Cain, who was of that wicked one, and slew his brother. And
wherefore slew he him ? Because his own works were evil, and his
brother's righteous. 1 John 3:12

I. THE Lord did not all at once finally reject Cain ; on the
contrary, he gave him an opportunity of finding acceptance
still, as Abel had found it.   The very intimation of his rejection was a merciful dealing with Cain, and ought to have been
so received by him, and improved for leading him to humiliation,
penitence, and faith.   Instead of being humbled, however, he
is irritated and provoked.   " Cain," it is said, " was very
wroth, and his countenance fell " (ver. 5).   Still, the Lord visits
him, and graciously condescends to plead and expostulate
with him.   He points out the unreasonableness of such a
state of mind : " And the Lord said unto Cain, why art thou
wroth ? and why is thy countenance fallen ?   If thou doest
well, shalt thou not be accepted ? and if thou doest not well,
sin lieth at the door.   And unto thee shall be his desire, and
thou shalt rule over him " (ver. 6, 7).

If we take " sin " here to mean " a sin-offering,"—as not a
few eminent scholars have done,—the Lord's expostulation is
very gracious.

Cain has no right to complain, and no reason to despair.
He has no right to complain of his not being favourably received, as if a wrong were done to him,—as if he were deprived of his due.   He knows, that " if he doeth well, he will
certainly be accepted ;" and if he stands on the footing of right,
this is all that he is entitled to claim,—that if his obedience be
perfect, he shall be rewarded.   But there is another alternative.
At the worst, be his case ever so bad, he has no reason to
despair.   If he will but consent to stand on another footing—

not of right but of grace—then, though he has failed in " doing well," or rendering a perfect obedience to his God, he may still, as one guilty, find acceptance. There is a " sin-offering." And it is not far to seek; it is near; it lies at " his very door." Nor is it difficult to obtain possession of it. He does not need to buy it, or to work for it; it is already at his disposal, and subject to him; it may be appropriated and used by him as his own; it is his for the taking. It is waiting his pleasure, and as it were courting his acceptance: " its desire is to him." And he may at once avail himself of it: " he may rule over it "* (iv. 7, iii. 16).

* I hesitate between this interpretation and another one suggested by a learned friend ; which also makes the Lord's remonstrance very gracious.

"Why art thou wroth ? and why is thy countenance fallen?" Wilt thou mend matters by thine angry and sullen gloom ? Nay, there is a more excellent way. Retrace thy steps. Do as Abel did. And if like him thou doest well, thou canst have no doubt of thine acceptance. Thy rueful and downcast looks will be changed into the radiant gladness of a spirit in which there is no guile. But, on the other hand, beware. If thou rejectest the only true and effectual remedy,—if thou doest not well, —think not that any passionate complaint or moody discontent of thine will avail for thy relief. Sin—the sin to which by complying with its solicitations thou hast given the mastery over thee,—is not thus to be got rid of. Nay, thou canst not keep it at a distance, or even at arm's length. It lieth at thy door ; ever crouching for thee ; ever ready to fawn upon thee for farther concessions, and then to grasp thee in its fangs of remorse and shame and terror. One only manner of dealing with sin can be either safe or successful. Treat it as thy father Adam was empowered to treat his Eve to whom he had so easily yielded. He is not again to be so fond and facile. He is to keep her in her right place. And whatever influence her blandishments may have over him as "her desire is toward him," he is to assert his manly prerogative of reason and conscience and "rule over her." Sin is to thee, Cain, what Eve, alas ! was to Adam. Nor canst thou shake it off, however angry and gloomy thou mayest be,—any more than Adam, if he had desired it, could have shaken off the temptress with whom for better and for worse he was irrevocably united. She was part of himself—his very flesh. But she need not on that account be suffered to

The enmity of his carnal mind, however, prevailed. Cain would not be subject to the law of God ;—nor would he submit himself to the righteousness of God. He thought that he did well to be angry. And as his wrath could not reach the great Being of whom chiefly he complained, he vented it on his brother, who was within his reach. Being of the wicked one, he slew his brother. " And Cain talked with Abel his brother ; and it came to pass, when they were in the field, that Cain rose up against Abel his brother, and slew him " (ver. 8).

exert a sway over him inconsistent with his manhood or injurious to his godliness. Let him assert the right that belongs to him, and wield even over the wife of his bosom, should he be in danger of becoming again too compliant, the power with which for that very end the Lord himself has invested him. So, in like manner, let Cain deal with what has now become his domestic foe. Let him stand upon his right as a man,—especially as a man acquainted with the great principle of the economy under which he lives ; "the seed of the woman shall bruise the serpent's head, while the serpent again shall bruise his heel." Let him cast himself manfully—believingly—into the deadly strife here depicted ; let him vindicate the power that belongs to him if he will but identify himself with that " seed of the woman ;" let him not suffer sin to have dominion over him, but rather enter into the great Redeemer's victory over sin ; and there need be no more dark thoughts and scowling looks, for all may yet be well.

It will be seen that in both of these interpretations, the latter clause of ver. 7 is not applied to Cain's relationship to Abel, as many expounders have applied it. The allusion which they suppose to be made to Cain having forfeited the birthright, and having an opportunity of recovering it, is not happy. On the other hand, whether we take "sin-offering," or "sin," to be the word in the preceding clause, there is great propriety and point in the comparison, either of a sinner's command through grace over the appointed victim, or of a believer's command over sin, to the husband's right over the wife. In either case, the objection to the feminine noun "sin offering," or "sin," having a masculine pronoun connected with it, is obviated by the personification "lying at the door" (Deut. ix. 21).

I do not venture to dogmatise ; but I own that after leaning a good deal to the second interpretation, my preference for the former has rather returned upon me.

He had been talking with Abel his brother, whether in friendship, or in controversy, or partly and successively in both ways, does not appear from the narrative. His talk may have been a subtle trap to beguile his unwary brother. If, as many think, Abel is to be viewed as the type of Him who was accounted "vanity"—a worm and no man—despised and rejected of men—who, at the same time, was meek and lowly of heart—being led as a lamb to the slaughter, and opening not his mouth against his persecutors ; we may be justified in applying to the first martyr the very passages in the Psalms which describe both the smooth treachery and the open violence of which Jesus—the faithful witness—was the object (Ps. lv. 21, lvii. 4). At anyrate Cain talked, smoothly or sharply, with Abel ; but not so as seriously to awaken suspicion or alarm in his brother's mind. They were together in the field. Abel having faith towards God, is ready to place confidence in his brother also. Cain adds to his ungodliness the sin of envy and hatred, and the crime of murder.

II. Returning from the field, Cain scruples not apparently to revisit the sanctuary—the very "presence of the Lord;" for it is afterwards said that upon receiving his sentence, he went out from thence (ver. 16). He seems to think that he may calmly meet both his parents and his God. He even assumes an air of defiance. He feels almost as if he were the wronged and injured party. When the solemn and searching question is put, "Where is Abel thy brother ?"—"I know not," is his impatient and unfeeling reply—"Am I my brother's keeper ?" (ver. 9.) My brother might have kept himself. Or his God, with whom, as it turns out, he was so great a favourite, might have kept him.

Thus the infidel regards religion, in the persons of its professors, as insulting and injurious to himself. He is not its keeper. It is no concern of his to save its credit or its character ; rather he may be justified in putting it out of his way as best he can. So Cain exults in his success, in thus easily getting the better of the feeble and unprotected simplicity of his righteous brother, and almost upbraids the Lord with the little care that he seems to take of his own.

But though the righteous is suffered to fall before the wicked, the wicked is not to be allowed to escape. His boasting is vain. Abel, indeed, was the unsuspecting and unresisting victim of his brother; silently and meekly he suffered wrong. But his "blood" had a "voice" (ver. 10); for "precious in the sight of the Lord is the death of his saints" (Ps. cxvi. 15, and lxxii. 14); and "He maketh inquisition for blood" (Ps. ix. 12). Abel is the first of that noble army of martyrs, "whose righteous blood" was to come on the generation that rejected the Lord (Matt. xxiii. 35); and whose souls, under the altar, still cry with a loud voice against the dwellers on the earth (Rev. vi. 9, 10). Cain, on the other hand, is doomed to be a castaway.

It is true, the first murderer does not immediately receive the doom of murder, which is death by the hand of man. On the contrary, his life is specially preserved. It is to be observed, however, that he is apprehensive of that doom. "It shall come to pass," he says, "that every one that findeth me shall slay me;" any chance passenger, recognising me as a murderer, will feel himself entitled to be my executioner (ver. 14). So strong, indeed, and so well founded is this apprehension of Cain's, that it needs to be allayed by a token of security given to himself—"The Lord set a mark on him, lest any finding him should kill him." Nor is even this enough. His life is still farther guarded by a threatening of aggravated judgment against any who should venture to inflict upon him that sentence of death which, but for this express prohibition, all his fellows might have felt themselves justified in inflicting —"Therefore, whosoever killeth Cain, vengeance shall be taken on him sevenfold" (ver. 15).

In all this it is evidently implied that the law, according

to which the murderer is to be slain by his fellows, is the original law of God and nature. Cain, when his conscience is in part awakened by the dreadful denunciation of divine wrath, has enough of feeling to convince him that his fellow-men will consider themselves entitled, if not bound, to slay him. And he does not—he dares not—quarrel with the justice of such a proceeding. God, on the other hand, clearly intimates that, but for an express prohibition, the murderer's fear would infallibly and justly have been realised. It is agreeable to the constitution of man's moral frame, and is in itself a righteous thing, that " whoso sheddeth man's blood, by man shall his blood be shed." This law, accordingly, God himself ordained after the flood (chap. ix. 6), not as a part of the Levitical code, which was local and temporary, but as a part of the universal patriarchal religion ; a standing law—the one only standing law—of capital punishment, for all ages and for all mankind. It was by a special act of grace that that law was in abeyance in the system which was established before the flood. God himself suspended it, in the exercise of his own sovereign prerogative. But ever since the flood it has been in force ; and man has no discretionary right to repeal it.

We read that the latter days before the coming of the Son of man are to resemble the days immediately before the flood (Matt. xxiv. 37). It will be a singular coincidence if men shall then be found proposing to bring back, by their own authority, that suspension of the law in question, which was formerly the act of God himself ; if the experiment of exempting even murder from the punishment of death shall be tried again, not with God's sanction, but in man's perverse wilfulness, setting God's prerogative at defiance. The trial was made, then, in the long-suffering patience of God ; and miserably was his patience abused. The murderer, in a subsequent generation, imitating Cain's example, gloried in his impunity (ver. 24) ; and soon the earth was filled with violence (chap. vi. 11). What may not be expected, if the trial shall be made again, in the mere wantonness of man's intellectual vanity;—especially if it shall be made when lawless infidelity again, as in the age which the flood surprised, rages against the truth, and against the scanty remnant of its witnesses!

III. But Cain, though thus spared, was made fully and terribly aware of the divine displeasure. He had hitherto been a tiller of the ground; and the ground, though cursed for man's sake, yielded a return to his toil. This employment of a cultivator of the soil seems originally to have possessed a certain pre-eminence of rank, and it had this manifest advantage that it was a stationary occupation,—a settled line of life. It permitted those engaged in it to remain quietly resident in their hereditary domains, and to exercise their hereditary dominion. Above all, it left them in the neighbourhood of the place where the Lord manifested his presence,—the seat and centre of the old primeval worship. But Cain was henceforth to be debarred from the exercise of his original calling; at least on the spot where he had previously enjoyed his birthright privileges. For not only is the ground cursed to him,—he is "cursed from the earth." It is forbidden to yield to him even the hard-earned return which it may still afford to others: "When thou tillest the ground, it shall not henceforth yield unto thee her strength; a fugitive and a vagabond shalt thou be in the earth" (ver. 12). Thus Cain is compelled to wander. He must abandon the simple and godly manner of life which he might have led, and seek his fortunes abroad,— at a distance from his early home, and from the presence of his father's God. It would seem that he is contented to do so. His anxiety at first, when his sentence was pronounced, arose chiefly from his selfish fear of death at the hands of his justly indignant brethren (ver. 13-15). When that fear is removed, he thinks little of his exclusion from the sanctuary of his God and the society of the faithful. He can still turn to account his natural talents and powers. He goes forth (ver. 16,

17), to live without God in the world,—building cities and begetting children,—himself and his seed prospering and prevailing—until the flood comes—to purge the earth of them all.

Here let us pause and trace the progress of unbelief in the soul. God draws near to sinful men, and proposes terms of free and full reconciliation. He so draws near to me, showing me the way of life. He does not require of me that I should purchase his favour by any oblation. He himself provides the sacrifice ; and he simply asks me to come on the footing of his favour being freely bestowed, and to present the offering of faith, as well as the offering of thanksgiving. But I care not for so close and intimate an intercourse with the Holy One, as is implied in this manner of approach to him. I am willing enough to render to him a certain measure of respectful homage ;—to present as an offering on the altar, such gifts out of my time and talents as I can afford;—but I see no necessity for anything more. I see, indeed, my neighbour making a far more serious business of his approach to God than I do—and laying far more to heart the whole question of his acceptance with God, and the state of his affections toward God. I see him very anxious and earnest, as one fleeing from wrath, and grasping mercy. And this may be very well for him. But for myself, I see no occasion for any such excitement. I duly go through my customary religious exercises ;—and is not that enough ?

It may happen, however, upon an occasion, that I am not altogether satisfied. My godly brother evidently has the advantage of me. He is better than I can pretend to be—he is happier. He is more at home with his God. There is an air of intense reality about his religion, which puts to shame my somewhat meagre and formal routine of duty. I am displeased and discontented—I am angry, I scarcely know why, or with whom. I have a secret feeling that all is not quite as it should be between my Maker and myself,—that, in short, there is something wrong in my spiritual state.

Ah! why do I not give this feeling its full scope and play? Why do I not come at once to close dealing with my soul, and with my God, and bring the matter promptly to an issue? If I am right—if I really do well—what have I to fear? And if I am wrong, if I am the very chief of sinners, have I not a way of peace with God and victory over sin at my very door?

Alas! my pride rebels,—I recoil from the humiliation of being a simple debtor to grace. I shrink from that complete union to God and thorough separation from sin which I shrewdly suspect would be the result of a full and fair settlement of the controversy between us. I choose rather to stand aloof, and to compromise the matter by a kind of formal understanding.

Still I am not at ease. I cannot but perceive the vast difference between the mere decency of my devout observances, and the evident heartiness of the man who really has peace in believing and joy in the Holy Ghost. I try to relieve myself, by venting my feelings of irritation against him. I may not indeed slay him—but I find a sort of satisfaction in speaking, or in thinking, ill of him. His high principles offend me; and I am interested in making him out to be no better than his neighbours. I am not the keeper of his reputation, or of his character—I am not responsible for his unblemished name. If he falls, what is that to me? Nay, even though the blame should be laid on me, and I should be the cause or occasion of his stumbling,—if I but escape immediate retribution, I can consent that my envious dislike and unjust treatment of God's servant should drive me, as it must practically do, further than ever away from God himself.

Beware, O my soul, of the great sin of Cain. If thy heart is not right with God, thou wilt assuredly be tempted to hate and harass the godly. The spirit of ungodliness is essentially the spirit of murder. It would, if it were possible, annihilate

God,—for he troubles it. The next best expedient is to annihilate all on the earth that reflects his image, and testifies of
him. Hence hard thoughts of the truly righteous—suspicions
—cruel surmises—evil speaking of their good and exaggeration of their evil—temptations offered to their principles—a
silencing and suppressing of their testimony—violence against
their persons. Let me take good heed lest the seeds of such
dispositions be in me. Let me carefully examine myself. Do
I feel any pleasure when the godly man stumbles? Do I join
with ready eagerness in the smile raised at his expense? Do
I experience relief when I seem to find him less perfect than
he once appeared to be?

If so, let me be awakened in time. Let me be convinced
that my real quarrel is not with him, but with his religion
and his God. Let me come at once to the question of my
own personal standing. I have nothing to do with my brother
—I am not his keeper. It may be so. But my own soul is
in peril. I have a matter personal to myself to settle. Alone
I have to deal with my God. If I am to justify myself, it is
not my brother's fall, but my own righteousness, that must
save me. But I am poor and miserable. I have nothing that
I can present to God for his acceptance.

Then let me end this controversy at once. Let me take
the offered Saviour as my own. He is mine, if I will but have
him to be mine ;—mine without money and without price. I
may at once, however unworthy and sinful, with all my guilt
on my head, whatever that guilt may be,—on terms altogether
gratuitous,—just as I am, appropriate his sacrifice and avail
myself of all its efficacy. In so doing, I honour God. Refusing so to do, I make him a liar. Let me no longer resist
his Spirit ; let me believe his testimony ; let me submit to
his righteousness, and receive remission, in the only way in
which it can be bestowed, through the shedding of blood.
Then, instead of seeking to brave out my continuance in sin
by means of anger or sullen discontent, I may meekly and

resolutely face the struggle against it and enter into the victory
over it which my Lord has won.

Thus shall I taste true blessedness and peace. Yes, even
though, instead of any longer persecuting the righteous, I
should now be myself persecuted as Abel was. Remembering
my own past feelings, I may well expect to be so, and I may
well take it patiently;—especially in the view of joining the
glorious company in which Abel was the first to be enrolled.
" Arrayed in white robes, and having come out of great tribulation, and washed their robes and made them white in the
blood of the Lamb,—they are before the throne of God, and
serve him day and night in his temple : and he that sitteth
on the throne shall dwell among them ; God shall wipe away
all tears from their eyes " (Rev. vii. 13-17).

8

THE APOSTATE SEED—THE GODLY SEED—THE UNIVERSAL CORRUPTION

Genesis 4:16-6:8

When the enemy shall come in like a flood, the Spirit of the Lord shall
lift up a standard against him.   Isaiah 59:19

PART FIRST —THE APOSTATE AND THE GODLY SEEDS

THE stream of the human family is now found to divide itself
into two channels, the one beginning with Cain, and the other
with Seth, who came into the place of righteous Abel. Around
these two heads, or centres, the growing population of the
world began more or less formally to range themselves ; and
in their distinctive characters and mutual relations, we trace
the progress of the struggle between the seed of the woman
and the seed of the serpent.

I. It is especially in the line of Cain that the arts of social
and civilised life are cultivated. The family of Adam originally settled in a kind of circle near the eastern gate of paradise.   Cain removed to a greater distance ; and having now
no longer the visible holy place as a centre round which his
household might rally, he set himself to find a centre of another kind. He built a city, not so much for security, as for
the gratification of his ambition and the aggrandisement of his
house (chap. iv. 16, 17). A stranger and pilgrim on the earth,
he sought not a heavenly, but an earthly city—desiring to
found a race and perpetuate a name. " He built a city, and

called the name of the city after the name of his son, Enoch"
—a name implying "dedication," or "high destination," applied to Cain's son in impious pride, as afterwards, in a
humbler and holier sense, it was fitly given to the patriarch
who was translated. It is the same name which is common to
both ; but while it is a gracious token in the family of the godly,
it is a profane usurpation in the household of the murderer.

In the sixth generation from Cain, his descendants are noticed as introducing great improvements and refinements into
the system of society. Not only farming and manufactures,
but music and poetry flourished among them. In farming,
Jabal gave a new form to the occupations of the shepherd and
the herdsman ; "he was the father of such as dwell in tents,
and of such as have cattle (ver. 20). In manufactures, Tubal
Cain promoted the use of scientific tools, being "the instructor
of every artificer in brass and iron" (ver. 22). Jubal, again,
excelled in the science of melody, standing at the head of the
profession of "such as handle the harp and organ" (ver. 21).
And Lamech himself, in his address to his two wives, gives
the first specimen on record of primeval poetry, or the art of
versification in measured couplets (ver. 23, 24) :

> "Adah and Zillah, hear my voice !
> Ye wives of Lamech, hearken unto my speech :
> For I have slain a man to my wounding,
> And (*or even*) a young man to my hurt.
> If Cain shall be avenged seven fold,
> Truly Lamech, seventy and sevenfold."

Thus, in the apostate race, driven to the use of their utmost
natural ingenuity and full of secular ambition, the pomp of
cities and the manifold inventions of a flourishing community
arose and prospered. They increased in power, wealth, and
luxury. In almost all earthly advantages, they attained to a
superiority over the more simple and rural family of Seth. And
they afford an instance of the high cultivation which a people
may often possess who are altogether irreligious and ungodly,

as well as of the progress which they may make in the arts and embellishments of life.

But there are dark spots in the picture. The introduction of polygamy marks the dissolution of manners which began to prevail. "Lamech took unto him two wives: the name of the one was Adah, and the name of the other Zillah" (ver. 19). And the impunity of which Lamech boasts (ver. 23, 24), shows the violence of a lawless age. He confesses the shedding of blood, and impiously exults in the solemn threatening by which Cain's life had been guarded; claiming for himself tenfold greater security. On what ground he rests his preferable claim does not very clearly appear. Perhaps he may have received provocation: "I have slain a man in retaliation for my wound, even a young man for my hurt"—so many render his song. Or even if, as others think, he had a double murder to answer for, he might still regard his crime as venial in comparison with the fratricide of Cain, and the fierce impiety which prompted it. At all events, he presumed on his exemption from the risk of death.

Thus the race of Cain, abusing the forbearance of God, began to deny his providence and to brave his judgment. And such seems to have been the character of the first apostasy —a natural following out of Cain's sin in refusing the sin-offering and rejecting the humbling doctrine of grace. It was not superstition or idolatry, but presumptuous scepticism. Men said, "God hath forgotten, he hideth his face, he will never see it." Or, "How doth God know? and is there knowledge in the Most High?" (Ps. x. 11; lxxiii. 11). This is very significantly intimated in the book of Job, where there is a description of the irreligion that prevailed before the flood: "Hast thou marked the old way which wicked men have trodden; which were cut down out of time, whose foundation was overthrown with a flood; which said unto God, depart from us: and what can the Almighty do for them?" (Job. xxii. 15-17). The apostate race perverted and abused that suspension of the righteous sentence of God, which prolonged the days of their father Cain, and even filled his house with good. In the bold spirit of atheistic unbelief, they gave a loose rein to their desire of pleasure and power. Hence, unbridled lust and bloody violence prevailed. Polygamy introduced the one, and the presumption of impunity the other. They became high-handed in vice and crime, and set at nought the prophetic warnings of the coming of the Lord in judgment (Jude 14, 15).

In this view, we have another feature of resemblance between the days before the flood, and the last times when the Lord is to appear. In both, we have an apostasy of the same character—the apostasy of scepticism, and an atheistic denial of Divine Providence, and of the day of retribution. For " there shall come in the last days scoffers, walking after their own lusts, and saying, Where is the promise of his coming ? " —men as ignorant and regardless of the judgments of God on the earth, as if he had not come forth to execute vengeance in the judgment of the flood, or were not again to manifest his wrath in the judgment of fire (2 Pet. iii. 3-7).

II. The godly seed was perpetuated in the family of Seth, whose name signifies " appointed, placed, or firmly founded ;" for on him now was to rest the hope of the promised Messiah. So God ordained, and so Eve devoutly believed. She no longer clung to Cain, though the first-born ; nor did she vainly regret the pious Abel, in whose death she must have received a sad warning and a salutary lesson. She recognised the will of God respecting Seth. " She called his name Seth ; for God, said she, hath appointed me another seed, instead of Abel, whom Cain slew " (chap. iv. 25).

The posterity of Seth maintained the cause of religion in the midst of increasing degeneracy. It is true they did not always maintain it very successfully—perhaps they did not always maintain it very consistently. Indeed, as if to remind us that this was really not to be expected, the historian at the very outset pointedly adverts to the difference between man as he came originally from his Maker's hand, and any race that can now spring from him. He was created " in the likeness of God " (chap. v. 1). A single blessed pair were thus created, that there might be a godly seed (Mal. ii. 15). But, when he had sinned and fallen, " he begat a son in his own likeness " (chap. v. 3). This is surely an assertion of the Psalmist's doctrine : " I was shapen in iniquity, and in sin did my mother conceive me (Ps. li. 5). And it is given as the explanation of the imperfect and inadequate manner in which now, at the very best, a godly seed can resist and stem the tide of ungodliness upon earth.

Still the race of Seth did testify for God, and in them the Spirit of God raised up a standard against the rushing force of prevalent iniquity. He did so especially in three successive eras of the world before the flood.

In the first place, in the days of Enos, the grandson of Adam, a signal revival took place among those who adhered to the true faith. For this is the import of the expression in the end of the fourth chapter,—whether we adopt the marginal reading of our English version, " then began men to call themselves by the name of the LORD," or, as is on the whole preferable, adhere to that given in the text, " then began men to call upon the name of the LORD " (chap. iv. 26).

The name " Enos," signifying poverty and affliction, seems to intimate the low state into which the cause and people of God had about this time fallen ; in consequence perhaps, partly, of the evil example or the violence of the now powerful political confederacy of the house of Cain. In these straits, an urgent appeal is made to God, and a spirit of boldness and union is infused into God's people, to counteract the lawless lust and pride of which the cities of Cain have become the centres. A more marked separation is effected between the followers of Abel's faith and the infidel apostasy. Men are

constrained to assume more distinctively the religious profession, and devote themselves more decidedly to the service of
God; avoiding worldly conformity, and giving themselves
more earnestly to prayer as their only refuge. It is a critical
season; a time of revival.

Again, secondly, several generations later, contemporary
with Lamech in the house of Cain, lived Enoch in the family
of Seth, the seventh from Adam. He was raised up as a remarkable prophet, and the burden of his prophetic strains is
preserved to us by the apostle Jude (ver. 14, 15). " And
Enoch also, the seventh from Adam, prophesied of these "
apostates and unstable professors, saying,

> " Behold the Lord cometh,
>> With ten thousand of his saints,
>> To execute judgment upon all,
>>> And to convince all that are ungodly among them,
>> Of all their ungodly deeds which they have ungodly committed.
>>> And of all their hard speeches which ungodly sinners have
>>> spoken against him."

This true prophecy of Enoch, like the vain-glorious boasting
of his contemporary, Lamech, is in the form and spirit of
poetry. May not the latter have been a profane mockery of
the other? Enoch announces the coming of the Lord in
judgment;—Lamech sets at nought the warning, and presumes
insolently on the impunity to be granted to his worst sins,—
encouraging himself in polygamy and murder. On the other
hand, as set over against Lamech's insidious poison, Enoch's
solemn warning is a seasonable antidote. In Lamech a new
height of daring impiety exhibits itself, and he openly assumes
the character of a prophet of infidelity. Enoch again is called
to be a witness to the truth; meeting the infidel in his own
line, with a divine poem matched against a ribald song.

But more than that. As the doctrines of the resurrection,
the final judgment, and the eternal state, were probably those
which a scoffing generation most sedulously corrupted or denied,

so Enoch was appointed to be a witness, in his person as well as by his ministry, to the truth of these vital articles of faith. His translation in the body, by the immediate and, perhaps, visible, hand of God himself—"for God took him" (chap. v. 24)—was a palpable proof of the reality of what he had been commissioned to teach to a gainsaying generation. The LORD, whose advent, as Judge of all, he announced,—of whom he spoke as surely coming to lay hold of the ungodly,—that same Lord came to lay hold of him ; and attested by an unequivocal sign the awful fact, that in the body all must at last meet and stand before their Sovereign Lawgiver and King.

This was the great truth which the men of that day set aside ; and by setting it aside, they emboldened themselves in all iniquity. Believing, or affecting to believe, that the body perished utterly, they deemed it of little or no consequence what they did in the body ; since, if the soul survived at all, it would be in a state into which the deeds of the body could not follow it. This is that "evil communication" of which the apostle speaks, as "corrupting good manners" in his day (1 Cor. xv. 33).* To meet it the servants of God have always preached the doctrine of the resurrection. In the body all shall meet the Lord. This truth Enoch's translation openly attested, not only for the terrible warning of the ungodly, but for the encouragement of believers, who must have found it no easy matter to walk with God, as Enoch did ;—not withdrawing himself into solitary seclusion, but continuing among his fellow-men, the father of a family, and a preacher and prophet of righteousness. Therefore, he was publicly acknowledged as faithful. He received a testimony that he pleased God ; and the signal privilege was conferred on him of exemption from the corruption of death, and immediate entrance, in the body, into the presence of the Lord.

The same, or at least a similar privilege, was afterwards bestowed on Moses. His death on Mount Nebo was, in all

* See this verse explained in "Life in a Risen Saviour."

probability, followed by an almost immediate resurrection. This may be gathered from the mystery of his unknown grave, —from the strife between the archangel and the devil about the disposal of his body,—and from his appearance in the glory of the resurrection state on the Mount of Transfiguration (Deut. xxxiv. 6 ; Jude 9 ; Matt. xvii. 3). The privilege of translation was also granted to the Prophet Elijah. Thus in each of the dispensations, the Patriarchal, the Levitical, and the Prophetical, there is, as it was fitting that there should be, a type and example of what is to be seen at the close of all things, when "the Lord himself shall descend from heaven with a shout, with the voice of the archangel, and with the trump of God." Then the dead in Christ shall rise first ; and they who are alive and remain shall be caught up,—as Enoch was,—together with the risen saints, to meet the Lord in the air : and so shall they both be ever with the Lord (1 Thess. iv. 16, 17).

Such was the import of Enoch's translation, to which Paul refers (Heb. xi. 6) as an instance of the power of faith. He takes the recorded fact as a proof that Enoch pleased God, and he argues that Enoch could please God only by believing. " By faith, Enoch was translated that he should not see death." It must have been by faith, as Paul proves in a formal syllo-gism. " Before his translation he had this testimony, that he pleased God." But "without faith it is impossible to please God." Therefore it follows that Enoch was translated as a believer. The articles of his faith are few and simple enough. The existence of God, and the acceptance in his sight of those that seek him, are the truths believed ; "he that cometh to God must believe that he is, and that he is a rewarder of them that diligently seek him." But, in fact, these are enough, if truly realised by that faith which is the " substance of things hoped for, and the evidence of things not seen," to account for the whole history of a sinner's conversion and a saint's walk with God. Let me see God as he is. Let me not merely hear of him with the hearing of the ear, but let mine eye see him (Job xlii. 5), vividly and brightly, as a present God. And let me, abhorring myself and repenting in dust and ashes, be constrained in downright earnest to ask, What must I do to be saved? Let me then know assuredly that God does reward them that seek him—that he rewards them by being found of them in peace—that I have but to believe in the Lord Jesus Christ and I shall be saved. I do believe, the Lord helping mine unbelief. Believing, I walk with God; and in me, as in my Surety, God is well pleased. So Enoch walked, accepted through faith, and waiting for the Lord's coming in judgment. He had present peace with God, and he rejoiced in hope of the glory hereafter to be revealed.

Once more, in the third place, still later in this melancholy period, the Lord raised up Noah; or Noe, as his name is often written. Either way, the name signifies " comfort " or " consolation ;" and certainly at the time the righteous family needed consolation. The delay of salvation and the wide prevalence of evil tried their patience, and embittered all their toil. Nevertheless against hope they continued to believe in hope ; and remembering the promise about the seed of the woman, they hailed this new heir of it as the harbinger of better days. In their expectations, they probably dwelt upon the time, when the curse being taken away, the face of the earth would be renewed (Ps. civ. 30) ; for they said of Noah, interpreting his name as prophetic, " This same shall comfort us concerning our work and toil of our hands, because of the ground which the Lord hath cursed " (ver. 28, 29).

Personally, Noah " found grace in the eyes of the Lord." He was accepted ; and still it was by faith. " By faith Noah, being warned of things not seen as yet, moved with fear, prepared an ark to the saving of his house ; by the which he condemned the world, and became heir of the righteousness which is by faith " (Heb. xi. 7). The proof of his faith was his " preparation of the ark ;" it was that which showed his faith to be real; his faith about the "things not seen as yet," of which he was "warned by God." For his faith was influential as well as real; influential because real. It worked, as was fitting, by fear; he was "moved with fear." He was cautious and provident; and so he prepared the ark for the saving of his house. But his faith worked also by love—it apprehended and embraced the free grace of the gospel. For, by his conduct in preparing the ark, Noah, renouncing the world, took the Lord alone for his portion. He thus constituted himself the sole ancestor of the promised seed, and served himself "heir to the righteousness which is by faith." He abandoned all confidence in the seed after the flesh which was to be destroyed, and consented to rely on the faithfulness of the Lord, by whom the true seed was promised.

Officially, Noah, like his predecessors, was a preacher of righteousness (2 Pet. ii. 5). Through him, Christ by his Spirit preached to the spirits in prison (1 Pet. iii. 19)—to those who, while the ark was a-preparing, were shut up as in a prison upon the earth. These Noah warned. He found them "disobedient," and doomed to the terrible punishment of disobedience. They were as criminals in the condemned cell, waiting the morning of their execution. There was no door of flight out of the prison in which the Almighty Judge held them under confinement—no possibility of evading the sentence of righteous retribution that awaited them. But one way of escape was provided. A holy man among them was commanded by God to prepare an ark. The long-suffering of God was waiting. The Spirit of Christ was in Noah—the Spirit by which, afterwards when Christ was put to death in the flesh, he was quickened and raised from the grave. By that same Spirit, in the days before the flood, Christ, through the teaching and testimony of his servant Noah, went forth and preached to these miserable spirits of the ungodly, imprisoned on the earth which the flood was to overwhelm.

Thus, in the name and by the Spirit of the Saviour, hereafter to be revealed as dying for men's sins, and rising again for their justification, Noah prayed these sinners to be reconciled to God. And he pointed to the ark as the sacramental seal and pledge, both of the certainty of coming judgment, and of the way of present deliverance. The ark then served the same purpose as the sacrament of baptism now; for baptism is expressly said to be a figure like the ark;—of the same kind with it (1 Pet. iii. 21). It saves believers in the same way ; not by itself, but by the death and resurrection of Jesus Christ, of which it is the emblem. For the ark figuratively represented Christ as, in his death and rising again, the refuge of those who must otherwise perish. It indicated a salvation, through a penal and judicial death for sin and a blessed and gracious resurrection to eternal life. The invitation to enter into the ark, like the call to submit to the water of baptism, was significant of the sinner's dying virtually and being buried with Christ ; and so putting away, not only the filth of the flesh, but also the guilt of conscious sin and the corruption of the old nature. And again, the assurance of his coming forth safely in the ark out of the water was the token of his being raised in Christ to newness of life. In one word, these sinners of the old world were exhorted, as sinners are still commanded everywhere, to repent and to believe. Entering into the ark, they would have been saved by water. Secure within that refuge, they would have gone down amid the raging billows of the flood, only to emerge again in triumph over all its fury. So believers now, shut up into Christ, die with him by participation in all his penal sufferings for sin, only to rise with him to a participation in his righteousness and its reward.

Thus, in three successive eras, the Lord remarkably interposed to arrest the progress of the apostasy. But apart from these occasional interpositions, it is to be kept in mind that the lives and deaths of so many patriarchs were continual testimonies against the sins of the times.

I. It is interesting in this view to consider the longevity of the patriarchs. The length of their days well fitted them for being the depositories of the revealed will of God, preserving and transmitting it from age to age ; and since so many of them survived together, not for years only, but for centuries, they must have formed a holy and reverend company of teachers and witnesses in the world.

The same circumstance, it is true, might tell also on the other side, and give a similar and corresponding advantage to the faction of the ungodly. The long lives of the fathers in the line of Cain, might tend to accelerate the progress of lawless impiety. Hoary patriarchs of infidelity, profligacy, and crime, surviving till the ninth or tenth generation, might lend the sanction of their accursed experience to the schemes of their more adventurous sons and grandsons. Still, upon the whole, the longevity of that ancient race must have proved a benefit to the cause of godliness. In regard to the wicked, not only would the curse of God, and their own violence, contribute to carry many of them off before their days were full— the most eminent in crime being often the earliest cut down ; but even if they were spared, they were as likely to meet for mutual strife among themselves, as for united efforts against the people of the Lord. The godly, again, enjoying the special blessing of Heaven, and having their peaceful days prolonged —honouring also the venerable worthies who could link together years so remote—Adam, sitting with Enoch and Methuselah, and Methuselah in his old age conversing with the men on whom the flood came—might be knit in one common faith and fellowship, and present an unbroken front to the adversary.

So, at least, it should have been. For surely this longevity of the fathers was a boon and privilege to the church. It served, to some extent, the purpose of the written word. It transmitted, not a treacherous and variable tradition passing quickly through many hands, but a sure record of the truth of

God. It was fitted to rally with no uncertain sound—not by the artifice of any dead and nominal uniformity, but on a trustworthy principle of living unity—the whole family of God. If the effect was otherwise—if the testimony of the long-lived fathers then, like the teaching of the abiding word now, failed to keep the sons of God at one among themselves and separate from the world,—their sin was on that account all the greater. The instrumentality was sufficient, being the truth authentically preserved, with as little liability to error or corruption as, in the absence of written documents, could well be guaranteed. Nor was the agency wanting which alone can give a spiritual discernment of the truth. The Spirit was throughout these ages continually "striving with men." By the Spirit, and through his long-lived servants, Christ was ever preaching to the successive generations of that antediluvian world.

II. But it is not the length of their lives only that is to be taken into account, when we would estimate the effect which the testimony of the godly patriarchs was fitted to have in stemming the torrent of ungodliness. Their deaths also must have been instructive and significant.

There is still something striking even to the most cursory reader, in the perpetual recurrence, throughout this record of protracted life (chap. v.), of the inevitable sentence of death. How often are these brief words repeated, after each long life, "and he died!" How startling is the reiteration of this announcement—how solemn its very uniformity! Little is told of the sayings, or doings, or sufferings of these men whose days were so long upon the earth. They were men of note in their generations—princes, probably, and priests, as well as patriarchs—taking a lead in civil affairs as well as in the things of God; but as to all their acts, in whatever spheres they filled, their memory has perished. That at a certain age he had a son, and thereafter lived a certain time, having many children

—this, and no more, is the history of every one of them. And whatever the allotted time of each, and with whatever stirring events filled up, the end of his brief biography is the same yet briefer epitaph—" and he died ! "

Adam lived nine hundred and thirty years, and he died. Seth, nine hundred and twelve, and he died. Enos, nine hundred and five, and he died. Cainan, nine hundred and ten, and he died. Mahalaleel, eight hundred and ninety-five, and he died. Jared, living longer than his predecessors, attained the age of nine hundred and sixty-two, and then he died. Methuselah, the oldest of all, was wellnigh within reach of a crowning millennium, but after living nine hundred and sixty-nine years, he died. The son of Methuselah, Noah's father, had almost seen the flood come ; but seven hundred and seventy-seven years being meted out to him, he, too, died !

It is the death-watch of that ancient and doomed world— the steady beat, as of a still small sound, striking at intervals upon the ear ; marking each footfall of the destroyer, as nearer and nearer, step by step he comes on. At each death of a saint, another hour of the world's day of grace is gone. As of patriarch after patriarch it is announced that he is dead ; there is a new alarum rung ; and a new call given forth. They depart one by one from the scene ; each leaving his dying testimony to a guilty world. And the single exception in the case of Enoch—who has this public token of his having pleased God—that suddenly " he is not, for God has taken him "— speaks even more eloquently than all the rest!

PART SECOND — THE UNIVERSAL CORRUPTION

> The fool hath said in his heart, There is no God. They are corrupt; they
> have done abominable works; there is none that doeth good. The
> Lord looked down from heaven upon the children of men, to see if
> there were any that did understand, and seek God. They are all gone
> aside, they are altogether become filthy; there is none that doeth
> good, no, not one. Psalm 16:1-3

THE seasons of revival from time to time granted to the people
of God, as well as the long lives and successive deaths of the
patriarchal fathers, might have been expected to have a wholesome influence on that early world. But the depravity of man
was to be proved, and the sovereignty of divine judgment and
divine grace was to be manifested.

I. The progress of corruption was not arrested. It increased as the tide of population rolled on.

For a time, the people of God, adhering to the house of
Seth, kept themselves unspotted from the world; but even
that barrier was at last overthrown. The sons of God, or the
righteous, sought alliances by marriage with the families of
the ungodly. For "it came to pass, when men began to
multiply on the face of the earth, and daughters were born
unto them, that the sons of God saw the daughters of men
that they were fair; and they took them wives of all which
they chose" (chap. vi. 1, 2). They followed their own inclination, without regard to the religious character of the
wives whom they chose; a grievous sin, which in every age
has marred the religion of many a household, and turned
many a fair promise of revival into a season of hopeless
declension and apostasy.

To this sad error, the godly seed had previously been
tempted by other considerations. There were very plausible
reasons for their cultivating a good understanding—at least
with the less abandoned of the ungodly faction.

The useful arts and graceful embellishments of social life

began to flourish, as has been seen, in the house of Cain (iv. 19-24). Agriculture, commerce, music, and poetry, were cultivated among his descendants, and brought to a high pitch of perfection. Were the children of Seth to forego the benefit of participating in these improvements and advantages ? Were they to deny themselves the profit and pleasure of well-directed industry and well-refined taste ? Was it not rather their duty to adopt and prosecute the laudable undertakings set on foot by the enterprise of the world—to rescue them out of the hands of God's enemies, and so make it manifest that religion does not frown on any of the lawful occupations and polite usages of society, but, on the contrary, ennobles and hallows them all ?

Then, again, the lawless violence of which Lamech's impious boast of impunity (chap. iv. 23, 24) was a token and example, and which soon became so general as to fill the earth, might seem to warrant, and indeed require, on grounds of policy, some kind of dealing between the persecuted people of God, and the more moderate of their opponents. Amid the distractions which must have prevailed in the ranks of the ungodly, it might seem a point of wisdom and duty that the righteous should avail themselves of any openings which occurred for an alliance with their neighbours, as well as of any advances which these neighbours chose to make to them. Might they not thus lawfully defend themselves with the aid of one portion of the world against another ? Might they not combine in a common cause with those who were not altogether at one with them in religion ? Nay, might they not thus detach their allies from the world, and by their friendly intercourse win them to God ?

Such plausible experiments, in the line of worldly conformity, naturally brought in a third kind of compliance. The intercourse of business almost insensibly led to a closer union in private life. The sons of God and the daughters of men were thrown much together. Other motives than a regard for

the glory of God and the salvation of the soul were allowed
to regulate the choice of companions and associates. The godly
were "unequally yoked together with unbelievers." Marriages
were contracted according to the dictates of policy, or the
fondness of passion, and not "in the Lord." It was no longer
deemed essential that husband and wife should be "heirs together of the grace of life, that their prayers might not be
hindered." The children of God "took them wives of all
which they chose," looking more to a fair countenance than
to a pious heart. The church and the world intermarried and
intermingled. And with what result? There ceased to be a
separate and peculiar people, testifying for God and reproving
sin. And ere long a race of giants, powerful and lawless men,
overspread the whole earth (chap. vi. 4).

II. At last, the patience of the Lord is represented as
worn out. The end of his long-suffering has arrived, and the
day of his wrath is at hand. His Spirit having been so long
grieved, is to be withdrawn—as if any further contending with
man's desperate depravity must needs be unavailing—and
judgment is to be executed. "The Lord said, My Spirit shall
not always strive with man, for that he also is flesh" (chap.
vi. 3). He is flesh and flesh only. It is needless to prolong
the use of means and opportunities, which only serve to harden
his heart, to deepen his guilt and aggravate his doom. He
must be suffered to show himself to be what he really is;
mere flesh; corruption and carnality.

The decree, indeed, is not instantly executed; the Spirit
of God is not suddenly withdrawn. A respite is granted.
"Yet," even yet, "his days shall be an hundred and twenty
years" (chap. vi. 3). Corrupt as it is, the race is to be spared
for a season. But it is only for a season. For the race is
incurably corrupt; not Cain's seed only, but Seth's also, is
become "flesh;" carnal instead of spiritual, living after the
flesh and not after the Spirit (Rom. viii.). It is all ripe and
ready for destruction.

Destruction, however, is the Lord's "strange work." He is represented as going about it reluctantly and with regret ; repenting of the very creation of a race on which he is under the righteous necessity of inflicting so terrible a doom. "It repented the Lord that he had made man on the earth, and it grieved him at his heart" (chap. vi. 6).

The expression here employed to describe the Lord's feeling towards the impenitent is in accordance with such language as that of the prophet—"How shall I give thee up, Ephraim? how shall I deliver thee, Israel? how shall I make thee as Admah? how shall I set thee as Zeboim? Mine heart is turned within me, my repentings are kindled together." But there is a peculiarity here, and it is a peculiarity singularly impressive. He repents and grieves, not merely that he is obliged to deal severely with his creatures, but that he has brought them into being at all. It is a bold figure. But, rightly understood, it enhances the tenderness of his compassion, while it aggravates the terror of his certain and inevitable wrath. The Lord speaks as if he would rather the earth had not been created, than that it should thus miserably perish. So the Lord Jesus, denouncing the crime of Judas, emphatically intimates that his having lived at all is a calamity— "Wo unto that man by whom the Son of man is betrayed. It had been good for that man that he had not been born." What a view does this suggest of the severity of God! What must that wrath be which the Lord so pathetically expresses his reluctance to inflict ; and in reference to which he so solemnly declares that it would have been good for the men of that old world that they had never been made, and for the traitor apostle that he had not been born!

Such is now the state of the world, lately so blessed. It is abandoned by the Creator, as unfit for the purposes for which it was created. He who saw every thing that he had made, and behold it was very good (chap. i. 31), now repents, as it were, of his having made the very chiefest and crowning part of all

—man, who was to be his image and glory on the earth. He changes, therefore, his work into a work of desolation. One man alone believes, to the saving of his house, and becomes heir of the righteousness that is by faith. "Noah finds grace in the eyes of the Lord." And his thus finding grace in the eyes of the Lord is a gracious encouragement to all the faithful in all generations. "For this is as the waters of Noah unto me: for as I have sworn that the waters of Noah should no more go over the earth; so have I sworn that I would not be wroth with thee, nor rebuke thee. For the mountains shall depart, and the hills be removed; but my kindness shall not depart from thee, neither shall the covenant of my peace be removed, saith the Lord that hath mercy on thee" (Is. liv. 9, 10).

9

THE END OF THE OLD WORLD BY WATER—
THE COMMENCEMENT OF THE NEW WORLD RESERVED
UNTO FIRE

Genesis 6:9-8:22; 2 Peter 3:5-7

THE demoralisation of the infidel world was now complete ; the corruption had now become universal ; " God
looked upon the earth, and, behold, it was corrupt ; for all
flesh had corrupted his way upon the earth " (ver. 12). The
measure of the world's iniquity was filled up, and the season
of God's forbearance exhausted. " The end of all flesh is come
before me " (ver. 13). It is come in a terrible sense and with
a terrible significancy.*

The Lord's resolution is irrevocable ; " I will destroy them
with the earth," or " from the earth." Orders accordingly are
given to prepare the ark wherein a few, that is, eight souls,
are to be saved : " Make thee an ark of gopher-wood : rooms
shalt thou make in the ark, and shalt pitch it within and
without with pitch " (ver. 14).

Of the form and size of the ark (ver. 15-21), it is enough
to remark that it had the shape of a chest or coffin—or, in
other words, of a vessel blunt in the front and stern, and flat
below ; and that, as almost all now confess who make the calculation on the common rules of Jewish measurement, it was
large enough for the temporary accommodation of the motley
crew and cargo that were to occupy it. That due provision
was made for their health and comfort, in respect of light, air,

*See Ezekiel 7:2-6 and Amos 8:2

and cleanliness, may surely be assumed, even although in this brief account the particular manner in which this was done is not stated. There were rooms and different storeys, as well as what is called a window, which perhaps was a sloping roof rising a cubit above the sides, and made of some transparent substance.* There were probably also other openings in the sides. There were the means, at all events, of suitably distributing the inmates of the ark, and preserving order and comfort among them.

When Noah received orders to make the ark, the Lord revealed to him the precise manner and extent of the coming judgment. He had before been generally warned; but now he is more particularly informed; "Behold, I, even I, do bring a flood of waters upon the earth, to destroy all flesh, wherein is the breath of life, from under heaven; and every thing that is in the earth shall die" (ver. 17).

It was an appalling announcement; how solemn and how stern! "I, even I." The repetition has in it an awful emphasis and force—"I, even I." It is the Lord who speaks, the Creator, the Preserver, now coming forth in wrath as the Destroyer. Thus, elsewhere, he swears by himself: "As I live, I, even I, am he, and there is no God with me: I kill, and I make alive: I wound and I heal: neither is there any that can deliver out of my hand. For I lift up my hand to heaven, and say, I live for ever" (Deut. xxxii. 39, 40). So here he confirms his word by an oath, "I, even I, do bring a flood of waters to destroy all flesh." And, as his counsel of love, confirmed by an oath in proof of its immutability, imparts strong consolation to the heirs of the promise (Heb. vi.

---

* The word rendered window, in a subsequent place, when the sending forth of the raven out of the ark is mentioned (chap. viii. 6), is different from that used when it is said, in the orders given for the building of the ark—"a window shalt thou make to it" (chap. iv. 1-6). In that other passage, the word may denote a window on the side, while here, in all likelihood, it is the roof that is spoken of.

17), so his purpose of wrath is, in the same way, shown to be unchangeable.

Then, again, as to its extent, how sweeping is the sentence —"I do bring a flood of waters upon the earth, to destroy all flesh, all wherein is the breath of life ; every thing that is in the earth shall die." This heaping up of words is full of terror. Surely there is, there must be an infinite evil in sin—it is indeed exceeding sinful.   One single offence opened by a small and solitary chink the flood-gate.   The tide rushed in.   And now the whole race of man—and not they only, but countless multitudes of unconscious and unoffending living beings made subject to vanity for man's sin—and the very earth itself, cursed at first with thorns and thistles, and now again doubly cursed with desolation on man's account—all are swept along in the impetuous torrent.   It might, indeed, seem as if the Lord had forgotten to be gracious—as if in this unbounded and intolerable provocation, his mercy were clean gone for ever (Ps. lxxvii. 8, 9).

It is not so, however.   God remembers his covenant : " But with thee will I establish my covenant ; and thou shalt come into the ark, thou, and thy sons, and thy wife, and thy sons' wives with thee " (ver. 18).   He is faithful and true ; and though terrible in his righteous vengeance, he keeps covenant and mercy.   And he has always some with whom he may establish his covenant ; if not seven thousand who have not bowed the knee to Baal, at least one who finds favour in his sight.   His purpose of love according to the election of grace stands sure, and all the unbelief of a world of apostates cannot make it void.   The gracious covenant, into which at first, when all seemed lost, he admitted Adam as a partner, he will now again, in this desperate crisis, establish with Noah.   And with excellent reason.   For it is neither with Adam, nor with Noah, that the covenant is made, else with Adam at the fall, and with Noah at the flood, it must have been for ever ended. What righteousness or what power had either Adam or Noah

in himself to save him from the general wreck and crash of a
ruined world, and sustain him erect and fearless before the
Righteous One? But the covenant is with his own beloved
Son; and with Adam and Noah only in him. Hence it stands
sure, being eternal and unchangeable. While the earth is
moved, and the mountains shake with the swelling of the seas,
the faith which God works by his Spirit in his chosen, enables
Noah calmly to lay hold of the promise, that the Seed of the
woman shall assuredly, in spite of all, bruise the head of the
serpent. In Christ the Son—whose day, even amid the
waste of waters, he sees, however dimly, afar off—he may
appropriate the Father's covenanted love as his portion; and
so doing he may be glad.

Thus God revealed his mind to Noah, when he was to
begin the preparation of the ark. And Noah, "warned of
God of things not seen as yet, moved with fear," or being
wary, proceeded to prepare the ark accordingly "for the
saving of his house" (Heb. xi. 7). He believed God. His
faith realised future and unseen things, and according as he
believed, so he did. "Thus did Noah; according to all that
God commanded him, so did he" (ver 22).

How long the ark was a-preparing is not said. But whatever was the date of its commencement, it is evident that it
was completed seven days before the flood was to come. At
that precise time, Noah received the order to take possession
of it;—"And the Lord said unto Noah, Come thou, and all
thy house into the ark, for thee have I seen righteous before
me in this generation. Of every clean beast thou shalt take
to thee by sevens, the male and his female: and of beasts
that are not clean by two, the male and his female. Of
fowls also of the air by sevens, the male and the female: to
keep seed alive upon the face of all the earth. For yet
seven days, and I will cause it to rain upon the earth forty
days and forty nights; and every living substance that I
have made will I destroy from off the face of the earth"
(chap. vii. 1-4).

These directions are more minute than those formerly given; in particular with reference to the animals. He had previously been told to take them in pairs. Now he is instructed to divide them into two classes, the clean and the unclean. Of the unclean he is to take single pairs; of the clean he is to take by sevens, three pairs and a half of each kind.

This is plainly not the first appointment of a difference between clean and unclean beasts; for the distinction is spoken of as familiarly known and recognised. And what was the ground of it? Not certainly any thing in the nature of the beasts themselves, for we now regard them all indiscriminately as on the same footing, and we have undoubted divine warrant for doing so; nor any thing in their fitness for being used as food, for animal food was not yet allowed. The distinction could have respect only to the rite of sacrifice. Hence arises another irresistible argument for the divine origin and authority of that rite, and a proof also of the substantial identity of the Patriarchal and the Mosaic institutions. The same standing ordinance of animal sacrifice,—and the same separation of certain sorts of animals as proper for that use,—prevailed in both. The religion, in fact, in its faith and worship, was exactly the same.

Seven days, then, before the tremendous catastrophe, the signal was given to Noah. With all that were to be saved, he was now on board. And "the Lord shut him in" (ver. 16).

In what a position did Noah now find himself! And in what a position did he leave his contemporaries!

Three successive eras may be noted in the years before the flood; three trials of the faith of Noah,—three signs and warnings to the world.

When the Lord first fixed the period of his long-suffering patience, and resolved to spare man on the earth for one hundred and twenty years, and no longer,—he doubtless intimated this purpose in some way ; announcing the destruction coming on all flesh, and giving some public pledge of the grace which Noah found in his eyes. This would be a new call to Noah to labour in his vocation of a teacher of righteousness, as well as a loud alarm to the world at large. Noah obeyed the call ;—the world set at naught the alarm. To Noah it was indeed a trying office that was assigned,— to testify for God in the midst of such a generation, to whose hatred and jealousy the very token of approbation with which God had honoured him, tended the more to expose him. He became a marked man, the object of scorn and contumely, of injury and insult. The people watched for his halting, and waylaid his path with subtle snares. It was a difficult part he had in these circumstances to perform,—a dangerous duty he had to discharge,—as he walked humbly with his God and went about warning the ungodly.

But the second era was far more critical than the first. The order reaches Noah to prepare the ark, and to gather food for the support of its destined inmates. The predicted judgment now assumes a more distinct form. Not only is it intimated that the world is to be destroyed, but the kind of destruction is specified. There is to be a flood. To a gainsaying and perverse generation, this makes the threatening appear even more improbable than before. Not considering how precariously their earth is poised, " standing out of the water and in the water" (2 Pet. iii. 5),—being wilfully ignorant of the facts of the creation, which doubtless had been revealed,—they laugh to scorn the notion of an overflowing deluge, as a chimera and a dream. They rely securely on nature's uniformity ;—as if the account of the primeval watery chaos and the division of the waters above and under the firmament, were an idle tale ;—as if there were no store of rain above and no great deep beneath. Hence Noah, with his endless reiteration and denunciation of terror, seems as one mad. And when they see him gravely setting to work on his huge unwieldy vessel, and gathering provisions for the motley crowd with which he means to stow her,—what are they to think? Can the man be serious and in earnest? Is it to be endured that he should so flagrantly outrage common sense, and so rudely offend his fellows, by his hoarse prophecy of evil, and the clank of his incessant hammer echoing his ominous and hollow voice of woe?

But now his task is done. One brief week is yet to elapse, and then–

Shall we say it is the eve before the Sabbath? The day has been spent in getting all into the ark,—his wife, his sons, his daughters-in-law, and the whole crowd of living creatures following. Noah himself enters, and "the Lord shuts him in." Thus the Sabbath begins, the last Sabbath of that old world. Within the ark there is Sabbatic rest, the quiet assurance of faith, chastened by solemn dread and awful expectancy. Without, on the earth, there are mingled sentiments of wonder, contempt, and bitter triumph; —sometimes a lurking fear, again a feeling of glad relief. Men have got rid at last of the preacher of righteousness. And if we assume, as is not improbable, that during this very week the aged Methuselah was taken from the evil to come, —it might seem to be the very jubilee of unrestricted and unreproved lawlessness that had now arrived.

True, it had been said, "Yet seven days and I will bring the flood." But how can this be? The heaven is serene; the earth is smiling; all nature is gay and joyous,—it being, as some reckon, the first breaking forth of spring. Now is the season of mirth, eating and drinking, marrying and giving in marriage. And Noah, the gloomy censor of the world's harmless joys, where is he now? Immured in a vast dungeon; buried alive; self-immolated; as good as dead; and at any-rate well out of the way!

What a contrast, during that awful week;—that mysterious pause ;—while the elements are gathering their strength for the sudden crash!

Look within the ark. There are prisoners there ; and to the eye of sense, they are apparently shut up to die. But they are prisoners of hope ;—they have fled to a stronghold ; —they have that all around them through which no floods of wrath can penetrate ;—their refuge is " pitched within and without with pitch" (chap. vi. 14). It is well protected against the worst weather. And what an emblem is the pitch ;—the very word meaning propitiation or the covering of sins by sacrifice ;—of their complete security from every kind of terror, whether temporal or eternal,—from all risk of perishing either here or hereafter ! They have pitch on all sides of their new dwelling ; pitch within and without, —pitch, making it effectually a covert from the storm and a hiding-place from the tempest—even such as A MAN is to the sinner,—the man Christ Jesus (Is. xxxii. 2).

Look again without the ark. There are prisoners there, too, " spirits in prison ;" condemned criminals, confined in the lowest vaults of that frail fortress on which the waves of wrath are about to burst. Do you see them, these prisoners, all alive and joyous, and affecting to pity the small company buried within the ark? Do you see them making merry,— or trying, by desperate gambling, to make gain?

Look once more and listen. There is a lightning flash, a rushing mighty noise. The flood comes.—In which of the two prisons would you have your spirit to be?

Thus, by the ark which he prepared, Noah " condemned the world." The warning which might have saved them, turned to their greater condemnation. But " he delivered his own soul" (Ezek. xxxiii. 9) ; and he prepared the ark to " the saving also of his house" (Heb. xi. 7).

I pass over the catastrophe itself, without discussing the various questions which have been raised concerning it. The

Apostle Peter, referring to the inspired account of the creation, has given the only explanation we have in scripture of the immediate cause and manner of the flood;—"By the word of God the heavens were of old, and the earth standing out of the water and in the water: whereby the world that then was, being overflowed with water, perished" (2 Pet. iii. 5, 6). So he connects the two miracles. In creation, the earth arose out of the waters; they partly retired into the deep places of the earth, and partly were gathered above in vapoury clouds, so as to leave the dry land. Convulsions from beneath, and incessant rain from above, conspired to bring back the waters, so that again they "stood above the mountains" (Ps. civ. 6).

The forty days of unceasing rain are now past, and the work of destruction is accomplished. The flood having risen to its utmost height becomes nearly stationary (ver. 17). These forty days form part of the hundred and fifty,—twice mentioned as the entire time of the flood's duration,—from the first day of rain to the day of the ark's resting on the mountains of Ararat. They were the days of the flood's increase; during which the ark was lifted up and floated safely on the surface of the rising tide of waters (ver. 18). About the end of the forty days, or perhaps nearer the middle of the hundred and fifty, the ark had reached its highest elevation. In sad and solitary majesty it rode sublime;— the only moving and living thing over the boundless ocean of death.

It is a time for the exercise of faith. Far down, in the unfathomable depths below, lies a dead and buried world. Noah, shut up in his narrow prison, seems to be abandoned to his fate. He cannot help himself. And in this universal visitation of sin—this terrible reckoning with sinners—why should he obtain mercy? What is he, that when all else are taken, he should be left? May he not be righteously suffered to perish after all ? Is he not a sinner, like the rest ? Does he not feel himself to be "the chief of sinners ?"

But the Lord, who " shut him in," has not forgotten him. With Noah, God has established his covenant; and for his own name's sake his covenant must stand. Therefore the Lord remembers Noah, and in his own good time brings the ship to land. The earth is again prepared for the habitation of man and beast. Once more it emerges out of the water; —never again to perish by the same means.

As the waters gradually subsided, Noah waited patiently where God had placed him ; only sending forth, at intervals, as the earliest visitors to the new world, the wandering raven and the domestic dove (chap. viii. 7-12). The raven was the first to find himself at home ; amid the remains, it has been supposed, of earth's former tenants. Upon the carcasses lying on the mountains or floating on the waves,—after his long abstinence from such food in the ark,—he might now greedily prey. Sad omen for the still cursed ground! But there is room also for the gentle dove ; and there is an emblem of peace which she may bear back to the ark, as the pledge of a better destiny awaiting this world after all.

In the successive intervals of seven days, marked by the sending of these winged messengers, we recognise, as we have had occasion to recognise already, the division of time by weeks. In the earliest worship after the fall, there is probable evidence of the continued observance of the weekly Sabbath. The entrance into the ark is measured by a single week from the beginning of the flood. The incidents that make the subsiding of the flood so interesting, are separated from one another by the same number of days. We can scarcely therefore fairly resist the conclusion that the Sabbath, as dividing time by weeks, was then known as a primitive institution ; and that the sanctification of the Sabbath formed a part of the divine service observed even in the ark. On the Sabbath, the dove brings to the weary prisoners of hope

the olive branch, which is to give them assurance of rest
(ver. 11). And accordingly Noah, seeing the face of the
ground to be dry, after waiting another week, goes forth with
his companions, by God's commandment, to resume possession
of the earth (verses 13-19).

The patriarch's first business is to erect an altar, and offer
sacrifices (ver. 20). Each kind of animal proper for sacrifice
successively furnished a victim; for of each kind there was
one individual, over and above the three pairs, provided
probably for this very end. Thus the new earth was cleansed
and consecrated for man's dwelling-place. "The Lord smelled
a sweet savour" (ver. 21). He was propitiated, reconciled,
well pleased:—having respect, undoubtedly, not to the heca-
tombs then slain,—the blood of beasts and birds,—but to
the more precious blood which theirs prefigured, the better
sacrifice of which the new earth was to be the scene. It is
that great sacrifice alone which suspends the doom to which
the world is otherwise every instant liable. It is in virtue
of that sacrifice that God purposes, in his heart, not again to
curse the ground any more for man's sake. If the Lord were
to act according to man's deserving, there would be no
interval, and no end, of his judgments. "The imagination
of man's heart being evil from his youth" (ver. 21),—no
threatenings, no terrors, no floods of wrath, can purge away
his guilt, or change and amend his nature. But where judgment is impotent, grace may prevail. There is to be blood
shed which shall cleanse from all sin, and a word of reconciliation preached, effectually to save the chief of sinners.
For the shedding of that precious blood,—for the preaching
of that blessed word,—the world is to be spared until the
end come. There is to be no more any violent shock of
nature, or universal destruction of life. The earth is to stand
secure during all the remainder of its appointed days; and
the seasons are not to cease.

But though its course is to be no more broken in the middle, it is to have a sudden and terrible termination at the last. The judgment of flood is but the type of the still more awful judgment of fire. The earth, saved from water, is reserved for fire. By both elements,—by the baptism both of water and of fire,—it must be purged, before it can be fitted for the habitation of the Lord and his redeemed. Meanwhile, the Lord is preparing a stronghold, an ark of safety. It is the ark of his everlasting covenant, to which all that will believe may flee. In this ark, or in other words, in Christ,—they are now dead and buried; though still they have a hidden life,—a life hid with Christ in God (Col. iii. 3). To the world, they may seem as fond and foolish as did Noah when he entered into his ark, and "the Lord shut him in." The men of the world, living at ease because all things continue as they were, may marvel and rage, when they see any of us, who once were of the world, moved by a wary fear of coming wrath, seriously betaking ourselves to the only hiding-place. But let us hear the word of the Lord: "Come my people, enter thou into thy chambers,"—the chambers prepared, made ready and set wide open, in the Lord's ark, which is his Christ, his anointed one,—"enter into thy chambers, and shut thy doors about thee: hide thyself as it were for a little moment, until the indignation be overpast. For behold, the Lord cometh out of his place to punish the inhabitants of the earth" (Isa. xxvi. 20). And who then may stand? Where shall the ungodly appear? Shut in, imprisoned, with no door of escape, while fire is devouring the earth! But let the Lord hide us now. Let him shut us up into Christ's blessed gospel of reconciliation:—let him shut us up into Christ himself. Then, although the elements should melt with fervent heat, and this earth and these heavens should be dissolved, we, in Christ, shall be hidden in security, floating in air above the fiery storm (1 Thess. iv.

16, 17).   And, finally, as the judgment passes away, an olive branch will be brought to us from the renovated world ;— and in the new heavens and the new earth, wherein dwelleth righteousness, we shall dwell for ever with the Lord, and offer the sacrifices of praise continually.

10

THE NEW WORLD IN ITS THREE DEPARTMENTS OF NATURE, PROVIDENCE, AND GRACE

1 THE LAW OF NATURE (Genesis 9:1-7)

Every creature of God is good, and nothing to be refused, if it be received
with thanksgiving ; for it is sanctified by the word of God, and prayer.
1 Timothy 4:4,5

THE law of nature is the rule which God has appointed for
the preservation of life on the earth. It embraces all the
arrangements, whether physical or moral, which are necessary
for that end. At first that law was very simple. It was
materially affected, however, by the fall ; and it was subjected
to still further modifications after the flood.

In its original simplicity, the law of nature provided for
the increase of the earth's inhabitants, for man's dominion
over the other animals, and for the supply of food ; and these
three objects it attained by the most suitable and effectual
means,—the distinction of the sexes, the native superiority of
mind, and the spontaneous fertility of the ground (chap. i.
28-30). The form of expression, in the first announcement of
this law at the creation, remarkably corresponds with what
is said on the renewal of it after the flood. In both instances
it is ushered in by a benediction :—" The Lord blessed them"
(chap. i. 28). " The Lord blessed Noah " (chap. ix. 1). Then,
having thus generally given his blessing ;—thereby consecrat-
ing as his own the law or rule which he is about to institute ;

—the Lord proceeds to lay down more particularly the details of his plan.

The plan is, I repeat, very simple. It provides first for the propagation of life ; and appoints the same rule, in the same terms, for the inferior animals (chap. i. 22) and for man (chap. i. 28), " Be fruitful, and multiply, and fill the earth." Afterwards that rule, as applicable to man, is more precisely and particularly explained, and takes the form of the ordinance of marriage (chap. ii. 23, 24). Next, for the protection of life and the safety of the earth's increasing population, the plan had in it a rule of order and subordination. Man, bearing the image of God, was to reign, as in God's stead, over all things here below, by the native superiority of intelligent mind, and by the influence of benefits conferred. While he restrained and commanded the creatures, he was to love, protect, and caress them. This was all the government that the yet unfallen world needed—God supreme over man—man supreme over the other animals. Lastly, for the support of life, and the sustenance of earth's teeming tribes, the Lord appointed the simple food which, as the God of nature, he bounteously furnished. The ground, as yet uncursed, grudged not the supplies which the creatures needed. With unstinted and spontaneous prodigality, the mother earth was to nourish from her own bosom all her children.

After the fall, the law of nature, in all its parts, is very considerably modified. The ordinance of marriage is still holy ; but the sorrow of the woman, greatly multiplied, is the token that, while human life is to be thus propagated, it is not now propagated in innocency, but in hereditary guilt and woe. For the safety and protection of life a new element of government and order is introduced. It is the subordination of the woman to her husband, and the consequent establishment of domestic rule. Law becomes indispensable, and power to enforce law. The husband and father becomes a head and lord. Formerly, the dominion of man over the creatures sufficed for every purpose of social harmony and security. Now, there must be the dominion of man over his fellows ; and that dominion begins in the family. The husband is the first king. Finally, as to the sustentation of life, the earth now yields her produce reluctantly ; and hard toil becomes the lot of man. The decree goes forth : " In the sweat of thy face shalt thou eat bread."

The law of nature, or of the preservation of life, as renewed after the flood, receives several new modifications. In its first branch, indeed, it is identical with what it was before. Life is to be propagated, and living creatures are to fill the earth ; the mode of increase, in each several kind, remains : and the ordinance of marriage stands in all respects unchanged. But there is a considerable alteration in reference to the second. Man receives a new power over the other animals, and has a new power set up over himself. The power, in both instances, is based on terror : but it is terror necessary and salutary.

Man's dominion over the creatures is henceforward to rest mainly on fear and dread :—" The fear of you, and the dread of you, shall be upon every beast of the earth " (ver. 2, 3). Originally, as it would seem, man's dominion was of a milder character ;—he ruled more by an influence of love ;—a good understanding, as it were, prevailing between him and his harmless subjects. By his kind demeanour, and his erect and noble bearing, he could sufficiently control them. But when sin marred the impress of his mental and moral majesty, and disturbed his friendship with the creatures under his sway— the very familiarity to which they were accustomed may have tended to introduce danger and disorder. His authority, based on love, being shaken—who shall say what part his once willing and obedient subjects may have had, in the violence with which the earth was filled ? Something like that is, perhaps, referred to in this very passage, when God, announcing what is henceforth to be the doom of murder, speaks as if beasts as well as men had been implicated in the antediluvian bloodshed ;—" Surely your blood of your lives will I require ; at the hand of every beast will I require it," as well as " at the hand of man" (ver. 5). After the flood, at anyrate, man's command over the creatures is not simply restored, but placed on a firmer footing. God inspires them with a dread of man. This instinctive fear has ever since characterised all nature's tribes—not the weak and timid only, but the savage and fero-cious also. Occasionally, indeed, it is changed by circumstances into the rage of hunger, or revenge, or despair ; but still it easily regains its habitual sway, and subjects them, in spite of all their strength and cunning, to their appointed master, either as servants or as victims, either to be tamed or to be con-quered, to do his work or be put out of his way.

Such is now man's dominion over the creatures ;—a do-minion painful in itself and apt to be abused ; bearing but too plain marks of that vanity under which, for man's sin, " the whole creation groaneth and travaileth together." Still, it is in mercy that God has rendered man thus formidable to the other dwellers on this earth. It is no enviable power, when rightly viewed, which he wields ; but, such as it is, it is the gift of God. It is the pledge, moreover, of his great plan of ultimate redemption. That man is still lord of this lower world, in any sense, and under whatever disadvantages, is the result of the covenant of grace and the mediation of Christ (Ps. viii. ; Heb. ii.) And the fact that he is so even now, gives assurance of the day when, in the terms of that covenant, the meek shall inherit the earth and all the creatures shall be at peace (Is. xi. 1-9).

But not only is there new power given to man over the creatures ;—there is new power set up over man himself. The power of the sword is instituted, and it is given into the hand of the magistrate. This is implied in the announcement which God makes of his determination to suppress violence, and to do so by the agency of a human arm :—" At the hand of every man's brother will I require the life of man. Whoso sheddeth man's blood, by man shall his blood be shed : for in the image of God made he man" (ver. 5, 6). Thus, " the powers that be are ordained of God" (Rom. xiii. 1-5). The magistrate has here his divine sanction. For this is not a mere acknowledgment of the instinct of private vengeance, far less a vindication or justification of it. It unquestionably refers to public judicial procedure, and places a high responsible power in the hands of the ruler of the people. For the protection of life, he is to hold the sword ; nor is he to hold it in vain : he is to be a terror to evil doers.

The government which was appointed after the fall, and vested in the husband, or the head of each house or family, bore the character of domestic discipline, or of that mild authority which is exercised in laying down rules for the order of a household, and inflicting occasional correction for the good of its offending members. It had nothing in it of a punitive or penal jurisdiction, properly so called ; and apparently it comprehended no power of life and death. On the contrary, we have seen (chap. 4 : 15) that the punishment of death, even for the crime of murder, was suspended, or kept in abeyance, by the express command of God, in the world before the flood. The experiment, as it were, was then tried of subjecting mankind to the least possible amount of coercion and restraint. And, alas ! it miserably failed. " The earth was filled with violence." Now, therefore, a new kind of government is to be introduced ; there must be a sterner rule than the mere discipline of home. Society must be more thoroughly organised and compacted ; law must speak with a more peremptory voice, and power must enforce with a higher hand the sanctions of law. Especially, and by all means, life must be preserved. The sentence of death for death must be recorded, and the sword must be unsparingly used against the murderer.

Such is the divine warrant for capital punishment ; very express and clear, but at the same time very limited. It is indeed true, that this announcement in the verse before us, is to be understood as virtually embodying the great charter of all civil magistracy, and sanctioning generally the exercise of that kind of power, of which capital punishment is the extreme infliction. It is to this charter doubtless, among others, that the Apostle Paul appeals, when he lays down the Christian doctrine respecting the power of civil rulers and the subjection due to them ; especially when he speaks of them as " bearing the sword," and as being " God's ministers, to execute wrath, as avengers upon him that doeth evil" (Rom. xiii. 1-4). But it is to be observed that the case of murder is here very particularly specified, and the case of murder alone, as the only crime for which that particular punishment of death is actually prescribed. The murderer, to the exclusion of all other offenders, is marked out for execution. By fair analogy, this may be held to warrant the visiting of all sorts of offences, not merely with salutary chastisement and corrective discipline, but with penal severities. But this precise kind of severity, the taking away of life, is of such a nature that it can scarcely be extended beyond the explicit declaration of God himself, the only Lord of life. The magistrate may not inflict death on any criminal without the command of God ; but having God's command, he may not suffer the criminal to live. Here, therefore, we have the divine statute of capital punishments for the world at large,—a statute altogether distinct from the provisions of the Jewish law, in which God, as himself the immediate sovereign of that people, in the exercise of his absolute prerogative, subjected other crimes to the same doom. This original statute remains in force, independently of any special and temporary enactments, as binding upon all governments ordained by God. The murderer must die by the hand of the magistrate, and except the murderer, none else.

This view is confirmed by what precedes, and what follows the ordinance in question.

In what goes before, God intimates his fixed determination to make inquisition for blood (ver. 5). He resolves, as it were, himself to look more strictly after the commission of this crime, and to see that it shall be visited more promptly than had been the case before. The murderer is no longer to experience so' much of his forbearance as in time past; for life, human life, is very precious in his sight. Even a beast that slays a man is not excused. The violence which filled the old world must be effectually restrained. God, therefore, will not let the murderer go; he must be taken and unhesitatingly put to death. Such is the divine purpose. And in fulfilment of that purpose, God demands the co-operation of human governments. He himself undertakes, as it were, for the discovery of the murderer; and then he gives him over to the civil magistrate to be slain.

That is the arrangement which the God of heaven makes with the powers which he has ordained on earth. He fails not in doing his part; for is it not notorious and proverbial that " murder will out ?" Divine justice, in the dealings of providence, dogs the heels of the shedder of blood, and hunts him down,—until his crime is brought to light, and either some " damning proof," or confession wrung out of the agony of remorse, discloses the criminal. Woe be to man if he abuses his trust when God has done his part;—if either not inflicting death at all, or inflicting it too frequently and indiscriminately for crimes of every dye, he makes void that stern and unrelenting ordinance of God, which, isolating from all others this one enormity of bloodshed, devotes and consecrates to it alone, and to it without fail, the doom of the accursed tree,— the malefactor's death of shame.

In what follows, also, God still further explains and enforces this ordinance, by the reason which he assigns for it. The life of man is to be thus guarded by so terrible a sanction, because God made him in his own image (ver. 6). It is true that the image is marred; but it is not marred beyond remedy. In every living individual it either is already or may be restored. Therefore every living individual is of inestim-

able value ; and his life, viewed in the light of heaven and
eternity, is beyond all calculation important.

How precious, when thus regarded, is man, simply as man!
How undeniable his claim, not only to protection at the hand
of his fellows, but to all good offices ! Here is one,—a unit in
the mighty mass of this world's crowded throng,—one of many
millions. What is he, that his fellows should go out of
their way to notice him ? Of what account is he, that all mankind should be obliged to give heed to him ? If he were lost,
what matters it ? A single grain of sand on the sea-shore is
displaced,—a drop of water from the ocean is amissing. Such
is the measure which infidelity would take of man, of the individual man. And so measuring him, what wonder if, instead of avenging slaughter, it slays men by thousands ? What
have conquerors, monarchs, and statesmen to do with individuals ? Their movements are on a great scale. Why should
they turn aside when I meet them, or pause to raise me when
I fall ? This single sentence,—what a change it makes ! " In
the image of God created he man ? "—this man ;—this particular man ;—myself for instance, or my outcast brother. This
is man's indefeasible charter, making the person of the meanest
as sacred as any king's ;—challenging for him, be he poor as
Lazarus, respect, reverence, regard. Let Christian magistrates
and Christian people look to him ;—not merely to require his
blood if he be slain ;—but to do him good while he is alive.
At anyrate, let them see to it that whoso sheddeth his blood,
shall have his own blood shed, in righteous retribution.

There yet remains the third branch of this law of nature
to be considered, the provision made for the support of life.
In this article, a very important change takes place at the
flood ; animal food being then, for the first time, granted for
the use of man ;—" Every moving thing that liveth shall be
meat for you ; even as the green herb have I given you all
things " (ver. 3).

The grant of animal food has a restriction imposed upon it ;—"flesh with the life thereof, which is the blood thereof, shall ye not eat" (ver. 4). This prohibition was probably intended to guard against certain horrors which prevailed when the earth was filled with violence, as well as to prevent wanton cruelty in slaying animals for food, and ensure that, previously to their being used, they shall not be tortured or mangled, but put to death in the same orderly way as when their life was taken for an atonement for sin.

A similar, but more precise injunction against the eating of blood, was subsequently enacted in the Jewish law ; and it was enforced by the Jews on their Gentile proselytes among some other precepts ascribed by them to Noah, and considered to be binding, apart from their national and ceremonial institutions. These last, it would seem, they did not require all converts from heathenism to observe ; but abstinence from the eating of blood was understood to be binding upon all. This may partly explain the sanction which the Jerusalem Council gave to the rule, in their judgment on the question submitted to them by the Gentile Church at Antioch (Acts xv. 29).

How far any such precept is applicable to Christians of subsequent ages, we need not now inquire. The prohibition, in the Levitical code, was undoubtedly connected with the rite of sacrifice ;—the blood being reserved exclusively for the purpose of expiation. That reason will not apply now, when blood is no longer shed for that end. And it is by no means clear that this Noetic rule is the same as that afterwards enacted in the Mosaic ritual. It does not appear to have any religious meaning ; on the contrary, it seems intended merely for the prevention of cannibal ferocity and wanton cruelty. And this view of it is made nearly certain, if we consider the relation which it bears to the general denunciation of blood-shedding. God speaks as the preserver of man and beast ; he gives the beasts into the hands of man, but it is with a limitation of his power over their lives to the strict necessity of finding food ; just as he gives man into the hands of his fellows, with a corresponding limitation of their power over his life to the single case of murder. If life is to be taken,— the life of a beast or the life of a man,—it must be exclusively for the end which God ordains ; with no aggravation of needless severity, and no accompaniments of rude or wild barbarity.

Such is the law of nature, or economy of life, as appointed by God for the world after the flood. It is, in part, a discipline of severity ; but it is to be viewed chiefly as a provision of mercy. It does not touch any of the endearments or refinements of social intercourse, as based upon the pure and peaceful affections of home. Men are still to dwell in families, and in families they are to fill and occupy the earth. But the dangers to which human society was exposed from the fearless familiarity of the subject animals and the growing anarchy of mere domestic rule, are to be remedied by the dread of man being forced upon the beasts ; and by the sword of magisterial authority being raised in terror against evil doers. And to meet the accumulating difficulty of obtaining supplies from the earth alone, the use of animal food is allowed. Then, to guard against the abuse of these beneficent arrangements, the sword of the magistrate is ordained to be used always for the protection of the life of man, and with a reverential respect to the image of God which man bears. And even the beasts given to man for food are to be the objects of a certain scrupulous care. They are not to furnish a bloody meal. They are to be so treated as to preclude the infliction of needless pain, and prevent any harm which the sanguinary use of them might cause.

How admirable is the wisdom of God, how great his goodness, in ordering the constitution even of a fallen world ! How manifold are the provisions of his care and kindness for alleviating the ills which sin has caused ! Far from leaving us to spend at random the season of his forbearance, as instinct or passion might blindly prompt,—God establishes a rule or system, whose salutary operation, even those who continue to set at naught its gracious design, are compelled practically to feel. It is that system—based on the principles of holy marriage, of lawful magistracy, and of laborious mastery over the soil that is to be cultivated, and the animals that may be slain, for food,—which alone hinders this globe from becoming a scene such as devils, and none but devils, could delight to witness. It is true that no mere external arrangements can of themselves secure the present or final welfare of any of Noah's children ; and all such arrangements are liable to perversion and abuse. Still, without their due observance, life is but a compound of license, disorder, and precarious subsistence or pining famine ! Purity, peace, and plenty flourish in any community, mainly in proportion as these ordinances are honoured and obeyed. And they place each individual man in the best possible position for escaping, through grace, the corruption that is in the world through lust, and laying hold on the blessed hope of everlasting life, to which, by the resurrection of Jesus Christ from the dead, believers are begotten again.

11

THE CONSTITUTION OF THE NEW WORLD, IN ITS
THREE DEPARTMENTS OF NATURE, PROVIDENCE,
AND GRACE

2. THE SCHEME OF PROVIDENCE (Genesis 9:8-17)

For this is as the waters of Noah unto me : for as I have sworn that the
waters of Noah should no more go over the earth ; so have I sworn
that I would not be wroth with thee, nor rebuke thee.   Isaiah 54:9

THE scheme of providence, in the world after the flood, is a
dispensation of forbearance, subservient to a dispensation of
grace, and preparatory to a dispensation of judgment.   Of
this forbearance, on the part of God, Noah receives a promise
and a pledge.   The promise is given in the form of a covenant
(ver. 9-11), while the pledge, as usual, is a seal of the covenant
(ver. 12-17) ; and the covenant thus sealed is the counterpart
of the decree or determination previously recorded, in connection with the acceptance of Noah's sacrifice (chap. viii. 21, 22).
The purpose which the Lord on that occasion formed, is now
openly announced (chap. ix. 8-17).   Then, " he said in his
heart ;"—now he speaks out, and binds himself by word and
sign.   It was then a secret intention : now it is a publicly
ratified and sealed covenant.   To Noah and his sons it is probable that the covenant alone, with its seal, was made public ;
—to us, the secret purpose also is disclosed.   We are admitted, as it were, into the counsels of God, in order that,
interpreting the covenant established with Noah by what we
are told of the previous mind of God, we may the better un-

derstand the nature and end, as well as the grounds and reasons of that covenant.

I. Looking, then, to the original purpose, of which we read as existing in the mind of God (chap. viii. 21, 22), his determination to spare the earth is explained on two principles, which it is important to observe. The first of these is the inveterate and desperate depravity of man : " I will not again curse the ground any more for man's sake ; for the imagination of man's heart is evil from his youth" (chap. viii. 21).

But how should that be a reason for the exercise of forbearance and long-suffering ? Or are we to adopt the marginal reading—" though," instead of " for,"—and conceive of God as resolving to spare the earth from another flood, not on account of man's corruption, but in spite of it ? It may be so ;—and indeed it matters little which of these two ways of rendering the phrase we prefer. At the same time, there is a peculiar force and significancy in the expression as it stands. " Why should ye be stricken any more ?" is the indignant voice of God to Israel by his servant Isaiah ; " ye will revolt more and more." " The whole head is sick, and the whole heart faint. From the sole of the foot even unto the head there is no soundness at all ; but wounds, and bruises, and putrefying sores " (chap. i. 5, 6). There is no sound part in you on which any chastening stroke can take effect. I will smite no more, for ye are too far gone to be thus reclaimed. So also the Lord says in his heart respecting the world after the flood ;—I will not again curse the earth—I will not again visit it with so desolating a judgment. Why should I ? What good purpose would it serve ? On man, on whom principally it is designed to tell, this kind of treatment can make no impression ; for his nature is too thoroughly depraved. Even the lesson of another flood would be thrown away upon him.

Thus this divine reasoning presents on one side a dark and ominous aspect. But on the other side it reflects a blessed gleam of light. It indicates the purpose of God, in his treatment of the world during the remainder of its allotted time, not to deal with its inhabitants according to their sins, nor to reward them after their iniquities. His providence is to be conducted, not on the principle of penal or judicial retribution, but on another principle altogether, irrespective of the merits or the works of man. What that is, appears from the relation which the Lord's decree bears to the sacrifices by which he is said to be propitiated (chap. viii. 20, 21). These undoubtedly derive their efficacy from the all-sufficient sacrifice of atonement which they prefigured. And it is that sacrifice which alone satisfactorily explains the Lord's determination to spare the earth. It does so in two ways. In the first place, the interposition of that sacrifice vindicates and justifies the righteous God in passing by the sins of men (Rom. iii. 25),—in exercising forbearance and suspending judgment; it renders his long-suffering consistent with his justice;—otherwise, as the righteous judge, he could not spare the guilty for a single hour. But, secondly, that sacrifice of Christ reaches beyond mere forbearance, and is effectual to save. Its direct and proper object is, not merely to provide that the barren tree may be let alone, but to secure that it shall be cultured and revived, so as to become fruitful. Therefore God spares the earth on account of the sacrifice of Christ, that, in the innumerable company of his believing people, Christ may see of the travail of his soul, and be satisfied.

Thus the Lord's purpose in regard to the sparing of the earth is explained by these two principles :—the first, negative, that he is not to deal with men according to their works ; the second, positive, that he is to deal with them according to his own grace and mercy, as embodied in the great sacrifice of atonement.

And as by these two principles the Lord's purpose of forbearance is explained and justified, so by them also it is restricted and defined. The first, while securing that the earth shall not again be visited with any universal retributive infliction, such as the general deluge, involves partial, temporary, and local judgments. These are by no means precluded. For it is of the very essence of a dispensation of forbearance, that while judgment, on the whole, is in suspense and in abeyance, significant hints and tokens of it shall frequently occur. The second again implies a limit to that forbearance. Connected as it is with an atoning sacrifice, it has a distinct purpose, and therefore also a definite period. There is an allotted time during which the earth is to remain ;—it has a certain season of grace. Already God has given one awful proof of the decision with which he inflicts judgment ; and if now he suspends judgment, it cannot be in mere indulgence. But seeing that judgment alone will not reclaim the evil heart of man, and having a plan of grace and reconciliation to accomplish, he grants an interval of respite. Still, it is only an interval, and an interval of limited and fixed extent. For the very provision of present mercy implies coming wrath; and the days of the earth are numbered.

Such is the decree or purpose of God, for the continued preservation of the earth ; and such is its connection with his acceptance of Noah's sacrifice.

II. In its publication to the human family (chap. ix.), this decree is embodied in the form of a covenant, and ratified by a significant seal.

In the first place, the Lord establishes a covenant on the earth. He might have kept his decree secret. He might have left men to learn from the result what his purpose was ; and they might have lived in continual apprehension of another desolating flood. But he dealt more graciously with them, and condescended to give, not merely an intimation, but an assurance, of his design of mercy. He bound himself by an oath, as he did when he announced the flood : " I, behold I, establish my covenant with you, and with your seed after you ; and with every living creature that is with you " (chap. ix. 9–11). Thus it is in the form of a covenant, and with the solemn ratification of an oath, that God intimates his purpose to spare the earth. And what covenant can be meant but only the covenant of grace? That and that alone, is pre-eminently his covenant—"my covenant;"—always the same in its character and terms, whatever may be the kind of salvation meant. In the present instance, it is exemption from the temporal judgment of a flood. But that is secured by the very same covenant in which the higher blessings of life eternal are comprehended. It is God's own covenant, —the covenant of free and sovereign grace, as opposed to any covenant of works, or merit, or express and stimulated condition,—it is that covenant which gives security against another flood;—an irrevocable covenant, standing sure, whatever may be man's doings and deservings, to the very end of earth's numbered days.

Then again, secondly, the covenant, as usual, has a seal or pledge; designed, as it were, to put the Lord in remembrance of his promise, and to settle and confirm the confidence of men :—" This is the token of the covenant: I do set my bow in the cloud, and it shall be for a token of a covenant between me and the earth " (ver. 12-17). It is not necessary to understand that the rainbow appeared now for the first time; but only that it was now, for the first time, assumed and adopted as a sign of the covenant of forbearance and grace. That end it might fully serve, although it existed before; for it is not any quality or virtue in itself, but the mere word of God alone, which gives to this, or any other token, its significancy and force. There is, however, an obvious propriety and beauty in the selection of such a token as this, for such a purpose. From amid the lowering and vapoury clouds, there suddenly emerges the fairest of all nature's sights, the many-coloured arch, spanning the dark earth, and reflecting the beams of the glorious sun. It is God's proof of his faithfulness to the children of men,—the pledge that he is keeping, and will keep, his covenant. He looks on the bow, that he may remember the covenant. And as the covenant, being made by sacrifice, not only secures a season of forbearance, but contemplates an end infinitely more important; so the rainbow becomes the seal of the covenant in this higher view of it also, —and is the token and pledge of its spiritual and eternal blessings. Hence, among the ensigns and emblems of redeeming glory, the rainbow holds a conspicuous place (Ezek. i. 28; Rev. iv. 3, x. 1); and hence, moreover, the covenant which it seals, gives to God's faithful people an argument of confidence, not for time only, but for eternity. He is true to his covenant, in sparing the world. Will he not much more be true to the same covenant, in saving those for whose sake the world is spared? (Is. liv. 9, 10; Jer. xxxiii. 20-25).

12

THE CONSTITUTION OF THE NEW WORLD, IN ITS
THREE DEPARTMENTS OF NATURE, PROVIDENCE,
AND GRACE

3. THE ELECTION OF GRACE (Genesis 9:18-29)

Charity rejoiceth not in iniquity, but rejoiceth in the truth.   1 Cor. 11:6
Salvation is of the Jews.   John 14:22

THE narrative which closes the history of the flood, introduces
the long history of grace contending with nature ; the seed of
the woman and the seed of the serpent, drawing off again to
their respective sides.   The enmity remains and the warfare is
resumed.   A single incident is selected to illustrate its re-
commencement ; an isolated picture is presented to us,—a
picture, however, most affecting and full of meaning,—as much
so as was the scene which began the struggle in the world
before the flood.   In either case, it is a domestic scene, a
family picture, that is exhibited.   In the one case, two brothers,
—in the other, a father and his three sons,—open the grand
drama of which the wide earth is to be the stage,—and of
which the issues are to be eternal.   Noah, with Shem, Ham,
and Japheth, and perhaps also Canaan, the son of Ham,—such
is the little household group, among whom we are to recognise
all the features of grace and nature respectively,—of the
church and the world,—as they mutually oppose, and at the
same time influence, one another.   How they usually lived
together, is not said ; how they acted on one memorable day,

is all that we are told. But that is enough. It reveals both Satan's malice and the power of the Spirit of God.

Noah is overtaken in a fault; he "began to be an husbandman, and planted a vineyard, and drank of the wine, and was drunken" (ver. 20, 21). It is an unwonted offence; the very use which Ham makes of it proves it to be so. But that such a blot should fall, even once only, on the character of such a man, is grief enough, and far more than enough. What can we say? What can we think? How could Noah be so left to himself, even in one solitary instance; and why, when nothing else in the history of his latter days is left on record, should this most painful narrative be preserved? Alas! is it not needed? Has wine ceased to be a mocker? or strong drink to be raging? or have men, even wise men, ceased to be deceived thereby? Are the servants of God,—heirs though they be of the righteousness that is by faith,—preachers of righteousness too,—never tempted now to tarry at the wine—to go to seek the mixed wine? (Prov. xx. 1, xxiii. 29-32).

But it is the conduct of Ham and Canaan on this sad occasion, that is emphatically stigmatised; for it would seem that Canaan had some share in the offence committed, as he certainly had a principal share in the doom pronounced. What precisely that offence was, can scarcely be gathered from the narrative; although we may partly guess its motive. It was obviously an instance of flagrant filial irreverence; for not even the last degree of unworthiness in a parent will justify the levity or cruelty of a son; far less a single instance of his being overcome when tempted. But the real explanation of his behaviour must be sought in some deeper motive. Mere wanton disrespect could never, of itself, carry a son so far as he went. Foolish, giddy, wilful as he might be, who that had not some more malignant end to serve, could find his father as Noah was found, and make the discovery a matter of jest or of exultation? But Ham had another quarrel with his father; he hated his religion. He not merely dishonoured him as a parent—he disliked him as a preacher of righteousness. Hence his satisfaction, his irrepressible joy, when he caught the patriarch in such a state of degradation. Ah! he has found that the godly man is no better than his neighbours ; he has got behind the scenes ; he has made a notable discovery ; and now he cannot contain himself. Forth he rushes, all hot and impatient, to publish the news, so welcome to himself! And if he can meet with any of his brethren who have more sympathy with this excessive sanctity than he has, what a relief—what a satisfaction—to cast this choice specimen in their teeth ; and so make good his right to triumph over them and their faith ever after.

The temptation presented to them by their younger brother, to join with him in his ribald mockery, the elder sons of Noah resisted ; and in doing so, they proved, not only the depth of their filial respect and duty, but the strength also of their religious convictions. They dared to be true and faithful to the cause of God, which they had espoused, in the most trying circumstances in which any man can well be called to maintain it. For how did they deal with the scandal which their unfeeling brother so recklessly exposed ? Did they treat it lightly ? Did they affect to get rid of it by some plausible excuse ? No. They do not give Ham the advantage which he would have had over them, if they had manifested indifference to their father's conduct, or had begun to palliate and defend it. They evidently show that they are alive to the full baseness and guilt of the offence. What they do, is their testimony and protest against the sin ;—the manner in which they do it, is the token of their continued attachment to him who has sinned, as well as to the faith which, notwithstanding this sin, they still believe that he truly holds. They treated Noah as one who had grievously fallen ; but, at the same time, they treated him as one who, before his fall, had been the upholder and representative of the cause of God, and who would still, by God's grace, be raised again and restored.

And now, when Noah awakes out of his wine, and knows what his younger son has done unto him, what may his feelings be expected to be ? If we read the verses in succession without a break or pause,—connecting the curse which Noah pronounced with his awaking to a knowledge of the manner in which he had been treated,—(ver. 24, 25), the narrative would suggest the idea of personal resentment and indignation ; and, doubtless, in the circumstances, such an emotion on the part of the father and the patriarch would be both natural and righteous. It is to be observed, however, that no such emotion is ascribed to Noah by the sacred history itself. It is not said that he uttered the prophecy which follows under the impulse of provocation or of passion. And the entire omission of the very name of Ham would seem intended for the very purpose of proving the absence of all personally vindictive feeling.

These two parts, indeed, of this narrative, are to be kept clear and distinct from one another. The fall of Noah is not at all connected with his prophecy ; except, perhaps, that it served to bring out the real character of his children, and so to reconcile him to the different destinies which he was to announce as awaiting their respective races. For it would seem that he had not previously discerned with sufficient clearness the antagonist principles of faith and unbelief, of godliness and worldliness, as they were at work in his own household, and were soon to divide the world.

Noah, we are told, awoke ; and immediately after, we find that he prophesied. This is all the account given us of his recovery from his grievous fall. But that he was humbled in the dust, as David was in the like case, who can doubt ? Of David's repentance, the notice in the history is very nearly as brief as what is here taken of Noah's—it is from the mournful strains of his psalms that we learn the secret experience of his soul. Noah, also, we may be sure, passed through a similar experience. His sin was now ever before him. And certainly if anything could aggravate his bitter sense of guilt and shame, as he thought of the just offence he had given to his God, it must have been the discovery which he made respecting the conduct of his sons.

That one of them, the youngest, and perhaps the best beloved, should have treated him so rudely, was sufficiently mortifying to his parental feelings ; but that was as nothing in comparison with the reflection, that it was his own father who had put a stumbling-block in his way, and proved the guilty cause of the profane outbreak which at last stamped the character and sealed the doom of his child. Nor could he fail to consider the very different conduct of the two elder brethren. To what a trial had he exposed their principles ! They had indeed stood the test ;—but how little could this have been anticipated; how easily might it have been other-wise ! The very reverence and awe, moreover, with which they executed their painful task, must have conveyed to Noah, when made aware of it, a terrible rebuke. Truly it could be no light matter thus to minister to the evil passion of him who sinned, and thus to wound also and lacerate the best principles and affections of those who did so well.

As the incident recorded respecting Noah and his family gives a picture of the church in its beginning, so the prophecy which follows (ver. 25-27) reveals to us the church in its pro-gress. The unequal struggle has commenced again between the church and the world ; and ominous enough has the com-mencement been. The ungodly son has gained an advantage; —the faithful are scandalised and discouraged. But he who "maketh the wrath of man to praise him," turns the worst actions to account for vindicating his honour and accomplish-ing his purposes. Thus, in this instance, he interposed to rebuke the proud and raise the lowly ; and he did so by the instrumentality of the restored patriarch himself.

Canaan is judicially condemned, and sentenced to a degrading servitude: "Cursed be Canaan; a servant of servants shall he be unto his brethren" (ver. 25). This may be viewed partly as a retributive judgment pronounced on Ham, dooming him to suffer in the tenderest part;—in those very parental affections which, in the case of his father, he had so cruelly mocked and scorned. It may be viewed also as an intimation of what, in the ordinary course of nature, must be the consequence of such sin as Ham had committed, and of such an evil spirit as he had shown. Himself an apostate, his son and his seed are cursed. But in the midst of deserved wrath, God remembers mercy; and, accordingly, the curse is here restricted to his seed in the line of Canaan.*

The punishment to which he is sentenced is servitude or bondage; a double bondage to both his father's brethren. It is thrice specified, and forms, indeed, the melancholy bur-

---

* There is no warrant for the liberty which some have taken, who have introduced into this prophecy the name of his father Ham, reading "Ham the father of Canaan," instead of simply "Canaan." Their reason for this seems to be, partly, that they think they see in history a wider fulfilment of the prediction than the limitation of it to the race of Canaan would indicate; and partly, also, that in the account given of the offence, the expression "Ham the father of Canaan" occurs (ver. 22). In regard to this last reason, it is far more likely that Ham is called the father of Canaan, from the very circumstance of his sin being avenged, and his seed cursed, in the single line of Canaan; as in a subsequent passage (chap. x. 21) Shem is called "the father of Eber's children," because in that line he was to be blessed. And in regard to the other reason, founded on the apparent signs and tokens of the curse in the history of other nations sprung from the other children of Ham, it may be observed, in the first place, that the prophecy says nothing against their participation in their brother's doom, although it does not expressly foretell it; and further, secondly, that the posterity of Canaan, mixing themselves by dispersion and by colonisation with the other descendants of Ham, may have carried with them, wherever they went, their liability to the curse, and may have involved in it, more or less, the people among whom they happened to settle.

den of this brief prophetic song. For the prophecy is in the form of a poem; and consists of three stanzas, in which the first line varies, while the last sadly reiterates the same solemn note of woe :

" Cursed be Canaan ;
      A servant of servants shall he be unto his brethren.
Blessed be Jehovah, the God of Shem ;
      And Canaan shall be his servant.
God shall enlarge Japheth, and he shall dwell in the tents of Shem ;
      And Canaan shall be his servant" (ver. 25-27).

In the first of these couplets, Canaan's doom is generally announced ;—he is to be a servant of servants. The expression is emphatic. He is to hold a position of peculiarly degraded subjection to both his brethren ; for so the doom is explained in the two following couplets, in the first of which subjection to Shem is specified, and in the second, subjection to Japheth. In addition to the couplet which opens the poem, and is expressly designed for Canaan, it is deemed necessary, in the two other couplets, to repeat the sentence, in the way of contrast or antithesis to the blessings pronounced on the two brothers respectively, who had been found faithful.

In this view, a special reason may be suggested, both for the selection of Canaan as the only one of Ham's seed who was cursed, and for the repetition of the curse, twice over, in connection with the blessings which Shem and Japheth were severally to receive. It was Canaan who, more than any other of Ham's descendants, was to come into contact with Shem and Japheth, and to interfere with them in their enjoyment of their privileges. For what were these ?

I. In the case of Shem, the blessing is indirect and reflex ; but on that very account it is the more precious ;—" Blessed be Jehovah, the God of Shem." The prophetic father, beholding afar off the highly-favoured descendants of his highly-honoured son, fixes his devout eye, not on their prosperous and happy state, but on the glory of that great and holy name, with whose honour their welfare is to be inseparably blended. What prerogative can equal that which this form of salutation implies ? I hail as blessed—not my son, but him who condescends to be his God ;—it is not, "blessed be Shem ;" but, "blessed be Jehovah, the God of Shem." Jehovah, the God of Shem, is the blessed One ; how blessed, then, he whose God Jehovah is ! "Blessed is that people whose God is the Lord." Evidently the blessing refers, in the first instance, to the line of Eber, who is singled out from all the other descendants of Shem (chap. x. 21) ; and ultimately to the family of Abraham, with whom the covenant was established (chap. xii.). But when the time came for the fulfilment of this prediction ; when the race of Shem, in the line of Eber and the family of Abraham, were to inherit the blessing ; when Israel was to possess the Lord's land and assume his position as the Lord's people,—who stood in the way ? Who but Canaan, by whom the land was preoccupied ? "The Canaanites were in the land" (chap. xii. 6 ; Exod. iii. 8, *et passim*).

II. Again, as to Japheth, what is the prophetic announcement ? "God shall enlarge Japheth, and he shall dwell in the tents of Shem." He is to be "enlarged ;"—or, as the word may be rendered, "persuaded ;"—and he is to "dwell in the tents of Shem ;"—to partake of his privileges and be adopted into his communion ;—in a word, to become one with Shem, in respect of that religious blessedness which is implied in Jehovah being his God. For "to dwell in the tents of Shem," is to have a common lot with the people whose God is the Lord, and amid whose habitations the Lord has his tabernacle. With a view to this, Japheth is to be "enlarged," or "persuaded." He is to be "enlarged"—invested with universal empire ; or, he is to be "persuaded,"—plied with influences fitted to open the way for the progress and diffusion of sound doctrine. And this is to be preliminary to his "dwelling in the tents of Shem," and having the God of Shem, the blessed Jehovah, as his portion.

Who can fail to recognise in this prediction the calling of the Gentiles, who spring from Japheth, and the preparation of the world for the first preaching of the gospel ? When the Gentiles were invited to be fellow-heirs with the Jews of the grace of life, Japheth began to dwell in the tents of Shem ; and when, previous to Christ's coming and the preaching of his gospel, the Roman power was peacefully established throughout the whole earth, and amplest means of communication and communion were thus afforded, and men's minds, in all Gentile nations, as well as among the Jews, were hushed into a state of strange expectancy,—then might be recognised that enlargement or persuasion of Japheth, which was foretold as appointed to precede and usher in his dwelling in the tents of Shem.

But it is especially remarkable, that in the course of this enlargement, or persuasion, on the part of Japheth, the main obstruction with which he met arose from Canaan. When Rome was laying the foundation of that wide dominion which, by securing peace, along with free and safe intercourse, through all the world, contributed more than any other external cause, to the early success of the gospel ; her only formidable rival was Carthage, a colony of Tyre, sprung from Sidon, one of the sons of Canaan. Canaan was to stand in the way of Japheth, as well as of Shem ; but his opposition, it was intimated, would be in vain,—his proud race would bend the knee to Japheth as well as to Shem. The conqueror of Rome's armies, himself at last defeated, would be compelled, at Rome's gates, reluctantly to recognise the fortune of Carthage. The curse of Canaan is upon the wealthy Tyrian colony,—while Japheth must continue to be enlarged and persuaded. Rome must reign, that the world may be Christianised.

Such is the meaning of the curse denounced against Canaan, and such its intimate bearing on the blessings which Shem and Japheth severally received. The curse is on Canaan, as representing his descendants generally,—it is upon his race, in their collective character. That multitudes among them might be individually saved, is quite compatible with this public doom ; the Syrophenician woman, to whom our Lord extended his kindness, furnishes an instance in point. Even in the Jewish dispensation, a Canaanite, after the third generation, might be received into fellowship ; and to all of every race the grace of the gospel is free. But the curse conveys a warning. If God intends to bless any people called by his name, or dwelling in the tents of those who are so called, Canaan may not oppose the Divine purpose with impunity. If he do, it is in vain,— it is at his peril. The mountain is removed and cast into the sea.

The world after the flood is now launched on the stream of time, having received its constitution, in its three departments or kingdoms, of nature, providence, and grace. In the kingdom of nature, wise laws are ordained, conducive to the purity, peace, and prosperity of social life, and to the best interests of each individual soul. In the kingdom of providence, again, a dispensation of forbearance is established, and the Lord waits to be gracious. And, finally, as regards the kingdom of grace itself,—the precarious and perilous standing of the church in an evil world is brought out in the dark commencement of the struggle, whose brighter issue, however, prophecy begins to unfold. That prophecy has already been partially fulfilled ; but the end has not yet come. Jehovah is once more to be blessed as the God of Shem, for he has not cast off Israel ; Japheth, still further enlarged, is to dwell in Shem's tents, when Israel's return shall be to the Gentiles as life from the dead ; and if Canaan is again to offer opposition, it can only be in order that the full meaning of that early curse may be seen, in all its terror, in the latter days.

13

THE EARTH GIVEN TO THE CHILDREN OF MEN, AND OCCUPIED BY THEM

Genesis 10:1-11:26

The heaven, even the heavens, are the Lord's : but the earth hath he given
to the children of men.   Psalm 115:16

THESE chapters might be expected to throw a flood of light
on the geography and chronology of the early history of the
world.   The tenth is very full and precise in its account of
the colonies and settlements into which the first families of
Noah's race spread themselves ; while the eleventh is no less
exact in marking the periods of the successive generations between Noah and Abraham.   Nothing, however, can be more
perplexing and embarrassing than the study of these chapters,
with a view to these very particulars.   Innumerable questions
arise respecting the nations and countries described in the one
chapter, and the dates indicated in the other ; and innumerable opinions are held on the subjects to which these questions
relate, supported by various arguments, upon whose comparative strength we have scarcely the means of deciding.

In regard, indeed, to the geography, something like
a general outline may be given, with something like a general
consent of interpreters, although the filling in of the details is
often little better than matter of conjecture, founded on remote
and doubtful analogies of words and names.   But the chronology is a more serious stumbling-block to the historical inquirer,
who would digest these brief hints of the inspired narrative

into full and formal annals. Not only are there occasional differences among our manuscripts and versions in minor and subordinate points of detail;—such as slight variations of a few years in some of the incidental dates, in which perfect accuracy might not be material. We have distinct and un-equivocal traces in the old copies and translations of this book, of two different modes of computation, varying from one another by whole centuries. And what is worse, the variations seem to be the result, not of accident, but of design, on one side or on the other; for there are, in fact, two systems, and the difference between them is itself very systematic.

To give an idea of this;—the dates, both before and after the flood, are determined by the age of each patriarch at the birth of his first son. Thus, before the flood, we have the succession of the patriarchs noted in the fifth chapter; and we may easily see how a very slight alteration in the reckoning of their years may effect a considerable variation in the entire antediluvian chronology. For instance, Adam, it is said (ver. 3), was 130 years old when he begat Seth; and he lived after he had begotten Seth 800 years. Add 100 years to Adam's life before the birth of Seth, and take away 100 from his life after that event, you make him 230 when Seth was born, and you allow him only 700 years for the remainder of his life. This leaves his whole life precisely the same, 930 years;—but it lengthens the chronology, adding 100 years to the time between the creation and the birth of Seth. This is the plan on which the longer chronology is formed; for the same thing is done with the notices of the other patriarchs. Thus Seth (ver. 6), instead of 105, is made 205 at the birth of Enos, and instead of 807, lives only 707 years after. So also Enos (ver. 9), instead of 90, is made 190 at the birth of Canaan, and lives, not 815, but only 715 years after. And this is done uniformly, except in three instances,—Jared (ver. 18), Methuselah (ver. 25), and Lamech (ver. 28), in each of which there are already, in our copies, 100 years more than

usual assigned to these patriarchs, before the birth of their respective sons.

Such, in general, is the system opposed to that which is
found in our present Bibles. And the difference is very much
of the same kind in the genealogies after the flood, as these
are given in the eleventh chapter; Arphaxad (ver. 12), being
made 135, not 35 years old at the birth of his son; and so on
throughout the list, down to the birth of Abram, Terah, and
Nahor (ver. 26).

It is clear that there is an intentional and methodical difference between these two schemes; but which is the original
and true one, it is by no means easy to say. The arguments
in favour of the prolonged chronology are drawn both from
ancient versions, confirmed by Josephus and some of the
fathers, and also from the nature of the case; the lengthened
periods enabling us better to explain the early increase of the
earth's population, and the early rise of cities and empires.
On the other hand, all the Hebrew copies, which have come
down to us, agree in giving the shorter dates; and unless this
very concurrence, which is even more exact than is usual where
the Hebrew manuscripts contain numerals or figures, be regarded as itself a suspicious circumstance, it ought to have
great weight. It is upon this system that the chronology of
our common English Bibles is reckoned; in regard to which
it may be observed, that while it is sufficient for all useful
purposes, when we come down to the events of later times, it
would be unsafe, to say the least, to accept it as quite certain
and trustworthy in the times between the creation and the
flood, and between the flood and the calling of Abraham. In
fact, so far as the practical benefit of chronology is concerned,
which is mainly valuable as it serves to unite and harmonise
different streams of history, it matters comparatively little
which of the two systems of dates we assign to events which
happened while the stream was as yet single and unbroken.
If we have a common point of measurement, it is enough; and

this is furnished by the chronology of our English Bibles, which is that in common use. Nor is there any thing in the doubt in which this unessential question is involved, which should at all shake our reliance on the genuine and authentic character, or on the verbal accuracy and inspiration, of this first book of Moses. It has been handed down to us in many manuscripts and a great variety of versions ; all of which, on the most searching scrutiny and collation, have been found, in every important particular, most thoroughly supporting and corroborating one another.

There are two considerations besides, which may partly reconcile us to our present uncertainty in regard to many of the names and dates which occur in these first chapters of the book of Genesis.

The first is, that they were probably better understood and ascertained once. These things were written for those who lived before us, as well as for us ; and the places and times specified in the history may have been well and certainly known to readers of this book in days of old, when the correct knowledge of them would be of more practical importance than it can possibly be to us now. The other is this,—that they may come again to be better understood and ascertained hereafter. They may have some bearing on the latter days, and may receive new explanations as these days draw near. It is not impossible that this ancient history may be found, before all is done, to have had a prophetic character, or at least to have had a prospective reference to events which prophecy foretells. The prophecies relating to the end of the world have their dates, and their names of places and nations, at least as obscure to us now, as are the delineations and computations of these early chapters of the Bible. The event, as the time of the restitution of all things approaches, will throw light on the dates and names of prophecy ; and it may also throw light on the delineations and computations of Genesis. The map sketched in the tenth chapter may be found useful, as a chart or plan, when some of the names noted there ;— such as Gomer, Togarmah, Magog, Meshech, Tubal, become again prominent ;—as prophecy seems to intimate that they shall (Ezek. xxxviii., xxxix. ; Rev. xx.)   And the chronological genealogies of the eleventh,—confessedly of doubtful interpretation now,—may then help to show on what terms, and according to what arrangement, the Lord, who retains "the heaven, even the heavens, as his own," hath " given the earth to the children of men ;"—in ideal, from the first, and in full realisation at last.

Thus, as a general principle, it may be observed, that if there are some few things in the Bible which do not appear to be very intelligible or very applicable to us now, they may have served a more useful purpose in time past, and may do so again in time to come.   Meanwhile, let us look at the early division of the earth, and the dispersion of mankind ; as to its manner and its results.

I. In regard to the progress of events connected with the occupation of the earth, we may mark four successive steps : 1. The exploits of Nimrod (chap. x. 8) ; 2. The division of the earth in the days of Peleg (x. 25) ; 3. The confusion of tongues at Babel (xi. 1-7) ; and 4. The consequent dispersion of the tribes and families of mankind (xi. 8, 9).

1. Nimrod, who " began to be a mighty one upon the earth " (x. 8), is the third from Noah, being the grandson of Ham, and the son of Cush.   Peleg, who was so called, because " in his days the earth was divided " (ver. 25), is the fifth from Noah.   It is probable, therefore, that the transaction, whatever it was, from which Peleg received his name, did not take place until Nimrod had at least begun his career, although it is quite possible that it may have occurred very nearly at the same time.   The earth, however, must have been as yet undivided when Nimrod entered upon his exploits.

In that view, we may understand the expressions about

Nimrod literally. He was powerful as a hunter of wild beasts; bent on clearing the fields and forests for the more enlarged habitation of man;—a lawful, and even laudable undertaking. The increasing numbers of mankind required room and space. They must break through the narrow limits within which they have been confined; and for this purpose, the lawless tenants of the adjoining territories must be dispossessed. In the bold undertaking, Nimrod leads the way.

2. At this precise stage;—omitting, in the meantime, what is said of Nimrod's kingdom in the tenth verse;—I am inclined to bring in the transaction alluded to in the twenty-fifth, respecting the division of the earth. When men were about to emerge from what had hitherto been their home, God interfered to direct them. It was not his purpose, either that they should issue forth in disorder, or that they should follow their own devices in their future settlements. He had a plan of his own for the division of the earth among the families of men; and it was probably at this crisis that in some way or other he gave intimation of his plan to the dispersing emigrants for whom Nimrod was opening the way.

He did so, as I suppose, by the instrumentality of Eber: "Unto Eber were born two sons: the name of one was Peleg; for in his days was the earth divided" (ver. 25). This patriarch, Eber, the fourth from Noah, is specially distinguished in the line of descent from Shem, and of ancestry to Abraham; for we find Shem called "the father of all the children of Eber" (ver. 21). He may have been, and probably was, contemporary, or nearly so, with Nimrod.

Thus, at the very time when the swarm, if we may so speak, is about to hive, and is on the wing—when, led by Nimrod, and inspired by him with a new spirit of enterprise, men are bursting the bounds of their former habitation—Eber receives a commission from God to divide the earth among them—to announce to the several tribes and families their appointed homes, and to lay down, as on a map, their different routes and destinations. This charge he executes, and in memory of so remarkable a transaction, he gives the name of Peleg, signifying " division," to his son, born about the time when it took place. In some such way the earth is allocated, by the command of God, as by a solemn act or deed, to which reference is more than once made in other parts of Scripture. It is of this transaction that Moses speaks in his memorable song, when, expressly appealing to " the days of old," he describes " the Most High as dividing to the nations their inheritance, separating the sons of Adam, and setting the bounds of the people," with an eye, especially, " to the number of the children of Israel " (Deut. xxxii. 8). And Paul, also, preaching at Athens, testifies of God, not merely as having " made of one blood, all nations of men for to dwell on the face of the earth "—but also as having " determined the times before appointed, and the bounds of their habitation " (Acts xvii. 26).

3. The plan of God, however, did not tally with the presumptuous projects of ungodly man. If Nimrod, after clearing, in his character of a mighty hunter, the regions around man's early home, chose to lead forth his fellows on an enterprise of discovery and high daring, were they to be immediately scattered to the four winds, so as to lose the advantage which a compact union gave them ? No. They must march in a body as a united band. So the emigrants thought and felt, as they eagerly followed their powerful leader, who himself, by this time, has tasted the cup of ambition ;—which, whoso touches it, must drain to the dregs.

Here, then, we have a vast host or army, journeying " from the east," or " toward the east "—for the expression (chap. xi. 2) is now ambiguous—moving probably along the course of the river Euphrates, eastward and southward, until they come to the vast plain of Shinar, where the famous Babylon afterwards stood. That this expedition, or emigration, is identical with the beginning of Nimrod's kingdom (chap. x. 10), may be certainly concluded from the circumstance, that the same spot is named, in both cases, as the seat of the enterprise—Babel or Babylon. Hence it is to be presumed that they are aware of the purpose of God respecting the division of the earth. But they cannot acquiesce in it ; for it comes across their path, at the very time when they are flushed with the expectation of achieving great things. What to them is the fine scheme concocted by Eber and his godly allies, who make such vain pretences to the favour of heaven ? They will take their own way—they will not be so foolish as to disperse themselves, and part company with their valiant captain—they will stand by him and by one another. They are on the look-out, accordingly, for a suitable place to be their centre of union and seat of power—and the plain of Shinar answers their purpose. It is of vast extent, and has most excellent materials for building—bricks as durable as stone, and slime or bitumen, which, on exposure, becomes harder and more tenacious than any mortar. Here, then, is the very spot—here they will build a city and a tower, " whose top is to reach to heaven. Let us make us a name, lest we be scattered abroad upon the face of the whole earth " (chap. xi. 3, 4).

Such was "the beginning of Nimrod's kingdom ;"—such was the building of Babel. It was an act of daring rebellion against the Most High ; and in particular, against his prerogative of dividing to the nations their inheritance ; being avowedly intended for the very purpose of preventing the orderly dispersion which God had manifestly appointed. It was, moreover, an act of apostasy from the primitive worship, and the first open avowal of heathenism, or idolatry. The building of the tower "unto heaven," had undoubtedly a religious meaning. What name they were to make, what gods they intended to worship in connection with the tower, —whether the heavenly bodies, or dead saints, or living heroes such as Nimrod himself,—or all the three combined,— it may be difficult to say. That their scheme was the consummation of their departure from the living God, too plainly appears, both from the spirit in which it was undertaken, and from the object which it was meant to serve. But " The Lord bringeth the counsel of the heathen to nought, and maketh the devices of the people of none effect." So, in the present instance, it proved.

The language used to denote the interference of God in this emergency is very peculiar, and strongly marks the importance of the whole transaction. There is first special notice taken of this enormous wickedness of man, and special inquiry made respecting it ;—" The Lord came down to see the city and the tower, which the children of men builded" (chap. xi. 5). Then there is, as it were, deliberation in the counsels of the Godhead ;—" The Lord said, Behold, the people is one, and they have all one language ; and this they begin to do : and now nothing will be restrained from them, which they have imagined to do" (ver. 6). And thereupon a solemn resolution is accorded ;—" Go to, let us go down, and there confound their language, that they may not understand one another's speech" (ver. 7). Immediately thereafter comes the swift execution of the decree ;—" The Lord scattered them abroad from thence upon the face of all the earth ; and they left off to build the city" (ver. 8). A physical obstacle is interposed in the way of their design. It is not merely a confounding of their plans, but it is so through a confounding of their tongues ;—" The Lord did there confound the language of all the earth : and from thence did the Lord scatter them abroad upon the face of all the earth" (ver. 9).

4. Thus the followers of Nimrod and builders of Babel are dispersed. But it is a regular dispersion. The confusion of languages is not what the name of Babel is often improperly used to denote,—a miscellaneous tumult and strife of tongues. It is a divine work, accomplished after the divine manner, decently and in order. He who gave man one language at first, now made, out of that one language, several ; but he did so systematically, and even sparingly. For, as some think that all the varieties of speech now on the earth may

be traced up to three original languages,—it is not improbable that these three alone were spoken at Babel; that being the real extent of the confusion of tongues there effected. Certainly that would be enough to defeat their scheme of union, and to scatter them abroad. Three languages suddenly brought into use instead of one, would effectually serve all the purpose intended. At all events, whatever was the number of radical languages introduced at Babel, it is plain that they were so introduced as to cause, not a confused, but an orderly dispersion; and, in particular, that they corresponded with the differences of race and of family. For, returning again to the tenth chapter, where the families of the sons of Noah, " by whom the nations were divided in the earth after the flood," are enumerated in detail, we find it expressly stated, of the descendants of Japheth, of Ham, and of Shem, successively, that the division took place " according to their families and their tongues, in their lands, and in their nations" (x. 32). The division of languages, therefore, was made subservient to an orderly distribution of the families of each of Noah's sons. They were scattered abroad; but it was in a regular manner, and upon a natural principle of arrangement,—with a joint regard to kindred and to language, —according to their families and their tongues.

II. The result of the dispersion, if it were to be minutely examined, would require a very elaborate and intricate discussion. Let a single observation suffice; it is one which, if well followed out, may lead to a clearer understanding of the geography of the tenth chapter, at least in its leading and general features, than ordinary readers are apt to gather from the apparently inextricable catalogue of names.

Let two lines be drawn; the one from the northern, the other from the southern extremity of Palestine; almost due eastward, through central Asia. Between these two lines lies the portion of Shem. Northward of the north line, partly in Asia, partly in Europe, lies the portion of Japheth.

Southward of the south line, partly also in Asia, and partly in Africa, lies the portion of Ham.

Japheth is mentioned first, as being the elder brother. His portion embraces a considerable district or tract of northern Asia,—the original seats of the Medes and Persians, —together with Asia Minor and the adjacent parts of Europe, called by the Jews "the Isles of the Gentiles," as they gave that name to all lands to which they were wont to go by sea (ver. 2-5). Next comes Ham, whose lot is cast to the south of the Mediterranean sea, both in Asia and in Africa (ver. 6-20). Shem lies between, and is appointed to occupy the fertile regions of which the holy land is the crown (ver. 21-31); an extent of territory nearly corresponding to the grant subsequently made to Abraham. Such generally is the arrangement.

But there are two remarkable exceptions.

The expressions used respecting Nimrod, that "he went forth," and respecting the families of the Canaanites, that "they were spread abroad," seem to mark a roving disposition, and a transgression of the allotted limits. And both of them occur in the line of Ham, encroaching on the portion of Shem.

1. Nimrod holds on in his ambitious career, "Out of that land," namely Babel, in the land of Shinar, "he went forth into Assyria, and builded Nineveh" (chap. x. 11, *marginal reading*). Babel is for a season abandoned,—and no wonder, after the dreadful miracle there witnessed. But in the spirit of lawless ambition, other towns are built. This mighty hunter lays the foundation of two mighty empires; the Assyrian, whose seat is to be Nineveh; and the Babylonian, whose vast metropolis is afterwards to be erected beside the gigantic and unfinished tower of Babel.

Both enterprises are encroachments on the portion of Shem; to whose race has been assigned the plain of Shinar, and indeed the whole of the region watered by the rivers of

Paradise,—the great streams that empty themselves into the Persian Gulf.*

But his ill-omened ambition has had signal mockery put on it by God. For many ages, indeed, the empires thus founded were allowed to flourish; and their founder received divine honours in both his capitals. But long since then they have been swept from the face of the earth; and of the trophies of Nimrod's greatness, the towers and cities which he built, to overtop the heavens and to outlast the world, scarce a vestige remains; except in the monuments only now brought to light—monuments which may well suggest the possibility of the ultimate realisation of the divine plan, in favour of the race of Shem.

2. Another son of Ham intrudes into the lot of Shem, and into that part of it, too, which is most sacredly his, where Jehovah was to be blessed as the God of Shem. It is the spot to which, in his scheme of division, God has special respect (Deut. xxxii. 8, 9). This very corner of Shem's allotted possession we find Canaan quietly preoccupying (ver. 19); not, however, to the frustrating of God's sovereign purpose, but to his own worse ruin when the time comes.

---

* That this was properly the inheritance of Shem, is inferred from various considerations. Thus, it is believed that the primeval language was preserved in the line of Arphaxad, the son of Shem and ancestor of Abraham; and that his family, accordingly, were appointed to continue in the original seat where Noah, after the flood, had settled. More particularly, the description given (ver. 30) of the region assigned to Shem's posterity, as reaching from Mesha, a mountain in the west of Mesopotamia, to mount Sephar, far eastward, in Susia, including the whole land in question,—and the circumstance of Abraham, when he was called, being found settled on that very spot, in Ur of Chaldea, evidently near the vale of Shinar itself,—make it nearly certain that the countries in which the empires of Babylon and Assyria took their rise, formed part of what was assigned, in the Lord's division of the earth, to Shem; and that Nimrod, therefore, laid the foundation of these empires in acts of unwarrantable aggression on territories which were not his own.

The race of Shem is to wait long before being put in possession of that pleasant region. Years of Egyptian exile and
bondage must intervene; and when at last the land is handed
over to Israel, it teems with powerful hosts of foes, such as,
in his own strength, he cannot venture to encounter (Numb.
xiii. xiv.) But the fault in their original title,—and their
subsequent iniquity which was then full,—made the nations
of Canaan an easy prey. God himself dispossessed them,
that the land, which is his own, rescued from vile pollution and
idolatry, might be given to the people whose God is the Lord.

This subject is somewhat speculative; but it may admit
of reflections for practical improvement.

I. How vain and disastrous is it for men to contend
against God! They cannot effectually resist him; they can
only destroy themselves. Especially, if their contention is
against any of the plans and arrangements connected with
his eternal covenant, how madly do they kick against the
pricks! For a season they may usurp what is his, or his
people's. But when their iniquity is full, they must be
removed out of the way, in answer to the prayer of faith;
they shall.be cut down, or cursed, as cumberers of the ground.

II. How wise is it to acquiesce in God's allotment of good!
and in his manner of bringing his purposes of good to pass.
The Lord is the God of Shem. But Shem suffers wrong, and
has to exercise long patience before deliverance comes. Still
it is enough that Jehovah is his God; let him not be careful
or anxious.

III. As regards the duty and destiny of nations, the purpose
of God is here revealed. On the one hand, schemes of conquest,
and of concentrated dominion, are not of God. He may make
them subservient to his own purposes; but he will always, in
the end, pour contempt on the proud ambition of man. On
the other hand—orderly dispersion and wise colonisation are of
God; especially in the line of Japheth. From the first, Japheth
was so situated as to have the best facilities and strongest in-

ducements to colonise ; and accordingly, in the early ages, even before he dwelt in the tents of Shem, he was thus enlarged. Colonies from Asia Minor, Greece, and Rome, successively overspread the best portion of the earth ; and by colonies as much as by arms, the way was prepared for the coming of Christ and the calling of the Gentiles. Since that time, Japheth, dwelling in the tents of Shem, has still been undergoing enlargement ;—and what is very remarkable, those branches of Japheth which have most truly dwelt in Shem's tents, have been most in the way of that enlargement. It is from free protestant lands that colonies and missions, carrying Christianity and civilisation with them, have chiefly gone forth. Can we fail to see a connection here,—intimating the purpose of God and our duty and responsibility ? But even if Japheth should prove unfaithful, there is hope for the world still. "Blessed be Jehovah, the God of Shem ;"—that is still, after all, the rallying watchword by which faith is quickened, and expectation stirred. For "salvation is of the Jews ;" and it is concerning the seed of Shem that the animating question is put,—"If their fall be the riches of the world, and the diminishing of them the riches of the Gentiles, how much more their fulness ?" (Rom. xi. 12).

Finally, the division of languages, though an obstacle to schemes of human ambition, will not be suffered to be an obstacle to the triumph of the cause of God. Of this, God himself gave a proof and pledge, in the miracle wrought on the day of Pentecost,—the counterpart of the miracle at Babel. The separation of nations will not hinder the unity of the faith. At this very time, the increasing facility of intercouse, the increasing use of our own tongue over vast continents in the East and West, and the familiar mingling of natives of various lands, are rapidly diminishing the difficulties which differences of language occasion. And whether these differences are literally to disappear, or are merely to become innocuous—assuredly, in the end, there shall be one utterance, as well as one heart and one Lord for all.

14

THE CALL OF ABRAM—HIS JUSTIFICATION—THE POWER OF HIS FAITH, AND ITS INFIRMITY

Genesis 11:27-12:20

Thou art the Lord the God, who didst choose Abram, and broughtest him forth out of Ur of the Chaldees, and gavest him the name of Abraham. Nehemiah 9:7,8

THE stream of history now flows from a new fountainhead; as before from Adam, and then from Noah; so now from Abraham, the father of the faithful, and the friend of God.

The nations descending from Shem, Ham, and Japheth, are in a general way disposed of in the tenth chapter. In the eleventh, one of the lines from Shem is more particularly traced, and is brought down to Terah. He becomes the beginning of a new set of generations, being the ancestor of the race with which almost exclusively the narrative is now connected. By and by, as the thread is drawn out, it becomes more and more slender, as, one by one, successive branches are struck off. Thus, of Terah's sons, Lot and his posterity are soon set aside, and Abraham himself takes the lead;—from among the children of Abraham, all of whom are noticed as the ancestors of great nations, Isaac is singled out;—of Isaac's sons, Jacob is preferred;—and from him the line of Judah is especially traced, and in the line of Judah, the house of David. Thus, by a process, the reverse of what occurs in the flowing of a river, the current of the stream of salvation,—instead of receiving as tributaries,—gives off as superfluous, successive streams or branches ;—becoming more and more limited as it rolls on, until it ends in the MAN CHRIST JESUS ; from whom again it begins to expand, until at last it covers the whole earth, and sweeps all nations in its mighty tide.

Terah, then, stands forth as the head of the chosen family, in that new section of the history on which we are now entering. " These are the generations of Terah"* (ver. 27). But he

---

* In adjusting the household of Terah, two difficulties occur. 1. Were his three sons born about the same period of his life, and was Abram the oldest, as he is the first named ? So we might at once conclude as we read ;— " Terah begat Abram, Nahor, and Haran" (ver. 27). It is to be observed, however, that Abram's standing first in the list is no proof that he was the first-born ; any more than Shem's being mentioned first among Noah's sons (chap. vi. 10) proves him to have been the senior. On the contrary, as we have reason to conclude that Japheth was the elder brother, so Abram, though named first among Terah's children, may have been actually the youngest. Then again, although it is said that " Terah lived seventy years and begat Abram, Nahor, and Haran " (ver. 26) ;—yet as the meaning obviously must be that his eldest son was born then,—the youngest, if Abram was the youngest, may have been born long after. He may even have been born, as some suppose, sixty years later, when his father was one hundred and thirty years old. This calculation would make Abram seventy-five years old when his father, " Terah, died in Haran" (ver. 32) ; and accordingly, we find (chap. xii. 4) that he was exactly of that age when he left Haran — the first stage of his pilgrimage to which he had removed with his father Terah. The coincidence is conclusive. If we suppose that Abram was born earlier, or in other words, that he was Terah's eldest son, then it would follow that he must have left his aged parent at Haran to spend sixty years of his declining life there alone. But, 2. another question occurs as to Sarai. Is she the same person with Iscah ? Of the three sons of Terah, Haran died young, in the land of his nativity, before the migration (ver. 28) ; leaving two daughters, Milcah and Iscah. Milcah married her uncle Nahor, another of Terah's sons, the brother of Haran and Abram ; and if Iscah is the same with Sarai, then Abram also, the third son of Terah, married his niece. In that case it would be plain that his brother Haran, whose daughter he married, must have been greatly his senior ; for Abram's wife, whoever she was, was only ten years younger

soon disappears from the scene : all that is said of him being
that he took Abram, his son, and Lot, and Sarai, and went forth
with them from Ur to go to Canaan (ver. 31). It might seem,
from this manner of intimating it, that the removal of Abram
from Ur to Haran was at the instance of his father Terah, since
no mention is made of any previous communication from God
to Abram. Looking to the narrative by itself, we might conclude that Terah and his family emigrated of their own accord,
in their first move at least. But this impression is corrected
by what Stephen says in his defence ; " the God of glory appeared unto our father Abraham, when he was in Mesopotamia,
before he dwelt in Charran," or Haran, " and said unto him,
Get thee out of thy country, and from thy kindred, and come
into the land which I shall show thee" (Acts vii. 2, 3). It is
to reconcile the Old Testament narrative with what Stephen
tells us, that our translators have adopted the expression in the
beginning of the twelfth chapter (chap. xii. 1), " The Lord had
said ;" not simply as they might have rendered the phrase—

than himself (chap. xvii. 17) ; and consequently, her father must have been
considerably older than her husband. On the other hand (chap. xx. 12),
Abram says of Sarai that she was his half-sister ; the daughter of his father,
though not the daughter of his mother ; and this would seem to indicate
that she could not have been his niece ;—and, therefore, not the same person
with Iscah, Haran's daughter. Still it is possible to reconcile these intimations. For, as it is common in Scripture to apply the term son or
daughter to the second and third generation, so Abram's meaning may be,
that Sarai was his father's granddaughter, of course by a different mother ;
in which case, she may still be held to have been the daughter of Haran,
and to be the same with Iscah.

These are barren speculations,—somewhat akin, as Luther hints, to the
endless discussions about genealogies against which Paul warns Timothy ;
and I pass from them with this remark, that as marriage was then necessarily allowed within the degrees afterwards prohibited, so, in the family of
Shem, and in the line of Eber, such domestic alliances may have been the
rather kept up, as the means of preserving a holy seed, uncontaminated by
the surrounding contagion of universal idolatry and crime.

"The Lord said," but,—throwing back the revelation to a previous part of the narrative,—" The Lord had said." And, upon the whole, this seems to be the best explanation and adjustment of the two passages. It is not unusual with the sacred writer thus to transpose the order of events. He finishes the subject he has on hand, and then begins a new one with the statement of some circumstance, which, according to its date, might have come in sooner, but has been postponed as bearing more immediately on the second subject than on the first. In the end of the eleventh chapter he is speaking of Terah, and of what happened in his time. Hence he merely mentions that Terah removed his family from Ur of the Chaldees to go to the land of Canaan, and that he came to Haran, where he died ; ascribing the emigration to Terah, as being the head of the house at the time ; and he does not say what occasioned it, until he comes to speak of Abram, who now, after his father's death, succeeds to the patriarchal principality. Thus we enter on the proper history of Abraham ; and we see him, in this twelfth chapter, in the first place, called out of Chaldea ; secondly, tried in Canaan ; and thirdly, recovered out of Egypt.

I. He is called by the Lord ; and the call is very peremptory, authoritative, and commanding ; it is very painful also,—hard for flesh and blood to obey. But along with the call, there is a very precious promise, a promise of good things manifold and marvellous ;—a great nation ; a great name ; the blessing of God on himself personally, making him a blessing to others ; so intimate a fellowship with God, that all his friends are to be God's friends, and all his foes are to be God's foes ; and, above all, the possession of what is to bless all the families of the earth (ver. 2, 3).

Let us picture to ourselves our father Abraham receiving this call and this promise.

1. The whole world around him is lying in wickedness ; as Joshua reminds the Israelites. "Your fathers dwelt on the other side of the flood," or the great river, "in old time, even

Terah, the father of Abraham, and the father of Nahor : and
they served other gods " (Josh. xxiv. 2).   By this time idolatry
had overspread the whole earth.   What was its original form,
it is extremely difficult to determine.   Joshua refers to it as
polytheism, or the service of other gods ; Job indicates the
worship of the heavenly bodies as common in his day (Job
xxxi. 26, 28) ; and in the question which Eliphaz puts—" To
which of the saints wilt thou turn ? " (Job v. 1)—there is,
perhaps, an allusion to another fruitful source of superstition,
—the reverence paid to departed worthies, and the notion of
their interceding as mediators, or giving help as gods.   These
two kinds of heathenism indeed,—the worship of dead men
and the worship of the hosts of heaven,—are intimately connected with one another; they both rise out of very
natural feelings in the corrupt heart of man, and they are
easily harmonised and fitted together.   Very probably they
began to prevail simultaneously, as parts of the one great
system of apostasy which came to a height at Babel.   At all
events, the earth was now idolatrous.   Some few indeed, in
different parts of the world, may have withstood the flood of
error and maintained the true worship of God ;—as Melchizedek did in Canaan and Job in Arabia.   But the declension
of mankind generally from the truth was universal ;   even
Terah's house was not pure ; and Abraham himself is en
tangled in the world's miserable plight.   If he has not become
conformed to a world lying in wickedness, he has at least
learned to tolerate its wickedness as a matter of necessity, or
a matter of course.   The old faith has grown lifeless and
inert.   To live in peace, and make the best of things as they
are, would seem to be the part of wisdom.

   2. Suddenly, after the silence of generations, the Lord
speaks out.   Instead of vague and uncertain tradition, his
WORD is again on the earth.   That LIVING WORD comes to
Abram, and like the Lord's appearance to Saul of Tarsus, it
takes him by surprise.   For when " God chose Abram " (Neh.

ix. 7), it was an act of free and sovereign grace. He did not choose Melchizedek, who was already in the holy land, and was faithfully maintaining there the good cause. The Lord is found of those who seek him not. He comes to Abram, dwelling afar off; and if not hostile, at least indifferent, to the truth. To him he reveals himself, him he chooses—him he calls. To Abram, while yet ungodly, God, intending "to justify the heathen through faith, preaches the gospel, saying, In thee shall all nations be blessed" (Gal. iii. 8). Such is the Apostle Paul's inspired commentary on this first call of Abram; and thus he explains the meaning of the word " blessed," as it occurs so often in the promise given to the patriarch. The blessedness is that of justification;—the free, gratuitous justi-fication of the sinner, without any works or righteousnes of his own, through faith alone in the appointed and accepted substitute, sacrifice, and surety. That is what the promise gives to the patriarch; what it conveys to him as the free gift of God; what it at once and summarily makes him. It makes him "blessed,"—blessed, in the sense of being "justi-fied through faith." And it makes him henceforth the de-positary of this gospel blessing,—this free gift of justification through faith,—for all the families of the earth. Abram be-lieved the promise; and on the faith of it, "when he was called to go out into a place which he should after receive for an inheritance, he obeyed; and he went out, not knowing whither he went " (Heb. xi. 8).

3. Such is the calling or conversion of Abraham. What a change does it work in his position, his character, and his destiny! Before it, what was he? An obscure and all but solitary man:—married indeed, but childless and hopeless of issue;—living very much like his neighbours, in an evil world and an evil age. But God has appeared to him—Jehovah, the God of glory; and the whole course of his life is changed. A word has been spoken to him,—a word of sovereign authority and sovereign grace. He has stood before the Eternal Word.

And what has he learned? That there is a blessing for him, and through him for others. And what a blessing! Justification without works, through a perfect righteousness freely imputed,—the righteousness of the Redeemer promised from the beginning,—the Seed of the woman, by whom the serpent's head is to be bruised. Surely he does well to obey such a call, peremptory and painful as it is, when he receives in it such a blessing! And yet, after all, his believing all this, so unhesitatingly, and so manifestly with all his heart;—his taking God so simply at his word, asking no questions and raising no difficulties—is a wonder. He might have started objections and made inquiries. How can these things be? How can he, whose wife is barren, be the father of a great nation? How can he, a poor sinner, a guilty man, be at once so graciously received into favour? And how is he to become so awful a sign of trial, and so fruitful a source of good, to his brethren, and to all men? But he does not stand upon any such scruples. He takes the plain testimony of the God of glory;—"I will bless thee;"—I, who alone can bless, and whose high prerogative and right to bless none may question; —I will bless thee. And if I justify, who is he that condemneth? It is enough. He believes, and is blessed in believing; blessed,—as having his iniquity forgiven, his transgression covered, his sin imputed no more, and his spirit freed from guile. And being thus blessed himself, he becomes a public and representative man; all-important issues depend on him. Not only has he a great nation and a great name now pledged to him, but a blessing and a curse are in him. Like the Saviour in whom he believes (Luke ii. 34), he is set for a sign,—a test, or touch-stone, to try the spirits of men, and bring out their enmity against God. Everywhere he will be spoken against; and speaking against him is braving the wrath of Heaven;—"I will curse him that curseth thee." But many also will rise up and call him blessed; and these God will bless with the same blessing with which he is blessed himself.

II. In this attitude, and in this character, Abram commences his pilgrimage. He does so amid many trials. (1.) The barrenness of his wife is a stumbling-block in the way of his trust in God, hard to be got over;—it troubles him often afterwards, and tempts him to grievous and aggravated sin. (2.) He knows not whither he is going. No doubt, it is said (chap. xi. 31) that the company went forth to go into the land of Canaan. But that is the historian's intimation of the end of their journey. They themselves, as the apostle testifies, were ignorant of their destination (Heb. xi. 8, 9). His way, and his final rest, are unknown to the patriarch. Nor does he seek to know them; he commits all to God. (3.) He breaks many ties of nature, the closest and the dearest. He must leave many beloved friends and kinsmen behind; and what is worse, he must leave them in the midst of the world's idolatry. Some, indeed, are partakers of his blessing;—his wife, his father, and his nephew Lot, are with him. But to many whom he would fain have carried with him, when he repeats the call of God, he seems as one that mocks. Already he is " a savour of death unto death," as well as " of life unto life ; " and hard as it is for flesh and blood, he must consent to abandon many a loved one to his doom,—a doom aggravated by the guilt of rejecting the Gospel invitation, and despising the Gospel grace. (4.) On the way, his little company is still further diminished. His father Terah is removed. This, indeed, is not so great a trial as the former ;—for his father dies in the course of nature, and as we may well believe,—for what else could have moved the old man to go along with his son at all ? —in the faith of the blessing, and in the hope of glory. Still it is a trial; and coming as it does, so soon after his separation from other friends, and leaving him now with no venerable counsellor to guide him,—with only his beloved wife and his young friend Lot spared to him,—it cannot but be grievously felt. He sorrows not as those that have no hope ; but still he sorrows. (5.) On his reaching Canaan new trials await him. He is not, as he might have expected, put into immediate possession of the land, or any portion of it. He is told, indeed, that the land will be given to his seed. When he has his second interview with the Lord in the plain of Moreh, he receives that express assurance (chap. xii. 7). But to himself nothing is as yet given ;—he is a stranger and pilgrim, wandering from place to place, from Sichem to Moreh, from Moreh to Bethel, pitching his tent at successive stations, as God, for reasons unknown, appoints his temporary abode (ver. 6-9). (6.) And wherever he goes he finds the Canaanites ; not congenial society and fellowship, but troops of idolaters (ver. 6). It is, as he may be tempted to complain, from bad to worse with him. In Chaldea it was bad ; and he might naturally hope that God was leading him out from among the ungodly, to bring him to the communion of his saints. But in Palestine it is still worse. He does not meet with many Melchizedeks in his wanderings ; the Canaanites are everywhere in the land ; and under exposure to their profane scoffing and persecution, he has to build his altars to the Lord. (7.) And as if all this were not enough, even daily bread begins to fail him. "There is a famine in the land" (ver. 10) ; and what now is he to do ? He has hitherto been steadfast ; —he has "builded an altar" wherever he has dwelt, and has "called on the name of the Lord" (ver. 7, 9). He has at all hazards avowed his faith, and sought to glorify his God. But it seems as if, from very necessity, he must at last abandon the fruitless undertaking. He is literally starved out of the land. Why should he not go back to his old home, and do what good he can ? There he would find peace and plenty, and ample room for work. But he is still faithful ; and rather than draw back, he will even encounter yet greater dangers. He will go down into Egypt for a time (ver. 10).

Truly "many are the afflictions of the righteous," and in various points is he wounded, as he passes on through his earthly pilgrimage. Disappointed hope,—ill-requited faithfulness and love,—the loss of dear friends,—the delay of promised good,—the uncongenial companionship of the wicked and the worldly, amid whose cold contempt and cruel hatred it is no easy exercise of faith to erect the family altar and make an open avowal of godliness,—the hard and biting pains of destitution and anxiety when bread and water seem to fail, —these are the allotted trials of him who, at God's command, goes forth as a stranger upon earth, seeking a better country. What wonder can it be, if, in such circumstances, his high principle should seem for once to give way, through Satan's subtlety, and his own evil heart of unbelief?

III. In Egypt, accordingly, for a brief space, the picture is reversed, and the fair scene is overclouded. This man of God, being a man still, appears in a new light, or rather in the old light, the light of his old nature. He is tempted, and he falls; consulting his own wisdom, instead of simply relying on his God. He falls through unbelief; and his fall is recorded for our learning, that we may take heed lest we fall. For the temptation, the sin, the danger, and the deliverance, are all such as, in Abram's circumstances, might have befallen us.

1. The temptation was a severe one. Egypt was at this time a flourishing nation; the fertile valley of the Nile supported a considerable population; and the country was already assuming the character which it afterwards bore, as the granary of the world. Its kings, boasting the hereditary name and title of Pharaoh, were wealthy and powerful. They affected the usual oriental state of a large retinue of consorts, and were far from scrupulous as to the means of adding to their number. That Sarai, distinguished by her fair beauty among the dark daughters of Egypt, would at once be coveted for that purpose, Abram seems to have taken for granted. With his limited band of followers, he could not resist any outrage that might be offered; nor would the laws of hospitality protect him. Nay, if she were known to be his wife, the Egyptians might even kill him, that she might be transferred to Pharaoh.

2. In these circumstances, it occurred to the patriarch that she might pass for his sister;—and so he might not only save his own life, but even do something to preserve her. He would then be in a condition to treat with Pharaoh as to terms of marriage,—and he might hope to prolong the negotiation, till, the famine in Canaan being over, he found means to escape with her out of Egypt. He sinned through unbelief. The falsehood which he put into Sarai's mouth was a grievous sin in itself; and it was sinful, also, because it indicated, as all falsehood does, the want of a just and reasonable confidence in God. He might have left it to God, in this trial, to make a way of escape, and provide for the safety of the promised seed; but he " would be wise " in himself, and " it was far from him " (Prov. vii. 23).

3. His scheme, accordingly, availed him little. He was not indeed killed ; but his wife was at once taken from him, without the ceremony of a previous treaty. She is already in Pharaoh's house; and though he loads her supposed brother with gifts, apparently that he may win his consent in due form (ver. 16), yet if he will not be satisfied, can it be supposed that the monarch will wait long for that consent, when he has the power in his own hands, and the bride already at his mercy ? Thus Abram's policy overreaches itself.

4. But God, whom he had better have trusted from the first, interferes to deliver him at last ; not dealing with him according to his sin. He averts the evil, and even turns it to account for good. He takes occasion, from this occurrence, to administer a just rebuke to this heathen king, whose lust and violence certainly deserved the chastisement which he received (ver. 17) ; and making known to him, by some special revelation, the cause of the plague which was sent, he teaches Pharaoh to respect Abram as a professor of the true faith, and as plainly enjoying the favour of heaven. At the same time, the very manner of the deliverance is a rebuke to Abram himself. The man of whom he thought so ill has fairly the ad-

vantage of him, both in reproving and in requiting him. The dignified remonstrance of Pharaoh, speaking as one wronged,— and in this particular instance, whatever might be his own sin, he was wronged,—is fitted deeply to humble the patriarch. There is no reason to suspect Pharaoh of insincerity here, as if he were merely pretending to be offended, and affecting a dread he did not feel of the offence he had been so near committing ; although even if it were so, still Abram must have stood rebuked before him. And when he saw the king so reasonable now ;—nay, when he even learned that if he had been told the truth at first he would have been as reasonable then ;—well might the patriarch be ashamed of his unnecessary and unprofitable falsehood,—his weak and wellnigh fatal act of unbelief. Had he trusted God, and dealt justly by Pharaoh, at the beginning, it might have fared better both with him and with his spouse ; they might have been spared what must have been to them an interval of intense anxiety ; and, as it now appears, an honest testimony might have told even upon one whom they regarded as beyond the reach of truth and righteousness. Still, as it was, God made the fall of his servant an occasion of good. He glorified himself in the eyes of Pharaoh and his court. A salutary impression was left on the king's mind ; and the Lord showed, that, notwithstanding the errors and infirmities of his people, for his own name's sake he would deliver them as "they went from one nation to another, from one kingdom to another people ; " that he would " suffer no man to do them wrong," but would " reprove kings for their sakes " (Ps. cv. 13, 14).

Thus, in the very beginning of Abram's walk of faith, the infirmity of that faith, as well as its power, is practically brought out. And may not this be done for the express purpose of thus early proving,—both that the continued exercise as well as the first production of faith must be the gift of God,—and also that it is not faith itself that really has in it any merit or any efficacy to save, but only that grace and strength of which faith lays hold? Abram is justified by faith; but the faith by which he is justified is as little to be trusted as any of his other virtues. It cannot, therefore, be on account of its own worth that it justifies or saves, but because, by its very nature, it looks to a worthiness or righteousness beyond itself, and rests on that alone for salvation. It was in the promise of God, and not in his own faith, that Abram trusted; and it was this alone which ensured his recovery from his sad fall; otherwise, when his faith failed, his only ground of safety must have been fairly and finally driven from beneath his feet. But the anchor of his soul was in God. Therefore, though cast down, he was raised up again;—and the salutary lesson which he learned was that of distrust in his own faith as well as his own wisdom, and reliance on the Lord alone. He had been tempted to presume upon his position, as chosen and called by God, and to think that he might himself take measures for averting evil, and securing the fulfilment of the divine promise. He is taught that he must leave all to God, and commit himself, as a little child, entirely to his guidance, who saves his people in a way altogether his own.

But though thus weak when he followed his own wisdom, how strong is Abram in the Lord! In Egypt his eye was not single; he became double-minded, and dealt in guile; and, consequently, he was unstable in his ways (James i. 8). But in his going out from Ur, and in his sojourn in Canaan, how full of light is his whole body,—how steadfast is his loyalty to God,—what trials does he endure,—what temptations does he resist! Surely his faith did work by love; it made him walk at liberty, when he had respect to all God's commandments.

15

THE INHERITANCE OF THE LAND PROMISED
TO ABRAM

Genesis 13:1-18 Hebrews 11:8-16

ON his return from Egypt to Palestine, a new trial awaited the pilgrim father. He returned, indeed, possessed of abundant wealth, for God had greatly prospered him (ver. 2);—but this very prosperity brought a new care along with it. He and his kinsman Lot,—who also had acquired great riches, (ver. 5),—found themselves straitened for room in the land. Their substance consisted chiefly in flocks and herds; and as the previous occupants of the country regarded them with a jealous eye, the two friends could with difficulty obtain accommodation in the same neighbourhood; especially when it would seem that after traversing the land, and moving from place to place, they were disposed to become more stationary (ver. 6). In these circumstances, it was wise and brotherly to part, before the misunderstanding among the servants extended itself to their masters (ver. 7, 8).

Like Paul and Barnabas, the uncle and nephew ended the contention by an amicable separation; and in the parting, Abram manifests at once his faith and his forbearance. He is not careful to choose for himself; but is ready to defer to Lot (ver. 9). Relying on the sure promise of God, and having good hope through grace for the time to come, he can well afford, so far as the scenes and interests of his present pilgrimage are concerned, to act disinterestedly and generously

Nor has he any cause to regret it afterwards. Lot, judging by sight and sense, rather than by faith, is attracted by the beauty and fertility of the plain of the Jordan,—its fruitful gardens and flourishing cities (ver. 10),—without sufficiently taking into account the wickedness of its inhabitants, which has already become notorious (ver. 13). He judges according to the world's judgment, and narrowly escapes the world's doom. Abram, walking by faith, and not anxious about an earthly portion, receives the promise of an eternal inheritance.

Being now left alone at the head of his domestic band, Abram stood in need of special encouragement; and special encouragement was afforded to him. The Lord appears to him, and makes him expressly the heir of the land (ver. 14-17). This is now the third occasion of the Lord's appearing to Abram; but it is the first time we find explicit mention made of what he himself is ultimately to possess. In his first interview with the Lord, before leaving the country of his fathers, he is assured generally (chap. xii. 1-3) of a signal blessing to be enjoyed by him, and to be dispensed through him to others. That blessing, as we have seen, is the Gospel privilege of free justification;—on the faith of which blessing, Abram goes forth a pilgrim to an unknown land. On his arrival in Canaan, he again sees the Lord who has brought him thither (chap. xii. 7), and is briefly told that this land is to be given to his seed. Now, at a third meeting with God, he is favoured with a fuller and more express communication. He is, if we may so say, infefted in the land. " Arise," says the Lord, look all around and see the land ; " go through it, in the length of it, and in the breadth of it." Take a survey of it ;—make a measurement of it ;—assume investiture in the lordship of it ;—it is thine. " To thee will I give it," as well as to that "seed" of thine which is to be as innumerable as " the dust of the earth."

It can scarcely be doubted that there is something more

here than the promise of the earthly Canaan to Abram's seed after the flesh. Twice the Lord repeats the express personal assurance to Abram individually,—" To thee will I give it." In the fifteenth verse, indeed, that expression may be held to be qualified and explained by what follows,—" and to thy seed for ever," which may seem to indicate merely the permanent or perpetual grant of the land to his posterity, as being all that is implied in its being given to himself. But in the seventeenth verse, the expression stands by itself,—" I will give it unto thee ;" without mention of his seed at all. Even this, however, may not be acknowledged to be at once decisive ; since some may still think that Abram is taught here merely to anticipate the possession of the land by his posterity, as being equivalent to its being possessed by himself. Let us turn, therefore, to the New Testament, always the best commentary on the Old, and inquire if there is any light there which may be reflected back upon this transaction. We shall then see that in all probability something more was intended, and was understood by Abram himself to be intended.

I. In the first place, that the hope of an inheritance for himself, individually, did actually form a part of the faith of Abraham, as also of the faith of Isaac and Jacob, the Apostle Paul most expressly testifies ;—" He looked for a city which hath foundations, whose builder and maker is God ;" and this was " the promise of which he was the heir." And the same is said of Isaac and Jacob, of Sara, and of all the " strangers and pilgrims " of that olden time (Heb. xi. 10, 13-16). They not merely expected a country and a city for their posterity ;— they expected a country and a city for themselves. To prove this, the apostle uses a very strong expression—" Wherefore, God is not ashamed to be called their God ; for he hath prepared for them a city" (ver. 16),—as if God would have been ashamed to be called their God,—as if it would have been unworthy of him to assume that title and that relation,—if he had not provided for them,—not for their posterity, but for them individually,—a country and a city. And what kind of country—what kind of city? A country, with reference to which they shall not have to confess, as they did in those former days with reference to the earthly Canaan, that they are merely strangers and pilgrims in it;—but " a better country, that is an heavenly,"—and a " city which hath foundations, whose builder and maker is God." Such a city, and such a country, the Apostle Paul distinctly assures us, Abraham looked for and desired, at a time when, as Stephen says (Acts vii. 5), " God gave him none inheritance in Canaan, no, not so much as to set his foot on." He died in the faith of such a city and such a country being his ; " not having received " in actual fulfilment " the promises, but seeing them afar off, and being persuaded of them, and embracing them."

It is plain, therefore, that Abraham had promises given to him of a country and a city, since he died in the faith of them. But no promises to that effect are on record in the Old Testament, unless we hold such an assurance as that now before us to be one. Nowhere does Abraham receive any promise whatever of future good, or of a future inheritance, for himself, if it be not in the announcement—" I will give thee this land."

II. Then, secondly, that this announcement does convey such a promise, may be further argued from an expression used by the apostle (Heb. xi. 8), when, speaking of Abraham's call, he says that " he was to go out into a place which he should after receive for an inheritance." It is to be remarked that the apostle makes no reference, in this whole passage, to Abraham's posterity, as inheriting the land ; he speaks throughout of Abraham as an individual. He cannot, therefore, mean that the place in question was one which Abraham was to receive for an inheritance, in a kind of virtual sense merely, and in respect of his seed receiving it. He describes it as a place which, though unknown to him at the time, he should yet himself after receive for an inheritance. And it is on this description of the place into which Abraham was called to go out, as a place which he was really, afterwards, to possess as his own, that Paul goes on to build what he has to say respecting the patriarch's hope. Upon any other interpretation we can scarcely see how the apostle's reasoning can have any force or meaning at all. Abraham "sojourned," he says, " in the land of promise, as in a strange country, dwelling in tabernacles, as did Isaac and Jacob ;" but it was the land of promise still, and the land of promise to him,—to himself personally. He had been called to go out into a place which he should after receive for an inheritance ; and this was that place. He knew and recognised it as such— as the place into which he had been called to go out, and which, therefore, he was hereafter to receive for an inheritance. On this ground alone he had to rest his personal and individual hope for eternity ; this was his warrant for expecting and " looking for a city which hath foundations, whose builder and maker is God" (Heb. xi. 8-10).

Thus we learn to connect the promise of a heavenly city and a heavenly country, which Abraham undoubtedly had, with the declaration respecting the place into which he was called to go out, that it was the very place which he should afterwards receive for an inheritance. And with this inspired commentary before us, we can scarcely hesitate to understand the words, " I will give thee this land," as conveying to himself, personally, the promise of a country and a city.

III. Still further, in the third place, the apostle's reasoning would lead us to postpone the fulfilment of the promise now in question till after the resurrection. Let us mark well his argument as it bears on this point (Heb. xi. 14-16). Abraham, and all the early pilgrim fathers, confessing that they were " strangers and pilgrims on the earth," still sought " a country" (ver. 14). Nor would any kind of country satisfy them; for, failing to obtain personal possession of the land of promise, they might have returned to " the country from whence they came out" (ver. 15). This, however, they declined to do ; and their declinature the apostle construes into a proof, not merely that they acquiesced in the arrangement by which their seed, and not themselves, were to own the earthly Canaan, but that their hearts were set upon an entirely different portion;—"they desire a better country, that is an heavenly" (ver. 16). Then, following up this exposition of their state of mind upon this subject, the apostle brings in the remarkable inference concerning God to which I have already referred;—" Wherefore God is not ashamed to be called their God : for he hath prepared for them a city" (ver. 16). The conclusion thus drawn is most precise and unequivocal. Nothing short of his " having prepared for them a city" could make it suitable on the part of God to take so peculiar a title, or to stand to them in so peculiar and intimate a relation. When he consents so condescendingly to call himself their God, it is because he has some great thing in store for them—something worthy of himself to bestow, something corresponding to so near a connection as is implied in his being their God, and their being his people ;—and what can that be but the " better country, that is the heavenly," which they " desire ?" Thus, according to the apostle, the title, " God of Abraham, of Isaac, and of Jacob," involves a promise of the continuing city, and the better country.

But, according to our Lord, this same title, " God of Abraham, of Isaac, and of Jacob," involves also a promise of the resurrection; for in his argument with the Sadducees, he emphatically appeals to it as proving the doctrine of the resurrection : " But as touching the resurrection of the dead, have ye not read that which was spoken unto you by God, saying, I am the God of Abraham, and the God of Isaac, and the God of Jacob? God is not the God of the dead, but of the living" (Matt. xxii. 31, 32). This reasoning of our Lord, though not at first obvious to a modern reader, is very beautiful and conclusive. It rests upon the use of the present, as opposed to the past tense, in the discovery which God made of himself on the occasion referred to, when he sent his message to the Jews, by Moses (Exod. iii. 6). God at that time announced himself, not as having been the God of Abraham, of Isaac, and of Jacob—but as being their God still, at the very time of his making the announcement. He did not say " I was their God while they were on earth." but " I am their God now." But what was it that made or constituted him their God while they were on earth ? Let the apostle answer. It was " his having prepared for them a city." It was in respect of this preparation of a city for them that he called himself their God ; and he continues to be their God still, even after their departure from earth : " I am the God of Abraham, of Isaac, and of Jacob." It is only, however, of Abraham, Isaac, and Jacob, as not dead but living, that he is, or can be the God. The promise or preparation of a city, in respect of which alone he assumes that title, was secured to them, not as disembodied spirits, but as living men in the body. If God, therefore, is still their God, even since their removal from this world—and if his being their God is connected with the preparation of a city for them—it plainly follows that God has still a city prepared for them, and that he has it prepared for them, in the view of their being again in precisely the same state in which they were, when first, on this very ground, he " was not ashamed to be called their God." Otherwise God would not be faithful. They must be identically the same persons, in body as well as in soul, to whom he places himself in this intimate relation. In plain terms, if God once becomes the God of Abraham, then, so long as he continues to be his God, he must have respect to him, as he was when the relation between them was first established. But Abraham was then in the body. It was with Abraham in the body, that God dealt so graciously as not to be ashamed to be called his God. Whatever privilege or promise that relation implies belongs to Abraham in the body, and must have reference to his living again in the body. " God is not the God of the dead." He never assumed this title, or gave any of its pledges, in relation to the dead, or to disembodied spirits. " He is the God of the

living." It is with the living—with men alive in the body—
that he has to do, in all that his being called their God can
be held to imply.

Such is the import of our Lord's argument. God not
merely was the God of Abraham while he sojourned as a pilgrim on the earth ; he is his God still, ages afterwards. But
this cannot mean that he is the God of Abraham's disembodied
spirit only, for he never constituted himself the God of Abraham in that sense. It was of Abraham in the body that he
condescended to become the God ; it is of Abraham in the body
that he is the God still ; and it is to Abraham in the body
that he is pledged to make good all that that relation denotes.
Abraham therefore must yet live in the body, to receive the
fulfilment of the promise which God gave him in the body,
and in respect of which, God says, not I was, but " I am, the
God of Abraham."

Thus this reasoning of our Lord, to which the Sadducees
could make no reply, evidently connects with the title, " God
of Abraham," the promise of the resurrection. And Paul, as
we have seen, connects with the same title the promise of the
inheritance—the country and the city—for which Abraham
looked. Plainly, therefore, beyond all doubt, the faith and
hope of Abraham had reference to what he was to receive after
the resurrection ; and accordingly the promise, " I will give
thee this land," must be understood as having reference to the
inheritance then to be enjoyed.

On these grounds, we are surely justified in regarding the
communication made to Abraham, after his separation from
Lot, as conveying to him personally the promise of an eternal
inheritance. And there is a special propriety in his receiving
such a promise at this particular time. He has already been
told (chap. xii. 7) that his seed are to have the land; and he
seems to have made up his mind to be himself a stranger and
a pilgrim in it all his days. In the true spirit of one who
feels that he is but a stranger and pilgrim, he is ready to defer

to his kinsman Lot in the choice of a dwelling-place. It is comparatively a matter of indifference to him where he sojourns, or how he fares, during the few years of his earthly course. In this land, however it may be with his posterity, he, at least, has no "continuing city." How suitable and seasonable, in such circumstances, to encourage him in seeking "one to come!" He is superior to those temporal and worldly considerations which usually create jealousy and envy, even among brethren. He is quite willing to give the best to his neighbour, and for himself to trust in God. And for what reason? Simply because he sets his affections on things above; because his treasure and his heart are in heaven; because God himself is his portion. Therefore he can afford to sit loose to the possessions of this present world. To one thus situated and thus minded, how little would the promise of a mere temporal and earthly inheritance, to be given to a nation yet to be born of him, seem at all in keeping, or in character, or to the purpose? But the promise of heaven—of the heavenly inheritance, the heavenly rest, the heavenly country, the heavenly city—how congenial, how appropriate, how soothing is it felt to be! Especially must it be so, if he is led to take a high and spiritual view— not only of the blessing promised, as a blessing so great that any temporary possession of a mere tract of ground, by himself or any number of his posterity, could be but a poor figure of it —but also of the persons to whom it is promised, as being, not his natural seed, but the countless multitude of the faithful, of whom he is to be the spiritual father. "To thee, and to thy seed," in this sense, "I will give the land." This, and nothing short of this, is the hope set before Abraham; this is the "recompense of reward" to which he looks forward; not the sojourn of his descendants in Palestine for a thousand years or so before Christ's first coming—nor even their sojourn there again, for some thousand years it may be, whether before or at Christ's second advent—but the resurrection of himself and his spiritual children to glory, and their full enjoyment of the everlasting inheritance of the saints in light.

But there are still two points, connected with this promise, which may seem to require explanation.

I. It may be admitted that it is to this, and other such promises, that the Apostle Paul refers as the ground of Abraham's hope, in looking for a heavenly city. And, indeed, if this is not admitted, there is really no promise of the kind recorded in the Old Testament at all ;—a conclusion very improbable ;—for how then should Paul, in writing to the Hebrews, refer to this matter so confidently, if it had not a place in their Scriptures ? But still it may be asked, how would the language employed by God on this occasion convey such an idea ? He speaks of giving to Abraham " this land," —the identical land in which he is at the time a sojourner. Is it by inference that this is to be understood as indicating, in a figure, the heavenly country, of which the land of Canaan is the type ? Or are we to take the words quite literally, and to believe that this very land may actually turn out to be, in part at least, that better country itself ?

If any lean to this last interpretation, it may be safely said that there is nothing very strange or improbable in it; nothing that does violence to right views respecting the future world, or the ultimate and eternal habitation of the redeemed. There is nothing unreasonable, or at all inconsistent with Scripture, in the idea that this material earth, itself redeemed and purified, may be fitted, after the great change which it is at last to undergo, for becoming their final and blessed abode. On the contrary, not a few passages in the word of God seem to favour that notion. The 104th Psalm, for instance, holds out some such prospect of the earth being renewed ; and the 37th Psalm, in several of its promises, may be most simply and suitably explained, according to the letter, on this same principle (ver. 11, 22, etc.) ; the precise recompense promised to the righteous and the meek being over and over again said to be their inheriting the earth on which now they suffer wrong. This, also, is consistent with what Job says of the resurrection to which he looked forward (chap. xix. 25, 26). And, once more, the final judgment of fire is compared (2 Pet. iii.) to the judgment of the flood, from which the earth emerged, anew prepared for man's habitation ; and so, accordingly, we read of there being new heavens and a new earth,—the earth still subsisting, only purified by fire and made new. Other expressions, no doubt, may be cited, which at first sight may seem to be at variance with this view ; but these, on a closer inspection, will generally be found to be irrelevant and indecisive as to the real question at issue. Certainly there is nothing contrary to analogy or to sound doctrine in the opinion, that the risen and glorified saints of God are finally to occupy this planet of ours—this spot, which of all creation is become the most remarkable,—" the holy fields,

> " Over whose acres walked those blessed feet,
> Which eighteen hundred years ago were nailed,
> For our advantage, on the bitter cross. "

According to this view, respecting the ultimate seat of the heavenly blessedness, it is easy to see how Abraham might understand the promise, " To thee will I give the land." Having been previously told that it was to be given to his seed, exclusive of himself, and now learning that it is to be given specially to himself and his seed, how can he reconcile these intimations ? How but by concluding that they refer to two distinct eras,—the one, to the life that now is, the other, to that which is to come ? In the present life, his natural posterity are to possess the land ; in the future life, " in the regeneration," or " in the resurrection," he himself, and his spiritual seed, are to occupy it. The soil which then he trode as a stranger, and where, almost by mere sufferance, his bones were to be allowed to lie, is to be part, and possibly the chief part, of the new earth, in which righteousness is to dwell ; and he and all the faithful, raised in glory, are to find there " the better, that is the heavenly country" which they " desired," and the "city which hath foundations, whose builder and maker is God."

II. Another observation remains to be made. The apostolic commentary, on which we have built so much, cannot possibly refer to any thing short of the final and eternal inheritance of glory. The heaven which Abraham looked for, may, as to its site, be on earth ; but at all events, it was what we mean by heaven that he did look for—the final and eternal state of the risen saints of God. For, mark again the apostle's argument. The whole force of it depends on the contrast which he draws between what was Abraham's condition when he got the promise and what is to be his condition when he gets the fulfilment of it. When he dwelt in the land, he confessed that he was a stranger and pilgrim on the earth; so also did his sons, Isaac and Jacob. Their descendants, too, the Israelites, when they came to inhabit Canaan, bore the same character (Ps. xxxix. 12 ; Lev. xxv. 23); the land was God's ; they were but strangers and pilgrims in it. Even if they come to be again restored, and possess the land on the footing of that better covenant, which Jeremiah and Ezekiel seem to announce,—on the footing of a free forgiveness, and the free gift of the Spirit (Jer. xxxi. 31-34 ; Ezek. xi. 19, 20)—still, if it is on this side of the general conflagration, their tenure of it will be but temporary. Nay, were the saints themselves, the patriarchs, and prophets, and martyrs, to be raised before the end of all things, and to dwell again in the land ;—after all, if any change yet awaited the earth, they would be strangers and pilgrims still. But, according to the apostle, what Abraham looked forward to was a state of eternal and enduring rest, a continuing city, as opposed to a condition of pilgrimage or temporary sojourn. And this can be nothing else than the heavenly inheritance, wherever placed,—the final gift of God to his redeemed, and the final fixing of their blessed lot.

Such is the hope set before Abraham. And now, to close this discussion, let the following remarks be weighed.

I. Some may think, that although we may gather all that we have been endeavouring to establish out of such a promise as that before us, it might not suggest so much to Abraham himself. The reverse rather is probable. It is to be remembered always, that the communications made by God to the patriarchs were not the beginning of his revelation; they all proceed upon previous discoveries. Hence much is taken for granted as already known; the knowledge of it needing only to be revived, corrected, and enlarged. The great leading truths of religion,—the being of God, the manner of his existence, the plan of salvation, the efficacy of sacrifice, the resurrection of the body, and the life everlasting,—these, having been made known from the beginning, are rather assumed than expressly taught in the subsequent intercourse of God with man. Hence, in all probability the patriarchs, with their previous knowledge and the views already familiar to them, would have a better apprehension of the full meaning of what God said to them, than, but for the New Testament commentary, we could have. In fact, the clear discoveries of the New Testament may substantially serve to us this very purpose of placing us more nearly in the same position in which the patriarchs were when the successive communications of the divine will reached them, and so enabling us to understand these communications more nearly as they would do. The idea of a resurrection and of a heavenly inheritance was not new to Abraham: it formed a part of the primeval religion which, amid all its corruptions, might still survive so far as to suggest the light in which he should regard this new promise. And above all, let it be considered that the Spirit who searcheth all things, yea the deep things of God, was as free to give a spiritual discernment of these things to the holy patriarch himself, as to any prophets, or apostles, or saints of all succeeding generations.

II. But further, however this may be, and whatever may be thought of the argument we have been pursuing, let it be carefully observed, that the main and all-important fact concerning Abraham's hope, rests, not on any reasoning of ours, but on the explicit testimony of an inspired apostle. We have endeavoured to explain how the promise of God might suggest the hope of Abraham. But that this was his hope, however suggested, is the express assurance of the Holy Ghost in the New Testament. He "looked for a city which hath foundations, whose builder and maker is God." He declared plainly that he sought "a better country, that is, an heavenly."

III. Now, therefore, believers, behold your father Abraham. In virtue of the two promises he has received,—the first, conveying to him the Gospel blessing of a free justification,— the second, the Gospel expectation of an eternal inheritance, —see him furnished at all points, and equipped from head to foot, for his pilgrimage and warfare now, and for his rest and triumph hereafter. He has his "feet shod with the preparation of the Gospel of peace, and for an helmet the hope of salvation." Ye, therefore, who are his children, assume your father Abraham's garb. Put ye on his greaves and his head-piece. The gospel of peace,—the gospel which gives peace, even peace with God through Jesus Christ your Lord,— that blessed Gospel will prepare your feet, as well as Abraham's, for walking as strangers, for warring as soldiers, and for suffering as pilgrims here on earth. The hope of salvation,— the good hope of everlasting life,—will guard and adorn your head. Raised erect above the smoke and din of this earthly scene, you will fix your steadfast, and ever-brightening and kindling eye, as heirs of God and joint heirs with Christ, on the glory to be revealed at the Lord's second coming;—being in the meanwhile " changed into the same image, from glory to glory, even as by the Spirit of the Lord."

IV. Nor let it be overlooked, as a practical improvement of the doctrine which would identify the eternal inheritance of the saints with the renovated earth,—and even Abram's peculiar portion of it, with the Holy Land,—that if, on the one hand, it may seem to attach something of the character of earth to the future heaven, it surely tends, on the other hand, to impart something of the holy elevation of heaven to this present earth. There may be a risk of making the eternal state, in our conceptions of it, too gross and material ; but there is danger also, in the dreamy and ideal spiritualising, which would refine away all matter, and which ultimately comes very near the notion of absorption into the Infinite Mind. The personal reality of hope, as well as the personal sense of responsibility, is thus turned into a dim abstraction. But the resurrection of the body and the renewal of the earth, realised as events still to come, stamp a present value and importance upon both ; and the reflection, that the very body which I now wear is to rise again, and the very earth on which I tread is to be my habitation hereafter, arrests me when I am tempted to make my body the instrument, or this earth the scene, of aught that would but ill accord with the glorious fashion of the one, or the renewed face of the other (Phil. iii. 21 ; Ps. civ. 30).

16

VICTORY OVER THE INVADERS OF THE LAND—
INTERVIEW WITH MELCHIZEDEK

Genesis 14:1-24

He teacheth my hands to war. Psalm 18:24   The less is blessed
of the better. Hebrews 7:7

THIS fourteenth chapter has the air and aspect of an episode
in the history;—it stands out, singular and unique.   The
warlike character which Abram assumes is a solitary exception
to the usual tenor of his life; and his subsequent interview
with the Royal Priest is altogether peculiar.

I. Abram, for the most part a man of peace, quietly
sojourning as a stranger in the land, suddenly appears at the
head of an army, and signalises his martial prowess in the
battle-field.

1. The occasion of his taking arms is the danger of his
kinsman Lot.   That righteous man, though he has imprudently
involved himself in too close a connection with the wicked, is
still reckoned as forming part of the household of faith ; and
while in this instance he pays dear for that selfish covetousness,
or reckless inadvertence, which had tempted him to associate
with men of the world, he experiences also the seasonable
benefit of having a man of God as his friend.

It would seem that, before this time, the land of the
Canaanites had been the scene of conquests and revolutions.
In particular, the remarkable fertility of the plain of the
Jordan, or "the vale of Siddim," together with the growing

wealth of the cities in the neighbourhood, made that portion of the country more especially liable to the scourge of war. Accordingly, it had attracted the cupidity of a foreign invader, who for a considerable time held undisputed sway over its petty princes;—" Twelve years they served Chedarlaomer" (ver. 3, 4).

Who this Chedarlaomer was, must now be almost entirely matter of conjecture. It is in the briefest and slightest possible way, and only in so far as it incidentally touches his main subject, that the inspired writer notices the contemporary history of the Gentile world. In the present instance, however, something may be fairly gathered from the designation given to the potentate in question. He is described as king of Elam, and Elam is the scriptural name of Persia; or at least it may here denote that part of Persia which was known in ancient history by the name of Elymais. At this period, probably, a Persian dynasty had arisen, in the race of Elam, who was one of the sons of Shem (chap. x. 22); and some have even thought that they could identify this Chedarlaomer with one or other of the early Persian kings, of whom a list is given in certain ancient annals.

That he was a conqueror, aiming at extensive empire, is very plain; and he seems also to have obtained an ascendency over the oldest and most powerful monarchies of the east. Among his three allies we find Amraphel, king of Shinar, which is the Babylonian plain (chap. x. 10, xi. 2);—evidently the head, at this time, of the Assyrian kingdom founded by Nimrod. Where the other two reigned, is quite uncertain. Ellasar, the country of which Arioch was king, is believed by some to be Syria; and Tidal, king of nations, is supposed to have been either the ruler over a few petty tribes, or the captain of a roving band composed of recruits from various countries. Of the four, Chedarlaomer plainly takes the lead on this occasion; and the expedition is mainly his. It was by him that this portion of Canaan had been subdued twelve years before, and to him it had continued subject all that time ; its inhabitants paying him tribute, and their native princes acknowledging his supremacy, and ruling as his deputies. Impatient, however, of a foreign yoke, they found occasion, in the thirteenth year, to rebel ; and as in these days an extensive empire could be but little consolidated, and the power of a conqueror over a remote province must have been very precarious, they succeeded in regaining their independence (ver. 4). But the very next year (ver. 5), Chedarlaomer with his allies undertook a new expedition into Canaan ; and after making a rapid circuit, sweeping along the very verge of the wilderness, so as to subdue the surrounding nations from whom the rebels might have looked for help, he came down with his victorious troops upon the devoted cities of the plain ;—prepared to dart upon his prey, and eager to avenge the revolt of this refractory portion of his dominions (ver. 5–9).

It may be presumed that the state of luxury and extreme dissoluteness of manners into which they had fallen, but ill fitted the effeminate inhabitants for resisting the army before which their neighbours had fallen. The kings of the five principal cities did, indeed, muster their forces ; but, in a pitched battle with the four invading princes, they sustained a total defeat (ver. 8–10). The nature of the country, full of slime pits, dug for the supply of pitch or mortar for building, rendered retreat difficult, so that nearly the whole of the vanquished were cut off, a few only escaping to the mountains. Thus the cities were left defenceless, and fell an easy prey to the conquerors. Accordingly, having satiated their lust for plunder by the spoiling of the houses, they departed, carrying with them goods and victuals, as well as the women and others of the inhabitants (ver. 11 and 16).

In this calamity Lot and his household shared. It does not appear that he was personally implicated, either in the revolt which provoked the vengeance of Chedarlaomer, or in the battle which ended so fatally for the native kings. But the disastrous issue of the contest affected him as well as the rest. The enemy made no distinctions ;—they had no respect of persons ;—they treated him with no ceremony ;—nor did they at all regard his character or his privileges, whether as a stranger or as a magistrate.* Still less did they stand in awe of his high calling, as a servant of the true God, and a man righteous in his generation. Why, indeed, should they? What did they know of his righteousness? Or what did they care for it? They found him among those who had rebelled against them, and that was enough for them.

So it will most commonly happen when a man of God, for worldly ends, joins affinity or makes alliances with the ungodly. Those with whom he immediately connects himself may at first seem to spare him, having some advantage to gain by his countenance or his help—and feeling that his presence among them is a kind of shelter to themselves. They may show him some deference, and exempt him from the necessity of co-operating in some of their most indefensible schemes. But he is in a false and suspicious position, and he cannot long escape. In the eyes of indifferent spectators,—still more in the eyes of inveterate opponents,—he is confounded indiscriminately with his associates. Their enemies become his ; and searching out the faults, and resenting the injuries, of those with whom he keeps company, they involve him alike in the blame and in the revenge. Nor can he with any decency complain ;—he suffers but what he might expect. Finding him among the rebels, will the conquerors be apt to hear or to believe that he is

---

* Some fancy that, his character having raised him to the office of a civil ruler in the city, he was on that account exempted from military service ; while others ascribe his exemption to his being regarded as a stranger or a guest, and perhaps respected for his worth even in so worth-less a community. It is all mere matter of conjecture ; and the point is of no consequence whatever.

innocent of the rebellion? Having been so unjust to himself, can he look for justice from them?

2. Such is the occasion on which Abram takes arms. But that he does so on the mere impulse of natural affection, however amiable, we can scarcely believe. He surely has divine warrant for what he does. He fights once, as he walks always —by faith. If it be to this affair that Isaiah refers (xli. 2, 3), his testimony is explicit as to the divine sanction given to Abram's enterprise. And even if the application of that passage in Isaiah be doubtful, we may safely judge that Abram would not have resolved beforehand on so unusual a step, and would not have received so remarkable a blessing afterwards, if it had been simply his own feelings, and not the express will of God, that he was obeying. For what right had Abram to wage this war? And what power had he to wage it successfully? Neither the right nor the power belonged to him naturally;—both were of faith. Both the right and the power flowed from him in whom he believed.

Thus as to the right,—what is Abram, viewing his position with the eye of sense, and apart from his peculiar character as the friend of God and the heir of the promise? He is merely a private individual, and a stranger too, in the land,—wealthy, indeed, but invested with no public or official authority. What title has he to levy arms? His kinsman's capture may be very grievous and offensive to him; he may be moved with compassion, and stirred up to anger; but is he at liberty, on that account, to put himself at the head of an army of his own, and to act as an independent captain or prince?

Besides, even if he should be so inclined, what power has he to give him any chance of success? What forces can he lead into the field? The males of his own household—three hundred and eighteen men—hastily prepared and armed;— for though three confederates are mentioned (ver. 13 and 24), it does not appear that they furnished any men for this enterprise. And with these he is to pursue a numerous army, flushed with victory, and headed by four valiant monarchs. The exploit of Gideon was scarcely, to all outward appearance more desperate.

But Abram believed, and in faith he went forth to battle. It is the promise of God which gives him both the right and the power. It is as the lord of the country, made so by the promise of God,—it is as the real owner and legitimate ruler of it, that Abram, on this occasion, exercises the royal prerogative of making war. This one passing glimpse God saw fit to give of the true character of him, who to the eye of sense seemed to be nothing more than a private man, a pilgrim and sojourner, comparatively obscure and unknown ; just as in the days of the Saviour's humiliation, it pleased the Father to show him once in the glory in which he is at last to reign. And as then, on the Mount of Transfiguration, there were three companions, eye-witnesses of Christ's glory, so it would almost seem as if the same number were purposely selected to be with Abram on the occasion of this unwonted manifestation of his high dignity. We read of three men, whether independent princes, or merely influential neighbours, does not appear,— though the last seems more probable,—who were confederate with Abram, who cultivated his friendship, and were disposed to make common cause with him ; recognising in him something more than met the eye—some mark of his actual position as blessed, and made heir of the land by God.

For that there were a few among those with whom the patriarch met, who had some idea of what he really was, and of what he had a right to be, this very chapter testifies, in the instance of Melchizedek. Possibly also the messenger who brought Abram tidings of Lot's calamity may have been one of these ; — "There came one that had escaped, and told Abram the Hebrew" (ver. 13). The message is brought to "Abram the Hebrew,"—a title which some have interpreted as referring merely to the patriarch's having come from beyond the river Euphrates, but which it is far more natural to understand as denoting his descent from Heber or Eber. We have already seen that Eber was specially distinguished in the line of Shem (chap. x. 21), and that very probably it was he who was commissioned to announce that authoritative division of the earth, from which his son, Peleg, received his name. Eber, therefore, might well be held in remembrance in these early times; and it could scarcely fail to be known that, in the division of the earth, this particular portion had been reserved for his seed. Accordingly, when Abram appeared in Canaan, to distinguish him as the Hebrew, or the descendant of Eber, might fairly imply an acknowledgment of his high hereditary claims; and such an acknowledgment he might naturally receive from those who duly marked the ways of the Lord in regard to him. Hence the propriety of his being saluted in this connection as " Abram the Hebrew." If he was to come forward in the matter at all, as the messenger seemed to suggest, and as his three friends were prepared to expect, it must be in the character indicated by this patronymic title, or name of descent. If they thought it natural or reasonable that he should interfere, it must have been because they discerned his right to that character and that title,—a right not only founded on his descent from Eber, but confirmed by special promises given to himself. Otherwise, indeed, the idea of his acting as a prince and leading an army would scarcely have occurred, either to them or to himself. He is justified in what he does by his consciousness,—they are reconciled to it by their perception,—of his true rank and final destiny. For once, in his pilgrim state, God glorifies his servant before the eyes of all, as the proprietor and lord of the land.

Not, therefore, as a private person, not as a stranger and pilgrim,—which character he usually bore,—but as the heir, did Abram on this occasion take the sword, and wage war against the invaders of the kingdom which was his own; and thus for himself he received, and to all who had a spiritual discernment he gave, a pledge and earnest of things to come

It was an anticipation of the promise; even as the transfiguration of Christ was a foretaste or foreshowing of the reward set before him, and the glory to be revealed in him.

3. Thus Abram for a brief space appears as a warrior-prince, and a conqueror. As a warrior, how just and generous is the cause of conflict! As a conqueror, how noble and disinterested is his use of victory!

To rescue a lost kinsman is his single aim,—a kinsman, too, deserving of no such kindness at his hands. The separation which had taken place, not, as it would seem, very reluctantly on the side of Lot,—his selfish choice of the fairest portion of the land,—his rashly-formed connection with the wicked, for the sake of gain,—and his consequent distance and estrangement from his best and truest friend,—these things might almost have justified Abram in leaving him to his fate. But all past unkindness is forgotten, in pity for his present woful plight. Abram makes haste to help him; nor does he fear, on his behalf, to encounter with a mere handful a mighty host. Such was the end of this war on the part of Abram— the deliverance of one of his own kinsmen and brethren out of the hands of the invading foe. That the men of Sodom shared for a season in the benefit of that deliverance, was an incidental consequence, not the main and primary purpose of his interposition. In rescuing Lot, he rescued also "their goods, and women, and people" (ver. 16). In their case, however, it was but a temporary respite that was thus procured for them; they only perished the more miserably at the last. Nor was it for their sakes that Abram interfered; whatever temporary advantage flowed to them was, as it were, by the way. The salvation of Lot was all that he sought.

In all this, who can fail to see a typical representation of the warfare of Christ himself? He comes to bruise the serpent's head,—to destroy the works of the devil,—to spoil principalities and powers,—to bind the strong man armed.

One result of his interposition is the respite granted to the impenitent and unbelieving,—who are rescued from immediate destruction and spared for a time on the earth. But, alas! it is only, like the men of these doomed cities of the plain, to "treasure up unto themselves wrath against the day of wrath, and revelation of the righteous judgment of God." Christ, however, has a people of his own, whose deliverance is the real end of his enterprise. For their sakes he came single-handed to encounter the foe, whose name is Legion; for their sakes he will not desist till, having followed up his conquest to the uttermost, he subdues even the last enemy, which is Death. Like Abram, he loves and will deliver those whom, in the face of ingratitude and estrangement, "having loved from the first, he loves to the last" as his own.

As the cause of war was just and generous, so the use which Abram made of victory was worthy of himself. Returning from this great exploit, he becomes at once a man of renown; he has acquired a name and power which nothing in the land can resist; great kings have fled before him, and have been destroyed. To the farthest corner of the land, even to Dan, he has pursued them with his little army of three hundred and eighteen men. Nay, beyond the borders of the land, he has penetrated even into Syria,—to the neighbour-hood of Damascus itself (ver. 15); and he has struck a blow in which, although he does avail himself of the arts of war,—having recourse to a night attack, made simultaneously at different points (ver. 15),—still, considering his comparatively feeble force, the hand of God is conspicuously apparent. Thus powerful and mighty in battle, why may he not instantly take possession of the land? It is at his feet; why may he not occupy its throne? Surely it is because he believes God; he is not impatient or ambitious; he seeks not an earthly, but a heavenly country. Having accomplished the single purpose for which he took this unusual step; and having on that one occasion asserted and manifested his true character, as lord and heir of the land ; he at once becomes a private man again. He is a stranger and pilgrim once more.

So scrupulous indeed is he, in his care to avoid the suspicion of a selfish or interested aim, that he refuses all share of the spoil. His companions, the three friends who accompanied him, he will not defraud of their portions ; but for himself he will take nothing ; nor will he suffer his young men to receive any recompense beyond the food they have eaten. Least of all, will he consent to receive hire from the king of Sodom, as though he were taking wages for the restoration of the persons or souls, by making the goods his own. " I have lift up," he says, " my hand unto the Lord, the most high God, the possessor of heaven and earth, that I will not take from a thread even to a shoe-latchet, and that I will not take any thing that is thine, lest thou shouldest say, I have made Abram rich : save only that which the young men have eaten, and the portion of the men which went with me, Aner, Eschol, and Mamre ; let them take their portion " (vers. 22-24). Nor is it in the mere affectation of a romantic and chivalrous independence that Abram thus rejects the king's well-meant proposal. His resolution had been formed before he undertook the expedition, and specially under the eye of him by whose authority he undertook it. From first to last the whole is of God and unto God alone. He is not the mercenary captain of a free company, to lend out his services to whoever will pay for them. It is as the independent head of a great nation, and the real owner of this whole territory, that he lays aside, as it were, for a few days, his disguise, or his incognito, and vindicates the title which belongs to him, as the heir of the divine promises, to the praise of the glory of divine sovereignty and grace.

Such is this memorable expedition. In its main and leading aspect,—the levying of war or the taking up of arms,—the conduct of Abram here is not a precedent for us. Still in its accompanying features this history is exemplary in a high degree. The brotherly-kindness of the patriarch, his disinterestedness, and his heavenly-mindedness,—are exhibited in this transaction for a pattern to us. Whatever power we have, let it be used for our brother's deliverance; for doing good to all, especially to such as are of the household of faith. Let all suspicion of covetousness or of selfish ends be carefully excluded in all our undertakings; and in the height of earthly triumph, let it be seen that we can forego the tempting prize, and live still as strangers and pilgrims, seeking a better, that is a heavenly country.

But it is chiefly in a spiritual and prophetical light that the affair is to be viewed.

Spiritually, it may well be held to represent the victory of the Lord Jesus, and his triumph over principalities and powers in his cross. He then rescued the captives of Satan, and recovered the prey from the mighty. As his atoning blood shed for the remission of sins has satisfied divine justice, and opened the way to the Father,—so, " through his death, he hath destroyed him that had the power of death, that is, the devil, and delivered those who, through fear of death, were all their lifetime subject to bondage" (Heb. ii. 14, 15). His people, therefore, are no longer under any necessity of making terms of precarious peace or compromise with "the father of lies" and " accuser of the brethren;" nor have they to wage with the "prince of this world" an unequal warfare, in which they are sure to be discomfited. Satan has lost his advantage over them; and, being no longer at his mercy, but standing on a firm footing in the free favour and almighty strength of their God, they may defy his malice, and make good their escape from his toils. But let none presume upon the victory which Christ has gained, as giving them warrant to live at ease. How many of those who were indirectly partakers in the fruits of Abraham's triumph, abusing the respite granted to them, perished miserably in the avenging fire which destroyed the cities of the plain. Let the impenitent and unbelieving, who continue in sin because grace abounds, beware lest, in the end, a worse thing come upon them. And let his own people be careful to improve the victory which Christ has gained on their behalf, to stand fast in the liberty with which he has made them free, and not again be entangled in any yoke of bondage. Let them not sleep, as do others, while the fire is kindling which is to consume the wicked; but let them watch and be sober.

Again, viewed prophetically, this incident presents to us the father of the faithful most vividly apprehending things to come. While as yet he has not a foot of ground that he can call his own, he assumes with all the calmness of undoubted sovereignty the right to act as the heir of the land. For a brief space, he exercises the functions of its lawful owner and ruler; thus truly living by the power of the world to come. It is a pledge of the glory to be revealed which is here given,—a passing glimpse of the scene which is to be realised, when the promise made to Abram shall be fully accomplished, and he shall be put in possession of his long-deferred inheritance. Like the heavenly brightness which overwhelmed the three apostles on the Mount of Transfiguration, this unwonted adventure in the lowly life of the pilgrim, points to another order of things, and serves to give substance and evidence to what is still hoped for and unseen. We do not therefore follow cunningly devised fables, when we anticipate the " power and coming of our Lord Jesus Christ," and of his saints with him. We are here, as it were, made " eye-witnesses" of the coming "majesty" of both. And we have the surer word of prophecy, unfolding to us the prospect of " many coming from the east and west, to sit down for ever with Abraham, Isaac, and Jacob, in the kingdom of heaven."

II. The interview with Melchizedek throws additional light on the faith of Abram. The endless questions which have been discussed respecting Melchizedek's person, as well as the fancies of some of the early Christian fathers respecting the bread and wine, may be left altogether unnoticed. They have all arisen out of the vague impression which the Epistle to the Hebrews gives of there being a kind of mystery about the man. And so there is, in the scriptural sense of the word mystery ; there is a spiritual and figurative meaning in his history ; he is a typical personage. But the evil is, that the mystery has been supposed to lie in particulars where Paul gives no hint of it ; as in the mere personal identity of Melchizedek, or in his selection of bread and wine as a refreshment for Abram. The whole real mystery of Melchizedek, the commentator himself clears up. It lies, not in his person at all, but exclusively in his office. It is as a priest and prince that he is a mysterious, or rather, simply a typical, personage. And he is so, chiefly in respect of these two particulars,—first the significant appellations which he bears as king (Heb. vii. 2) ; and, secondly, the singular and isolated order of his priesthood (Heb. vii. 3).

As king, he bore the personal appellation of Melchizedek, or " king of righteousness ; " and the seat of his kingdom being Salem, he held the title of " king of Salem," which means, king of peace. Whether this Salem was the city which after-wards became Jerusalem, or some other place nearer the vale of Siddim, and the river of Jordan (John iii. 23), does not appear ; nor, indeed, is it the precise locality, but the name, that is important. It was the King of righteousness and peace that Abram acknowledged in the very height of his own triumph, when he accepted Melchizedek's hospitality, and received at his hands the refreshment of bread and wine.

Again, as priest, Melchizedek stood apart from all other priests, isolated and alone ; and Abram availed himself of his sacred offices in that character. Melchizedek accordingly, on the one hand, blessed Abram on God's behalf,—" Blessed be Abram of the most high God, possessor of heaven and earth " (ver. 19); and again, on the other hand, he blessed God on Abram's behalf,—" And blessed be the most high God, which hath delivered thine enemies into thy hands " (ver. 20).

This brief and comprehensive form of benediction is, in truth, a summary of the entire priestly function ; and it brings out, as comprised in one single and simple act, the whole ministry proper to the priest, as interposing or mediating between the great God in heaven, and the servant or worshipper of God on earth. What is a priest, but one through whose effectual offerings and intercession the blessing of God comes down upon man ; and through whom, again, from man's deliverance, blessing, and honour, and glory, and power, redound to God " in the highest ? "

In a very inferior and subordinate sense, men may bless one another, and may bless God on behalf of one another ; but in the one case, it is merely the utterance of a desire or prayer ; and in the other, a becoming expression of reverence and gratitude. But the act of Melchizedek evidently implies something more ; it is authoritative and efficacious ; he blesses as one having right to bless—as one whose ministry really and actually does bring good to man, on the one hand, and praise to God, on the other. What good does it bring to man ? Is it not all the fulness of God ? What praise does it bring to God ? Is it not all the praise of man's salvation ?

How marvellous ; how full of meaning, is this alternation or reciprocation, this intercommunion between God and man, of which the priest becomes the minister ! Between the two parties, a transference or blessed exchange takes place, the highest property of each being imparted or ascribed to the other. For who, in this case, are the parties ? God, on the one side, "the most high God, possessor of heaven and earth ; " and Abram, on the other, saved in battle, and victorious over all his enemies. And what is this double blessing ? What does it imply ? What but this ; that the Lord's prerogative, as possessor of heaven and earth, becomes virtually

Abram's; and Abram's glory, as victorious over all his enemies, becomes truly the Lord's?

Oh, most blessed traffic, most profitable exchange! Who can hesitate about closing with so advantageous a treaty? Abram has the benefit of God being the possessor of heaven and earth; God has the glory of Abram's victory over his enemies. How gracious the arrangement! How reasonable, equitable, and righteous! What can faithful Abram say to it? Can he demur to the terms proposed; holding fast the praise of his victory as his own, and saying,—my own right hand has got it? Can he be for taking the credit of it to himself, and reckoning on the like success, as always at his command? That would be miserable policy,—poor economy indeed! Better far, even in a prudential point of view, to give it all over to God; and to receive instead of it a vested interest, if one may venture so to speak,—a right of property,—in God himself, the Lord, Jehovah, as " the most high God, the possessor of heaven and earth."

Besides thus blessing Abram, Melchizedek received tithes at his hand,—" tithes of all " (ver. 20)—whether tithes of all the spoil of his enemies, or tithes of all his own property, is not said;—probably it was the tenth of both. How the custom of paying tithes originated, and by what authority it was sanctioned in these early days, we stay not now to inquire. One thing, however, may be clearly gathered from the traces which we find of this usage, whether in the Bible or in other ancient writings, that it was intimately associated with the institution of the priesthood, and the offering of sacrifices. In his character of mediator, the priest received tithes. He received them as the pledge and token of the whole of what was tithed being the Lord's—of its belonging to God, and being freely dedicated and consecrated to him. For as the ordained and appointed medium or channel of communication between God and man, the priest not merely conveyed the gift of God to man, but conveyed also man's gifts to God.

The blessing bestowed on the part of God passed through his hands, and so also did the offices and services rendered on the part of man. Such is the priestly function, as discharged by Melchizedek and acknowledged by Abram.

But who or what is this Melchizedek, that he should be competent for such a function? He is, it is true, a king and priest together; but so were many heads of families and tribes in these days; and so, virtually, was Abram himself. Abram officiated as a priest when he built an altar—wherever he went —to the Lord; and on this one occasion, at least, the occasion on which he came in contact with Melchizedek, he acted as a king, going forth to battle and returning in triumph. In this respect, therefore, and in so far as the mere union of the two dignities of royalty and priesthood in one person was concerned, there was nothing very peculiar in Melchizedek's position; Abram himself stood almost on the same footing. What, then, does this transaction mean?

1. Melchizedek was undoubtedly an eminently holy man, a believer in the true God and in the promised Messiah; and accordingly the interview between him and Abram, considered merely as the meeting of two heaven-owned saints and patriarchs, is full of interest. The one is a remarkable example of the grace of God—preserving, amid the dregs of a general apostasy, an elect remnant; the other is an instance no less striking of that divine and sovereign grace bringing in, from without, a new seed. And the two, meeting thus as debtors to the same grace, cannot but rejoice in mutually recognising and acknowledging each other. It is as if the torch were here visibly handed over from the last of the former band, to the first of that which is to succeed. The church is transferred to a new stock or stem; the cause receives a new impulse, and is to have a fresh start; and this singular transaction between Melchizedek and Abram, is the connecting link between the two systems, or orders, or dispensations, of which the one is now waxing old, and the other is but just beginning

to appear. The general and unrestricted dispensation of religious faith and worship, transmitted indiscriminately by tradition among all the descendants of Noah, is about to give place to a dispensation limited to a particular family or race, to whom ultimately are to be committed the oracles of God. One form of the primitive order is to be superseded by another;—the patriarchal institute is to be succeeded by the Levitical and legal ordinances which are to be established in Abram's house. And the substantial identity of the two, the Patriarchal and the Levitical, is indicated by the meeting of their respective representatives. It is like aged Simeon, embracing in his arms the infant Saviour;—the last patriarch and prophet of the law not departing till he sees and hails the new-born hope of the Gospel; the lingering twilight of declining day mingling with the dawn of a better morn.

2. But a higher view still is to be taken of this transaction. This is plain from the use which the apostle makes of it, and the importance which he attaches to it (Heb. vii.). Melchizedek officiated as the type of the Messiah, who was to be a priest after the same order with himself; and Abram undoubtedly had respect to him in that character. It was not the mediation of a mere man that he acknowledged; it was not the ministry of an earthly priest in which he trusted. Melchizedek, king and priest as he was, could not really and effectually convey to Abram the blessing of the most high God, the possessor of heaven and of earth; nor was it through him him that the glory of Abram's victory, and the tithes of his spoil and of his goods, could be acceptably transmitted to God. But a greater than Melchizedek is here; present, surely, not indeed to the senses, but to the minds of both. In his name, Melchizedek acts, and to him, in Melchizedek's person, Abram does homage. The two patriarchs understand one another. Melchizedek, as the last preserver, as it were, of the primitive patriarchal hope, hands over his function to one more highly favoured than himself, in the very spirit of the Baptist—" He

must increase, but I must decrease " (John iii. 30). His own occupation, as a witness and standing type of the Messiah, is over; one newly called out of heathenism is to succeed and to take his place. Melchizedek is content. He hails in Abram the promised seed, and blesses him accordingly; while again, in Melchizedek, Abram sees, however dimly, the day of Christ, and Christ himself. Thus the Patriarchal, the Abrahamic, and the Levitical dispensations appear, all of them, in their true character, as subordinate and shadowy; and in the eye of faith Christ is all in all.

3. Let it be noted also that it is especially in contrast with the Levitical priesthood in the house of Aaron, that the apostle exalts and magnifies the priesthood after the order of Melchizedek. His object is to satisfy the Hebrew Christians as to the reality of Christ's priesthood, and to instruct them as to its nature. For this purpose he cites the deed or decree of nomination or appointment: "Jehovah hath sworn, and will not repent, Thou art a priest for ever after the order of Melchizedek" (Ps. cx. 4); appealing to this irrevocable oath as the warrant for regarding the Messiah as invested in perpetuity with the priestly office (Heb. vii.). Nor could exception be taken to his being held to be a priest, because he was not of the house of Aaron. This might have been an insuperable bar to his claim, had he sought to minister in the earthly sanctuary, and to be the mediator of the Levitical covenant. But as our forerunner, he has entered for us within the veil, into the true sanctuary, the heavenly place itself; and his ministry is connected with another dispensation altogether, and with another covenant. Neither, again, could it be objected that this was an after-thought—a theory devised by the followers of Jesus to serve a purpose and make the old Scriptures tally with the new faith of a crucified Messiah. For the very charter of the Messiah's priesthood, from the first announcement of it,—the very word of the oath by which it was solemnly declared that he was to be a priest,—intimated that

his priesthood was to be entirely distinct from that of Levi's house, and of another order altogether. It was not necessary that he should be of the Levitical order : it was expressly foretold that he was to be of the order of Melchizedek.

4. But even this does not satisfy the apostle, or exhaust the meaning of that marvellous oath of God on which he is authoritatively commenting. It is not enough to make out that it establishes, against all objections that might be taken to it, the unquestionable reality and validity of Christ's priesthood, as having undoubted divine sanction. It does that, but it does a great deal more. It opens up a glorious spiritual view of the nature of his priesthood ; and it suggests various particulars in respect of which his priesthood, being the one only Messianic priesthood, is pre-eminent in itself, and fruitful of all rich and heavenly blessings to his believing people.

Thus, in the first place, it is a royal priesthood, which that of Aaron's house and of the Levitical order was not, and could not be. Christ is " a priest upon his throne" (Zech. vi. 13) ; and as his priesthood effectually establishes " the counsel of peace " between God and man, so his kingdom is a kingdom of righteousness and peace (Ps. lxxii.). Again, secondly, as a priest, he has no pedigree or genealogy ; he has none going before or coming after him in the priestly office ; he is alone in his priesthood during all its time ; he continueth a priest for ever. Then, in the third place, the order of his priesthood is prior in point of date, and superior in point of dignity, to that of Aaron's or Levi's priesthood ; for when Levi, in the person of his ancestor Abraham, paid tithes to Melchizedek and received his blessing, he virtually acknowledged a higher priesthood than his own. And, fourthly, this acknowledgment of another priesthood, of a different order,—proved to be superior by the double test of blessing accepted and tithes given— evidently implies a certain imperfection in the Levitical priesthood, and therefore in the dispensation with which it was connected. The Levitical priesthood was not intended to be perpetual and permanent; it served a temporary purpose, until that other Priest of another order should arise.

From all this it follows, that when that other Priest of another order has come, his priesthood supersedes all that went before it; and being in the hands of one who continueth ever; and being ratified, moreover, by the divine oath; it cannot be changed. The Levitical priesthood was held by a succession of mortal men, infirm, and liable to death; and it was instituted without the solemnity of an oath. This last circumstance indicated the character of the economy to which that priesthood belonged, as being of the nature of a provisional, or, as it were, parenthetical, arrangement. It was not confirmed by an appeal to the two immutable things—the divine word and the divine nature, which enter into the idea of the divine oath. In other words, the Levitical dispensation and its priesthood did not form an essential part of that plan or system, to which the honour of God is committed, and with which his glory is inseparably blended and identified,—which, therefore, must be as irrevocably unchangeable as God himself is. The Levitical law was given, and the Levitical order of priests ordained, to serve a temporary purpose; and, accordingly, the formality of an oath was omitted. But the priesthood after the order of Melchizedek, enters into the very essence of the everlasting covenant. Hence, "not without an oath is Christ made an high priest;" and hence, also, as a high priest, he is the mediator, not of a shadowy and burdensome legal ritual, which was to wax old and vanish away, but of that grace and truth which came by him, and which in him endure for ever.

Such, in substance, is the reasoning of the apostle, in the seventh chapter of the Epistle to the Hebrews; and such is the exalted view which he gives of the priesthood of Melchizedek, as distinct from that of Levi, and identical, in its order, with that of Christ. Such is the High Priest, suited to the necessity of man's case; one who is not only touched with the feeling of our infirmities, but able also "to save them to the uttermost that come unto God by him, seeing he ever liveth to make intercession for them" (ver. 25).

In the person of Melchizedek, therefore, let us hail a present Saviour ; and in what passed between him and our father Abraham, let us recognise the reality and fulness of his ministry of love toward us. Receiving in him and through his mediation, the blessing of " the most high God, possessor of heaven and earth," we are filled with all the fulness of God ;—"All things are ours; whether Paul, or Apollos, or Cephas, or the world, or life, or death, or things present, or things to come ; all are ours." Then, again, in Christ, having "redemption through his blood, even the forgiveness of sins, according to the riches of the free grace of God," we are appointed to be "to the praise of his glory." In us, and on our behalf, Christ glorifies the Father. Our escape from guilt, and our consequent victory over all our enemies, form the theme of the new song of praise. With the whole multitude of the redeemed, we ascribe salvation to our God, who sitteth on the throne, and unto the Lamb ; and we present the first fruits of our deliverance, in the dedication of ourselves to the service of God for ever.

"I beseech you therefore, brethren, by the mercies of God, that ye present your bodies a living sacrifice, holy and acceptable unto him, which is your reasonable service" (Rom. xii. 1). "By him also, let us offer the sacrifice of praise to God continually, that is, the fruit of our lips, giving thanks to his name. And to do good and to communicate let us forget not ; since with such sacrifices God is well pleased" (Heb. xiii. 15, 16).

17

JUSTIFICATION BY FAITH—INSIGHT INTO
THINGS TO COME

Genesis 15:1-21

THE revelation recorded in this chapter closely followed the victory over the kings, and the interview with Melchizedek. It seems designed to bring out the patriarch in a new character; —that of a prophet, or an authorised and accredited depositary of the will and the counsels of God.

The announcement of the communication which God now makes to Abram is in peculiar language: " The word of the Lord came to Abram in a vision" (ver. 1). It is the first time this expression occurs, although afterwards it is extremely common in the Bible. In the use of it, there is generally, if not always, a special reference to the prophetic office. There are examples of this in the historical books (1 Sam. iii. 7 ; 1 Kings xiii.) ; and instances from the writings of the prophets themselves might be multiplied indefinitely. Their usual form of speech, indeed, is this, " The word of the Lord came ;" and of their " visions" we read continually. In fact, so continually is the phrase in question,—" The word of the Lord came," or " spake," or was " revealed,"—identified with prophetic inspiration, that we may partly see in it an explanation of the significant appellation given to the Son, " The WORD." He is so called as the revealer of the Father (John i. 18). His Spirit was in the prophets, and he spake by them. And it may be with reference to his immediate personal agency, as connected with all revelation, that this came to be the standing mode of announcing a prophetic oracle,—"The WORD of the LORD came."

Viewing, then, Abram as presented to us in this chapter in a new light—that of a prophet, properly so called—we are to observe, in the first place, his inauguration into that office as one personally accepted in the sight of God ; and secondly, the first prophetic disclosure, in circumstantial detail, of the future fortunes of the people of God.

I. That he may be qualified for receiving the prophetic communication, he must first be himself owned as on a right footing personally with God.   And he is so owned very emphatically and unequivocally.

" After these things," that is, after the events of the previous chapter, and very shortly after them, the vision of this chapter took place.   It was a vision of great compass and importance, and it occupied a considerable space of time ; reaching from midnight, or at least from before the earliest dawn of morning, till the darkness of another evening closed in.   For it was surely a real scene that Abram, though rapt in prophetic ecstasy, beheld, when God led him forth, and bade him look at the starry heavens (ver. 5).   This must have been before the sun arose.   As the sun is going down, we find the seer still watching beside the sacrifice he has prepared, and falling exhausted into the awful trance which is to be the means of giving him an insight into the sealed book of the providence of God (ver. 12).   An entire day, then, is spent in this vision.   Was it the Sabbath ?   Was Abram, like John, " in the Spirit on the Lord's day ?" (Rev. i. 10).   This first prophecy, beginning to unfold the peculiar history of the Old Testament Church, is in some sort parallel to that last Revelation of John the Divine, in which all the vicissitudes of the New Testament Church are opened up.   It is not, therefore, altogether a fanciful analogy which would connect the day here spent by Abram with that on which John records that he was in the Spirit.

1. In either case, the interview begins with the same gracious words of encouragement addressed personally to the prophet. "Fear not," says "one like unto the Son of man" to the apostle (Rev. i. 17)—"Fear not, Abram," is the corresponding salutation of the "WORD of the LORD" to the patriarch. John, indeed, mentions a loud voice previously heard by him, and a wondrous sight seen (Rev. i. 10-17); and, in doing so, does he not supply what is left to be inferred in this narrative respecting Abram? He accounts for the fear which, in his own case, the Lord made it his first business to remove. And may not the same explanation be understood to be intended in the case of Abraham? When it is said, "the Word of the Lord came unto him in vision" (ver. i.), must not this imply, not only an audible sound, but also a visible manifestation? And may we not with great probability suppose that Abram, like John, "heard behind him a great voice as of a trumpet;" and "turning, saw a glorious person;" and seeing him, "fell at his feet as dead?" (Rev. i. 10-17). Most certainly, whatever was the occasion of it, he must have been overwhelmed with amazement and terror, when the Lord found it necessary, in kindness and condescension, to say to him, as to John, "Fear not, Abram."

And the argument for the removal of fear is the same in both instances, being simply the gracious manner in which the person speaking discovers himself, and makes himself known: "Fear not, for it is I"—it is I, "thy shield and thy exceeding great reward" (ver. 1)—"it is I, the first and the last, the living one" (Rev. i. 17, 18).

In both cases, also, there is probably an appeal to the past. Thus, when the Word of the Lord says to Abram, "I am thy shield, and thy exceeding great reward," there is surely a reference to the battle and to the victory—to the fight and to the triumph. Dost thou not know me, Abram? It was I who shielded thee in the recent battle; it was I who rewarded thee in the victory. Didst not thou forego all other recompense for me? Didst thou not renounce all the spoils of conquest, and take me as thine only portion? And have not I been thy reward? And is it not a reward exceeding great? Then, "fear not," since it is I who speak to thee. "Fear not," though the voice be as a trumpet, and the vision terrible in its glory: "Be of good cheer, it is I, be not afraid." It is I, whom thou hast found to be not only able to save, but all-sufficient to bless. "It is I," thy shield in war, and thy reward in victory—thy Saviour and Redeemer, "thy God and thy portion for ever."

The simple discovery of himself on the part of the Lord is enough for John. But, in the circumstances in which Abram is placed, there is a special difficulty to be got over. When the "Word of the Lord came in vision" to John, the great battle was already actually fought, and the great victory won, of which Abram, in his successful encounter with the kings, had received but a remote and shadowy type. In particular, in the case of Abram, the very Being by whom the great salvation is to be accomplished, that mysterious person, of old announced as the Seed of the woman, and more recently, as destined to be of his own race, is still to come, and his coming has been made to depend upon a condition, growing daily, as it would seem, more hopeless. "I go childless" (ver. 2). I am childless now; childless I have passed through life hitherto; and childless, it would almost appear, I am to pass away. My time is running on, my years are drawing to a close, and still, alas! still "I go childless."

Is there impatience in this complaint? What wonder if there be? Abram begins to fear, lest his present earthly portion may turn out to be his all. He has become rich and prosperous notwithstanding the disinterestedness which he twice so remarkably practised—first, in ceding to Lot the best of the land, and then in refusing all the spoils of the war waged on Lot's behalf. In a temporal sense, he has received a large recompense for his generosity and forbearance; but is it with such a reward, or with more of the same kind, that he is to be put off, instead of the blessing promised in his seed? In a better spirit than that of Haman, he seems to say that all this availeth him nothing, so long as the one thing on which he has been taught to set his heart is withheld. Lord God, what wilt thou give me—what canst thou give me as my reward—what that will avail me any thing " seeing I go childless?" Nor is it merely an heir of his worldly possessions that he desires; that he can find—that he has already. This Eliezer of Damascus might suffice, if that were all he needed. But where is the promise of the Saviour? "To me thou hast given no seed."

Such is Abram's expostulation; thus he opens his whole heart to God. He does not keep silence when his sorrow is stirred,—painfully or sullenly musing when the fire burns (Ps. xxxix.). He may be obliged to restrain himself in the presence of the weak or the wicked among his fellow-men, who might have no sympathy with his anxiety and grief; but before his God he may lay bare his inmost soul, and make all his thoughts and feelings known. And even if they be thoughts of unbelief and feelings bordering on sin,—the suggestions of sense and sight contending against faith,—the groanings of the flesh lusting against the Spirit, better far that they be spread fairly out in the gracious eye of the blessed Lord, than that they be nursed and pent up in his own bosom to breed distrust and estrangement there.

Come, thou timid, shrinking, doubtful soul,—come forth and frankly, freely, fearlessly meet thy God. "Fear not." Speak, as his own Spirit moves thee, for his Spirit helpeth thy infirmities. But thou knowest not what to say. Then, with thy groanings which cannot be uttered, the Spirit will make intercession for thee, and the Searcher of hearts will know the mind of the Spirit in thee, as he takes thy secret sighs and tears, and lays them out as thy pleadings with thy God. Only "fear not." Let thy difficulty, thine objection, thy doubt, whatever it is, be imparted to the Lord, as Abram's was. What though it be thine infirmity? Will he not pity it ? Will he not teach thee to remember the years of the right hand of the Most High ? (Ps. lxxvii. 10).

2. So he teaches Abram. From his tent, where first he met with him,—from his bed, perhaps, which he has been watering with his tears,—the Lord raises the patriarch, and leads him out, and places him beneath the glorious midnight sky (ver. 4, 5). Seest thou these hosts of heaven? Canst thou reckon them? No. But he who speaks to thee can. He can count them. He telleth the number of the stars ; he calleth them all by their names; and to thee he saith, " So shall thy seed be." Here is the perfection of science—the highest sublimity of the most sublime of all the sciences—the most glorious lesson in astronomy the world ever learned. In the still and solemn silence of earth's un-broken slumber—under the deep azure arch of heaven—not a breath stirring—not a cloud passing,—then and there, to stand alone with God,—to stand with open eye, and behold his works,—to stand with open ear, and hear his word—his word to thee ! These stars ;—canst thou number them ? Look now toward heaven and tell them; these all I ordained, and even such a seed have I ordained to Abram ! Thus, in the undimmed glory of their multitudinous hosts, shining still, as they shone, when he talked with Abram, the Lord calls thee, on each returning night, to hail the renewed assurance of that promise on which all thy hope, as well as Abram's, must hang. So shall the seed of Abram—his seed, embracing Christ, and all that are his—and therefore not excluding thee—so shall the seed of Abram be.

The promise thus made Abram at once believed,—on the mere word of him who rules the starry host, and who " calls the things that are not as though they were." He believes, and " God counts it unto him for righteousness" (ver. 6).

Such is the testimony here borne concerning Abram,—that testimony of which Paul makes so much use in his two epistles to the Romans and the Galatians, when he is establishing the blessed doctrine, so glorifying to God—so gracious to the sin-

ner, on which it is his delight to dwell,—the doctrine of justification by faith alone without works. He quotes the verse
before us repeatedly as the scriptural evidence and assurance
of the way in which the patriarch was justified before God.
"Abraham believed God, and he counted it to him," or it
was counted to him for "righteousness;" or still more indefinitely, he believed God, and righteousness was counted or imputed to him. He believed, and was reckoned or accounted
righteous. For such, in substance, is the force of this important testimony. It is a testimony to the sole and exclusive
efficacy of faith, as the act by which a justifying righteousness
is apprehended and appropriated. It is in this light that Paul
regards the testimony here recorded, and it is for this purpose
that he uses it ;—as speaking not of the ground of a sinner's
justification, but only of the instrument of it.. The ground of
justification is not expressly mentioned in this record at all,
which is simply an attestation of Abram's faith, and of the
sufficiency of his faith alone, as the instrument of his justification. But the power or efficacy of faith to justify, cannot be
in itself; for, by its very nature, faith ever looks beyond itself,
and borrows all from without; if it rely on itself,—on any
worth, or value, or virtue, in itself,—it ceases to be faith,—it
becomes quite another act or exercise of mind. It is no longer
faith in God, but faith in some good work of my own; it may be
faith in my very faith itself, and not in what my faith should
grasp. But it is expressly said, "Abram believed God," and that
—namely, his simply believing God—that alone justifies him.

As to the origin and character, moreover, of the faith which
justified Abram, it is important to remark that we have not
here any explicit testimony. We gather indeed conclusively
from the frame of mind which its exercise must have implied ;
—from the entire subordination of the carnal to the spiritual
and the seen to the unseen ; above all, from the simplicity of
personal reliance upon God and the cordiality of personal submission to God, which may be traced in this marvellous act of

believing such a promise in such circumstances ;—that it could be no mere effort of human volition or bare conviction of the human understanding. Beyond all question, the faith called forth on this occasion is above all human capacity ; no reasoning or persuasive influence can command it ; no power of human thought or will can reach it. It is of divine workmanship,—created in the renewal of the whole nature by the immediate agency of the Holy Ghost. And it is divine in its character as well as in its origin ; uniting the soul to God ; assimilating the soul to God ; making it partaker of the divine fellowship and the divine holiness.

Being thus the work of God,—and a work so precious and heavenly,—such faith as Abram's might well be singled out as having an efficacy to place him on a right footing before God, and inspire him with a right heart towards God. Still let it be remembered that it is not this divine excellency of faith that forms the subject of the historian's testimony and the apostle's application of it ;—but the one only point of its being absolutely and entirely alone, without works of any kind, in this transaction of the patriarch's free justification through his simple trust in the bare and naked word of the living God. He had no thought on that night of his own faith at all,—or of any virtue, divine or human, that his faith might possess. But "he believed in the Lord, and he counted it to him for righteousness."

Precisely the same phrase here used respecting Abram, is repeated, but repeated once only, in the Old Testament, and is applied to Phinehas, in reference to the terrible vengeance which he inflicted on his guilty countryman ;—" Then stood up Phinehas, and executed judgment ; and so the plague was stayed, and that was counted unto him for righteousness unto all generations for evermore" (Ps. cvi. 30, 31). The act which Phinehas performed on that occasion, was performed in faith. He executed judgment, because he believed in the Lord; and it was exclusively on account of the faith in which he acted that it was counted unto him for righteousness, or, in other words, that he was personally justified, and that his service, consequently, was accepted also. But observe the difference between the two cases. It is the same faith ; but in Phinehas it wrought with his works, while in Abram, in this instance, it was alone. In other instances, this faith of Abram was not alone. His faith, as well as that of Phinehas, wrought with his works ; as when " by faith he went out, not knowing whither he went," and when " by faith he offered up his son Isaac." On these occasions, Abram, like Phinehas, had to work as well as to believe. But here he has simply and solely to believe. Hence the selection of this particular instance as that on the ground of which emphatic testimony is to be borne to the sole and exclusive efficacy of faith, in the justifying of the sinner. And mark how appropriate the selection is. Generally, faith is exhibited to us in active operation, prompting good works or acts of obedience ; and these may seem to have some share in procuring the benefit. Here, on the other hand, from the very necessity of the case, all working, all acting, is out of the question. There can be positively nothing, on Abram's part, but only faith—faith alone. On that starry night he has nothing whatever to do,—nothing whatever to suffer,—nothing whatever to sacrifice,—nothing whatever to undertake or pro- mise. He simply believes the Lord,—takes God at his word, —and closes with him in his free promise. That is all, and it is enough.

Doubtless, when occasion offers, this faith is found to be accompanied by works ; and then Abram is as truly justified by faith thus working, or by these works of faith, as Phinehas was by his act of faithful obedience. But, even then, though it is faith working, or faith doing good works, that may be rightly said to justify him, his justification after all depends on his faith alone. So the Apostle James teaches, when dealing with these very cases. For the practical purpose of his epistle, he takes examples of faith as it ordinarily exists and appears, not solitary and separate, but having in its train good works and holy graces ; his object being to show, that justifying faith must ever have such a train; and must ever, as opportunity occurs, be alive and alert for action. But still, in the view of the Spirit, even when these works and graces most abound, it is in respect of the faith round which they cluster, that Abram is justified ; and in respect of that alone. From first to last, Abram believed in the Lord, and through his faith alone, the divine righteousness on which it laid hold being imputed to him, he was accepted as righteous. But generally, he was called simultaneously to believe and to act ; his faith and his obedience were, as it were, combined and mixed up together ; and even to himself, the warrant of his peace and hope might not be always quite clear. It was fitting, therefore, that once, at least, he should be brought into a position in which all ambiguity must necessarily be cleared away, and the simple and glorious truth made plain and palpable to his soul. Such an era, such a crisis was this precious night, on which he stood alone with God, under the azure sky,—with no possible condition to fulfil, and no work at all to do. God speaks ;— Abram believes ;—and all is settled, all is sure.

A similar crisis, once, or it may be oftener, every believer must, in his own experience, know ;—a time when he is, as it were, shut up to the necessity of taking God simply at his word ;—believing what God testifies, and merely because he testifies it ;—without any, even the least respect, to any thing in or about himself, to any grace he may be exercising or any duty he may be doing or any purpose he may be forming. Blessed is such an era—doubly blessed,—whether you consider the past or the future. From how many dark thoughts and perplexing questions of unbelief, does it give instant and glad relief! What a preparation is it for whatever prospect may be opening before you! Groping in vain for some tangible ground on which to rest,—seeking to reconcile sense and faith,—walking still by sight, you cannot perceive how, on your behalf the promises of God can possibly be made good. Palpable contradictions, such as that in the case of Abram between his own childless state and the blessing centred in his seed, shake and stagger you. You see not how such sin as yours can be forgiven; you see not any thing in you to explain the marvel of its forgiveness; you are as unfruitful and barren as was Abram; and how, then, can you be blessed?

Oh, happy day, or night, when, after much weary toil, and many a device and expedient tried, you are led forth by the Lord himself;—you alone meeting with him alone; and are made to rest on his mere word; not asking how it may be, but believing that so it must be; believing this, because—simply because—HE says it,—HE, who calls the things that are not as though they were, and telleth all the stars! Then, the tossed soul returns unto its rest; and then, whether the future be shrouded in darkness or revealed in sadness, the mind, stayed on God, is kept in peace. Strengthened, settled, comforted and established by grace, it can stand any shock, trusting in the Lord.

II. Abram needs all the assurance implied in his being thus justified by faith, to nerve him for the insight into the future which, as a prophet, he is to receive. What is now to be revealed to him is not for himself or his household, but for remote posterity; that he may minister instruction and hope to the church of an age yet to come. For the sake of Israel, four hundred years hereafter, this prophetic vision is given to Abram;—while as to himself personally, it opens up a very mingled and chequered prospect.

At the very outset, however, God renews the promise of the heavenly inheritance. "I am the Lord," I am JEHOVAH, "that brought thee out of Ur of the Chaldees, to give thee this land to inherit it" (ver. 7).

Certainly God does seem here to lay weight and emphasis on his name, Jehovah, notwithstanding what is said afterwards; —"I appeared unto Abraham, unto Isaac, and unto Jacob, by

the name of God Almighty, but by my name Jehovah was I
not known to them" (Exod. vi. 3). Nor is there any real inconsistency here. It cannot be meant in that passage that
the name Jehovah was literally unknown to the patriarchs, or
that God, in his intercourse with them, never appealed to it.
The idea rather is, that as God appeared in their days chiefly
in the attitude of giving promises, whereas in the time of Moses
he appeared to fulfil them, his attribute of power was principally concerned in the former case, and his attribute of faithfulness and unchangeableness in the latter. The patriarchs
had to look to him as God Almighty; able, in due time, to
accomplish all the promises which he was then giving them.
Moses and the Israelites were to know him as Jehovah, un-
alterably true after the lapse of ages; truly fulfilling his promises given long before. But it does not follow from this
general rule that the view of God implied in his name Jehovah
was altogether concealed from Abraham, Isaac, and Jacob; or
that it was never used to impart to their souls strong consolation and good hope through grace. On the contrary, the
apostle, writing to the Hebrews, expressly tells us, that to
Abraham God "sware by himself;" or, as he explains it, in
support of his unchangeable word, appealed to his unchange
able nature or name (vi. 13-18). And if on any occasion his
name of immutability could be seasonably and suitably used, it
was at the opening of such a revelation as this. Referring,
accordingly, to his first dealing with Abram, while yet in the
midst of heathenism, and to the ultimate design of all his dealing with him, God assures him of the immutability of his
counsel, by pledging the immutability of his name. " I am the
LORD JEHOVAH," who called thee and promised to bless thee.
And whatever may be the darkness of the troubled scene now
to be set before thee, it is thy privilege still to know that he
who has brought thee out of Ur to inherit this land, is " the
same yesterday, to-day, and for ever."

The transaction which follows still further encourages

Abram personally, amid the clouds which are soon to gather over the fortunes of his race. It is the ratifying of a solemn covenant, by which he may know that he is to possess the land. That is the point on which Abram desires to have his faith confirmed ; " Lord God, whereby shall I know that I shall inherit it ?" (ver. 8). This is not the question of doubt or of unbelief, asked in the spirit of " an evil and adulterous generation seeking a sign ;" on the contrary, it is asked immediately after that exercise of faith concerning which such explicit testimony has been borne. And that makes all the difference. To ask or require a sign before believing, in order to believing and as the condition of believing, is unbelief and sin. But if I first believe the Lord, on his mere word, I may thereafter humbly hope to have some pledge of his promises. " Lord, I believe, help thou mine unbelief," is the fitting frame of mind for all of us. I believe in God now, for present pardon and acceptance in his sight. But the future is dark, and I am compassed about with infirmities ;—" Whereby shall I know that I shall inherit the land ?"

In reply, Abram receives an assurance, substantially the same as that to which the Apostle Peter refers as the assurance of his own hope of glory, and the hope of all like-minded with himself (2 Peter i. 16-21).

I. Like Peter and his companions " on the holy mount," Abram is an " eye-witness of the heavenly majesty." He beholds the " excellent glory" of the Lord ; and by this he knows that it is no " cunningly-devised fable" that he "follows," but a glorious and blessed reality. The Lord shows him his glory, in token of the inheritance in store for him. And the manifestation of that glory is through death ; through " an horror of great darkness falling upon him." It is through a propitiatory offering. For a sacrifice is prepared, consisting of the very victims, and what is remarkable enough, of all the victims subsequently used in the typical sacrifices of the Levitical dispensation. The animals are slain, and set in order, whether immediately by the hand of the Lord himself, or by Abram acting under his directions, does not very clearly appear;—though the latter is, on the whole, the most probable supposition (ver. 9, 10). In either view, the animals are slain; and the sacrifice is prepared and laid out. There is death,—the death of ordained and appointed victims. And what then?—what follows hereafter? Silence and suspense. Abram sits beside the dead limbs,—the divided fragments;—he sits and watches, scarcely saving them from the assaults of the devouring birds of the air;—"When the fowls came down upon the carcasses, Abram drove them away" (ver. 11). All through the live-long day he waits and keeps guard, warding off these ravenous invaders; and when the setting sun admonishes them to seek their nests, he too is weary, and a heavy slumber or trance falls strangely and dreamily upon him (ver. 12). It is, as it were, "their hour and the power of darkness;"—of darkness as of the shadow of death. But out of the darkness light shines forth, and in the death there is life (ver. 17).

"Between the pieces" of the slaughtered victims, "a smoking furnace and a burning lamp" are seen to pass. These are surely the visible emblems of the great God; corresponding to what was afterwards known as the Shechinah, or the GLORY OF THE LORD. In passing through, they probably consumed the pieces, as was usual on other similar occasions (Judges vi. 21, xiii. 19, 20). In the acceptance of the sacrifice, the glory of God is seen; and the heart of him who is thus an eye-witness of his majesty is reassured respecting "the power and coming of the Lord."

So it was in the case of Peter and his two companions on the Mount. In stating the ground of his confidence respecting the future glory, he appeals to his past personal experience;—to what he had already seen of that very glory at the scene of the Transfiguration. Then and there he beheld the glory of the Lord—"the glory as of the only begotten of the Father"—that glory of which, even when he dwelt on earth, Christ was thus once at least seen to be possessed, and in which, therefore, it might well be believed that he would come at the latter day. And it is to be particularly observed, that on the mount that glory was revealed in immediate connection with sacrifice—the sacrifice of the Lord himself; "the decease which he was to accomplish at Jerusalem." That was the theme of conversation between the Lord and his two heavenly companions there. Moses and Elias, representing the law and the prophets, thus attested the sufferings of Christ, and the glory that should follow; and it was with special reference to his mediatorial character and work, that the voice from heaven, out of the excellent glory, proclaimed;— "This is my beloved son, in whom I am well pleased." Nor is it unworthy of remark, as an additional coincidence, that as "a deep sleep fell upon Abram," so the three chosen witnesses on the mount were "heavy with sleep" (Luke ix. 32). That scene of mingled gloom and glory was as overpowering to them as this was to Abram; and the animating hope with which both scenes were full fraught, must have been as precious in the afterthought to Abram, as it was during all their lives on earth to them.

II. In connection with this sign, Abram receives "a more sure word of prophecy" (2 Peter i. 19)—more sure, or more clear and plain—more explicit and unequivocal.

The actual sight of the divine glory, illustriously displayed in the acceptance of the divinely-appointed sacrifice, confirms the believer's hope of the glory hereafter to be revealed. But it does so merely in the way of argument or inference. From the glory which he has seen already manifested, he concludes that a fuller manifestation of the same glory may be fairly anticipated—not as a fable or a dream, but as what has already been proved to be a reality. The word of prophecy, however, is more express. It not merely furnishes a presumption that so it well may be, or that so it probably must be—it gives positive information that so it shall be. Hence the apostle calls it a more sure word of prophecy. Such word of prophecy, accordingly, Abram on this occasion received. It was a word that spoke to him of hope deferred ; but not of that " hope deferred" which "maketh the heart sick ;" for it was none other than the hope which maketh not ashamed ;—the hope that is full of immortality.

Observe the sure word of prophecy in this connection ; as it affects the church or people of God generally, and as it affects Abraham himself individually. Mark how the hope is deferred, but yet not so as to make the heart sick.

1. In reference to his seed after the flesh, and the great nation of which he is destined to be the father, Abram's hope is deferred (ver. 13, 14). The patriarch is warned against cherishing the expectation of an immediate settlement of his children in the land ; and in so far as his expectation might be supposed to be of a temporal and earthly kind, this could not fail to strike his heart as a hard and cruel disappointment. Even the first instalment, as it were, of his allotted portion or recompense of reward, is not to be bestowed so soon or so easily as he thought. A period of exile, captivity, and oppression, is to intervene before the earliest possession of the land by any people bearing his name. Four hundred years of affliction must pass away before he or his seed can claim any property in the soil, beyond the grave in which his bones are, almost by mere sufferance, to lie.

This is the first instance which the Bible records of chronological prophecy, and considerable difficulty is found in determining the exact epoch intended. Thus there is a question whether the four hundred years should be reckoned from the days of Abram, or from the actual commencement of the Egyptian oppression, out of which the Israelites were rescued by the hand of Moses. And even if we adhere to the commonly received opinion, and consider these four hundred years as including the whole interval which was to elapse between Abram

and Moses, there is still some doubt remaining as to the precise
stage in the life of Abram from which we are to begin to count;
a doubt increased by the circumstance of this interval being
apparently referred to in other parts of Scripture, sometimes as
four hundred years, and sometimes also as four hundred and
thirty (Exod. xii. 40 ; Acts vii. 6 ; Gal. iii. 17).

It is unnecessary to enter into these inquiries; but there is
one general remark which it may be useful to make. The
matter may not have been by any means so uncertain in that
early age, as the perplexities and obscurities of chronological
science have since made it; although even then there might
be room for considerable latitude of interpretation beforehand,
and it might have been unsafe for any expounder of it, before
its actual accomplishment, to undertake to say, within a year,
or even several years, at what precise date the deliverance from
Egypt might be expected to take place. It was enough that
those who groaned under the tyranny of the Pharaoh "who
knew not Joseph"—those who continued to wait for the promised salvation—taking this prophecy as their guide, would
clearly conclude that the four hundred years were nearly expired
when their fiery trial was at the hottest; and would therefore
begin "to lift up their heads, seeing that their redemption was
drawing nigh." It must have been some such conviction
which led to that exercise of faith "by which Moses, when
he was born, was hid three months of his parents, because they
saw he was a proper child ; and they were not afraid of the
king's commandment" (Heb. xi. 23). They saw that he was
"a proper" or "goodly" child (Exod. ii. 2)—that he was "exceeding fair," or "fair to God" (Acts vii. 20); and knowing,
by a probable calculation of the four hundred years, that "the
time to favour Israel, even the set time, was come," they
believed that this goodly child was, or might be, the appointed
instrument of deliverance, and by this faith they were encouraged to brave the anger of the king. A similar faith, in regard
to the expiry of the appointed period of oppression, might be

cheering the heart of many a devout Israelite in that dark and dreary day of trouble. And cherishing this "sure word of prophecy," given to their father Abraham, they might still persevere "against hope, believing in hope."

It was thus that, in a subseqnent age, Daniel drew a similar conclusion from a calculation of the times marked out in preceding prophecy (Dan. ix. 1, 2). It does not appear that he could fix, beforehand, on the very hour, or day, or year, of the predicted restoration of Israel, any more than he could fix on the exact manner of its accomplishment. It was enough that, observing the signs of the times in the light of the prophetic dates, he arrived at the conclusion that deliverance was nigh, even at the door; and thereupon "he set his face unto the Lord God, to seek by prayer and supplications, with fasting, and sackloth and ashes" (ver. 3). In this devotional attitude he received that divine message which not only confirmed his own anticipations, but opened up to him a still more blessed prospect of the coming of "the Messiah, the Prince."

So also, in reference to the prophecy given to Abram, it was sufficient to put the church, and all its faithful members, into a posture of expectation and prayer, when the time foretold actually came near. But beyond such a general intimation, it may not have been the design of God to enable any one previously to say at what precise hour the deliverer was to appear.*

* A similar observation may be applied to the prophecies which predicted the era of Christ's first advent, as well as to those which announce events connected with his second coming. Devout men, among our Lord's contemporaries, were found "waiting for the consolation of Israel," and men observant of prophecy and of the signs of the times are now looking out for the dawning of the great day of the Lord. But as it would have been impossible then to settle accurately beforehand the very year or day of the nativity or the crucifixion, so it is surely rash now, to lay down too minutely the journal, as it were, or diary of the eventful and critical times that may be at hand. It is safer in itself, and equally conducive to the cherishing of a right frame of mind, to follow the example of the prophet

2. But while there is hope for his posterity at no very distant period, it might seem that the patriarch himself is excluded from all participation in it ;—" Thou shalt go to thy fathers in peace ; thou shalt be buried in a good old age" (ver. 15). Undoubtedly this is a blessed promise, so far as the circumstances and the manner of Abram's decease are concerned. His death is to be a release from trouble, and an entrance into rest,—the rest of God, into which the godly of ages past have entered ; for such seems to be the import of this touching expression, by which, as if to avoid the raising of a single painful image connected with the coldness and corruption of the tomb, it was customary to indicate the removal of pious friends. They are

> " Gone to the resting-place of man,
> The universal home ;
> Where ages past have gone before,
> And ages still must come."

Abram's departure is to be peaceful; nor is he to depart until he is satisfied with length of days. What more can the righteous man ask ? If he must die before the accomplishment of the Lord's gracious promises respecting the inheritance of the land, what can be more soothing than this assurance ? But that he is to die at all, before that happy consummation, might be a disappointment, or at least a deferring, of his hope ; and had he looked for a portion in the world that now

Daniel. The periods noted in the Revelation of John may be near their fulfilment. Like the parents of Moses, therefore, at the end of the four hundred years, and like Daniel at the close of the seventy, and aged Simeon, when the weeks of Daniel were expiring,—so let the church betake herself to confession and watching and prayer, giving heed to " that sure word of prophecy, which is as a light that shineth in a dark place," not clearly enough, perhaps, to satisfy a speculative curiosity as to the particulars of the approaching sunrise, but yet sufficiently for the exercise of faith and patience, " until the day dawn and the day star" appear, to usher in the glorious morn.

is, it must have been so. Rightly viewed, however, this
announcement of his death is a confirmation of his exalted
expectations. It shuts him out indeed from all participation
in that possession of the land which his descendants, after four
hundred years, are to enjoy. Whatever is implied in the
promise, " I will give thee this land," it is clearly not to be
realised by him on this side of the grave. It stands over as
a deed still unexecuted,—a pledge still unredeemed,—a promise still unfulfilled,—a debt still due, when he is buried in a
good old age. It cannot be said of him that he has had his
reward, or that he has, in his lifetime, received his good things.
Much as he has tasted of the Lord's kindness, and seen of the
Lord's salvation, he has not got all that he is entitled to claim.
The chief and crowning blessing to which God in his sovereign
grace has given him a right, still stands over. He has still
something more to look for. He may well therefore be reconciled to the prospect of his removal from this earth, which is
soon to be burned up, before he has received in it any inheritance. He may be content that his portion should remain to
be given to him in the new and better world which is to
endure for ever.

3. Nor, even as regards the occupation of the land by his
posterity in this present life, if that is an object of desire to
him, has the patriarch any cause to complain of the delay
which God intimates. In the end, their triumph is on that
very account to be the more signal ; they are to see their
tyrants and taskmasters terribly overthrown, and they are to be
themselves greatly enriched (ver. 14); and if there is to be delay,
there is a reason stated, which is sufficient at least to satisfy a
man of faith ;—" The iniquity of the Amorites is not yet full "
(ver. 16). The settlement of his descendants in Canaan is to
be connected with the execution of the fierce anger of God on
the present inhabitants of the land. But when judgment is
in question, the Lord will not make haste ; nor will the servant, who is of the same spirit with his Master, ask or desire

that he should. On the contrary, he rejoices in the thought of the long-suffering patience of God being extended to its utmost limits; and it is enough to reconcile him to the prolonged prosperity of the wicked, to be told that the divine forbearance towards them is not yet exhausted, that their day of grace is not ended, that there is still some space for repentance, and a remnant among them who may be saved. Well, therefore, may he consent, on such a ground, that his seed should have to wait. Alas! they will not have to wait very long after all. Too soon will the iniquity of the Amorites be full. " In the fourth generation" the land will be vacated for its rightful owners. Their patience is not much tried. The wilfulness of the wicked frustrates the forbearance of God, and too speedily brings it to a close. It is but a temporary obstacle which is thus interposed between Abram's children and their destined heritage. They shall early return to possess it.*

* The extent of the inheritance here indicated is wider by far than the territory which the Israelites, even in the days of Solomon's most enlarged empire, ever possessed or governed (ver. 18). From the Nile to the Euphrates it reaches in an unbroken tract, embracing the seats of many races or nations whom the Jews never thoroughly subdued or dislodged (ver. 19-21). How this matter is to be explained is a question of great difficulty, which falls, however, properly within the scope of investigations suggested by the later books of Scripture. Some are inclined to assume a certain degree of vagueness in the prophetic descriptions given beforehand of the extent and limits of the promised inheritance. They distinguish between actual possession and political ascendency. They hold that, when the actual possession, or inheritance proper, is spoken of, it is always Canaan alone that is defined; whereas, in a looser sense, inclusive of political influence and power as well as territorial sovereignty, the range of Israel's dominion might be stretched greatly beyond the bounds of his actual occupancy. On the other hand, to those who interpret the reasoning of Paul in the eleventh chapter of the Romans, as holding out the hope of a national conversion and restoration of Israel, as such, in the latter day, it is not wonderful that such a prophecy as this should suggest a different thought. In their view, it seems to imply that, in its full

Such, then, is the substance of the word of prophecy which accompanies the manifestation of the divine glory to Abram on this memorable occasion. And the whole transaction, in the end, takes the form of a most solemn ratification of an irrevocable covenant. For that is the principal import of the movement made by the symbol of the divine presence between the portions of the slaughtered victims (ver. 17, 18).

To this manner of confirming a covenant, the Lord, by the mouth of the Prophet Jeremiah, alludes when he indignantly reproves the men who had " transgressed his covenant, and had not performed the words of the covenant, which they had made before him, when they cut the calf in twain, and passed between the parts thereof, the princes of Judah, and the princes of Jerusalem, the eunuchs, and the priests, and all the people of the land, which passed between the parts of the calf" (Jer. xxxiv. 18, 19). It was customary thus to " make a covenant by sacrifice," the parties in the covenant passing between the limbs of the animals which had been slain and divided ; and hence, in the present instance, the Lord himself condescends to adopt this significant method of conveying assurance to Abram. He gives a pledge of his favour and his faithfulness in immediate connection with the shedding of blood and the offering of a propitiation for sin. And Abram, as the sun goes down, sees the sacrifice which he has saved from the devouring birds of prey, graciously accepted by the great God of heaven, and made the seal of his own heavenly hope, and of the inheritance to be bestowed upon his seed.

extent, the inheritance remains still to be bestowed upon the seed of Abram ; and that the nation, of which Abram was the father after the flesh, is literally to be put in possession of the whole wide dominion which these promises seem to convey. From Egypt eastward to the Babylonian plain,—from the shores of the Mediterranean into which the mouths of the Nile empty themselves, to the gulph which receives the waters of the Euphrates,—all is to be given to the seed of Abram.

18

THE TRIAL OF FAITH—ITS INFIRMITY

Genesis 16:1-16

Are ye so foolish? having begun in the Spirit, are ye now made perfect by the flesh? Galatians 3:3

And David said unto Gad, I am in a great strait; let us fall now into the hand of the Lord, (for his mercies are great,) and let me not fall into the hand of man. 2 Samuel 24:14

THE incidents recorded in this chapter form but a melancholy sequel to the preceding. The juxtaposition is one which an uninspired historian would probably have disguised, and which a mere fabulist would certainly have avoided. It seems strange and sad, that immediately after that remarkable scene in which the warrant of Abram's faith, and the sufficiency of it, are so expressly recorded,—in which we find the patriarch so unreservedly reposing in simple and honourable reliance on the divine word, and the Lord, on the other hand, condescending to give to him so explicit an assurance of his acceptance, and such sure and infallible tokens for good,—the very first circumstance related of him should be his falling into sin,—and that the sin of unbelief. But obnoxious as it may be to the cavils of the unreflecting and the ill-disposed,—and abused, as perhaps it has been, by not a few of the unlearned and unstable who wrest this, as they do the other Scriptures, to their own destruction,—the narrative is full of profit. In its origin, nature, and results, this sin of Abram may read us many salutary lessons.

I. It originated at such a time and in such a manner as may well enforce the solemn warning, "let him that thinketh he standeth, take heed lest he fall;"—while it painfully illustrates that other affecting saying, that "a man's worst foes may be those of his own household."

The patriarch's wife was undoubtedly a godly woman. She is commended as such by the Apostle Peter (1 Pet. iii. 6), who makes her an example to all Christian matrons; they are her daughters as long as they do well. She "obeyed Abraham, calling him lord." With him, she came out from among her kindred, and was willing to lead the life of a stranger and pilgrim. During all the time they had spent in the land of Canaan, she was constantly and faithfully with her husband, sharing his trials, and witnessing the great things which the Lord did for him. If, on one occasion, she became too readily a partaker of his sin, when she went into that plan of passing for his sister to which she had wellnigh fallen a victim,—she then experienced, along with her husband, the vanity and danger of every device of carnal wisdom;—while in the seasonable interposition of God, she received a new proof and pledge of his power to help in the time of need. Nor could the events which followed, marking out the patriarch so unequivocally as the friend of God and the heir of the promise, be lost on his affectionate partner, who herself was heir, together with him, of the grace of life, and by whom his prayers were not wont to be hindered (1 Pet. iii. 7).

Strange and sad, that at such a season, and from such a quarter, temptation should arise; that after a ten years' walk with God, in the very height of privilege, in the full assurance of faith, the faithful companion of his pilgrimage and helper of his joy, should beguile and betray him! After such an instance, who can be secure?—in what circumstances, or on what side, secure? Well may we lay to heart the warning, "Let him who thinketh he standeth take heed lest he fall."

II. The temptation itself is a very plausible one. It

bears all the marks of that subtlety which, from of old, has been the characteristic of that old serpent, the devil. Observe the spirit and manner in which the proposal is made by Sarai, and received by Abram. It is plainly such as altogether to preclude the idea of this step being at all analogous to an ordinary instance of sin committed in the indulgence of sensual passion. Most unjustifiable as was the patriarch's conduct, it is not for a moment to be confounded with that of David, for example, whose melancholy fall was caused by the mere unbridled violence of an unlawful appetite. There is no room for the introduction of such an element as this on the occasion of Abram's connection with Hagar. It originated in the suggestion of his faithful wife, and had, for its single object, the fulfilment of the divine promise, whose accomplishment otherwise seemed to be growing every day more manifestly and hopelessly impossible (ver. 1, 2).

The ungodly, indeed, who know but one kind of temptation, and that the lowest, may affect here to indulge in an incredulous smile or sneer. It suits their purpose better to give the narrative an interpretation as gross as their own tastes. Nevertheless, there are temptations of which they have no conception;—there are more things in the experience of a spiritual man than are dreamed of in their carnal wisdom. They know not, as he knows them, the wiles of the devil. Upon them Satan finds it enough to bring the coarser and more common inducements of his kingdom to bear;—and hence they can but ill imagine the rage to which he is provoked, and the arts to which he is obliged to have recourse, against those who have escaped, or are escaping, from his nets, and who now serve, or are striving with all their might to serve, another Master. To these last especially, he is compelled to assume the form of an angel of light, and his seduction of them may be expected to be peculiarly artful and refined.

So it was in the case of Abram. The patriarch is assailed

on the very ground of his spiritual privilege and hope. As one accepted in the sight of God, accounted righteous, pardoned, and justified ;—as one also made an heir of God, declared to be personally invested with a title to a glorious inheritance ; —and finally, as one sustaining a public character, ordained to be the father of a great nation, the source of blessing to all the families of the earth ; in all these particulars, Abram is peculiarly and eminently distinguished ; and in respect of them all, he is specially tempted. They are all dependent, let it be remembered, on "one who is to come forth out of his own bowels" —such is the Lord's express assurance—and still he goes childless. His wife, as she herself represents the matter to him, is barren ; and it would seem that she is contented to acknowledge her barrenness as hopless, and to acquiesce in it as a dispensation of God. She does not speak angrily or impatiently, as Rachel did to Jacob,—but meekly and submissively she says, " The Lord hath restrained me from bearing." It is his will ; and his will be done. But surely God can never intend that my barrenness should frustrate his purpose, and make void his promise. There must be some way of getting over this difficulty, and reconciling this apparent inconsistency between the promise that to thee a child is to be born,—in whom, as the great reconciler, thou, and thy posterity, and all the kindreds of men, are to be blessed,—and the providence which allots to thee a barren, and now aged, spouse. There must be some new expedient to be adopted ; some other plan to be tried. It may be that Sarai is to be a mother, as it were, by substitute and by proxy, and is to obtain children by her maid ; according to the custom already common, of which we have sad enough examples afterward in the family of Jacob. This will accomplish the divine word. And if there be any hesitation about the propriety of the course recommended,—may it not be justified by the manners of the age and country sanctioning the usage ; by the entire absence of every grosser motive ;—and by the necessity of the case shutting him up to some such plan ? Such was Abram's temptation. Such also, —of a similar nature, and indeed so far as regards the difficulty of reconciling sense and faith, substantially identical,—was the temptation of Abram's son and Lord. Jesus, in the lonely wilderness, was tempted as the Son of God, with direct and immediate reference throughout, on the part of the tempter, to what the voice of heaven, at his baptism, had declared. " If thou be the Son of God"—is the insidious insinuation of the devil, as if he would provoke him by reproach, or persuade him by flattery. " If thou be," or since thou art, " the Son of God." It is an insolent taunt, or a smooth and fawning hint. If thou be, or since thou art, as the voice declared, the Son of God, use thy power for thine own preservation,—appear in thy glory, as advancing in the clouds of heaven,—assume thy universal empire over all the earth. Make the stones into bread, lest thou perish. Cast thyself from the pinnacle of the temple, as coming gloriously in the air, lest the people despise thee as coming humbly on the earth. Take possession of the world's throne, lest the world give thee nothing but the cross. Thus the Lord was tempted in all points, like as Abram was, yet without Abram's sin. To the Lord, therefore, let us look as our example and our strength, that we may be saved. To Abram let us look as, in this instance, a beacon set before us by God for our warning, lest we perish.

Especially let us be warned against the two sins which are apt to beset us, in the view of our privilege and our hope as believers ; presumption and distrust, which, however opposite, are often found together. For there may be a lurking tendency to practical antinomianism in the heart of him who has tasted and seen that the Lord is good ; a sort of feeling as if he were a privileged person, raised above ordinary rules and restrictions, and, in difficult emergencies at least, entitled to judge for himself, to exercise a certain kind of discretion, and to take the matter at issue into his own hands. And along with this there may be a degree of impatience and distrust ; a weariness of waiting for the salvation of the Lord ; an undue anxiety, even on the part of him who should be always walking by faith, to "see his signs," and to have every stumblingblock removed. He is in straits ; troubled and perplexed ; and he casts about for some way of escape. He sees some kind of re-lief at which he may grasp,—some scheme for retrieving the loss he has sustained,—some decent form of self-indulgence which may dissipate his despondency and minister to his quiet. May he not avail himself of it ? Instead of looking for the deliver-ance or the good which he needs, as coming at some time still future, he knows not when,—and by some means still to be provided, he knows not how,—may he not arrive at his end by a shorter and more obvious road ? Instead of reckoning, for instance, on the long-deferred fruit of a barren womb, may he not be warranted at last in seeking the desired result by a more natural and usual course ? Then comes the insidious thought, that, as a child of God peculiarly situated, he may take some slight liberty, and claim a certain exemption and immunity from the strict rule of an exemplary walk. So he begins to walk after the flesh ; and too soon he loses the freedom and enlargement of heart which a calm and clear reliance upon heaven inspires, and feels the bitter subjection and enthralment of a renewed dependence upon earthly re-sources, and a renewed entanglement in earthly policy.

III. Accordingly, the sequel of this part of Abram's history is sufficiently sad. Viewed merely as a domestic scene which might be realised in any ordinary household, how true is it to nature ! And how emphatic is the warning which it holds out !

The jealousies, the heart-burnings and mutual reproaches which we now find disturbing the peace of this pious family, are such as might have been anticipated from the course un-happily pursued. That a woman so strangely and suddenly honoured, taken out of her due place and station, and admitted to the rank and privileges of a spouse, should forget herself and become high-minded,—was precisely such conduct as might have been expected on the part of a slave treated as Hagar was, and having a temper unsubdued and a mind uninstructed as Hagar's probably were. She could not enter into the plan which the heads of the house had formed, or into the reasons and motives which led them to form it. To their servant, if not to themselves, it must have been fraught with a most corrupting tendency ; and it is no wonder that it proved to her a temptation to insolence and insubordination, stronger than she could withstand. Hence Abram and Sarai had the greater sin. Even if they felt that they were at liberty, so far as they themselves were concerned, to do it,—and that they were safe in doing it,—were they not bound to ask how it might affect their dependant, whom they made a party in the transaction ? Was there not, now that the evil was done and its consequences were beginning to appear, too good cause of regret and repentance ?

And what of the effect on the godly pair themselves of the error into which they have fallen ? Sarai, provoked by the frowardness of Hagar, thought that she did well to be angry. She was loud in her reproaches, and spoke indignantly ; —" My wrong be upon thee :—I have given my maid into thy bosom ; and when she saw that she had conceived, I was despised in her eyes : the Lord judge between me and thee" (ver. 5). Alas ! had she forgotten that all that she complained of was but the fruit of her own device ; and that as she had sowed, so she reaped ? And what is Abram's predicament in so painful a family feud ? Has he, too, in part, and for a time, forgotten what is due to the partner of his pilgrimage and the wife of his youth ? Is he tempted to carry too far his indulgence towards one who is apparently to realise his anxious longing ? And under that natural feeling, has he become less sensitive than otherwise he would have been, in regard to her whom he was bound to honour, and more tolerant of insult shown to her ? We may almost gather something like this from Sarai's complaint.

If it was so, how sad an instance have we here of the difficulty of stopping short when a single doubtful step is once taken ? Abram, when he consented to the specious proposal made to him, thought that he was acting disinterestedly and for the best. But other and less worthy motives began to mingle with his better purposes ; and at all events he is now entangled in a net of his own making. He is no longer free : he is the slave of circumstances ; and he is compelled to make the best he can of a painful perplexity and hard necessity ; to do violence to his feelings, perhaps even to his convictions of duty ; and to consent to the degradation and disgrace of one whom, after what has passed, he is surely bound to consider as having strong claims upon his regard.

In this view, the treatment which Hagar received is all the more unjustifiable. The expressions, indeed, used in our translation, give a somewhat exaggerated idea of what she suffered (ver. 6). Strictly interpreted, they denote nothing more than that by Abram's command Hagar was again placed, as a servant, under Sarai's rule, and made to render to her obedience such as might be enforced by just discipline. Still, in all the circumstances, a milder and more generous way of dealing with Hagar might have been expected on the part of those who had themselves occasioned her offence, and might have prevented her from incurring greater guilt. Her flight is not excusable in her ; but surely it is a sad reproach to the godly family from which she is provoked to fly.

IV. In the wilderness the fugitive meets with a better friend. She wanders on in her solitary way, weary of the heat and toil of travel, and half repenting of the hasty step she has taken. At last she sits down beside one of those fountains of water which, with their little spots of freshness around them, form the grateful resting-places for the worn and fainting traveller in the desert, as the burning sun beats on his aching head, or the shades of evening invite his exhausted limbs to rest. There, as she meditates at leisure, and alone, the excitement of angry strife having passed away, many bitter thoughts crowd upon her mind. The pride which sustained her is gone, and her spirit is mortified and tamed. She cannot now find support in justifying herself and blaming others ; her sin has found her out ; and her heart is beginning to yearn towards the home in which she has dwelt so long in peace, and which, for all that had passed, might still, through God's mercy, and the mutual forgiveness and forbearance of his erring servants, have proved to her a refuge of holy tranquillity and repose. While feelings like these, perhaps, are swelling her bosom and dimming her eye, a heavenly stranger unexpectedly stands beside her, and a heavenly voice reaches her ear. Trained in the household of one familiar with such divine fellowship, Hagar easily recognises the Angel of the Lord ; the Being of whose visits she has heard her master speak. Hence she is not dismayed, although the appeal is one that seems only, in the first place, to convince her of her sin ;—" Hagar, Sarai's maid, whence camest thou ?" and then, secondly, to point out to her the utter helplessness of her state ;—" and whither wilt thou go ?" (ver. 8). Thus the Angel remonstrates with her as to the unwarrantable nature of her conduct, reminding her of her duty, as Sarai's maid, and causing her to feel how thoroughly she is now at a loss. Nor does Hagar resent the charge, or disguise the straits to which she is reduced. " I flee from the face of my mistress Sarai " is her frank acknowledgment, without one plea of self-justification, or any complaint even about her forlorn condition. And it moves the compassion of her heavenly friend ;—it is the very frame of mind with which he sympathises, and for which he delights to provide relief. " Return," he says, " to thy mistress, and submit thyself under her hands" (ver. 9) ;—virtually assuring her of a kind and gracious reception, or at least, of his own support and favour, should it unhappily be otherwise. And to give her still greater encouragement, he opens up to her the prospect of enlargement and prosperity awaiting the race of which she is to be the mother; the singular race that, with their wild and warlike spirit of jealous independence, standing aloof from the other families of man, are yet to keep their footing among them all,—to survive many a convulsion and outride many a sweeping storm,—still roaming the same vast plains, fresh and untamed as ever,—their fleet steeds scouring the Arabian sands, and their hands grasping the ready spear and flashing sword,—unsubdued, unsettled, unchanged,—and unchangeable, as it would seem, till the end come.

But the prophetical intimation which is connected with this transaction, as well as the allegorical or figurative meaning which the Apostle Paul attaches to Hagar's history, are brought out more fully in the subsequent narrative, and may at present be passed over. Meanwhile, the moral and spiritual lesson with which this incident ends is striking and affecting.

Hagar gratefully acknowledges the interposition of God, as a very present help in trouble. "She calls the name of the Lord that spake unto her, Thou, God, seest me,"—"thou regardest the low estate of thy handmaiden." And she dwells on the seasonable and unlooked for promptness of the help afforded,—"Have I also here looked after him that seeth me?" (ver. 13). Was I looking out for him? Or did his gracious providence surprise me, and his gracious eye almost startle me, when he sought out one, alas! too far gone in hardness of heart ever to have thought of seeking him? Truly may the well be called "the well of him that liveth and seeth me,"—of the living God, who looks on my affliction; and justly may the child be named "Ishmael," as the token that "the Lord will hear" the cry of the oppressed, and deliver the fainting soul (ver. 11).

Nor is the relenting offender slow in obeying the heavenly command. She has been led out into the wilderness, that the Lord might speak comfortably to her. Fleeing from the face of her fellow-sinners, who could but rudely aggravate, or, at the best, very slightly heal, the hurt they had themselves inflicted, she fell into the hands of one who could better treat her case. That she was here savingly converted, may be considered doubtful; although it is a great thing for her to speak of " Him that liveth, and seeth her." At all events, she is to abide a little longer in the household of faith, and to have an interest in the promise and the seal of the covenant. She returns, therefore, to the home she had forsaken, herself softened, and with an experience to tell that may soften her bitterest enemy. But her mistress is not her enemy, although misunderstanding may have arisen, and, alas! may arise again. The meeting may be supposed to be happy; and over the reconciled household, in which the wounds of sin are for the present closed, we may allow the mantle of hope and charity to drop.

19

THE REVIVAL OF FAITH—THE REPETITION OF THE CALL

Genesis 17:1

The steps of a good man are ordered by the Lord; and he delighteth in
his way. Though he fall, he shall not be utterly cast down : for the
Lord upholdeth him with his hand. Psalm 37:23,24

A NEW scene here opens before us—a new era in the patriarch's life. An interval of thirteen years is passed over in silence; but, alas! the silence is only too significant. Thirteen years ago Abram is seen to fall from his steadfastness; and now, for the first time, does he seem to be completely restored and revived. That he was altogether abandoned, during so long a period, it would be unreasonable to believe; the painful narrative of his sin and sorrow does not close without, at least, a partial glimpse of better things. The Lord has marked, with his unslumbering eye, the whole transaction; he has arrested the flight of Hagar; and in the restoration of comparative peace to this troubled household, in the preservation to the patriarch of the child for whom he longed so impatiently, and in the prospects held out respecting that child,— the Lord's hand bringing good out of evil, and graciously turning away from his servants the natural consequences of their own sins, is signally apparent. Still, the issue of that sad story is unsatisfactory. The patriarch, it would seem, is left very much to himself. No signal judgments, indeed, overtake him; but neither is he visited with any remarkable mercy, or any special instance of the divine favour.

In this doubtful calm, what is the patriarch's spiritual condition? How fares it with his soul? Is it prospering and in health? Or, is he saying,—Soul, take thine ease? Possibly the renewed enjoyment of domestic tranquillity, the increase of his worldly substance, his growing influence and reputation among the chieftains of the land, and, above all, the happiness that he now felt as a father,—in the supposed fulfilment of his long-deferred hope, and in the fresh light and love with which childhood's unconscious gladness ever fills a home,—all together might tend to lull his watchfulness asleep on the lap of a certain languid and luxurious repose, such as even piety itself might be tempted not to disown. He had got, as it has been well said, if not the very thing promised, at least something very like it; and he almost ceased to look or long very earnestly for more. In such a state, how great the need of such a revival as Abram now experiences; receiving, as he does, a repetition of his original call, as preparatory to a renewal of the covenant.

I. He saw the Lord again, and heard his voice calling him, as it were anew. "The LORD appeared unto Abram, and said unto him, I am the Almighty God" (ver. 1).

In this way the sinner is awakened at first. He is going to Damascus on some errand of his own, or of his master's, the prince of this world;—unconsciously, perhaps, walking contrary to God and opposing the Lord Jesus; dishonouring his name and persecuting his people. Suddenly a great light shines around him, and a loud voice reaches his ear; a light great—not outwardly, perhaps, but within, God shining into the heart, and giving the light of the knowledge of his own glory in the face of Jesus Christ;—a voice loud—not in the ear of sense, but in that of conscience, on which it strikes as a knell, breaking the very slumber of the grave—"Awake, thou that sleepest, and arise from the dead, and Christ shall give thee light." The sinner sees for the first time the real character of the God with whom he has to do, as the Holy

One and the Just, the great and terrible God, as well as also
the God whose name is love. He hears, uttered in thunder,
the inexorable threatenings of the law ; while in accents of
tenderest persuasion, the gracious but peremptory call of the
Gospel moves and melts his inmost soul. He falls on his face,
and when he rises he is a new man. " Who art thou, Lord ?"
is his eager question. " I am He whom thou persecutest "—
" I am the Almighty God," is the reply that goes to his heart.

Precisely similar is the process of revival in the soul on
which sin and the world have been exerting their blighting
and benumbing influence. The Spirit opens the eye anew to
behold God in his glory standing very near. He opens the
ear to hear God speaking home to the conscience, as one
having authority ;—" I am the Almighty God ; walk before
me, and be thou perfect."

II. Abram is called to be " perfect." Now, this word " perfect," or " upright," when applied to man, in the Bible, is not
absolute, but relative. It relates, for the most part, not to the
whole character of a man, but to some one particular feature
of his character, some individual grace or virtue specified, in
respect of which he is said to be complete or entire, consistent
and sincere.* In the instance before us, it is the duty of

* Instances of this use of the word are frequent in the Psalms. Thus, in
the 32d Psalm, the righteousness or uprightness mentioned, has reference
to the single duty of confessing sin to God (ver. 1-5) ; and denotes freedom
from guile, or the unreserved openness of a heart unburthening itself, in
the full and frank confidence of faith, to God. In the 64th Psalm, the
particular in respect of which perfection is ascribed to the man of God
(ver. 5), is his inoffensive demeanour towards his enemies,—the same particular which is referred to likewise in the 7th Psalm ; where also the
Psalmist appeals to his integrity in the same connection (ver. 4, 5, 8). So
again in the 139th Psalm, the Psalmist challenges to himself perfection, as
a hater of those who hate God (ver. 22), hating them as God hates them,
not personally, but for their wickedness' sake ; and hating them, in that
sense, perfectly, with no secret reserve in favour of what may be agreeable
or amiable in their sins,—no complacency in their company, nor any love

" walking before God," in respect of which Abram is exhorted to be perfect ;—" Walk before me, and be thou perfect."

To walk before God, is to walk or live as in his sight, and under his special inspection : to realise, at all times, his presence and his providence ; to feel his open and unslumbering eye ever upon us. To walk thus before God is impossible, if there be not redeeming love on his part, apprehended by faith on our part ; and to be perfect, guileless, and upright, in thus walking before God, is the great duty of the believer. He alone can discharge that duty. Others do not like to retain God in their knowledge ; they have comfort only when all serious thought of God is got rid of, and put aside ; and so they hide themselves from God amid secular vanities or sacred formalities. Their walk is not, and cannot be, in good faith, a walk before God, or with God, under his eye and subject to his control. But as to his own people,—why should they not walk before God ? Why should they not, with entire openness and uprightness, so walk ? Why should they shrink from so close a fellowship with God as such a walk implies ? Having peace with him, and making it their single aim to be like him —why should they not be perfect in such a walk ?

Alas ! for the unsteadfastness of faith, and the deceitfulness of sin ! The believer becomes involved in some device of worldly wisdom ; or he casts his eye along some forbidden path, on which he would venture but a few exploring steps ; or he is

of their conversation. In the same manner, in the 101st Psalm, where the Psalmist speaks of walking in a perfect way and with a perfect heart, he simply avows his determination, with unsparing and uncompromising impartiality, to discourage vice and countenance holiness, in the ordering of his household and the ruling of his court and kingdom. (See also Ps. lxxv.) And finally, in the preparation for the building of the temple (1 Chron. xxix. 9), David and the people are said to offer gifts to the Lord "with perfect heart," that is, with a heart perfect, in regard to this act of liberality, as an act springing from no unworthy motives, but done with a single eye to the glory of God. (So also in Matt. v. 48.)

tempted to take the measuring of his duty and the ordering of his lot into his own hands; or he falls under the spell of an indolent self-sufficiency. In some particular or other he compromises his integrity; and in the state of his affections or the habit of his life, there is something as to which he has not come to a clear and open understanding with God as his Father and his Friend. Then the hidden life of the soul begins to be disordered and deranged; the walk before God becomes unsteady and uncertain; the consciousness of something lying unadjusted between the conscience and its only Lord, creates uneasiness, suspicion, and reserve; there is guile in the spirit; and the fruit of guile is distance and distrust. The heart ceasing to be right with God, the walk is no longer upright before him.

So was it probably with Abram, when the loud call again aroused him, "Walk before me, and be thou perfect." Be thyself again;—return and do thy first works. Be perfect,—perfect in thy walk before me;—perfect as in the day when, with entire and unsuspecting confidence, thou camest forth out of thy father-land, not knowing, nor even asking, whither I was bringing thee;—perfect as in the night when I led thee forth under the starry heavens, and when upon my bare word, " So shall thy seed be," thou didst believe, and wast justified in believing. Be perfect,—not in any high or strange accomplishment, but in that in which a little child is the best specimen of perfection—in simply believing, trusting, confiding. Be perfect in walking before me, as a child may walk under the eye of parental watchfulness and love. That is perfection,—the perfection of walking before a father. No unbelief is there,—no selfishness, no reserve, no feeling of a separate interest, no secret consciousness of a double mind, or a divided heart, or an evil eye. Be thou thus perfect in thy walk before me.

III. Abram has a sufficient reason given to him for compliance with the command. It is a reason founded on the nature of God himself. God appeals to his omnipotence, as warranting his expectation that his servant's walk before him should be perfect ;—" I am the Almighty God." This is thine encouragement to act with entire frankness and unreserve in all thy dealings with me, and to let all be open and undisguised between us. I have all power and all sufficiency ; and all that concerns thee may be safely left to me. There is no need of any underhand or circuitous procedure, nor any occasion to resort to any doubtful walk of thine own for the accomplishment of all that thy heart desires. I am the Almighty God ; walk before me. Commit thy way to me, and I will bring it to pass. What is it that troubles thee, and would tempt thee to try some device of thine own for relief ? Is it sin ? Go not in any path of deceitful compromise, making a false truce with thine own conscience ; walk before me, and be perfect. Let thy sin, in all its blackness, be laid bare before me ; for I am the Almighty God ; I have a provision such as no resources but mine could furnish—a provision of infinite wisdom, power, and love, by which I freely cleanse thee from it all. Or is it that thy hope is deferred, and thy way is hid from the Lord ? " Hast thou not known, hast thou not heard, that the everlasting God, the LORD, the Creator of the ends of the earth, fainteth not, neither is weary ? There is no searching of his understanding." He is the Almighty God ; walk before him with perfect simplicity in thyself, and perfect reliance upon him. Take nothing into thine own management ; leave all to him. Nor be discouraged, or tempted to grow weary because of the way. " He giveth power to the faint ; and to them that have no might he increaseth strength. Even the youths shall faint and be weary, and the young men shall utterly fall : But they that wait upon the Lord shall renew their strength ; they shall mount up with wings as eagles ; they shall run, and not be weary; and they shall walk, and not faint " (Isa. xl. 29–31).

Thus did God appear to Abram, by the name of God Almighty ;—the name, as we have seen, most appropriate when he claims the confidence of his people, in giving exceeding great and precious promises, as the name Jehovah is the more significant when he is about to fulfil them (Exod. vi. 3). In promising, he appeals to his omnipotence ; in fulfilling, to his unchangeableness. As God Almighty, able to do whatsoever he says, he calls to a perfect walk before him. As Jehovah, the same yesterday, to-day, and for ever, he gives warrant for a patient waiting upon him, till all be accomplished. In the one character, God summons you to begin, or to begin anew, your course. In the other, he encourages you to hold on unto the end.

Thus the patriarch is called to be himself again,—seeing the Lord by faith as he really is,—emancipating himself from all guile in his spirit,—entering into the favour and fellowship of the Holy One,—and relying, as before, with implicit, unquestioning, and childlike confidence, on the almighty arm of him who can make all things work together for good, and bring the wanderer at last, after all the trials of sense and sin, into his own everlasting kingdom and glory.

20

THE RENEWAL OF THE COVENANT

Genesis 17:2-8

THE repetition of the call leads to a renewal of the covenant; and this accordingly is the fitting sequel of Abram's revival from the state of carnal peace and security into which he had been falling.

For ascertaining the import of the covenant as here renewed, the Apostle Paul is to be consulted. He is the best expounder of it; and he has given us no doubtful interpretation.

Thus, in the first place, in his Epistle to the Galatians, Paul refers to the seventh verse of this chapter of Genesis;— " And I will establish my covenant between me and thee and thy seed after thee in their generations for an everlasting covenant, to be a God unto thee, and to thy seed after thee " (ver. 7). The seed here spoken of, Paul expressly and very pointedly identifies with Christ, and with Christ alone; "to Abraham and his seed were the promises made;" to his seed; for special notice is taken by the apostle of the word being in the singular number, and much stress is laid on that circumstance; " He saith not, And to seeds, as of many; but as of one, And to thy seed, which is Christ." The covenant, therefore, is not with many, but with one, even with Christ. It embraces others, besides Christ, only as they are identified with him. On this footing Abraham himself is accepted, as being one with his seed, which is Christ. Christ, and all who, like Abraham, believe in him, are accounted one, being in the

Spirit really one. To Christ, then, as the seed of Abraham, are the promises of this covenant made; to Christ alone; to none but Christ (Gal. iii. 16).

Again, secondly, in regard to the assurance,—" Thou shalt be a father of many nations,"—which is repeated three several times in this renewal of the covenant (ver. 4, 5, 6), and is connected with the significant change of the patriarch's name, from " Abram," or " exalted father," to " Abraham," or " father of a multitude " (ver. 5)—the apostle, writing to the Romans, unequivocally interprets this promise, as referring, not to the natural posterity of Abraham, but to his spiritual family—to those, who, being of faith, are the children of faithful Abraham. Over and over again, he speaks of the promise which was confirmed by the seal of circumcision—that is, this very promise before us—as being a promise that Abraham " was to be the father of all them that believe;" even of those " who walk in the steps of that faith which he had," before his circumcision.

nd still more particularly, he founds upon this very view of the promise, an argument to prove that it cannot be a promise of the legal covenant, for then it would be limited to his posterity who were under that covenant. " Therefore," he concludes, it is not of the law, but " of faith, that it might be by grace; to the end the promise might be sure to all the seed; not to that only which is of the law, but to that also which is of the faith of Abraham, who is the father of us all "— of all who believe, whether of the law, or not,—" as it is written, I have made thee a father of many nations." Now this, it is added, was what Abraham believed, on the word of him " who quickeneth the dead, and calleth those things which be not as though they were." He did so on that memorable night when, as he looked to the stars to which God pointed, " against hope he believed in hope, that so," even as these stars, " was his seed to be;" as well as on this subsequent occasion also, when he was expressly told that he was to become " the father of many nations." Most plainly, therefore, the Spirit testifies, that both of these assurances,—that which the starry heavens were summoned by God to attest, and that of which the sign of circumcision was appointed to be the seal,—both the promise—"so shall thy seed be,"—and that other promise—"thou shalt be a father of many nations,"—were received, understood, and believed by Abraham, as referring to the multitude of his spiritual children—the innumerable company of believers of whom he is the father (Rom. iv. 11-18).

Once more, in the third place, Paul cites and explains the promise in this renewal of the covenant as to the inheritance of the land, or the world (ver. 8); and says of it exactly what he says of the promise respecting the number of the seed,—that it "was not through the law, but through the righteousness of faith." Now this excludes the possibility of the promise having reference to the possession of Canaan by the Israelites, from the days of Joshua till their last dispersion. Their occupation of the land during that whole period was really, whatever the ideal of it might be, "through the law;" it was on the terms of that legal dispensation, under which, as a nation, they were placed. Receiving the land, as they doubtless did, by an act of mere grace on the part of God, they practically held it on the condition of their own obedience; being, as it were, tenants upon their good behaviour. But, says the apostle, the inheritance promised to Abraham, and to his seed, was "through the righteousness of faith;" on the terms of that other covenant, not of works, but of grace, in which a righteousness is provided that is to be received by faith alone. To whatever inheritance, then, this promise may refer, it is at least clear that it cannot have received its fulfilment in the past history of Israel and of Canaan (Rom. iv. 13).

Now, taking together the three principles of interpretation suggested by the Apostle Paul, we may safely conclude that the promises of the covenant, as here renewed to Abraham, are not temporal and worldly, but wholly spiritual and eternal; having respect to Christ, the true spiritual seed of Abraham,

and to the spiritual offspring or family of Abraham, the faithful of many nations who are all one in Christ, though
they are as the stars of heaven for multitude, and who are all
in Christ called to the hope of an everlasting inheritance. So
these promises are understood by Paul ; and so they must
have been understood by Abraham, taught as he was by the
same Spirit.

How comprehensive, then, is this covenant ? With what
admirable fulness does it open up to us the number, the privilege, and the hope of believers !

First, the number or extent of the true Church of God is
largely set forth ; and on this particular special stress is laid.
It forms, indeed, the main or leading promise of the covenant,
being repeated frequently in different words, and with great
earnestness ;—" I will multiply thee exceedingly ;"—" Thou
shalt be a father of many nations ; "—" A father of many nations have I made thee ;"—" I will make thee exceeding
fruitful, and I will make nations of thee, and kings shall come
out of thee." To this, also, the change of the patriarch's name
from Abram to Abraham applies, being a pledge or token of
the vast and varied host that were to hail him as their sire.
The assurance is peculiarly well timed, and well fitted to
quicken and sustain his spiritual faith. What does he see before him ? Not a long line of earthly monarchs, and a great
variety of earthly communities, all tracing their natural descent
from him as their common ancestor ; but " a great multitude
which no man can number, of all nations, and kindreds, and
peoples, and tongues," gathered into one in Christ ; all justified
like himself by faith, and all rejoicing to be called his children,
and to be blessed as such along with him. He " saw the day of
Christ afar off," and in Christ he saw the exceeding increase and
fruitfulness of the great household of faith ; the countless host
of the elect, gathered into one out of all nations, united in the
same holy faith and heavenly fellowship with himself ; and
finally, nations themselves and their kings converted to the

knowledge of the Saviour in whom he believed, and so becoming his children indeed. What a prospect, to revive, elevate, and ennoble the patriarch; to break every worldly and carnal spell; to make the eye of his spiritual faith beem keen, and the pulse of his spiritual life beat warm and high and strong!

Secondly, the privilege of the patriarch's believing children is precious and peculiar, and throughout all ages it is one and the same. He who appeared to Abraham is to be their God; for he says :—" I will establish my covenant between me and thee and thy seed after thee in their generations for an everlasting covenant, to be a God unto thee, and to thy seed after thee" (ver. 7). God is to stand to them in a peculiar relation —the very relation in which he stands to him who is pre-eminently the Seed of Abraham. For it is in respect of their being one with that ONE SEED that they all enjoy this privilege. There may be many nations of them, and many generations; but still the seed is one; Christ is one, and they all are one in him alone. Hence the emphasis of this blessed promise, as applicable to all the faithful, in all ages, and of every clime. Its whole value lies in its primary application to Christ;—" I will be a God to him who is truly thy seed." Thence, by necessary inference, it follows, that to all who through grace are made one with him, and so become thy seed in spirit and in truth,—and to thee also as one with him,—I will be a God; in precisely the same sense in which I am to be a God to him who is my beloved Son, and in whom I am ever well pleased. Well, therefore, might that holy and elect one, with whom the covenant was really made, appeal to its promise in his last prayer; and, in terms of it, at least virtually, plead for all his believing people, as every where and always one in him. Well might he speak of the Father as loving them with the very same fulness of everlasting love with which he loves him. Most wondrous measure of the Father's love to you who believe! Hear these blessed words of the seed of Abraham : " Thou hast loved them as thou hast loved me." Who shall tell what love that is which the Father has to his own Son? Who shall estimate,—who shall exhaust it? And yet in respect of it all, they are one with him! How close, then, must be the union between those who, being of faith, are the children of Abraham, and that one Seed of Abraham in whom they all believe !—how complete their identity in respect of their joint relation to God, " as his Father and their Father, his God and their God !"

Still further, thirdly, the hope set before the spiritual seed of Abram is high and heavenly; it is none other than the hope of glory. It is true, the promise might seem literally to point to an earthly inheritance ;—" I will give unto thee, and to thy seed after thee, the land wherein thou art a stranger, all the land of Canaan, for an everlasting possession ; and I will be their God" (ver. 8). But that it has a reference to something beyond, is plain from the very terms in which it is conveyed. Abraham himself, let it be observed, has an interest in the promise,—he has personally a vested right in the inheritance, whatever it may be. " I will give it to thee "—is the unambiguous and unequivocal phraseology of the grant. Then, again, the land is said to be given " for an everlasting possession," not for a temporary occupation merely. And, above all, the crown and consummation of the whole promise would indicate something far higher and greater than ever was realised during the sojourn of the Jews in the land ;—" I will be their God." For we must never overlook the inference which our Lord has taught us to draw from this expression, when addressed to men living in the body ;—" I will be their God" —their God, as they are now, in the body. They may individually die, generation after generation may depart, and their bodies may moulder in the dust. But the promise stands sure, as belonging, not to their disembodied spirits, but to themselves as they were when they received it, in their compound nature, body and soul united ;—it is due, not to the dead, but to the living. And the apostle, it is to be remembered, has

put the matter beyond a doubt. He interprets the promise
as comprehensive of the world generally, or as a promise that
" Abraham should be the heir of the world ;"—not of the land,
but of the world,—for the original term here used is unambiguous (Rom. iv. 13) ;—and he places it on a footing that
will not at all agree with any mere settlement of Israel in
Canaan. Moreover, in the same passage, and in immediate
connection with this very promise, he seems to make a most
remarkable allusion to Abraham's faith in God as raising the
dead (Rom. iv. 17). He specifies two instances of divine
power, both of which Abraham believed, and the ·belief of
which would seem to be essential to his embracing the promise
made to him of a numerous offspring, and an everlasting inheritance. He believed that " God could quicken the dead,"
and that he could " call into being things which, as yet, were
not." The latter power God must put forth, in order to
Abraham's having a numerous offspring ; both naturally,
through the child of promise, as yet unborn, and his children
after the flesh ; and spiritually, through his seed, which is
Christ, to whom a people are to be given by the Father.
What need of the former, or the power to quicken the dead,
being so pointedly referred to, unless the resurrection be an
event involved in the grant of the inheritance ? And if so,
it must needs be the inheritance of heaven,—the only inheritance which lies beyond death and the grave.

Taking these considerations together, we may conclude
that the hope set before Abraham in this covenant is the very
hope of the resurrection for which, ages after, Paul was called
in question. That, for himself, Abraham looked forward to a
better land than the land whose soil he trod as a stranger,—
that he looked for a heavenly country,—is beyond all question.
He must, therefore, have understood the promise of the land of
Canaan as given to him individually, in a spiritual and heavenly
sense. It is possible, indeed, as before hinted, that that
sense may turn out to be more strictly literal than is often

supposed; if, as some think, and as is not improbable, the scene of the future heaven, the local habitation of the blessed, is to be this very earth, renovated and purified by fire. On that supposition, the meek shall literally inherit the earth; and Abraham, and his children in the faith, are yet to be the heirs of the world, and especially of that most hallowed spot of the world, where he who was pre-eminently the seed of Abraham died and rose again. But however this may be, Abraham most certainly saw in this promise the hope of an inheritance with God, to be reached by a resurrection from the dead; "an inheritance incorruptible, undefiled, and that fadeth not away."

Compared with this inheritance to be possessed for ever by himself and by all like-minded with himself; and to be possessed by them all as one with the true seed, "heirs of God and joint-heirs with Christ;"—compared with this, how poor the prospect of the occupation of Canaan for a few brief centuries. by a nation,—all born of him, it is true, but, alas! not all partakers of that faith by which alone he was justified, and by which alone either he or they could be saved. That, assuredly, was not the hope of Abraham's calling. No. He lived by the power of the world to come; he rejoiced in hope of the glory to be revealed; and in this renewal of the covenant he had his eye directed to no earthly prize, but to heaven itself, and to God as constituting the blessedness of heaven,—or, in a word, to the full enjoyment of God as his own and his children's portion for ever.

Such were the promises given for the revival of Abraham's faith. And what could be better fitted for that end? What objects of holy contemplation are here presented to Abraham! The countless multitude of his believing children, and their unity in him who is the true seed; the near relation in which God stands to this true seed, and to all that are one in him; and the glorious and eternal inheritance, of which, through the resurrection from the dead, a lively hope is given;—these are the elements of that spiritual food, that heavenly manna, by which the soul of believing Abraham is fed and refreshed. Such truths as these brought home to his heart anew, must recall his affections from earth, and fix them once more on God. His spirit is refreshed and quickened; his faith is re-animated; his hope is brightened; his first love burns again. And when the Lord "leaves off talking with him and goes up from him,"—it is with a fresh and glad appropriation of the opening assurance "I am the Almighty God," that Abraham sets himself, in all singleness of eye and earnestness of soul, to a hearty compliance with the command, "Walk before me and be thou perfect."

21

THE SEAL OF THE COVENANT—THE SACRAMENT
OF CIRCUMCISION

Genesis 17:9-27

And he received the sign of circumcision, a seal of the righteousness of the
faith which he had yet being uncircumcised. Romans 4:11

THE call and the covenant renewed, as has been seen, most
graciously to Abraham, are ratified on this occasion by the
additional confirmation of a sacramental pledge.

The nature of a sacrament in general, and of this sacrament in particular, is carefully defined by the Apostle Paul
(Rom. iv. 9-11.) Three things are distinguished by him ;—
the righteousness, the faith, and the seal.

The righteousness is that which is all throughout Scripture
called "the righteousness of God" (Isaiah xlvi. 12, 13 ; li. 5 ;
Rom. i. 17 ; x. 3). It is that perfect and all-sufficient righteousness, which consists of the voluntary obedience and atoning
sufferings of his own beloved son ;—or, rather, of the very
person of the Son himself, as manifested in our nature, and
satisfying on our behalf the righteous claims of the law, being
the Lamb of God and the propitiation for the sins of the
world. It is the righteousness which God has provided in his
Son,—and of which he is pleased to accept,—as the exclusive
ground of a sinner's justification in his sight.

The faith, again, is that "believing with the heart unto
righteousness" (Rom. x. 10), or that cordial appropriation of

this very righteousness of God, which brings the sinner near, and places him on a right footing with God.

The seal, which comes last, is something different from both. It is added as a token or pledge, a confirmation and assurance of the covenant-transaction with which it is associated. It does not itself constitute or make the covenant on the part of God. Nor is it that which, on my part, gives me an interest in the covenant. What makes the covenant, as the ground or reason of it, is the righteousness of God. What gives me an interest, or a personal right and concern in the covenant, is my faith—my simple acceptance of its blessings, or rather of him in whom, as being himself the righteousness of God, its blessings are all treasured up and stored. The affixing of the seal is an after-deed. It assumes, or takes for granted, the validity of the previous transaction. It proceeds upon the supposition, first, of the covenant being itself made and ratified, exclusively on the footing of the perfect righteousness of God ; and, secondly, of its being made over to me, and made practically and personally mine, exclusively through faith. Then comes in the seal, closing, and, if we may so say, crowning and consummating the whole procedure,—the entire negotiation of my peace and my fellowship with God.

According to this view, the expression (Gen. xvii. 10.) "This is my covenant" must be understood as elliptical, and interpreted by the explanation which the Apostle Paul suggests. It cannot be taken absolutely and literally as it stands ; for, in that case, not only is it at variance with all the teaching of Scripture upon the subject, but it has no clear or distinct meaning at all. It is evidently, therefore, a compressed and imperfect phrase, which the intelligent reader is to fill up. For circumcision is not itself the covenant, although in some sense it may be said to be "the keeping" of the covenant. "Thou shalt keep my covenant" says the Lord to Abraham in the preceding verse (ver. 9). And "this is my covenant which ye shall keep between me and you"—this is the keeping of it, or the way in which you are to keep it—" every man-child among you shall be circumcised."*

Many questions of detail, relating to circumcision as the keeping of the covenant, might here be raised, which the brief narrative before us does not enable us, with any certainty, to settle. A few points, however, may be simply noted.

I. As to the time of the appointment of this ordinance, it is important to observe that a visible Church is now to be constituted; a society is to be formed, which is to be separated from the world, consecrated to God, and destined, under different varieties of form and of economy, more or less spiritual, to continue to the end of time. That Church is now to stand out as authoritatively and sacramentally distinct from the world.

Before the flood, a similar distinction began to prevail in the days of Enos ;—spontaneously, as it would seem, on the part of men themselves (chap. iv. 26). As the world grew more and more corrupt, the true sons of God drew off from the rest of mankind, and by a peculiar profession and a peculiar walk, were

---

* It is the same phrase which is used with reference to the New Testament sacrament of the Lord's Supper;—"This cup is the New Testament," or the new covenant, " in my blood " (1 Cor. xi. 25.) And it is satisfactory to trace so exact a resemblance between the words of institution in the case of these two sacraments. It proves the substantial identity of all the sacraments, as seals of the same covenant,—the covenant of grace. It was that covenant which God confirmed with Abraham ; and to it the sacrament of circumcision stood in the same relation in which the sacraments of Baptism and the Lord's Supper stand to it now. " This is my covenant." Who does not see here the precise agreement of this mode of expression with the similar phrases—" This is my body,"—"this is my blood,"— " this is my blood of the New Testament," or covenant—" this is the New Testament," or covenant, " in my blood ?" These are, as it now appears, the customary and stated terms of a sacramental institution. How unreasonable to torture them into any more mysterious meaning ; since they denote, and really can denote, nothing more than the virtual identity which there is always understood to be between the seal and the substance of any solemn deed.

marked out as his. The line of distinction, indeed, separating the visible Church from the ungodly world, was but too precarious and uncertain. In course of time, fellowship was resumed, with most disastrous issue. After the flood, there was at first no visible society distinct from the general mass of men. The worship of God was in every house. And, although, even in the family of Noah himself, the elements of a division between the pious and the profane may be traced, no palpable selection of the one from among the other seems to have taken place. But as corruption again became general, God appointed a new centre, or rallying point, for those whom he would keep from the contagion of idolatry. The call of Abraham was the initial step towards the formation of a visible Church.

Now, to a visible Church, sacramental distinctions and pledges are appropriate. Hence the fitness of the time at which circumcision was instituted. And if we suppose, as we have ventured to do—no intimation of a divine appointment being given—that the association formed in the time of Enos was the act of the godly themselves, we see the reason why a sacrament should be instituted now rather than then. For now, God himself, by his own express authority,—not man by his voluntary choice,—is laying the foundation of a divine society. And, accordingly, he sets his own seal upon it.

II. The rite itself now instituted is not an unmeaning form or ceremony. It is significant of the great leading fact in the covenant of which it is the seal—the extraordinary and miraculous birth of him who is pre-eminently and emphatically the seed of Abraham, the holy child Jesus. It has obvious reference to Abraham's approaching paternity, his having a son, not after the flesh but by promise; and it is the sign and symbol of something peculiar and remarkable in the manner of the birth, as well as of some special purity and holiness in what is to be born. It has respect to the seed about to be begotten. It points to the Messiah, the Saviour about to be manifested as the righteousness of God—himself personally the very righteousness of God,—not less in his conception and birth than in his obedience unto death. It prefigures his assumption of humanity, in a way securing his exemption from the sinfulness of humanity. For of his miraculous birth as securing the sinlessness of his humanity, its being unstained by any participation in the hereditary guilt and corruption of man, the circumcision of the patriarch, and his house,—especially the circumcision of Isaac, in the view of whose birth the ordinance is instituted, is a fitting type and token.

Hence, perhaps, one reason for circumcision, as the initial or introductory seal of the covenant, being superseded, and another sacrament coming in its place. Circumcision pointed to the future birth of Christ,—his assumption of our nature, pure and perfect. That birth being accomplished, the propriety of circumcision as a sacrament ceases. Any corresponding rite now must be not prospective, but retrospective; not looking forward to the beginning of the Messiah's work as the righteousness of God, when in his birth he was shown to be his Holy One, and his Son, by his miraculous conception in the virgin's womb—but looking back to the end of his work, in his burial, when he was declared to be the Son of God with power, by his resurrection from the grave. Such a rite, accordingly, is Baptism; as explained by the apostle when he says, "We are buried with him by baptism into death: that like as Christ was raised up from the dead by the glory of the Father, even so we also should walk in newness of life" (Rom. vi. 4). Our baptism signifies our ingrafting into Christ, as not merely born, but buried and risen again. It refers not to his entrance into the world, but to his leaving it. It is the symbol, not of his pure and holy birth merely, but of the purifying and cleansing efficacy of his precious blood shed upon the cross, and the power of his resurrection to life and glory. Abraham and the faithful of old were circumcised into his birth, the redemption being yet future; we are baptized into his death, the redemption being now past. The one sacrament was an emblem of purity connected with a Saviour to be born; the other is an emblem of purity connected with a Saviour who "liveth, and was dead, and behold! is alive for evermore!" Both circumcision and baptism denote the purging of the conscience from dead works, or from the condemnation and corruption of the old nature, through the real and living union of the believer with Christ—with Christ about to come in the flesh, in the one case;—with Christ already come, in the other.*

III. Hence it appears that it is strictly and properly to the covenant of grace that circumcision, as instituted on this occasion, has respect. It is true that under the Mosaic economy it served a farther purpose. It became a national badge or mark of distinction—the pledge of the national covenant in terms of which God governed the nation of Israel. Even then, however, it did not lose its primary and original significancy. To a spiritually-minded Jew—to one who was an Israelite indeed—it was still the token of the better covenant, and the seal of the righteousness that is by faith. And as at first ordained for Abraham, it had absolutely no other meaning at all. It could have no other. For, in the first place, there is no limitation or restriction of it to the Jewish nation in particular. It is enjoined on Abraham, as the father of many nations; and on all, generally, who are of his house, or may be embraced, by whatever right, even the right of purchase, within it (ver. 9-13). And, secondly, the covenant with which it stands associated, is not temporal and national, but spiritual and universal. It is the everlasting covenant, in the one seed of Abraham, which is Christ.

* If this view is admitted, it sufficiently explains the language used concerning baptism in connection with Christ's burial and resurrection; and therefore cuts away the argument for dipping founded on that language; as if plunging into a watery bath and coming out of it were a fitting imitation of the lying in the new tomb and the glorious rising after three days.

For the reasoning of Paul, in his Epistle to the Galatians, will apply as strongly to the seal, as to the substance, of the covenant made with Abraham (Gal. iii. 15-17). Whatever modification the divine manner of dealing with his people might undergo in the days of Moses—whatever additional stringency of legal restraint might be rendered necessary " because of transgressions," and whatever additional reference circumcision might consequently come to have to the national Levitical institute—this could not affect its bearing upon the transaction with which alone it stands originally associated. And if that transaction is represented by the apostle as being substantially the covenant of grace " confirmed of God in Christ,"—which the law given four hundred years after could not disannul,—then it follows that the rite of circumcision, which is identified with it, must partake of the same character, and must be viewed as the seal of " the promises made to Abraham and his seed," which no subsequent economy could ever " make of none effect."

As the seal, therefore, of the covenant of grace, or of the righteousness that is by faith,—and in that view of it alone, —circumcision is on this occasion ordained. Hence, it must be in the same view of it that it is appointed to be administered to infants (ver. 12), and is made of indispensable obligation (ver. 14). Both of these observations are important in reference to the analogy between circumcision and baptism.

IV. The child, eight days old, was to be circumcised (ver. 12). Why then, we are accustomed to ask, should not children be baptised ?

To this question the opponents of infant baptism, among other things, reply, that circumcision was appointed for the Jews as a nation, and was the sign of their peculiar privileges as a nation, which, in consistency with sound principle, might be hereditary, and in fact were so. But grace, they say, is not hereditary ; and baptism is the pledge of grace. The answer would be conclusive, so far as to set aside the argument from analogy, were it well founded in point of fact—were circumcision a mere national distinction, and not, like baptism itself, the seal of a spiritual covenant, and of the very same covenant. But if, on the other hand,—whatever national application of it may have been subsequently made,—circumcision, as given originally to Abraham, had exclusively a spiritual meaning ; if it was to Abraham precisely what baptism is to us, the seal of his engrafting into Christ, and as such, was administered to the infants of his house ;—why, we may well ask, are the children of God's people now to be placed on a worse footing than in the days of old ? Is there any evidence of a change in this respect ? On the contrary, did not the Lord specially distinguish little children as the objects of his love, taking them into his arms, and affectionately blessing them ? And do not the apostles proceed all along on the principle, that the visible Church is to embrace not only all the faithful, but their children also ? Thus Peter (Acts iii. 39) speaks of the promise being to believers and to their children. Paul also (1 Cor. vii. 14) founds an argument on the assumption that the children of a believing parent are not unclean or common, but holy. And we read in the book of Acts (chap. xvi. 33, etc.) of entire households being baptised ; the expressions used being such as to render it very unlikely that the little children were excluded. Why, indeed, should they be excluded ? Without an express intimation to the contrary, the practice of administering the initiatory seal of the covenant to infants would be kept up, as a matter of course, under the gospel. It required no formal injunction to warrant its continuance ; but very explicit authority must be produced to entitle the Church to set it aside.*

---

* We may use this argument concerning other ordinances of divine appointment,—as, for instance, the Sabbath. The whole burden of the proof lies with those who contend that the Sabbatic ordinance is done away, or that the Lord's day is not the Sabbath. And so is it also in the instance of infant baptism.

But farther, the principle on which the circumcision of in-fants proceeded is equally applicable to their baptism ;—that principle being substantially the principle of a visible Church. For the permanent continuance as well as for the first forma-tion of such a society, provision must be made. And what provision can be more effectual, than that the children of those who compose it, should, from their very birth, be assumed into its fellowship—reckoned, accounted, treated, and trained as its members—served heirs, if we may so speak, to the privileges and responsibilities of their parents ? What can be more thoroughly in accordance with the whole analogy of the pro-vidence of God ? Does not his ordinary providence exemplify the hereditary transmission,—not indeed of good or evil,—but of the opportunities and probabilities of good and evil ? Our obligations, physical, social, and domestic, are largely made and determined for us by our birth ; and so also, to a great extent, are the means of fulfilling our obligations. All this must be acknowledged, apart from religion—as affecting, perhaps, and modifying, yet not at all superseding, our personal and indi-vidual accountability. And on the very same analogy, a religious brotherhood, destined to be perpetuated from age to age, is divinely formed.

I say divinely formed. For if the visible Church were a mere voluntary association—a union formed by men of their own accord—the idea of a transmitted right, or a transmitted duty, might seem unreasonable and unfair. To make me a member of such a body in my infancy and without my consent, might be held to be an unwarrantable infringement on my freedom of choice. But if the visible Church is God's ordi-nance there is no absurdity or injustice in the arrangement. If, while yet unconscious, and incapable of consenting, I am enrolled and registered, stamped, and sealed, as one of the household of God, visible on earth ; if, with his sanction, and by his authority, I am marked out from the womb as pecu-liarly his—his, in the same sense in which the Christian profession of my parents makes them his—his, by privilege, by promise, and by obligation ;—no wrong is done to me, nor is any restriction put on me, more than by the circumstance of my being born in a home of piety and peace, rather than in a haunt of profligacy and crime. If God makes me, by birth, the scion of a noble stock, the child and heir of an illustrious house, then by my birth I am necessarily invested with certain rights and bound to certain duties, in regard to which I have no discretion. When I am old enough to understand my position in society, I find it in a great degree made for me, and not left for me to make. I may refuse to take the place assigned to me ; I may never avail myself of its advantages ; I may never realise my rank, or imbibe the spirit and enter into the high aims of my honourable calling. Still, if I do not live according to my birth, the fault is my own, and my responsibility is great. And still, whether I take advantage of it or not, my birth, as ordered in God's providence, has a meaning which might stand me in good stead, if I so chose and so willed it. So also in regard to circumcision or baptism. If God owns me, by such an initiatory rite, as a member of the society on earth which bears his name, I may never be in reality what that rite signifies me to be ; but not the less on that account has the right a solemn significancy. And if afterwards I wilfully disown it, I do so with aggravated guilt, and at my own increased peril ; whereas, on the other hand, owning it, I obtain an ever fresh confirmation of my faith and good hope through grace.

V. On much the same principle on which this initiatory rite is administered to the children of God's people, it is declared to be of indispensable obligation (ver. 14). It is of course the wilful neglect of the ordinance that is here condemned ; and it is condemned as doubly sinful ; implying contempt, both of the authority by which the rite was ordained, and of the grace of which it was the seal. It involved the twofold guilt of disobedience to God's commandment and disregard of God's covenant. " He hath broken," or made void, "my covenant" (ver. 14). He who thus offended necessarily excluded himself from the society of God's people, and must be held as joining the ranks of the aliens and enemies. He was justly to be " cut off."

What that sentence meant, and how it was to be executed, is not very distinctly said. It would seem to indicate something more than excommunication, to which some have restricted it. The expression is a strong one, and in the Mosaic law it is certainly used to denote the punishment of death (Exod. xxxi. 14). It is possible, however, that before that law, as the national law of Israel, specified death as the ordinary mode of cutting off from the commonwealth, the sentence may have been otherwise carried into effect. But farther, if death is here meant, it is doubtful whether it was to be inflicted by the hand of man or by the immediate visitation of God. The warning, " He shall be cut off from his people," may intimate not the Church's duty, but God's purpose, in respect of the offender. In that age, there is no reason to believe that any crime save murder was made capital in the judicial procedure of men. But vengeance belonged to the Lord ; and in constituting a visible Church, and appointing an appropriate seal, he must vindicate the sanctity of his own ordinance against the despisers of his authority and his grace. There is a marked difference between the threatening of death, if that be meant, in the case before us, and the appointment of death as the punishment of murder ; (Gen. ix. 6) " Whoso sheddeth man's blood, by man shall his blood be shed." That is a far more express recognition of human agency, and a far more unequivocal ordination of it, than this ;— " He shall be cut off from his people." It is to be observed also, that in the view of this menace being an intimation rather of the divine purpose than of human duty, so far at least as any physical infliction might be concerned, there is a remarkable correspondence between the penalty here annexed to the breach of the law of circumcision, and the consequences that are represented as flowing from the sin of the Corinthians in profaning the sacrament of the Lord's Supper ;—" For this cause many are weak and sickly among you, and many sleep" (1 Cor. xi. 30).

Such, then, is the institution of circumcision, as the seal of the covenant which God made when he gave the promises to Abraham.

The patriarch's compliance with the divine command is recorded in the remaining portion of the chapter. And the narrative brings out the forbearance and abundant grace of God on the one hand, as well as the struggles of lingering unbelief on the other ;—while, in the issue, the triumph of faith appears, as made perfect by works. For it is no easy exercise of obedience that is required of Abraham, to prove and perfect his faith. A revelation awaits him, in the very act of complying with the injunction of God, that may well stagger his spiritual confidence, as it shocks his natural affection. Hitherto, in this renewal of the covenant, nothing has been said as to the line of descent in which it is to be established. Hagar's child is not formally set aside ; the covenant, as yet, is merely established generally in the seed of Abraham ; and the father's affections, despairing of any other son, may still be set on Ishmael. But he must be completely stripped of all confidence in the flesh, and made to live by faith alone. It is not to a son born after the flesh, but to a son by promise, that he is to look. Sarai herself is to receive strength ; and her name accordingly is changed. She is no longer " Sarai," my princess, as if she stood in that honourable relation to her husband alone ; but " Sarah," without limitation,—a princess, or the princess,—the princely mother of those of whom, in Christ, Abraham is the father (ver. 15, 16). The patriarch laughs, and of the laughter Isaac's name is a memorial (ver. 17).

Still there is a momentary revulsion of natural feeling.

His heart clings to Ishmael. The strange announcement of a child yet to be born he can scarcely comprehend or realise. But here is Ishmael ? May not he suffice ? Why look for another ? " O that Ishmael might live before thee" (ver. 18).

It is the last lingering look of sense,—the fond expostulation of the flesh still striving against the spirit. Is not Ishmael here alive before thee ? What better can come of Sarah ? There is a moment's hesitation ; but immediately there is an unreserved acquiescence in the Lord's will and way. Let him save me, let him bless me ; not as I would, but as he will; not in my way, but in his own.

Behold here the marvellous condescension of God. He is not offended by the outpouring of Abraham's natural longings and desires. He hears them, and, as far as may be, he meets and answers them. Ishmael is to be blessed, though Isaac still must be the heir ;—" As for Ishmael, I have heard thee : I have blessed him, and will make him fruitful, and will multiply him exceedingly. But my covenant will I establish with Isaac" (ver. 20, 21).

What encouragement have we, in this example, to lay aside all reserve in our intercourse with God. Freely and frankly we may unburthen our hearts to him, and unbosom all our grief. We may tell him, as if in confidence, all that we feel and all that we desire. If only there be submission to his will, he is not offended. For he is patient and pitiful. If it be possible, he will let the cup pass ; if not, he will mingle some drop of soothing comfort in it ; as he did in the case of Abraham.

22

ABRAHAM THE FRIEND OF GOD

Genesis 18:1-33

He was called the Friend of God. James 2:23

1. THE FRIENDLY VISIT

Behold, I stand at the door, and knock : if any man hear my voice, and open the door, I will come in to him, and will sup with him, and he with me. Revelation 3:20

(VERSES 1-8)

THE opening scene, in this chapter, is full of beauty,—having that peculiar charm which attaches to Eastern nature, and to the olden time. There is a new appearance of the Lord to Abraham, in the place of his ordinary abode, the plains of Mamre,—the plains which belonged to Mamre the Amorite, one of Abraham's allies in the war against the kings (chap. xiv. 13), and which probably on this account bore the original proprietor's name (chap. xiii. 18). Here are pitched the tents of Abraham's household and attendants,—the colony or company, by this time pretty numerous, over which he presides as chief. His own tent occupies a distinguished place among the rest,— standing near the path by which the casual wayfarer may be expected to pass. It is noon ; and Abraham is on the watch for any weary pilgrim, to whom its sultry and scorching heat may make rest and refreshment welcome. This, it may be believed, is his usual practice. The hour of noon, in that hot clime, suspends labour, and compels the exhausted frame to seek repose. Abraham and his people repair severally to their tents, and make ready the homely meal. But, first, the patriarch takes his place at his tent door, where usually is his seat of authority ; and there he waits to see if any stranger is coming whom it may be his duty and privilege to entertain. Perhaps some of the remnant of the godly, still holding fast their faith amid the abounding iniquity and universal idolatry of the land,—not protected and blessed, as Abraham once was himself, by any pious Melchizedek, but persecuted and cast out by those among whom they dwelt,—may be going about without a home, and may be glad of a day's shelter and a day's food. These the patriarch will delight to honour ; and the recollection of his own early wanderings, as well as his love to them as brethren in the Lord, will open his heart towards them. Thus he sits for a little in the heat of the day in his tent door, not idle, but intent on hospitable thoughts, " not forgetful to entertain strangers."

On this day he is well rewarded for his hospitality. " He entertains angels unawares " (Heb. xiii. 2). And not all of them created angels, even of the highest order. One, in the progress of this interview, discovers himself to be the Angel of the Covenant—the Lord himself.

While the strangers are yet unknown—having the aspect merely of ordinary travellers—Abraham manifests towards them, not only the somewhat elaborate homage of Eastern courtesy, but the sympathy also of a godly mind. He presses upon them his hospitality, as if their acceptance of it were a personal favour to himself. Water for their wayworn feet— a pleasant shade under which to rest—and a morsel of bread to comfort their hearts,—such are the kindnesses placed at their service. And still further to remove any feeling they might have on the score of encroaching on his liberality, or incurring irksome obligation, the devout patriarch puts his benevolence on the footing of its being not so much his own doing as the Lord's (ver. 5). Nothing, he would say, is due to me ; you need not consider yourselves to be indebted to me; all is of God. He has so ordered it that you should chance to come here, and that I should be waiting to help you; "Therefore are ye come to your servant."

Can finer or truer delicacy in the conferring of a benefit be imagined? Ah! it is godliness, after all, that is the best politeness; it is the saint who knows best how to be courteous. Other benefactors may be liberal, condescending, familiar. They may try to put the objects of their charity at their ease. Still there is ever something in their bountifulness which pains and depresses, and if it does not offend or degrade, at least inspires a certain sense of humiliation. But the servant of God has the real tact and taste which the work of doing good requires. And the secret is, that he does good as the servant of God. Like Abraham, he feels himself,—and he makes those whom he obliges feel,—that it is truly not a transaction between man and man, implying some greatness or merit on the one side, of which the want may be painfully realised on the other,—but that all is of God, to whom giver and receiver are equally subject, and in whom both are one.

The offer thus frankly made is frankly accepted. There is no empty form or idle ceremony on either side;—for God's saints and servants quickly understand one another. At a word, in God's name, they come together and are at home with one another. What is given in good faith is at once taken in good part. There are no affected declinatures or multiplied apologies—no exaggerated professions of humility or gratitude; but only simple acquiescence; "So do as thou hast said."

The hasty preparation which follows is exactly after the oriental fashion. The repast provided for the family will not suffice for these new guests; but the requisite addition is easily and quickly made. In the true primitive style, all in the house,—the heads as well as the servants of the household,—bestir themselves. Sarah prepares cakes.

Abraham himself fetches a calf, which one of his young men hastens to dress. Butter and milk complete the entertainment, to which the three seeming travellers sit down; Abraham, meanwhile, doing the part of an attentive host, and courteously standing by them, while they eat under the tree (ver. 6-8).

At first he knows not who or what they are whom he is entertaining. But be they who they may, in showing them this kindness, a glow of satisfaction fills his soul. And ere long he begins to discern under their homely appearance, some traces of their heavenly character. They are not of the common class whom business or pleasure brings across his path; they are not like the ordinary inhabitants of the land. Their holy air and holy demeanour cannot be mistaken.

One in particular seems to stand out from the other two, as commanding greater reverence. To him as the chief among them, Abraham had addressed his invitation :—" My Lord, if now I have found favour in thy sight, pass not away, I pray thee, from thy servant" (ver. 3). And soon, as the interview goes on, this Holy One reveals his real rank. From the first he conducts the conversation; and he speaks, not as any inferior or subordinate messenger, but as himself, in his own proper person, God. As God he makes a promise which God alone can fulfil (ver. 10, 14). Then again he is expressly called Jehovah (ver. 13); and in his detection of Sarah's secret sin—her unuttered thought of unbelief—he manifests the divine attribute of omniscience. He convinces and reproves, as the Searcher of hearts. Towards the end of the chapter also (ver. 16), it plainly appears, that of the three, who seemed to be men, only two go on to Sodom—the two angels who reach that city at even (chap. xix. 1). The third remains behind with Abraham, and speaks to him as the Lord Jehovah,—"face to face,"—"as a man speaketh to his friend" (Exod. xxxiii. 11).

The three strangers, therefore, whom Abraham entertains,

are none other than Jehovah himself, and two attendant angels. The Second Person in the Trinity,—who bears the double character of God, or the Lord, and of the Messenger of the Covenant, or the Angel of the Lord,—condescends on this occasion to be Abraham's guest, and becomes "known to him in the breaking of bread" (Luke xxiv. 30, 31).

It is a singular instance of condescension—the only recorded instance of the kind before the incarnation. On other occasions, this same illustrious being appeared to the fathers and conversed with them ; and meat and drink were brought out to him. But in these cases, he turned the offered banquet into a sacrifice, in the smoke of which he ascended heavenward (Judges vi. 18-24, xiii. 15-21). Here he personally accepts the patriarch's hospitality, and partakes of his fare,—a greater wonder than the other ; implying more intimate and gracious friendship,—more unreserved familiarity. He sits under his tree, and shares his common meal.

2. THE FRIENDLY FELLOWSHIP

The secret of the Lord is with them that fear him ; and he will show them his covenant. Psalm 25:14

(VERSES 9-17)

In the progress of the interview, as well as in its commencement, the Lord treats Abraham as a friend. He converses with him familiarly, putting to him a question which a mere stranger in the east would scarcely reckon himself entitled to put. He inquires into his household matters, and asks after Sarah, his wife (ver. 9). Then, in the pains he takes, by reiterated assurances, to confirm the faith of Abraham and overcome the unbelief of Sarah,—in the tone of his simple appeal to divine omnipotence as an answer to every doubt, " Is any thing too hard for the Lord ?"—and in his mild but searching reproof of the dissimulation to which the fear of detection led Sarah,—

"Nay, but thou didst laugh,"—in all this, does it not almost seem as if by anticipation we saw Jesus in the midst of his disciples, stretching forth his hand to catch the trembling Peter on the waters,—" O thou of little faith, wherefore didst thou doubt?"—or, after the denial, turning to look on Peter, and melt his soul to penitence and love!

Nor is it unworthy of remark, as an instance of divine grace and condescension, that from this very incident in Sarah's life, the Holy Ghost takes occasion to record her praise. Speaking of "the holy women" who, "in the old time" "trusted in God, adorned themselves with the ornament of a meek and quiet spirit, which is in the sight of God of great price, and were in subjection unto their own husbands,"—the Apostle Peter adds, by way of example,—"Even as Sarah obeyed Abraham, calling him lord; whose daughters ye are as long as ye do well, and are not afraid with any amazement" (1 Pet. iii. 6). He warns Christian matrons, indeed, against Sarah's great fault,—her "fear of amazement,"—or, in other words, her consternation at the discovery of what was passing in her mind when she "laughed within herself" in the tent-door. For it was that which tempted her to dissemble. The sudden searching of her heart by this mysterious stranger's all-seeing eye disconcerted and alarmed her. She lost her presence of mind,—her guileless integrity—and instead of a frank acknowledgment of the truth, which would have led to her being completely reassured, she had recourse, in her confusion, to an evasion and a lie (ver. 15). But with this exception, she is commended as "doing well;" and she is held up as a model of matronly simplicity and subjection. She found favour in his sight who is not easily provoked;— who does not break the bruised reed, or quench the smoking flax;—who reproves sin, indeed, even in his own people, but at the same time raises up them that fall.

It is chiefly, however, in the close of this interview, that Abraham is treated by God as his friend, being, as it were, admitted into his deliberations, and consulted in regard to what he is about to do.

The repast being over, the three divine guests arise to depart ; and Abraham bears them company, for a little way, as they turn their faces toward Sodom (ver. 16). Such a farewell compliment on the part of the host accords with the usages of hospitality, and especially with the kindness of brotherly love in the Lord ; and, accordingly, it is sanctioned by the practice of the early Church, as well as by the commendation of John the beloved (Acts xv. 3 ; 3 John 5, 6). By this time, also, Abraham has doubtless discovered who these travellers really are. And it is a singular proof of the intimate terms on which he is permitted to stand with God, that the discovery does not disconcert him. There is no appearance of confusion or alarm, as in the case of Isaiah (chap. vi.), when he saw the Lord ; or in the case of Peter (Luke v. 8), when the vivid sense of his Master's divinity flashed upon his mind. Abraham is calm and self-possessed ; he is at home and at ease in the presence of the Lord and his two heavenly companions. And, as if not presuming to break in upon the disguise which they thought fit to assume, continuing to treat them as ordinary wayfarers,—with true delicacy he suffers them to depart as they came.

Near the door of his tent, however, he overhears a strange consultation among the seeming travellers. One, who has already spoken as the Lord, and manifested the attributes and prerogatives of supreme divinity—detecting, rebuking, and pardoning secret sin—speaks, as it would appear, to the other two. He intimates that while they are to go on—for the purpose, as we shall presently see, of doing his errand to Lot in Sodom—he himself must tarry a little longer, having a communication to make to Abraham (ver. 17-19). Thereafter he announces to them his intention of joining them again, when his confidential business with Abraham is over. He will personally visit and inquire into the guilt of the devoted

cities, the cry of whose iniquity, like the cry of Abel's blood
(Gen. iv. 10), or the cry of the labourers defrauded of their
hire (James v. 4), hath entered into the ear of the Lord of
Sabaoth ;—" The Lord said, Because the cry of Sodom and
Gomorrah is great, and because their sin is very grievous, I
will go down now, and see whether they have done altogether
according to the cry of it, which is come unto me ; and if not,
I will know " (ver. 20, 21).

Perhaps these verses (20, 21) are to be taken as retrospective ; as being a parenthetical explanation of this whole scene,
which might have been given at the outset, but is now incidentally thrown in :—" The Lord had said, I will go down
now and see ;"—speaking after the manner of men, to mark
the perfect equity of his procedure, as not condemning hastily,
or without inquiry. This had been his purpose in coming down
to earth at all on this occasion. In the execution of this
purpose he had visited Abraham. And now sending on to
Sodom the angels who accompanied him, and who were
appointed to save Lot, he himself remains behind.

Thus Abraham stands alone before the Lord. And that
marvellous colloquy ensues, in which the Lord communicates
his purpose respecting Sodom to Abraham his friend, and
Abraham takes upon him, with unprecedented and extraordinary freedom, to speak to the Lord.

3. THE FRIENDLY AND CONFIDENTIAL CONSULTATION

Surely the Lord God will do nothing, but he revealeth his secret unto his
servants the prophets. Amos 3:7

(VERSES 17-19)

In announcing his intention to communicate his purpose
respecting Sodom to Abraham his friend, how strange and
singular is the Lord's language (verses 17-19) :—" Shall I hide
from Abraham that thing which I do ?" as if Abraham were

entitled to know it—as if he had a right to be consulted.
What condescension! That the sovereign Lord of all, who
"giveth not account of any of his matters"—to whom none may
say, What doest thou?—should feel himself, as it were, obliged
to open his mind to Abraham! "Shall I hide from Abraham
that thing which I do?" He speaks as if such concealment
would be a wrong not to be thought of—as if it would be unworthy of the relation in which Abraham stands to him;—
unworthy of it as a relation of high honour as well as great
responsibility.

1. The Lord refers to the honour or privilege already
granted to Abraham as a reason for having no concealment
from him now—"Seeing that Abraham shall surely become a
great and mighty nation, and all the nations of the earth shall
be blessed in him" (ver. 18). The rank to which the patriarch has been raised, the prospect of his increasing greatness,
and the blessing which in him all nations of the earth are to
receive, combine to warrant and explain his admission into the
divine confidence and counsels. He is in a position to be
trusted. He is not a stranger or an enemy, who must be kept
at a distance, and treated with stern and suspicious reserve.
He stands high in the favour and fellowship of God, and it is
not unreasonable that God should impart to him an intimate
knowledge of his works and his ways. "The secret of the
Lord is with them that fear him, and he will show them his
covenant" (Ps. xxv. 14). Hence the Lord speaks of his prophets as those who should stand in his counsel, or his secret
(Jer. xxiii. 18-22); and again, he says, "Surely the Lord God
will do nothing, but he revealeth his secret to his servants,
the prophets" (Amos iii. 7). And it is worthy of observation
that it is especially with reference to his judgments to be executed on the earth that the Lord thus speaks—such judgments
as he is about to bring on Sodom. It is indeed a very peculiar and precious privilege of this divine friendship, thus to
understand, from his own previous explanation of them, the

terrible visitations of the Lord. To the friend of God, these
visitations of vengeance are not, as they appear to other men,
mere accidents of fortune, or sudden outbreaks of capricious
wrath. To him they have a clear meaning—a distinct and
well-defined end. And hence, while others are distracted and
overwhelmed, he stands fearless amid the ruin.

What a privilege is this! See the ungodly, the worldly,
overtaken with swift destruction. Sudden calamity comes
upon them; they are stupified, they stand aghast; not knowing what to make of the dispensation; not knowing where to
turn. It is a mysterious, an inscrutable providence—is their
only cry. What means it? What shall we do? But the
friend of God is not thus, even in the worst storms, all at sea
and unprepared. He can form some idea of the meaning of
such visitations; he can put upon them a right construction,
and turn them to a right account. He can glorify God, and
kiss the rod; he can stand in awe, and not sin. So, when
the judgments of God are abroad in the earth, and men's
hearts begin to fail them for fear, the friend of God, understanding that these things must be—and understanding also
why they must be—to prove and to avenge his own elect—
can "make his refuge in the shadow of God's wings, until the
calamities be overpast" (Ps. lvii. 1). He is not alarmed, or
offended, or shaken in his loyalty, by all that he sees God
doing on the earth—most unaccountable though many of his
doings may be. He has been taken into the divine confidence,
so that now he "dwelleth in the secret place of the Most
High" (Ps. xci. 1) And "when the Lord cometh out of his
place to punish the inhabitants of the earth for their iniquity,"
they who are his friends hear his gracious call, " Come my
people, enter thou into thy chambers, and shut thy doors about
thee. Hide thyself, as it were, for a little moment, until the
indignation be overpast" (Isa. xxvi. 20).

2. The Lord, in communicating his purpose to Abraham
his friend, refers not only to the high honour and privilege

which that relation implies, but also to its great responsibility
—" For I know him, that he will command his children and
his household after him, and they shall keep the way of the
Lord, to do justice and judgment ; that the Lord may bring
upon Abraham that which he hath spoken of him " (ver. 19).
The same consideration is largely dwelt upon in the seventy-
eighth Psalm, as a reason for the recital of the Lord's mercies
and judgments which that Psalm contains (ver. 1-8). For the
transmission from generation to generation of the true knowledge and worship of God, it is essential that they who are to
command and teach their children after them, should themselves understand the scheme of God's providence, so as to be
well acquainted with what he has done, and is yet to do, on
the earth. Abraham is highly commended by God, as one
who will assuredly be faithful in this work of the godly training and godly discipline of his household. As the head of a
family—as a witness for God to the generation to come—as a
teacher of righteousness, he is intrusted with a most important
office, and he will not betray his trust. And that he may the
better and more effectually fulfil his trust, the Lord hides not
from him that thing which he is doing. He explains to him
the coming judgment upon Sodom, and the principle of that
judgment. For Abraham is to ply this as a weapon, and use
it as an argument, in dealing with those whom he instructs in
the ways of the Lord. Hence the value of this announcement
made to him beforehand of Sodom's doom. For now he can
speak of it, not merely as a historical fact—an event which
happened to occur in his day—but as a fact or event having a
special significancy, as a predetermined judgment of God. Nor
is he to speak of it merely as the result of natural causes,
whatever part these may have had in producing it, or however
in one view they may suffice to explain it. Abraham knows
that an additional explanation is to be given ; that the event,
by whatever instrumentality brought about, is to be regarded
mainly as holding a place in the moral government of God,

and as ordained by him for the special purpose of carrying
forward his righteous and holy administration over his intelligent creatures. In this light it is to be represented by Abraham to his children and his household ; and as the friend of
God, he is to turn it to account for causing them to keep the
way of the Lord, to do justice and truth.

"I will sing of judgment as well as mercy," says the
Psalmist. And if any one be indeed the friend of God, he
will enter with holy sympathy into the Lord's hatred of sin,
and not shrink from steadily contemplating and solemnly declaring his judgments to be executed on the workers of
iniquity. For to be the friend of God is to stand by him
against all his enemies—to resent with a holy indignation all
insults and injuries offered to him, and to approve of his purposes of wrath as well as of his plans and promises of love.
Other men may abuse or misinterpret the Lord's forbearance ;
putting a false construction on it, as if it implied either con-
nivance at the guilt of sin, or want of resolution to punish it.
But you who, as the children of Abraham are, like him, the
friends of God, are admitted into his councils. You understand the principle of his providential rule—the reason of that
long patience which he has with the workers of iniquity; and
you know that vengeance postponed but not averted must be
all the more terrible in the end. Having yourselves scarcely
escaped from the wrath to come, by fleeing for refuge to the
hope set before you in the gospel, you look forward with
trembling awe to the desolation to be wrought on the earth.
For the Lord does not hide from you that thing which he
does. You see him coming down to inquire into the great
wickedness of which the loud cry has entered into his ears.
He shows you his arm bared and uplifted to smite terribly the
earth. And he does so, that you may command your children
and your household after you ; that "knowing the terror of the
Lord you may persuade men."

4. THE LIBERTY OF FRIENDLY REMONSTRANCE

Then said the Lord unto me, Pray not for this people for their good.—
Jeremiah 14:11

(VERSES 23-33)

This pleading with God is the last and highest privilege of that divine friendship which is exemplified in the case of Abraham. He manifests, in the whole of it, the most profound deference and humility, as if deprecating the divine displeasure; " Oh let not the Lord be angry, and I will speak;" "Oh let not the Lord be angry, and I will speak, yet but this once " (ver. 30-32); and as if he were himself astonished at the liberty he has been emboldened to take, " Behold, now I have taken upon me to speak unto the Lord, which am but dust and ashes " (ver. 27-31). But he uses, at the same time, extraordinary freedom of speech, and an importunity that will scarcely take a denial. Nor is it for himself and for his own house that he pleads with the Lord. That would be much. But it is for a city, the cry of whose wickedness has brought the Lord down from heaven to search it out, and to visit it; which is more, greatly more, to be wondered at. That, on the strength of the friendship to which he was so specially admitted, the patriarch should have all boldness in asking favours on his own behalf and on behalf of all that were his, —might not be so very surprising. But that he should venture to come between the great and terrible God and the doomed objects of his righteous indignation; that with no personal interest at stake—nothing that could give him, as it were, a title to interfere—he should dare to arrest the uplifted arm of vengeance, and deprecate the descending blow; as if he affected almost to be more reasonable and more merciful than the very God of love himself;—what intimate, unbounded, most artless and fearless confidence of friendship does this

imply! Surely it is the perfection of that love which casteth
out fear!

Let it be observed, however, first, that there is no in-
trusive forwardness in this intercessory pleading ; no attempt
to pry into the secret things which belong to the Lord our
God (Deut. xxix. 29) ; no thought of meddling with the purposes or decrees of election, which the Lord reserves exclusively
to himself. The patriarch does not aspire to any acquaintance
with these high and hidden mysteries ; nor does he consider
that to be necessary in order to his offering such sort of prayer.
Why, indeed, should it be thought necessary? Why should
any of you ever feel yourselves hindered or restrained in
praying for the unconverted,—for the unconverted world,—for
unconverted cities,—for unconverted individuals,—because you
are ignorant of God's purpose of election respecting them ?
Does that ignorance prevent you from labouring for their good ?
Not unless your mind is wholly perverted by unprofitable
speculation. You have no embarrassment about addressing
yourself to the task of doing all you can for the conversion of
one, respecting whom you are sure there is a predeterminate
purpose of God, while yet you know not, and cannot know,
what that purpose is. You set yourself to the work, because
what you do know of the nature of the danger and the method
of deliverance is sufficient to warrant reasonable hope, and to
make exertion on his behalf, and the use of means, an anxious
labour indeed, but far from desperate. And what more is
needed in order to your praying for him ? You cannot but
desire his salvation, and assuredly, so long as he is spared, you
are not forbidden to desire it. And what is that very desire
itself but prayer ? Your "heart's desire," and therefore "your
prayer" for him, is that he may be saved (Rom. x. 1). Certainly Abraham stood on no other ground than you may
occupy, when he pleaded with God for the cities of the plain.
He was as ignorant as you are of the Lord's eternal decrees.
But he laid hold of the things revealed, as belonging to men

and to their children ; and therefore he longed, and, longing, he prayed that to each and all of the sojourners in the plain the long-suffering of God might yet in the end prove to be salvation (2 Pet. iii. 15).

Nor, secondly, does Abraham in this pleading arrogate any thing to himself. It is not an intercession on the ground of any merit of his own, or any title he may have to obtain favours for others. He does not ask the Lord, as for his sake, to spare or bless those for whom he prays. There is one in-tercessor alone to whom this is competent, the one only mediator between God and man, Jesus Christ the righteous. It is in a very different character, and in a very subordinate capacity, that Abraham ventures to plead for his fellow-sinners. "His goodness extendeth not to the Lord ;" "he is but dust and ashes." Nay, so far as he is himself personally concerned, he is lost and condemned. It is by grace alone, and through a righteousness not his own, that he has any footing at all in the favour and friendship of God. But the footing which he thus has is a very sure as well as a very exalted footing. He has "boldness and access, with confidence ;" he has liberty to converse with God familiarly as a friend ; and not for himself only, but for others, and indeed for all, to invoke the name of him whose "memorial to all generations" is this ;—" The Lord, the Lord God merciful and gracious, long-suffering, and abundant in goodness and truth ; keeping mercy for thousands, forgiving iniquity, transgression, and sin, and that will by no means clear the guilty " (Exod. xxxiv. 6, 7).

For, in the third place, Abraham's expostulation proceeds upon this name of the Lord ;—or in other words, upon the known character of God, and the known principles of his administration. Aspiring to no acquaintance with the secret decrees of God ;—and standing upon no claim of merit in himself ;—he has warrant enough for the earnestness of his intercessory pleading, in the broad general aspect of the nature and moral government of God, to which he

pointedly refers. He knows God as the just God and the
Saviour ; and on that twofold knowledge of God he builds his
argument.

1. "Is God unrighteous in taking vengeance ? " Far be
that thought from the devout and humble heart of believing
Abraham. He does not cherish the vain and presumptuous
notion on the strength of which not a few are inclined to
build their hope of an undefined measure of indulgence being
extended to the ungodly. They would oppose the infliction of
judgment altogether, as implying extreme severity and unreasonable harshness. Even Sodom, they think, may and ought
to be spared ; not for much good to be found in it, but because, after all, its wickedness is not so aggravated and inexcusable as to deserve so terrible a visitation. Much, or at
least something, may be said in palliation of the corruption of
its inhabitants ; and at the worst they have some redeeming
features. A merciful God may be expected to make some
allowances, and so far relent as to let them alone. In all such
pleadings there is a lurking disbelief of the righteousness of
God—an impeachment of the rectitude of his judgments—
an entire want of sympathy with that holiness which sin
offends, and that sovereign authority which sin sets at
defiance. Are such pleaders and plausible reasoners as these,
such smooth apologists of evil, with their feeble condemnation of God's enemies, and their sensitive recoil from the
idea of God's wrath coming down upon them ;—are they
indeed his friends ? Are they on the Lord's side ? Not
such is the spirit of Abraham. He acquiesces in the destruction of the wicked ; he acknowledges the righteousness
of the Judge of all the earth ; he is aware that judgment is
inevitable. Nor does the thought offend him. It is not from
any complacency towards the wicked, or any indifference to
the just claims of God, that he would have Sodom spared.
Let the wicked perish, rather than the divine justice be im-
peached. "Let God be true, but every man a liar ; as it is

written, that thou mightest be justified in thy sayings, and mightest overcome when thou art judged" (Rom. iii. 4).

2. What, then, precisely is his plea? On what is it that he rests his hope in these plaintive intercessory petitions?— "Wilt thou also destroy the righteous with the wicked? Peradventure there be fifty righteous within the city : wilt thou also destroy and not spare the place for the fifty righteous that are therein? That be far from thee to do after this manner, to slay the righteous with the wicked : and that the righteous should be as the wicked, that be far from thee" (ver. 23-25). What is it that he is so anxious about in this earnest pleading? Is it merely the temporal destruction of the righteous who may be in Sodom that Abraham deprecates so pathetically —their being involved in the judgment of fire which was to overtake the devoted city? Doubtless that is an evil against which, on behalf of his godly neighbours, the friend of God does well to pray. The desolating march of God's ministers of wrath here below,—the devouring fire and the raging storm,—war, pestilence, and famine,—cannot but affect most grievously the faithful people of God, who may be dwelling among the objects of his just indignation. And on that ground alone may one interceding for them desire and ask the suspension or removal of such wide-sweeping calamities impending over the cities of their habitation. But the righteous, after all, whatever may come upon the wicked, and however they may suffer along with them for a season, are safe in the end. It is not for their sakes chiefly that delay of the threatened doom, and a lengthened season of gracious forbearance, are to be sought. At any rate, Abraham's petition goes far beyond the mere exemption of the righteous from temporary suffering and trial. That might have been accomplished in another way than the one which he points out;—as ultimately it was accomplished by the deliverance of Lot. Such a manner, however, of saving the righteous from the evil to come, does not occur to Abraham ; not even when, in the progress of his singular

expostulation, he assumes, at every stage, a more desperate
case ;—not even then, does it enter into his mind as a last
resource—a final alternative. He does not so much as put it
forward as a forlorn hope. To the last, he is bent upon the
intercepting of the judgment altogether—the sparing of the
guilty thousands, in consideration of the ten righteous men
who may be found among them.

For he has got hold of that grand principle of the moral
administration of God, as applicable to this fallen, but not
irrecoverably fallen, world, that the righteous "are the salt of
the earth." He has learned the lesson which the parable of
the tares was intended to teach. So long as God may have a
single stalk of wheat in the field, which might be lost and
confounded among the tares in their premature destruction—
so long as he may have a single little one not yet gathered to
himself from among the crowd of the ungodly—so long as the
mass is not so hopelessly corrupt and putrid, but that the
savour of one holy man's zeal and love may yet keep some
small portion of it from decay—so long God will spare the
most abandoned city, and will not sweep the earth with his
besom of destruction. On this assurance Abraham plants his
foot. From this high ground he makes his assault, as it were,
knocking at the door of Heaven's mercy, and importunately
besieging the throne of Him who "would have all men every
where to be saved." Spare Sodom for fifty. Spare it for
forty-five. Spare it for thirty. Spare it for twenty. Spare
it even for ten. Why should even ten of thy children be partakers, though but as it were in passing, in so terrible a desolation ? And why should even Sodom, with all the greatness
of its cry, and all the unutterable enormities of its miserable
inhabitants, be given over as desperate while ten righteous men
are in it ? Are there still ten who " sigh and who cry for all
the abominations that are done in the midst of the city ?"
Are there " a few names, even in Sardis, who have not defiled
their garments ?" Let honour be put on these ;—a remnant,

a mere handful though they be. Let the salt, if it have not wholly lost its savour, still for a time season the mass. Let the light still shine. It may be, that even Sodom, through the continued shining of the light, be it ever so faint and flickering, may yet ere long turn to the Lord.

Such is the principle of Abraham's intercession for Sodom. And as it is founded on a right understanding of the nature and design of God's moral government of the world, so in the fourth place, it is combined with a spirit of entire submission to the divine sovereignty. Abraham's petition is persevering and importunate ; but all throughout he is most anxious to disclaim every thought of interfering with the supreme will of God; every idea of casting an imputation on his perfect equity and justice, or challenging his right to do whatever may seem to him good. The growing earnestness and intensity, we might almost say impatience, of his pleading, is tempered by a profound sense of the liberty he is taking, and a salutary fear of offending. In the very presence-chamber of God himself, speaking to him as a man speaks to his friend, he does not forget his own position ; he is but dust and ashes ; while God is the Judge of all the earth. He is sure that God will deal righteously and do right. He puts away, as repugnant to God's character, as well as to his own feelings, the very idea of the righteous and the wicked being placed on an equality : "Be it far from thee, Lord." He knows that that is, and must be, far from the Lord. Whatever may be the issue, he is sure that this will be made manifest, not perhaps in the very way he would suggest, but in the way most glorifying to God, and ultimately most satisfying to all who are his friends. Hence, in the end, he is contented with an answer, which, after all, seems to leave the matter still in doubt. In the holy boldness of his pleading—his bargaining, we might almost call it, with the Lord—he has brought him down to the very lowest point ;—" I will not destroy it for ten's sake" (ver. 32). And there he is satisfied to rest. He receives no explicit reply,—nothing beyond a general explanation and assurance; he asks no more; he commits all to God. If it be possible, he now clearly sees, the judgment will pass from Sodom. But the Lord's will be done. The case may be so aggravated and so hopeless, as to preclude the possibility of longer forbearance; —as was the case of the city, respecting which the Lord said by the mouth of Ezekiel (xiv. 14), "Though these three men, Noah, Daniel, and Job, were in it, they should deliver but their own souls by their righteousness;" or the people to whom he spoke by the mouth of Jeremiah (xv. 1), "Though Moses and Samuel stood before me, yet my mind could not be toward this people; cast them out of my sight, and let them go forth." Still the friend of God has discharged his own conscience and unburthened his soul. And with God, whom he has been addressing so confidingly as a friend, he confidingly leaves his cause.

And now, the Lord having communed with Abraham as his friend, and "gone his way," Abraham "returns unto his place" (ver. 33). With so many tokens of the divine friendship, he may well return in peace. He may well use the language of gratitude, "Return unto thy rest, O my soul, for the Lord hath dealt bountifully with thee" (Ps. cxvi. 7). Yes. For he has been enabled virtually, in faith, to use the language of submission—"Father, if it be possible, let the cup pass. Nevertheless, Father, not my will but thine be done."

Altogether this divine friendship has in it passages of most wonderful grace. 1. The Lord has condescended to visit Abraham on terms of very intimate familiarity,—accepting a common office of kindness, and sharing his simple and homely noonday meal. 2. He has blessed, by his presence, Abraham's heart and home; searching out, indeed, hidden unbelief, as well as timid, faithless guile;—but yet speaking a word in season;—speaking comfortably, speaking peace. 3. He has not hid from Abraham the thing he is doing.

He has made him acquainted with his judgments, that in the day of calamity his own soul may not be overwhelmed,—and that, knowing the terror of the Lord, he may persuade men. And (4.) he has permitted the patriarch to unburthen his soul, by pouring out his desires on behalf of the godly remnant in the midst of an ungodly city, as well as on behalf of the ungodly city itself.

Are not these the very privileges of that friendship in which we may rest and rejoice,—friendship with the same Lord who thus treated Abraham as his friend? Let us hear his own word :—"Ye are my friends if ye do whatsoever I command you." We are his friends, on the very same ground on which Abraham was called his friend, and to the very same effect. "Henceforth, I call you not servants; for the servant knoweth not what his lord doeth: but I have called you friends; for all things that I have heard of my Father I have made known unto you" (John xv. 15).

23

THE GODLY SAVED, YET SO AS BY FIRE; THE
WICKED UTTERLY DESTROYED

Genesis 19:1-26

If the righteous scarcely be saved, where shall the ungodly and the sinner
appear? I Peter 4:18

THE catastrophe recorded in this chapter is typical of the
final judgment of the world; while at the same time it
illustrates the principles of the divine administration, as connected with that solemn procedure. In both views, the
narrative is referred to and commented upon, not only by
our Lord in his discourse upon the downfall of Jerusalem,
but by the apostle Peter also, in his warning to the church
respecting the last times. In that warning he emphatically
quotes as a precedent this very visitation; briefly summing
up the lesson which it teaches;—"The Lord knoweth how
to deliver the godly out of temptations, and to reserve the
unjust unto the day of judgment to be punished" (2 Pet. ii.
6-9).

The expression, "the Lord knoweth how to deliver the
godly out of temptations" is very emphatical and comprehensive. He can, and he will deliver them; he is sure
to deliver them; and his deliverance of them will be in
a way of his own,—by mingled mercies and judgments, "by
terrible -things in righteousness." But while he is delivering
them, he keeps the wicked in reserve for final condemnation.

So the Lord "delivered just Lot." "He knew how to

deliver him;" the deliverance was of the Lord alone, and it was in a way of his own. This may be seen in several particulars connected with the preliminaries, the substance, and the sequel, of the great work achieved.

I. Among the preliminaries of the deliverance I notice first, what is implied in the very name given to Lot by the apostle. That, in the midst of all the ungodliness and iniquity of Sodom, Lot might still be characterised as "godly" and "just,"—is itself a remarkable proof that "the Lord knoweth how to deliver."

When Lot chose to dwell among the cities of the plain, he seems to have acted under the influence of worldly motives, and in the full knowledge that the people with whom he must associate "were wicked before the Lord, and sinners exceedingly." The well-watered valley of the Jordan, and the flourishing cities which already crowned its banks, attracted his longing eye. He would multiply his flocks amid the fertile fields round Sodom; and in Sodom itself his character and wealth might procure for him a name. Thus he ventured to come into contact with the world. That he suffered from the contact, in respect of his personal religion, is but too probable, or rather certain, as this very narrative proves. That he did not suffer more, was of the Lord's undeserved mercy. He has now been many years in Sodom; and he is still the godly, the just Lot.

How has he escaped the contamination? What is the sure sign that he has escaped it, as well as the explanation of his escape? What is the testimony of the Holy Ghost? He was "vexed with the filthy conversation of the wicked: for that righteous man dwelling among them, in seeing and hearing, vexed his righteous soul from day to day with their unlawful deeds" (2 Pet. ii. 7, 8). That was his security; he retained his spiritual discernment, his spiritual taste. He loved not them that hated the Lord; he had no sympathy with their ungodliness. He did not learn to palliate or excuse, either their unholy opinions or their unlawful deeds,—to call them by smooth names, affect a soft and serene charity, and hope the best even of the world lying in wickedness. He was vexed,—he vexed himself. The English word here is too weak by far. He was wearied, worn out, worn down, by the impieties with which the lawless were conversant. They were an intolerable burden to him. Thus the Lord knew how to deliver him, by keeping alive in his soul, amid abounding iniquity, an undiminished zeal for truth and righteousness, and an uncompromising hatred of all evil.

II. Secondly, That on the eve of this dread catastrophe, Lot is found in the way of duty, is a farther proof and illustration of the fact, that "the Lord knoweth how to deliver the godly out of temptations."

When the two angels came to Sodom at even, Lot was sitting in the gate of the city (ver. 1). As Abraham, at noonday, ere he sat down to his meal,—so Lot, at night, ere he retired to rest, remained on the look-out for those who might need his hospitality. Especially, if any of the remnant of God's people, persecuted and homeless, should be passing through the accursed city, it was indeed a most essential service to intercept them at the gate, to prevent them from falling into the hands of the crowd, whose companions or whose victims it was alike fatal to become, and to give them the shelter of a roof beneath which the Lord was worshipped. Thus Lot was employed, when all the rest of the city were probably either sunk in slumber, or abandoned to riot. Had he been asleep, like the others, or had he been indulging in vain and sinful dissipation, he might have missed the visit of the friendly angels ; they might have passed by his house. For even when he actually accosted them with the frank offer of entertainment, they made as though they would have declined it (ver. 2, 3). They needed to be pressed. It was only to Lot's importunity that they yielded. For he was not merely willing to do good as he had opportunity; he did not wait for the opportunity; he sought it and was on the watch for it. And when it did occur, he would take no denial. Not in his own dwelling, but in the gate of the city he was on the watch; not on those who sought, but on those even who were most reluctant to receive it, would he force his kindness. He would suffer none to fall unawares into the snares of the wicked, but would compel all to come in, and share the homely fare of his table, and the holy worship of his family altar.

Nor was this an easy exercise of godly charity, or one implying little personal risk. He made his house a mark for the assaults of "the men of the city," who could scarce endure that so godly a man should dwell among them,—far less that he should reprove or restrain their sins. That fearful night tried both them and Lot. "The wicked plot against the just." Doubtless they have an old grudge to gratify. And now they seize the opportunity of at once indulging their passions, and wreaking their vengeance on one whose faithful testimony and consistent life they have found to be an intolerable offence and provocation (ver. 4-6). The man of God, meanwhile, all unconscious of the gathering storm, is enjoying the rich reward of his seasonable hospitality. He has made a feast for his unknown guests. To his surprise and delight, he discovers their holy character, perhaps also their heavenly rank. An hour is spent in quiet and blessed fellowship; the evening service of devotion is over; the family of the godly are preparing to lie down in peace. But there is no peace to the wicked; they are as the troubled sea that cannot rest. Thus the wild tumult rages all around, while the house of the man of God is as a little ark of safety. Once, indeed, even that sanctuary is almost violated. "Just Lot" is pressed, and wellnigh overpowered. He is shut up in a terrible perplexity. He would make a sad, a dreadful compromise (ver. 7, 8).

Are the ungodly then to triumph? Is Lot to sacrifice all

for the sake of these servants of God ? And to sacrifice all in vain ? (ver. 9).

Suddenly Lot is rescued, and the people are smitten. They grope in the darkness, and weary themselves for nought, while the household of the man of God may retire safely to repose. So " the Lord knoweth how to deliver the godly out of temptations;" so he confounds the designs of their enemies ; so " he giveth his beloved sleep " (ver. 10, 11).

III. In the third place, that Lot is willing, at this crisis, to be still a preacher of righteousness, is a further token of the Lord's hand in his deliverance. The faith which could move him to go forth on the errand on which the angels sent him, was manifestly the gift of God (ver. 12-14). Lot at once believes what the angels tell him ; and he is not afraid to avow his belief. He has often before warned the ungodly to flee from the wrath to come ; but " who has believed his report ? " " All day long he has stretched forth his hands to a disobedient and gainsaying people." And as their conversation has vexed him, so his interference has only served to irritate them. Even his own relatives and acquaintances,— the very men who are, or are to be, his sons-in-law,—to whom his daughters are married or betrothed,—are led astray with the error of the wicked. Where are they during this memorable night, when Lot is entertaining his holy guests, and the people have arisen in their fury against him ? Have they turned their backs on the dwelling of the righteous ? Are they keeping company with sinners ;—if not encouraging, at least not disowning their iniquity ? Well might Lot hesitate in these circumstances, however warm his natural affection, and however strong his sense of duty. Well might he be tempted to conclude, that having enough to do at home, he need not venture on a fruitless experiment abroad. It is incurring deadly risk in vain. For how can he expect to be believed, when he has so incredible a tale to tell ?

As yet the night is calm ;—no sign is there of the fiery

storm. The unbroken earth is reposing under the serene and starlit sky.

What does this dreamer mean with his dismal cry of woe? Our fathers lived and died in these cities, and all things continue as they were in their days.

So might the scoffers say; forgetting already, in their wilful ignorance, the watery foundation, and the watery fate, of that old world, which the flood swept away; and not considering what magazines of explosive fuel their sulphureous soil even now concealed, ready, on the touch of a single bolt of heavenly fire, to burst forth and devour them. So will the scoffers of all ages say, losing sight alike of the recorded instances of God's past judgments in history, and of the appalling signs and symptoms with which even the present economy of the world abounds, ominous of more terrible judgments yet to come. For in the elements of nature the Lord has instruments and materials of his vengeance, whether through flood or flame, always prepared; "fire and hail, snow and vapours, stormy wind fulfilling his word" (Ps. cxlviii. 8) And in the bowels of this globe, as in a deep and vast storehouse, there is matter in abundance, with volcanic agency enough, to involve the whole, at any moment, in one burning ruin.

But, as it will be in the end of the world, so was it in that catastrophe by which the end of the world was foreshadowed. The crowded thousands in these cities, all unconscious of the charged mine on which they stood, laughed to scorn the voice of warning. But the godly man who uttered it lost not his reward. "Their blood was on their own heads; they died in their iniquities." But "he delivered his own soul."

IV. Coming now from the preliminaries of the deliverance to the actual deliverance itself, I remark,—in the fourth place, that the haste, the friendly violence, the stern command with which Lot was hurried out of the city, and on to the moun-

tain, are unequivocal marks of this deliverance being the
Lord's (ver. 15-17). For there is scarcely any surer or more
characteristic sign of the Lord's manner of delivering the
godly out of temptation than this. He uses a constraining
force, and teaches them to use it. The kingdom of heaven is
taken by violence.

For, first, he rouses them betimes, and hastens them to
depart, on pain of instant destruction (ver. 15). Again, when
they loiter and linger, loath to leave all the world behind, he
constrains, and, as it were, compels them (ver. 16). Nor will
he suffer them so much as to look back or to pause ; onwards,
still onwards, for your lives, is his word (ver. 17). Thus decisive and peremptory is the Lord's dealing with those whom
he would save. But it is not more peremptory than the case
requires.

1. To snatch a brand from the burning—to apprehend a
soul just about to be consumed with the wicked—to get Lot
out of Sodom—to bring you, brother, out of Babylon—
demands not a soft and gentle touch, but a prompt, powerful,
and commanding grasp. "When the morning arose, the
angels hastened Lot" (ver. 15).

Are you in danger of perishing in the midst of those on
whom the wrath of God lies? Are you entangled in the
world's friendship, and is the world swiftly to be judged?
Is the morning almost already risen—the morning of the
judgment day? And are you still to be delivered? Is "the
harvest past,—the summer ended,—and you not saved?" What
time is this for delicacy and dalliance—that your couch should
be very cautiously approached, and your rest very softly and
smoothly broken, lest some pleasing dream should be too
rudely interrupted, and the shock of an abrupt awakening
should ruffle and discompose you! And, when you open your
drowsy eyes, and listlessly catch the hasty summons to arise,
—will you still complain that it is too soon to be up, murmuring your sluggish wish—"yet a little sleep, a little slumber?"

Bless the Lord, if in such a crisis he has not taken you at your word, and let you alone, as you desired him to do; if he leaves you not to repose, but cuts short your half-waking and dreamy musing; if he " hastens you." " Awake! Arise! Lest thou be consumed in the iniquity of the city! "

2. But, when all is ready, and you are now at the very point to flee, do you linger still? Is there a moment's halting —a moment's hesitation? Are you wavering? Are you undecided? It is Satan's golden opportunity. Another instant of doubt or of deliberation, and you are lost.

Bless the Lord again,—who, being merciful to you, seizes you by the hand, and, scarce allowing you time to think, brings you quickly forth, and sets you without the city! " While he lingered, the men laid hold upon his hand; the Lord being merciful unto him; and they brought him forth, and set him without the city" (ver. 16). Oh, how many of God's people have found and felt,—in the very act of their turning their back on an evil world, and quitting its snares for ever,—a kind of infatuation or spell coming over them;— like that fatal torpor, which, creeping upon the frozen limbs of the wanderer amid the snows, tempts him to lie down for a seductive rest! Were there but a companion near, to take him at that critical moment by the hand, the doomed man might be made to move on; his lethargic apathy would be shaken off. Let but a few paces be briskly traversed, and he would be safe. So God apprehends the fugitives from Sodom, when he sees them lingering. He constrains them to make a movement in advance. Let but one decided effort be made— one irrevocable step taken, under the leading of God's providence, and by the power of his word and Spirit—and the Rubicon is crossed; the better part is chosen; the city of iniquity is finally forsaken.

3. Is there, after all this, danger still? Have the fugitives not escaped? May they not conclude that all is safe? Alas, no! They have escaped indeed, but how narrowly!—

by what a hair's-breadth! And they must make good their escape; they must "make their calling and election sure." Moved and led by heavenly power, they have been brought forth, and set without the city. But the command still is, " Escape for thy life;" and the warning is, "Look not behind thee, neither stay thou in all the plain" (ver. 17).

But may not the exile, now that he is fairly out of the city, relax his speed, and proceed a little more leisurely? May he not cast his eye once more on the scene he is forsaking, and indulge one last, lingering, farewell look? At his peril be it if he do. One who should have shared his flight to the last has tried the experiment. She cleaves to her old home; she loves the world, and in the world's swift judgment she is miserably engulphed. " His wife looked back from behind him, and she became a pillar of salt" (ver. 26). One look behind is fatal; to pause is ruin.

Who is there who has been persuaded and enabled to come out from among the ungodly,—escaping the corruption that is in the world through lust? " Remember Lot's wife." Say not, Let me go and bury my father,—let me return to bid farewell to my friends,—but one more embrace, but one more look! Tempt not the Lord. He who says, " Follow me," utters also these solemn words:—" No man having put his hand to the plough, and looking back, is fit for the kingdom of God." " If any man draw back, my soul shall have no pleasure in him." Be not " of them who draw back unto perdition, but of them that believe to the saving of the soul." And let the voice of Him who has led you forth ring continually in your ears;—" Escape still for thy life;"—" Look not behind thee, neither stay thou in all the plain."

V. In the last place, one other feature of this deliverance, and of the manner of it, is to be noticed, as especially marking it to be of the Lord. Not only is the sovereignty of the Lord manifest in the very peremptory tone of authority, as well as in the constraining hand of power, which, in a manner, force

Lot out of Sodom;—the grace of the Lord also remarkably appears in the seasonable personal interview vouchsafed to him, and the tender and paternal solicitude evinced for his immediate comfort, not less than for his final safety. For the Lord manifests himself to Lot in another way than he does unto the world,—in a way of peculiar favour,—listening to his remonstrance and conceding his request (ver. 18-21).

That it is the Lord himself who now confers with Lot, may be fairly gathered from the use of the singular pronoun instead of the plural, indicating the presence of one distinct from the " two men," or angels, who at first ministered to him, —as well as also from the style of Lot's address, and of this divine person's reply. Lot speaks to him as to the Supreme God, and in that character also he speaks to Lot ; taking upon himself the divine prerogatives of accepting the person of the godly, hearing his prayer, and determining the time of judgment on the wicked. Thus it would seem that he who had remained behind with Abraham, while his two attendants went on to Sodom, now himself appears again to take part in the awful scene. For his elect's sake he comes ; and amid the terrors of that dark day he is welcome.

1. Lot stands accepted before him, and boldly pleads his privilege of justification ; " Behold now, thy servant hath found grace in thy sight, and thou hast magnified thy mercy, which thou has showed unto me in saving my life " (ver. 19). He is " strong in faith, giving glory to God." And to what does he look as the ground of his confident assurance ? Simply to that rich mercy which God has magnified on his behalf, and that great salvation which God has wrought for him. The acceptance, the justification, on which he relies, is altogether gratuitous and free. It is of the Lord's mercy that he is not consumed. By grace he is saved ; by grace " his heart is established." He has lost his all ; his corn and wine no longer abound ; his fondest earthly hopes are blighted, and his dearest affections torn. Still, amid dreariness and desola-

tion, he can appeal to God and say,—" I have found grace in
thy sight, and thou hast magnified thy mercy in saving me."
The light of God's countenance shines upon him ; his Redeemer, his Saviour, is with him ; and that is enough.   He
believes ; and he has peace in believing.   " Although the fig-
tree shall not blossom, neither shall fruit be in the vines ; the
labour of the olives shall fail, and the fields shall yield no
meat : the flock shall be cut off from the fold, and there shall
be no herd in the stalls : yet I will rejoice in the Lord, I will
joy in the God of my salvation" (Hab. iii. 17, 18).

2. Nor is this all. His Saviour is one who is touched with
a feeling of his infirmities, and will not refuse his prayer.
" Lord, I believe, help thou mine unbelief," is, after all, the
best profession for a feeble soul to make.   The faith of Lot,
simple and sincere as it was, could not be considered perfect ;
he had his misgivings and doubts.   The distance and danger
of the refuge whither he had to flee, filled him with anxiety
and alarm ;—" I cannot escape to the mountain, lest some evil
take me, and I die" (ver. 19).   Might no nearer, no safer, no
less dreary shelter be found ?   It is hard to be all at once cast
out upon the solitary wild.   Such thoughts vexed the rescued
soul of Lot.   But in the Lord he found relief.   He did not
nurse these melancholy musings sullenly and suspiciously in
his own bosom.   He poured them forth into the ears of the
Lord.   With humble and holy boldness he ventured to represent his case to a present and sympathising God ;—to plead, to
reason, to expostulate,—with a touching and pathetic, a childlike earnestness, such as only the spirit of adoption, the spirit
that cries Abba Father, could inspire ;—" Behold now, this city
is near to flee unto, and it is a little one : Oh, let me escape
thither (is it not a little one ?) and my soul shall live" (ver. 20).
The appeal was not in vain.   He who knows our frame was not
offended by the liberty which his servant took ;—" See, I have
accepted thee concerning this thing also, that I will not overthrow this city, for the which thou has spoken" (ver. 21).

The boon, indeed, though granted, would, as the Lord knew well, stand Lot in little stead. The ruin of the cities was to be so much more appalling in reality than imagination could anticipate, that even Zoar would soon be felt to be unsafe, and Lot himself would be glad at last to escape to the mountain (ver. 30). It is possible that, foreseeing this, the Lord granted merely a temporary respite to this little city; which, indeed, was all that Lot's petition required. But at all events, how graciously was that petition heard, even though it might seem needless and unavailing in the end! As a temporary halting-place, at the least, for the harassed pilgrim, it was a seasonable act of kindness to spare the little city,—an act which stands as a signal instance of the Lord's care, not merely for the final salvation of his people, but for their refreshment and consolation by the way,—like the washing of the disciples' feet, as preparatory to the hard pilgrimage on which he is about to send them.

Thus always, in little as well as greater matters, we may see the Lord's goodness in the land of the living. Even at the worst, the world is not all barren. In the most sweeping desolation, levelling the houses and cities of our habitation to the ground,—in the wide waste beneath which all things bright and fair seem buried,—some little Zoar is left, some haven of rest in which the weary spirit may recruit its strength. Such earthly refreshment the redeemed child of God, who has turned his back on Sodom, may lawfully ask,—such green spot in the desert,—such little city of refuge amid the storm ;—in the bosom of domestic peace, and the endearments of a quiet home ;—that he may not be tried above measure. Only let his request be moderate ; " See now it is a little one,—is it not a little one?" Let it also be a request offered in faith, as to a friend and father, with submission to his wisdom and trust in his love. And if the request be granted,—if the object of his fond regard, for which he speaks, be spared to him,—if he get a little Zoar to flee to,—let him not set his heart on it too much. For a brief space he may rejoice in it ; but let him be ready to quit it soon, as Lot did, and if need be, to dwell in the mountain and in the cave. That may be the Lord's way of thoroughly humbling and proving him, for the very purpose of his salvation being seen to be all of grace.

3. For yet, once more, the Lord has a sad lesson to teach the patriarch,—that it is not merely deliverance from Sodom, whether in Zoar or in the mountain, that he really needs, but deliverance from himself. For, alas ! after all, what security is there either in Zoar or in the mountain,—what shelter from fear,—what safeguard against the assaults of sin ? Even in Zoar fear overtook the patriarch ; and as to the mountain, the shameful incident with which this affecting narrative closes is on record to teach a bitter but a salutary truth.

Let not him who is a fugitive from Sodom ever lay aside his watchfulness, or abandon his attitude of onward and hasty flight. A moment's relaxation of his vigilance,—and Satan has him at an advantage ; all the more in consequence of the excitement of his recent deliverance, and the calm seclusion of his present solitary retreat. Neither his experience of the Lord's salvation, nor his entire separation from worldly temptations, will of itself avail him. Rescued from the world's doom, driven forth from its vain joys, amid such touching mercies and such desolating judgments,—surely his heart will be all the Lord's ! Alas ! that a man's worst enemies should be those of his own household. His own flesh and blood,—the sole surviving pledges of his past love and partners of his present sorrow,—his most cherished earthly treasures—moved, not indeed by horrid passion, but by a carnal policy,—having recourse to devices of their own, instead of leaving all to that God who has already done so much for them—his own daughters betray him into foul sin, and transmit his dishonoured name as a beacon of warning, if not a byword of infamy, to all coming generations.

Strange and startling issue of so wonderful an interposition on the part of God ! And yet it is the very issue fitted to crown the whole deliverance, and prove it to have been the Lord's. "By terrible things in righteousness " God answers the prayers of his people. And especially when the risk they run is of their own seeking,—as it was in the case of Lot,—the escape is literally like the plucking of a brand out of the burning, or the rescue of a sinking disciple out of the waves of the stormy deep. Is the brand plucked out of the burning to have no singe upon it ? Is the disciple rescued from the waves to have no damp cleaving to his garments ? Can Lot come out of Sodom,—even by a Divine interposition,—untainted by its lusts ?

The whole history of Lot is a precious lesson to the humble believer, whatever ground of triumph it may give to the proud scoffer. And it is a lesson to the one, in the very particulars in which it is a cause of boasting to the other. That a godly man should have volunteered to be a resident in Sodom—and upon such manifestly worldly considerations—is enough to win a smile from the profane, while it costs the pious a tear. That in his very escape out of Sodom's doom, he should show the taint of Sodom's foul fellowship—may turn the sneering smile into a broad laugh on the one hand. But, on the other hand, will it not deepen the pious tear into a gush of inward conviction—prompting the eager cry—"Cleanse me, O Lord, from secret faults ! " " Who shall deliver me from the body of this death ?" " Create in me a clean heart, O Lord, and renew a right spirit within me."

THE SEQUEL OF THE DELIVERANCE

The end of this whole transaction is the destruction of the ungodly. During the process of delivering just Lot, they are " reserved ;" the sentence impending over them is suspended. But it is suspended only that the godly may be delivered—

and it is suspended only until they are delivered. Hear the amazing words—"I cannot do any thing till thou be come thither" (ver. 22)—marvellous words of grace to the godly! But how terrible as words of wrath to the wicked! For, mark the terrible announcement—"The sun was risen upon the earth when Lot entered into Zoar" (ver. 23). It is the signal for the punishment to begin. Up to this point the doomed people have dwelt securely, reckoning on all things continuing as they are. The voice of the preacher, indeed— perhaps also that of the magistrate (if Lot ever held such an office)—has been testifying to the last against them ; and, on the very eve before their doom, the hand of God himself, smiting them in the act of sin, may well warn them to beware. But to-morrow, they say, shall be as this day, and much more abundantly. Day after day has the sun shone upon them in his splendour, and the shades of evening have gathered peacefully over them. What idle rumour is this, as if the sun were not to rise on the morrow ?

The sun, indeed, rose on the morrow. But he was just " risen on the earth when Lot entered into Zoar."

Then comes the end ; the judgment for which the wicked have been reserved ; inevitable and inexorable. For this is the manner of God. Long time his hand seems to tremble, as if he were reluctant to strike. But he is waiting for the day—the fixed and appointed day. So soon as that day's sun is risen on the earth, the stroke descends. And, when it does de- scend, it is with terrible decision. There is no relenting then ; no apparent hesitation ; no more tender reasoning with himself—" How shall I give thee up, Ephraim ? How shall I deliver thee, Israel?" The Lord waits long to be gracious, as if he knew not how to smite. He smites at last as if he knew not how to pity.

For he is the Lord ;—he changes not. He changes not, either in his purpose of saving love, or in his purpose of right- eous retribution. Not in mere weak and fond compassion does he spare the guilty—but on a set plan of righteousness—for a set end—during a set time. And not in sudden anger,—but in the terrible calmness of deliberate judgment,—he awards the punishment to which they are reserved. Up to the very moment when the day of grace is expired, all things continue as they were ; it would seem as if neither earth nor heaven were ever to be shaken. " But the sun is risen on the earth, when Lot enters into Zoar ;" and then comes the end.

Into the details of the catastrophe, it is not my purpose to enter. It may have been brought about in a great measure by the agency of natural causes—by the electric flash, perhaps, and sulphureous and volcanic explosions. The miracle of wrath lay in the foresight and adaptation of all the physical as well as the moral circumstances of the scene, for the accomplishment of the will of God.

It is a scene to be repeated, on a vastly enlarged scale, at the end of the world. For, " as it was in the days of Lot, they did eat, they drank, they bought, they sold, they planted, they builded ; but the same day that Lot went out of Sodom, it rained fire and brimstone from heaven, and destroyed them all ; even thus shall it be in the day when the Son of Man is revealed" (Luke xvii. 28-30). And what will all their vain expedients for dissipating thought and pacifying conscience avail the unjust then ? They have " lived in pleasure on the earth, and been wanton ; they have nourished their hearts as in the day of slaughter." They have been reserved unto that day ; shut up, so that none can escape.

Viewed thus, what a spectacle does the ungodly world present ! A pen in which sheep are making themselves fat for the slaughter—a place of confinement—a condemned cell —in which sentenced prisoners are shut up—sinners held fast in the hands of an angry God !

In that final catastrophe also, as in this type of it, a refuge is provided for the godly. The Lord himself comes, and the dead in Christ rise, and the living are changed. Together they are " caught up to meet him in the air." And then, but not before, " the heavens shall pass away with a great noise, and the elements shall melt with fervent heat ; the earth also, and the works that are therein, shall be burned up."

But not as with the cities of the plain is it to be with the world then. The desolation is not perpetual. No Dead Sea, no unwholesome lake, remains as a monument of the terrible doom. "Behold new heavens and a new earth, wherein dwelleth righteousness,"—wherein the righteous dwell for ever with their righteous King. "Behold the tabernacle of God is with men, and he will dwell with them, and they shall be his people, and God himself shall be with them, and be their God. And God shall wipe away all tears from their eyes ; and there shall be no more death, neither sorrow, nor crying, neither shall there be any more pain : for the former things are passed away."

24

THE IMPRESSION OF THE SCENE WHEN ALL IS OVER

Genesis 19:27-29

Thou shalt not be afraid for the terror by night ; nor for the arrow that
flieth by day ; nor for the pestilence that walketh in darkness ; nor
for the destruction that wasteth at noonday. A thousand shall fall at
thy side, and ten thousand at thy right hand ; but it shall not come
nigh thee. Only with thine eyes shalt thou behold and see the
reward of the wicked. Psalm 91:5-8

THE deliverance of Lot, amid the ruins of Sodom, is specially
connected with the favour God had for Abraham ; " And it
came to pass, when God destroyed the cities of the plain, that
God remembered Abraham, and sent Lot out of the midst of
the overthrow, when he overthrew the cities in the which Lot
dwelt " (ver. 29).

The patriarch, let it be remembered, was at this time living
within a few hours' distance of the devoted cities ;—probably
within sight of them. Of the three divine guests who rested
with him at noon, two were at the gate of Sodom before
evening—having gone thither, as we are led to believe, in the
guise and at the common pace of ordinary travellers. The
third, who remained behind, and who turned out to be the
Lord himself, conversed with Abraham, on a spot at a little
distance from his tent, overlooking the plain which was so
soon to be laid waste. To this spot, where he had " stood
before the Lord," Abraham betakes himself early in the morning. And what a sight meets his eye ? " He looked toward

Sodom and Gomorrah, and toward all the land of the plain, and beheld, and, lo, the smoke of the country went up as the smoke of a furnace" (ver. 27, 28).

What desolation has the Lord wrought on the earth! The fertile and smiling fields are as one vast furnace ; a noxious sulphureous vapour clouds all the sky. Of the cities which but yesternight were thronged with countless thousands of thoughtless sinners, not a trace remains. So sure, so sudden, so terrible, is this judgment of the Lord. Has Abraham been indulging some vague and uncertain hope—as if the threatened doom might yet be averted—as if, when the hour came, the Lord might relent ? One glance in the early morning puts to flight the imagination.

It is hard, even for God's faithful people, to realise the certainty and the terror of his coming wrath on the children of disobedience ; it demands a certain unquestioning and uncompromising loyalty, to which it is difficult indeed to attain. To sympathise with God in his purpose of judgment ;—to recognise the righteousness of the doom he inflicts, with feelings free from all alloy of vindictive satisfaction or personal revenge ;—is no easy exercise of faith. Even they who, on their own account, have no longer any interest in deceiving themselves on this point, are too prone to do so on account of others. For it is a coarse and senseless imputation which is sometimes cast on the people of God, when it is alleged that the comfortable sense of their being themselves safe may make them look with great complacency or indifference on the doom of their neighbours who are lost. The real tendency of their hearts—the actual temptation to which they are liable—is precisely the reverse. In their own experience,—taught by a quickened conscience—and the Spirit convincing them of sin, of righteousness, and of judgment,— in their own apprehension, they know the terror of the Lord so well,—so vividly do they realise his terrible indignation against all iniquity,—that they almost shrink from the thought of any one of their fellow-creatures enduring even the convictions to which they have themselves been subjected. Much more do they recoil from the idea of his suffering what these convictions foreshadow and foretell—the gnawing of the worm that never dies, and the burning of the fire that never can be quenched.

Little do the scoffers know of the deep movements of a believer's soul, when they would represent him as exulting over the world that knows not God, or feeling anything in the least like a zest or relish in the anticipation of its fate. In point of fact, he is in nothing more apt to yield to his evil heart of unbelief than in the cherishing of a kind of latent incredulity respecting the punishment of the ungodly. He can scarcely think so very badly of them,—adorned as they may be with many amiable and friendly qualities,— as to be quite satisfied that they must inevitably perish. He would fain persuade himself that judgment will not be so inexorable and severe. He cannot bring himself to conceive of their being all—in one common ruin—swept remorselessly away. Thus even the friend of God, in the tenderness of his heart, may be tempted to feel; and this lurking feeling tends sadly to lower the tone of his own piety, as well as to enfeeble the voice of his testimony against the world's sin, and his pleading for the salvation of the sinner's soul.*

It is good for him, therefore, to gaze on the desolation of that smoking plain. How many fond surmises—how many indistinct and half-unconscious presumptions respecting God's indiscriminate clemency—how many relenting emotions of false pity and false hope—what deceitful pleadings for ungodliness—what inclinations towards the palliating or justifying of evil—what notions of sin's possible impunity and the relaxing of judgment at the last hour—notions most dangerous alike to the cultivation of personal holiness

* See *Exposition of the First Epistle of John*, Lecture 13.

and the discharge of the public duty of rebuke and persuasion,—does that one glance dissipate and dispel for ever!

Does Abraham retire to rest at night, tempted, in spite of all that he has heard of Sodom's intolerable wickedness and the Lord's stern purpose of wrath, still to entertain the fancy that the case of these sinners may not be, after all, so very bad, and judgment may not be so very terrible and so very near? Does he go out in the morning to the spot where, on the previous day, the Lord had communed with him on this very subject, almost expecting to see the green valleys smiling and the lofty turrets shining, as of old, in the sun's rising splendour? A single look is enough. Too surely does he see that the Lord's word is true; that judgment is certain; that "it is a fearful thing to fall into the hands of the living God."

There is a spectacle in this view more solemn still. It is the cross of our Lord and Saviour Jesus Christ. The judgment which took effect and was executed upon him is the most affecting of all proofs of the severity of God;—the only proof that will silence every misgiving, and awe into submission every lax and rebellious thought of the evil heart of unbelief. If ever the friend of God is conscious of an inclination to yield to the insidious suggestion of a sentimental pietism and spurious charity—to think that, after all, there may be no such wide separation between the godly and the unjust—between the Lord's people and the world from which they have come out—and that possibly, in the end, there may be no necessity for the actual infliction, on all who will not come to Christ that they may be saved, of so terrible a sentence as that of eternal death;—if ever any follower of Jesus detects himself thus falling into the vague reasonings of carnal wisdom, and beginning to confound the essential distinctions alike of the law and the gospel,—to become the apologist of them that hate God, and to question even the

word of the Most High, which dooms the wicked to hell;—
let him go out betimes in the morning. Let him take his
stand on an eminence—apart, by himself alone. Let him behold and see,—not a smoking plain, filling the air with
unwholesome vapour,—but darkness on the face of the earth,
and amid the darkness, One who knows no sin pouring out
his soul unto the death for sin—the well-beloved Son of God
enduring the wrath of heaven! Then and there let him
learn a humbler, a sounder faith. What must that judgment
be from which the blood of Jesus alone could redeem! What
that aggravated doom which must inevitably await those who
crucify the Son of God afresh, and put him to open shame!
"If these things were done in the green tree, what must be
done in the dry?" (Luke xxiii. 31).

But in the midst of wrath the Lord remembers mercy.
The prayer of his friend and servant Abraham is not forgotten; it proves not to be unavailing. At first, indeed, it
might seem as if the only answer he was to receive was the
sight of this universal desolation. But let him look more narrowly, and he may see one little city exempted for a time
from the fiery storm. Let him wait a little, and tidings will
reach him of his friend's marvellous escape.

For Lot's sake, for the love and friendship he bore him,
Abraham had pleaded with the Lord, in earnest, repeated,
importunate supplication. He besought the Lord to spare
these cities, that the righteous might not be destroyed with
the wicked. He could think of no other way in which the
righteous could be saved, except by the wicked, among whom
they dwelt, and with whom they seemed to be mixed up,
being also spared along with them.

But "by terrible things in righteousness" the Lord
answers prayer. Abraham's kind interest in Lot is not in
vain, though what he asked on his behalf is not literally
granted. God did indeed, notwithstanding Abraham's plead-

ing, overthrow the cities of the plain in which Lot dwelt. But
" he remembered Abraham, and sent Lot out of the midst of
the overthrow." And Abraham, thus edified and comforted,
learns the blessed lesson that the Lord's ways are all just and
true ; for " the Lord knoweth how to deliver the godly out of
temptation," while " the unjust are reserved unto the day of
judgment to be punished."

25

CARNAL POLICY DEFEATED—EVIL OVERRULED FOR GOOD

Genesis 20; 21:22-33

A man's heart deviseth his way ; but the Lord directeth his steps.
Proverbs 16:9

For the rod of the wicked shall not rest upon the lot of the righteous ; lest
the righteous put forth their hands unto iniquity. Psalm 125:3

THE curtain has closed upon the tragical catastrophe of one
act in the divine drama; commencing with the first arrival of Abraham and Lot within the borders of Canaan, and
ending with the fatal storm that turned a smiling valley into
the Dead Sea. A new act is opened, when the curtain rises
again ; and alas ! it opens darkly.

The transition is marked by a removal, on the part of
Abraham, from the place where he had hitherto pitched his
tents ; he "journeyed from thence toward the south country,
and dwelt between Kadesh and Shur, and sojourned in Gerar"
(Gen. xx. 1). His change of residence was probably connected
with the terrible disaster which he had witnessed. It was
high time to move from the accursed neighbourhood, and it
was good for him to be reminded that he was but a pilgrim
in the land. He had now sojourned for many years in the
plains of Mamre (xiii. 18 ; xviii. 1), and he had seen much of
the Lord's goodness, as well as of the Lord's terror, there.
But still greater things await him ere his pilgrimage finally

closes. The last stage of his earthly journey is to be the most signally blessed and the most remarkably tried of all.

Over its commencement indeed there hangs a dark cloud, into which it would be painful, as well as unprofitable, to search too carefully. It is a repetition of the patriarch's previous sin, in connection with his wife (chap. xii.) ; and it is, therefore, all the more inexcusable. To account for his conduct, without at all extenuating it, some probable explanation may be gathered from the narrative.

I. In the progress of religious apostasy and corruption, a frightful dissolution of manners seems to have extensively overrun the nations ; and, in particular, the inhabitants of Palestine, or the land of Canaan. They had at first usurped possession of the land, contrary to the allotted plan of division announced in the days of Peleg (Gen. x. 25 ; Deut. xxxii. 8) ; and this very circumstance, vitiating their original title, may have led them all the more to cast aside the authority of God. At any rate, in Abraham's day, they were making fast progress to that excess of wickedness which was to justify their ultimate extermination. Abraham, therefore, might well expect to find the people, wherever he went,—not, perhaps, so flagrantly wicked as the dwellers in the cities of the plain,—yet at least so regardless as to warrant no confidence in their sense either of religion or of justice. The very fact of his imagining that he could defend his partner and himself in the character of a brother better than in that of a husband, speaks volumes. Under that impression Abraham acted. In this instance of Abimelech, as well as probably also in the previous case of Pharaoh, he was mistaken. He wronged Abimelech in thinking so ill of him ; and the king's warmth is good (ver. 9-10). As it proved, he might have been trusted ; and it would have been better for the patriarch if he had been less suspicious. Abraham might have believed and hoped that there were some in the world who had not lost all sense of rectitude and honour ; the judgment of charity would have been the judgment of safety. Still it is melancholy to observe that this is to be viewed as an exception. That the expedient to which Abraham had recourse should have been, on any occasion, thought necessary,—still more, that it should have been thought necessary, not once only, but repeatedly,—is a sad proof of the prevalence of that impious and lawless wickedness which, in the end, made the land "spue out" (Lev. xviii. 28) the nations which defiled it, that in terms of God's original purpose Abraham's posterity might possess it.

II. In accordance with this general impression as to the nations with whom his wandering life was to bring him into contact, the patriarch had adopted at the outset a general rule, which he explains to Abimelech : " I thought, Surely the fear of God is not in this place ; and they will slay me for my wife's sake ;" therefore, "when God caused me to wander from my father's house, I said unto her, This is thy kindness which thou shalt show unto me ; at every place whither we shall come, say of me, He is my brother" (ver. 11-13). This does not justify his evasive policy ; it rather aggravates it, as showing it to have been systematic and deliberate. But it explains the repetition of the incident, and the reason why a single check did not suffice to prevent it.

On the former occasion, the Lord did not expressly condemn Abraham, or explicitly forbid the offence of which he had been guilty. That he was virtually reproved, and in a way fitted to humble him to the dust, is plain enough ; but the reproof was indirect and inferential. For God does not rule believers by mere precepts and prohibitions, precisely and literally laid down. He " guides them with his eye." They are not " like the horse or the mule," who can be turned or restrained only by positive coercion—" by bit and bridle." They are expected to watch the very look of the Lord ; the eye with which he guides them ; any indication of his will which conscience, exercised in prayer upon the leadings of his providence, may give. Such is God's discipline of his people.

It is a discipline which hypocrites and formalists cannot understand ; a hint, therefore, is lost on them. And even on true believers, a hint is apt to be lost. They might often gather from circumstances what the Lord would have them to do ; as Abraham might have learned, from that previous incident, the lesson of straightforward and single-eyed simplicity in serving God. But it was an old preconcerted plan which would have been thus broken through ; and there was no specific injunction given. The patriarch was not alive and alert enough to note and be guided by the Lord's eye. In consequence, he was led to persevere in a practice evidently reproved by God, and to repeat conduct which the Lord had marked with his displeasure ;—conduct which all the rather should have been abandoned because the displeasure was indicated indirectly in a way so full of grace and kindness. This want of discernment, this failure in the watchful docility and tact which ought to characterise the walk of a justified sinner and reconciled child with a gracious God and father, brought sin a second time upon Abraham himself ; and formed the double precedent which, it is to be feared, occasioned subsequently Isaac's similar offence.

III. The poor evasion which the patriarch tries to plead in excuse of his conduct might be less discreditable, according to the usages of that age, than when tried by the standard of an entirely different state of society and of the social relations. "And yet indeed she is my sister ; she is the daughter of my father, but not the daughter of my mother ; and she became my wife " (ver. 12). Marriage was then lawful within degrees since forbidden ; and the term sister was commonly applied to any female as nearly related by birth as Sarah was to Abraham. So far, he is warranted in what he says. His real fault was his concealment of his marriage ; a point on which he might consider himself at liberty to exercise his discretion. That he did wrong in resorting to this expedient of concealment is certain ; nor does it appear that he means to justify himself in the explanation which he gives to Abimelech. He may rather be regarded as merely wishing to show what it was that suggested to him the policy he had adopted, and made it possible for him to follow it. But for the relationship which actually subsisted, he could not have thought of this mode of hiding what he did not think it safe to avow.

IV. The root of bitterness, however, in this melancholy instance, was an evil heart of unbelief. His faith failed him exactly where the faith of many a believer fails ;—not in any fundamental article of the Lord's covenant, nor in the main and essential characteristics of his walk with God ;—but in the practical application of the promises of that covenant and the principles of that walk to some one or other of the details or the difficulties of his ordinary worldly condition. He forgets that he is to bring the high principles of his loyalty to heaven to bear upon the minutest incidents of his state on earth. He begins to consult and act for himself, instead of leaving all to God. It is this infirmity of faith which occasions so many inconsistencies in his daily walk—which entangles him so often in unworthy schemes of compromise and evasion—which mars his peace, and makes him, as a double-minded man, unstable in his ways. And it puts him too often at the mercy of those to whom his disingenuous reserve gives an advantage over him. Like Abimelech, they may have cause to reproach him for the want of that manly and open frankness which it had been better for all parties if Abraham in this emergency had shown.

Still it was good for Abimelech, on the whole and in the end, that a servant and prophet of the Lord was brought into his neighbourhood. God made even the infirmity of the patriarch the occasion of a blessing to the king.

I. It procured for Abimelech the advantage of an immediate visit from God himself. That visit was partly in severity, and partly also in kindness. The king, in this matter, though not aware of the actual state of the case, was by no means free from blame. The judgment, therefore, which the Lord sent on his house (ver. 18) was not undeserved. But it was mainly with a merciful design that God interposed to warn him. He acknowledges Abimelech's plea of ignorance and innocence in regard to the heinous crime which he was in danger of committing ; while he orders him to redress the wrong which he had undoubtedly done (ver. 5-7).

II. This untoward occurrence was in another way over-ruled for good. It procured for Abimelech the friendship and the intercessory prayer of one of the chosen servants of God. This was to him a signal benefit, and he was evidently taught gratefully to avail himself of it.

When these two distinguished persons—the prince and the patriarch, mutually both sinned against and sinning—met after the incidents of that memorable day and night, there was much in what had passed to knit them closely together ; and in the frank explanation which ensued between them, there is much that is honourable to both. The king, indeed, has some cause of complaint, and he does complain. He asks what offence he had given to Abraham, or what wickedness Abraham had seen in him, to provoke or warrant the course of conduct he had thought fit to adopt towards him ? And he puts forcibly to Abraham the evil of that conduct, as not only insulting to himself personally, but fitted to "bring on him, and on his kingdom, a great sin" (ver. 9, 10). This honest expostulation must have humbled the patriarch ; and both he and his partner must have felt some shame under the well-merited and delicate hint implied in the gift of the veil.* But

* Such a hint seems to be intended in the somewhat obscure language —"And unto Sarah he said, Behold, I have given thy brother a thousand pieces of silver : behold, he is to thee a covering of the eyes, unto all that are with thee, and with all other. Thus she was reproved" (ver. 16). The king intimates, by way of gentle reproof, that he has made a present to her brother, or husband, of a sum of money for the purchase of coverings for the head, for herself and for her attendants, to be worn in token of their

they do not recriminate. On the contrary, Abraham seems to acquiesce in the king's censure, simply venturing to offer an explanation, rather than an apology, for his conduct. And the king must have condemned himself—all the more because the patriarch abstained from retaliating his accusation. He could not but be touched by the thought of the difficult and dangerous pilgrimage to which Abraham was called, and the sad and peculiar hardship of his position, which seemed to render necessary such an expedient as he had adopted. He could not fail to sympathise with the perplexities and embarrassments which led so holy a man to have recourse to such arts. Thus Abimelech might be prepared to make a friend of this prophet of the Lord, whom he had unwittingly proposed to injure in so tender a point. He deals with him on terms of princely liberality; loading him with favours; and he reaps a rich reward.

He obtains an interest in the prophet's prayers. This was the inducement held out to him by God: "Restore the man his wife, for he is a prophet, and he shall pray for thee, and thou shalt live" (ver. 7). Accordingly the patriarch "did pray unto God, and God healed Abimelech and his house" (ver. 17). Abraham thus redresses his share of the wrong. Of the two parties who have offended, each, according to his station and office, seeks to requite the other. The prince bestows his royal bounty, the prophet gives his prayers.

The friendship thus begun is at a subsequent period matured: and on that occasion it still more signally turns to Abimelech's account (xxi. 22-34).

This incident is chiefly remarkable as illustrating the progress of Abimelech's faith, and the consummation of his union with Abraham. It occurred after the birth of Isaac; when

being under Abraham's protection and authority; whence, it has been thought, we are to trace the custom to which the apostle Paul refers, as sanctioned by the proprieties of nature, and therefore comely in the church of God (1 Cor. xi. 3-15).

Abraham, having dismissed the son of the bondmaid born after the flesh, has now centred all his hope in the son whom he had received by promise. In these circumstances, Abimelech pays him a visit in state, and proposes to make with him a hereditary alliance. In this proposal he has respect to Abraham's near relation to God. He recognises him as a prince; and evidently anticipates his future possession of the land. He assumes that Abraham and his seed after him are to have an inheritance in Canaan, and to exercise power and authority. Nor is it at all impossible that he may have had his eye on the spiritual as well as the temporal promises connected with the seed of Abraham. For if we consider all the circumstances, it is a very enlarged and enlightened faith that the king here manifests. He seeks to participate in Abraham's favour with God, and to lay hold of God's promises in Abraham. He covets the blessing of those who bless Abraham; he would have himself and his children recognised as fellow-heirs of that righteousness and that salvation which belonged to Abraham. Hence probably his acknowledgment, "God is with thee in all that thou doest;" and his proposal, "Now, therefore, swear unto me here by God, that thou wilt not deal falsely with me, nor with my son, nor with my son's son: but according to the kindness that I have done unto thee, thou shalt do unto me, and to the land wherein thou hast sojourned" (ver. 22, 23). Nor was the king's request preferred in vain. The patriarch promptly and frankly consents—"Abraham said, I will swear" (ver. 24).

First, however, he tests the sincerity of Abimelech, by appealing to him on a point of ordinary justice about a disputed right of property in what was then and there of great consequence (ver. 25-26). It relates to the possession and use of the well named Beersheba, or the well of the oath (ver. 31). Abraham takes the king, as it were, at his word, and in his character of a prince, which Abimelech ascribed to him, asserts his title to equal and equitable treatment at his hands—a title which Abimelech evidently acknowledges, by consenting at once to redress the injury complained of.

Then, this little preliminary being happily adjusted, Abraham proceeds to ratify the covenant of friendly alliance by a transaction which seems to partake of the nature of a sacrificial offering (ver. 27-31). For the seven lambs set apart by Abraham, to be " taken of his hand " by Abimelech—that quantity being too small for a mere present, and being the well-understood sacred and sacrificial number—were probably designed to be victims. The patriarch and the king, therefore, by engaging jointly in that solemn rite, confirmed their compact, as not a civil and political treaty merely, but one that was religious and spiritual also. It would even appear that provision was made for their continuing afterwards to join in occasional acts of worship. The grove planted in Beersheba (ver. 33),—whether by Abraham, as our translators have made it, or by Abimelech, as some suppose,—might be designed for common use. And there, from time to time, the two friends might meet, as members of the same communion,— having now a common faith, a common hope, a common love, —to call in common " on the name of the Lord, the everlasting God" (ver. 33).

Thus Abraham blessed Abimelech: not merely giving him, as a prophet, an interest in his prayers, but, as the heir of the land and the father of the promised seed, admitting him into a participation of the privileges and prospects of his faith. It is truly, in all views of it, a signal instance of evil overruled for good ; it is a remarkable illustration of the Psalmist's devout utterance, " Surely the wrath of man shall praise thee ; the remainder of wrath shalt thou restrain" (Ps. lxxvi. 10).

And not merely in its bearing upon the individual interests of the parties principally concerned is the issue of this transaction significant and important. It is to be considered also in a larger and wider point of view. It is an early example of the fulfilment of the assurance, that in Abraham and in his seed all the families of the earth were to be blessed. It is not for himself alone that Abraham has found favour in the eyes of God, and has become the father of the one seed to whom all the promises are made (Gal. iii. 16); but for others also, not of his natural lineage, if only they are willing to receive all covenant blessings on the same footing with himself. For this end he is brought in contact with Abimelech; for this end the incidents of their intercourse, so painful and yet so blessed, are placed on record; that the comprehensive character of the dispensation of God towards the patriarch may receive an early illustration, and that the one spirit animating the church from the beginning may be seen to be what is expressed in the glorious missionary psalm :—" God be merciful unto us, and bless us; and cause his face to shine upon us; that thy way may be known upon earth, thy saving health among all nations. Let the people praise thee, O God; let all the people praise thee. O let the nations be glad and sing for joy: for thou shalt judge the people righteously, and govern the nations upon earth. Let the people praise thee, O God; let all the people praise thee. Then shall the earth yield her increase; and God, even our own God, shall bless us. God shall bless us; and all the ends of the earth shall fear him " (Ps. lxvii.).

26

THE SEPARATION OF THE SEED BORN AFTER THE
FLESH FROM THE SEED THAT IS BY PROMISE

Genesis 21:1-8

Of the three pictures which this chapter brings before us,
especially in the first twenty verses, the last is by far the most
interesting and attractive to the eye of natural taste, and the
sympathy of the natural heart.

The festivities attendant upon the birth, the circumcision,
and the weaning of Isaac, are contemplated with a feeling of
decent and respectful acquiescence, such as seems due to the
venerable character of the parties chiefly concerned (ver. 1-8).
The strife, again, which some time after ensues in the household, irritates and offends the onlooker;—recalling, as it does,
to his mind that former most unseemly female brawl (chap. xvi.),
whose smothered embers seem to be now breaking out afresh
into a still more outrageous heat (ver. 9-14).   But the scene
of the poor wanderer, with her helpless boy, in the wilderness
of Beersheba, is a very gem for the poet and the painter.   The
little incident of the child's thirst, and the mother's despair, is
one of exquisite truth and tenderness ; nor can any thing
exceed the pathos of these simple words :—" And the water
was spent in the bottle, and she cast the child under one of
the shrubs.   And she went, and sat her down over against him
a good way off, as it were a bowshot ; for she said, Let me not
see the death of the child.   And she sat over against him, and
lift up her voice, and wept " (ver. 15, 16).   Her simple and

plaintive utterance of despair may well affect us, since it
attracts the compassionate interest of the Lord himself. God
listens to the cry of Ishmael and the weeping of his mother.
And the angel of God comes to the rescue with salutation full
of tenderness—" What aileth thee, Hagar? fear not ;" with
promises for the future large and liberal—" Arise, lift up the
lad, and hold him in thine hand ; for I will make him a great
nation ;" and with present relief most seasonable and satisfying—" And God opened her eyes, and she saw a well of water :
and she went and filled the bottle with water, and gave the
lad drink" (ver. 18, 19). Thus, the narrative of this transaction would seem to be so constructed as to enlist our sensi-
bilities rather on the side of the rejected, than of the chosen ;
and to draw out our affections far more towards the wilderness
where Hagar and Ishmael wander, than towards the home
where the patriarch, and his holy partner, and the child of
promise, dwell. But while freely admitting this, we must
remember, that in respect of the place they hold in the
grand economy of the divine providence and grace, the first
two incidents have a prominence and pre-eminence all their
own.

Thus, as to the first, if there be an occasion on earth fitted
to call forth the songs of heaven, next to the birth of Jesus,
and not second to the birth of his forerunner John, it is the
birth of Isaac. Upon no event, between the fall and the incarnation, did the salvation of men more conspicuously depend.
And yet few verses of the Bible are more commonplace, and
less awakening—at least in our modern view of them—than
those that describe the entertainment with which the child of
promise was welcomed (ver. 3-8). Nevertheless, Sarah's song,
" God has made me to laugh, so that all that hear will laugh
with me," is the brief model, first of Hannah's (1 Sam. ii. 1-19),
and then of Mary's (Luke i. 46-56). And the whole ceremonial
here briefly indicated has its antitype and accomplishment in
the advent of the Messiah.

As it stands in the history, and as it would appear at the time to the contemporary dwellers in the land, the incident that stirred Abraham's household was insignificant enough. It was a wonder, no doubt, fitted to awaken some attention, that the pilgrim pair should, after so long a childless sojourn together, be blessed with unexpected offspring. But it was a wonder that might soon pass into forgetfulness. Little notice, after all, would be attracted by it then beyond the lowly tent of the patriarch; and little heed may be given by superficial readers now to the summary record of it in the Scriptures; so analogous are the methods of the divine procedure, in providence and in revelation. Let us enter, however, by faith into the mind of the faithful patriarch, as it must have glowed with holy gratitude on the three successive holidays of his son's birth, his circumcision, and his being weaned from his mother's breast;—let us feel as Abraham on these occasions must have felt. And let us seek to catch the spirit of the hymn then virtually anticipated in Sarah's exulting note of joy—the hymn of the heavenly hosts rejoicing in the assurance of salvation to a lost world, "Glory to God in the highest, and on earth peace, good will toward men" (Luke ii. 14).

It is the central incident, however, the expulsion of Ishmael, which chiefly staggers our natural judgment, while it is that very incident of which the most emphatic use is made in other parts of Scripture for the purposes of the spiritual life.

Beyond all question, the thing here done is felt, at first sight, to be harsh; and the manner of doing it perhaps even harsher still: "Sarah saw the son of Hagar the Egyptian, which she had born unto Abraham, mocking. Wherefore she said unto Abraham, Cast out this bondwoman and her son: for the son of this bondwoman shall not be heir with my son, even with Isaac" (ver. 9, 10).

Surely never was slight offence more spitefully avenged! An unmannerly boy vents some ill-timed and ill-judged jest; —and his mother as well as himself must be cast helpless on the wide world on account of it! It looks like the very wantonness of female jealousy and passion. No wonder that the proposal vexed and shocked the patriarch. No wonder that he needed a divine communication to make him recognise in his irritated partner's unrelenting demand—" Cast out the bondwoman and her son "—the very mind and will of God himself ;—" God said unto Abraham, Let it not be grievous in thy sight because of the lad, and because of thy bondwoman ; in all that Sarah hath said unto thee, hearken unto her voice ; for in Isaac shall thy seed be called " (ver. 12, 13).

Now, it is not necessary to acquit Sarah of all personal vindictiveness, or to consider her as acting from the best and highest motives, merely because God commanded Abraham to " hearken unto her voice." It may have been in utter uncon- sciousness of its being a heaven-directed and heaven-inspired voice, that Sarah, yielding to an impetuous temper, called for the removal of a rival out of the way of her son's succession and title to the inheritance. At the same time, even if it was so, there are certain circumstances which should be taken into account, not for the vindication of Sarah's conduct, but for the better understanding of the divine procedure.

I. Thus, in the first place, let the actual offence of Ishmael, now no longer a child, but a lad of at least some fourteen years of age, be fairly understood and estimated. The apostle Paul represents it in a strong light—" He that was born after the flesh, persecuted him that was born after the Spirit ;"—and he points to it as the type and model of the cruel envy with which the " children of promise " are in every age pursued, for he adds, " even so it is now " (Gal. iv. 28, 29).

From the history itself in fact, it is plain enough that Ishmael's " mocking " had a deeper meaning than a mere wild and wanton jest. The " children," the lads or young men, who " mocked " Elisha after the translation of his master in a chariot of fire, " saying unto him, Go up, thou bald-head ; go up thou bald-head,"—knew what they were about better than we are apt to think (2 Kings ii. 23, 24). It was no boyish frolic—no senseless insolence to Elisha personally—no idle mockery of his grey and scanty locks—that was so promptly and terribly punished ; but a profane and ribbald outburst of blasphemy against the stupendous miracle which had just taken place. They mocked, not the prophet, but his God ; when scoffing at Elijah's glorious ascension into heaven, they taunted his venerable follower with impious scorn ;—Thou, too, "thou bald-head, go up," as he did ! The mockery of Ishmael was probably of a similar kind. That it had respect to the birthright is evident, both from Sarah's reasoning, and from the Lord's. She assigns, as the cause of her anxiety to have Ishmael cast out, her apprehension lest he should claim a joint-interest with Isaac in the inheritance. And the Lord sanctions her proposal on this very ground, when he says to Abraham, " In Isaac shall thy seed be called."

It was a quarrel, therefore, about the birthright, that the mockery of Ishmael indicated or occasioned. And if we suppose him, as is all but certain from the whole tenor of the scriptural references to this transaction, to have been instigated and encouraged by his mother, — considering the prize at stake, and the impetuous blood that boils in the dark veins of Africa's daughters.—we can assign no limits to the extremities her desperate maternal ambition might prompt. It may have been little more than an act of self-defence on the part of Sarah, when she seized the first opportunity of overt injury or insult, to put an end to a competition of claims that threatened consequences so disastrous.

II. Again, secondly, it is to be remembered that the competition in question admitted of no compromise ; and that, whatever might be her motives, Sarah did, in point of fact, stand with God in the controversy. She believed God, when in accordance, not more with her own natural feelings than with the known will of God, she determined to resist every attempt to interfere with the prerogative of the child of promise. Her determination also would be the more decided, and her announcement of it the more peremptory, if she saw any indication of hesitancy in the mind even of the patriarch himself. For Abraham may have been swayed by his affection for his first-born child, as well as Sarah by her fondness for the son of her old age. In point of fact, Abraham felt great reluctance to give up his hope of Ishmael being his heir and successor in the covenant. Before the birth of Isaac, he clung to that hope with great tenacity, and pleaded hard with God on behalf of Ishmael that he might have the birthright blessing (chap. xvii. 18). And even after that event, he seems still to have had a leaning towards Ishmael. He can scarcely persuade himself to hazard all on so precarious a risk as the puny life of an infant who has so strangely come and may as strangely pass away. He would fain keep Ishmael still in reserve, and not altogether lose his hold of that other line of descent. He would be for combining, in some way, their joint claims, and so doubling his security for the fulfilment of the promises.

That this may have been partly Abraham's state of mind is not at all improbable ; nay, it receives countenance from the pains which the Lord takes to remove the last scruple of lingering unbelief ;—to reconcile him to the destiny of Ishmael, and persuade him to acquiesce in the purpose of sovereign election—"In Isaac shall thy seed be called" (ver. 12, 13). If it was so, not only may the knowledge or suspicion of such a leaning in their favour have made Ishmael and Hagar more presumptuous in their insolence ; but some light is thus thrown on the circumstances of very peculiar difficulty in which Sarah was placed, and the very trying part she had to act towards Abraham. She was wont "to obey him, calling him Lord." But now, a regard to her own rights,—and still more a regard to the will of God and the wellbeing of her husband's soul,— constrain her, however affectionately, yet uncompromisingly, to remonstrate with him and to resist.

III. In the third place, it should not be overlooked that the severity of the measure resorted to is apt to be greatly exaggerated if it is looked at in the light of the social usages and arrangements of modern domestic life.

It was no unusual step for the head of a household, in these primitive times, to make an early separation between the heir, who was to be retained at home in the chief settlement of the tribe, and other members of the family, who must be sent to push their way elsewhere.* It would appear, indeed, that the expulsion was in this instance hurried and abrupt, at least at first. The case being urgent, Abraham sends the young man and his mother somewhat hastily away. But it does not follow that they were sent away cruelly or carelessly. Nor are

---

* Abraham himself adopted this course with reference to his other sons whom he had besides Ishmael. He " gave all that he had unto Isaac ; but unto the sons of the concubines, which Abraham had, Abraham gave gifts, and sent them away from Isaac his son (while he yet lived), eastward, unto the east country" (chap. xxv. 5, 6). This statement occurs in the general summary of Abraham's history that ushers in the account of his death. It can scarcely be doubted that the persons referred to as the mothers of his sons, are simply Hagar and Keturah ; for with none else is there the least hint of his having lived in marriage. They are both called by the name commonly given to women occupying a subordinate place in a man's household, as if to mark the unquestionable pre-eminence of Sarah, the one gracious spouse of the patriarch, with whom neither any partner while she survives, nor any successor after she is gone, is to be for a moment put upon a level. The sons of both Abraham is represented as treating exactly in the same way ; his conduct towards Ishmael did not differ at all from what his conduct afterwards was towards the children of Keturah. But there is no question as to his just and liberal treatment of them ; "he gave them gifts." He made provision for their settlement, under his own eye, being both comfortable and reputable ; furnishing them with the means of well-doing. The presumption surely is, that he meant to deal upon the same terms with Ishmael when he and his mother were cast out, and that this is intended to be indicated in the brief description subsequently given of his manner of disposing of his children generally.

they sent away to a far country. They are to wait for further
orders on the very borders of the place where Abraham himself is dwelling. The wilderness of Beersheba is almost at his
very door; and long ere the bread and water they take with
them are consumed, it may be expected that Abraham will be
in circumstances to communicate with them more fully as to
what they are to do.

By some mistake or mischance, however, it would seem
that it unfortunately happened otherwise. Were a conjecture
here warranted, it might be surmised as not improbable that
the proud spirit of the Egyptian, stung by disappointment, may
have become reckless and regardless, both of any provision her
master may have promised to make for her, and of any directions he may have given as to the course she was to follow.
After roaming thus heedlessly and aimlessly for a time, she
may have begun to suffer from the reaction of high excitement; losing her way and her presence of mind, and so bringing upon herself an unnecessary aggravation of her trial. It
is some confirmation of the view now suggested, that when
Hagar's tears and the lad's cries are heard on high, and the
angel comes to administer relief, the manner of that relief is
so very simple; " God opened her eyes, and she saw a well of
water; and she went and filled the bottle with water, and
gave the lad drink " (ver. 19).

IV. Once more, in the fourth place, a presumptive proof,
at least, of the patriarch's continued interest in Ishmael is to
be found in the account given of his interview with Abimi-
lech, king of Gerar. That interview must surely have had
some connection with the immediately preceding incident.
And the precise link of connection may be found in what gave
occasion to Abraham's remonstrance; he " reproved Abimelech
because of a well of water, which Abimelech's servants had
violently taken away " (ver. 25).

It appears from Abimelech's reply that he was not aware
of this cause of complaint (ver. 26);—a circumstance not a

little remarkable, if the well in question was upon the ground occupied by Abraham's own household. But if it was a well that had belonged to Ishmael ;—especially if it was the well which God caused Hagar in her distress to see, and around which her son might naturally form his earliest settlement, Abimelech's ignorance and Abraham's anxiety are simply and naturally explained.

For we may assume some little time to have elapsed before this visit was paid by Abimelech to Abraham. And indeed but very little time would be needed to give Ishmael a position among the companies that roamed the desert. "God was with the lad ; and he grew, and dwelt in the wilderness, and became an archer. And he dwelt in the wilderness of Paran ; and his mother took him a wife out of the land of Egypt" (ver. 20, 21). He might thus very soon assume his place at the head of such a household, or such a troop of volunteers, as his daring spirit was sure to gather round him; and all the sooner if he was still recognised as in alliance with Abraham, and still largely enjoyed the benefit of Abraham's patronage and name. And if we suppose him, as the captain of a band of archers, to have had an interest in the well which became matter of discussion between Abraham and Abimelech, the whole narrative becomes singularly vivid.

The King's servants have taken forcible possession of a well that has been frequented by a small tribe of adventurers. That is an affair in itself too insignificant to attract notice ; nor, in ignorance of the relation of the new tribe to Abraham, could Abimelech be expected to know or care much about the matter. But when Abraham explains that relation ; and, taking advantage of Abimelech's friendly visit, asks redress for the wrong that had been inadvertently done, he gains more for Ishmael than the mere recovery of the contested well. He secures to him a footing of acknowledged independence among the princes of the land.

For the ratification of the treaty by sacrifice has special

reference to the well which Abraham claims as having been dug by himself; and which Abimelech accordingly cedes to him for ever (ver. 27-30). The well itself is called Beer-sheba —the well of the oath; and it gives its name to the wilderness in which it is situated. It is not therefore carrying conjecture too far to suppose,—if our previous supposition as to the ownership of the well be allowed,—that the Ishmaelites may have had a share, not only in the covenant which was made at Beer-sheba, for the securing of the right of property that had been in dispute, but in the common worship also which was set up there,—for calling " on the name of the Lord, the everlasting God" (ver. 32, 33).

27

ALLEGORY OF ISHMAEL AND ISAAC—THE TWO
COVENANTS

Genesis 21:9-12   John 8:33-42   Galatians 4:21-31

" THESE things are an allegory," says the apostle Paul, referring to the two sons that Abraham had—Ishmael and Isaac—
and to the difference that there was between them, first in
their respective births, and afterwards in the positions which
they held in the family of the patriarch.   " It is written that
Abraham had two sons ; the one by a bondmaid, the other
by a freewoman.   But he who was of the bondwoman was
born after the flesh ; but he of the freewoman was by promise.   Which things are an allegory " (Gal. iv. 22-24).   And
the " allegory " is continued down to the expulsion of Ishmael.
For the apostle adds, " Now we, brethren, as Isaac was, are
the children of promise.   But as then he that was born after
the flesh persecuted him that was born after the Spirit, even
so it is now.   Nevertheless, what saith the Scripture ?   Cast
out the bond woman and her son : for the son of the bond
woman shall not be heir with the son of the free woman.   So
then, brethren, we are not children of the bond woman, but
of the free " (Gal. iv. 28-31).

This history, then, is allegorical ; it was written with a
view to its being allegorically interpreted and applied ; and
the facts which it registers were ordained and ordered with
that view.

And yet the facts themselves are real ; and they have a

real and literal importance apart from all allegory. As incidents illustrative of human nature and life generally—as incidents, in particular, bringing out the actual experience of believers in the circumstances in which the church was placed at the time—they are significant and valuable. Their significance and value, in that view, have been already opened up. They are not a mere allegory; far from it; they are the real actions of living men.

Still they are an allegory. And they are so, not because an inspired apostle has said it, but because that is their real character. Nor is it a character which belongs to them in common with all events that have happened or are happening upon earth. All things may be said, in one sense, to be allegorical; all objects and all events. Not a blade of grass grows —not a sparrow falls to the ground—but an allegory may be made of it. But the peculiarity here is that the facts recorded have a spiritual meaning in themselves—substantially the same with the appplication which they suggest. Ishmael and Isaac—Mount Sinai and Mount Zion—Jerusalem which now is and Jerusalem which is above—are all of them contrasted pairs; not artificially, but naturally. The principle of antagonism or contrast is the same throughout; and it is exemplified completely at each stage. In Abraham's twofold seed— the one after the flesh, the other by special promise—we have the germ of the whole gospel as a system of free and sovereign grace. And the germ is only expanded and unfolded in the subsequent revelations of Sinai, and Zion, and Calvary.

Thus this transaction of the expulsion of Ishmael and Hagar is an allegory; not merely because Paul has used it allegorically, but because, in its very nature, it is evidently designed and fitted to be allegorical. "For these are the two covenants;" they are allegorically or spiritually the two covenants—Ishmael and his mother Hagar representing the one— Isaac, again, typifying the other.

The contrast turns upon the distinction between Ishmael's

footing and Isaac's in the house or family of Abraham ; a distinction real and significant in itself, and therefore capable of being selected to represent, spiritually and by allegory, an equally real and significant distinction in the dealings of God with men under the two contrasted covenants.

For, in point of fact, the position of Ishmael in the household did differ widely from that of Isaac. It differed, especially, in two particulars ; in respect of the liberty enjoyed, and in respect of the permanency secured. The son of the bond woman had no such right of freedom, and no such sure standing, as belonged to the son of the free woman. His position was both servile in its character, and precarious in its tenure of duration. Still farther, this twofold difference between them is traced up to the manner of their respective births. The one was born according to the ordinary course of nature, the other by special promise. Whatever claim Ishmael had to be acknowledged as a member of Abraham's household rested merely on the ordinary laws of human nature and society. Isaac's claim, on the other hand, flowing from the terms of the divine promise, was very directly and immediately of God (Gal. iv. 22, 23).

Now all this is exactly analogous to what constitutes the characteristic difference between " the two covenants." For what are the two covenants ? They are the law and the gospel ;—the method of salvation by works and the method of salvation by grace;—the one which says, Do this and live, and the other which says, Believe and live. And how are men connected with these two covenants respectively ? By birth ; in the one case natural ; in the other, spiritual, or by promise. Under the first covenant, men are naturally, by their very coming into the world, placed. Under the second covenant, they have no standing by nature, but only through grace alone.

But, still further, how do these two covenants tell upon the position which men occupy in the house or family of God ? That is the main and vital question.

What position can men have under the first or legal covenant? At the best, a position partaking much of the nature of a servitude, and precarious, moreover, being contingent on the issue of a probation or trial that cannot be indefinitely prolonged. For the legal covenant " gendereth to bondage " (Gal. iv. 24). It puts us and keeps us in the position of servants,—exacting high service under a heavy penalty,—and chafing the earnest soul with an increasing feeling of helpless subjection; and that too in very proportion to the spiritual insight it obtains into the excellency of the divine commandments, and the inevitable certainty and righteousness of divine judgment. Nor is that all. Servile as our footing is and must be under that covenant, it is precarious also. We abide in the house, in terms of it, only by sufferance and for a brief season. Any shortcoming in the fulfilment of the conditions of our continuance may at any moment be fatal to us; the time given to test our character and conduct may come to a swift and sudden end. And then the impending sentence may be deferred no longer; we must be cast out.

But now, suppose that we are in the house upon another footing; born, not after the flesh but by promise; and placed, therefore, under the evangelical covenant,—saved by grace through faith.

Then, in the first place, we are in the house, as not bond but free. We have the rights of freedom and the feelings of freedom. We have not to work for our liberty; we are already free. For the gospel-covenant giving us life, not conditionally upon certain terms prescribed, but gratuitously—for the taking, as men say—emancipates us on the instant from legal bondage; breaks the yoke of servile obligation, and severs the fetters of conscious guilt. The despairing worker under the law, the condemned criminal vainly toiling to win his release, is now pardoned freely; nay, more than pardoned; accepted and justified. At once, and once for all, he is placed upon a footing of free favour in the household which none can ever challenge or question. For "if God be for us, who can be against us? It is God that justifieth, who is he that condemneth?"

A second privilege, accordingly, of our birthright under the gospel-covenant, is the security of our position in the house. We are no longer in it as being merely tolerated, or put upon trial; we are in it as already and once for all approved. Our standing, upon the terms of the legal covenant of works, must always be precarious, contingent, and conditional. Even beings capable of fulfilling exactly all the terms of that covenant could never divest themselves altogether of the feeling that they might yet be cast out; they could never attain to the assurance of their "abiding ever." The unfallen angels themselves, who stood firm and faithful when their companions were lost, could not realise their own security, had they continued still to be placed upon probation. Some change must have taken place in their tenure of the divine favour after that sad catastrophe. They were elevated, doubtless, to a higher rank than had previously belonged to them, and brought into such a relationship of filial love to the Most High, as would carry with it a sense of safety they never otherwise could have enjoyed.*

But if even sinless creatures must feel their footing in the house insecure under the covenant of works, how much more the guilty! Any period of probation allowed to us for trying the experiment again of our ability to win life by our own obedience to the law, must be precarious indeed! What thanks, then, are due to the God and Father of our Lord Jesus Christ, who receives us into his house, and takes us home to his bosom, on very different terms indeed! What praise for his free and sovereign grace, in the exercise of which, " of his own free-will he begetteth us by the word of his truth, that we should be a kind of first-fruits of his creatures;"—placing us upon a rock which neither earth nor hell can shake, and sur-

* See Lectures on the *Fatherhood of God*—Appendix i. and v.

rounding us with the shield of his everlasting favour, so that we are his for ever—never to be cast out!

Such, then, are the two covenants allegorically represented in the family of Abraham.

Hagar, in the apostle's view, typified, first Mount Sinai in Arabia, and, secondly, Jerusalem as it then was. In other words, she is the symbol, first of the legal dispensation, and, secondly, of the Jewish Church under that dispensation. Of the former, it is said that it gendereth to bondage; of the latter, that she is in bondage with her children. For whatever might be the meaning of the old economy, spiritually apprehended, and whatever might be the intimations of gospel truth conveyed by it to a spiritually enlightened mind,—the law given by Moses was virtually and practically to the nation at large a method of salvation by works. As such, it laid upon the conscience a heavy load of unfulfilled obligation and uncancelled guilt; and the people, looking for life according to its terms, were helplessly bound under its yoke of service and its sentence of condemnation. Their standing before God, therefore, is fitly compared to that of the bond-maid's son in the family. Thus, if Hagar represents the legal covenant, Ishmael naturally stands for those whose life, such as it is, flows from that covenant, and of whom the church, constituted according to that covenant, is the mother.

Over against that condition and channel of life the apostle sets one higher, freer, and incorruptible. And it is remarkable that in doing so, he partly loses sight of the symbol. He speaks not of Sarah, the proper antithesis to Hagar, in his ascending series of contrasts. But, reaching at once the summit, he brings the Jerusalem which is above into antagonism with the Jerusalem which now is. He confronts " the church of the first-born, which are written in heaven," with the church constituted in terms of the law.

For it is not any personal pre-eminence on the part of Sarah that entitles her son to a preference over Ishmael; it is simply his being the child by promise. It is as the child by promise that he is no servant, but emphatically the son, and therefore free. It is as the child by promise that he continues in the house, when the bondwoman and her son are cast out. So they whose mother is the Jerusalem which is above,—who hold their spiritual life and standing before God, not by derivation from any visible earthly church, but by fellowship with the spiritual economy of the unseen world above,—are born, not after the flesh, but by promise. Hence their title to a free footing in the house. That economy which is their spiritual mother is itself free; and it is the source of freedom. It is the system of free and sovereign grace ; and, as such, it ushers into life a vast family of new-born and free-born souls. "It is the mother of us all."

Barren as it may seem in the eye of sense; incapable of forming and preserving a collective or organised body of worshippers; greatly less efficacious for that end than "the Jerusalem that now is," the apparatus of an earthly church, with its baptismal unity and outward pomp of service ;—still the gospel plan of salvation by free grace, carried home by the Holy Spirit, and laying hold of the conscience, the mind, the will, the heart,—the whole inner man, in short,—gives new life to multitudes of the lost race of mankind, and heralds into glory such a company of the redeemed, as no family, or tribe, or nation, could ever count as its own. "For it is written, Rejoice, thou barren that bearest not ; break forth and cry, thou that travailest not ; for the desolate hath many more children than she which hath an husband" (Gal. iv. 27).

These are the countless throng described as meeting around the throne, and singing the song of Moses and the Lamb : "A great multitude, which no man could number, of all nations, and kindreds, and people, and tongues, stood before the throne, and before the Lamb, clothed with white robes, and palms in their hands ; and cried with a loud voice, saying, Salvation to our God which sitteth upon the throne, and unto the Lamb"

(Rev. vii. 9, 10). For they all disown any earthly Jerusalem as their mother, or any birth after the flesh as their title to life. They are all scions of a higher stock, deriving their spiritual being from a more heavenly source. They are born by promise ; " By grace are they saved through faith, and that not of themselves, it is the gift of God." And displacing and dispossessing all whose claim rests merely on their connection with the Jerusalem that now is,—they come forth at last to crown the Jerusalem that is above with the joyful acclamations of a united family, all gathered together into one in Christ, and all to the praise of the glory of his grace.

28

THE TRIAL, TRIUMPH, AND REWARD OF
ABRAHAM'S FAITH

Genesis 22:1-19

By faith Abraham, when he was tried, offered up Isaac.   Hebrews 11:17-19
Was not Abraham our father justified by works, when he had offered
    Isaac his son upon the altar?   James 2:21-23
Your father Abraham rejoiced to see my day; and he saw it, and was glad.
    John 8:56

THE temptation of our Lord in the wilderness occurred immediately after his being declared to be the Son of God by the
voice from heaven at his baptism (Matt. iii. 17). And all
throughout, the temptation turns upon the privilege and prerogative which his being the Son of God implies. The tempter
would fain persuade him to stand upon his right, as the Son
of God,—to avail himself of the power belonging to him, in
that character, for his own relief and his own aggrandisement,—
and to snatch the inheritance to which he is entitled, as the
Son whom God hath appointed heir of all things, without
waiting the Father's time and fulfilling the Father's terms.

It is not Satan, but God, who "tempts Abraham," or puts
him to the proof. So far there is a difference between the
patriarch and the Saviour. The trial of the one is gracious
and paternal; the other has to stand a more fiery ordeal.
Abraham has to listen to God, and obey; Jesus has to encounter Satan, and resist.

In other respects, however, there is a remarkable analogy

between the two events. The father of Isaac is tried concerning his son, at the very time when that son has been emphatically owned from above as the heir. The Son of God is
tempted upon the precise point of his sonship, just when it
has been most signally and unequivocally acknowledged by
the voice from heaven. Jesus is solicited to grasp impatiently
the inheritance of his birthright, without passing through the
preliminary stage of his deep humiliation and painful death.
Abraham, again, is expected to acquiesce patiently in the
putting off of the promises, even though the sacrifice of his
beloved child, and the darkness of that child's tomb, be
brought in between his hope and its fulfilment. In the one
case, the question is,—Will the Lord Jesus anticipate prematurely the immunities and glories of the heritage ultimately
designed for him ? In the other case, the question is,—Will
Abraham, on the part of his son, and as bound up with his
son, consent to their being indefinitely postponed ?

In this connection, the trial of the patriarch's faith may be
viewed in two lights, as bringing out, first, the general principle of his faith, and, secondly, its more specific character and
reward.

I. Let the general principle of Abraham's faith, as here
exercised, be considered.

If we look at the bare fact of a father offering up his son
in sacrifice, we can see little to distinguish the conduct of the
patriarch from that of too many unhappy men who, in the
dismal infatuation of superstitious fear, have " given their first-
born for their transgressions—the fruit of their body for the
sin of their souls." We search in vain in such a work of delusion for real faith ;—that meek and holy trust which alone can
be either honourable to God, or saving in its influence on the
soul of man. A faith indeed of a certain kind we may discover—a faith in the existence and the power of God—a faith
also in the terror of his unknown judgment. But it is such
a faith as the devils have, who " believe and tremble." We

discover no sense of the divine love, no enlightened and manly confidence, in the father's severe and gloomy resolution. All in his soul must be doubt and darkness ; doubt inexplicable, darkness impenetrable. And in the horrid deed of blood at which we shudder,—by which the frantic parent would appease the wrath of an inexorable and implacable Deity,— we see no hopeful reliance on an unseen benefactor, but only abject and servile fear, grasping at a lie ! We must look, therefore, beyond the naked fact that " Abraham offered up Isaac," if we would rightly understand his faith.

Let us look, accordingly, to the occasion of the deed ;— " Abraham, when he was tried, offered up Isaac." He made this sacrifice of parental affection at the express command of God, and sought, perhaps, to conciliate the favour of God, not indeed by the costliness of his offering, but by his ready and implicit submission to the divine will. Perhaps that may be a full account of Abraham's views and feelings in this act, as well as of the motives from which he acted. So far it may be so. He certainly did well to submit to the declared will of his Creator, however mysterious that will might be. We see in such obedience plain evidence of faith ; and of faith more enlightened in its nature than what we formerly observed in this sacrifice ;—faith in the righteous authority and moral government of God, who commands, and requires obedience to his commandments, however inexplicable they may be. But we do not see faith confiding, clinging, living ; for we might conceive of the heart of the forlorn parent inwardly rebelling, while his trembling and reluctant hand was stretched out to execute the stern decree. Again, therefore, we must take into account some other circumstances of the case, if we would truly estimate either the intense severity of Abraham's trial, or the unconquerable energy of his faith.

It was " he that had received the promises " who did all this. In full and faithful reliance on these promises, while as yet he was childless, Abraham left the land of his fathers, and went out, not knowing whither he went. By faith in these promises, he sojourned as a stranger in the land which his descendants were to possess. On the birth of Hagar's son, despairing of any other child, he cries, " O that Ishmael might live before thee ;" but when the long-expected heir is born at last, God, renewing the promises, expressly confines them to Isaac :—" In Isaac shall thy seed be called ;" and as if to cut off all room for doubt, Ishmael is expelled altogether from the patriarch's house. All his hope now is centred exclusively in Isaac. Thus the promises which Abraham had received were all closely and necessarily bound up in the life of Isaac. And it was that " only begotten son "—in whom " his seed was to be called "—on whom the promises depended—whom, nevertheless, by faith in these very promises, he was ready at the command of God to offer up !

In the light of all these past proceedings on the part of God, we can now better understand the trial and the faith of Abraham, as they are recorded with such affecting simplicity ; —" And it came to pass that God did tempt Abraham, and said unto him, Take now thy son, thine only son, Isaac, whom thou lovest. And get thee into the land of Moriah, and offer him there for a burnt offering " (ver. 1, 2).

Was this, then, to be the end of all the patriarch's hopes ? —this the fate of that son—the heir of so many promises, the child of such persevering faith, the destined father of a mighty people—in whom all the families of the earth were to be blessed ? Was it thus that the old man, who had given up to God his youth, his friends, his home, his country, was to give up even Isaac, the child of his old age, the son of his love and his tears, his last and only stay ?—to give him up, too, to the God in the fond faith of whose promises he had already sacrificed so much, and sacrificed all so vainly ? Were all his long-cherished expectations to be thus cruelly mocked, at the very time when they seemed to be at last realised ?

Yet we read of no hesitation—no natural regret—no

murmur—no thought even of remonstrance. The patriarch did not delay or deliberate an instant. He rose up early in the morning, and took Isaac his son, and went unto the place of which God had told him. Then, leaving his attendants behind, and going on with Isaac alone, he "built an altar there, and laid the wood in order, and bound Isaac his son, and laid him on the altar upon the wood"—and these arrangements being deliberately made, " Abraham stretched forth his hand and took the knife to slay his son" (ver. 3-10).

Here let us pause to contemplate the patriarch at this tremendous moment. Let us observe the conflict between sense and faith.

In the eye of sense, he was by one rash act casting recklessly away the tardy fruit of a long life of obedience, and sternly sacrificing on the altar of his God the very hope which that God had taught him to cherish. Visions of grace and glory which had fed his soul during the years of his weary exile were fast vanishing from his view, and his high prospects were by his own hand now dashed for ever to the ground. Henceforth he was to linger out his days, childless and hopeless; his faith turned into despair, his joy into heaviness; since, in the excess of his self-denying devotion, he was obeying God, and yet, by the very act of obedience, putting utterly beyond his reach all the blessing which he had been so fully warranted by God himself to expect.

But, in the eye of faith, the venerable patriarch was still, even in this hour of terror, looking up to God, and reposing with unshaken confidence on that goodness which, during a long and harassed life, had never deceived or forsaken him. The same humble and holy trust in God, as his benefactor and his friend, which had thus far led him in safety, still triumphed over every doubt. Harsh as the decree might appear, he knew by much experience that God had never yet commanded him to his hurt; and he felt that the faithfulness of God must be as secure in the time to come as he had ever found it in time past. The cloud, indeed, might be dark which veiled the divine proceedings from his view; but it was not so dark as to cast a single shadow over his heart. He still trusted in the Lord as implicitly as when first he abandoned his father's house, casting himself on the Lord's protection. It mattered not to Abraham that by sacrificing his only son, he was, to all appearance, sacrificing his hope of a future people and a future Saviour to spring from him through that son. It mattered not that what God commanded seemed most inconsistent with what God had promised; and that, according to human judgment, by obeying the command, he was making utterly void the promises. He presumed not to question the wisdom or truth of God. He simply confided in his faithfulness and love; being well assured that God would reconcile all difficulties in the end, and justify his own ways, and accomplish his own word.

Thus, "against hope he believed in hope." The language of his obedience was the language of Job: "Though he slay me, yet will I trust in him."

Such was the spirit in which Abraham, on this occasion, unreservedly obeyed God; such the principle of that faith by which he was rendered willing to offer up Isaac. He did not offer up Isaac in order that by so costly a sacrifice, he might purchase or propitiate the love of God; nor in order that by so signal an instance of obedience to the divine will, he might merit the divine favour. He had already received from God "exceeding great and precious promises" which, from the first, he implicitly believed, and which, from the first, warranted him in placing full reliance on the love of God as already his. He did not seek to make out, by his obedience, a claim to the favour of God, for the promises of God had already given him a claim sufficiently clear and sure. From the first and all along, his faith was altogether independent of his obedience, resting simply and solely on the promises of God; it was not the consequence but the cause, not the result but the motive, of his obedience. It was not because he obeyed God that he felt himself entitled to trust in God; but because he trusted in God, therefore he obeyed him. And his trust rested not on any thing he had done, or was willing to do, but exclusively on the promises he had received. That was the faith which made him cheerfully consent to leave the land of his birth, and carried him safely through all his trials—even the present trial as by fire; not a vague, doubtful, contingent faith, timidly venturing to deprecate wrath, and hoping, by good behaviour, to find acceptance at last; but a strong assurance of God's faithfulness, and a blessed sense of acceptance in his sight, springing out of the simple credit which he gave to the free and gracious promises made to him. Had he not had such faith in God, he never would have taken a single step in the pilgrimage of toil and trouble which God prescribed. But God promised, and Abraham believed; God commanded, and Abraham obeyed. Long before this crowning instance of his obedience, Abraham believed;—"He believed God, and it was counted unto him for righteousness;"—a justifying righteousness was imputed to him. It could not, at that time, be on the ground of his own obedience that he felt himself warranted to believe, but simply on the ground of the promises. And still, to the last, even after this crowning instance of his obedience, his faith was of the same simple kind; resting not on any service of his own, as if that were the condition of his peace and hope, but on the promises he had long before received, and still continued to hold fast.

Such is the explanation generally of Abraham's faith, as exemplified in the most memorable instance of its trial and its triumph. It is reliance, confidence, consent; taking God at his word; closing with his proposals; resting upon his known character and revealed will; laying hold of himself. Thus viewed, it has a double efficacy, as a bond of union and a motive of action. It unites him who exercises it to the Being upon whom he exercises it; they are one; and the oneness implies justification, reconciliation, peace. So far faith is receptive, appropriating, acquiescing. But it is an active and moving force, as well as an acquiescent uniting embrace. It not only clings closely to the stem in which it finds its inner life ; it works powerfully upward and outward, bringing forth fruit. Hence, while in one view, it justifies by apprehending a righteousness not its own, in another, it justifies by verifying and vindicating itself. It justifies, as resting upon God and receiving the promises ; it justifies, also, as proving itself to be genuine, by obeying the command. By faith alone Abraham was justified as a sinner before God ; by faith alone he obtained acceptance in God's sight ; he believed, and he was accounted righteous. But his faith wrought by works ; believing the promises, he obeyed the commandment. And by this obedience, he was justified as a believer ; nor without it could he be justified in that character. By works, his faith was verified and completed ; and his acceptance, as the result of that faith, sealed and secured for ever. Thus we may understand the question of the apostle James—" Seest thou how his faith wrought by works, and by works was his faith made perfect ?"—in harmony with what he immediately adds —" And the scripture was fulfilled which saith, Abraham believed God, and it was imputed unto him for righteousness " (Jas. ii. 22, 23). That very Scripture was fulfilled when " by faith Abraham, when he was tried, offered up Isaac : and he that had received the promises offered up his only begotten son, of whom it was said, That in Isaac shall thy seed be called."

II. Let the specific character and reward of Abraham's faith be now considered. Its simplicity, viewed generally as a habit of reliance on the promises of God, and its power, as a motive of implicit obedience, are sufficiently brought out in the mere narrative itself of his trial relative to the offering up of Isaac. But we seem to obtain a deeper insight into its exercise and reward on this occasion, when we look at it in the light of allusions made to it in other parts of Scripture. In particular, both the apostle Paul (Heb. xi. 19), and our blessed Lord (John viii. 5, 6), lead us to an understanding of the precise truths which Abraham believed, more definite than a perusal of the history, without the benefit of their commentaries, might of itself suggest. They speak to the question of the What? as well as the How? It is not now merely—How did Abraham believe? how strongly, unhesitatingly, unreservedly? but, What did Abraham believe? what facts and doctrines had such a hold over his convictions as to make him willing "against hope to believe in hope," and to slay his only son—the very son "of whom it was said that in Isaac shall thy seed be called"?

One article of his creed is not obscurely indicated as having some bearing on this act of faith. He did it,— "accounting that God was able to raise him up, even from the dead; from whence also he received him in a figure" (Heb. xi. 19). What gave him courage for the offering up of Isaac, was his "accounting that God was able to raise him up, even from the dead."

But a question arises. Was it a return to this present life that Abraham had in his view, or a resurrection to life in the world to come? Did he contemplate the possibility of a miracle similar to that performed long after by our Lord in the case of Lazarus? Or, was he thinking of his lost child as Martha thought of her departed brother, when, in reply to the assurance of Jesus, "thy brother shall rise again," she said, so simply—"I know that he shall rise again, on the resurrection, at the last day."

It may have been upon some such event as the raising of Lazarus that Abraham reckoned. The God who commanded him, at one instant, to slay his son, was able the very next to restore him again to his arms. Abraham could not doubt that. So far, this may appear at first sight a credible and consistent enough account of his conduct.

But on farther consideration, it will probably be felt by
most men to savour somewhat of refinement; it makes the
apostle's explanation of the patriarch's faith somewhat far-
fetched and artificial. Such a raising of Isaac to life again,
was not a natural idea to enter into the mind of Abraham; if
it had, it would have been fitted to give rather an unmeaning
character to the whole scene in his eyes. The intense reality
of it is upon this supposition gone; and a sort of theatrical
stroke, or piece of stage effect, is substituted in its stead. We
have the impression that God is not acting in his usual manner, or in a way altogether worthy of himself, in thus commanding a deed to be done, on the implied understanding that
he is instantly to undo it. And Abraham putting his son to
death upon the faith of God being able to restore him again
to life, is subjected to a physical rather than a moral trial—
to the mere instinctive pain of embruing his hands in kindred
blood, rather than to any exercise of the higher and more
spiritual faculties or affections of his soul. Surely, when having built the altar and laid the wood in order, and having
bound Isaac his son, and laid him on the altar upon the wood,
the venerable father stretches forth his hand, and takes the
knife to slay his son—it is with no expectation of ever seeing
him in this world again; it is a long last look of love that he
casts upon that dear face, and a fond and final farewell that
he sadly whispers in that ear, as he nerves his hand for the
fatal, the irrevocable stroke!

And then, on the other hand, the idea of a resurrection to
life in a future state was as familiar to Abraham, as that of a
return from death in this world must have been strange and
inconceivable. Had any one sought to encourage him concerning his son, by telling him that it was not impossible for
God to reanimate the mangled body, and recall the departed
spirit; had some Eliphaz, or Bildad, or Zophar been schooling
him to patience by some such discourse on the divine omnipotence, and the abstract possibility of a dead man being

restored to life ; Abraham, like Job, might have winced under the commonplaces of his miserable comforters ; but as to the notion they would insinuate into his imagination,—he must have rejected it as a temptation, not from God, but from Satan ; he must have felt it to be a fond delusion and a dream.

But it could not "be thought" by him " a thing incredible that God should raise the dead " (Acts xxvi. 8). On the contrary, that is " the very hope of the promise made of God unto the Fathers," as Paul speaks in his defence before Agrippa ; — " unto which promise," he adds, " our twelve tribes, instantly serving God day and night, hope to come " (Acts xxvi. 7). In the very passage, moreover, in which his reference to the sacrifice of Isaac occurs, he celebrates the faith of the patriarchs generally, and especially the faith of Abraham, as a faith which made them feel that they were strangers and pilgrims in the land, looking for a more permanent order of things beyond the tomb (Heb. xi. 9-16). And it is in immediate connection with this explanation of the hope which animated Abraham, as well as all that went before him in the heavenly race, that the apostle introduces, as a specimen and choice example of it, the incident of the offering up of Isaac.

Surely, therefore, we may conclude, on all these grounds, that what Abraham in this instance relied on, was not generally the power of God to raise the dead, but specially his power to fulfil his promise about the resurrection and the inheritance of the world to come. It was no vague notion of the divine omnipotence,—or of God being able to do any thing, however strange,—that sustained the patriarch ; but a hope far more express and unequivocal ; a hope having respect unequivocally to the world to come.

Thus veiwed, the trial of Abraham's faith receives a meaning not perceived before.

He had been warned, that with respect to himself personally, the promise of " the land which God was to show him "

(Gen. xii. 1) ;—" the place which he should after receive as an inheritance " (Heb. xi. 8) ;—the very promise on the faith of which he left the country of his birth and the home of his fathers ;—was to have its fulfilment in the resurrection state, or in the world to come. He had been told that he should " go to his fathers in peace, and be buried in a good old age," and that several generations must elapse before the land was to be taken from its present possessors and vacated for his posterity (Gen. xv. 15, 16). Thus far he had been taught to abandon the prospect of his being himself put in possession of the promised inheritance on this side of time, and had been led to regard it as a hope for eternity. But he might still be clinging to the present—the seen and temporal—in reference to his seed. Contented to die himself before receiving the promised inheritance, he might still be dwelling on the bright future that stretched itself out before his children in the land. And now that Isaac was born, he might be willing to say, as Simeon said, " Now lettest thou thy servant depart in peace," —not from any spiritual apprehension of eternal things, but because he could now leave behind him one who, even in a temporal point of view, might elevate his name and lineage among the families of men.

The command to offer up Isaac is the test of his faith upon this very point. Is he willing, not merely to have his own inheritance postponed till after the resurrection, but the inheritance of his seed also ? Can he bear to have, not only his own expectation, but that of Isaac, deferred to the future state ?

He can ; for he believes in the resurrection. He "accounts that God is able to raise him up, even from the dead." He can forego, therefore, all his fond imagination of being the founder of a family and father of a great nation, in this present world. He can consent to the arrangement that after his decease there is to be no farther trace of him excepting only in the line of Ishmael that has been so unequivocally disowned.

He is to die in a good old age; and it may be that he is to survive the son of whom it has been said, "In Isaac shall thy seed be called." After his decease, there may be no genuine representative of his house left behind; and to the end of time it may be matter of wonder and reproach that neither he, nor any child of his, has ever actually got possession of the inheritance, on the faith of which he went out, "not knowing whither he went." But none of these things move Abraham. He looks not to the things which are seen and temporal, but to the things which are unseen and eternal; being well assured that "if our earthly house of this tabernacle were dissolved, we have a building of God, an house not made with hands, eternal in the heavens" (2 Cor. iv. 18; v. 1).

Great indeed, in this view, is the faith of Abraham—great almost beyond our power of sympathy or insight. And yet we may partly measure it by the universal instinct which prompts men to aim at leaving a name, or building a house, that shall survive their own removal. One of the most painful thoughts connected with death is that "the place which once knew us shall know us no more;" and one of the strongest natural desires in a parent's bosom is to live again in his children. Not a few of us can make up our minds to our own obscurity; but we yearn after distinction in the race we are to leave behind. It is often the last weakness even of a spiritual man to cherish such prospects of posthumous renown; and it is no trifling trial of his spirituality when he must submit to his not having, either in his own person, or in his posterity, a high position in the world. But if this is trying to a man having only ordinary expectations in this life, what must it have been to Abraham? No common parent is he; nor is it any common hope that is bound up with the son for whose birth he has waited so long. The child of promise is the heir of no common birthright. A glory coextensive with the blessing of all the families of the earth is in store for his seed; a mighty nation is to hail him as their honoured sire; and the

whole world is to own him as the source or channel of its regeneration.

And are the whole of these bright anticipations to stand
over till time gives place to eternity? Is the patriarch, after
having been taught to see glorious visions of temporal greatness
and spiritual good hovering over the head of his dear child,—
visions reaching to long ages and embracing the entire family
of man,—not only to depart himself ere they are realised, but
to have the realisation of them made impossible in the present
world, and possible only in the world to come?

Then so be it. "Lord, not my will but thine be done."
Abraham believes that God is able to raise the dead; and
therefore he is willing to have the entire inheritance of
himself and of his seed laid up in that unseen and eternal
heavenly state to which the faithful dead are to be raised.
His faith in the resurrection reconciles him to the loss of all
his possessions and prospects in the life that now is, and
enables him to lay hold of the treasure that is in heaven.

Such, then, is the precise and specific character of
Abraham's faith, as brought out in the greatest trial it had
to undergo. It embraces the doctrine of the resurrection.
And it embraces that doctrine with a cordial preference of the
state that is beyond the resurrection over the state that is on
this side of it. There is thus plain evidence in it of that
transference of the affections from earth to heaven, which a
divine agency alone can effect. It obtains accordingly a
suitable as well as signal reward. Being made perfect by
works—having its consummation in the act of obedience
which it prompted—it has its appropriate and congenial recompense also in that very act itself. He "received" Isaac
"from the dead, in a figure" (Heb. xi. 19). He "saw the
day of Christ, and was glad" (John viii. 56).

In the first place, "he received Isaac from the dead,
in a figure." In the signal and seasonable deliverance of his
son he had a vivid representation of the resurrection which

he had believed that God was able to effect. To all intents and purposes, Isaac had been dead, and was now alive from the dead. It was an emphatic rehearsal of the real and literal resurrection ; nor could the patriarch, having been thus brought to feel the power of the world to come, ever afterwards lose the vivid sight and sense he had got of its eternal realities. Isaac has been spared to him ; and, in acknowledgment of his obedient faith, the promises are renewed to him of a numerous family through Isaac, as well as of the Saviour in whom all the nations of the earth are to be blessed (ver. 15-18). But the blessings thus graciously secured to him in time, must have a peculiar meaning now in his eyes, when viewed in the light of the resurrection and of eternity. For the lesson he has been taught is really this ;— that the promises reach beyond this present life, and have their chief fulfilment in the life to come ; that, even if he should see no fulfilment of them here, this need not surprise or grieve him, since there is a greater and better fulfilment of them in reserve hereafter ; and that any fulfilment of them he may see on earth is altogether subordinate to the fulfilment awaiting him in heaven. The birthright of which Isaac is the heir, is now seen to have its principal seat—not in this world, where all is change, and where, in a moment, the child of promise may be suddenly cut off—but in the world to come, where there is no more sorrow or separation, because there is in it no more sin.

Thus, in the second place, "Abraham saw the day of Christ" in this transaction, "and was glad." For we can scarcely doubt that it is to this transaction that the Lord refers in his controversy with the Jews on the subject of their boast of liberty, and their standing in the house or family of God (John viii. 34-59).*

It is an animated controversy. The Lord drives them back from one point of defence to another. He proves that

* See Lectures on the *Fatherhood of God*, Appendix 5.

they are the servants of sin ; so that they can have no footing but that of servants in relation to God. He meets their proud boast of descent from Abraham, by an appeal to their entire want of sympathy with Abraham. He meets their still prouder boast of having God as their father, by the exposure of their family-likeness, not to God, but to Satan. And at last, in answer to their challenge—" Art thou greater than our father Abraham, which is dead ?"—he announces himself as the object of Abraham's faith : " Your father Abraham rejoiced to see my day ; and he saw it, and was glad" (John viii. 56).

Now, the day of Christ which Abraham "rejoiced"—or earnestly desired—to see, must be the day of which he himself speaks ; " I must work the work of him that sent me while it is day." It is the day of his sojourn on earth ; when he glorified his Father, and finished the work given him to do. More particularly, it is the day on which his work was finished, and he was himself acknowledged, accepted, and glorified by the Father ; according to the prophecy of the second psalm—" Thou art my Son ; this day have I begotten thee." For " this day," as the apostle Paul expressly explains it, is the day on which God " raised up Jesus again" (Acts xiii. 33). That is the day of Christ which Abraham desired, and was permitted, to see.

But the sight which he longed to have of it must have been something more than was ordinarily granted to the saints and patriarchs of old. They, indeed, living by faith in a Saviour yet to come, looked forward to his day, and anticipated the time when the Seed of the woman should bruise the head of the serpent. But what the Lord refers to would seem to have been the peculiar privilege of Abraham ; for Abraham is very specially represented as desiring to see " the day of Christ ;" and as on some special occasion seeing it, and being fully gratified with the sight.

But what occasion in the history of Abraham can we fix

upon more probably than the occasion now before us ?   And does it not give a very beautiful significancy to that most mysterious transaction, if we regard it as the appointed means of affording to Abraham that glad sight of " the day of Christ" for which he had longed and prayed ?   Regarded in no other light than as a trial of Abraham's faith, the narrative of the offering up of his son Isaac is abundantly interesting and affecting.   But it becomes still more so, if we look at it in the light of our blessed Lord's commentary.

Abraham had desired to see " the day of Christ ; " and a sight of it, more full and distinct than believers of that time ordinarily had, is to be granted to him.   He is to see in vivid reality the details of that event, the general outline of which alone was then communicated to others.   For this end, he is to stand on Mount Moriah, which, as some think, is the very spot subsequently called the hill of Calvary.   And he is to behold the scene of the atonement accomplished there.

He beholds it in a threefold figure.   First of all, when he takes the knife, and stretches forth his hand to slay his son, he is made to realise the intensity of the love of him who spared not his own Son, but gave him up even to the death. Again, secondly, in the ram provided for Isaac's release, there is a vivid representation of the great principle of the sacrifice of Christ—the principle of substitution.   A ransom is found for the doomed and condemned—an acceptable victim is put in their place.   But, thirdly and especially, in the reception of Isaac again by Abraham virtually from the dead, and his welcome restoration to his father's embrace ;—not, however, without a sacrifice, not without blood ;—the resurrection of the Son of God, and his return to the bosom of the Father—after really undergoing that death which Isaac underwent only in a figure—might be clearly and strikingly discerned.   And in Christ's resurrection, his own resurrection also was involved, as well as the resurrection of all his true children, to the inheritance of eternal glory.

Thus the very transaction which so severely tried the faith of Abraham showed him all that his faith longed so much to see. He saw the day of Christ—the day of his humiliation and triumph—not darkly and dimly as others then saw it, but clearly, distinctly, vividly. He saw the very way in which the salvation of man was to be accomplished, and the blessing purchased for all the families of the earth, by the atoning death and glorious resurrection of the beloved Son of God. And seeing thus gladly the day of Christ, he saw Christ himself as the Living One;—dead indeed, and sacrificed once for all, yet still living, and by his very death enabled to be the author of life to the " many sons whom he bringeth unto glory " (Heb. ii. 10).

These, then, are the gracious fruits of this trial of Abraham's faith. They are such as the trial of our faith also may yield. For we are tried in the very same way with him. We are called to give up to God the desire of our eyes—the beloved of our hearts—some dear partner, or child, or friend, around whose brow, in our fond esteem, the halo of many a bright anticipation shone. It is a bitter parting; and it is hard to acquiesce in it,—to consent to it. But it is God's will; and we submit. And what sustains us, but our accounting that God is able to raise him from the dead ? Yes; let him depart to be with Christ—and let the once beauteous body rot in the silent tomb to which my own hand consigns it. I know he is not lost after all. My own inheritance now is not on earth but in heaven ; and in heaven he will rejoin me again. For myself and for him, I place all my hope beyond the grave. It is but a little while. " This corruptible must put on incorruption." " The Lord shall appear, and all that are his shall appear with him in glory."

Is my heart wrung with the anguish of that parting hour ? Is the bitterness of death felt in my desolate home, and my still more desolate heart ? Ah ! do I not now enter as I never did before—with a new insight and new sympathy—into the agony of the death endured by him who bore my sins in his own body on the tree? And as I lift my thoughts from this shadowy scene to the region of realities, how does my bosom burn with adoring gratitude and love to that Saviour who has spoiled death of its sting, and the grave of its victory,—who has abolished death, and brought life and immortality to light!

He calls me to suffer with him now, that we may be "glorified together" hereafter. He would have me to be partaker of his cross, that he may make me partaker of his crown. Through his own day of suffering and shame, issuing in his return to the Father's bosom, he summons me to the hope of that heaven where he dwells. Am I contented to have all my hope there—and there only? Can I bear to have my portion postponed—my expectation deferred—till the hour when time gives place to eternity? Can I resign myself to the surrender of every thing dearest to me here below—friendship, love, happiness,—honour, wealth,—a husband's or a wife's embrace,—a child's fond smile,—a friend's sweet counsel,—not in gloomy submission to fate ;—not in stoical and stubborn pride ;—not in heartless worldly unconcern ;—but in firm reliance upon that blessed Redeemer, who has himself passed through much tribulation, and gone to prepare a place for me among the many mansions of his Father's house? And he cometh again,—his risen saints all with him,—to receive me to himself, that I may be with him for ever! Even so, come, Lord Jesus.

29

TIDINGS FROM HOME—THEIR CONNECTION WITH
SARAH'S DEATH AND ISAAC'S MARRIAGE

Genesis 22:20-24; 23; 24

The three events recorded in the end of the 22d, in the
23d, and in the 24th chapters respectively, are more nearly
connected than might at first sight appear ; they have all a
common bearing on the settlement of Abraham's family in the
line of Isaac.   They form the last chain that binds the race
from which the father of the faithful sprung, with the race that
is to spring from him.   First, the patriarch hears news of his
kindred whom he left behind when he began to be a pilgrim
(xxii. 20-24).   Secondly, the tent of Sarah is made sadly vacant
(xxiii.)   And thirdly, as the issue of both events, a wife is
found for Isaac (xxiv.)   It is a kind of historical syllogism,
with its two suggestive premises and its legitimate conclusion ;
—not that there is any thing formal or artificial in the arrangement ;—on the contrary, the story is told so naturally, and as
it were unconsciously, that it requires a clue to trace the under-
current of connection throughout.

The mention, for instance, of Abraham's relatives, at the
close of the 22d chapter, seems to ordinary readers unmeaning
and abrupt.   It has nothing at all to do with the preceding
narrative ;—although the chance of chapters has bound it to
that narrative in modern editions and translations.   The previous act in the divine drama is complete ; the incident on
Mount Moriah being its catastrophe and close.   An entirely

new act begins at the twentieth verse ; the act of which the climax is the marriage of Isaac. And it has its appropriate successive scenes :—the first, common and preliminary, the household receiving apparently indifferent intelligence ; the second, tender and pathetic, implying deep domestic woe ; and the third, affording a welcome relief, in the advantage taken of the news that came first, and the consolation administered to the sorrow that followed after. In this connection, let the three scenes be successively considered.

I. The tidings from the old home are briefly narrated (chap. xxii. 20-24) :—" And it came to pass after these things, that it was told Abraham, saying, Behold, Milcah, she hath also born children unto thy brother Nahor ; Huz his firstborn, and Buz his brother, and Kemuel the father of Aram, and Chesed, and Hazo, and Pildash, and Jidlaph, and Bethuel. And Bethuel begat Rebekah : these eight Milcah did bear to Nahor, Abraham's brother. And his concubine, whose name was Reumah, she bare also Tebah, and Gaham, and Thahash, and Maachah."

It is a catalogue of strange and hard names that we have here. But it is introduced for a particular purpose, and that no unimportant one. For the information thus brought to Abraham, respecting the friends he had so long ago left behind in the country from which he migrated, has more in it than a mere matter of ordinary domestic intelligence might seem to imply. It has reference to the transaction afterwards recorded ;—the approaching marriage of Isaac.

Doubtless, in itself, simply as reminding him of those from whom he had now been parted for more than half-a-century, the tidings could not fail to be welcome to his affectionate heart. In the wandering and unsettled life which he led, so far from his father's house,—with the rare and difficult means of communication which then existed,—he seldom, or more probably never, during all this interval, had heard any certain report of his father's household—his kinsmen according to the flesh. The yearnings of that natural affection which he had been willing to subordinate to the command of him in whom he believed, but which had never been extinguished or diminished, must have been gratified by hearing of his brother's welfare ;—for, " as cold waters to a thirsty soul, so is good news from a far country."

But the particular juncture at which this message came, must have made it to him and to his partner peculiarly seasonable.

Isaac was now growing to man's estate ; and his parents were very naturally beginning to be anxious about his permanent establishment in life. They felt the necessity of the sacred family, the chosen seed, being kept separate and distinct from the surrounding worldly tribes. They shrank from connecting their son with even the best of the households among whom they dwelt. They dreaded the contagious influence of the growing impiety and corruption of the nations ; and they believed that it was God's purpose and desire that they should not intermingle or intermarry with the people of the land. But, at the same time, what could they do ? Here they were, isolated and secluded ; and it might seem that, in the circumstances, neither they nor their son had any choice.

Considerations like these must have cost the believing parents of Isaac many an uneasy thought. And as they could not but know that they must themselves ere long be removed, the situation of their son, so soon to be left alone in the world, must have been the frequent subject of their earnest communings and their united prayers.

At the right time, the apparently casual intelligence reaches them ;—" And it came to pass after these things, that it was told Abraham, saying, Behold, Milcah, she hath also born children unto thy brother Nahor ;" (xxii. 20)—among the rest, " Bethuel," who has become the father of " Rebekah " (ver. 23).

Is this not a hint from heaven—to relieve their anxiety and direct their conduct ?

To Sarah, in particular, now about to depart, how gracious is this kindness of the Lord! Her last and only care is removed. She owns the Lord's hand—leading her and her household by a way that she knew not. She may commit all to God—to him who "will provide" (Gen. xxii. 14)—whether it be a lamb for a burnt-offering, or a chosen handmaid to be a mother in Israel. She, too, sees "the day of Christ" afar off. Every obstacle to the fulfilment of the promise being taken away—"her eyes see the salvation of God." She is contented. "Lord now lettest thou thy servant depart in peace." It is all well. "The Lord will provide."

Thus we trace a connection between the short genealogy of Nahor's family in Mesopotamia, and the eventful history of Abraham and his household in Canaan. Nor is the connection to be regarded as a strained or far-fetched one. On the contrary, it is essential to the right understanding of what otherwise must be felt to be an unseasonable and unmeaning interruption in the narrative. And a lesson may be derived from the analogy that is to be traced, in reference to this particular, between the word and the providence of God. For in actual life, may not instances be noticed of incidents occurring, which at the time appear to be very casual and insignificant—parenthetical and insulated circumstances, coming in as it were by the way, in the onward course of more important events—which ere long, however, are found to have a material bearing upon what God in his providence is about to bring to pass? A mere flying rumour may drop seed that is soon to spring up and bear fruit—fruit for good or for evil—that may endure even beyond this present world and reach into eternity. The whole complexion of a man's life may be affected by an occurrence, as slight and seemingly immaterial, as "its being told Abraham" that his brother had had children born to him.

Surely, therefore, it is the part of wisdom as well as of

devotion, if we believe in the exercise of a particular providence on the part of God over human affairs, not hastily to conclude concerning any thing that befalls us, or any thing that we happen to learn—however trivial and accidental it may seem to be—that it is unworthy of remark or of remembrance. Let us rather be on the watch "to regard the works of the Lord and the operation of his hands,"—to notice the minute evidences of design which even the details of his dealings with us afford. For we may be sure that every thing which he does, or which he would have us to know that he has done, has a meaning; which we "may not know now, but which we shall know hereafter" (John xiii. 7). "Whoso is wise, and will observe these things, even they shall understand the loving-kindness of the Lord" (Ps. cvii. 43).

30

THE DEATH AND BURIAL OF A PRINCESS

Genesis 23:1-20

IN the announcement of Sarah's age at her death, the minute and literal criticism of the Jewish expositors takes notice of a peculiarity of expression. Exactly rendered, the text speaks, not of the life, but of the lives of Sarah: "Sarah was an hundred and seven and twenty years old: these were the years of the life" or lives "of Sarah" (ver. 1). To these fanciful and ingenious fabulists, the slightest hint is enough: and accordingly they tell us of three lives, or stages of life, in Sarah's career, distinguished according to the numbers employed in summing up the whole;—"a hundred; and seven; and twenty." The conceit is childish, if not profane.

There is, however, some reason to suppose that in the latter years of her pilgrimage, she renewed miraculously her youthful beauty, as well as her youthful capacity of conceiving seed, when the time for the birth of Isaac drew near;—what passed in Abimelech's land may be some confirmation of that idea. Nor.is it unimportant to observe that it is not said of Sarah at her death, as it is usually said of the other patriarchs, and as it is said at a former period of herself, that she was "well stricken in age." Moses, we are told, retained the freshness of manhood to the close of his extreme old age—"his eye was not dim, nor his natural force abated" (Deut. xxxiv. 7). Sarah, in her old age, "received strength" (Hebrews xi. 11); and it may be that she continued in the enjoyment of that strength, and in her restored prime of life, to the last.

That her end was blessed, we cannot doubt. She was, indeed, highly favoured among women ; second only to the mother of our Lord—of whom, indeed, in the extraordinary birth of Isaac, she was an evident type, as Isaac himself prefigured the favoured virgin's Son. Her name was significant of her character and fame. To Abraham, from the beginning of his pilgrimage, she was " Sarai,—my princess ;" so he delighted affectionately to honour her. To the church at large, the vast multitude of Abraham's believing children, she is " Sarah—the princess ;"—to whom, as to a princess, they are gratefully to look, and whom in all generations they are to call blessed (chap. xvii. 16, 17).

Yet the tenor of Sarah's life was very private, unostentatious, and unassuming. She tarried at home. The leading features of her character which the word of inspiration commends are these :—her holy and unadorned simplicity ; her meek and quiet spirit—an ornament in the sight of God of great price ; and her believing and loving subjection to a believing and loving husband (1 Pet. iii. 1-6). She was devoted to Abraham ; not in the mere blindness of natural and fond affection, but with an intelligent apprehension and appreciation of his high standing, as the friend of God and the heir of the covenant. She did not indeed always act wisely. Her false step in giving Hagar to Abraham, through despair of the fulfilment of God's promise—her harshness in resenting the frowardness of her maid—her incredulous laughter at the announcement of the Angel—her attempt, in the confusion occasioned by the Angel's sudden discovery of her offence, to prevaricate and to deny it,—these are blemishes over which we may breathe a sigh. Let devout women by all means be warned against such sins, and against the unbelief which is their source. In his very commendation of Sarah, the apostle points to what her daughters are to avoid, as well as what they are to imitate, in her example. He makes mention of that " amazement of fear " which led her to conceal by a false-hood the deviation from " well-doing " into which she had been betrayed, and so to add sin to sin (1 Pet. iii. 6). Still, these errors need not detract altogether from the sincerity of her faith, and her meek devotedness to her husband,—or rather to him in whom both she and her husband believed.

For she too walked by faith, having favour with God, and waiting for his salvation. In faith, being like-minded with Abraham, she left her early home and her father's house. In faith, she bore him company through the long years of his exile, cheering him amid many troubles, and upholding him under many disappointments. Through faith she received strength to conceive seed ; and afterwards, when even Abraham himself was perhaps too much divided between the child after the flesh and the child by promise—between his own righteousness and that of God—between the covenant of legal bondage and the covenant of grace and liberty,—she seems to have had a more spiritual discernment than he had. She be-lieved salvation to be in the line of Isaac alone ; and her counsel, to " cast out the bondwoman and her son," obtained the sanction of God himself. Finally, she stands enrolled among those " of whom the world was not worthy ; " and it is in immediate connection with her, and with " the strength she received to bear seed because she judged him faithful who had promised," that the apostle introduces his comprehensive testimony to the humble walk and high hope of all the patriarchs ;—" These all died in faith, not having received the promises, but having seen them afar off, and were persuaded of them, and embraced them, and confessed that they were strangers and pilgrims on the earth. For they that say such things declare plainly that they seek a country " (Heb. xi. 11-14).

Such was Sarah, living in faith and dying in faith ; whose daughters the matrons of Israel are,—even as their husbands are the children of faithful Abraham. The two " dwelt with one another according to knowledge, being heirs together of the grace of life," so that their " prayers were not hindered " (1 Pet. iii. 7). Such is the Scriptural model of marriage in the Lord, and such the high and holy honour that is to be attached to that estate, among all Abraham's sons and Sarah's daughters.

Thus " Sarah died in Kirjath-arba ; the same is Hebron in the land of Canaan : and Abraham came to mourn for Sarah, and to weep for her " (ver. 2).

From the expression in this second verse, " Abraham came to mourn for Sarah, and to weep for her," it has been supposed by some that he was absent at the time of his wife's death. At this period, in consequence of the size of his household, the multitude of his cattle, and the difficulty of removing them all at once, he very probably had two establishments ; the one at Beersheba and the other at Hebron ; both on the borders of the territory of the Philistines, and the country of Abimelech, king of Gerar ; and both within the limits of the promised land. His affairs having called him away from Hebron, he found, on his return,—recalled by the tidings of his beloved partner's illness,—that all was already over ; and that his house being turned into a house of mourning, nothing now remained for him but to weep !

To watch beside the bed where parting life is laid—to cool the throbbing brow and smooth the restless pillow—to whisper soothing words of consolation and catch the latest breath of expiring love—to press the cold hand, and close the eye now bright no more,—such offices of tenderness even the breaking heart would not forego. It is a sacred privilege to render them. It is a sad aggravation of the pain of separation to be away when they fall to be paid.

Whether Abraham was called to endure this additional bitterness of sorrow or not, we cannot tell. The phrase, " he came," is not conclusive. It may mean merely that he left his own tent, or private chamber, and betook himself to that of his deceased wife, to mourn,—or generally, that he set himself to discharge the usual functions of a mourner. But at all events, it is clear that he gave himself to this exercise of mourning ;—and that he did so of deliberate purpose and systematically.

There is much to be learned from this. Mourning for the dead is natural. When the tie of mutual affection is severed by the rude hand of the destroyer, tears spontaneously flow. It is a relief, it is an indulgence to weep—to weep for the dead ! But on what footing does this mourning for the dead stand, according to the estimate of faith and the rule of godliness ? Is it merely permitted—tolerated and allowed—as an infirmity ? That would be much. The assurance that he may sorrow without sinning, is an unspeakable consolation to the believer in his bereavement. The fact that Abraham " came to mourn for Sarah, and to weep for her,"—still more the fact that " Jesus wept,"—is as oil poured into the wounds of the heart's lacerated and torn affections. But that is not all. Still more complete—still more wonderful—is the adaptation of the Gospel to man's nature and man's trials. The patriarch evidently made conscience of his mourning. He gave himself to the exercise, not merely as to a privilege but as to a duty. His sighs and tears were not simply regarded by him as lawful, for the relief of his overcharged and overburdened soul ;— even into this department of his experience he carried his sense of obligation. In a religious and spiritual sense, he made a business of his grief. He went about the indulgence of it as a work of faith ; he allotted to it a fixed and definite time ; he came to Sarah's tent for the express purpose ; he gave up for this work his other avocations and his other employments. His occupation was " to mourn for Sarah and to weep for her."

There is therefore a time to weep ; there is a time to mourn. There is a season during which to mourn and weep

is not merely the allowed license, or tolerated weakness, of the
believer, but his proper business—the very exercise to which
he is called. This instance of Abraham is not only a warrant
and precedent, but a binding and authoritative example. It
not merely sanctions a liberty ; it imposes an obligation.

The custom, indeed, of all ages and nations has borne testimony to the obligation. At all times and in all places, the
usage of society—ancient as well as modern—eastern and
western alike—has prescribed a certain period and certain
forms of mourning. The mourner is expected to seclude
himself for a while from the tumult and gaiety of life, and to
be conversant with symbols significant of sorrow. To transgress these rules is accounted unseemly and unfeeling. To
rush from a domestic deathbed to the public gaze of the garish
world, whether in the way of business, or in pursuit of pleasure
and excitement, is confessedly an outrage on the common
decencies of society, as well as on all the sympathies of our
social nature. Doubtless, the usage may become a form—a
mockery—a farce. The rueful look—the managed tears—the
ostentatious solitude and elaborate retirement—the weeds and
trappings—the sighs and sentiments,—all may be mere ceremony—as repulsive to true delicacy of taste and feeling, as
were the cuttings and howlings of the hired mourners at
heathen funerals of old. Still, the practice has its foundation,
not only in the natural sense and sensibility of mankind, but
in reason and in faith. It is in itself right. It is fitted to
serve a spiritual and sacred end ; if only in a becoming spirit
we consider in connection with it, first the past, and secondly
the future.

Thus as to the past,—in looking back along the vista of
years, there is pregnant matter for most profitable meditation.
One natural thought may perhaps be suffered for a moment—
the thought that had it been possible, we would have had the
event itself, or some of its circumstances, differently ordered.
But in this, let there be no sinful reproaching, either of the

decree of Heaven, or of second causes and subordinate accidents on earth. Let us look on the past—not in discontent or melancholy musing merely—but in deep self-abasement and lowly gratitude.

Ah! what questions, reaching far back in life's varied history, does the breaking of a fond tie of brotherhood force on the startled memory? How old is that now broken tie? When and how was it first recognised as a tie of nature, or formed as a tie of love? When and how did it become a tie closer still,—a tie of grace? For how many years,—for what portion of a century,—a quarter, or a half, or more,—has the tie subsisted? And during all that period how have you lived and walked together,—you and the loved one now gone to return no more? You thought that you dwelt together in unity; that you had enough of mutual esteem and love; that you had few occasions of difference or dissension, and little or no unkindness with which to reproach one another. The current of your natural affection,—your wedded happiness—your parental tenderness—your social joy—flowed smoothly and equably along. There might be occasional waves and eddies; but there was no serious obstacle to trouble or to break the stream. Do you think so now? Do no bitter regrets and recollections haunt you? Is there no painful handwriting on the wall? Especially in regard to your spiritual fellowship together, have you no uneasy misgivings?

It is a humbling lesson which this mourning may teach,—pricking the conscience with a new sense of sin,—touching the heart with a profounder feeling of the vanity of all earthly things. But it is not all dreariness and woe. Think of the way by which God has led you and your partner together, and trace his fatherly hand in his manifold dealings with you. Review and revive, in your saddened memory, scenes of tenderness long past and gone; hours, perhaps, of holy and blessed communion in the Lord; days when you and your beloved went up to God's house, taking sweet counsel together; times of refreshing, when "your souls prospered and were in health," and you were knit one to another, as by a new bond of heaven's own love! Instead of dwelling only on what is dark and gloomy in the lines which recollection sadly traces, allow the brighter spots to refresh your eye. Recall the Lord's goodness towards those whom you have lost;—the gifts with which they were endowed, the services they were enabled to render to the commonwealth or the church, the long lives of usefulness they were permitted to lead on earth, and the indications their last days may have afforded of mellow ripeness for heaven. So you will be stirred up to new aspirations of faith and prayer, that you may be "followers of them who, through faith and patience, have inherited the promises" (Heb. vi. 12); and that you may meet them at last, when "the Lord shall appear," and all that are his "shall appear with him in glory" (Col. iii. 4).

The future, however, as well as the past, is to occupy the thoughts in the season of mourning. We are to look forward, as Abraham was fain to do.

His happiness on earth was now well nigh at an end. The delight of his eyes, the beloved of his heart, is no longer fair and pleasant to look upon. She can no more share his dwelling. The green earth must cover what else would be offensive;—"Let me bury my dead out of my sight" (ver. 4).

And is this, then, all? Is this the close of that long and endearing fellowship of Abraham and Sarah in the Lord? Has it passed away "as a tale that is told?" Is Abraham to put away his dead for ever? Is he to have done with this severed tie of sanctified love as with a broken potsherd, or with water spilt on the ground?

That can scarcely be. For, in the first place, he is very careful of the lifeless body; he is much concerned about its being decently disposed of. Why should he be so, unless that body is to live again? Why is he so anxious for the comely interment of what, to the eye of sense, is but a mass of clay ? Why is the very dust of his beloved so dear to him ?—her body so sacred, and to be sacredly handled ? It is not mere sentiment and fancy, but rather strong and hopeful faith. This thy sister, thy spouse, shall rise again. Her remains, therefore, may well be precious in thy esteem.

Such, probably, is the origin of that care for the burial of the dead which has prevailed so universally from the earliest ages among all men. It is to be traced to the primeval and traditionary revelation of a resurrection. The practice, no doubt, degenerated into a superstition ;—as witness the ceremonies connected with the burning and embalming of the lifeless remains of departed friends,—the reverence paid to their relics and their ashes,—as well as the multitude of sepulchral rites, alike frivolous and abominable, to which blind fanaticism has everywhere and always had recourse. Nevertheless, there is a foundation of divine truth, not less than of human affection, for the universal concern of survivors as to the disposal of their dead. It is a testimony to the doctrine of the resurrection of the dead.

But this is not all. For, in the second place, Abraham is not merely anxious about the decent and comely interment of his beloved Sarah; he is concerned also about the place where she is to be buried, and especially about having it as his own. He is smitten suddenly and strangely with the desire of being a proprietor in the land (ver. 3, 4). How is this, at such a time ? Hitherto he has been contented to be a stranger and pilgrim, not owning a foot of ground in the country which God had promised to give to himself personally, as well as to his seed, for an inheritance. Now he must have some possession in it that, by the strictest and fullest right, he can call his own. He covets, indeed, no very wide domain ;—no large and productive estate. A barren rock, a hollow cave, is all he cares for; not fields whose rich harvests may fill his barns, but a solitary sepulchre to receive the dust of his dead. Still such

as it is, he must have it as his own.   He insists on that with
not a little pertinacity in his conference with the people of the
land ; and he must be supposed to have some good reason for
insisting on it.

The narrative of this remarkable conference (ver. 3–20) is
singularly graphic and picturesque.   Abraham appears in a
peculiarly interesting light.   It is pleasing to see the esteem
in which he is evidently held, as well as the sympathy which
his domestic misfortune awakens.   And the somewhat stately
and elaborate, yet graceful interchange of courtesy between
him and the sons of Heth, is in the finest style of oriental
manners.   It is a vividly painted scene of the olden time.
We see the whole negotiation going on before our eyes ; and
as we listen to the formal compliments that pass between the
parties,—with such studied dignity, yet withal such real cordiality and kindness,—we feel as if we actually witnessed the
solemn gravity of countenance with which they mutually
saluted one another,—and as if, for all that solemnity, we
could yet clasp them in a genuine embrace of brotherhood.

But the spiritual meaning of the transaction, and its bearing upon Abraham's faith and hope, should interest us, as
believers, even more than its simple and natural beauty.

Why does Abraham refuse the proposal of the children of
Heth, that he should make use of one of their sepulchres ?
(ver. 6-9.)   And why does he decline the second proposal
made to him by " Ephron the Hittite, the son of Zoar,"—who,
finding that the patriarch has set his heart on a particular
cave which he wishes to purchase, offers frankly and heartily
to make it over, with the field in which it is situated, as a
free gift for ever ? (ver. 10-13.)   But no ! nothing will satisfy
him but his being allowed to make the property his own by
right of purchase.   Accordingly the bargain is struck ; the
money is paid ; the transference is made in due form of law,
and in presence of a sufficient number of witnesses.   Abraham
weighs to Ephron the silver, and receives a sure right to the
field (ver. 14-20).

There is something very singular in all this. It is more than a mere contest of politeness between persons unwilling to be outdone by one another in the exchange of mutual courtesies. Might not these men of Heth, and this Ephron the Hittite, have with some reason charged Abraham with something like churlishness in thus refusing so peremptorily to let them show him any kindness? It was as if he was determined to misunderstand and distrust them; and it really argued, one would say, almost as high a tone of generous feeling on their part that they did not take Abraham's refusal amiss, as that they made to him the proposals which he so obstinately declined.

Abraham could not mean to offend these kind and friendly neighbours. Nor could he have any silly scruple about being under obligation to an honourable man for a slight token of respect—a natural and simple office of good will.

The explanation of his conduct must be found in the light in which he regarded the land in which he was a sojourner. For let it be remembered, as I have already explained, that the only hope connected with the future world which Abraham had, was bound up in the promise that he was himself personally to inherit that land. There is no trace, in all the patriarch's history, of any other promise whatever, relating to the life to come. What Abraham was taught to expect was the inheritance of the very soil on which he trod, all the long years of pilgrimage. It was to be his at last; his personally.

Does not this hope give a peculiar and very precious meaning to Abraham's determination that Sarah shall not be buried in a strange, or in a hired, or even in a lent or gifted tomb, but in a sepulchre most strictly and absolutely his own? He is taking infeftment in his inheritance. It belongs not to him living; but it belongs to him, and to his, when dead. Living, he can but use it as the strange country of his pilgrimage; but dying in the sure prospect of rising again, he claims a proprietor's right in it; and his kindred dust is entitled to repose in it as a home.

True,—the patriarch may almost be imagined to say to the friendly children of Heth,—True it is, that while I and my household pitch our tents among you, we are for the present, as it were, your guests ; we are in the position of casual visitors, accidental sojourners. You are the proprietors of the country. You are our hosts, and we thankfully accept of your hospitality in all that relates to our present residence within your borders. But death makes a mighty difference. Living, I dispute not with you the possession of the land. But dying, I claim it as my own ; and this lifeless body of my spouse has a better right to it ultimately and in the long run, than you or any others can ever have so long as time endures. True, it is a right that will not be asserted until time gives place to eternity. Not till then will she, and I, and all our faithful seed, stand on our feet again to receive our final inheritance of glory. But nevertheless, the right to it belongs by divine covenant to that clay-cold corpse ; and so far as regards its needful accommodation till that day comes,—it shall have a place really its own to rest in.

Such might be Abraham's feelings, though not, of course, expressed in words, in reference to the proposals which his kind and courteous neighbours made to him. And such, probably, were the views with which, sad and sorrowing, yet not despairing, he consigned his beloved one to the tomb.

I would not dogmatise upon a subject so very obscure as that of the future habitation of the blessed ; the final abode of the risen saints of God. That their inheritance is to be material as well as spiritual, is expressly revealed ; and indeed follows almost as a necessary consequence from the doctrine of the resurrection of the body. Nor are there wanting indications that seem to point to this very material creation that is now their temporary dwelling-place, becoming in the end their everlasting home. Be that, however, as it may, this instance of Abraham's faith and hope, in connection with Sarah's burial, may be profitable to all believers.

It is a strong faith that he exercises ; it is an animating hope that he cherishes. In laying Sarah where she is to lie till the last trumpet sounds, Abraham anticipates the raising of her buried frame, in glorious beauty, once more to share his love. And for himself and for her he claims investiture in the promised inheritance of the "better country—even the heavenly,"—which they both alike earnestly longed for.

And is not this the very exercise of faith and hope, to which I am called when I bury a dear friend in the Lord ? I sorrow not as those who have no hope. True, my departed brother has now no portion in all that is under the sun ; nothing of all this fair and goodly earth can he claim as his own, save only the narrow cell that I have purchased for his sepulchre. But what living man really possesses such an inheritance as his lifeless clay may claim ? What ruler over a hundred kingdoms—what owner of thousands of acres—has an estate or property like that which belongs to his mouldering dust ? These proprietors are but tenants for a day ; at any moment they may receive notice to quit. But the dead body of a saint of God, destined to rise again, has an indefeasible right to an everlasting inheritance.

Ah ! it is the dead—the dead in Christ—who are the only legitimate possessors of this whole creation of God. To the redeemed dead belongs the entire property of the redeemed world. The rich man, clothed in purple and faring sumptuously every day, must be content with six feet of soil at last ; and even that is not his own ; the earth is to cast him out. But Lazarus, as angels carry his soul to Abraham's bosom— the beggar Lazarus, with his sores that the dogs were wont to lick—tossed carelessly into a reeking charnel-pit, where all vile things are contemptuously cast aside,—takes quiet possession bodily, by anticipation and in part, of what ultimately and in full is to belong to him for ever.

31

A MARRIAGE CONTRACTED IN THE LORD

Genesis 24:1-69

Whoso findeth a wife findeth a good thing, and obtaineth favour of the
Lord. Proverbs 18:22

House and riches are the inheritance of fathers ; and a prudent wife is from
the Lord. Proverbs 19:4

THE incidents recorded in this chapter are in themselves, viewed
simply in the light of a story of human life, full of interest.
The scene is one of homely and primitive simplicity ; its romance fills the imagination; its pathetic beauty affects the
heart. As a picture of manners, it has the blended charm of
classical and oriental grace ; as a domestic tale, it carries our
best and purest sympathies along with it.

The solicitude of the venerable father, and the affecting
solemnity of his charge to a long tried and trusted servant—
the oath so sacredly imposed, and with such scrupulous con-
scientiousness accepted—the departure of the messenger on his
singular errand—his honest devotedness to his master—his
unbounded reliance on his master's God and his own—these
preliminaries of this transaction are conceived and described
in the simplest and most touching style of pious faith (ver.
1-9). Nor does the interest of the narrative diminish as we
follow the old man—or rather go along with him—in his
strange embassy. All throughout, this chosen servant of the
chosen friend of God manifests his unbounded reliance on the
divine goodness and grace ; and we delight to connect his

tenderness of conscience in undertaking the mission beside Abraham's bed at first, with his committal of himself and it to the special providence of God, in that prayer at the well, so bold and at the same time so humble, in which he almost ventures to prescribe how his errand is to be accomplished—leaving the matter, however, unreservedly in his hands whose wisdom is as unerring as it is unsearchable. Thereafter, in quick succession, we mark, as if we saw them, the meeting at the well—the courtesy of the opening interview—the frank exchange of kindly greetings and good offices—the admirable delicacy of the servant's introduction of himself to the daughter of his master's kinsman—and his pious acknowledgment of the hand of the Lord in ordering the whole affair. Then passing on, we enter the brother's house. And we are touched by the servant's impatience to discharge his trust, and his simple recital of what the Lord had done for him, as affording, without argument or remark, or any pleading at all of his own, sufficient warrant of his suit. The promptness with which all is arranged, and the consent of all parties obtained—with no questioning or debate, but with a single eye to the manifest leadings of the divine providence, and a believing acquiescence in the divine will—this also forms a striking feature in the scene, and prepares us for the hasty departure of the maiden, with her faithful nurse as her single attendant. She willingly leaves her father's house—recognising the call of the same Lord who had called Abraham, and casting herself on him alone, with a noble confidence, worthy of one who is to be Abraham's daughter. Last of all, we trace the homeward journey—the approach of Isaac in his meditative evening walk—the vail modestly taken for a covering by his betrothed—the servant's recital to Isaac of all that he had done—and the cordiality with which Isaac welcomes the wife so evidently sent by God, and receives her into the tent of his lamented mother—" loving " her, as the history with touching simplicity concludes, and " being comforted."

All these circumstances combine to make this portion of the sacred record peculiarly attractive. In reading it, we feel at home amid these patriarchal incidents and descriptions, realising them as if they were familiar. The stately pomp and ceremony—the reserve and coldness and suspicion of a more artificial social state—pass away. The freshness of nature's early truth and tenderness returns—artless, guileless, fearless. We breathe a purer and freer air. We are touched with a deeper sense, at once of a special providence in heaven, and of a real and true sympathy on earth. We feel that there can be such a thing as the exercise of a frank and generous trust, relying both upon God and upon man; and that it is possible to act upon the belief, both of God's superintendence, and of man's sincerity.

A narrative like this is marred rather than illustrated by minute exposition. A few leading points may be selected as indicating its moral and spiritual bearings. Faith, and the prayer of faith, are here signally honoured.

I. Abraham in this matter is evidently guided by a higher wisdom than his own; although he is left apparently to consult and act for himself. There is no direct and immediate revelation of the divine will given for his guidance, as in many former instances of his difficult pilgrimage; he must exercise his own judgment. He is not, however, on that account, abandoned by God. He has signs enough to direct him; and using his best endeavour to discover and ascertain what the Lord would have him to do, he may, without anxiety, commit to him all his way.

He finds himself in circumstances which call for some step being taken. The mourning for Sarah is over; but sadness and desolation still reign in the patriarch's household. Her tent is still empty, and the grief of Isaac is still unsoothed. He is reminded also of his own approaching dissolution; his course on earth is drawing to a close; he is " old and well stricken in age;" but his cup is full,—" the Lord has blessed him in all things" (ver. 1). There is only one care remaining —one duty to be discharged, ere he depart in peace. Isaac's union with a suitable partner must if possible be secured ; " an help meet for him," as the son and successor of the patriarch, must be found.

It is a subject that may well perplex him. For it is not merely a private matter of personal and family arrangement, involving Isaac's individual happiness and the honour of his father's house. It is a public concern, intimately affecting the covenant of which Abraham is the earthly head, and the countless millions who are to be blessed in his seed. Isaac sustains a peculiar, an almost sacred character. It is his to inherit and transmit, not worldly possessions merely, but the hope and promise of salvation. Hence his marriage has an importance reaching far beyond himself ; and, in arranging it, there is a difficulty or dilemma.

For the conditions of the problem might seem to be irre-concilable. On the one hand, Isaac must contract no alliance with the daughters of the land ; and, on the other hand, he must not leave the land to seek a bride elsewhere. The for-mer condition is essential to the preservation of the holy seed pure and uncontaminated by any intermixture with strange and idolatrous nations. The latter is indispensable to his sharing with his faithful father, not only the future inheritance, but the present pilgrimage as well. For Isaac is to share his father's trial as well as his reward ; he is to walk by faith in an inheritance to come ;—living and dying in the land destined to be his, but without a portion in it that he can call his own, —except his grave. Hence he must continue among the people from whom he is not at liberty to select a wife ; he may not go in search of one to the ancient seat of his race. Here is a perplexity and a hard question ;—what is to be done ?

Abraham had, indeed, received intelligence from his early home, which he might well regard as a seasonable hint from

God; and had he been younger, he might himself have managed the affair. Now, he must leave it in other hands. But happily he has one in his household whom he can fully trust, an old and confidential servant;—the steward, as we may probably conjecture, who has been already noticed in this history,—Eliezer of Damascus (ver. 2-4). He, too, however, when the commission is first proposed to him, sees the difficulty. He is not to marry his master's son to any daughter of the Canaanites; neither will he be allowed to take Isaac back to the land from whence Abraham came. And yet he may be unable to persuade any woman of the country and kindred to which Abraham limits him,—any daughter of Terah's family, —to leave her home; to commit herself to the care of a stranger, and share the fortunes of an unknown husband. In these circumstances, he will not bind himself by an absolute and unconditional oath (ver. 5); nor is it until he is not only encouraged by Abraham's strong expression of his faith in the guidance of Jehovah, or the Angel of Jehovah,—but relieved also by the arrangement that, in the contingency he apprehended, he is to be free from his vow,—that he consents to undertake, under so solemn a sanction, so responsible a mission (ver. 5-8).*

* The manner of the oath is singular, having respect probably to the covenant of which Abraham had received the sign and seal;—the covenant ratified by the rite of circumcision, "And the servant put his hand under the thigh of Abraham his master, and sware to him concerning that matter" (ver. 9). Both Abraham and his servant regard the transaction in which they are now engaged as essentially connected with the covenant of which Isaac, or rather Isaac's seed, was to be the heir; and hence, by an appeal to the covenant, and to its seal, they hallow it. Or it may be that the party thus taking the oath swears by him who is to spring out of Abraham's loins,—the promised Saviour of the world;—if indeed the ceremony be not rather, as some think, a mere token of leal and loyal subjection, without any such peculiar spiritual significancy. At all events, this is manifestly a transaction of great and solemn import: and the pledge is to be regarded as one of no ordinary force.

II. Such being the spirit in which this commission is given by the aged patriarch, and undertaken by his confidential servant,—the execution of it is in entire harmony with its commencement.

The preparation for the journey being simply made, and the journey itself being well and happily accomplished (ver. 10), Abraham's ambassador and plenipotentiary sets himself to consider how the extraordinary treaty of marriage he has on hand may be most hopefully opened ; and after a somewhat strange manner does he proceed to open it He follows a course in which we may discern, perhaps, some traces of shrewd practical wisdom, as well as still more certain evidence of simple reliance on the providence of God—a course, as it turns out, proved to be as prudent as it is primitive and pious. The well beside which he has halted—now that he knows himself to be near the country of his destination—may afford a test of character as well as an occasion of prayer.

For the token which he asks of God is not wholly arbitrary (ver. 11-13) ; there is more in his appeal than the mere demand of a sign. It is not a parallel case to that of Gideon with his fleece (Judges vi. 37) ; still less is it like the haphazard venture of the Philistines, as to the disposal of the Ark of God (1 Sam. vi. 9). It resembles rather the arrangement Jonathan made with his solitary attendant, in his assault on the garrison of the Philistines :—" If they say thus unto us, Tarry until we come unto you ; then we will stand still in our place, and will not go up unto them. But if they say thus, Come up unto us ; then we will go up : for the Lord hath delivered them into our hand ; and this shall be a sign unto us" (1 Sam. xiv. 9, 10). For in both instances we may trace a reason for the token fixed upon. That which Jonathan proposed to his armour-bearer was fitted to indicate the actual state of the army to be assailed ;—whether so alert as to repel invasion, or so secure and careless as to encourage it. And the wise old ruler of Abraham's house, with admirable sagacity, adopted a measure calculated to prove the kindly nature of the woman whom he sought, as well as to secure the guidance of that God in the faith of whose providence he sought her.

But, after all, it is to be observed that Abraham's servant, in this entreaty for a sign, is by no means either peremptory or presumptuous. He does not arbitrarily stipulate for a miracle ; he does not even suspend his own procedure on a previous assurance being given of the interposition which he desires. He forms a plan of conduct,—the most expedient and most likely to be successful that could well be devised. He spreads it out before God ; and humbly seeks divine countenance and co-operation.

III. It is a striking and singular scene that now presents itself. Wearied with his journey, a stranger stands by the well ; and his camels at a little distance kneel down exhausted. There is nothing in his own appearance, or in his retinue, to distinguish him from an ordinary traveller. A solitary woman draws near (ver. 15-16). Suddenly she hears the wayfarer, —whom probably she has scarcely, if at all, observed before,— addressing to her a simple petition :—" Let me, I pray thee, drink a little water of thy pitcher" (ver. 17).

Ah! little thinks that fair young damsel of the issues that depend upon her reply ! How is it, she might have answered, that thou, being a foreigner,—and for anything I know, a foe, —askest drink of me, a native of this country,—a daughter much honoured in my father's home,—a lady entitled to be waited upon by my father's menials ? What am I, that I should minister to thee ? Or what art thou to me, that thou shouldest expect this favour at my hands ?

It was good for Rebekah that she did not answer thus. No other opportunity would probably have been given to her ; no second appeal would have been made to her ; no farther parley or pleading would have ensued.

Yes ! And it was good for another woman, who, long after, met another stranger, " wearied with his journey," at another

well,—that when she met his request, " Give me to drink,"
with the churlish question, " How is it that thou, being a Jew,
askest drink of me, which am a woman of Samaria ?" she had
a different person from Abraham's servant to deal with. A
rude reception of that sort might have ended at once and for
ever the negotiation for a marriage-treaty which this messenger
from Canaan was about to open. But that other messenger
from the heavenly Canaan is not so easily repelled ! " For
my thoughts are not your thoughts, neither are your ways my
ways, saith the Lord" (Isa. lv. 8).

The maiden, in the present instance, manifests that very
bountifulness of spirit which the woman of Samaria not only
wanted, but thought it strange that she should be expected to
possess. Without suspicion or inquiry, without upbraiding, she
is impatient to respond to the stranger's call and minister to
his wants. " She hasted," it is said ;—and said, not once, but
twice,—as if to indicate emphatically her ready mind, " She
said, Drink, my lord : and she hasted and let down her pitcher
upon her hand, and gave him drink. And when she had done
giving him drink, she said, I will draw water for thy camels
also, until they have done drinking. And she hasted, and
emptied her pitcher into the trough, and ran again unto the
well to draw water, and drew for all his camels" (ver. 18-20).

No wonder the good man marvelled ! Such alacrity of
attention to a poor wayworn traveller did indeed betoken a
gracious disposition. And the circumstance fitted in so aptly
to his previous train of holy meditation, that he could not fail
to recognise in it an answer to his prayer. Accordingly, " the
man, wondering at her, held his peace, to wit whether the Lord
had made his journey prosperous or not" (ver. 21). Encouraged,
however, by so plain a sign—using also his privilege of age,
and accepting frankly the damsel's frank cordiality of welcome,
—the servant of Abraham presents the gifts which the usages
of the times warranted (ver. 22). Availing himself, moreover,
of the introduction so graciously arranged and ordered by his

master's God, he asks and obtains the customary rites of hospitality (ver. 23). And finally, overcome with the emotions which the Lord's marvellous guidance of him awakened, the old man unreservedly pours out his soul in the utterance of grateful praise :—" Blessed be the Lord God of my master Abraham, who hath not left destitute my master of his mercy and his truth ! I being in the way, the Lord led me to the house of my master's brethren !" (ver. 26, 27).

Such a sight is fitted to move deeply the soul of the guileless maiden. The venerable aspect of the stranger, surprised into a sudden act of most profound devotion, could not but strike her heart : and the mention of the name of Abraham, of whom doubtless she had often heard in her father's house—and with whose migration, narrated as a household tale, she had been taught to associate something of the mysterious and the supernatural,—could not fail to call forth in her breast feelings of wonder, expectancy, and awe.

Who is this to whom she has been rendering what appears to be received as so remarkable a service ! It is but a little cold water that she has been giving ; a boon that she would not withhold from the poorest pilgrim she might chance to meet with at any well. But what a burst of pious gratitude does it cause ! And what a discovery does it occasion ! The old man who is the object of her apparently trifling courtesy and kindness, as if bent under the weight of an insupportable obligation, " bows down his head and worships God." And the words he utters in his ecstasy of thankfulness, bring home to her as a present reality all that from her childhood she has doubtless been wont to hear, of what was probably the most remarkable event in the family history,—the strange adventure of the ancestral patriarch called so mysteriously away long ago into a distant and a sort of dreamy land. Well may she be in haste to communicate the surprising intelligence she has so unexpectedly obtained. And well may her brother Laban, scarcely pausing to hear her rapid account of the strange interview, hasten forth to welcome the man who has thus wonderfully introduced himself:—" Come in, thou blessed of the Lord " (ver. 28-32).

IV. The preliminaries of this affair having passed off so auspiciously, the negotiation proceeds happily to its issue. The faithful servant, true to his master's interest and his own oath, refuses even to take the refreshment that he needs until he has delivered his message and received his answer. He acts upon the principle laid down by our Lord for the guidance of his ambassadors (Luke x. 8-11). For Abraham's ambassador, also, has in a sense the gospel to preach ; he has to speak of the kingdom of God being brought nigh to this house. He comes from a family in which the fear and worship of the Lord are to be found ; nay more : he comes from the family which alone has had an authentic revelation of the covenant, and which alone has received its seal. And he comes to offer to Laban's household a share in the privilege of Abraham's calling, as well as in the blessing of Abraham's God. Will they believe the good news he has to deliver ? Will they so believe as to be willing to let their young sister go upon the venture of what they now hear ? To this point the faithful messenger must first address himself. To press for a decision upon this point is his first and chief concern, to which even the supply of his necessary food is altogether subordinate. He is in earnest,—as the great Messenger was in earnest, when he too had to deal with the woman whom he met at the well about her spiritual good,—her separation from old connections that she might be the Lord's handmaid,—and found the task so engrossing as to make him forget his own most pressing wants (John iv. 31-34). So Abraham's servant felt in reference to the commission with which he was charged. It was his meat also, as it was the Lord's, to get his commission well executed in obedience to his master and his master's God ; and the execution of it took precedence with him even of his necessary food.

And how simply does he go about the execution of it! He does little more than narrate the Lord's dealings with Abraham in Canaan, and with himself on his journey thence. As a matter of course, we may be sure that he dwells somewhat more at length on the details of his master's pilgrimage than the brief summary given of his discourse might indicate (ver. 34-36) : nor can we doubt that he opens up, at least in part, the fulness of the blessing with which "the Lord had blessed his master greatly," as having in it a rich store of spiritual as well as temporal benefits. At all events, it is the Lord's blessing upon Abraham and his seed that this devout and upright man holds out as the chief, and indeed the only, recommendation of the suit he has to urge. For, in what remains of his address (ver. 37-48) beyond a plain recital of the things that had befallen him, with a pious reference throughout to the manifest grace and goodness of the Lord in the leadings of his holy providence,—the good man uses no arguments whatever to enforce the proposal he has to make to Laban's household. If his mission is to be successful, their "faith is not to stand in the wisdom of men, but in the power of God." For himself, he simply awaits such result as the Lord may be pleased to appoint (ver. 49).

The effect of his appeal is not merely an instance of the confiding hospitality of these times, but a proof that the same divine interposition in which this whole procedure originated was continued down to its close. The brother and father ; the latter in all probability being now, in his old age, represented to a large extent by his son ; the relatives, in short, of the woman thus strangely courted as the bride of a Prince Royal, whose person and whose kingly heritage are alike unknown,—cannot withstand the evidence of a divine warrant which the whole transaction bears. They frankly own their conviction. It is the Lord, what can we say or do ? (ver. 50, 51). Again, the old man is overpowered in spirit by the marvellous goodness of God : "When he heard their words, he worshipped the Lord, bowing himself to the earth " (ver. 52).

Then follows on the part of the overjoyed messenger, a display of the rich presents which he had been authorised to distribute, if his message was crowned with success. He had already, on the first opening of his conversation with Rebekah, used the oriental liberty of enforcing his address by adding a slight but substantial token of respect; "a golden ear-ring of half a shekel weight, and two bracelets for her hands of ten shekels weight of gold" (ver. 22). Now that his overtures have been so well received, he has no occasion for reserve, but may freely disclose all his ample stores, and endow the destined bride of his master's son with the whole princely presents that he has had in keeping. Accordingly, he "brought forth jewels of silver, and jewels of gold, and raiment, and gave them to Rebekah: he gave also to her brother and to her mother precious things" (ver. 53).

V. Thus, as to all that is essential to it, the treaty of marriage is fully ratified, according to the usages of eastern hospitality; and in a sense, too, with the munificence of princely state. It is now merely a question of time and circumstance;—as to when and how the treaty is to be carried out to its consummation.

Very natural is the remonstrance which the brother and the mother of the bride addressed to the impatient servant of Abraham (ver. 54, 55). Whether it be a delay of ten days, or as some say, of ten months, or even years, that the mother joins with her son in soliciting, before her daughter bids her a last adieu,—it is a touch of genuine tenderness such as we would not willingly lose in this narrative. Nor in such circumstances is it a trifling evidence of the chosen virgin's faith, that she is herself enabled to withstand this pleading (ver. 57, 58). She has taken the decisive step when she has resolved to peril her all upon the truth of the singular embassy that has come to her. And now, when it is left to her to say how soon the step shall become irrevocable, her reply is prompt. She balances the fond reluctance of her family to part with her—a reluctance which, however grateful to her feelings, has no force at all as an argument addressed to her faith—against the clear appeal which the holy man who has called her makes; " Hinder me not, seeing the Lord hath prospered my way; send me away that I may go to my master" (ver. 56). And she cannot hesitate for a moment. Having made up her mind to a painful sacrifice and serious risk, she feels that " now is the accepted time; now is the day of salvation." What is to be done, had best be done quickly ;—no halting between two opinions ;—no hesitancy ; —no yielding to the temptation that would gain time and prompt dangerous postponement and procrastination. Having put her hand to the plough, she will not draw back. She hears a voice powerfully speaking to her, and saying, " Go forward"-

—And she is gone; gone for ever from her father's dwelling, and from the love and sympathy of her mother and her brother !

With an ample benediction do her friends dismiss her (ver. 59, 60) ; and with entire resignation and hearty good-will, in simple faith—really not knowing whither she goes—she turns her back on the home of her childhood and the land of her birth (ver. 61). Truly it is a wife worthy of Abraham's son that the good providence of Abraham's God has selected. It is a faith not unlike that of Abraham himself which animates and sustains the appointed wife of Isaac, the destined mother of the promised seed.

VI. And now, the strange embassy is well ended. The journey back to Canaan is without adventure or interruption. The caravan, with its attendant camels and bands of servants, is drawing near to the place where Abraham's tents are pitched. What tumultuous thoughts are filling the bosom of the young stranger ! Her venerable friend is not unmoved himself. The first glimpse of his master's encampment, in the distance afar off, stirs his soul to its warmest depths. He has right joyous news to impart to the aged pilgrim ; he has a gracious daughter to present to him. And that daughter— may she not well be agitated as she approaches the unknown scene of the great crisis of her life, in profoundest darkness as to what the colour of that life is to be ?

It is a calm summer evening. The oxen have been lodged in their stalls, and the implements of husbandry are at rest in the furrows of the field. Not a breath of wind rustles in the noiseless leaves. Not a stray sheep wanders in the dark shadow of the hills. It is a time of profound repose. One solitary figure is seen slowly pacing the sweet-scented meadow path. Unconscious of nature's charms, although his soul is melted into sweet harmony with the peace that reigns all around,—he is rapt in holy fellowship with the God of his salvation. Suddenly, as it happens, he lifts his eyes ; and what a sight meets his view !

Can he fail to guess what cavalcade it is that is crossing the plain towards his father's tents ? Are his meditations rudely interrupted ?

Nay rather, his prayer is now graciously answered. The aged servant of the household is evidently not returning alone. He has not been unsuccessful in his suit. Again Isaac is to have an illustrious instance of the truth of that blessed word : —" Jehovah-jireh—The Lord will provide."

What a meeting on that serene summer night ! It is faith meeting faith ;—faith venturous and bold, meeting faith meditative and meek ! On the one hand, there is the faith that not all the perils of a long journey and an unknown issue can daunt ; on the other hand, there is the faith that seeks quiet rest in communing with the God of nature, as the God also of covenanted grace. Rebekah, dropping thy modest veil, as if half-afraid or half-ashamed, of thine adventurous spirit,—and thou, Isaac, lifting thine eyes, as if awakened out of a trance,—ye two are now one in the Lord ! Your different characters,—already perhaps slightly indicated in the

different actings of your common faith,—may cause, alas! some
dispeace and sin in your future course, when they come to be
more fully unfolded and brought into collision with one
another, amid the cares and trials of your common pilgrimage.
But in the main, ye are congenial souls. And the marriage
thus arranged by divine wisdom and grace and love, has its
fair share of the happiness which that blessed estate is fitted
to yield to those who " marry in the Lord."

At all events, the commencement of this matrimonial
alliance is auspiciously announced, when the narrative, connecting the declining shadow of the past with the opening
dawn of the future, intimates with all simplicity that " Isaac
brought her into his mother Sarah's tent, and took Rebekah,
and she became his wife ; and he loved her : and Isaac was
comforted after his mother's death" (ver. 67).

32

THE DEATH OF ABRAHAM

Genesis 25:1-10

Precious in the sight of the Lord is the death of his saints.
Psalm 116:15

THE eventful career of Abraham is drawing to a close. The purposes being now fulfilled for which God raised him up,— and another being ready to take his place,—he passes from this stirring scene, and is permitted to depart in peace. The circumstances connected with his departure are very briefly noticed ; but they are suggestive of some profitable thoughts.

I. Of the last few years of his life little is recorded, excepting only that, after Sarah's death, he contracted a second marriage, and had, as the issue of it, a new and considerable family (ver. 1-4).

It does not appear that in Abraham's second marriage there was anything discreditable or sinful.* Living as he did

* It is a groundless notion which some rash expositors have invented, that this Keturah was none other than Hagar. Abraham, it is imagined, took Hagar back to his home, after her temporary flight from Sarah, and had by her the children here named ;—and that, too, before the birth of Isaac. Any necessity for such a theory as this that might be supposed to arise out of Abraham's age, and the improbability of his having a family after Sarah's death, is met by the consideration already suggested in connection with the birth of Isaac. Nor is there a single other argument of the least force upon this point. For we cannot have any sympathy with the delicacy of those morbid ecclesiastics who, condemning in every case a

for years after the loss of Sarah,—and seeing his sons Ishmael and Isaac settled in households of their own,—it was not un-natural, nor in the circumstances unjustifiable, that he should seek another partner. That the promise might be fulfilled literally as well as spiritually, he became the " father of many nations " after the flesh;—even as in Isaac, and his seed through Isaac,—the seed which is, " not many, but one, that is Christ,"—he was destined to be the " father of many nations," spiritually and by faith. Nor is it unimportant to observe, in the near prospect of Abraham's decease, how pointedly the sacred history adverts to the timely settlement which he made of his earthly affairs before his end came (ver. 5, 6). The particulars of the settlement are not indeed detailed. But while the divine decree constituted Isaac his principal heir, the other parties having claims upon him were by no means overlooked. The patriarch was careful, not only to make suitable provision for them during his lifetime, but also to leave such instructions as might prevent disputes after he was gone.

Thus Abraham passed the latter stage of his troubled journey,—in privacy, apparently, and in peace,—waiting till his change came.

II. In peace also he departed, his eyes having seen the salvation of God (ver. 7-8). The pilgrim's journey is over; the wanderer has found repose ; the stranger has reached his

second marriage as unholy, would acquit the patriarch of that factitious sin, by charging him with the real guilt, either of systematic polygamy, or of continued and deliberate adultery. Certainly Keturah was not Hagar. The sacred history is not here resuming a dropped thread, and introducing out of its place what should have been mentioned before, as these inter-preters allege. They would read the first verse of the chapter thus :— " Abraham had taken a wife "—and so forth. But the history is not thus retrospective in this instance. It is evidently carrying on the narra-tive in its simple and natural order, and mentioning what occurred after Sarah was dead. It was after her death that Abraham lawfully entered into a second matrimonial alliance.

home. There is no more trial of faith,—no anxious feeling with the hand if by any means it may grasp "the substance of things hoped for,"—no straining of the eye to catch "the evidence of things not seen." The difficulty of laying hold of the intangible and realising the invisible is now for ever at an end. The eternal economy is at last unvailed. Shadows and phantoms are gone ; and this material world, as well as the bodily frame which connected him with it, are for a season left behind. So Abraham, as to his soul or spirit, " gave up the ghost and died,"—departing to be with the Lord. And as to his body or flesh, he went the way of all living, to the "long home" to which " man goeth," while " the mourners go about the streets" (Eccles. xii. 6). The patriarch was " gathered to his people," until that day when the dust shall live again at the sound of the last trumpet, and all the buried dead,—Abraham and his people to whom he is gathered,—shall hear the voice of the Son of Man, and shall come forth.

" Precious in the sight of the Lord is the death of his saints" (Ps. cxvi. 15). It was so in the case of Abraham. His death was matter of concern to the God in whom he believed. The Lord specially looked to it, and made it on one special occasion the subject of a special promise. His death, as he is then assured, is to be full of calmness and contentment. He is to die, indeed, as his fathers have died, and to be buried. But he is to " die in peace, and be buried in a good old age." For even his death and burial are cared for by his covenant-God ; and all the circumstances are ordered by him, so that the patriarch, departing, enters into rest.

III. The departure of Abraham, thus calm and peaceful in itself, was not premature or untimely in its date. He did not die too soon. He died " in a good old age "—" an old man, and full of years." " He was satisfied with length of days, for his eyes had seen the salvation of God" (Ps. xci. 16). He had experienced enough of the Lord's loving-kindness in the land of the living.

For it is not by the ordinary measures of the successive seasons as they roll on, that this fulness of years is, in a spiritual point of view, to be estimated ;—nor even by those public or domestic events which men often set up as landmarks beside the stream of time or the beaten path of life ;—but by what the faithful and patient pilgrim has seen of the salvation of God, and what he has tasted of the divine goodness during his sojourn on the earth.

Is he full ? Is the pilgrim satisfied ? Is he ready to depart ? It is not because he can reckon some threescore and ten revolutions of the sun ; or it may be fourscore ; or even like Abraham, " an hundred, threescore, and fifteen" (ver. 7). Nor is it because he can say of the various sources of interest and pleasure upon earth,—I have drunk of them all. But it is because he has eaten the bread of heaven and drawn water out of the wells of salvation ; because he has been filled with the fulness of God ; because he has been partaker of the unsearchable riches of Christ. He has lived long in the earth—his days have been many in the land ;—not in pro-portion to the anniversaries of his birth that he has celebrated ; or to the varied casualties of infancy, childhood, manhood, and old age, that he has experienced ; or to the changes all around him, that make him feel as if it were a new world in which he is now dwelling. No ! It is by the tokens of the divine love that he has received, the gracious dealings of God with his soul that he has noted, and the wonders of grace and mercy that he has witnessed in the church of the redeemed, that the believer reckons himself to have lived long on the earth !

Has he but this very moment acquainted himself with God, and found peace ? Has he only now for the first time tasted and seen that the Lord is gracious ? Then already, let him be ever so young in the estimate of time, he is old enough, by the measure of eternity, to depart in peace to his heavenly home. "He is satisfied with length of days, for his eyes have seen the salvation of God."

Is he, on the other hand, doomed to a long sojourn on the earth ? Is he spared to grow grey in the service of his Lord ? Is he worn and wasted with the burden and heat of a lengthened pilgrimage ? Has he length of days reaching to the extreme limit of life, and surviving all contemporary sympathies and friendships ? And is he left alone among strangers, like a stranded vessel when the tide has ebbed ? Even with such length of days he is satisfied, for " his eyes have seen"—and continue still to the last to see—" the salvation of God." " To him to live is Christ" (Phil. i. 21). And when at last the hour of his departure comes, it is not as if he were laying down the burden of years of vanity, but as thankfully owning a well-furnished table and a full cup, that he utters the language of faith and hope :—" Surely goodness and mercy shall follow me all the days of my life : And I will dwell in the house of the Lord for ever" (Ps. xxiii. 16).

33

THE LIFE AND CHARACTER OF ABRAHAM

Genesis 25:1-18

So then they which be of faith are blessed with—FAITHFUL ABRAHAM.—
Galatians 3:9

THE notice of the death of a distinguished man is usually regarded as incomplete without at least an attempt to sum up
his history and delineate his character.   In the instance of
Abraham, this is no easy task.

The recorded life of the patriarch might almost seem to be
left to the church as an exercise and trial of the very faith
upon which he himself was called to act.   In every view he is
a test, as well as an example, of believing loyalty to God ;—
both in what he did and dared, and in what he sacrificed and
suffered, during his eventful career.   The outward aspect of
his course is exhibited in a few of its most striking particulars ;
but we have scarcely any key to its inward interpretation.
We have little or no insight into his private and personal experience.   He is presented to us as a public character ; and
the incidents of his pilgrimage are narrated with an obvious
reference rather to the general information of the church than
to the prolonged remembrance of the individual.   The notes
and explanations are rare.   No private diary remains to
open up the secret springs of thought and action ; nor has
any intimate friend withdrawn the curtain of confidential intercourse, and unfolded to us the mysteries of the closet, the
study, and the unbent hour of familiarity.   There is no access

behind the scenes ; no unfolding of those hidden movements of soul which have their external types, and nothing more, in the vicissitudes of a strangely-chequered history. One advantage, however, we have ;—and it is a great and most important one. It is the authoritative announcement of the general principle or category under which the whole is to be classed. Abraham lived and walked by faith ; and therefore what is required in a brief recapitulation of the leading events of his life is simply to trace the working of that believing reliance upon God which furnishes the solution and explanation of them all.

Consider then, this " FAITHFUL ABRAHAM " in the successive eras of his history, as these may be grouped under two, comprehensive heads ;—the one reaching from his first call to the remarkable crisis of his full and formal justification (chap. xi. 27–xv. 21) ; and the other, from his unsteadfastness in the matter of Hagar to the final trial and triumph of his faith in the sacrifice first, and then in the marriage, of his son Isaac (chap. xvi. 1–xxiv. 67). During the first of these periods, his faith is chiefly exercised upon the bare promise itself made to him by God. During the second, it has to do mainly with the manner in which the promise is to be fulfilled.

First Part - Genesis 11:27-15:21

In this first period, we have a deeply interesting and almost dramatic series of events,—beginning with a very commonplace transaction, but ending in what elevates the patriarch to a high rank in the sight both of God and of man.

I. Abraham comes before us as an emigrant, but an emigrant in very peculiar circumstances ;—an emigrant, not of his own accord, but at the call of God (chap. xi. 31–xii. 5). The first stage of the migration, from Ur to Haran, is accomplished without a breach in the family ; but at Haran the oldest member of the company is cut off ; Abraham there loses his venerable father. He does not, however, shrink from this trial and its accompanying increase of responsibility. He might have taken it amiss, and counted it a bad omen, that the very beginning of his pilgrimage should be marked with so sad a stroke. His father might surely have been spared to witness his triumphal entry into the new territory which he was to possess for an inheritance; or at least he might have been allowed to depart in peace in the old country where his lot had been so long cast. Why should Abraham's movement be so ordered that his father's bones must rest,—neither in the place from which he goes, nor in the place which God has promised to him,—but as it were by the wayside? Surely it is not for nothing that he is appointed to set up as his first milestone a parent's tomb. It is an emphatic initiation into his calling, as destined henceforth to be a stranger on the earth.

II. As a stranger, accordingly, we find him entering Canaan, and beginning his migratory sojourn in that country (chap. xii. 6; xiii. 4). It is not, in his case, an ordinary removal from one settled habitation to another; the emigrant arrives at the place of his destination, and finds it a place of wandering. Nor is this a result ascertained by experience; he is warned beforehand that he is to have but a wayfarer's passing use of the land, although ultimately, in connection with it, a rich inheritance awaits him. In such circumstances, the incidental failure as well as the habitual firmness of his holy trust in God is to be made manifest. Wherever he went, Abraham "built an altar unto the Lord," and "called upon the name of the Lord" (chap. xii. 7, 8; xiii. 4). Everywhere and always he openly observed the worship of the true God, to whatever misunderstanding or persecution it might expose him. One only blot disfigures the picture. The transaction in Egypt is the first sad instance of that infirmity which led him on rare occasions to walk by sense rather than by faith; and to consult for himself, instead of leaving all to him in whom he believed. It is easy to condemn these instances of

weakness; although if we place ourselves in Abraham's position,—with a just estimate of that fearful dissolution of
manners which alone could suggest or account for the expedient he adopted,—we shall be far more ready to sympathise
with his embarrassment than to censure his unsteadfastness.
And our very sympathy will all the more dispose us to profit
by the example of his otherwise unshaken faith.

III. The shifting scene next presents to us the patriarch
in an aspect of bright moral beauty (chap. xiii. 5-18) ;—for
never, perhaps, does Abraham appear in a more attractive
light than in his courteous and kindly dealing with his kinsman Lot.   The wisdom of his attempt to allay domestic strife
by the proposal of an amicable separation, is cleared from every
suspicion of a sinister or selfish policy by the admirable disinterestedness with which he leaves the choice of the whole land
to Lot, and the cheerfulness with which he acquiesces in Lot's
preference of the better portion.   And we may well trace these
noble qualities to no ordinary motive of mere human virtue,
but to that divine grace which alone enabled Abraham, as a
stranger and pilgrim on the earth, to sit loose to the attractions
of earthly possessions and earthly privileges, and to have his
treasure and his heart alike in heaven.   For it is a great instance of heavenly-mindedness that is here exhibited ; and
as such, it is owned and blessed by God at the time, while all
the subsequent history attests the divine approval of it.   By
the example of his gracious dealing with Abraham, the Lord
ratifies the assurance which his believing people in all ages
may have, that they shall fare none the worse, either in this
world or in the next, for any sacrifices they may make, or any
sufferings they may endure, in the interest of holiness and
peace and love—since " godliness is profitable unto all things,
having promise of the life that now is, as well as of that which
is to come " (1 Tim. iv. 8).

IV. The plot of that moral drama, if we may so call it,
which opens with Abraham's offer and Lot's choice, very

speedily develops itself. The war of the kings (chap. xiv.), in
its origin and issue, is a striking commentary on that transaction. The plain where Lot settles, well watered by the Jordan,
sheltered by sunny hills on either side, and basking in the full
smiles of a most genial clime, has become populous and rich ;
but the moral does not keep pace with the material improvement of the land. The too common accompaniment of abundant
prosperity is to be traced among the people ; unheard-of profligacy characterises their manners ; crime and effeminacy are
in the ascendant. The usual consequences soon follow. A war
of petty principalities breaks out ; and Lot suffers in the tur-
moil. In spite of all the past, Abraham hastens to the rescue ;
thinking only of the sad calamity which has befallen his brother's son. It is an instance of no common generosity ; and
it is an evidence, moreover, of the patriarch's deep spiritual
insight into the promises of which he is the heir. For it
was his faith which moved Abraham to assume so strangely
the unwonted character of a prince entitled to levy war ; and
it was his faith also which led him to give so remarkable an
expression of his willing subjection to the illustrious being
whom Melchisedec prefigured—and to whom, as " a priest
upon his throne," all the spiritual seed of Abraham are ever
willing to give the undivided glory of all their victories.

V. The transition from the most palpable and almost ob-
trusive publicity to the deepest privacy—which forms the next
era in Abraham's life—is also eminently fitted to bring out the
spirituality of his faith (chap. xv.)

In any case to combine these two—public action for the
Lord and private communion with him—is no easy exercise.
But in the case of Abraham, the combination is peculiarly trying. Look at him, and mark the contrast. On the one side
you see a brave general at the head of a conquering army,
risking all for the recovery of a kinsman's household goods,
and playing a right royal part among this world's potentates
and princes. On the other hand, you seem to see a melancholy

recluse, wandering alone at midnight, a star-gazer, imagining ideal glories in some visionary world to come. The transition is most startling, from the hostile din of tumultuous strife to the serene solitude of a colloquy with God beneath the silent eloquence of the starry heavens! But Abraham is at home in either scene. After his brief experience of worldly renown, he is found in secret and most confidential communion with his God.

It is the hour of universal slumber; every eye is closed; every busy foot is at rest. But near that silent tent two figures may be seen; one like unto the Son of God—the other a venerable form, bending low in adoration of his divine companion. It is the hero who but yesterday on the field of successful battle might have reared a throne to defy all the pride of eastern empire. But he has another and a far different calling. Not the garish pomp of military triumph, but the secrecy of midnight fellowship with heaven, has charms for him. And as we listen and overhear the strange colloquy that ensues—in which, apart altogether from any corroborative sign on which he might lean, the patriarch simply believes the divine assurance that, childless and aged as he is, a progeny as numerous as the stars awaits him—we cannot but own that it is indeed a mere and simple exercise of faith alone, without works or services of any kind whatever, that is the instrument of his salvation, and the means of his finding favour with God. And we cannot but acquiesce in the divine testimony respecting his justification—so frequently repeated with reference to this single and solitary incident in his history:—" Abraham believed in the Lord, and he counted it to him for righteousness" (chap. xv. 6; Rom. iv. 3, 9, 22; Gal. iii. 6).

But though faith alone is the hand by which Abraham on this occasion appropriates the justifying righteousness pledged to him, in the person and work of the yet unborn Saviour who is to spring from him,—it is not a faith that is content indolently to acquiesce in the darkness of entire ignorance respecting the ways of that God upon whose mere word it so implicitly relies. On the contrary, as the Lord follows up his assurance respecting Abraham's posterity—" so shall thy seed be," with the repetition of the promise more immediately affecting Abraham in his own person, " I am the Lord that brought thee out of Ur of the Chaldees, to give thee this land to inherit it ;"—so the patriarch on his part follows up his believing submission with the earnest inquiry, " Lord God, whereby shall I know that I shall inherit it ?" In reply, he has the covenant of his peace ratified by a very special sacrifice ; and he obtains a gracious insight both into the future fortunes of his seed, and into the destiny awaiting himself. As to his seed, he is informed that though the delay of four centuries is to intervene, through the long-suffering of God, until " the iniquity of the Amorites is full"—they are at last to possess the whole land ; while as to himself, he is to understand that his inheritance is to be postponed to the future and eternal state, and that the utmost he has to look for in this world is a quiet departure when his pilgrimage is over. Thus, justified by faith, the patriarch is made willing to subordinate all the earthly prospects of his race to the will of him in whom he has believed ;—and as for himself, to live by the power of the world to come.

I look upon the midnight scene, with the remarkable covenant transaction which closes it, as the climax of what we may call the first part of Abraham's walk of faith ; in which he is led onward and upward to the highest pitch of expectation, while as yet not a hint is given of the way in which his expectation is to be realised. Thus far the Lord has been training him to the exercise of implicit faith in the promises of salvation, altogether irrespective of any clear information as to the means of their fulfilment. And it is the triumph of Abraham's faith at this crisis of his history that he acquiesces with unhesitating confidence in these promises, though not the slightest ray of light is cast upon the momentous and most difficult question, how it is possible, in his case, old and child-less as he is, to have them ever made good.

Second Part - Genesis 16:1-24:67

But now, in the next stage of his pilgrimage, it is upon that very point that the faith of Abraham is to be tested and proved. The trial is to turn upon the manner in which the promises previously announced are to be accomplished.

I. In this new trial, the patriarch's faith appears at first to fail. Impatient of the Lord's delay, he listens to the plausible suggestion of his partner, and suffers himself to be betrayed into that sin in the matter of Hagar, which brought ere long so much domestic dispeace in its train, and proved even at the time so sad a root of bitterness to his soul ; marring the pure joy and interrupting the even tenor of his holy walking in covenant with his God (chap. xvi.)

For the offence, though not in his case prompted by carnal appetite, bore nevertheless the fruit which the like offence always bears ;—blunting the conscience, hardening the heart, and unfitting the whole inner man for the divine fellowship and communion. In the dreary blank, accordingly, of the long interval between the birth of Ishmael and the next re-corded communication from on high,—a period of no less than thirteen years (chap. xvi. 16 ; xvii. 1), during which a dark cloud seems to rest upon the patriarch, such as nothing short of a fresh call and new revival can dispel,—we trace the miserable fruit of his backsliding. The Lord thus signalises his holy jealousy of the purity of the nuptial tie, by the hiding of his countenance for a time from the man whom he had chosen to be his friend, and the suspension of that intimate intercourse into which, as his friend, he had so graciously ad-mitted him.

II. But "the steps of a good man are ordered by the Lord ; and he delighteth in his way. Though he fall, he shall not be utterly cast down : for the Lord upholdeth him with his hand" (Psalm xxxvii. 23, 24).

The revival is eminently gracious. There is a mild rebuke of his former unbelief and guile, in the announcement, " I am the Almighty God," and in the invitation, " Walk before me and be thou perfect ;" but there is relenting tenderness in the assurance—" I will make my covenant between me and thee" (ver. 2). It is as if the Lord were weary of the restraint which he had put upon himself, and could no longer refrain from returning to visit and bless his faithful servant. Yes ! In spite of all that has passed, " I will make my covenant between me and thee." This unwonted estrangement has been long enough continued ; we must be friends again.

The interview that follows is one of the spiritual epochs of Abraham's life. Viewed in connection with the renewal of the covenant, and the institution of the sacramental seal,— it was fitted to recover Abraham out of the depths into which he had been falling through his attempt to realise the divine purposes in a way of his own ; and to bring him back to the safe and simple attitude of waiting patiently for the Lord's own fulfilment of them, and meanwhile addressing himself, in all humility, to the keeping of the Lord's commandments.

III. The culminating point of Abraham's exaltation, during the second period of his pilgrimage, is again to be found, as in the former, in connection with his conduct towards Lot. And the exaltation is on this occasion more signal than at the first. Then he manifestly had power, as a prince, to prevail over princes ;—now he has power, as a friend, to prevail with God. The Lord visits him as a friend, and along with two attendant angels, accepts his hospitality, and sits familiarly at his table. He converses with him as a friend, not only on what personally concerns the patriarch himself,— the terms of the covenant, and the near approach of the time when Sarah is to have a son ; but, what is a still more special proof of friendship, on his procedure as Governor among the nations ;—as if he could hide nothing from Abraham. Thereafter, in the liberty of speech granted to the patriarch, as he pleads for the doomed cities, and in the assurance that what was done for the deliverance of Lot was done for his sake, the highest honour is conferred on him of which human nature can well be considered capable. And we stand in awe as we contemplate him thus illustriously signalised as "the friend of God."

IV. But, alas! the next "varying" scene of this "changeful life" presents the patriarch in another light. The catastrophe of Sodom having led to the breaking up of his establishment in that neighbourhood, he is cast abroad as a wanderer again ; and in another part of the land of his pilgrimage, he is brought into contact with the people and the princes from whose lawless corruption of manners he has so much to apprehend. The new "strength" which "through faith" Sarah is at this time receiving "to bear seed," implying probably the return of somewhat of her former attractiveness, is an additional embarrassment to the wanderer. His old expedient unhappily suggests itself to him again ; and though the same overruling hand that had brought good out of evil before, interposes now to avert a calamity that might have marred the whole design of the covenant as established in the promised seed, still the patriarch himself is sufficiently rebuked.

V. The actual fulfilment of the promise, in the birth of Isaac, might seem to be the fitting occasion for ending all strife between the flesh and the spirit,—between sense and faith. It is not so, however ;—at least not entirely. The joyous festivities at the birth and circumcision of Isaac are strangely blended with a sad domestic misunderstanding. The patriarch is seen halting between two opinions, and manifesting a sort of lurking preference for "the son of the bond-woman born after the flesh," over "the son of the free-woman, born after the Spirit." But at last he makes a final surrender of the confidence he has been tempted to build upon Ishmael.

He acquiesces in the arrangement,—so characteristic of the divine sovereignty, but so contrary to nature,—that the elder shall be postponed to the younger. He is made willing to commit the entire hope of his own inheritance, and of the world's salvation, solely and exclusively to the frail ark of that precarious life which has just begun to flicker in the feeble frame of one " born out of due time."

VI. The scene on Mount Moriah forms the climax in this second part of Abraham's walk of faith,—as that midnight colloquy with the Lord under the starry heavens formed the climax in the first. Then the patriarch,—every outward adminicle of faith being absent, and not a ray of light shed on the means by which the divine word is to be made good,— has to take that bare word as his sole and sufficient security ; and believing, he is declared to be justified before God. Now, after he has actually seen how God intends to fulfil his promise, and his faith on that point has become sensible experience, he is to forego all the advantage and help that sight and sense might afford ; and once more he is required, in still more trying circumstances than before, " against hope to believe in hope." For to believe before Isaac's birth was really not so hard a thing as to continue to believe in spite of Isaac's death. Then the trial turned upon the question,—Can Abraham trust God for the making good of his promise while the child of promise has not yet come ? Now it turns on the far more testing question,—Can he hold fast his trust even when the child of promise is taken away ? He stands the test, and is rewarded in standing it, for he " sees the day of Christ afar off, and is glad."

VII. The closing incidents of Abraham's eventful history— his grief for Sarah's death and care for her burial,—the blessedness of securing a suitable wife for Isaac,—his own entrance a second time into the marriage-state, and becoming thus literally as well as spiritually the father of many nations,—his timely settlement of his worldly affairs,—his quiet death in a good old age, and his burial, at which both his sons, Ishmael and Isaac, took part,—these several particulars might all admit of separate notices ; but a single general remark may suffice.

It is the sunset of a hot day of trial,—the heat and burden of which have been spent in the searching furnace of divine light and love. The quiet domestic chronicle comes in with a sad yet soothing charm, to wind up the wanderer's agitated career. The crisis is now over. The power of faith has been tested to the uttermost. The patriarch has been enabled to " overcome when he is tempted." And now he calmly makes preparation for his departure, and for the accomplishment of the Lord's will when he is gone. It is a peaceful twilight, coming after a long troubled day,—ushering in the repose of a serene night —that awaits a brighter dawn.

I pass from this summary of the life and character of " the father of the faithful" reluctantly, and with a feeling of utter inadequacy to do justice to the theme. Running the eye again over the successive vicissitudes of his history,—all minute criticism and special pleading apart,—we must note faults and failings for which we ought not to apologise ; but we must also close the survey with a deeper impression than ever of the majesty with which, in the hands of a spiritual and poetic word-painter, this great example of faith might be invested. Of the original and natural temperament of Abraham, independently of his call as a believer, but few traces can be discerned. He was already an old man when he received the summons to forsake all for the Lord's sake ; and of what he was and what he did, before that era, Scripture says not a word, beyond the bare intimation that he was beginning, at least, to be involved in the growing idolatry of the age. I am persuaded, however, that if the devout students of God's word and ways would throw themselves into this history of Abraham's pilgrimage, with more of human sympathy than they sometimes do,—and with less of that captious spirit which a cold infidelity has engendered,—they would see more and more of the patriarch's warmth and tenderness of heart, as well as of his loyalty to that God whose call and covenant he so unreservedly embraced.

One word more in conclusion as to the faith of Abraham, viewed in its objective, and not merely in its subjective aspect. The truths on which his believing confidence laid hold are plain enough. A present justifying righteousness, and a future heavenly inheritance—these were the objects which his faith grasped, with a tenacity all his own. As a sinner, he apprehended a divinely-provided righteousness on the ground of which he had pardon and peace. As a child of God, he looked for a city that hath foundations, whose builder and maker is God ; he walked as an heir of unseen glory. And in both particulars, he is an example to all believers. Nor is it of any material consequence to speculate on the amount of knowledge which Abraham may have had, with regard either to the righteousness which by faith he appropriated, or to the inheritance which in hope he anticipated. How far he had a clear and definite view of the great principle of substitution upon which the believer's acceptance, through the blood of an atoning sacrifice, depends—still more, how far he had any adequate conception of the person and work of the Substitute who was, in the fulness of time, to live on the earth, and die, and rise again—may be matter of doubtful disputation. And it may be impossible to determine with absolute certainty whether he identified the inheritance promised to him with the land in which he sojourned, or merely looked in a general way for a portion in the resurrection-state, or in the world to come, that might fairly be regarded as an equivalent. The main facts as to his faith and hope are these two :—first, that Abraham trusted in a righteousness not his own for his justification in the sight of God—and secondly, that he sought his rest and reward in a heritage of glory beyond the grave.

We may have clearer light on both of these points ; if so, then so much the greater is our responsibility. And it will be good for us if, by the grace of God, we are enabled to live up to our clearer light, as conscientiously as Abraham lived up to his more imperfect illumination—walking before God in uprightness, as he did—and as strangers and pilgrims on the earth declaring plainly that " we seek a better country, even a heavenly."

34

THE FAMILY OF ISAAC—THE ORACLE RESPECTING JACOB AND ESAU

Genesis 25:19-27

AFTER noticing the death of Abraham, the sacred narrative proceeds to trace the two principal lines of succession in which his name and memory are to be perpetuated. These lines are at the very outset found widely diverging. The patriarch's two sons, Isaac and Ishmael, met indeed at the funeral of their aged parent, and united in paying the last tribute of filial respect to his remains (ver. 9, 10). But thereafter, as it would seem, they finally separated from one another.

To Ishmael and his " generations," the sacred history devotes but a brief space (xxv. 12-18). It simply notices the first steps towards the actual fulfilment of the prophecies that had been given respecting him to sustain the drooping spirits of his mother (xvi. 10-12 ; xxi. 18) ; and to reconcile Abraham to the " casting out " of his first-born (xvii. 20 ; xxi. 13). In two particulars, especially, these prophecies began to be accomplished to the very letter in Ishmael's own day. In the first place, he became the father of " twelve princes " (ver. 16). And, secondly, he " fell," or in other words, his lot fell " in the presence of all his brethren." He was put into secure possession of that independent footing—on the very frontiers of the territory occupied by " his brethren," and as if in defiance of their power—which his descendants, the roving tribes of Arabia, have ever since continued to maintain.*

The inspired narrative, however, is chiefly occupied with the transmission of the covenant birthright ; and accordingly, after this brief glance at " the generations of Ishmael," it returns to the more congenial task of tracing the line of Isaac.

The period during which that patriarch was the head of the chosen family is comparatively one of repose ; it comes in as a sort of quiet calm between the manifold trials of his father Abraham's life, and the still more agitating career that awaited his son Jacob.   The course of Isaac's life appears to run smooth ; his own character is tranquil ; and so also is his history.   Whatever disturbance vexes that tranquillity, belongs rather to the opening of Jacob's troubled experience than to the placid routine of his father Isaac's pilgrimage.

The key to this portion of the history is to be found in the divine purpose respecting the birth of Isaac's sons ; and in dealing with the matter historically, it is with the oracular promulgation of that purpose that we are chiefly concerned. The reason moving the divine mind to prefer the younger to the elder,—or justifying and accounting for the preference, —is not within the scope of any inquiry suggested by the narrative.   It is not with the prophet Malachi's use, or the apostle Paul's use, of this divine decree that we have now to concern ourselves,—but solely and exclusively with its publication, and·the result of its publication, as given to us by the inspired historian.

For the decree was embodied in an oracle to the house of Isaac, and so became one of those " things that are revealed" which " belong to us and to our children ;" although still the reason of the decree, continuing to be unrevealed, is one of the

* I prefer the marginal reading "fell" to that of the text "died." The passage is obscure ; but it seems to indicate the beginning of Ishmael's occupancy of the position assigned to him in the prophecy.

" secret things belonging to the Lord our God," which we can but reverently adore (Deut. xxix. 29).*

An anxious wife, who, with her husband, has waited long and prayed for the blessing, is about to become the mother of the promised seed. Moved by signs that seem to betoken either personal danger to herself, or something strange respecting her offspring, she hastens to consult and inquire of the Lord (ver. 21, 22). In reply, she is told that she is to be the mother of two nations, that are to differ widely from one another in " strength," or in other words, in spiritual privileges and secular power. And farther, she is warned that in the transmission of the birthright the order of nature is to be reversed :— " The elder shall serve the younger " (ver. 23).

This announcement to Rebekah was surely intended to be made known. The pious mother was not, like Mary, to ponder all these things in her heart ; she was to speak of them to all her house. And, accordingly, the subsequent history, with its sad indications of human infirmity, sufficiently shows that

* This distinction between the announcement of the decree in the history, and the use made of it in the prophecy of Malachi and the epistle of Paul, it is most important to observe throughout. The announcement in the history is prospective ; the reference to it in the prophecy and epistle is retrospective. In the history, it takes its place among the things at the time revealed, which belong to God's people and to their children ; in the prophecy and epistle, it is considered as ranking among the secret things which belong to the Lord their God. Doubtless, it is the same divine decree in both instances. But in the one case, it is the decree, as it was made known beforehand to the actors in the scenes or incidents to which it relates ; in the other, it is the decree, as it existed from all eternity in the divine mind, brought forward, as it were, by way of an after-statement, to vindicate the divine procedure and silence cavilling objectors, long after these actors are all off the stage. In the one case, it is the commandment issued in good time to the parties personally interested,—to be obeyed ; in the other, it is the comment or reflection, suggested subsequently to their successors,—to be improved.

this divine oracle was no secret in the family; the whole interest of it, painful as it is, turns on that fact.

And the knowledge of the decree was really, to all the
parties concerned, a proclamation of the gospel. It directed
them to the quarter from whence the Saviour was to come. It
pointed out Jacob as virtually for the time the representative
of the Redeemer; and in him, the far-reaching eye of faith
might have seen, with more or less distinctness, the day of
Christ afar off. By that faith, accordingly, the household
might have been regulated. If it had been so, all would have
been benefited.

Jacob himself, had he rightly and spiritually apprehended
the prerogative conveyed to him, would have been humbled,
rather than elated, by the distinction. He would have counted
all the other privileges of his birthright as loss, for the excellency of the knowledge of that Saviour who was to spring
from him. Esau, again, would neither have envied nor
despised the blessing centred in his brother Jacob. Acquiescing in the sovereignty of God, he would have been contented
to acknowledge his dependence, for all spiritual and saving
benefits, not on Jacob, as personally his superior, but on
that promised " Seed of the woman," of whom it now appeared
that Jacob was to be the father. And the parents, understanding and submitting to the will of God, would have agreed
together in assigning to Jacob his proper place, as not in himself, or on his own account, to be preferred to his brother, but
only in respect of his being the root of that elect " Branch," in
whom, with the whole multitude of the redeemed of every
age and clime, they are all one. Favouritism, partiality,
rivalry, deceit, strife,—all might have been averted from this
house, if only the declared and revealed counsel of God had been
believed and acted upon.

Alas for the infirmity of faith and the deceitfulness of
man's desperately wicked heart! The very word of God,
which should have been a bond of union, became a root of

bitterness and an element of unholy contention.   In Jacob, a selfish and self-righteous spirit appropriated the covenant-blessing as a matter, not of grace, but of right.   It became, in his eyes, a personal distinction, to be vindicated by the usual methods of worldly force or fraud.   The fitful mind of Esau alternated between moody and sullen discontent on the one hand, and those softer relentings on the other—those gushes of childlike tenderness—those outbursts of passionate grief—to which the most rugged nature is often most easily moved and melted.   A mother's fond partiality made Rebekah turn the oracle, given as a ground of spiritual faith and hope, into a warrant for gratifying her own natural affections ;——and tempted her to believe that in accomplishing God's ends by her own craft, she was doing God service.   While in regard to the patriarch Isaac himself—a man of God from his youth—a man of prayer——what shall we say ?

Would that this pious man had understood aright the footing on which the oracle placed both Jacob and Esau, and indeed all the household !   Would that he had used his influence, and exerted his parental authority, to enforce com-pliance with the oracle in its true spiritual meaning !   Then he might have removed all occasion of self-righteous compla-cency on the part of Jacob, as well as of dark jealousy on the part of Esau.   Then he would have superseded, by a timely and equitable settlement, the whole wretched train of plots, stratagems, and wiles that make his household history so sad. From the first he might have taught Jacob to regard the birthright so specially given to him by divine decree, as chiefly valuable, not only on account of the spiritual blessings which it bestowed, but also on account of its bestowing them all so freely as to embrace his brother Esau, if Esau will consent to have them.   No occasion would have been given for Rebekah's crooked policy ; for she would have been satisfied to fall in with his faithful teaching.   And at last, in his old age, he might have had something better than a remnant of earthly good to give, in answer to Esau's pathetic pleading, "Bless me, even me also, O my father!" True, he had but "one blessing,"—one real blessing worthy of the name,—the blessing of Abraham with which he had just blessed Jacob. But the salvation that was to come through Abraham's seed, though it was to be of Jacob, was yet to be for all that would believe. And in Jacob's blessing,—as the patriarch might have taught his weeping and groaning son,—even he need not despair of having a share, if he will but believe. For "it is a faithful saying, and worthy of all acceptation, that Jesus Christ cometh into the world to save sinners," and thee, too, Esau, if thou canst but bring thyself to add, "of whom I am chief" (1 Tim. i. 15).

The true secret of family peace is to be found in setting up Christ, and Christ alone, as all in all. Let father, mother, sisters, brothers, all submit themselves to Christ ; and they will be ready in Christ to submit themselves to one another. Members of Christ's body, and members one of another, they will together, as a household, "keep the unity of the Spirit in the bond of peace."

35

PARENTAL FAVOURITISM AND FRATERNAL FEUD

Genesis 25:28-34

"THE boys grew" (ver. 27); and it would seem that, as they grew they were suffered very much to follow the bent of their own inclinations in the choice of their respective occupations. Their natures were different; and the difference, apparent in their very birth, was significantly indicated in their names. The rough and ruddy aspect of the first-born led to his being called by a name denoting rugged strength; while the seemingly accidental circumstance attending his brother's entrance into the world—"his hand taking hold of the other's heel"—suggested the name to which Esau afterwards so bitterly alludes (chap. xxvii. 36): "Is not he rightly named Jacob," or supplanter; one who takes his brother by the heel.

With these names the brothers, as they grew up, soon began to show that their natures remarkably corresponded. Esau's bold spirit found its fitting sphere of exercise in the excitement of the chase and the wild sports of the field. Jacob, again, being of a milder disposition, addicted himself to more domestic pursuits. He was disposed to lead a quiet pastoral life. He dwelt in tents, following the profession of a shepherd-farmer, tending his flocks and herds, and tilling the soil (ver. 27-28).

But the difference between them was probably one of rank as well as taste. Esau's manner of life was not only the result of his own inclination, but the indication also of his being accounted the elder son and heir. The pursuits to which he was devoted were of that noble character which the first-born of the earth have always affected; while Jacob, on the other hand, appears to have had the drudgery of a more servile and menial toil imposed upon him. He was thus early familiarised to such service as that which he afterwards rendered for his two wives to his kinsman Laban.

In fact, before his father's death, Jacob did not derive any temporal advantage from the privilege of the prior title to the birthright, which the oracle had conveyed to him. So far as his position can be gathered from the brief notices of the history, he is seen from the first occupying a subordinate place in the household,—engaged in the offices and duties of domestic service; while Esau assumes the air of a prince, and addicts himself to princely sports. Thus " the boys grew."

How their parents discharged towards them the parental duties is not told; one thing only is revealed—that " Isaac loved Esau, but Rebekah loved Jacob " (ver. 28). The silence of the Holy Spirit respecting all except this single fact is a solemn and emphatic warning. It is as if the Spirit meant to indicate that all the good of the godly rearing which these parents gave to their children was marred by the indulgence of their favouritism.

Let the real fault, however, which Isaac and Rebekah committed in the rearing of their sons, be quite understood. Let it be considered once again what their conduct would have been, had they rightly apprehended and acted upon the oracle which pointed out to them the line of the future Saviour.

They were taught to see in their younger son Jacob the father of the Messiah—of him who was to bruise the serpent's head and bless all the families of the earth; and doubtless this would have warranted a certain kind and measure of preference for Jacob. But it would not have been after the flesh. On the contrary, as they looked in faith on the fair child who was constituted to them, as it were, the representative of Christ —Jacob would have faded away from before their eyes; and a greater than Jacob would have appeared. And calling to mind the scene on Mount Moriah, in which he himself bore so great a part, Isaac might have directed Rebekah, and the rude Esau, and plain Jacob also, to fix their spiritual contemplation on the one Redeemer, the one propitiation for sin, whose day his father Abraham rejoiced to see afar off.

For who then is Jacob?—or who is Esau ?—that might have been the humble exclamation of the united household. Jacob may be honoured on account of the Saviour who is in his loins. But personally, what is Jacob the better for that distinction, or what is Esau the worse for wanting it ? To be the ancestor of the Messiah is to be indeed great. But to be "least in the kingdom of heaven" is to be greater still. And that distinction might have been reached by Esau !

Thus, in this family—in which there was too much disputing "who should be the greatest," it had been good for all parties if a little child had been set in the midst of them, and it had been said to one and all of them—Be as this little child. And how good beyond all calculation would it have been for them, if the little child so set in the midst had been none other than the "holy child Jesus;" the very Saviour of whom Jacob was to be the sire ! Then it might have been seen "how pleasant a thing it is for brethren to dwell together in unity ;" in the unity which is like "the precious ointment" flowing over the whole body of the high priest, from the head to the lowest members, making all one ; the unity which the Spirit, poured out from heaven inspires, as "the dew of Hermon descends on the mountains of Zion," enriching all with one common blessing—the unity, in a word, of faith and love.

Set up, ye Christian parents, in the midst of your children, Christ and Christ alone. Set not up one child above another, but set up Christ above all. Let not Isaac love Esau because he "eats of his venison,"—sympathising in his venturous trade, and enjoying the fruit of it. Let not Rebekah love the more peaceful Jacob, because, dwelling in tents, he gives her more of his company and companionship. But let both learn to love their children in the Lord. Isaac need not withdraw his affection from Esau, nor need Rebekah greatly moderate her attachment to Jacob. But let Isaac direct Esau, as a poor sinner, to the salvation which is to be of Jacob. And let Rebekah commend that same salvation to Jacob, as standing equally in need of it with his brother Esau. So shall they all—husband, wife, and children—be truly one—one in their sense of their own great poverty and sinfulness—one in their apprehension of the righteousness and the unsearchable riches of Christ. Alas! that it should turn out otherwise, and with such disastrous results.

The first evil issue of the opposite course pursued is the transaction of the sale of the birthright (29-34); a melancholy instance of the manner in which trifles may bring out deep-seated springs of action, and may lead to serious consequences. For what could be apparently more trifling than the occasion here described?

A weary and hungry hunter, returning home from the exploits of the field, finds a savoury mess prepared, as if seasonably to meet his wants. It is the very food which he most relishes at any time; and at this time it is doubly welcome. It is provided also by his own brother's hand; and certainly his brother stands in no such need of it as he does. What more natural than that a brother should ask food of a brother? What need of any terms of purchase, or any driving of a hard bargain?

"Sell me this day thy birthright." What a proposal! How unkind, ungenerous, unbrotherly! What has this pottage,—this same red pottage of thine, brother Jacob,—to do with the privilege of succeeding, as the first-born, to our father's inheritance? Especially if, as thou sayest, thou hast that

envied distinction already by decree of the oracle at our birth,
—and if thou valuest it, as thou professest to do, not as a
temporal and earthly, but as a spiritual and eternal blessing,
—wilt thou make it a commodity exchangeable for a morsel of
perishable meat?

Most justly might Jacob have been thus answered; and if
thus answered, he must have been silenced. For he had put
himself in a false position. Doubtless, in this negotiation
with his brother, he considered himself, not as purchasing
what did not previously belong to him, but as barring a claim
which Esau wrongfully set up, and in the setting up of which he
had the countenance of a too partial parent. The birthright was
Jacob's already;—by the divine decree, solemnly promulgated.
That in spite of this decree Esau was allowed to enjoy the
privileges of the first-born, Jacob might truly regard as a
usurpation. And now he might think an opportunity offered
itself for putting an end to Esau's claim for ever, by his own
consent, and by express stipulation. Nor was it really taking
any unfair advantage of Esau's peculiar straits; since, even if
the concession were extorted from him by sheer physical
necessity, it was a concession strictly due.

Vain apology! Does Jacob really believe that the birthright is his, by the express destination of God? Then, may
he not leave it to God himself to make good his own word?
Is it not the most presumptuous and offensive form of unbelief
to adopt expedients of our own for bringing to pass the counsels of the Most High? Yes; it is unbelief; Jacob sinned
through unbelief. He did not simply trust in God, and leave
it to God to effect his own designs in his own way. Heir as
he was of the birthright, he would make assurance doubly
sure, and would have the decree of Jehovah countersigned and
sealed by the covenant of a frail brother of the dust;—a
covenant, too, extorted by a scheme most revolting to natural
affection, as well as to spiritual uprightness and truth.

Can it indeed be a spiritual blessing which Jacob thinks,

by such a carnal and worldly policy, to secure? It may be so. And indeed it does not appear that Jacob here assumed or possessed the right of primogeniture, in a temporal sense. It would really seem that he valued the birthright chiefly as a spiritual privilege and prerogative. But if so, surely his sin in this instance is all the greater. Does he think to purchase the Holy Ghost with money,—the heavenly inheritance with a mess of pottage? Or, viewing the transaction in the least offensive light,—as a bargain, not for the possession of a blessing already his, but for the setting aside of an unwarranted claim to it by another party,—what a poor spirit of compromise does it display! Let it be even persecution that Jacob suffered at the hands of Esau,—is persecution to be bought off by a mess of pottage? Is the antagonist of our spiritual principles, or the enemy of our spiritual peace, when he applies to us for help and we have the means of doing him a service, to be refused, or be kept waiting, until we adjust with him the terms of a conventional truce, and bargain with him at least for neutrality? Is that the spirit of Christian brotherhood or of Christian charity? Were it not better that Jacob, wronged and injured by having his birthright withheld, should " heap coals of fire on the head " of the usurper? Might he not thus have "overcome evil with good," and so gained his brother?

As it was, what did he gain? The bargain is concluded, —the price is paid. Is the blessing more securely his now than it was before? On the contrary, does not the very sinfulness of the expedient resorted to,—the wretchedness of the device by which he sought to make the blessing his own for ever,—only serve to show that if it ever actually become his at all, it is not by his might or merit or wisdom, but altogether and exclusively by the sovereign decree, the free grace, and the free Spirit of God alone.

But Jacob's fault will not make Esau guiltless. His great sin stands condemned in both Testaments. "He despised his birthright," says the historian (ver. 34). As " a profane person, he for one morsel of meat sold his birthright," says the epistle to the Hebrews (Heb. xii. 16).

" He despised his birthright ;"—selling it for a mess of pottage,—" that same red pottage,"—as he himself describes it, with all the emphasis of genuine epicurean longing,—" that red—that very red pottage "—so tempting in its appearance —of which the hunter was so fond that its very name stuck to him as a distinction, and he was called Edom, or " the red," from this very incident (ver. 30).

Feed me, he says, abandoning himself to the delights of appetite,—as the keen sportsman will crown his day of hard exercise in the field with an evening of indulgence at the table ;—feed me with that same red pottage, whose savoury odour already overcomes me. And then, when he hears the condition so artfully proposed to him,—instead of resisting the tempter and seeking relief elsewhere, how contemptuously does he speak ! " The birthright!" he exclaims. What good will the birthright do to me, if in the meantime I starve and die ? Will it feed me ? Will it gratify my taste and satisfy my hunger ? Nay, rather let me have that same red pottage,—which is a present and substantial good. And take thou, if thou choosest, that birthright, whose shadowy and remote advantages it seems thou prizest so highly !

That it was in some such way, and in some such spirit, that Esau " despised his birthright," may appear, not only from the inspired testimony, but from the very circumstances of the case. For, in the first place, Esau could scarcely, on this occasion, be really in very great straits for food. He was not a prodigal perishing with hunger,—but an elder son, treated as such, returning from a day's sport. Had he been actuated by a right spirit,—had he even felt that high sense of honour of which men of the world, like himself, make so much boast, —would he not have spurned the pitiful proposal of his brother Jacob, and preferred a dry crust of bread and cup of water to all the dainties with which this " plain man " would seduce or bribe him? Then again, secondly, it was evidently the spiritual blessing implied in the birthright that Esau held in such light esteem; there is no appearance of his meaning to resign any of its temporal advantages. Had it been merely a secular or worldly distinction that he bartered for the gratification of his appetite, there might have been folly in the transaction,—and sin also,—but not the sin of profanity with which he is unequivocally charged. The presumption is, that both the brothers understood the bargain to relate to the much coveted honour of being the ancestor of the Messiah, and sharing in the blessings which the Messiah was to bestow. That privilege Esau despises; using the argument of profane unbelief;—Who or what is the promised seed that I should wait for him at the expense and sacrifice of this red pottage? What profit shall I have of this spiritual faith and hope? What gain will this godliness be to me?

In this view, what a solemn lesson may we learn from Jacob's conduct; especially in its bearing upon his brother Esau's character and fate!

Jacob was probably even now professedly a more spiritual man than his brother Esau; apprehending in some measure his need of spiritual blessings, and the value of these blessings, as they were to flow from the Messiah destined to spring out of his loins. But what then? By what means did he seek to secure these blessings to himself? And what pains did he take to commend them to his brother? Ah! if he had simply trusted in the sure word of God, and left to God himself the fulfilment of it,—how little did it really matter whether Esau recognised his character and claims or not? If Christ were indeed " formed in him, the hope of glory,"—was it for him to be careful about the esteem in which his brother might hold him? Rather, might he not present to that brother the same Christ in whom he himself believed? And instead of the language which he virtually used to Esau:—Take thou this earthly portion and leave me the better birthright;—his invitation might have been to him to share with him freely and fully in both. In pursuing a very different course, he cannot be held guiltless of a participation in his brother's sin ; he is in fact his tempter. He uses means, and adopts a line of conduct fitted to bring out his brother's contempt of spiritual things. And whatever he may say as to its being merely for the purpose of securing what is already his by divine right,— he cannot be acquitted of cruelty and crime, in seeking to profit by his brother's straits, and turn his brother's fleshly desire to his own account.

But after all, every man must bear his own burden ; and Esau must not escape censure, even though it may have been a brother's infirmity of faith, or defect of love, that proved the occasion of his apostasy. It was in his heart to " despise the birthright," when he sold it. And the deed, alas ! admitted of no recall ; for " he found no place of repentance, though he sought it carefully with tears " (Heb. xii. 17).

What may be the full meaning of that ominous and appalling statement, I do not now inquire ; but one thing it unequivocally attests. Whatever may have been Jacob's sin in the matter, the Lord intended, through his instrumentality, to bring the question of Esau's spiritual state to a prompt and peremptory decision. The alternative is plainly proposed to him. He has to choose between the birthright blessing—in which he still might have found an interest, if he had been willing to own Jacob in the character that the oracle assigned to him—and the carnal indulgence on which his heart is set. It is a decisive choice he has to make ; he is shut up to an instant and final determination, one way or other. He does determine. And it is without the possibility of any recall.

Is there no such crisis in the experience of a sinner now ? May not one who has long been hesitating between God and Mammon be brought at some anxious moment to a point at which the irrevocable choice must be made ? Can any one be sure that his very next choice may not be that irrevocable one ? Dare any one, considering this, trifle with such scriptural exhortations as these?—" Choose ye this day whom ye will serve ;" " How long halt ye between two opinions : if the Lord be God, follow him ; but if Baal, follow him ;" " To-day, if ye will hear his voice, harden not your hearts," lest the sentence go forth against you, " I sware in my wrath that they should not enter into my rest."

36

Genesis 26:1-35

THE CHOSEN FAMILY UNDER ISAAC—HIS PERSONAL ADVENTURES IN HIS PILGRIMAGE

I PASS hastily over the incidents of Isaac's pilgrimage recorded in this twenty-sixth chapter,—not because they are void of practical interest,—but partly because they are so similar to corresponding events in Abraham's career as to be almost literal repetitions of them,—and partly also for another reason ;—to concentrate attention on the special peculiarity of the believing household's history during this period, as we have the key to it in the oracle accompanying the birth of the twin brothers.

The resemblance of Isaac's experience, during the brief space of time which he spent as a pilgrim, to the previous experience of his father Abraham in similar circumstances, is not a little striking.

We have a famine, breaking up the establishment at Lahai-roi, where, after the death of Abraham, Isaac dwelt (xxv. 11). And this circumstance leads to a temporary sojourn at Gerar among the Philistines (xxvi. 1). There the Lord appears to him, to arrest him in the purpose he seems to have formed of going down for greater plenty to Egypt, that granary and storehouse of the ancient world ; and at the same time to renew to him the promises, temporal and spiritual, which had been ratified by the divine oath to Abraham. Thus " Isaac dwelt in Gerar" (ver. 2-6) ; and in Gerar the son repeats the sad offence twice committed by his father.

In the very place in which, on the second occasion, Abraham had recourse to the expedient of an evasive policy, through fear of the corrupt manners of the age, Isaac is tempted to equivocate respecting his wife, in the very same way, and with the very same result too ; scarcely escaping death, or dishonour worse than death ; and exposing himself to the humiliating and indignant reproof of the prince whom he so unjustly distrusted (ver. 7-11). Thereafter, we have an account of Isaac's growing prosperity, and of the increase of his wealth in flocks and herds (ver. 12-14) ; an increase which leads to the usual consequences that were wont to follow in these days. We read of jealous heartburnings on the part of the people of the land ;—" The Philistines envied him." Then we trace the fruit of this envy in proposals of separation, for the sake of peace, on the part of their prince ; frequent removals in search of room ; and interminable misunderstandings and strifes among the herdmen about wells (ver. 12-22). And there is this aggravation,—that besides the ordinary disputes apt to arise between parties feeding large quantities of cattle near one another,—questions of hereditary right are raised, and complaints have to be made on behalf of Isaac, as to the wrong done by the Philistines, in stopping the wells which his father Abraham's servants had digged (ver. 18).

At last, after a vexatious, though not lengthened course of wandering and contention, Isaac returns to the vicinity of his former dwelling-place ; and at Beersheba receives anew a personal visit from the Lord ; has the covenant again confirmed to him ; and prepares, as it would seem, permanently to take up there his henceforth unmolested abode (ver. 23-25).

And, to complete the parallel, the narrative closes with the transaction between Isaac and the ruler of the country where he had been sojourning. That prince, with the chief captain of his army, hastens, evidently in some alarm, to appease the patriarch's resentment and conciliate his favour, by a friendly overture :—" Let there be now an oath betwixt us, even betwixt us and thee, and let us make a covenant with thee ; that thou wilt do us no hurt, as we have not touched thee, and as we have done unto thee nothing but good, and have sent thee away in peace" (ver. 26-29). Whereupon Isaac enters once more into a treaty,—identical with that to which his father Abraham had consented to swear,—on the same precise spot, and beside the same precise well,—which thus a second time merits and regains its appellation of " Beer-sheba" —the well of the oath (ver. 30-33).

So exact a similarity, even down to minute particulars, between the story of the son's pilgrimage and that of the father, may very possibly create difficulty in certain minds. And at this distance of time, both from the occurrence of the events and from the recording of them, it may be beyond our power to account for it altogether satisfactorily. That the king of Gerar and his prime minister, or commander-in-chief, should bear the same names that the corresponding personages bore in Abraham's time,—Abimelech and Phichol, —may be easily enough explained, according to eastern usage, upon the supposition of these being hereditary titles of hereditary offices. But it does seem somewhat strange that the very details of the adventures which the father and the son respectively underwent, should be to so great an extent identically the same. Let it be observed, however, that the picturesque and graphic annals of that older time are apt to cast into the same type or mould analogous events, and successions of events. They seize upon the features that are identical, without dwelling upon circumstantial differences ; and thus they give to the whole narrative a somewhat artificial appearance of even literal repetition. Then, again, let it be remembered, that the domestic manners of the East have always been far less liable to change from generation to generation, and have always had far more of a sort of stereotyped character, than the manners of other countries and later ages with which we are more familiar.

And, above all, let it be considered that there was a wise purpose to be served by the plain and palpable identification of Isaac, as the heir, with Abraham, whose successor and representative he was. It was important that he should be recognised and acknowledged by the nations and kings with whom Abraham had been called to mingle. And it may well be ascribed to the immediate and special ordering of the providence of God, that the younger patriarch was appointed or allowed to retrace and revive the footsteps of his predecessor's pilgrimage;—as well as to re-open the wells which, under his father's auspices, had been dug.

One thing, however, distinguishes the experience of Isaac.· His career as a wanderer is a kind of episode in his history ; for the most part, his life is settled and sedentary. Sixty years at least, and probably more than sixty, had passed over his head before he was called to remove from the place where Abraham had latterly pitched his tent ; for we may safely conclude that Isaac did not go to Gerar until after the birth of his two sons, and the transaction between them respecting the sale of the birthright. Then we must certainly suppose him to have been settled again at Beer-sheba before Esau's unhappy marriage with two daughters of the proscribed race. Thus the years of Isaac's wandering must be reduced to some eight or ten at the utmost. And we find him restored, in his eightieth year, to that comparatively quiet course of life which for nearly a century thereafter he continued to follow,—until he died peacefully at the age of an hundred and fourscore years (chap. xxxv. 28, 29).

How that long period of an entire century was spent— what was Isaac's habitual occupation, and what vicissitudes were apt to vary the uniformity of its routine—we have no means of even conjecturing. All that we learn with respect to it, in so far as Isaac himself is concerned, is comprised in the memorable incident of his final and decisive bestowal of the blessing (chap. xxxvii.) Nor is it easy to fix exactly the date of that incident, so as to adjust it to the prolonged continuance of Isaac's life and sojourn in the land. That he lived some considerable time after the scene of the benediction, is evident from the fact that Jacob found him still alive when he returned from his residence in Laban's family ; for he joined with Esau in rendering the last offices of filial love (xxxv. 29). But at the same time it is equally evident that it was upon his deathbed, at least in his own opinion, that Isaac transacted the affair which led to Jacob's exile. It was as a dying man that he meant to dispose of the birthright-blessing. And however long he may have lingered afterwards on the earth, we are to consider the twenty-seventh chapter, the chapter with which we have next to deal, as virtually recording his dying bequest—his final and irrevocable legacy.

37

THE TRANSMISSION OF THE BIRTHRIGHT-BLESSING

WE now enter upon the most pathetic of all the narratives in this book—if we except, perhaps, that of Joseph's discovery of himself to his brethren.   And we enter upon it, not to mar it by any paraphrastic commentary, but merely to apply to it the key furnished by the oracle of God ;—" The elder shall serve the younger."   In the light of that oracle let us review the history.

The struggle between sense and faith is nowhere in all the Bible more painfully brought out than here ; it might almost seem, indeed, as if the scene were meant to be as much a trial of those who are mere spectators of it, through the perusal of the inspired narrative, as it was of those who were originally and personally engaged in it.

In general, it may be observed that the sacred history, especially in the Old Testament, often makes a strong demand upon the faith of readers ; at least it makes a demand on that peculiar exercise of faith which consists in obedience to the peremptory injunction—" Be still and know that I am God." The sovereignty of God, as the direct and immediate cause of whatsoever comes to pass,—together with the absolute vanity of all subordinate agents,—fills the mind with awe ;—while the open and undisguised, nay, as it would seem, minute and elaborate exposure of human weakness and sin, would almost make one echo in sad earnest what the Psalmist said in his haste, " All men are liars" (Ps. cxvi. 11). It happens too, here, as in other instances in which the divine and human elements are combined, that the balance, in the comparison of character and conduct, is often felt to be in favour rather of those who are opposing, than of those who are carrying out, the divine will. The blessing reaches him for whom it is intended, in a way that is apt to connect it, in our esteem, with the idea of ill-gotten gain ; and sympathy is enlisted on the side of the real usurper. His impiety in aspiring to that rank which, by the divine declaration as well as by his own consent, now belonged to another, is lost sight of in the generous indignation with which we resent the fraud put upon him, and the deep compassion with which we listen to the plaintive pleadings of his despair.

Hence, in estimating aright the moral and spiritual bearing of such a narrative as this, we have to guard against a double danger. On the one hand, we may be tempted to extenuate or excuse the sins of those who are taking part with God, and seeking to fulfil his purpose ; and, in so doing, we may run the risk of compromising God's holy law, and lowering our own sense of truth and right. Or again, on the other hand, we may allow our just indignation against the faults into which we see the professing people of God betrayed, to carry us too far in the direction of an unjust and uncharitable judgment of their whole profession. We may thus strengthen in ourselves and others a prejudice, not only against the godly, but against their godliness itself, such as may be any thing but conducive to the spiritual prosperity either of our own souls or of theirs. The last error is the most natural of the two to the natural mind ; and it is an error which the perusal of this story, under the influence of merely natural feelings, is very apt to foster. A generous heart revolts from the meanness of Jacob's poor trick— and lavishes all its sympathy on Esau's bitter disappointment.

There is a lesson in all this of much practical importance. To those who would be accounted the people of God, it says emphatically : Consider in what light your conduct will appear to the world of onlookers around you. At the very best, they are not apt to be prepossessed in your favour ; and if they do not actually watch for your halting, you need not at any rate expect them either to break your fall, or to cover your nakedness. Nor are they to be altogether blamed. Not only are the sins that may be found in you more offensive to a correct natural taste, than the same sins in others who do not make your profession ; but the kind of sins to which religious men are tempted, are often such as the natural conscience more instinctively condemns, than it does the open excesses of the thoughtless children of pleasure. The virtues of nature—although for the most part merely constitutional—the frankness, bravery, lightheartedness, and good humour that spring from an easy temper, and a large flow of animal spirits, command universal sympathy. Even the vices of nature, unbroken and untamed—its honest outbursts of passion—its frailties leaning to virtue's side—are frequently such as to attract rather than repel the lover of what is generous, manly, and sincere. On the other hand, the meek and lowly graces which religion cultivates have but little comeliness in the sight of eyes dazzled with more gaudy colours. The deep exercises of soul, again, that religion occasions, are not always favourable to that equanimity which it is so easy for one believing neither in heaven nor in hell to assume. And it must be confessed, also, that the vices which a religious profession admits of, or tolerates, as not flagrantly inconsistent with itself, are apt to be such as a man of worldly honour most indignantly repudiates. The mere name of godliness is at variance with the more splendid follies which the world conspires to idolise ; while alas ! that name, and even the reality, is sometimes found to be but too compatible with other violations of the strict rule of honourable conduct, such as the world itself is foremost to disown.

What a motive is thus presented to watchfulness over their whole conduct on the part of the people of God ! But for the ungodly, it will be but poor consolation that in their resentment of Jacob's inexcusable fault, they exclude themselves from the covenant of Jacob's God.

In my brief review of this affecting narrative, I mean to notice the persons interested in it, in the order in which they come upon the stage, after the purpose of Isaac is formed in his own mind, intimated to his son Esau, and by some means or other reported to his wife Rebekah. According to this arrangement, Rebekah herself is the first to claim attention; then, secondly, her favourite Jacob; in the third place, the patriarch Isaac himself; and lastly, the unhappy Esau.

I. Of all the parties concerned, Rebekah is the one most easily given over, by ordinary readers, to summary and condign condemnation; nor would it be safe to call in question the all but unanimous verdict of the church, as well as the world, against her conduct in this case. But it is important that the real nature of her offence should be ascertained and recognised. It is not merely the indulgence of a fond mother's doting and unreasonable partiality that we have here to deal with. It is a sore trial of spiritual faith that this mother in Israel has to sustain.

The divine oracle is, to all human appearance, on the point of being frustrated and made void—Isaac is about to thwart the revealed purpose of God. The known will of her God, and the known intention of her husband, are irreconcilably at variance. God has destined the Abrahamic promise to the line of Jacob; Isaac is about to vest it in the lineage of Esau. And the crisis is urgent. The transaction for which Isaac is preparing himself is understood to be decisive. It is no ordinary or everyday occurrence. The head of the chosen household is, or imagines himself to be, on his deathbed; and what he may say or do now, especially with reference to the transmission of the birthright, is believed to have the force of an infallible and irrevocable bequest. What, in these circumstances, is the believing wife to do?

To remonstrate either with Esau or with his father would be, as she may well imagine, altogether in vain. They had gone too far, and committed themselves too deeply, to be now arrested by the warning of one whom they might suspect—perhaps with some justice—if not of malice, at least of partial counsel. The weakened mind of the old man, and the wilful mind of the young man, might seem alike to preclude any hope of success, if Rebekah had been inclined to try her influence with either. The case then seems desperate. It is true that she may safely leave it in the hands of him whose oracle is in danger, and rely upon his wisdom and power to baffle all attempts that may be made to turn his purpose aside. But it is difficult to remain inactive when a great evil is about to happen, and the means of preventing or averting it seem to be at hand. Shall I see the declared mind of God thwarted before my eyes, when a little ingenuity can suggest a way of turning the very endeavour to thwart it into the means of its accomplishment! Is not any device justifiable for such an end! May not fraud itself, in such a crisis, be regarded as almost pious?

Such is the probable and fair explanation of the mother's part in this miserably complex family sin.

II. The conduct of Jacob is little else than an aggravated repetition of his cold-blooded negotiation with his brother Esau about the sale of the birthright. He hesitates, indeed, when he is first asked by Rebekah to become a partner with her in her fraud ; not, however, from any righteous abhorrence of the crime, but from doubt of its practicability (ver. 11, 12).

Accordingly, when he is reassured by the urgency of the tempter's solicitation—alas! that he should have had such a tempter !—he goes about the work of guile with a deliberation that shocks our sense of decency as well as of virtue (ver. 13). He suffers himself without remonstrance to be arrayed in the skin borrowed from a senseless animal, and the robes stolen from an unwitting brother. And led by the false fondness of a mother into the chamber which the seeming approach of death, as well as the solemn transaction then on hand, should have hallowed with an awful reverence of truth and righteousness,—he heaps lie upon lie with unscrupulous effrontery; abuses the simple confidence of the blind old man; and almost, if we may so speak, betraying his father with a kiss,—steals from him the birthright-blessing,—and then hastens out of his sight, as if he were not only afraid to meet his brother, but impatient to exult in secret over the success with which his daring stratagem has been crowned (ver. 14-30).

Nor is it any palliation of his offence that he is leading his father in this matter to act according to the will and purpose of God. My father, he might say within himself, is infirm of purpose,—he is in his dotage. He has all along had a wrong bias with regard to the disposal of the birthright; and now in the failure of his mental as well as bodily powers, he is scarcely to be held accountable for what he does. He must be managed for his own good as one manages a froward child in its days of unintelligent infancy. Miserable excuse! as idle with respect to God, as it is cruel with respect to Isaac! The oracle of God—the dotage of Isaac,—are these valid reasons for this crooked policy? Nay, should not the very fact of God's purpose having been so unequivocally announced, supersede the necessity of all human plotting and contrivance? Will the wit, any more than the wrath of man, work the righteousness of God?—Let us stand still and see the salvation of God.

And then as to Isaac's imbecility, and the necessity of keeping him right by craft if not by reason,—does the interference of his wife and son really mend the matter? Will Isaac's sin be the less, if by mere mistake he does one thing when he means to do another? Is there no other method that may be tried? Where is the use of prayer?

The patriarch is about to convey the blessing by a deed implying a divine sanction and divine inspiration. May not God be asked to interpose, and the issue thereafter left to him?

On whatever side we view it, the crime into which Rebekah hurries her favourite child Jacob is a very sad one; and deeply have they both occasion, all their life long, to rue the day when they were tempted to take into their own hands the execution of the plans and purposes of the Most High.

III. Of Isaac himself, as his conduct on this memorable occasion illustrates his general character, there is but little to be said. An important inquiry, however, suggests itself on the subject of the faith which he is expressly said to have exercised. For it is with special reference to the transaction which we are now considering, that he is enrolled in the catalogue of the men " of whom the world was not worthy," the "great cloud of witnesses;" this emphatic testimony being borne of him;—" By faith Isaac blessed Jacob and Esau concerning things to come" (Heb. xi. 20). What, one may ask, does the testimony mean?

I. Let it be remembered in the first place, that in this whole transaction, Isaac understood himself to be the depositary and transmitter of the great covenant-promise which his father Abraham had received. It was in that character that he blessed Jacob and Esau, and to realise that character implied an act and exercise of faith. In that faith, Isaac never wavered. Very early in his lifetime he was initiated into the most sublime and spiritual of the articles of its creed; for the part he bore in the scene on Mount Moriah,—when he was young indeed, but not too young to apprehend the meaning of what he saw,—must have made him familiar with them all. The incidents of his life tend to confirm the impression which that scene is fitted to make, of Isaac's believing acquiescence in the terms of the covenant made with his father Abraham. The whole circumstances of his marriage—his contentment under the delay which his father's scruples occasioned—his unreserved surrender of himself into his father's hands—the ready consent he gave to what must have seemed to the eye of sense a perilous venture for a spouse—and the attitude of de-

votional meditation in which he is found waiting for the issue
of the expedition,—all concur to give a strong conviction of
the personal piety of Isaac, and his vivid apprehension of his
high calling as the heir of the covenant and the ancestor of its
great Mediator and Surety. Nor can there be room for doubt
that, in his final testamentary arrangement, Isaac acted upon
the faith which he had all along professed and cherished.

It may be a question indeed whether or not he chose the right
time and adopted the right method. Misled by the failure of
his sight, and other growing infirmities, he may have proceeded
to the discharge of what should have been the last duty of his
life, before he had any indication from God of his end being
near, or any legitimate warrant to expect that divine inspiration which was wont to prompt the dying utterances of the
prophetic patriarchs of old. In the manner also of pronouncing the decisive benediction, Isaac may have been, and probably was, in fault. That something like a feast should be
associated with the solemn act of conveying the birthright-
blessing ; and that on such an occasion the pontifical robes
belonging in hereditary succession to the first-born should be
worn—we may be prepared to admit. But surely the feast
should have been of a religious character, and the investiture
of the first-born in his robes should have been a public and
solemn religious act. A mere savoury mess of venison, the
fruit of a day's hunting in the field, could have no appropriate
relation to the prophetic act which the dying head of the
household had to perform. And as to the investiture of the
priestly and royal robes, for such the " goodly raiment" of the
elder son is with great probability supposed to be, surely it
should have been arranged beforehand with such open formality as would have rendered the assumption of them by stealth
impossible. The entire ceremony, in short, in all its three
parts,—in the eating of meat, the putting on of the garment
of primogeniture, and the pronouncing of the solemn covenant-
blessing,—should have been a devotional service in the presence

of all the household ; and not the pitiful stealing of a march on the part of one parent against the other.

It is on both sides a deplorable game of craft. If Rebekah is blamed, and justly blamed, for her cunning plot in favour of Jacob,—let Isaac's procedure also be duly scanned. Is the patriarch called to execute, as he believes, the last solemn deed of his earthly career? And is he to do so, not merely in the character of an ordinary parent, but in the official capacity of a priest and prophet, entitled to look for special divine inspiration in this closing act of his life? Then how does he set about it? Not openly, in the face of all his family, and with the customary observance of all the appropriate sacrificial rites ; but clandestinely, without so much as communicating his purpose to the wife of his bosom. Certainly the conduct of Isaac, in seeking furtively, by an underhand manœuvre, to secure the envied and sorely-contested prerogative for Esau, does not indicate much more of truth and integrity than we are accustomed to ascribe to the plan of Jacob and Rebekah.

Nevertheless, it was by faith that Isaac was moved to dispose of the blessing.

For, in the second place, it is chiefly in the sequel of the scene that the faith of Isaac appears. When first he discovers the imposition that has been practised upon him, the patriarch is altogether overwhelmed. And no wonder! His whole plan has miscarried. All the pains he has been taking to get the business done quietly, without the knowledge of the rival claimant and his partisan, have been thrown away. He has hurried it on in the hope that all would be over, and all securely settled on behalf of Esau, before Rebekah or Jacob could hear any surmise of what was on foot. No wonder, therefore, that when he finds himself so signally and shamefully foiled, he "trembles very exceedingly." But through this trembling his faith manifests its power ; first in the broken accents of his passionate exclamation,—"Who? where is he that hath" surreptitiously got the blessing?—and next, almost before the outburst is over, in the calm language of acquiescence, "yea, and he shall be blessed" (ver. 33).

It is the very agony of faith, sorely shaken, but yet recovering itself. The patriarch's eyes are opened ; it is as if a long dream were dispelled. All at once, and all around him, a new light flashes ; showing the past, the present, the future, in new colours. He has been trying to overreach ; but he is himself overreached. Above all, he has been "kicking against the pricks ;" and he finds that to be "hard." But now his faith signally triumphs. If he had given way to natural feeling, anger must have filled his bosom. If he had looked merely to second causes, he must have revoked his blessing on the instant, and turned it into a curse ; for he could not be held bound by anything he had uttered under a mistake or misapprehension, as to the party to whom he uttered it. What has passed, he might have said, between me and Jacob is essentially null and void. He got the birthright-blessing under a false pretence. I did not really mean to convey it to him.

Isaac maintains no such plea ; he owns the blessing as beyond recall.

And on what ground ? Simply on the ground of its being manifestly of God.

Here is the faith of Isaac ; the faith by which he "blessed Jacob and Esau." "Let God be true, and every man a liar," is the principle upon which now at last he acts.

There has been falsehood among all the parties concerned in the transaction ; they have all been trying to forestall and overreach one another. On all hands it is a miserable confusion and complexity of deceit ; and instead of the calm and holy beauty of a saint's departing hour,—a venerable patriarch in the presence of all belonging to him, and under the guidance and inspiration of his God, sealing with his latest voice the covenant and counsel of heaven,—the household is scandalised by a spectacle of domestic feud fitted to shake all confidence in human truthfulness, and make God's chosen family a very by-word for disunion and dispeace, among all the dwellers upon the earth. But for his own name's sake, God overrules the evil for good, and on the ruins of man's manifold lies establishes his own truth. Signally does he visit upon the guilty parties, in their after-life, the plot in which they have been concerned. But in the first instance he disconcerts the plot itself. The well-devised scheme of the stealthy hunting, the hasty meal, and the secret blessing, is frustrated ; and Isaac, awaking as from a dream, owns that it is the doing of the Lord ! With fear and trembling he acknowledges at last the divine sovereignty, and acquiesces in the righteousness and salvation of God. He no longer resists God ; he believes, the Lord helping his unbelief ; and by faith he confirms the birthright-blessing anew to Jacob. He consoles, indeed, as best he can, the passionate grief of Esau ; but he does not now question the divine purpose in favour of his younger son. He recognises in him the heir of the promise made to his father Abraham, and the ancestor of the expected Messiah. He sets to his seal that God is true. It was thus that " by faith Isaac blessed Jacob and Esau concerning things to come (Heb. xi. 20).

IV. The saddest of all the pictures in this dismal domestic tragedy is that of Esau. There is nothing extant in the whole range of literature, sacred or profane, more heart-rending than the wild and passionate outburst of his sorrow ; his cry, his " exceeding bitter cry,"—" Bless me, even me also, O my father !" (ver. 34). His keen complaint against his brother ;—" Is not he rightly named Jacob ? for he hath supplanted me these two times : he took away my birthright ; and, behold, now he hath taken away my blessing" (ver. 36) ; his pathetic pleading with his father " Hast thou not reserved a blessing for me ?" (ver. 36) ; and finally the uncontrollable vehemence of his despair, when replying to the feeble question of the agitated old man ;— " What shall I do now unto thee, my son ?" (ver. 37)—he

abandons himself to the utmost agony of woe, crying, " Hast
thou but one blessing, my father? bless me, even me also, O
my father!"—and then "lifting up his voice, and weeping"
(ver. 38);—the whole constitutes a more melting scene by far
than poet ever fancied or painter ever drew. And if we
isolate it from all consideration of the spiritual relations in
which the parties stood to one another, our sympathy is carried
along in full flood with the whole swelling torrent of the
injured man's wrath and grief. But it will not be wise to
suffer our sympathy with him, or our resentment of the pitiful
trick that baffled him, to blind our minds to the real character
of Esau, and of the course of conduct in which he was defeated.

Tried even by the standard of worldly honour, Esau is on
this occasion found grievously wanting. If Jacob succeeded
in circumventing him, did not he, in the first instance, seek to
steal a march upon Jacob? Setting the oracle of God aside,
—was there not enough in his own compact and covenant with
Jacob to preclude the idea of this underhand procedure in the
mind of an upright and conscientious man? Even if he
thought that he had been hardly used in that negotiation,—
and that he ought to recall the foolish bargain by which he
sold his birthright for a mess of pottage,—he might have
remonstrated with his brother instead of seeking to outwit
him by a secret stratagem. Surely that is not exactly the
behaviour that might be expected from a frank and manly
spirit; it is not quite the conduct of one who "sweareth to
his own hurt, and changeth not" (Ps. xv. 4).

But it is chiefly in a spiritual view that his conduct is here
again to be regarded,—in the light of the inspired commentary of the Epistle to the Hebrews, in which the writer speaks
of Esau as "a profane person, who for one morsel of meat
sold his birthright;" and who "afterward, when he would
have inherited the blessing, was rejected; for he found no
place of repentance, though he sought it carefully with tears"
(Heb. xii. 14-17). So the apostle testifies with reference

evidently to the passionate pleading of Esau with his father Isaac. Esau really did seek a place of repentance. Not merely did he seek to change his father's mind, as some understand the expression; he sought to recall and reverse his own rash act in consenting to the sale of what now at last he had learned in some measure adequately to value. The apostle manifestly alludes to Esau's own change of mind, to which the wretched man sought to give effect; not to any change he needed or tried to work in the mind of Isaac. For he had indeed changed his mind upon the subject, and he would have made good that change of mind now, if he had been able. How far he was in earnest desirous of the spiritual blessings of grace and salvation involved in the birthright,—is another question; at all events he was so far awakened as to be alive to the preciousness and importance of that which he had once despised,—the birthright-legacy which he had consented to sell, and which now at last he sought in vain to recover. Yes! it was, alas! in vain. He had taken a decided step. The issue was beyond recall. Neither toil, nor craft, nor importunity, nor tears could revoke the deed.

Nor could he take refuge in the oracular decree. That decree made the sale unmeaning as regards the purpose and will of God; but it did not make it unmeaning as regards the intention of Esau. His consent to sell the birthright, and his desperate attempt to recover its blessing, were alike irrespective of the oracle. If he had owned at first that revelation in the exercise of a true faith, he never would have negotiated the sale at all; he would have made common cause with Jacob, upon a different footing altogether; upon the footing of a common interest in the Messiah, of whom Jacob was to be the father. Or, if he had really come now to recognise and believe the revelation in its real significancy, he would have sought to recall and review the past transaction, with all its sin and shame, in a very different spirit, and to a very different effect. He would have sought for a place of repentance with even deeper and bitterer sorrow than he did ; but it would have been with sorrow " after a godly sort ;" and he would have sought for it in the way of fulfilling the very terms of the oracle. He would.have looked to Jacob, or rather to the Messiah of whom Jacob was to be the ancestor, for any interest in the birthright or its blessing to which he might yet hope to aspire. If he had thus sought for a place of repentance, or an opportunity of effectually changing his mind, he would not have sought for it in vain.

It was not, however, this, but something far short of this, that Esau after all desired. He was awakened, indeed, so far as to see and bitterly lament the folly he had committed in consenting to barter all that was precious in his hope for the future in exchange for a present morsel of meat. Fain would he have repented now of that folly. And if a very agony of carefulness and floods of tears could have availed, he would have recalled the past. But that was all. To the last, there was no real acquiescence in the divine method of salvation,— no real seeking of the blessing in the only direction in which it could be found, and through the only name in which it was treasured up.

And is not this the very awakening that often haunts the dying hour, or the dreary solitude, of the unhappy child of earth, when he is startled to find that he has made a miserable bargain in consenting to gain the whole world and lose his own soul? Remorse,—rage,—revenge,—madden his breast and fire his brain ! He has committed a fearful mistake in living for the world, and bartering for the world's mess of pottage all that might have brightened his immortal hope! What energy, even of despair, agitates his frame ! If cries and tears could suffice, he would yet recall, and cancel, and undo the past. But in all this, there is no real bringing of his soul into subjection to the sovereign will of God, or the saving righteousness of Christ, or the sanctifying work of the Spirit. He is stung to the quick as a disappointed, befooled, and outwitted man ;—not converted to the meekness of a little child. There is no acquiescence in the appointed way of mercy ; no seeking of a Saviour for his lost and guilty soul. But poignant regret of the past, and blank terror of the future, extort the cry of expiring agony ; and extort that cry in vain.

It is the appointed nemesis of the despised voice of wisdom —the slighted gospel call ;—" Because I have called, and ye refused ; I have stretched out my hand, and no man regarded ; but ye have set at nought all my counsel, and would none of my reproof : I also will laugh at your calamity ; I will mock when your fear cometh ; when your fear cometh as desolation, and your destruction cometh as a whirlwind ; when distress and anguish cometh upon you. Then shall they call upon me, but I will not answer ; they shall seek me early, but they shall not find me : for that they hated knowledge, and did not choose the fear of the Lord : they would none of my counsel ; they despised all my reproof : therefore shall they eat of the fruit of their own way, and be filled with their own devices."

38

Genesis 27:41-28:15

THE BEGINNING OF JACOB'S PILGRIMAGE
THE VISION

Whither shall I flee from thy presence ?—When I awake I am still with thee.   Psalm 139:7,18

Are they not all ministering spirits, sent forth to minister for them who shall be heirs of salvation ?   Hebrews 1:14

THE divine testimony concerning Esau's state of mind towards his brother Jacob—his bitter hatred and bloody purpose—is the most authentic commentary upon his previous conduct ;— "Esau hated Jacob, because of the blessing wherewith his father blessed him : and Esau said in his heart, The days of mourning for my father are at hand; then will I slay my brother Jacob" (ver. 41)? Surely if Esau had really been seeking either true repentance, or any spiritual blessing which the godly sorrow of true repentance can command, he would have been humbled for his own sin before God, and anxious to have a share in the covenant-blessing on any terms that God might appoint.   And towards his brother, he would have cherished such a sentiment as the oracle from the first should have awakened; and now much more after even his too partial father had acquiesced in it.   Certainly, it is conclusive proof against the genuineness of that "repentance" for which Esau "sought a place, and found none," that he harboured so deadly a hatred against Jacob, and formed so deliberate a plan of fratricide. But as in other instances, so here, persecution is overruled by God for good ; it leads to a more decided separation of the church from the surrounding idolatrous world. The violent threatening of Esau is the means of preserving Jacob from such alliance with the ungodly as that into which Esau himself has unhappily fallen. First of all, it brings Jacob into nearer and more confidential fellowship with God than he had ever before enjoyed ; shutting him up in the bonds of a gracious and holy covenant. And then it puts him in the way of forming a connection somewhat better than the marriages which Esau had contracted with the daughters of Heth (xxvi. 34-35 ; xxvii. 46).

The movement towards Jacob's departure from the paternal roof, originates with his mother. A twofold motive animates her ; she acts partly under the impulse of natural affection, and partly also under the guidance of religious belief or spiritual faith. She would save Jacob from falling a victim to his brother's anger ; she would save him at the same time from falling into his brother's sin. The two motives are by no means incompatible. Rebekah dreads the double bereavement she must experience if Jacob should die by Esau's hand, and Esau also should die as a murderer, by the hand of the avenger of blood, or of the Lord himself making " inquisition for blood." " Why should I be deprived also of you both in one day ? " (ver. 42-45). But besides, she perceives the necessity of the chosen family being kept holy and uncontaminated by heathen admixture : and she feels that the time has come for a wife being found for Jacob, to be the mother of the promised seed, not from among the daughters of the land, but from the kindred out of whom the Lord had so evidently selected herself as a spouse to Isaac. Hence her suggestion to her husband ;—" I am weary of my life because of the daughters of Heth : if Jacob take a wife of the daughters of Heth, such as these which are of the daughters of the land, what good shall my life do me ? " (ver. 46). And hence

Isaac's charge to his younger son ;—" Thou shalt not take a wife of the daughters of Canaan ; arise, go to Padan-aram, and take thee a wife from thence of the daughters of Laban thy mother's brother" (xxviii. 1, 2). With this charge,—after receiving anew his father's blessing,—Jacob is sent away (ver. 3-5).

Stung by the implied reproach cast on him by his parents, Esau vainly tries to repair his error, and only succeeds in adding sin to sin by the connection which he forms with the rejected race of Ishmael ;—" Seeing that the daughters of Canaan pleased not Isaac his father ; he went unto Ishmael, and took unto the wives which he had Mahalath the daughter of Ishmael to be his wife" (ver. 6-9). Under better auspices, blessed by his aged parent, and led by God himself, Jacob goes forth on his lonely journey. Surely he goes forth in faith.

The outward circumstances, indeed, of his departure from home and his entrance on his solitary pilgrimage, are by no means such as to indicate or prove the high rank he holds in the estimate of heaven. Alone and unattended,—flying from the resentment of his brother,—he finds himself, as darkness closes in, without house or hut to shelter his weary head. No dwelling is near ;—no hospitable hand is ready to open the willing door and spread the welcome couch. Under the broad roof of the heavenly vault, and on the bare earth, he is fain to lie down; the wide expanse his chamber, and the rough stone his pillow (ver. 10, 11). But that night is to be a crisis in his history. "God found him at Bethel" (Hos. xii. 4). Now for the first time,—at least now for the first time decidedly,—he is to be apprehended, or laid hold of, by the Lord. He falls asleep on his hard, uncurtained couch; but it is to awake as a new man; with new life and energy, and new assurance of the divine favour and protection. Here, for the first time, so far as we can gather it from the history, by a formality, not of man, but of God, Jacob is served heir to the Abrahamic covenant, and the birthright-blessing of the Abrahamic family (ver. 12-15).

The manner, as well as the matter, of this communication from God to Jacob, is remarkable; indeed, the manner is even more so than the matter.

The key to it is to be found in a transaction long subsequent,—connected with the opening of our Lord's ministry on the earth. There can be little or no doubt that it is Jacob's dream which the Lord has in view when he makes the otherwise strange and inexplicable announcement to Nathanael;—"Hereafter ye shall see heaven open, and the angels of God ascending and descending upon the Son of man" (John i. 50, 51).

Let the circumstances of that memorable interview be considered. Nathanael is told by Philip that he and some others have "found him of whom Moses in the law, and the prophets, did write, Jesus of Nazareth, the son of Joseph" (ver. 45). Upon this he first interposes the objection, "Can there any good thing come out of Nazareth?" and then, with the docility of a candid and earnest mind, he complies with Philip's invitation, "Come and see" (ver. 46). He is somewhat strangely welcomed; "Jesus saw Nathanael coming to him, and saith of him, Behold an Israelite indeed, in whom is no guile!" (ver. 47). A salutation like that must have surprised not a little one whose acquaintance Jesus was now for the first time making. He puts a simple question, and receives a reply that carries his conviction in a sort of ecstasy of gladness;—"Nathanael saith unto him, Whence knowest thou me? Jesus answered and said unto him, Before that Philip called thee, when thou wast under the fig tree, I saw thee. Nathanael answered and saith unto him, Rabbi, thou art the son of God; thou art the King of Israel" (ver. 48, 49).

What, we may well ask,—what is there in this brief colloquy,—to convince Nathanael so quickly, so effectually, so enthusiastically and joyously?

To say merely that Jesus gave a proof of his omniscience by referring to the fact of Nathanael having been recently under his fig-tree,—is by no means satisfactory. It is not to the accidental circumstance of an ordinary visit to a fig-tree that the Lord alludes; in that case, his allusion could scarcely have told so promptly and powerfully as it did upon Nathanael's mind. There was more in the hint, as Nathanael himself evidently caught it up. It was a swift electric and telegraphic interchange of intelligence between Jesus and this new inquirer. Not to the place where Nathanael happened at a particular time to be,—but to what was then and there passing in his mind,—does the Searcher of hearts appeal. And therefore the appeal comes home with point and efficacy to the conscience.

Let it be remembered that "under the fig-tree," was the oratory or place of prayer,—the "closet,"—for a pious Jew in the middle rank of life;—whence the sort of proverbial expression employed to denote a state of tranquillity and religious freedom: "They shall sit every man under his vine, and under his fig-tree; and none shall make them afraid" (Micah iv. 4). In that genial climate, and with the scanty accommodation furnished in their ordinary dwellings, the grateful shade of the vine or the fig-tree in the garden might be resorted to, as was also the enclosed house-top, for the purposes of secret prayer and meditation; and we can scarcely doubt that it is to an exercise of that sort that our Lord alludes, when his allusion carries such swift conviction to Nathanael's soul:—"When thou wast under the fig-tree, I saw thee." I saw what thou wast doing; I saw what was passing in thy mind. And it is upon the ground and warrant of what then and there I saw in thee, that upon thy very first coming to me I pronounce the sentence which not unnaturally surprises thee so much :—"Behold an Israelite indeed, in whom is no guile!"

But there must have been something special in Nathanael's exercise of soul under the fig-tree, to which the Lord so significantly points ; and there is one hypothesis which seems to possess no inconsiderable amount of inherent probability.

Let it be supposed that it was the thirty-second psalm that had been engaging Nathanael's devout thoughts. He has been passing through some such experience as the psalmist in that psalm describes. There has been previously a season of de- cline in his spiritual life ; there has been more or less of reserve in his intercourse with God. Especially in regard to sin,—either the general sin of his heart and life, or some spe- cific sin in particular,—he has been restraining confession and prayer ; excusing perhaps and justifying himself. " Going about to establish a righteousness of his own," he has been dealing unfairly and deceitfully with the holy law of his God, as well as with his own guilt and corruption ; trying to soothe his soul by means of palliatives,—to pacify his conscience with the usual opiates that lull worldly men asleep. But he has not succeeded ; in very mercy, God has not suffered him to find rest. He has been harassed by misgivings and fears, until he has been constrained to try " a more excellent way ;" the way of an unreserved unburthening of his whole heart to God. He has been driven to confession, and the simple, child-like, utterance of all his wants and all his griefs.

Such had been David's experience. " When I kept silence, my bones waxed old, through my roaring all the day long. For day and night thy hand was heavy upon me : my moisture is turned into the drought of summer." Then I changed my plan. " I acknowledged my sin unto thee, and mine iniquity have I not hid. I said, I will confess my transgressions unto the Lord ; and thou forgavest the iniquity of my sin."

It is in the fulness of that instant and glad relief which he found in unbosoming his whole soul to God, that David pours out the burst of grateful joy with which the psalm be- gins,—connecting the assured pardon of sin with the entire abandonment of all reserve,—" Blessed is he whose transgres- sion is forgiven, whose sin is covered. Blessed is the man unto

whom the Lord imputeth not iniquity, and in whose spirit
there is no guile" (ver. 1, 2).

Let us say that in the soul-exercise under the fig-tree of
which our Lord shows himself to have been cognisant, Nathanael had just been brought to the precise point to which the
psalmist came ; that self-convicted and self-condemned he had
come to the conclusion,—"I will confess my transgressions
unto the Lord ;"—seeing nothing for it but a frank and full
casting of himself on the mercy of his God. Then, what
an adaptation to his case,—what a word in season,—what a
message of peace directed personally and pointedly to himself,
—might his broken and contrite spirit recognise in the testimony of Jesus,—"Behold an Israelite indeed, in whom is no
guile"—applied as it was to a scene which none but the
Searcher of hearts could know!   And calling instantly to mind
the connection in which the emphatic condition of guileless-
ness stood, in that experimental psalm, with the full and free
forgiveness of all iniquity,—how must he have exulted in the
assurance thus indirectly, but only on that account the more
effectually, conveyed to him of pardon, acceptance, and peace!
"Be of good cheer, Nathanael, thy sins are forgiven thee!"
With what unutterable emotions of relief, gratitude, and joy,
must he have hailed this Omniscient One, so evidently having
power on earth to forgive sins ;—"Rabbi, thou art the Son of
God ; thou art the King of Israel" (John i. 49).

Now, it is to Nathanael, thus convinced and thus quickened,
that Jesus addresses the stimulating appeal : "Because I said
unto thee, I saw thee under the fig-tree, believest thou ? thou
shalt see greater things than these" (ver. 50).   And it is as a
sequel to this blessed negotiation of forgiveness and peace that
he introduces the promise so plainly borrowed from the record
of Jacob's vision ;—"Verily, verily, I say unto you, Hereafter
ye shall see heaven open, and the angels of God ascending and
descending upon the Son of man" (ver. 51).

Here, therefore, we have the interpretation of the vision.

The angels ascending and descending upon the Son of man represent the restored intercourse between heaven and earth which his mediation secures. The guileless believer not merely obtains the forgiveness of sin,—tasting "the blessedness of the man to whom the Lord imputeth righteousness without works" (Rom. iv. 6). "Being justified by faith, he has peace with God through Jesus Christ his Lord, by whom also he has access into that grace wherein he stands" (Rom. v. 1, 2). He has an insight into the unseen economy that now knits heaven and earth in one; and enjoys the benefit of that friendly commerce of reconciliation, love, and confidence, that upon the ladder of mediation is ever kept up, between the throne on high where the Son now sits and the simple heart of the poor smitten sinner here below, who has been converted and has become guileless as a little child.

But not only may we interpret Jacob's vision by the Lord's allusion to it in the promise given by him to Nathanael. We may not unreasonably carry back with us what we have gathered as to Nathanael's previous exercise of soul that it may throw light on Jacob's state of mind, during the night he passed on the bare ground and stony pillow at Bethel.

It is something more, as I cannot but think, than a plausible conjecture—that Jacob may have been undergoing an experience very similar to that of David and Nathanael, when he beheld what the Lord intimates that it would be the high privilege of Nathanael also to see. He leaves his home, as we may but too truly assume, not only with guilt on his conscience, but also with guile in his spirit. His sin has not yet found him out. He has been justifying himself and blaming others. Standing upon his divine title to the birthright-blessing in a self-righteous frame of mind, he has been insensible to the evil of that sad train of cruelty and craft which has made his father's household so unhappy, and in which, from first to last, he has himself had so great a share. And so long as he has been buoyed up by his mother's sympathy and his own repeated successes in his schemes, he has felt little sorrow and little shame for all that has taken place. But it is altogether otherwise now. He is alone; and the hand of God is heavy upon him. His dream of self-confidence and self-complacency is at an end. His sin is now "ever before him." He can restrain his voice no longer from confession and prayer. He can no longer "keep silence." He can but say ;—"I will confess my transgressions unto the Lord!" And may it not be that, through the gracious inter-position of the blessed Spirit applying to his now opened wounds the healing balm of the gospel of peace, he has cause immediately to add :—"And thou forgavest the iniquity of my sin?" May not this have been the manner of the Lord's dealing with him, and the course of his own experience, as preliminary and preparatory to the vision on which the promise to Nathanael is based ; " Hereafter ye shall see heaven open ;" —not opened occasionally, now and then, but open always ;— so open always that, not at any particular Bethel, but anywhere and everywhere, " ye may see the angels of God ascending and descending upon the Son of man."

39

Genesis 28:16-22

THE BEGINNING OF JACOB'S PILGRIMAGE—THE VOW

Vow, and pay unto the Lord your God : let all that be round about him
bring presents unto him that ought to be feared. Psalm 76:11

It would seem that this was the first occasion on which
Jacob was recognised, directly and personally from heaven,
as the successor of Abraham and the representative of the
chosen seed. His mother had received an oracular intimation
at his birth; and his father had been led at last to bestow
upon him the patriarchal blessing. But this midnight transaction is Jacob's formal inauguration, by God himself, into
the high and holy position of the child of the promise.
Henceforth Isaac is as one virtually dead; the entire rights
and responsibilities bound up in the Abrahamic line of descent
being transferred to Jacob.

There is a growing clearness in the divine utterances concerning Jacob which is worthy of a passing notice. The
oracular announcement to Rebekah is vague enough; and
even the two benedictions pronounced upon him by his father
Isaac are by no means very explicit. The distinctive promise
in the one is simply that of superiority over his brother (xxvii.
19); with the accompanying assurance that to bless or to curse
him is to be a test of men's minds, such as the Lord's own
advent afterwards was declared to be (Luke ii. 34, 35). In the
other benediction, again, the point of the promise turns upon
these few and general words: " God Almighty give thee the

blessing of Abraham" (xxviii. 4). Now, however, the Lord himself renews with him the Abrahamic covenant in all its breadth and fulness (ver. 13-15). Favoured in such circumstances with such a vision, and receiving so gracious a renewal of the covenant, Jacob might well awake with a vivid sense of the divine presence;—"Surely the Lord is in this place, and I knew it not. How dreadful is this place ! this is none other but the house of God, and this is the gate of heaven" (ver. 16, 17). And he might well accompany his awakening not only with a solemn act of dedication, turning his stony pillow into a sacred memorial, and calling the place Bethel (ver. 18, 19), but also with a solemn acknowledgment of obligation. Accordingly "Jacob vowed a vow, saying, If God will be with me, and will keep me in this way that I go, and will give me bread to eat, and raiment to put on, so that I come again to my father's house in peace, then shall the Lord be my God : and this stone, which I have set for a pillar, shall be God's house : and of all that thou shalt give me, I will surely give the tenth unto thee" (ver. 20-22).

I. This vow, or covenant, is a strong confirmation of the opinion already indicated, that the night of Jacob's sojourn at Bethel was the era of his new birth, or of his spiritual awakening to an apprehension of the unseen world, and of his own position with regard to it. We seem to have here the instinctive impulse of the new creature, under the regenerating or reviving influence of the Spirit. Snatched from impending ruin, which now for the first time he has in some measure adequately discerned,—tasting the fresh gladness of unlooked-for hope in the visit of the great deliverer who has so seasonably interposed to relieve him,—he can scarcely pause to collect his bewildered thoughts ;—so eager is he, and so impatient, to bind himself by new obligations, or, at least, by a new and formal recognition of obligations that have been overlooked before. Nor is it mere impulse that prompts such a step at such a crisis ; it is dictated also by sober reason. Conscious of weakness and fearful of temptation, the new convert, or the newly recovered backslider, feels a kind of security in the entire and absolute committal of himself which a vow or covenant implies. It is like burning his ships, now that he has landed on the shore where the onward march is to be ordered and the battle is henceforth to be fought. Being irrevocably pledged, as by military oath, he has nothing for it but to press manfully on, till his faithfulness unto death win for him the crown of life. Thus discretion, as well as enthusiasm, may recommend a covenant or vow.

II. But the vow must be made in faith; and this faith must characterise equally the motive, the matter, and the object of the vow. Thus, as to the motive,—to be either lawful or expedient, the vow must be an expression, not of future, contingent, and conditional compliance, but of present trust, absolute and unreserved. Vows made in a spirit of superstition or self-righteousness,—as if man might stipulate or make terms with the Sovereign Lord of all, are impious and vain. Again, the matter of the vow,—the thing vowed,— that which I bind myself by covenant to render to my God, —must be of his own selection, not mine. To think that I may go beyond what God himself requires in my voluntary vow, is to assume the attitude, not of a debtor to grace and a dependant upon grace,—but of one in a position to lay God himself under obligation, and almost gain an advantage over him. Nor must it be any selfish end that I seek in my vow; not mere relief from some impending calamity or exemption from some unwelcome service; far less any compromise of the spiritual affection and hearty loyalty and love which I owe to my God.

The vow of Jacob will stand these tests; especially when considered in connection with the position in which he was when he made it. To some readers, it is true, it may seem as if the language used by him indicated doubt, and some disposition to make terms with God—rather than faith, and an acquiescence in the terms already made by God with him. The apparently conditional form of the vow, and the apparent postponement of what is vowed, may occasion to their minds some little difficulty. But in reality there is no ground for it.

As to the first point, the form of expression—"If God will be with me, and will" do so and so—does not necessarily imply contingency or suspense; on the contrary, it denotes the absolute certainty of the conviction upon the faith of which the vow proceeds. The particle "if" often bears the sense of "since," or "forasmuch as;" instances in proof might be multiplied indefinitely (Rom. viii. 17; Gal. iv. 7; Phil. ii. 1; Coloss. ii. 20; iii. 1, etc.) In the case before us, we may confidently gather from the correspondence between the Lord's promise (ver. 15), and Jacob's recital of it (ver. 20), that the meaning of his vow is not, "If it shall turn out that God is with me," as if Jacob considered that blessing to be still uncertain; but "if it be so," or "since it is so," that "God will be with me." It is not the language of scepticism but of faith; faith echoing and appropriating the pledge which God had given. Yea! hath God said that he "will be with me, and will keep me in this way that I go, and will give me bread to eat, and raiment to put on, so that I come again to my father's house in peace!" (ver. 20, 21). Can it be? Is this, in truth, his communication to me? Then, if so—that being the case—however beyond all expectation and all belief such goodness manifested to such an one as I am may be—I hesitate, I doubt no more. I take thee, O Lord, at thy word. And as thou givest thyself in covenant to thy servant, so in the bonds of the same covenant I venture to give myself to thee!

Then again, as to the other point, affecting the matter as well as the manner of the vow, it is unquestionably a prospective engagement under which Jacob binds himself. He is anticipating—not however doubtfully but in lively hope—the actual accomplishment of what God had been pleased to promise. And he is simply owning beforehand what will then be his duty, and pledging himself to its discharge. When the Lord shall have fulfilled all that he has said, as to his care of me in the way that I go, and as to my return to my father's house in peace, what will be the fitting return of gratitude for me then and in these circumstances to offer ? What the peculiar obligation under which I must then feel myself to lie ? Am I then to be wanting in a suitable acknowledgment ? Nay, then more than ever "the Lord shall be my God." And in token rather of his faithfulness to me, than of my loyalty and love to him, "this stone, which I have set for a pillar, shall be God's house : and of all that thou shalt give me, I will surely give the tenth unto thee" (ver 22).

Such is the real import of this transaction between Jacob and his God—corresponding and fitly answering to the previous transaction between his God and him. The two are connected as cause and effect : they stand in the relation of antecedent and consequent to one another. Jacob's act is the response of faith to the divine promise. Because thou, Lord, dealest graciously, and hast dealt graciously, and dost promise to deal graciously in all time to come, with thy most undeserving servant, therefore, with thy help, I also will deal truly and faithfully with thee. Thy covenant with me is sure : let my vow to thee also stand. Surely a better model of a spiritual and evangelical vow is nowhere to be found than that which the rude pillar was to attest and commemorate at Bethel.

III. The service which Jacob here performed had its accompanying external rites. A hastily-constructed altar was made of the stone on which he had laid his head ; and, in default of other sacrifice,—for he who erelong was to pass again that way with flocks and herds enough and to spare, had not a kid or a lamb that he could call his own,—oil was poured upon the stone (ver. 18). A new name also was given to the spot, to make it ever memorable in after years—Bethel, or the house of God—a name destined to survive some notable revolutions (ver. 19). The Canaanites, when they built a city there—for in Jacob's time it was a mere field—ignorant or careless of the patriarch's intention, gave it the appellation of Luz. But the Israelites, on their taking possession of the land, carried out the patriarch's purpose, and called the place once more Bethel.

These external and formal accompaniments this vow had. And it may be noted that, being better remembered and understood than the covenant itself, they became afterwards a snare. The stone set up, with the oil poured on it, was probably one occasion, among others, of that aggravated kind of idolatrous worship which consisted in adoring, with abominable rites, anointed pillars like that of Jacob. And the superstitious regard paid in after years to the mere name and locality of Bethel, so moved the indignation of the holy prophet that he gave it—instead of Bethel, or house of God—the ignominious and contemptuous nickname of Beth-aven, or house of vanity (Hos. iv. 15 ; Amos v. 5). But apart from the formalities of Jacob's simple ritual,—so simple that one might have thought it scarcely possible ever to misunderstand or pervert it,—the essence of this transaction is not ceremonial, but altogether spiritual and moral; and its spirit is not legal, but on the contrary highly evangelical.

It is in fact the very type and model of the believer's consecration of himself,—with all that he now has, all that he ultimately hopes for, and all that he may receive by the way, —to the Lord. His person, as accepted in the beloved, is to be the Lord's. His final inheritance is to be to the praise of the glory of God. The very stone that upheld his weary head when the Lord first visited him in mercy upon earth, will be ever freshly anointed for praising God continually when he reaches his home in heaven. Every cross he has borne, as well as every deliverance he has experienced, will have its own song to be sung in it as in a consecrated temple. And the whole will be one everlasting hallelujah to the Lamb that was slain.

Meanwhile, between his present acceptance and the coming rest, he casts himself on the providence of his God; and whatever may be the amount of the Lord's liberality, he offers a pledge and proof of his accounting all that is given to him by the Lord to belong to the giver alone, by freely devoting to holy purposes such a portion of his time, his talents, and his substance, as may afford evidence of his holding the whole from God and for God—evidence which shall be at least equally conclusive with the literal tithing of all that he has.

40

JACOB'S SOJOURN IN SYRIA—ITS GENERAL ASPECT

Genesis 29-31

And Jacob fled into the country of Syria; and Israel served for a wife,
and for a wife he kept sheep.   Hosea 12:12

THE exact meaning and object of Hosea's reference to Jacob's
flight from Canaan, and his sojourn and service in Syria, are
not very obvious.   The style of that Prophet is abrupt; his
transitions are often rapid, and his allusions brief and sudden.
In this chapter, he is apparently contrasting the present sunken
state of Israel with its former greatness, and the place which
it once occupied in the divine regard.   To give point and
vividness to his representation of the past, he selects incidents
in the early history of the nation, and especially in the life of
the father of its twelve tribes.   He reminds the people of the
power which Jacob had to prevail over the angel, as well as of
the Lord's gracious acknowledgment of him at Bethel (ver.
3, 4); and he exhorts them to make trial for themselves of the
divine faithfulness;—" Therefore turn thou to thy God: keep
mercy and judgment, and wait on thy God continually"
(ver. 6).   Then, after a solemn reproof of their iniquity,—
their deceit and oppression,—their pride and self-righteousness
(ver. 7, 8); and a renewed intimation of the Lord's purpose of
mercy (ver. 9-11); as if in confirmation of that intimation, he
brings in again this other passage in Jacob's experience, his
flight and servitude.   And he contrasts with it the great

national deliverance long afterwards wrought out by the hand of Moses;—"Jacob fled into the country of Syria, and Israel served for a wife, and for a wife he kept sheep. And by a prophet the Lord brought Israel out of Egypt, and by a prophet was he preserved" (ver. 12, 13). Thus over against Jacob's suffering of reproach and oppression, the prophet sets,—not Jacob's own escape from Syria,—but, as answering his purpose better, the deliverance of his descendants out of Egypt. In Jacob's degradation, Hosea sees the type, and as it were, the beginning of Israel's bondage. He fitly therefore passes at once, in the way of contrast, to the crowning interposition by which that bondage was ended. And he does so, that his countrymen may on the one hand be brought low, in the remembrance of Jacob's being brought low, and may, on the other hand, be moved to return to the Lord ; believing that " he is the Lord their God from the land of Egypt" (ver. 9), and that there is no saviour besides him.

Such is the connection in which the prophet's allusion to Jacob's Syrian experience stands; and such its fitness, taken along with the accompanying allusion to the Exodus, at once to humble the people under a sense of their degradation, and to lead them anew to repentance.

Before going into a detailed examination of the incidents of Jacob's sojourn in Syria, it may be useful to suggest a few general considerations regarding it, which must be borne in mind all through the narrative.

I. In the view of the romantic adventures which Jacob met with, and the spirit and manner in which he met with them, in the country of his exile, it is important to bear in mind his singularly strange position as he left his paternal home.

Compare Jacob's lot with that of his father Isaac. There was no question in Abraham's house as to the title of Isaac to inherit the birthright ; there was no misunderstanding on that point between Isaac's parents. Abraham and Sarah were at one in owning him as the child and heir of the promise. And when it was needful to find a wife for Isaac, that the covenanted line might be prolonged, there was no proposal made to send him away. He was not destined to be an adventurer, taking his chance of success in life, as well as of a partner for better and for worse to share it. His piety, which was both of early growth and of mature strength, had no family jars or jealousies to contend with; and the even tenor of his quiet domestic life was for the most part unbroken.

Very different is his son Jacob's entrance into the world, and the world's busy strife. He goes from home a fugitive, with a wide commission to push his fortune and seek a wife, in what had been once indeed the country of his fathers, but was now to him a strange land. And he goes with a home experience and home life but little calculated to keep alive the home feeling abroad.

In the home which he is leaving, there ought to have been no room for misunderstanding; the oracle of God which preceded and announced the birth of Isaac's two sons, should have made strife impossible. The recognition of Jacob, as the heir, in terms of that oracle, and on the ground of that submission to the sovereign decree of God which it demanded, would have obviated all risk of domestic rivalry and partizanship, and ensured peace and order in the household. But Isaac's favouritism for Esau, which blinded him to the divine purpose preferring Jacob,—and Rebekah's favouritism for Jacob, which was too much of the same carnal or merely natural sort,—led Jacob to use subtlety in the purchase of the birthright, and issued in the last melancholy plot. Isaac's unbelief, disregarding the divine oracle, and in spite of it treating Esau as the heir; and Rebekah's unbelief, aiming at the fulfilment of the oracle by means of her own policy, are alike fitted to have an evil effect on Jacob's moral nature

From first to last, it was a poor training that the chosen son and heir had in the house of his parents.

And now, suddenly, we find him far away from home. He carries with him, no doubt, his father's blessing, twice repeated ; the first time pronounced unwittingly—his father intending it for Esau—the second time given expressly and unequivocally. But this late recognition of him as the heir, wrung so reluctantly from his father, and given, too, in immediate connection with his mother's trembling haste to get him out of the reach of his brother's vengeance, could not undo the mischief of an education under influences and associations very different from those which, in holy and happy homes, minister to the growth of a manly character, and the due development of truth and love. Certainly, the school in which he has been brought up has had in it too much of the world's craft and jealousy, and too little of honourable, not to say heavenly, singleness of eye and generous warmth of heart. And his own natural disposition being originally, as we may suppose, inclined rather to a quiet than an active life,—inclined consequently to diplomacy rather than to daring and adventure,—he has had a home-training but too congenial to his constitutional temperament, and too well fitted to nurse and foster his tendency to aim at success in his enterprises,—by art rather than by arms,—by cunning stratagem, rather than by manly openness and boldness.

II. Thus born and bred he is thrown upon the world ; experienced enough,—alas ! more than enough,—in domestic intrigues and broils ; but as regards the world's ways, rude and raw as any of those " home keeping youths " who, as the poet says, "have ever homely wits." And the world on which he is thrown is more than a match for him.

Laban, its representative and type, is the impersonation of worldly shrewdness and unscrupulousness. In the family of such an uncle, Jacob is tempted, by the very craftiness and cold selfishness of the kinsman with whom he has to deal, to try a game of policy. From first to last, as we may say, it is diamond cut diamond—Greek meeting Greek ; a trial of skill —a keen encounter of wits.

The record of it is not pleasant ; it is a painful narrative of subtlety and sin. The elder of the two players has for a long time, as it would seem, the best of the game. The veteran man of the world out-manœuvres more than once his less experienced relative. In the end the tables are turned. Jacob rights himself, and he is, as I think the history indicates, divinely taught and authorised to do so. But it is not a satisfactory issue ; it is too much like the extrication of an overreached man out of an ugly scrape,—the rescuing of him, not too creditably, out of the hands of a partner or customer, whose cool cunning has proved too much for him.

Can we doubt that it would have been better for Jacob if he had dealt with Laban throughout more frankly and more boldly ? He might have entered his kinsman's house, not as one needing to be hired and to receive wages, but as the heir of the promise, on the faith of which his great ancestor Abraham had left these parts for a better portion in Canaan. He did not come to buy a wife by years of servitude. He knew well how his mother Rebekah, this Laban's sister, had been wooed and won for his father Isaac. The confidence and courage of good old Eliezer in courting a wife for Isaac might have inspired Jacob with the like confidence and courage in courting a wife for himself. He was entitled to take high ground, as the son and heir of Isaac and of Abraham. He might have made his demand to be at once acknowledged in that character. He had his commission and his credentials, with their blessing, from both his parents.

More than that, he had warrant and witness from above. A vision and a voice from heaven had owned him as proprietor of the promised land and father of the promised seed. Fresh from the scene at Bethel,—strong in the faith there begotten or revived,—he might have avowed his rank and destiny, on his first introduction to Laban's household. And not as a mendicant wanderer, at Laban's mercy, and fain to take service with him on any terms ; but as the heaven-destined and heaven-declared inheritor of the covenant birthright and covenant blessing, he might have proclaimed the errand on which he came, and asked at once the spouse of his choice with as simple a trust in his God as that which Abraham's servant had manifested long years ago.

Surely if Jacob had behaved thus, in keeping and consistency with his position, as it was attested by the Lord at Bethel, and accepted by himself in the vow which he so solemnly made,—things might have turned out far otherwise than they did. Even worldly Laban might have been so awed or won, as to respect the man whom God honoured, and who honoured God. He might never have thought of proposing meanly to barter for hired service a hospitality which, on such a footing, Jacob would have refused to accept at the hands even of his mother's brother. The unworthy trick of substituting Leah for Rachel ; the guilt of the double marriage, with its consequent polygamy and domestic profligacy ; the thrice repeated change of wages ; the plan for redressing the wrong by securing the strongest of the flock ; the furtive flight ; the pursuit ; the discreditable incidents of the meeting when Laban overtook Jacob ; and the questionable truce or compromise which ended their connection ; all, perhaps, might have been avoided ; and a very different course of mutual confidence and esteem might have marked the history ;—if Jacob, in his intercourse with his uncle and his uncle's house, had acted less as the timid and temporising man of expedients,—the politic man of the world,—and more as the acknowledged friend of God,—the believing child of believing Abraham,—the heir of the covenant that is by faith.

The whole history of Jacob's sojourn in Laban's country, is an illustration of the mischief and misery resulting from an opposite line of conduct. He certainly but ill sustains the

character of one favoured with such heavenly communications
as had so recently been granted to him. His solemn vow is
too little in his mind. He accommodates himself far too easily
to the world in which he lives, learns too well its lessons, and
becomes too familiar with its ways. A second gracious vision,
and a long night of severe wrestling with the Lord (xxxii.), as
well as also a fresh visit to Bethel (xxxv.), are needed to rid
the patriarch of his Syrian tastes and tendencies, and revive
his soul again for his pilgrimage and walk with God in
Canaan.

III. The redeeming feature in the picture of Jacob's life at
Padan-aram, otherwise far from pleasing, is his love for Rachel.
It was of quick growth ; but it was strong, and it lasted long.
When he serves for her, the seven years seem to him but a few
days for the love he has to her. When she dies in childbed, his
affection touchingly appears. He will not give her child a
name of grief, but one almost of joy ; not Benoni, son of my
sorrow, but Benjamin, son of my strength. He would have
associated with his beloved, when she is gone, no word of evil
omen, but rather a token for good. And how he cherished
her memory is evident from what might seem a trifling circumstance in his parting interview with Joseph (xlviii).

The old man is sick and dying. He strengthens himself,
however, to welcome his favourite child once more. He sits
up on his bed to bless Joseph and Joseph's sons. As he proceeds in blessing them, the image of Joseph's mother, his much-
loved Rachel, is before him. He interrupts his speech to tell
how, " when he came from Padan, Rachel died by him in the
land of Canaan in the way, and how he buried her at Bethlehem" (ver. 7).

What has that to do with the matter in hand ? Rachel's
death and burial have no bearing on the blessing which Jacob
is conveying to Joseph, and Ephraim, and Manasseh.

But the old man's heart is full. Something in Joseph's
look,—some trace or lineament of his mother's pale fair face

as he last saw her, travailing and expiring,—brings back the sad scene to the patriarch's dim eye. Simply, as if almost unconsciously, he gives utterance to his recollection. And having paid this last tribute to one he loved so dearly, he calmly resumes the interrupted thread of his benediction.

There is something, to my mind, irresistibly affecting in this proof, so natural and incidental, so true and tender, of the hold which Rachel had of Jacob's heart. It constrains one to exclaim—Behold how he loved her.

Oh! that this love had been allowed to reign alone in Jacob's home, pure from the contamination of polygamy and concubinage! So one is apt to wish. And one is apt to think that if Jacob had been left to himself, to take his own way, it might possibly have been so. Jacob might have been happy with Rachel alone, as Isaac was with Rebekah. His household might have been a pattern of wedded faithfulness and affection, and his seed might have been all holy. It was not his own choice, but Laban's craft, that imposed upon him Leah. It was sad sisterly jealousy, the natural fruit of so melancholy a partnership, that introduced to him his concubines. But it is vain to speculate on what might have been Jacob's family history, if he had been more fairly treated by others, or had done more justice to himself. The history, as it actually unfolded itself, is before us; and it is written for our learning. It is a history of error and sin on every side. All parties are culpable. And the emphatic moral of the whole is surely this; that any deviation at all, upon any plea, from the primeval law of marriage, ordaining the union of one man with one woman only, is fatal to domestic purity and domestic peace; that there can be neither holiness nor happiness in the house in which that law is set at nought; and that the word of the Lord, by the mouth of the Prophet Malachi, denouncing the man who violates the marriage ordinance of God, stands irrevocable and sure; "Did not he make one?" one single pair, in Eden, one woman for one man. "Yet had he the residue of the Spirit "—the spirit of life. Had it so pleased him, he might have made more. But he made only one. "And wherefore one?" and one only. "That he might seek a godly seed." "Therefore take heed to your spirit, and let none deal treacherously against the wife of his youth" (ii. 14, 15).

Some practical lessons may be suggested here.

1. The influence of home training, home habits, home associations,—how deep and lasting is it! If that influence is unfavourable to the cultivation of honourable principles and kindly affections,—if it fosters the development of evil passions and low arts of deceit,—how may it, in after life, eat as a canker into the very heart even of a sincere Christian profession! Conversion itself may not undo the evil. The child whom you send out from home may be a child of God when you send him ; or he may become a child of God at some Bethel after he has left your roof. But if, through the sad infirmity of parents, perhaps of godly parents, or through the faults of rude brothers or unkind sisters, he has become familiar with strife, disorder, and cunning craftiness,—his character may have got a taint, his moral nature a bias, which may not indeed hinder his being converted and becoming a Christian, but which, even after conversion, may stunt the growth of his Christianity, and cause it to wear an aspect the reverse of amiable or honourable in the eyes of those before whom he should be "adorning the doctrine of God his Saviour in all things." How important, in this view, is it that the home in which youth is bred, be a home of pure peace, and truth, and love ; a home of frank manliness, where every eye "beams keen with honour;" a home of genial souls and warm hearts ; a home of gratitude, of gladness, and of joy. Oh! let the boy and girl you send out into a cold, cruel, deceitful world, have no coldness, cruelty, deceit, at home, on which to look back as having fashioned their characters beforehand too much in harmony with that world's ways. Send them forth

with a substratum of such manly honesty, and womanly truth and tenderness, as will recoil instinctively from all that is mean,—all that is selfish or false. Let it be seen in them, wherever they go, what sons and daughters can be reared for God's service, and their country's, in a Christian's pure and peaceful home.

2. How needful is it for Christians to know and vindicate their true position in all their intercourse with the world and with worldly men; to live always fully up to their Bethel experiences, their Bethel privileges, their Bethel obligations, their Bethel visions, prayers, and vows. They gain nothing by giving in to any churlish Laban, accepting his terms, accommodating themselves to his ways. Enter into no house, brother, sit at no table, form no intimacy, contract no alliance, otherwise than as avowedly a Christian man, determined by God's grace to act out thoroughly your Christianity. Ah! you are apt enough to be drawn into worldly conformity, even when you have your Christian standing most clearly in your view. But how much is the danger increased when you mix with men, and do business or take pleasure with them; they not recognising your Christianity; and alas! you making it but too plain that for the time you have almost ceased to recognise it yourself.

3. "Hail wedded love," sings our divine poet; and his strain is in highest accordance with the mind and heart of God. "Rejoice with the wife of thy youth. Let her be as the loving hind and pleasant roe. Be thou ravished always with her love." Yes, it is a holy ordinance, a blessed institution, which makes man and wife no more twain but one flesh. Oh! then, what vile ingratitude is there,—what foul shame, —in all that tends to make that ordinance void,—the ordinance on which all the charities of life hang,—around which all its best blessings cluster. Who art thou, who under whatever pretence, or for whatever end, darest, most unthankful as thou art, to treat this ordinance with contempt, to set it aside, to

turn it into an affair of traffic instead of a bond of love, or to countenance practices with which it is incompatible ? Hast thou no fear of the vengeance of that God whose best earthly gift thou art abusing ? Wilt thou not hear his word ? "Marriage is honourable in all, and the bed undefiled ; but whoremongers and adulterers"—whatever men may think or say of them—"God will judge" (Heb. xiii. 4).

41

JACOB'S SOJOURN IN SYRIA—ITS SPIRITUAL MEANING

Genesis 29:1-35

And Jacob fled into the country of Syria ; and Israel served for a wife, and for a wife he kept sheep. Hosea 12:12

THE transition, or descent, is a great one, from Bethlehem to Padan-aram ; from the position assigned to Jacob from heaven, to the position accorded to him on earth. Nor is it a brief degradation to which he has to submit,—like the brief scene of grace and glory which prepares him for it. One cold dreary night, when a stone was his only pillow, sufficed for the testimony from above. Years, not fewer than a score, were needed to exhaust the toil and trial of his humiliation. Leaving his father's house, in lowly guise, he is once, and once for all, declared by a vision and a voice from heaven, to be the son and heir. It is the act of a few moments. It is as a vivid flash of lightning across the starless gloom ; and then all is dark once more. Thereafter, in the dark, nearly a quarter of a century is to pass before the son and heir again emerges out of obscurity. And all the while he is to be suffering wrong ; and he is to be suffering wrong, that he may see his seed—the seed in which the foundation of the family and Church that is to be called after him is to be laid. In his humiliation, he purchases for himself a spouse, and a seed to bear his name.

It would be unwise to run the risk of pushing fanciful

analogies and types so far as some of the older interpreters of
the Old Testament Scriptures, patristic and mediæval, were
accustomed to do. The story of Jacob's sojourn in Syria may
easily be allegorised and spiritualised by a dreamy imagination,
so as to become a rehearsal, as it were, or a sort of shadowy
anticipation, of the Lord's incarnation and the Church's
redemption. The double marriage is, in this view, supposed
to be significant ; the elder sister, who must be first espoused,
representing the Jews, to whom the gospel must first be
preached ; the younger and favourite spouse standing for the
Gentiles, who are preferred, and in favour of whom the Jews
are comparatively disparaged and set aside. Even in its
minute details, as regards the connection of Jacob with the
concubines, as well as the births and names of the children—
whether the children of the wives, or of their maids—the
history has been turned into a figure of better things to come,
and each separate particular has received its own small mite
of spiritual application.

It is well to be on our guard against such refinements
upon the plain and homely,—the intensely real and personal,
—narratives of the Old Testament, as would emasculate them
of all manly sense and spirit, and turn them into the senile
drivellings of a morbid, and sometimes prurient sentimental-
ism. At the same time there are certain broad analogies or
resemblances not to be overlooked. Even in creation, as the
volume of nature is more and more clearly read, it appears
that God reveals himself upon a plan of typical forms. It
would be strange if we had not everywhere traces of the same
method in that providential history of redemption which it is
the object of the Bible to record. If the forms of creation are
cast in typical moulds, why not also the events of providence ?
—especially those events of providence which form part of
that onward march of the gracious plan of salvation to which
both creation and providence are subordinate and subservient.
In a general way, surely, and without undue merging of the

real in the ideal, or losing the plain and useful practical history in recondite and far-fetched spiritual figure,—it is right to notice such coincidences between the experience of the Patriarchs and that of him who sprung out of their loins, as are fitted to throw light on the principles of the divine procedure in the great economy of redemption.

I. "Israel served" in Syria ; he served as a shepherd ; he "kept sheep." "He who by his strength is to have power with God,"—" he who is to have power over the Angel and prevail," served ; he must needs serve. That is the law of his position, the condition of his deliverance and exaltation.

All throughout the history of the chosen people, it is made manifest that they,—the nation Israel, as well as the man Israel,—are under this condition and law. Servitude in exile is the indispensable preparation and preliminary if there is to be either grace or glory; it is the price to be paid for subsequent prosperity and peace at home. They served as fugitive exiles in Egypt, in order to their taking triumphant possession of the land at first. They kept sheep in Goshen, that they might reap the fruits of Canaan. They served also as captive exiles in Babylon, in order to their resuming the land in the presence of all their enemies. They hung their harps on the willows beside the rivers of Babel, that they might have their mouth filled with laughter, and their tongue with singing, at the recovered sight of their own glorious Zion.

Thus Israel, as a nation, was subject to the law or condition of dark banishment and dreary servitude being the way to light, liberty, and life. How fitting then that the founder of the nation,—the man Israel, from whom the nation derived its birth and took its name,—should exemplify in his history the same law, the same condition. Owned by God as the son, the heir,—he is not immediately glorified. He is not on the instant declared to be the son with power, or invested with the honours and prerogatives of the heir. He has first to flee and serve,—to banish himself to Syria, a strange land, and there to be a servant, keeping sheep.

Can we stop short of the conclusion that—whether exemplified in the people Israel or in the man Israel—the law or condition in question has a deeper root than either accidental coincidence or mere discretionary appointment? And where can such a root be found but in him of whom either Israel is the type?

"The man Christ Jesus" is the true Israel of God. He was hailed in that character in the waters of Jordan,—as Jacob was at the stone of Bethel. He was saluted as the Son, the Heir. The seal of the covenant was upon him and in him. Why should he not, then, as the Son, the Heir, assume at once his rank and assert his power? Why should not the stones become bread to feed him? Why should not the angels wait on him to keep him from harm, as, casting himself from a pinnacle of the temple, he appears gloriously as King in Zion? Why should he not take possession, not of Canaan only, but of all the kingdoms of the world, as their rightful proprietor and lord? So Satan would tempt him to do. And he would help him to do so, upon the terms of a very moderate compromise. But no. Israel must recognise his position as for the time a sojourner in Syria. Nay more. Israel must serve,—keeping sheep. He must "take upon him the form of a servant." "Being made in the likeness of man, and found in fashion as a man, he must humble himself and become obedient unto death, even the death of the cross." All this must come before God highly exalts him, and gives "him a name which is above every name: that at the name of Jesus every knee should bow, and every tongue confess that he is Lord, to the glory of God the Father" (Phil. ii. 9-11).

Have we not here the root, the ground, and reason, of that rule of the divine procedure which we find exemplified in the history of the nation Israel, and of its founder the man Israel or Jacob? May we not now contemplate his low estate in

Syria, as well as the Egyptian bondage and Babylonian captivity of his posterity, in the light of a far more wonderful and awful humiliation,—in the light of the principle which that humiliation expresses and embodies? That principle is one which could only very inadequately be made apparent in the case of either of the two types,—Israel, the nation,—Israel, the individual; but it comes out emphatically in the case of the antitype. He must banish himself from his heavenly home, and become a servant in a strange land, because he makes common cause with us, places himself in our stead under the law which we have broken, redeems us by obeying and suffering on our behalf, and as the captain of our salvation brings many sons and daughters to glory. Thus he comes into Syria, and serves, keeping sheep; being "the good shepherd, who lays down his life for his sheep." Thus our Jacob, through the tribulation of his condescending from heaven's glory to a low estate on earth, and the service of his obedience and propitiation in that estate, comes forth as our Israel, having power with God, "able to save to the uttermost all that come unto God by him, seeing he ever liveth to make intercession for them" (Heb. vii. 25). So the principle applies to him as the Saviour. And so it must apply to us, if we are to be saved by him. For he saves us by making us one with himself. Israel now—the true Israel of God—is Christ; not Christ, however, isolated and alone, but Christ identifying himself with his people, and identifying them with himself. In Christ therefore, the rule or principle which governed his experience and determined his history, must govern and determine ours also. We in Christ must consent to serve in Syria, if we would be free in Canaan; to suffer in Egypt and in Babylon, if we would be exalted as sons and heirs in the promised land; to be humbled in him if we would be glorified with him. There must be the same mind in us that was also in him. We must be crucified with him, and be obedient with him, if we would hope to live and reign with him.

Thus far, guided by the Prophet Hosea, we can scarcely go wrong in taking a large and comprehensive spiritual view of Jacob's banishment to Syria and service there, as involving a principle in the divine administration which is exemplified in other dealings of God with Jacob's race ; in Egypt, for example, and at Babylon ; but of which we have the full development, as well as the real explanation in the humiliation, obedience, sufferings, and death of Christ—and of all who are Christ's—his for them, theirs in him.

II. Is it pressing unduly the analogy suggested, as I think, by the Prophet—or overstraining it—to go one step farther, and observe that, as in his low estate in Syria, Israel served for a wife, so in his humiliation the true Israel purchased for himself a spouse ? Before he got home again to Canaan, Jacob saw in his household the foundation laid of that Church of the twelve tribes which was to be built upon the foundation of his twelve sons. Before he passed from earth to heaven, Christ had laid the foundation of a better church, in the twelve apostles whom he chose to build the spiritual habitation, "the habitation of God through the Spirit," of which he himself is the head corner-stone. Jacob, in Syria, served well and worked well for a wife. The family he got at Padan-aram was purchased at no ordinary price ; it cost him years of much servile toil, and of not a little suffering and shame. But the years passed swiftly, for the love he had to the wife of his bosom. Christ also "loved the church, and gave himself for it." It is the church which "he has purchased with his own blood." It is the church which he "nourisheth and cherisheth as his own body." It is the church which he "sanctifies and cleanses with the washing of water, by the word ; that he may present it to himself a glorious church, not having spot or wrinkle or any such thing ; but that it should be holy and without blemish" (Ephes. v. 25-27).

For here, this marriage, divine and heavenly, shines forth in bright contrast with these Syrian nuptials, alas ! too earthly and impure. Jacob, fleeing into the country of Syria, and serving there for a wife, finds himself in the midst of an evil age, " a wicked and adulterous generation." He cannot even extricate himself out of its snares, or keep his own hands and his own heart clean. How then can he rescue and redeem the objects of his choice? The ties which bind them to him are close and endearing; his love to them may be ardent and strong. But ah! how impotent is he to save either himself or them from the bondage of corruption! But mark the true Israel! See how he can deal with the spouse, the church, for which in his humiliation he serves, at such a cost of patience and of blood! When he comes in contact with the objects of his choice, he finds them in the midst of a world that is lying in wickedness; themselves as deeply sunk in pollution and guilt as the very vilest of those among whom they dwell; the victims, like others, of its lying vanities; the heirs, like them, of " the wrath revealed from heaven against all ungodliness and unrighteousness of men." Such and so situated are the objects of our Israel's choice, in this Syria in which he, exiled for a time from heaven, has to serve for his bride. And into how close contact does he come with these miserable objects of his election, making all their misery his own, and all their guilt—the guilt of that estrangement from his Father and theirs which has rendered it needful for him to come into a far country, to seek and to save the lost! But being himself uncontaminated and free, he is able to be a ransom for them. Purchasing their release from condemnation—redeeming them to be his own peculiar people—he raises them out of the depths out of which, when for their sakes he had gone down into them, he has himself been raised. He makes them partakers of his own rising—his own resurrection. Nay more, he makes them partakers of his own nature. His Holy Spirit beautifies, purifies, ennobles them. " The king's daughter is all glorious within; her clothing is of wrought gold."

Yes! in that day of the full and final consummation of our

divine Israel's espousals—when the wife for whom he served in his humiliation is to be revealed as one with him in his glory—when he shall appear and all his hidden ones with him ; ah! in that day there will be no dark deceit, no fraud, no guile—no plot that needs the cloud of thickest night to cover it. Before all intelligences, in the eyes of an assembled universe ; Lo, a great sight! New heavens and a new earth ; the first heavens and the first earth passed away. And what do I see, as the rapt apostle saw it in his lonely isle of Patmos ? " The holy city—the New Jerusalem coming down from God out of heaven, as a bride adorned for her husband." And hark! a great voice out of heaven! " Behold the Tabernacle of God is with men, and he will dwell with them, and they shall be his people, and God himself shall be with them and be their God, and God shall wipe away all tears from their eyes, and there shall be no more death, neither sorrow, nor crying, neither shall there be any more pain ; for the former things are passed away " (Rev. xxi. 1-4).

42

JACOB'S SOJOURN IN SYRIA—RETROSPECT

Genesis 29:1-30:26

THE interval between Jacob's leaving Bethel for Padan-aram, and his proposal to return home again, is in many respects a dark and unsatisfactory subject of study. It is not necessary, as it is not pleasant, to dwell on its incidents in detail. Some leading features, however, must be noted.

It may be convenient to fix upon a sort of central point, —such as that between Jacob's first two seven-years' services, and his third and last ;—his first two services, almost enforced, for his wives, and his last, more spontaneous, for his fortune. From this central point, a retrospective glance may be cast on the fourteen preceding years, before proceeding to the remaining seven. Such a retrospective glance, from some central point, it is often very useful to cast on the bygone part of life. How does it look now ? An occasion arises for a kind of count and reckoning as to the past,—with ourselves, or with some one with whom we have had dealings,—a friend, a relative, with whom we have been living familiarly. It is time that we should part, or come to an understanding. Old scores are to be inquired into and disposed of. A new footing is to be adjusted.

So Jacob at this crisis feels. He must be off. It is high time for him to go home. He has tarried long enough in Padan-aram ; longer far than he at first intended; as long certainly as was good for himself ; as long as his grasping relative had any shadow of right to keep him. His heart

yearns to embrace his parents once more. His duty calls him
to make the land of promise his abode. It will not do to
have the chosen family all bred, as well as born, in Syria.
Let them learn to breath the air of Canaan. Therefore, at
the end of fourteen years, " Jacob said unto Laban, Send me
away, that I may go unto mine own place, and to my
country." In thus asking his dismission or discharge, Jacob
appeals to Laban's sense of equity. In all fairness he is quite
entitled to what he asks. He has honourably fulfilled the
terms of his engagement ; as he can call Laban himself to
witness ;—" Thou knowest my service which I have done
thee" (xxx. 25, 26).

It has been a service on which the two men may look back
with very mingled feelings.

I. Jacob's first introduction to Laban's family must be
fresh in the memory of both. It was not of such a sort as
would have led either of them at the time to anticipate the
nature of the connection that was to subsist between them,
or the manner in which it was to be developed.

That first meeting with Rachel—how vividly is it before
Jacob's eye ! He is a weary pilgrim once more,—way-worn,
foot-sore, and thirsty. He sees three flocks and their keepers
gathered round a well. He hails them courteously as
brethren. He gathers from them that he is at his journey's
end. They are of Haran : they know Laban ; they are expecting his daughter, and the sheep she has to tend. He at
once calls to mind how old Eliezer found a wife for his father
Isaac, perhaps at the very same well. The coincidence strikes
him. Silently he breathes Eliezer's prayer, that it may please
the Lord to show him her whom he has appointed for him.
It is the prayer of faith. That he may be alone while waiting
for the answer, he would be rid of the men whose presence
may be embarrassing : for such, perhaps, is the reason of his
suggestion that they should at once water the sheep and lead
them off to pasture — a suggestion, however, which they

decline to follow, on the plea that they must wait "until all the flocks be gathered together, and till they roll the stone from the well's mouth." Suddenly Rachel appears with her father's sheep, following her lead. Jacob hastens anxiously and eagerly to serve her,—rolling the stone from the well's mouth and watering the sheep for her. His heart is full.—Hast thou heard me, Lord, as thou didst hear that good old man, whose way of executing his commission from home I so well remember? Is this indeed the answer to my prayer?—Regardless of onlookers, he sees Rachel only. Saluting her with a holy kiss, he cannot refrain himself. He gives vent to his emotions in irrepressible tears—"Jacob kissed Rachel, and lifted up his voice, and wept" (xxix. 1-11).

How strange, after fourteen such years as he had spent with Laban, to recall, as if it were yesterday, that first interview with Laban's daughter, and those first gushings of love! Could it ever have entered into his mind then to fancy it possible that so tender a scene was to be so followed up; that a moment of such simple faith and pure joy was to usher in so long a train of humiliation? And Laban too, has he no recollection of that day? Does he not again see his daughter running to him with the eager tidings that his sister's son has come? Does he not remember how the tidings then affected him?—how "he ran to meet Jacob, and embraced him, and kissed him, and brought him to his house," and made much of him, because—so he said, "Surely thou art my bone and my flesh." There was no thought in Laban's heart that day of the frauds he was to practise on his kinsman, or the service he was to extort from him. For the time, he was as truly and deeply moved as Jacob was himself. Who that saw the family group round Laban's board that evening, and listened to their talk of home memories and home ties, could have anticipated such a domestic history as that which Jacob is looking back upon, when he says to Laban, "Thou knowest my service which I have done thee?" (xxix. 12-14).

II. The double marriage, and the manner of it,—what are
father-in-law and son-in-law thinking of that whole matter
now ? "I have served for my wives," says Jacob, as thou
didst stipulate ;—our bargain is fulfilled. It was a strange bargain ; and now that, on the eve of a proposed parting, they
recall all the circumstances of it,—not very creditable to either.
How came they to fall into it ? Surely Laban, when he so
affectionately embraced Jacob, had no idea of treating him as
he did. He is at first sincere in his kindness to his kinsman,
his sister's son, when he invites him to abide with him as a
guest for "the space of a month." But as the month rolls on,
he begins to be disappointed. He had expected, perhaps, that
Jacob, being Abraham's grandson, and claiming to be his heir,
would produce some evidence of his birthright-title to the
temporal wealth of that patriarch, as well as to the spiritual
blessing. True ; Jacob does not come with that rich and im-
posing retinue which formerly made Abraham's servant welcome
in that worldly house. Still he may have some more private
means of attesting his rank and riches. No. Jacob confesses
he has none. He came away in haste and by stealth ;—leaving his elder brother, as Laban would naturally think, in possession of the worldly privilege, at least, of which he accused
Jacob of having defrauded him. Laban is no believer in divine
oracles, or in deathbed patriarchal benedictions; he would have
something more tangible. Jacob may turn out to be the son and
heir; made the son and heir by some sort of spiritual covenant or
arrangement of which Laban has no evidence, and can form no
idea. Meanwhile, by his own acknowledgment, he has been a
deceiver or supplanter, and is now little better than a runaway
and a beggar. The least that can be expected, therefore, if he is
to remain in his uncle's house, is that he should be willing to
work as his uncle's servant. It does not, after all, seem very
unreasonable that a man like Laban should assign to him that
position. Nay, Laban may even consider himself to be deserving of some credit for generosity, when he proposes to recom-

pense Jacob for his service. I will not take advantage of your relationship to me, as if it entitled me, while you are an inmate of my house, to set you to such offices as the other members of my family, and even my own daughters, gratuitously discharge. " Because thou art my brother (my kinsman), shouldest thou, therefore, serve me for nought? tell me, what shall thy wages be?" (ver. 15). So far this Laban, as it might seem, is not much to blame. And when, still farther, upon learning that Jacob sought, as the only wages he then cared for, his younger daughter in marriage, Laban accepted, in lieu of the dowry which it was customary for a suitor to offer for his bride, a term of service proffered by the suitor himself,—he cannot well be considered seriously censurable. It was not wonderful that as a careful, if not tender, father, he should, for his daughter's own sake, acquiesce in Jacob's proposal to serve for her seven years ;—that during that time of probation he might know more of one who, though allied to him by blood, had reached his house as a stranger, and a stranger not free from circumstances of suspicion. Even this part of the transaction, therefore, is not by any means unnatural or unjustifiable. Laban might reflect on it afterwards without much regret or self-reproach. Would that he had nothing worse to reflect upon! (xxix. 14-20).

But, first, the false nuptials, the fraud practised on the marriage night ;—how practised, we cannot tell—by what fell tyranny over the affections of the one daughter—by what threats forcing to her dishonour the other—by what vile arts practised on the outraged husband ; the remorseless and unscrupulous plotter himself alone could reveal the secrets of that dark deed of shame ;—then, secondly, the cool effrontery of his vamped-up excuse, when he is challenged for the base trick ;—and, lastly, what is almost worse than all, the infamous offer of redress,—the proposal to repair the wrong by a new iniquity; making true love, unjustly and most scandalously baulked, minister to that incestuous bigamy in which alone it can now

find its gratification ; bartering both his children for the service of a man whose chief recommendation in his eyes manifestly was, that he was making him rich ;—what complication
of cruelty and crime, of low cunning, sordid avarice, gross
impurity, and unfeeling oppression ! And what has come of
it ? Laban has got a double seven years' lease of a most valuable servant, in whose diligent and faithful hands his affairs
have prospered as they never prospered before. But has he
no misgivings ? Ah ! might he not have some, now that Jacob
talks of leaving him—as he thinks on the sort of home he has
made for his son-in-law ; the jealous rivalry of the sisters, unnaturally associated as wives ; with all the unseemly strifes
and unholy devices to which that rivalry gave inevitable occasion ? And Jacob—what of him ? How does he feel in looking back to the short week within which his double marriage
was consummated ? After one seven years' service, he found
himself suddenly, and against his will, committed to another ;
with the wife he loved, indeed, in his bosom,—but under a
sad drawback upon his anticipated domestic joy. He sought
none other than Rachel. Left to himself, he would have been
content with her alone, and what pure happiness might have
been his, but for that outrageous stratagem of Laban of which
he was the victim ! The first term of his service for Rachel
seemed to him but a few days for the love he had to her.
And if, at its close, he had been allowed, as he intended, honourably to espouse the object of his chaste choice,—he might
have walked in the steps of his father Isaac ; and whether remaining in Syria, or returning to Canaan, waited until it pleased
God to crown the union with the promised issue. It is vain,
however, to wish to recall or undo the past. The second seven
years' term of service is over.* It has not gone so smoothly
as the first ; there have been family feuds and family faults.

* I adopt the opinion of those who place the marriage of Jacob and
Rachel at the beginning of the second seven years' term of service. It
seems all but impossible otherwise to harmonise the narrative.

The sisters, in their jealousy of one another, have led their husband into still grosser conformity to the loose manners of the age and country than he would himself have dreamt of. At the end of it he finds himself rich in children ; he has a household large enough. But there is something significant in the close connection between Rachel's bringing forth, after years of barrenness, her first-born son, Joseph, and Jacob's instantly proposing to return to Canaan. It is almost as if he recognised, not indeed as regards Laban, but as regards the Lord, a sort of *nunc dimittis*,—" now lettest thou thy servant depart in peace ; for mine eyes have seen thy salvation." It is as if he felt that, had he been allowed to act according to his own choice and his own sense of duty alone, he would have gone home more gladly with this one solitary pledge of the love that knit his heart and Rachel's in one, than with the large family which he owes to mothers whom, of his own accord, he never would have sought (xxix. 21 ; xxx. 25).

Yes ! the full enormity of Laban's treatment of him is now apparent. For a long time, while Rachel's womb is closed, Jacob may have been tempted to congratulate himself on his having been tricked into a previous marriage with her sister Leah. He evidently has satisfaction in Leah's fruitfulness ; and while piously reproving Rachel's impatient demand, " Give me children or I die," he seems to acquiesce in her conclusion, that she is not likely to be a mother,—" Am I in God's stead, who hath withheld from thee the fruit of the womb " (xxx. 1, 2). So hopeless is he of issue by her, that he consents to take her handmaid as her substitute ; that, according to the views then prevalent, he may lighten Rachel's reproach and abate Leah's triumph. Still, by herself or by her handmaid as her proxy, Leah has the best of it in this most sad and unseemly emulation. Rachel continues, as it would seem, hopelessly barren. Jacob is more and more inclined to count it a happy circumstance that he has got other wives to be the mothers of his children. His indignant sense of the wrong which he sustained, when that arrangement was at first so fraudulently forced on him, is abated; so also is his sense of his own sin in consenting to it afterwards. He begins to feel as if he could not have trusted the promised seed to Rachel alone; and as if he had done well to make sure of it by accepting Leah, for whom he had to thank the cunning of her father;—and the handmaids whom he owed to the evil passions of the sisters. They were not of his seeking,—these other spouses,—Leah, Bilhah, and Zilpah; they have been in a manner imposed upon him; and Rachel's continued childlessness seems to explain the reason. At last, however, Rachel's womb is opened; quite as soon after her marriage as either Sarah's or Rebekah's;—nay, sooner. Jacob is rebuked. He sees that the flattering unction he has been laying to his conscience is vain. However he may be justified or excused for his polygamy, his defence or apology cannot rest on the ground on which Rachel's prolonged barrenness has been tempting him to place it. With her alone, as his only spouse, his faith would not have been tried so much as was the faith of his father Isaac;—the trial of it would have been as nothing in comparison with the trial of his grandfather Abraham's. It is altogether according to the manner of God thus to open Jacob's eyes, if in some such way as has been indicated, he has been tempted to deceive himself, and to think well, or at least not so ill, of those miserable matrimonial expedients on which he has been beginning, perhaps, to look with some measure of complacency.

Nor is it Jacob's eyes only that this event, the birth of Joseph, is fitted to open. The whole household, including Laban himself, might be the better for the lesson, if they could but lay it to heart. If, from the beginning of these transactions, faith had been allowed to regulate the counsels and proceedings of all the parties concerned,—if when Jacob sought a wife in faith, with a view to the promised seed, Laban, in the same faith, had given him the wife manifestly appointed for him by the Lord,—Rachel would have been to him what Rebekah was to Isaac, and Sarah to Abraham. Faith would have waited patiently in their case, as it did in the case of these other holy pairs, for the promised issue. And as it now turns out, faith would in due time have received its reward.

Who are these poor worms of the dust, Laban, Leah, Rachel, Jacob himself, and all the rest of them, that they should go about plotting and planning, after so vile a fashion, for the building of the house or family in which the God of Abraham is to record his name, and out of which the Son and Lord of Abraham is to spring, for the saving of the nations? What mean these wretched bickerings and jarrings in that ill-assorted home? To what purpose is this indecent haste of these women? Why all this miserable game of rivalry, defiling honourable marriage,—this pitiable trade and traffic of mandrakes,—and all the other incidents which so offend us;—enacted beneath the roof of a professed man of God? Does the Lord stand in need of such devices and doings as these for the raising up of a seed for Abraham?—the Lord, who is able "out of these stones to raise up children unto Abraham?" Nay, let Isaac's birth in Abraham's house, and Jacob's in that of Isaac,—and now the opening of Rachel's womb in the birth of Joseph,—give the emphatic reply.

Yes! the Lord might have been trusted to work out his own ends in his own good way. He may be pleased, now that the thing is done, to turn to account the issue of these unholy devices, as "he makes the wrath of man to praise him." He may use Jacob's sons, however Jacob has got them, for the founding of his church in Israel. So he manifests his sovereignty and power, his electing grace and overruling providence. But surely, for Jacob himself, and for all concerned in these strange and sad affairs, it would have been better far, if faith had all along from the first been allowed to rule; if Jacob, in faith, had dealt more frankly and more boldly with

Laban ; if Laban and his house had, in faith, received Jacob ; if all parties had, in simple faith, followed the Lord's guiding eye,—in simple faith, leaving the event to him.

" Fret not thyself because of evil-doers, neither be thou envious against the workers of iniquity. For they shall soon be cut down like the grass, and wither as the green herb. Trust in the Lord, and do good ; so shalt thou dwell in the land, and verily thou shalt be fed. Delight thyself also in the Lord ; and he shall give thee the desires of thine heart. Commit thy way unto the Lord ; trust also in him, and he shall bring it to pass. And he shall bring forth thy righteousness as the light, and thy judgment as the noon-day. Rest in the Lord, and wait patiently for him : fret not thyself because of him who prospereth in his way, because of the man who bringeth wicked devices to pass. Cease from anger, and forsake wrath : fret not thyself in anywise to do evil" (Ps. xxxvii. 1-8).

43

JACOB'S SOJOURN IN SYRIA—THE LAST BARGAIN

Genesis 30:27-43

And the man increased exceedingly, and had much cattle, and maid-servants, and men-servants, and camels, and asses. Genesis 30:43

THIS is a summary of Jacob's manner of life during the third and last term of his service in the household of Laban.   Some six or seven years have passed away since he consented to renew his engagement with his father-in-law ; and the close of it finds him prosperous, thriving, wealthy.   He has been " providing for his own house," as he intimated at the time his intention of doing (ver. 30), and God has blessed his provision. He has got more than he covenanted for in his vow at Bethel, which was simply bread to eat and raiment to put on.   He has large store of what chiefly constituted the riches of these days ;—" much cattle, and maid-servants, and men-servants, and camels, and asses."   The bargain which he made with Laban, when after two weeks of years spent in his service he consented to a third, has turned out to be profitable.

Into the terms of that bargain and its issue, we need not inquire very particularly ; it is not made very clear by the narrative, not at least to us, at our distance of time and place. From our point of view, the reason and propriety of it are not very apparent ; according to our modern and western notions, the whole affair appears strange, not to say fantastic.   Possibly those who lived nearer the date of this history, being familiar with primitive patriarchal habits and the manners of nomadic

tribes, may have been better able to enter into the meaning of
the transaction. It may have had lessons to teach them,
which we can but imperfectly learn. For though all Scripture
is written for our learning, it is not all equally so. Nor is it
any disparagement of the perfection of the Bible, but rather
the reverse, that being given for the use of successive generations, it should contain waymarks of these generations which
the foot of time partially obliterates. In all essential matters,
in all things pertaining to life and godliness,—to grace and
glory,—the light shines more brightly as, from age to age,
revelation rises from its dim and morning dawn to its meridian
fulness,—so that its latest beams shed lustre on its earliest
discoveries. But in what relates to times, and seasons, and
circumstances,—the incidents and outer garments, rather than
the essence and inner spirit, of the truth which it has to disclose,—the Bible, being all throughout human as well as divine
—and that is its perfection—may be expected to contain
passages in its history, and paintings in its poetry, which distance makes comparatively obscure to us, though to the men
of the day they may have been interesting and edifying. It
would be well if this consideration were kept in view, as in
common fairness it ought to be, by those who hunt for difficulties in these old sacred records, or who stumble at them.
It would be well also if it were kept in view by those who
study or expound these records for the purposes of moral instruction and the spiritual life. It might lead the former to
be more modest and diffident in their criticism ; and the latter
to be more reserved sometimes in their moralising and spiritualising.

But to return. There is one thing about the bargain now
in question that cannot fail to strike an attentive observer. It
was singularly disinterested and unselfish on the part of Jacob.
He himself makes it a test of his " righteousness" (xxx. 31-33).

It must be allowed, indeed, that that is not the notion
which, on a cursory reading of the history, we are apt to take

up. The whole thing looks like trick ; Jacob defeating Laban on his own ground, and with his own weapon ; plot against plot ; stratagem against stratagem. But it is not really so. The appearance of craft is on the surface. If we look a little below the surface, what have we ? At the best, or at the worst, Jacob offers to lay a bet, or make a wager, with Laban. And he gives his father-in-law most extraordinary advantage —such advantage as no speculator would give now. I do not say that Jacob's affair with Laban was of that character ; all I say is, that in that view of the matter, he gave Laban all the chance,—all the advantage,—of the trial as to the different kinds of sheep and goats. The whole transaction is so arranged that Laban cannot well lose, while the probability of Jacob gaining is extremely small.

But is it Jacob's craft that so arranges it? Or is it so arranged according to the will of God? What was the bargain? its occasion ? its character ?—

1. As to its occasion,—Jacob, having gained his end, and being all but complete as the ancestor of the twelve tribes, proposes to Laban that he should be suffered to go home to his father Isaac's house, and to the land of his inheritance. Surely it is a reasonable proposal, and one in which Laban should in all fairness have been willing to acquiesce. If he hesitates, it certainly does not appear to be from any reluctance to lose the society of his son-in-law, his daughters, and their children. There is not much evidence of friendly feeling or natural affection in Laban's dealings with them. Nor, indeed, to do him justice, does he make much profession of any thing of the sort. He frankly owns his motive for wishing to keep Jacob in his employment to be a selfish one ;—" I pray thee, if I have found favour in thine eyes, tarry ; for I have learned by experience that the Lord hath blessed me for thy sake" (ver. 27). He knows the value of a faithful servant, and plainly avows his love of gain. Jacob, on the other hand, when his conduct on this occasion is fairly judged, appears in

a comparatively favourable light. Evidently he has not been
covetous of wealth ; at the close of a fourteen years' service,
he is as poor as he was at the beginning : and in that condition of poverty, he is willing to quit the service (ver. 26). No
doubt there had been opportunities within his reach of better-
ing his circumstances,—such opportunities as many in his place
would not have scrupled to take advantage of. And, indeed,
considering how he was situated, and how he had been used,
I am apt to feel as if I could scarcely have blamed Jacob
much, if I had seen him bent, not merely on enriching Laban,
but on laying up something for himself. Without anything
like what the world stigmatises as dishonesty,—if he had been
disposed to do what many another man in his position would
have had no hesitation in doing, and would have been held
entitled to do,—Jacob must have had it frequently in his
power to transact a little business on his own account. For
can we doubt that the chief herdsman of a powerful and
wealthy Sheik like Laban must have come in contact with
parties ready to oblige him,—that he might have had capital
advanced to him on which to commence trading for himself,—
and that without prejudice, as it might have been represented,
to his master's interests, he might have had his own private
stock of cattle meanwhile accumulating and thriving on his
hands ? But Jacob acts otherwise. Faithful to his trust,—
not as an eye-servant, but as one fearing God,—he conscientiously devotes himself to Laban's work. He uses no arts or
methods of self-aggrandisement ; nor does he make any complaint about the poor state in which his father-in-law, growing
wealthy by his means, so ungenerously keeps him. Quietly
he pursues the even tenor of his way ; and when at last he
proposes to leave his greedy kinsman, it is without one word
of upbraiding about the past, and with no demand upon him
now for more than his wives and his children for whom alone
he has thus faithfully served during these long fourteen years.
Surely that does not look like the conduct of one making haste

to be rich, and not very particular as to the way. And surely it affords some ground for thinking that in making his new
bargain with Laban, and in carrying it into effect, Jacob is
not the party lightly to be suspected of underhand policy or
fraud.

2. The bargain itself, so far as its tenor can be gathered
from the somewhat obscure account which we have got of it,
would seem to have been briefly this. All the purely white,
or all that are of one uniform colour, among the cattle, the
sheep, and the goats, are henceforth to belong to Laban ;
Jacob is to have as his hire the party-coloured among the
goats, and the brown among the sheep. Under the bargain,
a division is immediately made,—certainly most favourable to
Laban, and scarcely equitable or fair to Jacob. All the cattle
of the kind for which Jacob had stipulated are removed from
under his care and consigned to Laban's sons. Jacob is
left in charge exclusively of those that are of the sort Laban
is to claim. And a space of three days' journey being interposed, every possible precaution is taken to prevent the two
separate portions of the cattle from mixing and breeding
together. For as yet the whole stock belongs exclusively to
Laban. Jacob has not a single sheep,—not a solitary goat.
The bargain applies only to the offspring of the existing generation of these animals ; and so far as appears, only to the
offspring of those of them left with Jacob—to the exclusion of
the others carried away by Laban and his sons.

Here, then, is Jacob left with a handful of sheep and goats,
not one of which is of the colour that is to distinguish the
cattle that are to belong to him. And from among the lambs
and kids that may be born of them, he is to pay himself his
hire as best he may.

Who has the best, humanly speaking, of this novel sort of
engagement ?

One can fancy the grasping household of Laban chuckling
as they led away the only portion of the flock or herd that

could have afforded Jacob any chance, as it might be thought, of making anything by his bargain, and exulting in the prospect of the whole property continuing to belong to them. For surely the cattle left with Jacob will produce offspring like themselves. Our simple kinsman will soon find that he has notably miscalculated, and is finely taken in.

How far this procedure on the part of Laban and his sons, —the removal from under Jacob's care of all that were of the sort that he was ultimately to have as his,—was part of the bargain as intended by Jacob, or was consistent with it, is not very clear. It is by no means improbable, when the character of Laban is kept in view, that it was an after-thought. It may be one of the instances to which Jacob refers when he says to Leah and Rachel,—" Your father hath deceived me and changed my wages ten times ;" an exaggeration, doubtless, but not unnatural in the circumstances (xxxi. 7). If so, then we can see a special reason for that interposition of God on his behalf of which he tells his wives (xxxi. 8-12). It was upon the suggestion of God,—such virtually is Jacob's protest, —it was at his instance and in compliance with his directions, —that I adopted the expedient which he has so greatly blessed. In fact, how he should have thought of such a device without some impulse or instruction from above, it is extremely difficult to imagine. It is true that much learned and ingenious speculation has been expended on making it out that he adroitly availed himself of a natural law of the animal economy ; but the result of all such attempts has been anything but satisfactory. The success which the scheme met with cannot well be explained upon any principle of nature's ordinary operations ; it seems both wiser and safer therefore to refer it at once to divine agency and superintendence ; and to regard it as a case analogous to that of the blind man whose cure the Lord chose to effect by means equally unlikely to succeed (John ix). What Jacob did he did by faith. Why his faith was tried in this particular way,—why God chose to interfere on behalf of his servant in a manner so strange, and as it might seem, so out of all accordance with natural sense or reason,—we cannot of course tell, any more than we can tell why Jesus cured the blind man as he did; we can only acquiesce in God's sovereignty, working when and where and how he pleases ; and recognise his purpose to test and prove, with a view to strengthen, the trust which a believer puts in him. We can well imagine, however, Laban and his sons, watching with supreme contempt, and the supercilious smile of calm and complacent incredulity, the fond and foolish experiment Jacob was trying. Jacob too, might sometimes be out of countenance, as he heard their sneers and felt the ridicule of his situation. But patience for a little. The scoffers are put to shame, and simple faith is owned and requited. For " the man increased exceedingly, and had much cattle, and maid-servants, and men-servants, and camels, and asses" (xxx. 43).

44

THE PARTING OF LABAN AND JACOB

When a man's ways please the Lord, he maketh even his enemies to be at
peace with him. Proverbs 16:7

THE parting between Jacob and Laban is better than, in the
view of all the previous intercourse between them, might have
been anticipated. In so far as it is so, it is very manifestly
the Lord's doing. Little or nothing of what is decorous and
peaceful, not to say friendly, in the closing scene, is to be
ascribed to the goodwill or the good sense of those engaged in
it. Jacob's stealthy and felon-like flight was fitted to awaken
Laban's wrath. Laban's pursuit, again, was the sort of last
offence that makes the trodden worm turn round and show
fight, as Jacob does in his angry chiding. But for the special
interposition of God, disastrous consequences must have marked
the meeting of the fugitive son-in-law and the incensed father
of his wives. That interposition, however, made the meeting
safe, and the farewell in which it issued decent, if not amicable.

I. Jacob's resolution to return to Canaan is of the Lord.
He says so himself expressly, when he tells his wives of
what the Angel of God had said to him :—" I am the God of
Bethel, where thou anointedest the pillar, and where thou
vowedest a vow unto me : now arise, get thee out from this
land, and return unto the land of thy kindred" (xxxi. 13).*

* There is a difficulty, though not a serious one, in clearing up the
vision, or visions, which Jacob relates to his wives, when he is persuading

He is bent on reconciling his wives to his purpose of leaving Syria. It was a purpose which he had announced to his father-in-law seven years before, on the birth of Joseph (xxx. 25). At that time, it was a purpose of his own,—natural, in the circumstances, but not of God. He had been persuaded to postpone the execution of it. He now resumes it; and he is anxious to satisfy his household that he has divine warrant for resuming it. In doing so, he briefly notices the whole history of God's dealings with him during the closing period of his service under Laban. God has been manifestly protecting and prospering him, for it was by express divine direction that he adopted the course which has so greatly enriched him. And now it is the command of the same God that he shall " arise, get him out of this land, and return unto the land of his kindred " (ver. 13). He who during these last years has defended me against the wiles of my crafty father-in-law,—

them to quit their father's house, and accompany him to his own home (ver. 11-13). He appeals to God as having given him two distinct and separate revelations. They seem to be one, as he cites them to his wives ; but if we look closely into them, it is manifest that they are really two. They are joined as one, because they are the beginning and the end of the Lord's communication of his will to Jacob, with reference to the supplementary period of his sojourn with Laban, after he had served fourteen years for his wives and children. Now that after another seven years' term of service he again, for the second time, proposes to leave Syria, it is reasonable that he should satisfy his household as to the divine warrant which he had both for remaining seven years before, when he had meant to go, and for going now, when there was much that might have induced him to stay. He intimates to his family that it is the same divine authority which sanctioned his renewed bargain with Laban for other seven years after the first two periods were ended, that now indicates the path of duty, as lying in the direction of Canaan and of home. Hence he recites as if it were all one vision, what really resolves itself into two ; the one having reference to the manner in which he grew rich in cattle during the last seven years of his sojourn with Laban (ver. 12) ; the other having reference to his return to the land of his kindred (ver. 13).

" not suffering him to hurt me,"—and who, in spite of an unequal bargain, unfairly kept, has "taken away his cattle and
given them to me,"—he, my father's God, now bids me seek my
father's home.

The order, as Jacob cites it, is given with great solemnity.
An appeal is made to the memorable scene at Bethel, and the
transaction which was consummated and ratified there. Jacob
is reminded of the Lord's grace and of his own obligation. The
time has come for him to pay his vow (ver. 13).

It is possible that he may have been inclined to forget it.
During the fourteen years of his poverty, when "he served for a
wife, and for a wife kept sheep," he was not in circumstances
to redeem his pledge ;—God, the God of Bethel, gave him
food and raiment, but nothing more.   It is but yesterday, as
it were, that he has begun to acquire the means of carrying
his devout and liberal purpose into effect ; he is only now becoming wealthy.   The sudden change may be apt to operate
injuriously ; reconciling him, perhaps, to his sojourn far off
from Bethel.   He may not now be so ready as he was when
he was poor to say to Laban, Send me away that I may go
unto my own place, and to my country ; he may be willing to
tarry a little longer.   The impression of that night when first
he tasted and saw how good the Lord is, may be growing
somewhat faint ; and when his own voluntary engagement is
brought to his recollection, he may be tempted to persuade
himself that the fulfilment of it had better be postponed for a
season, till he is better able to show his gratitude to him
whose blessing is making him rich.

If it be so with Jacob, as alas! it too often is even with
men of God similarly situated,—if thus the world is getting
hold of his heart, and causing him to be content in Syria, and
unmindful of Canaan,—how graciously is his case met!   The
very murmuring of Laban's sons, and the change of Laban's
countenance towards him, are in this view special mercies.
They make him feel how precarious his position is, and how un-

certain is his tenure of all that he has got. They reawaken his sense of the bitterness of his exile, and set him upon thinking of his home, and his father, and his father's God. And when, at that precise crisis, just as his soul is becoming weary under the feeling of the utter vanity of the very success he has attained, God once more comes specially to deal with him,— what can be more fitted to drive home the blow which has been already struck,—what more likely to give a gracious turn to the disappointment and resentment naturally rankling in his bosom,—what more certain to touch a tender chord, and revive in him the freshness of his first love—than so affecting a reference as the Lord is pleased to make to that old fellowship between himself and his broken-hearted servant ;— " I am the God of Bethel, where thou anointedst the pillar, and where thou vowedst a vow unto me : now arise, get thee out from this land, and return unto the land of thy kindred " (ver. 13).

II. The manner of Jacob's departure is not, as it would seem, of the Lord. It savours too much of Jacob's own disposition towards guile.

In the first place, there was no reason for his having recourse to the stratagem of a secret movement, or clandestine flight. Laban had no claim upon him,—he was not Laban's bondsman. As an independent man, who had certainly got nothing from Laban as a favour,—nothing for which he had not paid full value,—Jacob might have stood up manfully for his right to go where he pleased, and to manage his household in his own way. If he retained any sense of his high position as the representative of believing Abraham,—the heir of the promise,—he ought to have taken a firmer and more worthy stand with his worldly father-in-law. And having express divine warrant for the step, he was inexcusable in not acting upon that warrant, openly and boldly. He might thus have left behind him such an impression of God being with him as could not fail to lead to good in many ways, beyond all that his calculations of expediency could forecast. But alas! he is radically and essentially a schemer; manœuvring is his forte and his fate. He must needs play the part of a cowardly fugitive,—escaping as a thief under the cloud of night. As it turns out, his plot is both unnecessary and unavailing. It is made evident that God would have interfered, at anyrate, to help him; and it is made equally evident, that without God's interference, his plan for helping himself was vain. Nor is this all.

For, secondly, his plan proved itself to be full of mischief. Not only did it tend so to lessen him in the eyes of Laban as to make it impossible for him to exert any wholesome influence on that churlish man,—which he might have done, if he had gone forth boldly, at the Lord's call;—it wrought sore evil in himself and in his household. For himself, it made him too much what he had been before, when he won the blessing by a stratagem; and it works disastrously in his family. Would his beloved Rachel have cut so poor a figure in this world-wide and world-lasting history as she does when her father questions her about the secreted gods (ver. 34, 35), —would there have been idols in the chambers of his wives and children, hindering afterwards his payment of his Bethel vow (xxxv. 2-4),—if Jacob had not stolen away so slyly, but had insisted on his liberty to go forth in face of day, as a worshipper and servant of the most high God alone?

Certainly the manner of Jacob's departure from Syria, is not of God, but of man.

III. The peaceful end, however, of what threatened to become a violent and warlike collision, is of the Lord.

The clandestine flight of his son-in-law naturally provokes Laban. Considering indeed his past treatment of Jacob, and what we may with great probability conjecture to be his present intentions with regard to him,—now that his sons have awakened his covetous jealousy, and his countenance is not towards Jacob as it was before,—one would be disposed to say that he has no great reason to be surprised and no right to be displeased. Nor, whatever he may afterwards affect, can we give him much credit for being moved by fatherly affection. But he has lost a valuable servant. And with no misgivings of conscience as to the way in which he has dealt with him, feeling himself to be deceived and defrauded, he thinks that he does well to be angry. For none are more apt to be resentful of wrong than the sharper outwitted, or the biter bit.

What the meeting would have been, if the parties had been left to themselves, may in some faint measure be gathered from what, even under the restraint which the. Lord's command to Laban imposed, it actually was. Certainly it was at one time passionate and stormy enough. It begins indeed with tolerable decency and smoothness. The wily and plausible man of the world assumes a bland countenance and uses fair words. It is his honour, as it seems, that is touched! His tender feelings as a parent are wounded! He is hurt because Jacob has suspected and distrusted him; and he resents his having had no opportunity of handsomely dismissing him, if he was determined to go, loaded with benefits, —and carrying with him the daughters he had got for wives, not as poor captives taken with the sword, but as women of rank suitably attended and attired. Above all, it is hard that a loving father should not be suffered to imprint a last kiss on the lips of children whom it is not likely that he is to see on earth again. Truly the good Laban is a sorely injured man (ver. 26-28).

But the specious dissembler cannot be consistent with himself. As if to let out the cloven foot, he must needs make a boast of what he might have done; and that in such a manner as to indicate pretty clearly that but for a divine arrest laid on him, he would have actually done it ;—" It is in the power of my hand to do you hurt: but the God of your father spake unto me yesternight saying, Take thou heed that

thou speak not to Jacob either good or bad" (ver. 29). Jacob
shrewdly and rightly gathers his worthy father-in-law's real
meaning (ver. 42). Laban has unconsciously dropped the
mask. He had been bent on mischief. But, as he says,
"the God of your father spake unto me." The God of your
father! For Laban will not own and worship him as his
God, although he is constrained to stand in awe and obey.
It is not true faith but slavish dread that stays his hand. He
is at heart a persecutor,—restrained neither by a conscientious
reverence for God, nor by a kindly feeling towards man, but
only by a sort of servile and superstitious apprehension of
some evil coming upon himself from the wrath of that being
whom his intended victim worships. So he betrays his real
purpose; giving a hint, at the same time, of the ground he
might have alleged that he had for picking a new quarrel if
he chose; "though thou wouldest needs be gone, because
thou sore longedst after thy father's house, yet wherefore hast
thou stolen my gods (ver. 30)?

Jacob's reply is, in the circumstances, as calm and dignified
as it well could be. For his flight he has no occasion to
apologise; at least not to Laban. He had too good reason to
be apprehensive of wrong at his hands, not to be justified in
taking the step he took, so far as his father-in-law might think
he had any cause of complaint. He avows his fear, as a fear
for which he had too good ground; "I said, Peradventure thou
wouldest take by force thy daughters from me" (ver. 31).
He is not to be taken in by a hypocritical show of friendship.

As to the other charge about the theft of the gods, Jacob
treats it with a sort of summary contempt. He may well
regard it as an accusation got up by Laban to be the occasion
of a fresh act of treachery and wrong. The unscrupulous
Syrian, while pretending to obey the divine voice,—that he
should not, either by flattery or by threats, attempt to stay
Jacob as a fugitive servant,—is trying to get round him
another way. I have nothing to say, good or bad, as to the

manner of your quitting my service. Your God, it seems, the God of your fathers, forbids me to reckon with you, as otherwise I might have a good right to reckon with you, for that. But the impunity thus secured to you for your flight cannot be meant to cover theft or sacrilege. Why hast thou stolen my gods? (ver. 30).

This looks at least very like a subterfuge or an afterthought on the part of Laban; and Jacob so regarded it,—putting upon it, naturally enough, a construction fully warranted by his knowledge of the man, and his experience of his consummate skill, as a master in the school of cunning. Hence his bold reply. First, he simply defends himself, and challenges his accuser to the proof—" with whomsoever thou findest thy gods, let him not live" (ver. 31, 32). And then,—Rachel's device (ver. 32-35) keeping him as well as her father in the dark,—he vehemently speaks out his mind in the honest indignation of injured innocence; giving vent at last in one burst of invective to his pent-up feelings.

" Jacob was wroth, and chode with Laban," saying to him, " What is my trespass? what is my sin, that thou hast so hotly pursued after me?" The hunted victim stands at bay. He rehearses his wrongs; he taunts the wrong-doer; he will own no obligation to him or to his forbearance; the Lord alone has been his helper. " Except the God of my father, the God of Abraham, and the fear of Isaac, had been with me, surely thou hadst sent me away now empty. God hath seen mine affliction and the labour of my hands, and rebuked thee yesternight" (ver. 36-42).

True to his character to the last, the wily Laban receives Jacob's torrent of invective with affected meekness. Assuming an air of moderation, making allowance for his son-in-law's vehemence, he professes himself willing to waive his rights. These wives of thine and their children are indeed all mine; I might claim them as mine. And the cattle are all mine. But what then? What can I do now? Far be it from me to proceed to extremity. Come, let us be friends. If we must part, let us part in peace, and let us ratify a parting covenant of peace (ver. 43, 44).

The ratification of the covenant is effected by a succession of solemn ceremonies (ver. 45-55).

First, on Jacob's suggestion, he himself setting up the first stone for the central pillar, a monumental or memorial heap is raised. Both parties acknowledge the pile,—each in his own tongue giving it a name significant of its object,—" the heap of witness,"—the "beacon or watch-tower." It marks a locality which,—under the name of Mizpah, and as some think also, Ramoth in Gilead,—became afterwards, in the days of the Judges and the Kings, a place of no mean importance,—a kind of frontier town, serving even then a similar purpose to that with a view to which it is here signalised (Joshua xiii. 26 ; 1 Kings xxii; 2 Kings viii. 28, 29, etc.). Next, " this heap of witness," this "pillar of witness," is constituted by Laban in a very solemn manner the seal or symbol of an appeal to the Most High: " The Lord watch between me and thee, when we are absent one from another" (ver. 49). God is to be witness, if Jacob afflict or wrong the daughters of Laban (ver. 50). And he is to judge between them if either party pass this limit for hurt or harm to the other (ver. 51.) The oath is taken by each according to his faith. Laban's adjuration is, " The God of Abraham, and the God of Nahor, and the God of their father judge betwixt us ; while Jacob sware by the fear of his father Isaac " (ver. 52). Some common ground they have. Each of them believed that the God he worshipped was the God of Abraham. But Laban knew him only as the God of Abraham's father ; Jacob knew him as the God of Abraham's son. Laban recognised him as he was wont to be traditionally recognised in the family to which Abraham originally belonged. Jacob acknowledged him in the character which he had assumed, by a new revelation, as the God of Abraham's seed,—" the Fear," therefore " of his father Isaac." Thus they understood one another, as mutually binding themselves, by the most solemn vow that each could take. The transaction is completed by a sacrifice on Jacob's part, and a sort of sacrificial feast : "Then Jacob offered sacrifice upon the mount, and called his brethren to eat bread: and they did eat bread, and tarried all night in the mount" (ver. 54).

And now nothing remains but the bidding of a long and last farewell :—"Early in the morning Laban rose up and kissed his sons and his daughters, and blessed them: and Laban departed, and returned unto his place" (ver. 55). It is a quiet ending of a troubled history. The curtain falls on the Syrian act of the drama. And the last we see of it is the kiss of charity and the blessing of peace.

45

THE TWO ARMIES—THE FEAR OF MAN—THE FAITH
WHICH PREVAILS WITH GOD

Genesis 32:1-23

The company of two armies. Song of Solomon 6:13

As Jacob had been dismissed from the land of promise by a vision of angels, so a troop of angels are in waiting to welcome his return. " The angels of God met him. And when Jacob saw them, he said, This is God's host: and he called the name of that place Mahanaim ;" that is, " two hosts, or camps " (ver. 2).

Why a name signifying "two hosts," or "two camps," or " a double army " (*mahanaim*), is used to denote what Jacob saw—for he meant evidently to call the place from the event, —is a doubtful matter of inquiry. That the angelic company divided themselves into two bands,—so as to cover the patriarch's train in front and rear, or on either flank,—is a view suggested by such expressions as that of the Psalmist, " The angel of the Lord encampeth round about them that fear him, and delivereth them " (Ps. xxxiv. 7), and that of the prophet, " I will encamp about mine house because of the enemy " (Zech. ix. 8). On the other hand, Jacob seems to regard the angels as one single body, when he says, " This is God's host ;" and it is at least as probable a supposition as the other, that the duplication of this host, or its branching into two, indicated in the name he gives the spot, may arise from his associating with the heavenly attendants visible from above, his own array of pilgrims treading the earth below. "We are two camps,—two hosts!"—he may be regarded as gladly and gratefully exclaiming, for the encouragement of his followers and himself. We are not a mere feeble and defenceless handful of women, children, and cattle, but two armies! This retinue of angels is God's host; and it is on our side. And they and we together form a double encampment, and a double line of battle. How great then is our security! How invincible are we! How strong may we be!

The only other instance in Scripture of the use of the term here employed is to be found in the Song of Solomon; and the two uses of it, there and here, may throw light on its meaning, and on the meaning of the passages in which it occurs. Referring to the spouse, an appeal is made; "Return, return, O Shulamite; return, return, that we may look upon thee. What will ye see in the Shulamite? As it were the company of two armies"—or "Mahanaim" (Song vi. 13).

The image in that passage is undoubtedly a strange one; the spouse compares herself to an army. Or rather, perhaps, she is compared to an army by the bridegroom and his associates;—"Who is she that looketh forth as the morning, fair as the moon, clear as the sun, and terrible as an army with banners?" (ver, 10). So they hail her as an army; and she is content to be viewed in that character. But it must be a double army that she consents to personate;—she cannot otherwise be terrible to any adversary, be he human, or satanic, or divine; she cannot otherwise, as an army, display her banners in successful battle or triumphant victory. Her being saluted thus, as an army, is a plain enough indication to her that she has a warfare to wage,—a fight to sustain. It may be to meet the onset of an angry brother; it may even be to bear the brunt of an assault on the part of the Lord himself, to chasten or to prove her. But whether it is man's violence that she is to withstand, or the close onset of the Angel Jehovah wrestling with her vehemently, she can make

head only as a double army. Alone, she is too feeble to
stand in battle array ; but when the angels of God meet her,
she is two hosts. And it is only as two hosts that she can
prevail. Therefore if the spouse is to be an army at all, she
must be a double army,—having, as it were, a heavenly
duplicate of herself associated with her. Only thus can she
face a hostile Esau. Only thus can she stand the encounter
of her loving Lord.

But the heavenly fellowship of angels, in so far as it is
matter of sense and sight, is rare and brief ; their visits are
few and far between. The patriarch is still in the flesh ; and
" the life which he has to live in the flesh, he has to live by
faith,"—and the prayer of faith. Once, in some fourteen, or
twice fourteen, years, the believer may be " caught up into the
third heavens," to behold inconceivable glories and overhear
unspeakable words (2 Cor. xii. 4). On some critical occasions
the heavenly hosts may meet the weary wanderer. But he
must be made to feel that earth is still the scene of his pilgrimage and probation, and that earthly work and warfare
must be attended to. The business on hand is the earthly
walk and the earthly struggle. The land of promise is to be
reached. And Esau is in the way.

Into the feelings of Jacob with reference to his brother, it
may be difficult for us to penetrate ; for on the surface of the
narrative, little appears that can throw light on them.
That he was honestly anxious to adopt measures of conciliation, is plain from the embassy he sent, and from the words
he put into the mouths of his ambassadors : " Thus shall ye
speak unto my lord Esau ; Thy servant Jacob saith thus, I
have sojourned with Laban, and stayed there until now :
and I have oxen, and asses, flocks, and menservants, and
womenservants : and I have sent to tell my lord, that I may
find grace in thy sight" (ver. 3, 4, 5). The message in itself,
and particularly as explained by the subsequent interview,
amounted virtually to a concession to Esau of all the temporal

benefits of the disputed birthright. Jacob was in haste to give up to him the title of superiority, and the higher rank belonging to the first-born,—and to intimate that he neither needed nor sought any part of the hereditary patrimony. He had enough of his own, through the kind providence of God, and had no wish to interfere with anything that Esau cared to claim ;—for as to the spiritual privileges of the birthright, Esau had made it too plain that he felt but little concern.

On the other hand, we cannot but gather from the report brought back to Jacob, that Esau's approach was of a hostile character ;—such at least was the impression conveyed to Jacob ;—" The messengers returned to Jacob, saying, We came to thy brother Esau, and also he cometh to meet thee, and four hundred men with him. Then Jacob was greatly afraid and distressed" (ver. 6, 7). Notwithstanding what we cannot but admire in his reception of his brother when they actually met, there is no meaning in the inspired account, if it is not to be understood as implying that Esau did at first intend measures of hostility and revenge. No doubt,—as an evil conscience makes cowards of us all,—Jacob's sense of the offence he had formerly given to Esau may have rendered him suspicious and apprehensive ; that may be true. But he must have had more to go upon when his fears prevailed so much. And unless we suppose Esau to have dissembled for the purpose of surprising his brother by unexpected kindness—and there is not a trace of any such refinement in the record, nor does it agree with the impetuous character of the man—he must be viewed as hastily rejecting Jacob's proposals of friendship, and continuing his adverse march towards him.

No wonder, then, that in the circumstances Jacob experienced a bitter feeling of disappointment, and was put into serious alarm. He was unaccustomed to battle. He was familiar only with pastoral and peaceful occupations. And now he was about to encounter one who had been a man of stern action, involved in the strife of war, or of the chase, from his earliest youth. Nor was he provided with an armed convoy, or any sufficient means of resistance. One part of the army he had around him might consist of the invisible hosts of heaven ; but the other was composed of "the mother with the children" (ver. 11). In these straits, what does Jacob do ?

First, he takes measures for securing the safety of at least a portion of his company ;—" He divided the people that was with him, and the flocks, and herds, and the camels, into two bands ; and said, if Esau come to the one company, and smite it, then the other company which is left shall escape" (ver. 7, 8). His plan is in accordance, as we are told by some writers, with Eastern usages ; it would be considered a wise and proper precaution in a similar emergency even now. But it does seem to savour somewhat of Jacob's natural disposition to calculate and scheme for himself, instead of simply doing his duty, and trusting implicitly in the Lord. The separation of his household, especially in the view of the reason assigned for it, does not commend itself to our ideas of what is chivalrous and brave. We would rather that all should have run the same risk together. But we cannot well judge, at so great a distance of time, and at a still greater distance of manners, how far Jacob's policy might be justified.

His second expedient we can better estimate. He has recourse to prayer. And his prayer has several evident marks of its being really the prayer of genuine faith.

In the first place, he lays hold of the covenant ;—" O God of my father Abraham, and God of my father Isaac, the Lord which saidst unto me, Return unto thy country, and to thy kindred, and I will deal well with thee" (ver. 9). He thus appeals to God as in covenant with his fathers and himself. He relies on the promise made to Abraham and to Isaac ; and he appropriates it as his own. Secondly, he confesses his unworthiness, and his obligation to free and sovereign grace alone ;—" I am not worthy of the least of all the mercies, and of all the truth, which thou hast showed unto thy servant; for with my staff I passed over this Jordan; and now I am become two bands" (ver. 10). Thirdly, he looks to the Lord, and none else, for deliverance out of his brother's hand;—" Deliver me, I pray thee, from the hand of my brother, from the hand of Esau : for I fear him, lest he will come and smite me, and the mother with the children" (ver. 11). And in the fourth place, he takes his stand on the sure word of God;—putting the Lord in mind of his own express assurance with reference to the future fortune of his race; —" Thou saidst, I will surely do thee good, and make thy seed as the sand of the sea, which cannot be numbered for multitude" (ver. 12).

If anything amiss is to be noted in the prayer, it is the tendency which it indicates, on the one hand, to regard the opposition of Esau as the only obstacle in his way to Canaan, and on the other hand, to reckon,—somewhat too much in the spirit of self-righteousness,—on a sort of hereditary and personal title to the favour and help of God. It is Esau who has a controversy with him; and in that controversy the Lord must needs be on his side. He is soon to be taught, by a very sharp lesson, how inadequate a view this is of his true position in the sight of God.

For the present, however, he is thinking only of Esau as his adversary; and he carries out his plan of operation upon that assumption. He sends on successive droves, to be offered one after another, as propitiatory presents to his brother. That was his scheme;—" For he said, I will appease him with the present that goeth before me, and afterward I will see his face; peradventure he will accept of me" (ver. 20). So the day was spent. "The present went over before him : and he himself lodged that night in the company" (ver. 21). Under cloud of darkness, he effected the passage of his family; and he was "left alone" (ver. 24).

But the Lord has a controversy with Jacob; he is to be made to feel that Esau is not his most formidable adversary.

The Lord is to deal with him as an adversary ;—first turning
his strength into weakness ;—and then causing him to know
by experience that " when he is weak then he is strong " (2
Cor. xii. 10). Hence the scene of the wrestling.

When Christ says that " the kingdom of heaven suffereth
violence, and the violent take it by force,"—he may be referring, in part at least, to this transaction. He is describing the
ministry of his forerunner ; and he is describing it as a crisis,
not only in the history of the church, but in its bearing also
on the duty and destiny of individuals.

" What went ye out into the wilderness to see ? " What
did your going out into the wilderness mean ? Was it an idle
jest ? Did you go to be befooled by a reed shaken with the
wind ? Or was it a holiday excursion ? Did you go to have
your eyes dazzled by a man clothed in soft raiment ? Was it
as light an affair as the taking of a careless ramble in the
common ? Or was it as mere a matter of form as the paying
of a stately visit at court, where gorgeous ceremony dwells ?

No! You knew that you had more serious work on hand ;
you felt that the hour and the man were come ; it was indeed
a critical time. A new and fresh era had arrived. It was to be
now or never. The old routine of a mere passive yielding
to impulse, or devotion to etiquette, would suffice no longer.
Listless, half-awake, childish curiosity, pleased with every
shaken reed, will not do. Vacant wondering after a sumptuous or solemn dress, such as piety may wear in kings' houses,
will not do. Both must give place to something sterner and
more real. Religion, as John's preaching forces it on our
regard, is neither sport nor show, but close conflict and strife.

That is the lesson which Jacob is now taught. Left alone,
and preparing to follow his family and goods across the brook,
he is suddenly and forcibly stopped. An unexpected antagonist
meets him, and a sort of death-struggle ensues. Who his assailant
is, Jacob cannot at first even guess ; but the force of the onset is

felt. The two parties grapple in right earnest ; and there is wrestling, as between man and man, till the breaking of the day.

Jacob makes a stout resistance ; he is not to be intercepted on his way to Canaan ; he is determined to possess the land ; and be his adversary who he may, he shall not hinder him. The struggle waxes desperate, and Jacob yields not an inch. He who has thus attacked him as a foe gains no advantage.

But all at once, upon a single touch from the hand of this mysterious combatant, there is a shrinking of Jacob's sinews, a halting upon his thigh, a trembling of his knees,—a "piercing," as it were, "even to the dividing asunder of the joints and marrow" (Heb. iv. 12). Helpless, lame, and ready to fall, he can but cling with desperate tenacity to the very Being who has so sorely smitten him.

Not to prolong the conflict, however, does he cling to this strong adversary, now discovered to be divine ;—no, nor even to beg for his mere life, though now so evidently at the mercy of his seeming foe ; but—oh wondrous importunity in such a case !—to deprecate his departure,—to insist on detaining him when he would be gone,—to crave his blessing !

Surely, O Jacob, "great is thy faith !" Might it not be enough for thee to escape death at the hands of this formidable "man of war," as he with whom thou hast to do proves himself to be? (Exod. xv. 3). Thou mightest be too thankful to be left by him prostrate on the ground, and to get rid, on any terms, of his contending with thee. But no. Jacob has discovered who this "man of war" is, and he will not let him go until he get his blessing.

The opposition which God offers to Jacob, and Jacob's resistance,—the sudden weakening of his strength, and his subsequent importunity,—are all spiritually significant.

God takes the attitude and aspect of an adversary, fighting against Jacob ; and Jacob stoutly resists and maintains his ground. There is vehement wrestling all the night ; and there is this peculiarity in the wrestling, that it is the heavenly combatant who acts the part of the assailant ; Jacob stands on the defensive. At first he might be inclined to regard the interruption as rather vexatious and impertinent than serious. It must be some idle fellow bent on mere annoyance or a frolic ; it will cost but a moment to chastise his insolence and be rid of him. But he finds that this is more than a mere holiday wrestling-match, and that it is not to be so soon or so easily ended.

Who then can this mysterious adversary be, coming between me and the work I have to do? Can it be a secret emissary of Esau's—a hired bravo or assassin, or one of his followers bent on carrying that old threat into execution—" I will slay my brother Jacob ?" No. That is not Esau's mode of warfare. Is it Esau's guardian angel interposing to prevent any injury being done to him ? So the later Jews have fabled ; but no such belief belonged to the age or the faith of Jacob. Is it, then, the great adversary of God's people, who would fain prevent the entrance of the patriarch into the promised land ? Even if it be, Jacob will not give way.

No ! Not even when he finds out that it is the very " Angel of the Covenant himself,"—the " Fear of his father Isaac,"—the God who had twice appeared to him in Bethel, who is now stopping the way, and, as a mighty man, seeking to overthrow him,—not even then will he gave way.

When he makes that discovery, he may have many misgivings ; and were his desire less intense, and his faith less strong, in reference to the country he seeks and the promises he has received, he might be inclined to call back his family and flock, and wend his way again to the luxurious pastures and the sumptuous dwelling of his kinsman Laban ;—or to some new home among earth's many vacant places, where he might hope to win ease and honour. If he wanted an excuse, he had it now. It was not Esau only who threatened him ; God himself was against him. After a decent show of reluctance and pretence of resistance, he might have submitted to necessity, as it might have appeared, and turned his back on Canaan.

But he would not. His longing for Canaan was too intense,—his warrant for claiming it too clear,—to admit of his giving it up. God had taught him to look for it ; God had given him the promise of it. And now, not even when God himself seems to be against him, will he be beaten back. He may wrestle with me, but " though he slay me, yet will I trust in him." He shall not hinder me, while I have life, from passing this brook.

Again I say—O Jacob! great is thy faith! It is like the faith of one who, though not thy child after the flesh, was yet like-minded with thee, in the days when that divine Saviour who wrestled with thee dwelt on the earth, and went about doing good. The woman, who was " a Greek, a Syrophenician by nation " (Mark vii. 26), coming to Christ on behalf of her poor daughter, met with much the same treatment with thyself; and like thee, she was not to be overcome. Jesus wrestled with her,—dealt with her harshly,—spurned her, it might almost seem with his foot,—and called her dog. But she stood her ground. The divine Wrestler saw that he prevailed not against her ; he was as it were forced to give in ; the kingdom of heaven suffered violence, and this violent assailant took it by force ;—" O woman, great is thy faith ; be it unto thee even as thou wilt " (Mat. xv. 28).

This wrestling of God their Saviour with those who seek his salvation, is not uncommon in the experience of his saints. Nor is it, as they can testify but too sadly, a mere show or feint on his part. It is not that he makes as if he fought ;—as it is said when he was with the disciples on the way to Emmaus that " he made as if he would have passed on." It is not what we might call a make-believe fight, got up for the mere trial of their spirits. No. It is a real antagonism and opposition that they have to encounter. The Lord has a controversy with them, and does really set himself against them.

Is any sinner, for instance, moved to quit the land where he has been dwelling too long, and to take the staff of a pilgrim, and set out on the path to heaven ? He has every encouragement in doing so—" exceeding great and precious promises, whereby he is made partaker of the divine nature." Still he must lay his account with difficulties. He may be hotly pursued by those who fancy themselves injured by his going away,—persecuted by old companions,—harassed by old claims, and outstanding engagements and entanglements. Before him, also, he may anticipate coming evil ; and reaping the fruit of former offences, he may have fears and misgivings as to enemies to whom his conscience tells him he has given an advantage. All this he may be prepared for.

But on some dreary night of watching and anxiety, I have to encounter a higher foe. God, the very God who has moved and encouraged me to take the decisive step, comes out as wrestling with me. He, too, is felt to be turning against me ; and it seems as if it were all over with my chance of ever reaching heaven. I may as well give up the unavailing struggle and return to my worldly ease and unconcern again. So Satan and the world would have me resolve ; so also does my own heart tempt me to resolve ; and if my sense of eternal realities be faint, and my care for the salvation of my soul slight,—so unhappily I may resolve.

But far be such a thought from the man who is in earnest. God may buffet me, if it so please him ; yes, he may slay me. But I cannot do without the salvation of my soul. Nay, now that God has put it into my heart to care for the salvation of my soul, not God himself, even when he meets me in his wrath, shall make me willingly give in.

46

JACOB'S TRIAL ANALOGOUS TO JOB'S

Genesis 32:24-32

THIS mysterious duel or single combat,—this marvellous wrestling-match,—may be viewed as having two stages. In the first, Jacob is put by his divine adversary upon his defence. In the second, he appears as the assailant.

The scene opens with a violent and prolonged assault upon Jacob, on the part of an antagonist in human form, at first unknown. He turns out to be no other than the Angel of the Covenant, the Lord himself. And it is that discovery which gives its peculiar point and interest to the incident.

It is an instance, in its first stage, not of man wrestling with God, but of God wrestling with man ; the Lord striving, in an attitude of opposition,—not feigned but real,—and striving vehemently, in a protracted encounter, with a poor child of the dust,—who yet, so far from yielding, even under the onset of so mighty an antagonist, stoutly resists and stands up to him manfully. This, Jacob felt, was the fight in which he was engaged.

And others also have felt the same thing. In particular, more than one or two of the Old Testament saints describe a certain crisis of their experience in such language ;—borrowed, perhaps, from this very record of Jacob's memorable duel ;—as plainly indicates that they regarded God as dealing with them precisely as he dealt with Jacob. No doubt, it may be a spiritual combat to which they refer, and not one that is merely physical and bodily. But surely, in Jacob's case, there must have been an apprehension of some spiritual meaning being connected with the bodily wrestling; and in the case of the others, there is often some affection of the body associated with their spiritual frame.

The language of Hezekiah, for instance, as to the sickness from which he got a temporary respite, is remarkable in this view. He describes the dealings of the Lord with him under this very image of a violent onset;—" He will cut me off with pining sickness: from day even to night wilt thou make an end of me. I reckoned till morning, that as a lion, so will he break all my bones: from day even to night wilt thou make an end of me." Thus he complains; while at the same time he cries, " O Lord, I am oppressed; undertake for me " (Is. xxxviii. 12-14). So also Jeremiah speaks ;—" Surely against me is he turned ; he turneth his hand against me all the day. My flesh and my skin hath he made old ; he hath broken my bones. He was unto me as a bear lying in wait, and as a lion in secret places" (Lam. iii. 3-10).

But it is chiefly Job's experience that is here relevant. For perhaps the closest parallel, in a spiritual point of view, to the Angel's wrestling with Jacob and its gracious issue, is to be found in the sharp trial which Job had to undergo as he describes it graphically and most pathetically in one of his sorest experiences ;—" Thou huntest me as a fierce lion : and again thou shewest thyself marvellous upon me. Thou renewest thy witnesses against me, and increasest thine indignation upon me ; changes and war are against me." " Are not my days few ? cease then, and let me alone" (Job x. 16-20).

Consider, in this view, the case of Job.

There was a terrible onset made on him at the instigation of Satan. " Doth Job fear God for nought ?" is Satan's challenge to Jehovah ;—" Put forth thy hand, and touch all that he hath, and he will curse thee to thy face." In answer to this challenge, Satan is allowed to have his own way ; he is to see the Lord putting forth his hand against Job. All that Job has is touched ; messenger after messenger pours into the patriarch's ear the tidings of oxen, asses, sheep, servants, sons, daughters,—all, as by one fell stroke and sweep of doom, gone ! In the twinkling of an eye, the rich householder, the fond father, is a beggar, and childless ! Whose doing is that ? Satan's, in one view ;—for it is done on his suggestion ; and therefore it may be said,—as the Lord says,—that "Job is in Satan's power." But strictly and truly, it must be held to be the Lord's own doing. It is the Lord himself who smites ; —otherwise Satan's challenge is not met. He meant the trial to be that the Lord—not he, but the Lord—should put forth his hand and touch all Job's possessions. That must be the character and aspect of the procedure against Job. And in that light, accordingly, Job regarded it when he said ;—"The Lord gave, and the Lord hath taken away ; blessed be the name of the Lord " (i. 21).

This is true also of the still closer onset on Job's person which the malignant spirit is permitted to suggest, and in which he is permited to have some part (ii. 1-10).

The Lord says indeed to Satan :—"Behold he is in thine hand ; only save his life." The patriarch is in Satan's hand,— inasmuch as it is upon his motion, as it were, that this second part of the trial, like the first, is appointed. And in it, as in the former, Satan is active and busy. But, if it is to answer his purpose, it is as an infliction of God that he must use it ;—the trial must be felt by the poor sufferer to come immediately from the Lord.

Doth Job fear God for nought ? Will he fear God, when God is not for him but against him ? So Satan, this second time, moves the Lord against Job. And Job, when he is smitten from head to foot, understands it to be the Lord's doing. What ! he says, in answer to what he calls the foolish speech of his wife,—"Shall we receive good at the hand of God, and shall we not receive evil ?"

Thus all throughout it is the Lord who is dealing with Job, and Job apprehends it to be so.

Now observe Job's bearing under this fierce onset of the Lord against him ;—instigated by Satan, and embittered by Satan's interference in the fray;—but still felt to be the Lord's. Observe it in connection with the advice given him by his wife on the one hand, and his three friends on the other.

I. The wife of his bosom entices Job to one sort of bearing under this onset ; " Dost thou still retain thine integrity ? curse God and die " (ii. 9). That is what Satan said Job would do ; and that is what his own wife would have him to do. He whom thou hast been accustomed to reverence and love is against thee now. Of what avail is thine integrity ? Plainly thou art no more a favourite with him ; he could not treat thee worse if thou wert his worst enemy. Thou must perish after all, it seems, in spite of all thy fear of him, and all his seeming goodness to thee hitherto. Be it so. Let there be an end of this fond dotage of thinking thou canst gain anything by holding on by one who so uses thee. Accept thy fate ; cursing, for thou canst not help cursing, as thou acceptest it, the Being who has led thee thus far, on the faith of assurances thou never couldst doubt,—and who now, as thou must feel, is so unrelentingly destroying thee.

That is one way of meeting the Lord's wrestling with me to which I may be tempted ; but it was not the way of Job. He met God in the erect and upright port of a manly faith. He is resolved not to take amiss anything that God permits or does. He will hold on and stand firm, even when, as it might seem, the Lord is most against him. And he fortifies his courage by that argument which so well becomes the lips of a dependent creature,—undeserving of any good,—deserving of all evil—" Shall we receive good at the hands of the Lord, and shall we not receive evil ?"

" In all this Job sinned not, nor charged God foolishly " (i. 22). " In all this did not Job sin with his lips " (ii. 10).

II. The same testimony is not recorded as to Job's bearing up against the onset of the Lord against him, under the advice given him by his friends. They would have him to meet the divine wrestler in a different frame of mind from that which his wife has been recommending. Their reasoning is all in the line, not of despair and defiance, but of abject prostration.

They start from the principle that great suffering is a proof of great sin (John ix. 2 ; Luke xiii. 1-5) ; their whole object being to make it palpable to Job, that because he is a great sufferer, he must be a great sinner. They urge him to confess some great crime. They insist upon his acknowledging that the Lord's present mode of dealing with him,—his wrestling with him so terribly,—is a proof that all his previous walk with God has been hypocrisy, and all his experience of God's favour a delusion and a dream. All their lengthened and elaborate dissertations on the providence of God, with which they wearied the afflicted patriarch,—" talking to the grief of him whom God was wounding,"—turned upon the one strain, in which they would have their suffering friend to acquiesce, that because he was a sufferer more than other men, therefore he was more than other men a sinner. It was not that he should say, irrespectively of this wrestling of the Lord with him, what might be equivalent to the saying, long after, of one nearly as sorely tried as he was, and proved by trial to be as true :—" This is a faithful saying, and worthy of all acceptation, that Christ Jesus came into the world to save sinners ; of whom I am chief." No. It was not that. They would have him to interpret this wrestling of the Lord with him as in itself a sure evidence and mark of his having no standing at all before God as a righteous man,—a man justified and accepted in his sight.

This Job refuses to do. He combats the arguments of his friends, by calling in question their fundamental principle, according to which they would square the manifold and varied

aspects of the providence of God to their own rigid notion of
what we have learned to call poetic justice,—that every man
must be held to be treated by God, even in this life, exactly as
he deserves. As a general principle, the patriarch controverts it.
And in reference to its application to himself, he stoutly and
indignantly refuses to let go his consciousness of his uprightness. He would not listen to the impious suggestion of his
wife that he should let go his integrity, and renounce the fear
and service of one who seems to be so dead-set against him.
Neither will he listen to the poor special-pleading of his friends,
who would have him to own that he has no integrity to let
go,—that all his fear and service of God has been false and
hollow,—and that it is proved to be so by his present trouble.

The controversy is long ; the contrast striking.

See these three men, Eliphaz, Bildad, Zophar. They " come
to mourn with Job and to comfort him." They weep and
rend their clothes and sprinkle dust upon their heads. They
sit with him seven long days and nights in silence. Surely
they sympathise with him. It may be so ; but they must
search him also. Sleek they are themselves, and smooth ;
having a comfortable opinion of their own righteousness and
their right standing with God. In their personal experience,
godliness is literally gain ; virtue is its own reward ; they are
religious and prosperous citizens ; prosperous, perhaps, because
religious. And here is one who has been more prosperous than
any of them, and who has had the character and reputation of
being more religious also. And how do they find him now ?

Ah! we must be faithful to him. We must tell him
plainly that the Lord's present wrestling with him is sure evidence that all along, as regards his relation to God and his
acceptance in God's sight, there has been something radically
wrong. It must be so. To account for so formidable an assault of God upon him, we must assume that there is some
dark criminality lying at the bottom of our friend's religion,
and vitiating it all. For some hidden fault or falsehood, God

is thus setting himself against him, and it must be our task to bring him to confession. While we comfort him, we must deal truly with him. He must be made to see and feel what this wrestling of God with him means;—how it should smite him, as a deceiver of others and of himself, to the ground, and make him own that his whole walk with God hitherto has been a dream or a lie. That is the end which the friends have in view, in all their conversations. For that end, they enlarge on the common-places of the doctrine of providence. Their speeches have in them many sound and valuable thoughts and observations on the subject of man's subjection to a righteous government, and the certainty of good and evil being ulti-・ mately extricated from the complications in which they are now involved. There is truth, and important truth, of a general sort, in their reasonings. That indeed was what fitted them for being the apt ministers of Satan, in causing the Lord's sharp wrestling with him to bear so heavily as it did on Job. They were so sound in the faith as to God's government being a government under which the distinction between good and evil never can be lost sight of; they said so many admirable things in praise of virtue and uprightness, as being always honoured and rewarded, and in condemnation of vice and hypocrisy, as sure to be detected and exposed;—that it must have been very hard indeed for the unhappy victim of their consolation to bear up against their reiterated assertion or insinuation, that the Lord, in wrestling with him, was rejecting him as false-hearted, and condemning him as still a guilty and guileful sinner.

But he does bear up; he stands upon the consciousness of his integrity. He will not allow the Lord's present dealing with him, however painful and however humbling, to overthrow his confidence. He will not, to please his friends, confess himself a hypocrite or self-deceiver; he cannot believe that that is what the Lord, who is wrestling with him, would have him to do. He knows both the faithfulness of his God

and the honesty of his own heart too well, to put such a construction on the treatment which he is now receiving, however
adverse and hostile a look it may have. He will not so stul-
tify himself and make void his faith. Even when God is rushing upon him as an antagonist, he will maintain his ground,
and make good his cause. He will not be beaten down ; he
will not give way or give in.

It is this high-spirited assertion of his uprightness,—running through all his speeches, mingling itself with all his woeful
lamentations, his sad and bitter complaints and cries,—it is
this that imparts so deep a pathos to the plaintive utterances
of this sorely afflicted man. We see him sitting alone, desolate and bereaved, covered all over with a loathsome malady,
writhing under intolerable pain of body, tortured in spirit, the
wife of his bosom turned against him to tempt him, his familiar friends pouring dreary platitudes into his vexed and
aching ears. Most touching are his melancholy wailings, expressive of present unutterable grief, as well as his tender
reminiscences of better and brighter days. But more touching still is his stern determination to refuse for one moment
to abandon the footing he has got for himself, as a true and
upright servant of the living God. Plied to utter weariness
with all satanic temptations,—solicited on religious grounds to
admit that God is casting him away as a false professor,—
pressed by the endlessly reiterated common-places of his three
" miserable comforters " to acknowledge himself to be one
whom for some great sin God is justly punishing and rejecting ;—they would make him out to be a murderer, or secret
criminal, whom, though he had escaped man's notice and judgment, God's vengeance would not suffer to live ;—still the
smitten patriarch stands up for himself and for his God. He
knows that his righteousness is not a lie. He has not been
false in serving God ; he repudiates the imputation. Even
when God is moved to be against him, he will not admit so
foul a charge.

So far it is a noble as well as an affecting spectacle ;—like what the heathen poets said was a sight worthy of the gods, a good man suffering adversity. So far also it is acceptable to God ;—more acceptable at all events than if Job had assumed the other attitude which his friends urged him to assume,— and, false alike to God and to himself, had consented to count himself a castaway.

But yet the lesson of this wrestling is not fully learned— its object is not fully gained—until, rescuing him out of the toils of the three messengers of Satan who were so vehemently buffeting him,—first a true apostle of the Lord, Elihu,—and then the Lord himself in person,—open up to him the mean-ing of this whole procedure ; causing him to see the glory of him who is smiting him, and in the light of that glory to see himself.

For Job needs to be humbled ;—not as his false friends would have had him humbled,—in false and unbelieving abjectness of soul ;—but as the Lord alone can humble. Elihu's testimony to this effect is true. Job, in the eagerness of his self-vindication against the cruel surmises of his perse-cutors, has been justifying himself rather than God. He has indeed done well in refusing to write such bitter things against himself as these men would have had him to write ;—to put the interpretation they would have had him to put on the Lord's wrestling with him ;—as if it meant that the Lord was condemning him utterly as a hypocrite. Still the Lord has something to say to him. His wrestling with him is designed and destined to leave behind it upon the soul of Job as deep and lasting a mark of God's majesty and the creature's weak-ness, as his wrestling with Jacob left on Jacob's body. The Lord will not indeed cast off, or cast down, his servant Job. But neither will he let him go, or cease from wrestling with him, until he brings him, in the view of the glory of the divine majesty, and under the apprehension of his own weakness and vileness, to cry out,—justifying himself no longer but justifying God,—" I have heard of thee by the hearing of the ear ; but now mine eye seeth thee ; wherefore I abhor myself, and repent in dust and ashes" (xlii. 5, 6).

Thus spiritually the Lord touches the hollow of Job's thigh, as literally he did in the case of Jacob ; and Job, like Jacob, halts on his thigh,—his bones being out of joint. And to Job, as to Jacob, that penetrating touch,—overmastering, overpowering, prostrating him altogether,—is the beginning of his power with God. It is the crisis of the conflict ; " when he is weak, then is he strong." Subdued, smitten, helpless, lost,—at that very moment, his defence against God being beaten down, he assumes the offensive, taking the kingdom by storm. It is not now any longer God wrestling with Job ; it is Job who wrestles with God ;—" Hear, I beseech thee, and I will speak : I will demand of thee, and declare thou unto me ;" for " I have heard of thee by the hearing of the ear, but now mine eye seeth thee ; wherefore I abhor myself, and repent in dust and ashes" (ver. 4-6).

It is the very experience of David. When he is thoroughly worsted, he waxes valiant in this fight ;—" I acknowledge my transgressions : and my sin is ever before me.—Behold, I was shapen in iniquity ; and in sin did my mother conceive me" (Ps. li. 3, 5). So he cries, in his distress. He is at his last extremity, unclean, undone ! But that is God's opportunity ; and David knows it to be so when he becomes importunate in prayer :—" Purge me with hyssop, and I shall be clean : wash me, and I shall be whiter than snow. Make me to hear joy and gladness ; that the bones which thou hast broken may rejoice" (Ps. li. 7, 8).

47

THE MEETING OF JACOB AND ESAU—BROTHERLY RECONCILIATION

Genesis 33:1-16

WHEN Jacob got the name of Israel (xxxii. 28), it was explained to mean that not only with God, but with men also, he had power as a prince to prevail. His power, as a prince, to prevail with God appears in this, that the Angel,—the Lord who came upon him as an adversary to wrestle with him,—is constrained by his vehement and prolonged importunity to bless him. His power, as a prince, to prevail with men appears in this, that his brother,—advancing towards him in hostile array and with hostile intentions,—is moved, on the first sight of the man whom he meant to crush, to shed tears of fraternal love. This last instance of his power is indeed but another form of the first. When God is against him, dealing with him so as to weaken his strength and smite him to the dust, Jacob cannot face an angry Esau. But when, weakened and smitten, with broken bones and broken heart, Jacob is yet enabled to keep hold of the very Saviour who is wrestling with him;—to "weep and make supplication to him," and refuse to let him go until he receive his blessing;— then, this very weakness being his strength, Israel may boldly say : "The Lord is my helper, I will not fear what man may do unto me." Having overcome even God himself, he will not now shrink from the face of Esau.

That Jacob is now prepared to meet Esau in a very different frame of mind from what he felt but yesterday, may be gathered from a slight circumstance in the narrative. He does not arrange his household as he had proposed to do.

In his first consternation on receiving the tidings of his brother's advance, he thought of adopting an expedient, savouring too much of that tendency to cowardice, and craft as the weapon of cowardice, which formed an evil element in Jacob's natural character, and had been aggravated by his early training (xxxii. 7, 8). There may be wisdom in it, but it is the wisdom of carnal and selfish prudence. The division of his company into two bands, with his reason for it, we cannot reconcile either with the simplicity of faith in God, or with the affection which would have moved a right-hearted husband, and father, and householder, to keep the objects of his love and care together, in the time of danger,—gathering them as, when the storm is brewing, a hen gathereth her chickens under her wings. But now there is a change. He marshals his family, not upon the miserable principle of risking one half for the chance of saving the other ; but altogether ; in the order of his customary mode of arrangement (xxxiii. 1, 2). And instead of keeping in the rear himself, as apparently he had meant to do, he takes his proper position at their head (ver. 3).

At all events, whether we are justified or not in supposing him to have thus changed his plan, and in putting this construction upon the change, Jacob approaches Esau, not "greatly afraid and distressed," but with confidence and courage. He approaches him, indeed, with gestures significant of deepest courtesy, after the usual oriental fashion. But there is nothing abject or degrading in the salams or salutations which he offers. He is simply carrying out the purpose which, by his first embassy, he had intimated to his brother (xxxii. 4, 5) ; the purpose of acknowledging him, in all temporal respects, as the first-born ; leaving him in possession of the civil rights and prerogatives of primogeniture ; asking no surrender of the patrimonial inheritance ; but simply desiring, as a younger brother, to be allowed to render to him the tribute of an acceptable compliment or service. His manner now is in entire accordance with his intention then. Holding fast whatever spiritual benefit the conveyance of the birthright to him and his seed may imply,—and about that there was no likelihood of any quarrel,—Jacob is careful to show in act, as he had said virtually in words, that as regards all else, he waives and foregoes his claim. Hence he humbles himself before Esau. And surely we may give him credit for doing so sincerely—not to serve a purpose, but in good faith. Fresh from that wondrous midnight wrestling,—" bearing in his body the mark of the Lord" (Gal. vi. 17),—Jacob was in the very mood to be truly humble in any human presence ; to cede any-thing, to cede all things, except the divine favour and the promise of the covenant ; and not in fear, but in faith, to take anywhere contentedly the lowest place. Thus, not in fear but in faith,—all selfish pride and policy apart,—he " bowed himself to the ground seven times, until he came near to his brother " (ver. 3).

The conduct of Esau is irresistibly affecting ; and the simple, artless manner in which it is narrated adds exceedingly to the charm. The man breaks down under the impulse of fraternal emotion ; " Esau ran to meet him, and embraced him, and fell on his neck, and kissed him " (ver. 4). After a separation of more than twenty years, during which few, if any, messages could be interchanged, he sees his long-estranged and long-lost twin-brother again. He sees him drawing near, in an attitude of confidence and friendship, soliciting his favourable regard ; not presuming on any right which past events,—the divine oracle and the paternal bene-diction,—may be supposed to have given him ; nor on the other hand shrinking and hanging back as if he were afraid or ashamed ;—but coming, as brother to brother, younger brother to elder brother, seeking only reconciliation and peace. The generous soul of Esau is touched. All the wrong he thinks he has received,—all the wrath he has been nursing,—all is on the instant forgotten. An unarmed man, at the head of a number of unarmed men, and women, and children, and flocks, and herds, is casting himself on his pity and honour. The brother with whom his days of pleasant childhood were spent, is at his feet. Long years have passed since offence was given and taken between them. Far older recollections rush in upon the memory. The brothers are twin children once more ;—" and they wept " (ver. 3).

One fears to mar the pathos of a scene like this by raising any questions as to Esau's state of mind ; but something must be said in the way of explanation.

That his intentions were hostile up to the very time, or about the very time of the meeting, it is scarcely possible to doubt. He meditated revenge. He had heard of Jacob's proposed return to Canaan, and of his being on the way. He had himself now got a position in " the land of Seir, the country of Edom," such as enabled him easily to intercept his brother's homeward journey. Estranged by his marriages and other causes, he had removed from the land of promise and become an independent chief. In that character he has been dwelling in Edom after his own manner, little mindful either of his brother Jacob or of his father Isaac. But now he learns that Jacob is returning from his long exile in Padan-aram, and is seeking again the paternal home. The information stirs up all his old jealousy and anger ; the buried and forgotten injuries of the past rise again in his memory. He may have been thinking little of the rights and privileges of that standing in the paternal establishment about which he was so sensitive some quarter of a century ago. But is he to allow a younger brother, who, once and again, long ago, injured him so deeply, to step quietly into the possession of them ? Not if he has the power to intercept him. And he has the power ; he can come in between the banished one and the home and heritage which he seeks. He may himself be caring little about the inheritance in the meanwhile; but at anyrate Jacob shall not again supplant or forestal him. With an armed force at his command, he will call his brother to account for the past, and effectually prevent his doing him any farther wrong.

Such, if we fairly interpret all the circumstances of his position, together with the unmistakeable indications of the narrative,—such was Esau's state of mind when, rejecting Jacob's embassy of conciliation, he came to meet him with his army of four hundred men.

But the first sight of his brother, casting himself on his kindness, is too much for Esau; a man, at all events, of most true and tender nobility of natural character,—whatever else might be wrong about him. Doubtless he who has the hearts of all men in his hands has been preparing Esau's soul for this softening influence and impression. The same divine wrestler who thoroughly humbled Jacob, has been beginning to humble Esau too. Jacob's power to prevail with men, like his power to prevail with God, is to be proved to consist in his own weakness; and to make that clear, the relenting of his adversary is to be manifestly the Lord's doing; the result, not of any measure of policy or persuasion on the part of Jacob, but of the Lord's immediate interposition to change the mind of Esau. Still the occasion and manner of the change, when it becomes manifest, are characteristic.

For it cannot be denied that of the two brothers, Esau seems in this interview to act the better part, and to present himself in the better light. Generosity is on his side, and magnanimity; and above all, nature.

Yes! Esau is natural;—so far as appears hitherto, merely natural;—a natural man;—yet also natural in the best sense of that term. All throughout this whole transaction his conduct is natural; it is all an affair of impulse. There is no planning beforehand, no forecasting and pre-arranging, as there was on the part of Jacob. The apparently studied obsequiousness of the one brother brings out in pleasing relief or contrast the spontaneous and impulsive warmth of the other. Esau prevents and outdoes Jacob in the reconciliation. It seems to be nature against art ; it might almost seem to be nature against grace ;—nature acting naturally against grace apparently artificial and even artful.

The natural acting out of nature is always sure of sympathy ;—hence the charm of such characters as Esau. It is impossible, and it would not be right, to be insensible to that charm. Our Lord himself was moved with love to the young man in whom he perceived many amiable and admirable qualities, although unhappily the love of riches caused him, when told what he lacked, to go away grieved. Let full justice then be done to the conduct and character of Esau, and let the touching and tender interest of this scene be thoroughly relished and enjoyed. Whatever memory of old grievances may have been rankling in his mind,—whatever temptation he may have felt to execute his old threat,— whatever purpose of violence he may have been meditating,— one glance at his brother's form and face, altered by years of trying toil, yet still the same,—is enough to chase them all away. The strong, stern man of war is a child again. He cannot, he will not, restrain himself. He suffers himself to be overcome. His tears flow fresh as he falls on his brother's neck and kisses him. And in the mutual embrace of long-forgotten kindness, the breach of years is healed, and the renewed brotherly friendship is complete.

What the future course of this renewed brotherly friendship was, the inspired history does not say. The progress of the conversation would seem to indicate, on Esau's part, a strong desire to prolong the fellowship so auspiciously resumed.

After receiving the homage of Jacob's family and attendants, Esau is for declining the present, which Jacob had sent on before (ver. 8, 9), and is only induced to accept it by the apprehension that his refusal may be considered ungracious. For Jacob urges him on that score. The present is no longer needed to propitiate Esau's favour. That was the original design of it,—but for that design it is now superfluous. Jacob thankfully acknowledges this : " I have seen thy face as I saw the face of God, and thou wast pleased with me " (ver. 10) ; —so the original expression may best be understood. I have already, independently of any gift of mine, found grace and favour in your sight ; your face I have now seen friendly to me, even as I saw the face of God friendly to me, when my importunity extorted the benediction. For Jacob connects the present scene with that of the wrestling. It was before the wrestling that he sent on the present, when he was greatly afraid and distressed ;—probably, after the wrestling, he would not have sent it. He would have dispensed with so poor an attempt to bribe his brother into forbearance, and left all to God, whose face he had seen in peace ; not doubting, but believing that he would bring him to see his brother's face also in peace. And so it has turned out. Your face, my brother, I have seen, as I saw the face of God. I ask you not now to take my gift if it were to pacify you towards me. But it may serve to seal the peace which God has established between us. On that footing Esau takes it (ver. 11). But he is not inclined to take it as a parting gift; he is not willing to let his brother away from him again ; he assumes, as it would seem, that they are to continue together, and at least for a time travel together ; —" Let us take our journey, and let us go, and I will go before thee " (ver. 12).

What does this proposal mean ? Has some faint notion of revisiting, along with Jacob, their aged father's dwelling, flashed across Esau's mind ? Is his heart drawn towards Canaan again ? Is he almost inclined to renounce his high position in Edom, and resume the patriarchal and pilgrim life of his father Isaac. and his grandsire Abraham ?

It may be so ; who can tell ? But if it was so, it was in

all probability, a mere passing emotion,—the natural effect of the meeting which had so melted him; it could not be relied on as likely to be lasting. Jacob, therefore, acted wisely, and doubtless under divine direction, when he courteously declined Esau's invitation,—calling his brother's attention, as if in explanation of his doing so, to the difference of their modes of life, as indicated in the very difference of their modes of travel (ver. 13, 14). Still the proposal surely indicated good feeling; —as did also the modified form of it, the offer of an armed convoy to see Jacob safely through the disturbed territory that lay before him on his way home: "Let me now leave with thee some of the folk that are with me" (ver. 15). That offer also, Jacob feels himself precluded from accepting: "What needeth it? let me find grace in the sight of my lord" (ver. 15). He is not to be indebted even to his brother for his safety. Thankful for the revival of friendly feeling between them, and desiring Esau also to be satisfied with that, he thinks it best that they should pursue their different paths in life apart.

And so the brothers part in peace.

Whether or not they often met again does not appear. Jacob seems to point to his visiting his brother Esau at some future time, when he speaks of "coming unto my lord, unto Seir" (ver. 14). He may have fulfilled his intention, and the friendly relations, now auspiciously re-established, may have been confirmed and made closer by occasional intercourse from year to year. Or it may have been otherwise. They may have continued to live apart, with little or no interchange of communication, either personally or by message. Perhaps it was best that it should be so. The tender meeting may have told upon Esau,—reflection deepening the impression of it on his mind. He may have been led, after Jacob was gone, to think over the circumstances of the scene,—to recognise the finger and the Spirit of the Lord, rather than any merit of his own, as the true cause of the good feeling which prevailed,— and to ponder his brother's saying, "I saw the face of God."

If any salutary effect was wrought by the interview, on either side, it may have been all the deeper and more lasting for the separation that followed. Had the brothers continued long in one another's company, or come much in contact afterwards, their differences of taste and temperament might have led to disagreements again,—old grudges might have been revived in new causes of offence,—their mutual influence on one another might not have been for good. We may be reconciled, therefore, to the thought of their living still apart, until we find them once more together, as they should be, at their father's funeral. In all likelihood, they must have met at Isaac's deathbed, and jointly closed his eyes. At all events, it is a not unpleasing close of a painful family story, to read how "Isaac gave up the ghost, and died, and was gathered unto his people, being old and full of days,—and his sons Esau and Jacob buried him" (xxxv. 29).

48

PERSONAL DECLENSION—FAMILY SIN AND SHAME

Their heart was not right with him, neither were they stedfast in his covenant.   Psalm 78:37

On parting with Esau, Jacob resumed his march—" journeying to Succoth."   There he was within the border of the promised land once more ; so far he had obeyed the voice of the Angel who had spoken to him in a dream, enjoining his departure from Syria, and his homeward movement to Canaan (xxxi. 13).   But the obedience was very stinted ; it was according to the letter, rather than the spirit, of the divine commandment.   It was such as to indicate on his part a certain halting or hesitancy, not consistent with " following the Lord fully."   And it may be too truly surmised that it gave occasion for the saddest and blackest page being written in the annals of his chequered domestic history.

I. The Angel who had spoken to him had announced himself in these words : " I am the God of Bethel, where thou anointedst the pillar, and where thou vowedst a vow unto me."   That was the preface to the command ; " Get thee out from this land, and return unto the land of thy kindred." Fairly interpreted in the light of the preface, the command pointed to Bethel as his first resting-place in Canaan, and to the paying of his vow there as his first business.   If Jacob's heart had then been quite right with God, he would have "made haste and not delayed to keep his commandment."   He would have felt as David felt when he " sware unto the Lord, Surely I will not come into the tabernacle of my house, nor go up into my bed ; I will not give sleep to mine eyes, or slumber to mine eyelids, until I find out a place for the Lord, an habitation for the mighty God of Jacob." But Bethel and its vow,—and alas ! must we not add its God ?—are for the time forgotten or postponed. A border residence is preferred.

There may have been plausible reasons for the delay. Perhaps he thought that, by-and-by, he and his house might be better prepared for meeting the Lord in his own appointed place and way,—that the taint or leaven of idolatry, of whose working Rachel's conduct about the images gave too convincing a proof, might be gradually purged out,—and that it would be time enough, after they had got settled in their new abode, and Syrian recollections and associations had been got rid of, to carry his family up to the spot of which he had himself been constrained to say, " How dreadful is this place ! this is none other but the house of God, this is the gate of heaven."

But such special pleading could ill disguise the indifference or estrangement of his own heart. What he had to do at last he might have done at first (xxxv. 2-5) ; he might have been as decided now as then, in purifying and preparing his household for Bethel's holy service and joy. But his mind does not as yet lie in that direction ; he is otherwise occupied and attracted. He is tempted first to linger at Succoth, and then to pitch his tent, or set up his establishment, at Shalem (xxxiii. 17, 18).

For the world has taken, and is still keeping, too strong a hold of the patriarch's affections. He is rich in flocks and herds ; and he is delighted with the ample accommodation which Succoth offers. It is the very place in which to set up stalls for his cattle ; it deserves the name of " Booths." Here then he will dwell in the commodious house he builds for himself,—surrounded on every side by the hard-earned trophies of his painful and protracted Syrian service. But even Succoth does not content him long. It is not enough that he finds there abundance of vacant room, in which he may lodge himself and his cattle. for as many days or years as he may choose to remain. He must be not a sojourner merely, as his fathers were, but a proprietor; he must needs purchase a permanent habitation for himself. Hence he removes a little way and comes to " Shalem, a city of Shechem," or comes " in peace to the city of Shechem,"—for so the words have been rendered. It may be that he gives the name of Shalem, signifying peace, to the " parcel of a field " which he " buys at the hand of the children of Hamor, Shechem's father, for an hundred pieces of silver " (ver. 19). At all events, the arrangements which he makes betoken a purpose to settle quietly here, as well as an expectation that here, his pilgrimage being over, he may take his rest in peace. This is to be his home. As such it is to be secured to him and his seed by the indefeasible hereditary right of property which purchase is understood to give. As such it is to be hallowed by the customary rites of worship ; " he erected there an altar " (ver. 20).

This last act may seem to be an act of pious faith ; and it is doubtless meant to be so. But may it not also be a means of self-deception, tending to reconcile him to his neglect of duty,—his unsteadfastness in God's covenant ? Was it here that he should have erected an altar ? Was there not still waiting for him at Bethel the hallowed stone of which he had vowed that it was to be " God's house ?" And is not the name which he gives to the altar at Shechem a name of somewhat doubtful omen, as expressive of his state of mind ? " He called it El-Elohe-Israel " (ver. 20),—God, the God of Israel,— referring, doubtless, to the recent scene of the wrestling, and the change of his name, by divine authority, from Jacob to Israel. Is he trusting in that new name,—perhaps presuming upon it ? Is it as a prince, having power to prevail with God, that he claims him as his God ? Might he not have done well to remember that other title which God assumed when he called him out of Syria, from Padan-aram, to come back to Canaan,—" I am the God of Bethel "? It is with the God of Bethel, not the God of Israel, that he ought to be at present dealing. Instead of standing on his high prerogative as acknowledged to be Israel on the night of the wondrous wrestling,—he might rather have been recalling and resuming his low condition, when, as Jacob, he was a fugitive on the night of the lonely sleep and heavenly dream. Has Israel forgotten Jacob's vow? Has Israel's God ceased to be the God of Bethel? Has the man who once lay trembling on his stony pillow,—the man whose strength God weakened by the way,—waxed so confident in his princely rank, as to shake off the memory of the past,—with all its sense of dependence and all its debt of gratitude? This is his infirmity. " When I am weak, then am I strong ; " twice had he proved that great truth in his own experience. Now, when he is strong, he is weak. It were better for him still to be " the worm Jacob " than " the prince Israel,"—if this last distinction is to issue in his buying land, building houses, and rearing altars with proud names, at Sychem,—when he should be hastening, at the call of Bethel's God, to pay his vow at Bethel's pillar.

II. This decline of Jacob's own personal religion, of which we seem to have but too conclusive evidence, must be viewed as having an immediate and very close connection with the dismal family history that follows. Beginning himself to fall away, he cannot be ruling well his household. The traces of this want of rule thus occasioned are not far to seek ;—they lie on the surface of the melancholy narrative (xxxiv.)

1. Dinah's fall is explained in one emphatic statement,—" She went out to see the daughters of the land" (ver. 1). For it is not a solitary incident that is thus indicated, but a customary course of conduct. Instead of being a " keeper at home," as a " discreet and chaste " maiden would have done well to be, especially in the neighbourhood of seducing worldly

society, at once ungodly and impure,—this fair and frail child of a pious parent is suffered to be on terms of familiarity with the giddy throng frequenting the haunts of heathen pomp and pleasure. Surely Jacob is to be blamed. It is one of the untoward consequences of his halting on the border of Canaan and stopping short of Bethel, that his family are in such circumstances of exposure to temptation as might not otherwise have surrounded them. And it indicates relaxed discipline at home,—if not even perhaps a fond and foolish disposition to feel pride and take pleasure in his daughter's success among the gay and fashionable abroad,—that Dinah is found mingling, as it would seem, freely and without reproof, in the gay circle in which female beauty is apt to be a snare to its possessor, and female innocence is in danger of falling a prey to the arts and flatteries of the seducer (ver. 2).

2. Jacob's way of receiving the tidings of his daughter's dishonour is not creditable to him as the head of a family professing godliness; at least it does not commend itself to our notions. For one thing, he seems afraid or unwilling to judge and act for himself. He is inclined to defer too entirely to his sons; he will say nothing and do nothing without consulting them. They were away upon their usual occupation "with his cattle in the field; and Jacob held his peace until they were come" (ver. 5). This may have been a proper and necessary measure of precaution; to strengthen himself, by means of their support, before treating with the man who had so grievously wounded him in so tender a point. Or it may have been according to the usage of the patriarchal polity, that such an offence should be regarded as a wrong done to the community, and in that view, should be considered only in a common council of the tribe. Still we cannot but regret that there should be so little of the grave authority and ripe wisdom of venerable age, and so much of the heady rashness of impetuous and unbridled youth, in the management, on Israel's part, of this miserable affair. And above all, we miss that

reference to the divine will and law in the disposal of it, which surely we might have expected to find in the family deliberations of a man of God.

3. Hence partly, or rather chiefly, the sad contrast which here once more appears, between the goodness of mere nature, in its kindlier mood, and the evil of grace,—or gracious privilege and gracious profession,—perverted and abused. For, as between the two parties brought together in this transaction, —the Hivites and the Israelites,—the prince and people of the land, and the prince and people of the Lord,—who can hesitate to say on which side the preponderance of right and amiable feeling lies? If only such allowance as the manners of the world ask is made for the young man's sin at first, what is there in the narrative that does not redound to his credit? Instead of despising and hating his victim,—as is too often the case in such circumstances as his,—he continues to be attached to her more than ever. It is simply and touchingly told that "his soul clave to Dinah the daughter of Jacob, and he loved the damsel, and spake kindly unto the damsel" (ver. 3). He is most anxious to repair the injury he has done to her; nothing will content him but honourable marriage. In spite of the fault in which he has been overtaken, —and which he is so willing, as far as possible, to undo,—all our sympathy now is with the generous and faithful lover. His father too we cannot but admire. His frank consent to his son's proposal, when he says, "Get me this damsel to wife" (ver. 4), and his earnest appeal on his son's behalf to Jacob and his household, "The soul of my son Shechem longeth for your daughter: I pray you to give her him to wife" (ver. 8), bring this Hivite king before us in an aspect very pleasing. Nor can we put any other than an honest and generous construction on the larger overtures which he goes on to make, for a permanent friendly union between the two houses (ver. 9, 10). Let this matrimonial treaty,—this union of my son with your daughter,—be the auspicious inauguration of pros-

perous and peaceful times for both our tribes. It is in good
faith, we cannot doubt, and with all his heart, that the chief
holds out thus frankly the right hand of fellowship. And it
is a conclusive proof of his own and his father's earnestness
that Shechem gives, when he hastens to add,—speaking "unto
her father and unto her brethren,"—"Let me find grace in
your eyes, and what ye shall say unto me I will give. Ask
me never so much dowry and gift, and I will give according
as ye shall say unto me : but give me the damsel to wife" (ver.
11, 12).

We need have no scruple in allowing ourselves to be
charmed with so artless and touching a picture of love and
honour. It is good to mark the traces of high-minded and
amiable feeling among those who are still children of nature
merely. We cannot but be drawn towards such characters,
although they may be nothing more than earthly and worldly
after all ; and we cannot but on that account be all the more
grieved that dispositions so genial and upright as those manifested by these Hivite princes, were not met far otherwise than
they were on the part of the family that should have proved
itself to be the Church of the living God. Surely the
advances so honourably made by these mere men of the
world should have been differently received by men who were
professedly the Lord's people. Either they should have been
courteously declined, and the reasons for declining them faithfully and kindly stated, so as to impress the heathen with a
sense of the sacredness of the chosen family, and the blessing
that was ultimately to come to all nations through its being
kept separate, in the meantime, and apart. Or else, if it had
been considered lawful to entertain these advances favourably,
the terms of alliance might have been deliberately adjusted,
and its pledges ought to have been scrupulously kept. If one
or other of these courses had been adopted in good feeling
and good faith, who shall say what impression might have
been made on these noble-minded chiefs and on their nation,

—and what an influence for good might have been exerted on the whole of the ungodly world, in the midst of which the chosen ones were sojourning? Alas! that so precious an occasion should have been lost,—so favourable an opportunity thrown away! The very opposite effect must have been produced by what was seen and experienced of Israel's ways.

4. That Jacob was privy, or was consenting, to the horrid plot by which her brothers avenged Dinah's fall, cannot for a moment be imagined. The idea is contradicted by all we know of Jacob's general character, as well as by the express terms of the narrative. But he erred greatly in leaving the matter too much in the hands of his sons,—committing the whole negotiation to them, and allowing them to have their own way. He might have known them better than to trust them so implicitly. He ought to have transacted the business himself; if he had, the foul crime could not have been committed. But he has let go the reins of government in his own house;—his sons have evidently got the upper hand. Hence they are in a position to concoct their vile stratagem without his knowledge, and to carry it into bloody execution without his being able to prevent them.

Their device is very base; doubly so because it is in the name of religion that it is practised. Religion! Much wronged, deeply insulted, religion! What frauds, what foul abominations, what unutterable cruelties, art thou not invoked to cover! And the true religion too! the religion of the one only living and true God! With what smooth hypocrisy do these villains propound their nice scruple of conscience! Most anxious are they to have their sister married to so generous a prince, and to be "one people" with such worthy neighbours (ver. 14-16). There is but one small obstacle, not, however, insurmountable. They cannot waive the objection, but their friends can easily remove it. A little bodily suffering, a few days' delay, that is all. And then the holy rite of circumcision makes us all one. That is our condition, say these reli-

gious men—comply with it or not as you please. If you see
your way to comply, you are ours and we are yours, in a sacred
covenant, for ever. If not, "we take our daughter and are
gone" (ver. 17). No farther harm is done; you and we part
in peace. So the trap is laid. And the honest, unsuspecting
parties on the other side simply walk into it. The princes
warmly recommend the alliance to their people. The men are
so "peaceable with us" (ver. 21)—"honourable men" surely
and peaceable—not resenting violently an affront that might
have provoked them greatly, but rather inclined to overlook it
and be friends with us. And then commerce with them will
be so profitable, and dwelling together with them so pleasant.
The condition, moreover, is so simple—it indicates such a sense
of religion in them, and may be so great a religious benefit to
us! There ought to be no hesitation. And there is none.
The men are all circumcised, and for the time therefore rendered helpless.

Suddenly, as at a St. Bartholomew signal, "on the third
day," holy mother church lets loose her dogs of war. The
righteous avengers,—for is it not a righteous crusade?—with
bloody swords in their hands, make the night hideous indeed.
Ere morning dawns, the massacre is complete, and the spoil is
gleaned (ver. 24-29).

5. And how does Jacob feel when the terrible fact bursts
upon his knowledge? He is deeply moved, no doubt. The
discovery of the atrocity is to him both a shock and a surprise
—and he does not hesitate to express his mind to the two
who had been the ringleaders in the exploit, Simeon and Levi
(ver. 30). But even here, the traces of the lowered moral and
spiritual tone of his own mind come out. The remonstrance,
after all, is but a feeble one; it indicates no high principle—
no holy indignation—no righteous wrath; it turns mainly on
considerations of selfish policy and prudence. It is a false
step that has been taken—a step false in point of expediency.
A blunder, rather than a crime, has been committed; and it

may lead to unpleasant consequences. It may rouse the resentment of the neighbours and allies of the suffering tribe—and so endanger the fortunes, and even the lives, of himself and his family. Surely this is a kind of expostulation far below the occasion—not such as one who "feared God and regarded man" would have been apt to utter. And he seems but too ready to accept the lame apology of the culprits—"Should he deal with our sister as with an harlot" (ver. 31). For it was a lame apology, and false as well as lame. It was an apology exaggerating the original offence, and suppressing all that was so honourable to his heart in the subsequent conduct of the offender. It was, in truth, a shameless justification of the foul deed, in all its foulness. And Jacob, by his silence, appears to make himself almost a party to the deed—a sort of accomplice after the fact.

Long afterwards, Jacob spoke very differently concerning this transaction. On his deathbed, looking at it in the near prospect of eternity, he stigmatised it with somewhat more severity;—"Simeon and Levi are brethren; instruments of cruelty are in their habitations. O my soul, come not thou into their secret; unto their assembly, mine honour, be not thou united! for in their anger they slew a man, and in their self-will they digged down a wall. Cursed be their anger, for it was fierce; and their wrath, for it was cruel!" (xlix. 5-7). By that time the patriarch had come to view the matter more in the light of God's holy law, and less in the light of human policy and passion. But alas! for the close of the present chapter of his history. It leaves him a dishonoured and degraded parent,—reaping the bitter fruit of unsteadfastness in ruling his own household, and giving sad evidence of that unsteadfastness being the result, in large measure, of his own heart not being right with God.

49

PERSONAL AND FAMILY REVIVAL — MINGLED GRACE
AND CHASTISEMENT—AN ERA IN THE PATRIARCH-
AL DISPENSATION

Genesis 35:1-29

I have somewhat against thee, because thou hast left thy first love. Remember therefore from whence thou art fallen, and repent, and do the
first works. Revelation 2:4,5

THE scene here changes for the better. The patriarch experiences a revival ; a new crisis of his spiritual life occurs. His
heart is graciously made right with God once more, evidently
in the prospect of his being called, upon the death of his father
Isaac, to assume formally the position of the head of the chosen
family in Canaan.

The first step in this quickening movement, is a sovereign
and effectual interposition on the part of God (ver. 1).

So it must ever be. Left to himself, the sleeper will sleep
the sleep of death. But the Lord in great mercy awakens him;
—"God said unto Jacob, Arise." It is a startling call, as addressed to the Church, or to any of the people of God, in any
circumstances, in any mood of mind. "Arise ye and depart,
for this is not your rest; because it is polluted; it shall destroy
you with a sore destruction !"—such is the Lord's warning
voice by the mouth of the prophet Micah. And through Isaiah
he gives the word of comfort ;—"Shake thyself from the dust,
arise and sit down, O Jerusalem. Arise, shine, for thy light

is come, and the glory of the Lord is risen upon thee." These calls may be held to indicate the full meaning of the call to Jacob. In his case also, it is a call to depart out of the midst of what is polluting and destroying himself and all that are his. It is a call to awake to righteousness and not sin ; to shake himself free from the dust of worldliness, security, and sloth ; and to be on the look-out for new light coming, and a new rising upon him of the glory of the Lord.

For it is a call to Bethel, the house of God ;—"Arise, go up to Bethel." He should have gone up thither long ago, and should have been dwelling there now. He has been remiss and dilatory,—he has been worse,—he has been ungrateful to his God, and faithless to his vow. And were he now, of his own accord, proposing to repair his error and make up for lost time, it could be no matter of surprise to him if the Lord should lay an arrest upon him, and tell him it is too late. But the Lord "waiteth to be gracious." Nay more. His grace outruns and anticipates Jacob's purpose. And as he takes the initiative in this movement, so he makes it a movement worthy of himself, and like himself. He interferes to rescue his servant from backsliding and its bitter fruits. And he interferes in a manner that accords with his own great name, as "the Lord God, merciful and gracious, long-suffering and slow to anger, forgiving iniquity, transgression, and sin, though he will by no means clear the guilty." Bethel, though sadly neglected hitherto, is still accessible. The call is still free,—the warrant ample ;—"Arise, go up to Bethel." Nor is it open only to a passing visit, an occasional pilgrimage and brief act of homage. It is to be thy habitation,—"Go up to Bethel and dwell there." It is a better dwelling-place than thou hast been choosing for thyself,—safer and more blessed,—for it is the dwelling place of thy God. And it is still at thy service,—as much at thy service as if, on first quitting Syria, thou hadst sought it with all thy heart ;—"Dwell there, and make thee an altar unto God." Let it be thy rest, because it is the rest of God ;

—of that God who "appeared unto thee, when thou fleddest from the face of Esau thy brother." (ver. 1.)

What can be conceived more condescending and kind,— more touching and tender,—than this summons to Jacob,— in all the circumstances? It is in fact virtually an act of amnesty and oblivion, as regards all that has passed since the night of his flight from home. It obliterates the intervening period, and blots out all its sins. It is almost like the Lord's question to Peter,—"Simon, son of Jonas, lovest thou me?" That question must have been felt by the fallen disciple to carry in it a sentence of full and free pardon,—for it proceeded upon the principle, with which his master had made him familiar,—"To whom much is forgiven, the same loveth much." Lovest thou me? I am the Lord who called thee from being a fisher of fish, to be a fisher of men. I am the Lord who said, "Blessed art thou Simon Barjona." I am the Lord who promised that "on this rock I would build my Church." Thou hast denied me. But here am I, asking thee, "Lovest thou me?" Could I ask thee such a question, except on the footing of all that has come in between us being to me as if it had never been? I ask thee to be all to me that thou wast before thy backsliding,—all that and more,— all that thou wast when thou saidst that I was "the Christ, the Son of the living God." Substantially like this, is the Lord's call to Jacob. It annihilates the recent past, and goes back to the more remote. And it does so on the strength of a present act of grace,—forgiving all, forgetting all,—and proposing to have all again adjusted as at the first, when the first fresh gleam of the light of God's reconciled countenance broke the gloom of midnight,—and the worse gloom of a moody spirit,—as the exile lay forlorn on his stony pillow. It is indeed a call to him to be as he then was,—in spite of all that he has since been,—"to remember from whence he has fallen, and repent, and do the first works."

Jacob's response to the call is prompt and decided. He

takes immediate measures for complying with it,—and for complying with it in the spirit, and not merely in the letter. As the head of the family, and the prince and priest of the community, he issues suitable orders and enjoins special preparation, with a view avowedly to a very solemn act of worship. The preparation is twofold. It consists first of what is moral and spiritual,—the purging out of the old leaven of idolatry from among them ;—and secondly of what may seem to be more of a ceremonial and ritual character, the special cleansing of their persons, and the changing or washing of their garments (ver. 2). So Jacob would present his household before the Lord at Bethel, with no taint of the world's idol-worship cleaving to them, and with "holiness to the Lord" stamped alike on their bodies and on their souls. And he enforces his injunction by a consideration that might well reconcile them to its observance. The God with whom we are about to meet,—is the God "who answered me in the day of my distress, and was with me in the way which I went" (ver. 3). It is in acknowledgment of that first and most seasonable interposition of his grace when I was in my sorest straits, even more than of all his kind providence towards me since, that I,—who have hitherto, alas ! but ill requited his love,—now go to worship him at his own appointed place, taking you along with me. You cannot but feel that we must go, with no strange gods among us,—with clean hands and pure hearts.

The appeal of Jacob is effectual. The "strange gods that are among them are put away" (ver. 4). These were probably idols or teraphim, instruments of some sort of modified idolatry; —the true God not being altogether disowned, but false deities associated with him, or false methods of worship practised,— for that seems to have been the sort of religion prevalent in Syria, in Laban's house. But whatever they were, they are all, together with the ornaments of jewellery that were more or less identified with the use of them, unreservedly given up to Jacob, and buried by him in the earth, under an oak at Shechem ;—not surely to be afterwards brought to light, and made the occasion of heathenism in the kingdom of the ten tribes,—as some have feigned ;—but rather to be hidden and lost for ever (ver. 4).

Thus, the preliminary steps being all rightly taken, the journey towards Bethel begins.

It is accomplished in safety. That it should be so, is almost more than could have been anticipated as possible. It was, humanly speaking, far more likely that what Jacob feared would be realised (xxxiv. 30),—that, roused by the atrocity of the Sychem massacre, all the neighbouring tribes of "the Canaanites and the Perizzites," outnumbering many times over the little band amid which Jacob presided, would combine to follow after and destroy them. That it fell out otherwise, was wholly of the Lord. "The terror of God was upon the cities that were round about them, and they did not pursue after the sons of Jacob. So Jacob came to Luz, which is in the land of Cannan, that is, Beth-el, he and all the people that were with him. And he built there an altar, and called the place El-beth-el" (ver. 6, 7).

Yes! It is "El-bethel" now,—not as before (xxx. 20) "El-eloi-Israel." It is God, the God of Bethel, not God, the God of Israel ;—not God with whom he is a prince and prevails, but God who "appeared to him when he fled from the face of his brother" (ver. 7). The stone which had been his pillow, and which he had set up as a pillar on that night long ago, is now, according to his vow, the house of God to him. It is as if all the intervening space of years were obliterated, save only for his grateful remembrance of the Lord's kindness and faithfulness in fulfilling all his promises so abundantly. The patriarch takes up the dropped thread of his former Bethel experience, in continuation as it were, and in supplement of the worship then begun.

Of the three incidents that follow (ver. 8-20),—the death of Deborah, the appearance of God to Jacob, and the death of Rachel, in giving birth to Benjamin,—the central one is of course the chief. It is God's gracious act owning his servant's revived and quickened faith, and it is the conclusion of the series of personal divine communications to the patriarchs.

Viewed in the former of these two lights, it is a significant circumstance that it is preceded and followed by a note of domestic woe. The return to Bethel first, and thereafter the departure from Bethel to join his father Isaac, are both saddened by the funeral pall. As he reaches the holy place, he has to bury his mother's faithful nurse ; as he leaves it, he has to bury his own loved wife. The afflictions are not equal ; the second immeasurably outweighs the first. But the first is heavy enough. The relation in which Deborah, as Rebekah's nurse, stood to her mistress, and her mistress' favourite son, was, according to the usages of the East in these primitive times, a very close and endearing one. She was no ordinary servant, and was not treated as such ; she was a favourite and friend in Jacob's house, in which she seems to have been domesticated. Probably her death occasioned the first breach in the family circle, and was felt as a family bereavement. She was mourned with genuine tears ; and for a memorial the oak beneath whose shade her remains were laid got the significant name of " The oak of weeping " (ver. 8). Thus Jacob's first business at Bethel is to be chief mourner at a household grave. And his last, as he quits Bethel, is the same. It is the same, however, with aggravation unspeakably severe. Rachel is about to be a second time a mother. The doting husband's hopes are raised high. It may be that this child is to be born at his father's home,—in his mother's tent. He would fain see the wife he loves thus honoured, and one of his seed at least cradled in the hereditary patriarchal couch. Perhaps it is with a view to this that he hastens from Bethel to go to

Isaac his father. Alas! he is doomed to bitter disappointment. The journey is not well begun when travail comes suddenly on the woman with the child. Rachel is in hard and fatal labour. In vain the attendant tries to comfort her with the joyful tidings of " a son born into the world." In vain the broken-hearted father,—refusing to take in the terrible fact passing under his eye,—determined to be sanguine to the last and let no evil omen touch either mother or child,—whispers hope in the dull ear of death, and welcomes the last pledge of an undying love as no "son of sorrow," but " the son of the right hand." He is Benoni to her still,—the child of her grief,—however she may try to accept, with a languid smile of thankfulness, her husband's hope, in another sense than he meant it, as a hope that he is to be something very different to him. Her soul is departing,—let us say in peace. She has given him whom she loves a Benjamin ; she is content that he should be to herself a Benoni. And so she dies, and is buried on the way from " Uz, or Bethel," to " Ephrath which is Bethlehem." Jacob rears a pillar to perpetuate her memory. Then all is over. The curtain falls on the bereaved husband's unutterable woe (ver. 16-20). Surely it is not without a meaning that the gracious visit paid by God to Jacob comes in between two such calamities as these.

In the visit itself there is not much that is specially remarkable. It is announced in the usual simple and solemn form : " God appeared unto Jacob again, when he came out of Padan-aram, and blessed him" (ver. 9). The change of Jacob's name to Israel is confirmed (ver. 10) ; and the promise of a numerous posterity, and of the inheritance of the land, is renewed (ver. 11, 12). Then the close of the interview is intimated : " God went up from him in the place where he talked with him" (ver. 13); and it is followed up by a suitable act of worship on the part of Jacob, and a formal, public ratification of what before had been simply a private act or purpose of his own,—determining how the place was afterwards to be known among his seed (ver. 14, 15). In all this there would seem to be little or nothing beyond the recognition and renewed sanction of former covenant promises and pledges.

The only very notable circumstance is, that this is the last of what we may call the personal interviews with which God honoured the patriarchs. Henceforward that mode of communication between heaven and earth ceases. The next we read of is that by dreams, and the interpretation of dreams. Of the "appearing" of God to the party visited; his "talking with him;" his "going up from him;" of that direct, face to face, mouth to mouth, kind of intercourse, which these descriptions must be understood to signify,—we do not discover any traces in any of the subsequent revelations of which Old Testament Scripture speaks. The nearest approach to it is to be found in the case of Moses, concerning whom, on the occasion of the murmuring of Miriam and Aaron against him, the Lord bears emphatic testimony "If there be a prophet among you, I the Lord will make myself known unto him in a vision, and will speak unto him in a dream—my servant Moses is not so, who is faithful in all my house, with him will I speak mouth to mouth, even apparently and not in dark speeches; and the similitude of the Lord shall he behold" (Numbers xii. 6, 7, 8). But what Moses enjoyed of this direct communication with the Most High would seem to have been, not so much in the way of the Lord visiting him on the earth, as in the way of the Lord calling him up, as it were, into heaven, on the mount to commune with him there. And at all events, the Lord's way of making known his mind to Moses is declared to be exceptional; and the ordinary manner of divine revelation is represented as being altogether different. Revelation by a personal visit,—as when Jehovah, assuming the appearance of a man, sat with Abraham in his tent, eating meat with him—and talked with him as a man talks with his friend,—came to an end with this second interview between the Lord and Jacob at Bethel; which indeed was, more clearly

than the first, of the same sort with those which his fathers
had had with God. Here, therefore, is a critical change in
the administration of the covenant on the part of God,—and
here accordingly it may with not a little probability be con-
tended that, strictly speaking, the patriarchal dispensation, in
so far as it is of the nature of a revelation, comes to a close.
The patriarchal religion may now be said to be complete,—
the last contribution to it being now made in the Lord's
renewed ratification of the covenant with Jacob. Whatever
intimation of his will God may be pleased to make for the
guidance of his servants by visions and dreams ;—and whatever prophetic insight into the future may be vouchsafed to
gifted seers and dying saints ;—all that is rather in the way
of applying in detail to persons and circumstances, a revelation
already given as for the time final, than in the way of adding
to it, or repeating and confirming it. Henceforth the family
of Jacob and their descendants are to live under the patriarchal
dispensation, as a finished religious code,—very much as the
Israelites lived under the Mosaic dispensation after the death
of Moses, and as we live under the Christian dispensation,
since the death of Christ and his inspired apostles and evan-
gelists.

We seem, therefore, to be about to turn over a leaf at this
stage of the history. The signal for doing so is the death of
Isaac,—with which event the present chapter ends. It has all
the appearance, especially towards its close, of what may be
called a winding up ; making even, as it were, the odd ends
and remnants of the preceding narrative,—and clearing the
stage for a new act of the drama, to be inaugurated when
Jacob, on his father's death, becomes the patriarchal head of
the chosen tribe. Hence, probably, there is introduced at
this stage, the account of Reuben's crime (ver. 22), as well as
the catalogue of Jacob's now completed family (ver. 22-26).
The church visible, as its development is about to be traced
from a new starting point, or fountain source, is now before

us, in its heads, complete,—Jacob or Israel, and the twelve sons whose names are here enumerated. It has been formed and nursed in exile; it is now to take its place in Canaan. All is told about it that is needful for our understanding its future course ;—how it has, to begin with, some foul blots,—bloody treachery staining two, and vile lust a third, of the men who are to be its representatives ;—how human sin and shame are thus blended at the outset with divine grace and love ;—and how, therefore, it need be no matter of surprise, if a history of a very chequered character, even while Jacob lives, prepares the way for the equally chequered prophecy which he is constrained to utter ere he dies.

Thus then, in the circumstances which are here brought together in this chapter,—experiencing a gracious revival,—chastened and afflicted in his dearest affections,—honoured with a last visit of God to renew and ratify his covenant,—with his family of twelve sons now complete,—but alas ! completed at the cost of Rachel's loss ;—and with Reuben's incest now superadded to the cruelty of Simeon and Levi ;—thus does Jacob find himself once more in his father's house. There he is soon, along with Esau, to close his father's eyes, and consign his last remains to the silent tomb. And thereafter he is to take his father's place as the heir of promise, and to fulfil, as best he may, with such materials as he has, the functions which that high character involves.

50

A NEW ERA—THE BEGINNING OF A NEW PATRIARCHATE

Genesis 37:1-11

These are the generations of Esau. **Genesis 36:1**
These are the generations of Jacob. **Genesis 37:2**

" THESE are the generations of;"—such is the formula—the title or heading—that ushers in each new branch, whether lineal and descending, or collateral and diverging, of the great genealogical chart or tree, which the Book of Genesis unfolds. It is the sign which marks, at successive stages, the gradual contraction of the narrative into a few, and ultimately into one alone of the innumerable streams in which the flood of human life rolls on.

Thus, first, it heads the record of the original destination of our world and our race (ii. 4). The creation of the heavens and the earth,—of all the earth's living tribes, and especially of him who is to have dominion over it and them,—having been previously narrated in the first chapter ;—history proper begins in the second. And it begins comprehensively enough ; with the all-embracing phrase ; " These are the generations of the heavens and of the earth." Again, secondly, after notices of the fall and its first fruits, applicable to all mankind ; when the genealogical history of the fallen race is to be traced in the one line of Adam through Seth ; the same formula is used,— " This is the book of the generations of Adam " (v. 1). So also, thirdly, when a new start is to be made, and amid universal defection, a fresh fountain-head of life is to be selected, it is announced in the same way,—" These are the generations of Noah " (vi. 9).

After the flood, the genealogical tree springs again from one parent stem, in a threefold ramification ; " These are the generations of the sons of Noah, Shem, Ham, and Japheth " (x. 1). But Ham and Japheth being suffered to drop aside, the interest is fixed in the lineage of Shem ; " These are the generations of Shem " (xi. 10).

Soon the choice is still farther narrowed,—and the name of Abraham's father, as representing his son, becomes the starting-point of the new branch in which the progress of the tree is to be traced ; " These are the generations of Terah : Terah begat Abram " (xi. 27).

Of Abraham's two sons, Ishmael's line is first briefly sketched ; " These are the generations of Ishmael, Abraham's son " (xxv. 12). And then, in Isaac the history of the election of grace starts afresh,—" These are the generations of Isaac, Abraham's son " (xxv. 19).

Upon the death of Isaac, the same principle of elimination out of the sacred historic stream on the one hand, and selection for it on the other hand, comes to be applied. Each of his two sons, Esau and Jacob, has his place in the genealogical tree.

The genealogy in the line of Esau is very briefly and summarily traced ; " These are the generations of Esau who is Edom " (xxxvi. 1) ; but like that of Abraham through Ishmael, it is traced with sufficient clearness to admit of its being at last historically identified. The two, indeed, as branch genealogies,—the one from Abraham through Ishmael, and the other from Isaac through Esau,—are recorded mainly with a prophetic view to such future historical identification. But, even apart from that consideration, the chapter which records the progress of Esau's house is an interesting study,—especially when viewed in the light of Isaac's dying benediction.

Look along the advancing course of Esau's posterity. See him in his families, multiplied and enriched; these families rapidly becoming dukedoms or principalities; these dukedoms, again, gathered up into a kingdom; and that kingdom reaching its culminating point, long before the kingdom for which Moses made provision in his law was even looming in the distance for Israel; for the history speaks of "kings reigning in the land of Edom, before there reigned any king over the children of Israel" (ver. 31). Such is the general outline of the rise and progress of the Idumean power which this brief and bare list of Esau's generations may suggest; and it is enough for any practical use. The minute discussion of its details, in a genealogical or ethnological point of view, is unnecessary, and would be out of place.

Esau being thus withdrawn, Jacob remains (xxxvii. 2); and along the line of Jacob's seed, the entire subsequent stream of sacred history is to flow. No more branches are to be given off,—and the branches already given off are to be noticed only in so far as they come across the current of Israel's wondrous course. The formula, as now used, "These are the generations of Jacob,"—stands henceforth alone; being the title or heading of the whole accumulating mass of inspired narrative, prophecy, proverb, and song, in which Israel's varied fortunes are embodied; till the time comes when once more the old formula is to be used to usher in a new branch of the family tree;— "The book of the generation of Jesus Christ, the son of David, the son of Abraham" (Mat. i. 1).

Jacob is now the acknowledged head of the chosen family. Isaac is dead, and Esau has removed from Canaan into the territory which his race are to occupy and inherit. It is not improbable that he had begun to look in that direction shortly after he sold his birthright to Jacob, and before the transaction of the blessing. At all events, on Jacob's return from Syria, Esau is found, not where his father Isaac is dwelling, but in settlements of his own, more or less fixed, in the country with which his name is ever afterwards to be identified. Jacob resumes his place in his father's household, and upon Isaac's death takes the position of patriarchal head over the now considerable tribe into which Abraham's seed has expanded itself. It might seem, therefore, that the dark shadows of his life should now give place to sunshine.

Alas! no. The trial of his faith is not yet complete. The old man's heart is to be pierced with fresh and bitter pangs. "These are the generations of Jacob. Joseph"— (ver. 2).

Joseph! So this new section begins,—this new stream of the genealogical history,—having its new fountain in Jacob. Joseph! With the alarm of that name is the new patriarchate or headship of the chosen family, in the person of Jacob, rung in;—even as with the alarm of the same name, after a romance of history unparalleled before or since, it is to be rung out. Joseph! The first and last, the alpha and omega, the beginning and the end, of Jacob's whole patriarchal reign!

For the interest of that patriarchal reign, (1.) as a story of human character and life, giving insight and calling forth sympathy, as no other story, either real or feigned, ever did;— (2.) as embracing a world-wide revolution, attested to be so by world-wide footprints, lasting till this day; (3.) as determining the condition of Israel's national development as a people sold into bondage and redeemed; (4) as all bearing on what really fulfilled the prophecy—" out of Egypt have I called my son ;" the interest I say in all these views of it, of the patriarchal reign of Jacob, is all centred in Joseph. "These are the generations of Jacob. Joseph"—

But in the first instance, the history of Joseph is to be viewed in its bearing personally on his father Jacob. Let the state of the patriarch's household therefore be, as far as possible, realised.

1. Before Joseph's dreams, there is a root of bitterness in

the family. Two reasons are assigned for the jealousy that
sprung up. Joseph was dreaded by his brethren as a tale-
bearer; and he was envied by them as a favourite. This
double cause of offence did the stripling of seventeen give to
his brothers, now grown to manhood.

He was a tale-bearer; "Joseph brought unto his father
their evil report" (ver. 2). Rather he was a truth-teller. As
one who was always "in simplicity a child," he naturally told
his father the incidents of each passing day. If his brethren,
—old enough, some of them, to be his father,—were accustomed, while away from home, ostensibly on the business of
tending their flocks, not only to familiarise themselves, but to
attempt to familiarise their youthful brother, with scenes and
doings which they cared not to submit to the scrutiny of the
parental eye; so much the worse for them; his mouth however cannot be shut.

But he was a favourite; "Israel loved Joseph more than
all his children" (ver. 3). Did these sons of Jacob consider
what cause might be pleaded for their aged father making a
favourite of Joseph? He was "the son of his old age;" the
first-born of his beloved Rachel,—now, alas! no more. Had
they no allowance to make for so natural a fondness?

Very evidently, however, as the whole narrative shows, it
is not as a tale-bearer, nor as a favourite, that Joseph is hated
by his brethren. The real ground of their dislike is that he
will not be one of them, and go along with them in ways
which they know that their father condemns. Their quarrel
with him is that his truth and simplicity, his piety and worth,
commend him to their father's special confidence and regard.
At all events, "when his brethren saw that their father loved
him more than all his brethren, they hated him, and could not
speak peaceably unto him" (ver. 4).

Possibly Jacob may have manifested his warm esteem for
his beloved son in an injudicious way. To listen to his reports of the evil he witnessed, instead of at once withdrawing

him from its contagion, and from the temptation to become a mere spy and informer,—that may have been Jacob's weakness or mistake. And it was a poor conceit that led him to express his affection by a costly garment (ver. 3);—if indeed it was not something worse,—conferring on the youthful object of his fondness a foolish mark of rank and distinction, that could not fail to expose him to the ridicule or rage of his older brothers. Still, there lies at the bottom of the rankling sore in Jacob's household, as its chief cause, the evil conduct of his sons; which Joseph could not tolerate or conceal; and which Jacob himself perhaps did not, or could not, control.

2. The two dreams which Joseph had introduced a new element of disquiet into the family. What weight Joseph himself attached to them, when he first told them, does not appear;—but his very openness in telling them shows that he could mean no harm. He might have kept them to himself, and watched for opportunities of realising what they seemed to foreshadow. He might have made a confidant of some shrewd adviser or crafty tool, who, being entrusted with his secret, might be a safe accomplice in any ambitious scheme his dream-heated brain might devise. But Joseph has no reserve. His brethren, whom alone it can concern, are to know all about the first dream (ver. 5-7). And as the second dream, if it means anything, points to the heads as well as the members of the family, it is dutifully communicated to his father also (ver. 9, 10).

Such fraternal and filial frankness should have disarmed suspicion and hostility. Whatever there may be in these dreams, beyond midnight fancy's fairy and fantastic tricks,— whatever of supernatural significancy, and anticipation of the future,—Joseph surely is not to be blamed. He could not help having the dreams;—and he does all that could be asked or expected of him, when he hastens to put all the household in possession of them.

That Joseph did right in communicating his dreams,—

seeing that they were meant not only for himself but for the whole household,—can scarcely be doubted. The communication of them, however, was not welcome ; it gave dire offence to his brethren (ver. 8). His father also was at first displeased, or rather perhaps only surprised. For, one is inclined to ask, was it really in anger, or was it by way of dissembling, under colour of irritation, a secret satisfaction at the high prospect opening up before his favourite son, that the patriarch so mildly "rebuked" the lad's seemingly insolent aspirations— "What is this dream that thou hast dreamed ? Shall I, and thy mother, and thy brethren, indeed come to bow down ourselves to thee to the earth ?" (ver. 10). At all events, while " his brethren" simply " envied him," " his father observed the saying" (ver. 11). Jacob kept it in his mind, treasured it in his memory,—pondered what might come of it, and whereto it might grow ;—as Daniel did with reference to the vision of the four beasts, and as Mary did with reference to the visit of the shepherds at the birth of Jesus, and the saying of Jesus himself, when he was twelve years old, in the temple. Evidently, therefore, he attached importance to the intimation given in the dreams as to things to come. And the reflection is apt to arise,—If he and his other sons had received the intimation in faith, as coming from the Lord, and so far acted upon it as to wait in humble patience for the issue—what sin and suffering might have been averted from the chosen family ! But, alas ! unbelief prevailed. Jacob may perhaps have been prepared to bow to the will of God ; but the brethren of the good and godly youth, so evidently favoured of the Lord, envied him and hated him the more. For these great divine lessons were still to be taught by the eventful history of Joseph,—that the heart is deceitful above all things, and desperately wicked,—that they who will live godly in Christ Jesus must suffer persecution,—that the righteous must through much tribulation enter into glory.

51

THE MISSION TO DOTHAN—THE PLOT—THE SALE

Genesis 37:12-36

He came unto his own, and his own received him not.   John 1:11

In the history of Joseph's strange career the particular providence of God is most signally illustrated.   There is, indeed, evidence enough in the previous narrative of a wise and holy providence watching over the actions and affairs of men,—and carrying forward, by means of human agency and instrumentality, a vast and comprehensive plan for undoing the mischief of the fall, and bringing about the predicted result, that " the seed of the woman is to bruise the serpent's head."   But the march of that providence has hitherto been, as it were, along the highway of that great general divine purpose and promise, —individual and family interests being manifestly subordinate. Now, however, in the life of Joseph, what is personal carries it over what is public.   The march of providence is, as it might seem, through a bye-way.   The varied fortunes of one man, Joseph, as unfolded, not in the inheritance, nor in any movement connected with it, but in a region remote and in events remote,—not in Canaan but in Egypt ;—the vicissitudes of his chequered course ;—his biography ;—that is now the groove in which the church's history is to run.   Hence it is a biography doubly important.   It constrains us to observe the footprints of God's providence, as very specially exercised in the case of Joseph himself.   And by analogy it points to an era when once again biography prevailed to usher in and mould a new church-development.

In the manner of Joseph's descent into Egypt, — how remarkably may the typical providence of God, if one may so call it, be traced and noted.

I. Take, first, the mission of Joseph, on his father's behalf, to his brethren (ver. 12-14). That Jacob should send Joseph on an errand of inquiry about his other sons, and that Joseph should be so ready to go, might seem natural enough, did we not remember the relations in which the members of this uneasy household stood to one another. But has Jacob forgotten the evil report which, in his honest and childlike simplicity, Joseph had brought of his brethren, and the offence which that had given? The robe of honour, also, with which his partiality had adorned his favourite son, and the jealousy and envy which that mark of distinction, however well deserved, had occasioned,—and the dreams, so artlessly told and so angrily listened to—is all that overlooked? Has the previous conduct of these men been such as to warrant Jacob in relying on their generosity and forbearance, when he commits to their tender mercies the object of his own love and of their hatred?

But perhaps he thinks to melt them by this proof of his interest in them, and of his beloved son's interest in them. They have been away from home—possibly for a considerable time. It would appear, too, that they have been in trying circumstances. The necessity of going farther than they intended, and the dryness of the pit into which they let down Joseph, point to drought, or scarcity of some kind, as having forced them to move on and seek food for their cattle. They had thus been, in a sense, exiles from the parental roof, and they had encountered difficulties. The father's heart yearns towards them. Their hard and stubborn nature may have been melted by what they have had to undergo. A visit of their young and amiable brother, charged with a message of tender fatherly affection, may be the very thing to put an end to all misunderstanding and animosity, and to effect a cordial and complete reconciliation. So Jacob proposes, and Joseph accepts, this mission of family peace. So "he came unto his own, and his own received him not."

II. There is a special providence also in the fact or circumstance of Joseph's brethren having gone away beyond the place where he first expected to find them (ver. 15-17). Possibly, if they had remained at Shechem, they would not have ventured on the crime which they committed. They could not have so easily concealed it from their father. He was a proprietor there; and in spite of the horrid cause of offence given in the case of Dinah, he must by this time have so far accommodated matters with prince and people, as to have his right of occupancy in the land which he had bought acknowledged and respected. Considering the means of communication which their father must have had open with Shechem, the brethren of Joseph, if it had been there that he had fallen into their hands, could scarcely have hoped to keep their cruel treatment of him secret. But it was so ordered that they had to move farther off. Had they Jacob's sanction for the movement? Apparently not. Whatever reason they might have for quitting Shechem, they should surely have either returned home, or sought instructions from home, before resolving on a journey beyond it. They were not found where their father had a right to expect that they would be found, when he sent their younger brother on his errand of affectionate inquiry about their welfare. And if he had been his father's unwilling messenger, or if he had been indifferent about his brethren to whom he was sent, he might have stopped short at Shechem; he might have been justified in going back from thence to his father, and simply reporting his having failed to find his brethren there. But no. He acts not merely according to the letter, but in the spirit, of the commission which he has received. He longs to carry to his brethren, however far away, the tidings and tokens of a father's loving care for them.

He will not desist from his undertaking, or give up his errand, to whatever destiny it may lead him. He must go to his brethren wherever they may be, and cheer them with a voice from home. He wanders up and down in search of them ; and hearing, as it were, by chance, to what place they talked of removing when they quitted Shechem, the tenderly nurtured youth, fresh from his father's bosom, and with the fond pledge of his father's affection upon his shoulders, hesitates not a moment :—" Joseph went after his brethren, and found them in Dothan" (ver. 17).

III. It is noticeable that Dothan should be the place to which Jacob's sons had gone, and at which Joseph found them. It was in the line of the ordinary traffic between Syria and Egypt. Already there was a brisk trade carried on, chiefly by the Ishmaelites and other Arab tribes, such as Midianites, associated with them, for the exchange of oriental, perhaps Indian, commodities,—chiefly spices and such like luxuries,— with the costly and curious fabrics of Egyptian manufacture. Then, as now, the trade was conducted by merchants travelling in companies, with camels and caravans, fully furnished and equipped for defence as well as for the march. It was of the Lord's special ordering surely, that, unintentionally on their part, and against what either Jacob or Joseph could have anticipated, the men of Israel had betaken themselves to the very spot where the means of conveyance into Egypt were to come in their way. It is the spot where Joseph, by a providential coincidence as to time also, as well as place, can best be delivered into the hands of the Gentiles.

IV. The manner in which he came to be actually delivered into the hands of the Gentiles, is, in all its details, specially providential (ver. 18-20).

(1.) The conspiracy against him, before he joins them, is in this view to be noted. It is very emphatically put—" And when they saw him afar off, even before he came near unto them, they conspired against him to slay him" (ver. 18-20).

They would not wait to learn what he had to say ; they would not give him a hearing. And yet they could not but know and feel that it was in no unfriendly, or unkindly, or unbrotherly spirit, that he was coming to them. A mere stripling, unarmed and unattended, he commits himself to them, without suspicion and without fear. The very simplicity of his having on him the much-grudged robe of honour, the badge of his father's love, might make his brothers sure that it is on an errand of love his father has sent him. Why is he here, so far from home ? Can it be for any other than a purpose of love ? But these dreams ! This dreamer ! He to be our Lord ! He to be king of the Jews ! Away with him ! Crucify him ! So there is a conspiracy. And it is of the Lord's special providence that there is a conspiracy. His typical purpose, if one may so call it, is thus accomplished.

For it might have been otherwise ; the rage of Joseph's brethren might have broken out suddenly in an outburst of violence after he had come among them. Joseph's peaceful approach might have disarmed for the moment their hostility ; and the movement against him might have been the result of a subsequent storm of passion.

But that was not to be the manner of Joseph's being delivered into the hands of the Gentiles ; there must be deliberation, contrivance, treachery ; a plot ; a sale. It is neither by being cast from the brow of the hill on which Nazareth stands,—nor by being tumultuously stoned,—that he whom Joseph represents and typifies is to go down to the depths. He is to be conspired against ; plotted against ; betrayed ; sold.

(2.) The stratagem of Reuben is also of the Lord (ver. 21-25) ;—not of course in the sense of its being suggested or inspired by the Lord, but in the sense of its being providentially ordered and overruled by the Lord. It serves the purpose of gaining time. He deprecates the shedding of blood, and suggests the casting into the pit ; intending, though of course he concealed his intention, "to deliver Joseph to his father again."

That it should have been Reuben who in this instance showed such consideration for his father is not a little remarkable. The last thing we read of him is his commission of his horrid sin ; the sin which lost him his birthright prerogative, and brought upon him, long after, his dying father's sad prophetic denunciation (chap. xlix. 3, 4). It may have been the recollection of that very wrong ;—and something perhaps in the way his father took it,—for the narrative of the crime, though very brief, has a certain strange significancy,—" And Israel heard it "—betokening the agony of silence, shame, and sorrow ;—it may have been this that occasioned the relenting of Reuben's heart now. He will not inflict a new stab in his father's tortured bosom. He will not do him a second wrong, —more cruel, in some aspects of it, than the first. He will be no party to the child's murder. He will deliver him out of the hands of those who thirsted for his blood.

But how ? Remonstrance, he well knows, will be vain. No appeal to their brotherly affection, their human pity, their filial duty, will avail. But their prudence may be called into exercise ; their fear may be aroused. By all means let this dreamer of dreams die ; surely it is meet that he should perish rather than dream himself into domination and us into bondage. Yes ! Let him die. But not after the coarse and clumsy fashion you propose. You would slay him with your own hands, and so stain them with blood which may betray you. Nay, rather, let his death be such as may pass for accidental. Here is a pit, or well—dry, for it is summer, and there has been drought. What more likely than that the boy, wandering about in search of us, should have stumbled unawares upon it and fallen into it ? When we are gone from the place, no marks of violence will remain to witness against us. Possibly none may ever discover the body but the birds that are to prey upon it. Or if any passer-by should hear a faint dying moan, and, looking down, should see a fair child breathing his last in solitary anguish,—he will but lament his inability to help him, and with a sigh of sorrow over his sad and untimely fate, go on his way musing on the vicissitudes of human life.

The suggestion of Reuben pleases the brothers and is promptly acted upon. Joseph, amid what tears and entreaties on his part, it is left to imagination to conceive,—enough to melt a heart of stone, any hearts but those that should have been the most open to embrace him,—Joseph lies deep down, along the cold and slimy bed, on which he is to experience the lingering torment of thirst and hunger, till nature sinks and death relieves him. The brothers at the pit's mouth sit down to their repast with what appetite they may.

"Woe to them that drink wine in bowls, and anoint themselves with the chief ointment; but they are not grieved for the affliction of Joseph" (Amos vi. 6). Such is the indignant utterance of the prophet, referring, ages after, to this old historical scene, as the type of the worst kind of spiritual insensibility, and carnal, selfish, devilish hardness of heart.

(3.) The arrival of the caravan of travelling merchants is clearly of the Lord (ver. 25-28). They come in good time. The heartless and unfeeling murderers,—for they were so in intent, and virtually, even in act,—are beginning to have some misgivings. Judah probably speaks the mind of all,—at least he carries their consent. He does not propose that they should undo what they have done; he is no preacher of repentance; to such preaching they will not listen. But a compromise may be expedient. They will not be the actual crucifiers of their brother; Joseph leaves their hands unharmed. All that they do is to rid themselves of one whose presence has become intolerable. Let those who receive him now be answerable for him. "Judah said unto his brethren, What profit is it if we slay our brother, and conceal his blood? Come and let us sell him to the Ishmeelites, and let not our hand be upon him ; for he is our brother, and our flesh. And his brethren were content."

So the sin of man-selling is palliated. The men take credit for not slaying, but merely selling Joseph,—because, forsooth, "he is our brother and our flesh!" And so, in after years, Judas and the Jews may have tried to satisfy or silence conscience ;—Judas, when he sold his Master for thirty pieces of silver ;—and the Jews, when they first made themselves parties to the sale, and then gave Jesus over into the hands of Pilate !

52

SINFUL ANCESTRY OF " THE HOLY SEED "—GRIEF IN CANAAN—HOPE IN EGYPT

Genesis 38 (and 37:25-36, 39:1)

Let God be true, but every man a liar. Romans 3:4

THE narrative of sin and shame in the thirty-eighth chapter comes in as a somewhat strange parenthesis, or interruption, in the history of Jacob's patriarchate, or patriarchal reign, as it unfolds itself in the adventures of Joseph.   There is, however, a break at the stage at which this sad story about Judah is introduced.   The scene is about to be shifted from Canaan to Egypt.   From this point Canaan, as it might seem, is, in the meanwhile, lost sight of.   What is going on there is noticed only incidentally, as it were, and in subordination to the march of events and the fortunes of Joseph in Egypt. No doubt, as is soon made evident, the reverse of that is the real truth of the case.   It is only in relation to Canaan, as the inheritance of Abraham's seed, that Egypt has any importance at all, in the view of inspiration.   Still, in fact, for a season Egypt, and not Canaan, is to be the arena on which, as " in the heavenly places," there is to be " made known to the principalities and powers, by the Church, the manifold wisdom of God " (Eph. iii. 10).

The account of this affair of Judah's finishes and disposes of the Canaan line of march.   It is indeed a melancholy finale for the present—a most dishonourable close.   Dating from the time of Abraham's first setting his foot in Canaan, to the time

of Joseph's first appearance in Egypt, it is an eventful and interesting voyage along the stream of time that has been presented to our view. And now, when the vessel that carries
the Church and her fortunes—may I not say Christ and his
fortunes,—passes or is transported from the land of the Jordan
to the land of the Nile, a dismal catastrophe occurs,—a sad
enough wreck or waste is left.

The story told in the thirty-eighth chapter very probably
had its beginning before the events recorded in the thirty-
seventh ; for we cannot interpret very strictly the phrase " at
that time," or about that time (ver. 1) ;—unless, indeed, we
hold it to intimate, what we may regard as true, that the consummation of the story occurred cotemporaneously, or nearly
so, with the sale of Joseph.

Reuben, Simeon, and Levi, the three elder brothers of
Judah, having justly incurred the forfeiture of their privileges,
—Reuben by his invasion of his father's bed,—Simeon and
Levi, by their cruel treachery in avenging Dinah's fall,—Judah
stands now, naturally, first in the order of hereditary preference among the sons of Jacob. The pre-eminence, judging
after the flesh, belongs to him. But, as if to make it conclusively and clearly evident that the flesh must give place to the
spirit, and nature to grace, Judah also is found to have made
shipwreck of his integrity. He too has fallen.

How he was led astray at first, being induced to quit the
company of his brethren, by his fond and rash preference for
one of the people of the land (ver. 1); how that unwise and unwarrantable friendship issued in his marriage with the daughter
of a Canaanite (ver. 2-5) ; how the fruit of that marriage was
foul and loathsome sin, bringing two sons in succession to
an untimely end (ver. 6-10) ; how his breach of engagement
as to his third son moved his widowed daughter-in-law to
have recourse to so scandalous a stratagem as to be almost
unparalleled, for redressing the wrong done to her (ver. 11-16);
how Judah's unbridled lust, he being now a widower, and

no longer young, laid him open to the woman's wiles (ver. 15-23); how he was compelled to own his sad fault, and if not to justify his partner in guilt, at least to condemn himself more than her (ver. 24-26); and how ultimately he seems to have so far repented as to avoid any repetition of his iniquity (ver. 26);—all these things are written for our learning; being fitted to suggest practical lessons of private and personal morality as important as they are obvious. But there are two points of interest to be noted as regards the more public bearing of this narrative on the divine plan of providence and grace.

1. The practice afterwards sanctioned in the Mosaic economy, by what is called the law of the Levirate (Deut. xxv. 5), is recognised as already in use in the chosen family;—and the reason of it is not obscurely indicated. It would seem that it was not a practice that commended itself as suitable or welcome to the natural man,—to a mind imbued with merely natural notions, and without faith in the Messianic promise which Abraham and his house had to grasp. Judah's sons by his heathen wife were themselves, we may well suppose, more heathen than Israelite. Hence the younger brother did not care to take his elder brother's widow to wife, on the understood condition of his first-born being reckoned that elder brother's child,—so "raising up seed to his brother." The unnatural crime by means of which the wicked and wretched young man sought, and sought successfully, to defraud his deceased brother and defeat his father's ordinance —or rather the ordinance of his father's God,—while it stands out conspicuously, in the record of its swift and terrible doom, as a warning against all abuse of appetite,—is, at the same time, a proof of the depth and strength of his repugnance to what was required of him as an act of fraternal duty. And hence it may serve to show that the chosen family of Israel must have been reconciled to the custom, and to the enactment of it in a statute, by some peculiar consideration.

Nor is it difficult to see what that was. Every true-hearted son of Abraham cherished the eager hope that he might be the ancestor of the promised Messiah—the seed of the woman that was to bruise the head of the serpent. To die childless, therefore, was not merely the disappointment of a natural desire and expectation,—it was a cause of regret in a far higher point of view. Hence the suitableness of the younger brother being commanded to repair the defect, by taking his elder brother's widow to wife, and raising up seed to him by her. It was an appropriate office of brotherly love, inasmuch as it substantially secured to one prematurely taken away, his name and standing among the fathers of the families of Israel. Thus there was a special reason for the practice among the posterity of Abraham before the birth of Christ ;—a reason, however, manifestly partial and temporary ;—not applicable to mankind universally, nor to any portion of mankind, now that Christ is born.

In the present instance, the reason comes out very clearly. The family in which the practice was to be observed, was that of Judah, of whom Christ was actually to be born ; so that, over and above the sin, in the sight of God, of the pollution done to himself, the offence of Judah's second son, as against his deceased brother, was very highly aggravated. It went to rob him of the honour, which he might otherwise have had, of being held in law to be the progenitor of the promised Saviour,—even of him in whom all the families of the earth were to be blessed. To make this still clearer—

2. As it turned out in point of fact, it was through this very woman, the widow of Judah's first-born, whom the younger son so infamously wronged, that the descent of the Messiah, according to the flesh, was to be traced. This woman of Canaan is to be the mother of the promised seed (Mat. i. 3).

Strange! That from such an incestuous connection, to which she knowingly tempted her father-in-law, and into which he unwittingly fell, there should spring—" such an high priest as became us, holy, harmless, undefiled, and separate from sinners!" Is it not strange indeed?

Strange! Nay, not more strange than that he should have compassion on that other woman of Canaan, who in the days of his flesh wrestled with him, and refused to let him go, until he blessed her. That in his genealogy he should be mixed up with human sorrow and human sin, is a fitting type of his being, when he comes, a man of sorrows,—a friend of publicans, and sinners,—calling not the righteous but sinners to repentance. This blot upon his escutcheon,—this bar-sinister across his crest,—this blight in his family tree,—this taint of heathenism and of harlotry in his ancestral blood,—is ordained of set purpose. It is ordained, to abase the lordly pride and pomp of lineage the most renowned,—to put a mockery on earth's highest glory. It is ordained also, to mark the grace and condescension of the Most High,—who gives his holy and beloved Son,—that Son most freely consenting,—to be one of our unclean and guilty race, and to come—all holy and righteous as he is in himself—into personal contact and conflict with its guilt and its uncleanness;—" his own self bearing our sins in his own body on the tree, that we being dead to sins, should live unto righteousness " (1 Peter ii. 24).

And now, look, on the one hand, at the closing scene of one act of the drama in Canaan; and on the other, at the opening of the next in Egypt.

I. (xxxvii. 29-36), Joseph is gone. The feast at the pit's mouth is over. The bargain is struck and the money paid. The captive boy,—with what tears and struggles on his part! with what specious apologies on the part of his brothers!—is carried away. He may be thankful that it is no worse; that instead of being left miserably to perish amid slime and filth, he is only sold into bondage in Egypt. It is the finest country in the world,—with the widest scope for action,—where surely,

if there be anything in those dreams of his, he may somehow
find the means of distinguishing himself ;—and without claiming any unseemly lordship over his father and his father's
house, gratify his ambitious aspirations to the utmost. At all
events, they are well rid of him now, for good. And the best
of it is that they are rid of him without having his blood upon
their hands.

But their task is not over. They must devise some cunning tale,—some plausible lie,—to account for Joseph's disappearance.

First, Reuben must in some way be satisfied. For he, as
it would seem, had withdrawn from their company, after he
had succeeded in persuading them to use the pit, rather than
the knife ; and in all probability without waiting to see them
act on his advice. For, even though he means to rescue his
young brother (ver. 21, 22), he shrinks from witnessing the
cruel treatment he is to receive. He cannot stand by while
these strong men so roughly seize and strip the lad, and cast
him helpless into so loathsome a dungeon. On some plea or
other, he excuses himself from joining in their plot and their
repast, and retires into some secret place, intending to return when they are gone,—to save the lad's life and restore
him to his father. He does return, after allowing them, as he
supposes, time enough to finish their feast. He comes upon
them still where he had left them,—their business with the
merchants having detained them. Perhaps they are in the
very act of counting or concealing their gains. He expects to
discover Joseph in the pit ; and when he finds the pit empty,
it is a cry of real and bitter anguish that bursts from his lips,
as, "rending his clothes, he returns unto his brethren and
says, The child is not ; and I, whither shall I go ?" (ver. 30).

How is this cry to be met ? How are these murderers in
heart, man-sellers in act, to evade the keen questioning, and
face the righteous wrath, of their elder brother ?—now, especially, when his vehement grief confirms, what from his absence

they may have begun to suspect before,—that he meant to assume the office of Joseph's protector and deliverer? Do they make him privy to the transaction of the sale? Do they tell him that Joseph lives, and is on his way to push his fortune in Egypt? That is not said, and does not appear from the narrative. On the contrary, long afterwards, when Reuben is bringing home to their consciences,—and they are taking home to their consciences,—this crime of theirs, as explaining and justifying the Lord's judgment upon them, he assumes apparently the death of Joseph (xlii. 22). Perhaps they tried to deceive him by the same trumped up falsehood by which they were soon to impose upon their father. And it is possible that Reuben may have been thus deceived, and that he may have again left their company, under that impression, sad and sorrowful, to weep alone, before they proceeded to put their vile trick into execution (ver. 31, 32). At the same time, it is not easy to acquit him of all blame ; for he could scarcely be altogether satisfied by such a story. He was well aware of the murderous intentions of these men, and must have had some suspicion that in some way or other they had found means to carry them into effect. He may not have been a party to the device of the kid's blood staining the coat, any more than to the crime which that device was meant to cover. He may have believed that the blood was really Joseph's. But was it indeed shed by a wild beast, and not by those who avowedly sought the child's life? At all events, Reuben does not reveal at home all that he knows. He allows his brothers to tell their tale, and lets it pass for the truth, and all the truth, in silence. Is not his silence, however procured, sin ?

Thus with the intent of blood upon their consciences,— the price of blood in their hands,—and a cruel lie in their lips, these patriarchs and heads of houses in Israel return home to their father.

Their story is at once believed: "It is my son's coat; an evil beast hath devoured him; Joseph is without doubt rent in pieces" (ver. 33). Such an accident is but too probable,—considering the wild country into which Joseph, in pursuit of his brethren, had wandered. The bereaved parent is utterly cast down: "Jacob rent his clothes, and put sackcloth upon his loins, and mourned for his son many days" (ver. 34).

In vain his family gather round him to suggest the ordinary topics of consolation,—some of them hypocritically perhaps at first,—but soon even the worst of them, after a sort, sincerely (ver. 35). For they are scarcely prepared, these hard and cold men, for the deep and lasting grief into which they have plunged their father; they had not anticipated that the blow would fall so heavily. It was, as they represented it, a providential dispensation; a sad enough affliction, no doubt, but one "common to man,"—the loss of a darling child, by a calamity that could not have been prevented or helped by any human foresight, skill, or strength. So, they imagined, the event must have looked in their father's eyes; and they might have expected therefore that he would manifest the meek patience and submission of faith, and say, "It is the Lord, let him do what seemeth good." And then it is but one of a large family that is gone. His house is still firmly established for generations to come. He has even one pledge left of his lost Rachel's love,—her Benoni,—his Benjamin. And the promised seed continues to be safe.

But the bereaved father "refuses to be comforted;" the hurt is not lightly healed. The wound inflicted on his tenderest affections is incurable on this side the tomb: "And he said, For I will go down into the grave unto my son mourning. Thus his father wept for him" (ver. 35).

Ah! have his sons no misgivings now—no relentings? Would they have done what they did, if they had foreseen all this agony of a parent's soul? But the deed is beyond recal. They cannot bring Joseph back; they dare not even hint that he may be yet alive; they will not retract their lie. Could they hope to be believed if they did? Joseph, at all events, is as much lost to his old father as if he were " without doubt rent in pieces." It would be no kindness to undeceive Jacob, and so substitute for a painful sense of irretrievable loss, a still more painful suspense, never to be either satisfied or ended. Therefore they may think that they do well to keep silence. Even Judah holds his peace. They can but join their efforts to those of Reuben. His sympathy at least is real. But alas! is his offence forgotten? Can the wronged and outraged parent listen to the soothing words of one who has so recently wrought him such disgrace? And can he fail to detect, under the soothing words of the others,—however they may now be, on the whole, sincerely anxious to comfort him — occasional gleams of satisfaction in their countenances, at the thought of Joseph being got rid of?

So, in spite of sons and daughters rising up to comfort him, the bereaved father continues to weep for Joseph.

For Judah also he is now called to weep, if possible, still more bitter tears. The fruit of his miserable transgression is now coming to light. All in the chosen household is sin, sorrow, shame.

One only sign of good is there in it, and that is as yet secret. The ancestor of the Messiah is born ; alas ! under no promising auspices, judging after the flesh. The holy seed is still the substance of the smitten and ravaged tree (Isaiah vi. 13).

Thus the curtain falls on the last scene of the drama for the present in Canaan.

II. It rises,—and another scene, or succession of scenes, opens to view. Lo ! a company of merchants marching through the wilderness ; and in the midst of them a young lad, with bleeding feet and streaming eyes, bound, footsore, weary, a servant, a slave (xxxvii. 36). And lo ! again, a

youth of promise, in a lordly mansion, on the road to preferment and the highest honour (xxxix. 1-6.)

But first, once more, Behold a prisoner, falsely charged
with crime,—wearing out long days in a prison-house, and yet
even there seen and known to be without fault.

And finally, Behold this wronged and afflicted one,—
justified, exalted, raised to reign over all the land, to wield all
royal sovereignty and power,—to be " a light to lighten the
Gentiles, and the glory of his own people Israel."

53

HUMILIATION AND TEMPTATION YET WITHOUT SIN

Genesis 39:1-23

He sent a man before them, even Joseph, who was sold for a servant;
whose feet they hurt with fetters; he was laid in iron. Psalm
105:17,18

THE lessons to be learned from the life and adventures of
Joseph, considered simply as a matter of human history, or of a
divine history of human experiences, lie on the very surface of
the narrative; so much so that the business of drawing them
out, and setting them in formal didactic array, is apt to
become trite and tedious. For the most part, indeed, comment serves rather to weaken than to enforce the teaching of
the Spirit in this matchless biography. It really tells its own
tale, and suggests its own moral throughout, so clearly and so
pathetically, that it might seem best to leave it to make its
own impression, undiluted and unadulterated by the reflections, however sound, of ordinary exposition.

But Joseph can scarcely be considered simply in his individual character or capacity. He must be viewed as standing in
a very peculiar relation to the church of God, as then represented
by the chosen family of Abraham. In a very special sense,
and in a very unusual manner, the church is bound up with
him;—her history with his, and her prospects with his. In
him and through him, she is to undergo a very special course
of discipline, and to pass through a most momentous and significant change or crisis. Virtually, for a time, the church, as

to her trials and hopes, is identified with him. Joseph in Egypt is working out the problem of her earthly progress.

Hence, it is almost impossible not to regard Joseph as sustaining, more than any of the other patriarchs, a sort of Messianic character, executing Messianic offices, and passing through Messianic experiences.

It is not merely that ingenuity may trace in what befel Joseph much that may be represented as analogous to what we find recorded in the gospels concerning Christ. Resemblances of a more or less typical character cannot fail to be observed between him and Christ, and between his varied life and Christ's, by the most literal and unimaginative commentator. I cannot but think, however, that we have to recognise a closer bond of union than that which such incidental coincidences might establish between Joseph and Jesus. Beforehand, we might anticipate, I apprehend, a parallelism between the two biographies, because the two subjects of them are themselves closely parallel, and intimately associated with one another. In this view, it might almost be said, with literal truth, that Joseph is the Jesus of the Old Testament church's history. In him, as in Jesus, the church is represented and developed.

The full truth and meaning of this virtual identification of the two may come out more clearly as the examination of the sacred narrative proceeds. I advert to the subject now, as explaining the method which I adopt in opening up the record which the chapter under review contains—I. of Joseph's first appearance in Egypt in a low estate; II. of his nobility of nature being even there, from the beginning, recognised; III. of his manifold and complex temptation; IV. of his suffering what was to him almost worse than death, through his refusal to yield when tempted; and V. of his being owned—even in the lowest depths—as one chosen and beloved of the Lord.

Thus the humiliation of Joseph in Egypt may be traced in several of its successive features and stages somewhat significantly.

I. Joseph first appears in Egypt in the low estate of a servant ; "Potiphar, an officer of Pharaoh, captain of the guard, an Egyptian, bought him of the hands of the Ishmaelites, which had brought him down thither" (ver. 1). His being found in that condition at all is noticeable. It is not his original, natural condition ; it is one into which he is brought in a specially remarkable manner,—by a train of events and circumstances altogether out of the ordinary course of things,— by his being subjected to treatment to which, in his own proper sphere, he never could have been exposed. He himself, after-wards, in looking back to it, ascribes his coming into the position of a servant in Egypt to a special divine act or appoint-ment,—when he says to his brethren :—" Be not grieved nor angry with yourselves that ye sold me hither ; it was not you that sent me hither, but God" (xlv. 8). It is noticeable, too, that he puts this construction upon his being made a servant, in subordination to a divine purpose of mercy and salvation to be accomplished by that means ;—" to preserve life ; to save your lives with a great deliverance." In point of fact, as we have seen, this change in his condition took place when he was on an errand of kindness to his brethren,—and an errand of kindness, moreover, voluntary and spontaneous on his part. His going on to Dothan, instead of stopping short at Shechem (xxvii. 12-17), was, so far as appears, his own act. Doubtless, he was obeying the spirit, if not the letter, of the command-ment he had received from his father. But he might have returned home from Shechem, with the report that his brethren were not there, where he had been instructed to look for them. His going farther, alone, in search of them, through a wild and savage region, involved no little toil and risk, and was a proof at once of loyalty to his father, and kindly affection towards his brethren. He was not bound to go ; it was altogether of his own accord that he went. God, as it would seem, had so arranged matters that in his visit to his brethren he should be manifestly a volunteer ; and it is in the very act of visiting them as a volunteer, that he becomes a servant. His becoming a servant may thus be viewed as forming part of a divine plan of salvation. And it is not remotely connected, so far as he himself is concerned, with an act indicating both willing obedience to his father and spontaneous goodwill to his brethren.

II. In his humiliation as a servant, his nobility of nature early and conspicuously shone forth (ver. 2-6). The grace of God,—a certain divine gracefulness,—was upon him. A certain glory also,—a certain air of distinction,—bespeaking a higher origin and rank, distinguished the young Hebrew from the beginning. He grew in favour with God and man. " The Lord was with Joseph, and he was a prosperous man." In person and accomplishments, in mind and body, he excelled. In whatever he undertook he prospered. In the pursuits and exercises of the youth about him,—in the discipline and learning of the Egyptians,—in the tasks imposed upon him and the trusts committed to him,—he proved himself eminently successful. Evidently he was one on whom fortune smiled propitious. He won men's hearts too. He found grace in his master's sight, as he served him, and was subject to him, in all dutifulness and respectful obedience. So, in the years of ripening boyhood and opening manhood, his character unfolded itself. Through the disguise of his low servile state, glimpses of what he really was appeared. It was no ordinary personage who had come from afar to take his place among Egypt's swarthy children,—but one fairer than any of them, —one, moreover, whose very presence brought a blessing with it, in house and field,—one to whom all things that his lord had, at home and abroad, might be safely left,—one high in the esteem of heaven,—" a goodly person" also, " and well-favoured."

III. Joseph is exposed to solitary temptation,—led, as it were, by the Spirit into the wilderness, into solitude, to be tempted,—and tempted truly of a devil (ver. 7-9).

The temptation is, in the first aspect of it, an appeal to appetite,—to carnal or bodily desire,—to the hunger of youthful lust. Strong in itself, it is strengthened by its being an insidious compliment to his high birth and concealed nobility. It is as one who, although in form a servant, is really something more,—as it were, a son of God,—that he is asked to take this course,—a course ordinarily unlawful, but in the case of one such as he is, and situated as he is situated, surely not unwarrantable,—not too great a liberty. Why should not this son of God, if needful, turn stones into bread? So the terms of the trial might virtually run. It was not every one, or any one, of the servants in the house that would have received such an invitation from such a quarter. The proposal is a flattering acknowledgment of his superiority; it is a challenge to him to take advantage of the position which his acknowledged superiority entitles him to assume; to avail himself—so the matter might be plausibly represented—of the privilege which it brings within his reach. Thus subtle is the temptation as it deals with natural appetite, or the lust of the flesh.

But in another view, it is even more subtle still. Compliance might have set him on a pinnacle of luxury and pomp, from which, when he chose to condescend, or cast himself down, he would have been received by his old familiars almost as one coming from a higher sphere. The prospect doubtless was held out to him, of some exalted and brilliant position to be reached through the influence which, if he had consented, would have been at his command. Nor is it difficult to see,—if those acquainted with the ways of Eastern courts, from of old till now, tell us true,—how whatever we would think disgraceful to either party in the transaction might have been cautiously covered, or ingeniously got over, and a lavish grant of honourable place and title might have come through the tempter's wily ascendency over the very man who, as a husband, would have been so cruelly wronged by her.

Nor is even this all. If the spirit of ambition as well as the love of pleasure and of show has place in Joseph's heart, —if the possession of " all the kingdoms of the world and the glory of them" is a prize worth the having, in his esteem,—if such pre-eminence of power and influence over the civilised earth as he afterwards reached through a very different experience,—although he could not in his wildest dreams imagine it possible then,—yet if that, or more than that, in the line of universal empire, would gratify him,—what limit can be set to his tempter's ability to place him,—if only he will take counsel of her, and can keep it,—on the ladder of promotion to the right hand of what was then the throne of all thrones among mankind?

I am persuaded that I do not greatly err, in ascribing to the temptation of Joseph this complex, threefold character,—making it turn on these three principles or elements of the world's antagonism to God,—"the lust of the flesh, the lust of the eyes, and the pride of life." In the view of the relative position of the parties, and the whole circumstances of the case, it may be regarded as all but certain that such prizes as I have indicated were held out to the Jewish captive as the rewards of compliance, and held out by one who might well be believed to have the power of making even so great promises good.

On the other hand, it is equally obvious that the too probable consequences of declinature must have been present to Joseph's mind. He was too clear-sighted not to perceive that such blandishment, if withstood, might, or rather must, turn to resentment and revenge. Satan, the prince of this world, having tried the wiles of flattery in vain, will have recourse to threats and violence. The short and easy road of pleasure, pomp, and power, being in faith and godly fear conscientiously declined, it is but too obvious, as the only other side of the alternative, that Joseph must lay his account with meeting wrath to the uttermost. And if ever the promise of those early dreams of his, which he so simply told, and which his father counted so worthy of observation, is to be realised, it can only be through even deeper shame and sorrow than he has yet endured. It can only be through much tribulation that he is to enter into his glory. He is to be tried and perfected by suffering.

IV. The narrative of Joseph's disgrace (ver. 17-20) is not to be discredited because similar narratives occur in profane or uninspired literature, whether poetical or historical,—legendary or authentic. That only shows how true, alas! to nature,—to female nature, corrupted, abandoned, and debased, —is the conduct ascribed to the foiled and disappointed agent in this crafty plot of Satan against the righteous.

Charged with odious and heinous iniquity; laden with the accusation of a crime against the God whom he professed to serve, and an offence against the ruler in whose house he was; condemned, not justly,—for "this man has done nothing amiss,"—but on false testimony, Joseph has to bear the doom of the sin imputed to him, and to expiate its guilt, by enduring a sentence almost worse than death. For to his pure mind and tender heart,—to a soul so sensitively alive as his was to the honour of Jehovah and the sanctity of his law, and so prompt in its recoil from the very idea of disaffection or disloyalty to the master under whom he lived,—the disgrace of such an infamous imprisonment,—the reproach of such a cross,—must have been little short of prolonged agony and torture of the cruellest kind.

Whether or not the abridgment of his liberty was accompanied with any of those aggravating circumstances of cruel barbarity which are but too common, in such instances, under tyrannical power, subordinate or supreme, would be comparatively a small matter for him. The history speaks of his being put in a part of the prison " where the king's prisoners were bound;"—and again, of his being in "the dungeon" (xl. 15; xli. 14). The Psalmist represents him as having

" his feet hurt with fetters," and as " being bound in iron."
And what sort of punishment confinement in the dungeon of
a king's prison was, may be learned from the experience of
Jeremiah (Jer. xxxviii. 6-13). In every view of it, Joseph's
fate is, at this crisis, hard and sad enough. He is brought
very low. Not only are his fair and warrantable hopes of an
honourable extrication, by the well-won favour of his patron,
from the state of servitude into which he had come, nipped
and blighted: but there he lies, prostrate, helpless,—plunged
in the mire of a loathsome cell, and the still more intolerable
mire of a vile reproach which his whole soul abhors,—himself
loaded with unmerited obloquy, and the name of that God
whom he sought to honour in the heathen's sight, wickedly
blasphemed on his account. He is indeed, as it might seem,
forsaken of all, abandoned by earth and heaven alike, and left
all alone in his anguish and agony. The arm of the ruler,
which ought to have shielded him from injustice, is by a lying
witness turned against him. Home memories rushing in
upon his heart only madden him with the thought that by
this time, where he had been so fondly cherished, so favourite,
so well-beloved a son, his name is probably never heard. All
evil mouths are open, and all evil tongues are busy, against
him. Lovers and friends have gone from him. The iron is
entering into his flesh and into his spirit. The earth is shaken
beneath him. The heavens are darkened over him. " My
God," he may cry, " my God, why hast thou forsaken me ?"
(Ps. xxii. 1.)

V. But even in the utmost depths of his humiliation, his
glory is seen (ver. 21-23). In the midst of all his sufferings
as a reputed sinner, something of the essential glory and
beauty of his nature, something of his exalted character and
rank, appears. "Certainly this was a righteous man;"—"Truly
this was the son of God; (Luke xxiii. 47 ; Mat. xxvii. 54)—
such, in substance, is the impression made on the keeper, in
whose sight the Lord gives Joseph favour. For " the Lord

was with him, and showed him mercy." He was not to be left without some witness from on high of his being indeed, in spite of all outward appearances, the Lord's chosen servant. He has the witness in himself; the Spirit witnessing with his spirit that he is a child of God, and enabling him, in the strength of conscious innocence and integrity, and in the still greater strength of the divine approval and support consciously enjoyed,—" the love of God shed abroad in his heart by the Holy Ghost being given to him,"—to resist almost "unto blood, striving against sin," and to "endure the cross, despising the shame." And out of himself, in his being recognised and acknowledged by one and another, given to him by the Lord to be the first-fruits of his pain,—won over to him in his affliction and by his affliction,—he has a testimony that, however he may be despised and rejected of men generally, he is owned by some as accepted of God. His trial, and his manner of bearing it, tell upon a few, at least, among the onlookers. From the very officer appointed to guard him,—as if it were from the Roman centurion beside the cross,—this admirable sufferer wins sympathy and approval. And soon it is to appear that his fellow-sufferers in the same condemnation are not all to prove insensible to his claims. Joseph in prison, like Jesus on the cross, is still beloved by God. And his very imprisonment, his very cross, is the occasion of his being seen and felt and owned to be so.

These, surely, are sufficiently significant indications of parallelism between the humiliation of Joseph and that of Jesus ;—enough to warrant us in viewing the events in Egypt as eminently, and in a very special sense, typical of the incarnation at Bethlehem, and the crucifixion at Jerusalem.

But the narrative, considered simply as a narrative of life and character, must not be dismissed without some notice of the double lesson which it is fitted powerfully to enforce.

1. See, young man, where your strength must lie in resist-

ing temptation ;—" How can I do this great wickedness and sin against God ?"

Joseph's previous remonstrance seems intended to influence the weak or wicked woman who is soliciting him ;—" Behold, my master wotteth not what is with me in the house, and he hath committed all that he hath to my hand ; there is none greater in this house than I ; neither hath he kept back any thing from me but thee, because thou art his wife " (ver. 8, 9). He suggests considerations which, even apart from the motives of pure religion, might have been expected to tell on an uninstructed heathen mind. The rights of his master, sacred in his eyes, ought to have been sacred in the eyes of his tempter also,—all the more because that master evidently reposed such honourable confidence in both.

But his defence for himself lies in God ;—in a prompt, abrupt, instant, and, as it were, instinctive appeal to God, as in his law forbidding this sin, and all sin, peremptorily and without room for evasion, or exception, or compromise.

It is that which puts all casuistry and sophistical special pleading aside. Joseph does not deliberate, or parley, or debate. He takes the sword of the Spirit, which is the word of God. His reply virtually is, "It is written." I dare not take into my own hands the gratifying or pleasing of myself. I dare not presume to tempt the Lord my God by venturing on unwarranted pleasure or promotion, and challenging him to keep me. I worship the Lord alone, and him only do I serve. "How shall I do this great wickedness, and sin against God?"

Ah ! let me beseech you, brother, in this spirit, to "flee youthful lusts, which war against the soul." Flee, as this tempted Israelitish youth did. Stand not to argue, or even to contend. Flee for your life. And that you may flee, at once, resolutely, with fear and trembling,— with haste and horror, —put the matter plainly, as Joseph did—" How shall I do this great wickedness, and sin against God ?"

This swift word is your only safety in any temptation.

Beware of going beyond it. Beware of beginning to question and to reason. Beware of raising specious arguments of expediency, or of possible lawfulness or excuseableness. Be decided. Be firm. And be sure that "whatsoever is not of faith is sin." Enter into no doubtful disputations. " He that doubteth is condemned if he eat." Stand fast in the only stronghold of integrity,— the abrupt, strong, honest outburst of holy zeal and indignation,— "How shall I do this great wickedness, and sin against God ?"

2. Learn to endure and hope, however dark the dungeon may be in which, through no fault of your own, perhaps for your faithfulness to God, and his law, and his truth, you may be plunged. Be sure that occasions and opportunities for glorifying God in your tribulation will open up before you. Be patient, be meek, be submissive. And wait, and watch ;— " Weeping may endure for a night, but joy cometh in the morning."

Praise the Lord then, "even in the fires;" in prison, a large room may be opened. From the cross, which you share with Jesus, a word, or voice, or influence in season, may go forth to win souls to Jesus, as well as to win friends to yourself. Be not then slow of heart to believe such gracious assurances as these ;—" Ye have not received the spirit of bondage again to fear; but ye have received the Spirit of adoption, whereby we cry, Abba, Father. The Spirit itself beareth witness with our spirit, that we are the children of God : and if children, then heirs ; heirs of God, and joint-heirs with Christ ; if so be that we suffer with him, that we may be also glorified together. For I reckon that the sufferings of this present time are not worthy to be compared with the glory which shall be revealed in us " (Rom. viii. 15-18). And think for what end it may please the Lord that you should be brought low ; what good may come to men, and what glory to God, through your being brought low. "Look not every man on his own things, but every man also on the things of others.

Let this mind be in you, which was also in Christ Jesus: who, being in the form of God, thought it not robbery to be equal with God: but made himself of no reputation, and took upon him the form of a servant, and was made in the likeness of men: and being found in fashion as a man, he humbled himself, and became obedient unto death, even the death of the cross. Wherefore God also hath highly exalted him, and given him a name which is above every name: that at the name of Jesus every knee should bow, of things in heaven and things in earth, and things under the earth; and that every tongue should confess that Jesus Christ is Lord, to the glory of God the Father" (Philip. ii. 4-11).

54

THE SUFFERING SAVIOUR—THE SAVED AND LOST

Genesis 40:1-23

This child is set for the fall and rising again of many in Israel ; and for a sign which shall be spoken against ; that the thoughts of many hearts may be revealed. Luke 2:34, 35

Then were there two thieves crucified with him ; one on the right hand, and another on the left. Matthew 27:38

THE successive steps or stages of Joseph's humiliation may be briefly recapitulated. 1. He is sent by his father on an errand of kindness to his brethren—and with his whole heart he goes on that errand, determined to seek and find them, however far they may have wandered from home. 2. He comes to his own, and his own do not receive him. A plot is formed against him the moment he appears in sight. The dreamer must be got rid of. " This is the heir; come let us kill him." 3. They will kill him, if needful, themselves. But they think it better to deliver him into the hands of the Gentiles. It is a shrewd device—like that of the Jews long after—to make Pilate do their work—to get him who came to visit them in love disposed of, not by them, but by the men of another nation. 4. Joseph is valued and sold — cheaply valued, treacherously sold. 5. As a servant he is found in Egypt, dwelling among Pharaoh's servants — and yet so dwelling among them as to give evidence of his being a child of heaven, gracious, true, and fair ; and to give promise, also, of some high destiny in store for him. 6. He is led into solitary temptation, assailed with solicitations appealing to three of the strongest principles in our human nature— appetite, ostentation, ambition;—the lust of the flesh, the lust of the eye, and the pride of life. He is virtually offered all that can gratify his utmost wishes for pleasure, pomp, and power—if he will only worship a devil. 7. His tempter, foiled in flattery, tries persecution. A liar, like him who is "a liar from the beginning, and the father of it," Joseph's assailant prevails against him by false testimony, and so succeeds in having him condemned. 8. Brought under condemnation, having guilt imputed to him, laden with obloquy, doomed to a servile punishment, Joseph is still so marked as God's own child, that amid all the darkness of his unmerited suffering, he is recognised, by the very officer appointed to carry out his sentence, as a righteous man.

Thus, with mingled evidences of grace and degradation— of a high character and a lowly state—Joseph comes to sound the depths of his appointed humiliation. And now we find him, even in the lowest of these depths—as it were, on the cross itself—still owned and honoured by God; appointed to be an arbiter of destiny, if I may so speak, to those between whom his cross stands; and that in such a manner as evidently to prepare the way for his own approaching exaltation.

It is the close of his humiliation, therefore, that is now to be considered.

Joseph in prison, at the extreme point of his humiliation, appears as the dispenser of life and death among his fellow-prisoners. He is the instrument or occasion of a decisive separation between the two whom he finds involved in the same condemnation with himself. He fixes authoritatively and conclusively their opposite destinations.

From the first, he is not altogether under a cloud; what he really is in himself, shines out from beneath his prison-garb, in spite of the drawbacks of his prison-state (ver. 1-4). Not only does he find favour,—the Lord being with him and showing him mercy,—in the sight of the keeper of the prison, —but even the captain of the guard, Potiphar himself, seems to have relented.

For it must be Potiphar who, receiving from the king the two officers with whom he is wroth, puts them where Joseph is confined, and charges Joseph with the care of them. As commanding the king's body-guard, he had charge of the state-prison,—which was indeed part of his own house,—with a subordinate keeper under him;—a common arrangement in old eastern despotisms. That being his position, it was easy for him to consign Joseph to imprisonment without trial, or with such trial as he might choose to count sufficient. And it was equally easy for him to have other state prisoners associated with Joseph, and placed under his superintendence, if he so chose. That he should have so chosen in this instance, need not appear strange or surprising. Perhaps he doubted all along the truth of the accusation against Joseph, and suspected its unworthy motive, although he felt himself constrained to yield to influence and importunity that he dared not withstand, and sacrifice to the malice of disappointed desire, one in whom he had no fault to find. Or if at first credulous, and naturally inflamed with sudden wrath, he may have begun, on cooler reflection and better information, to change his mind. Or he may have received such reports of Joseph's demeanour in prison, from his subordinate officer, as to cause a revulsion of feeling,—and his old confidence may thus be beginning to return. At all events, it is by his order and with his consent that Joseph is placed,—as it was by Pilate's order that Jesus was placed,—between the two malefactors.

In that position he was " charged with them and served them " (ver. 4). It was a double function. He waited upon them and was their attendant,—responsible doubtless in that capacity for their safe custody,—but not authorised to act as their superior,—only entitled to officiate as their servant. For they were evidently persons of some rank and consideration in Pharaoh's court,—although the precise position of each is about as hard to be ascertained as his offence ;—and as unimportant and irrelevant, for any practical purpose, if it could be ascertained. They were chiefs in their respective departments. They may have been guilty of fraud,—of what in meaner men would be called theft. Under some such accusation probably they were suffering, having Joseph between them, ready to serve and be of use to them. Thus "they continued a season in ward."

The day, however, now dawns that is to decide their respective fates. In the morning, Joseph visits them, as usual ; and finding them discomposed, he naturally asks the reason, "wherefore look ye so sadly to-day ?" Carelessly perhaps, and as a mere matter of civility, they inform him,—"We have dreamed a dream, and there is no interpreter of it." And they are somewhat startled, we may be sure, by Joseph's reply:—"Do not interpretations belong to God ? tell me them, I pray you" (ver. 6-8).

For it might well be deemed a strange reply from such a one as Joseph must have appeared to them to be. Who was he that he should dare to speak in so high a tone, and undertake so confidently what he avows to be a divine office ? A servant,—one who ministered to them in humble guise,—a prisoner,—a convict,—one whom they may have been disposed to treat with supercilious indifference or despiteful indignity,— a poor degraded Israelite,—in their proud eyes contemptible. What wonder if both of these more reputable victims of the frowns of power should have laughed to scorn the lofty pretentions of one who was more a victim than themselves ?

They may have done so, both of them, at first. But if so, one of them at least speedily relents. For we begin here to recognise a distinction between them. And the distinction is vital and fatal.

I. The chief butler, at once and unhesitatingly, told his

dream (ver. 9-15). His doing so, and the result of his doing so, are in several views not a little remarkable.

1. He acted in faith. He believed Joseph's own assurance, —for it was virtually an assurance on Joseph's part,—of his having a commission from God to interpret the dream. And it was this faith that made him tell it. It was no child's play, or holiday-sport, between Joseph and these men—no mere trick of ingenious riddle-reading and guess-work. It was not an affair of magic, or legerdemain, or vulgar fortune-telling— a conjuror practising his sleight-of-hand manœuvres and manipulations—an oneiromantist, or dream-prophet, with his jargon of symbols and occult senses, affecting to weave the idle thoughts of a tossing bed into a plausible web of fate. Joseph at least is in earnest. His trumpet gives no uncertain sound. He assumes the prophetic character, as decidedly as Daniel did when he stood before Nebuchadnezzar—or Christ when he comforted the dying thief. He undertakes to speak for God —to speak as the oracle of God. It is avowedly on that footing that he invites his companions to tell him their dreams ; he would not on any other footing encourage them to expect any satisfaction from him. And therefore, when the chief butler proceeded to act upon the invitation, it must have been from a decided persuasion, on his part, of the reality of Joseph's claim. But for some such conviction, we cannot imagine that he would have received Joseph's proposal otherwise than with ridicule and abuse. There was that, however, about Joseph which inspired confidence in his divine mission. " He spake as one having authority," and not as the soothsayers—" not as the scribes."

2. The faith thus exercised meets with an immediate recompense ; as well it may, for it is of no ordinary sort. In opening his mind to Joseph, the chief butler virtually acknowledges him as a chosen servant of God, entitled to declare his will, and on his behalf to show things to come. He does so, in spite of outward appearances and outward circumstances.

He sees through the veil of suffering and shame a divine grace and glory shining forth in this seeming culprit. The truth being its own witness—the divine Spirit in Joseph's soul making his presence there even outwardly manifest—the man perceives that he is a prophet, one whom God has sent and sealed. And he makes known to him his dream accordingly.

3. The dream and its interpretation are both of God; being God's method of revelation—the method of revelation which he saw fit on this, as on other occasions, to adopt. It is idle to be speculating about the principles and laws of this sort of divine communication; estimating the probability of the dream beforehand, or laying down the supposed rules of its subsequent explanation. To dream about a vine, with its buds, and blossoms, and clusters, and ripe grapes, and to connect all the particulars of the dream with a scene in Pharaoh's palace—the dreamer himself doing his office as cup-bearer, pressing the grapes into the cup, and giving the cup into the monarch's hands—all that may seem natural enough, and well fitted to suggest sage remarks as to the working of the mind in sleep. Any shrewd deceiver, we may be apt to think, might take the hint and gratify the credulous dupe consulting him, with a flattering prediction in the line of what was obviously running in his head. But nothing of that sort will suit the parties here, or fit into their relation to one another. There is no room for the supposition of this being anything like an ordinary case of dream-telling and dream-interpreting, after the fashion of what has sometimes been reduced almost to a system or a science—the art of turning to account man's inveterate superstitious proneness to pry into futurity. The whole must be accepted as altogether the Lord's doing.

4. It is so accepted by the chief butler himself. If it was in faith, believing Joseph to be what he professed to be, that he told him his dream at first, much more now, in faith, he must have received the interpretation of his dream as from heaven. Joseph had not said, Tell me the dream, and I will

see if I can find a possible or likely meaning in it. He had appealed to God, and announced himself as able and authorised to put God's own infallible meaning on it. It was on that understanding that the man had placed his case in Joseph's hands. Clearly, therefore, Joseph's word must have been to him as God's. "Within three days" thou shalt be, as it were, "in paradise,"—taken from the prison to the king's palace and the king's presence—no longer languishing in the torture of condemnation, but safe from wrath and high in favour. Such salvation does Joseph announce to his fellow-sufferer.

5. Is it too much for Joseph to couple with the announcement of this salvation, so simple and touching a request as this :—" But think on me when it shall be well with thee, and show kindness, I pray thee, unto me, and make mention of me unto Pharaoh, and bring me out of this house : for indeed I was stolen away out of the land of the Hebrews : and here also have I done nothing that they should put me into the dungeon " ? Can anything be more reasonable ? Can anything be more pathetic ?

It is not here, as it was in the instance of one greater than Joseph, when he spoke peace to the poor criminal hanging on a cross beside him. Then the petition to be remembered in the kingdom came from the malefactor to the Saviour; here it comes from the saviour to the malefactor. The situation is simply reversed. It is his fellow-sufferer who says to Jesus, " Lord, remember me when thou comest unto thy kingdom ;"—it is Joseph who for himself makes virtually this same request of his fellow-sufferer,—" Think on me when it shall be well with thee." There is no risk whatever, in the case of the one petition, of its being forgotten or overlooked. Alas ! there is but too much risk in the case of the other. When it is the deliverer, the saviour—for such, to all intents and purposes was Joseph's position here—who begs a favour of the party delivered, there is but too great a likelihood of his finding that he has begged it in vain. What ground for thankfulness is ours when we reflect, that the party needing deliverance, when he begs a favour of his deliverer, can never incur the hazard of any such sad disappointment!

Joseph might doubt whether the man who owed so much to him would indeed think of him when he was once himself out of the fellowship of suffering which had made them so much akin. We may be very sure that Jesus in his exaltation will remember us. It is not that we can make out a better case, or show more cause why we should be remembered. Joseph's plea is stronger far, upon the merits, than any plea of ours can possibly be. He can appeal to his blameless innocency, his spotless righteousness. He has done nothing to deserve the dungeon; he is well worthy of a better destiny. And the man to whom he appeals is surely bound to him by most affecting ties, of communion in disgrace and sorrow, and communion also in sympathy and kindness, given and received. What, in comparison, is our plea? We have well merited the worst that can befall us. And the Man to whom we appeal is he whom we have pierced! But he will not neglect our appeal to him, as we, like Joseph's friend the butler, might be found but too apt to neglect his appeal to us.

Did it depend on our remembering him—had it depended even on that penitent and pardoned thief remembering him—to fix and determine how soon Jesus should come to his kingdom,—who can tell but that he might have been left dying, or dead,—as Joseph was left languishing in the prison,—aye! to this very hour. Thanks be to God, it was the Father's remembrance of him, and not ours, that was to bring our Joseph out of his dungeon to his royal court;—to bring Jesus from his cross to his crown.

It is ours to ask him to remember us in his kingdom. Nor will he ever fail to do so.

He will not forget his having shared our imprisonment, our condemnation, our guilt and doom. All that he endured with us and for us, when he took his place beside us, and accepted as his own our criminality and our curse, must ever be fresh in his mind and heart. Joseph's fellow-sufferer might cease to think, in his prosperity, of the pains of their common distress; but our fellow-sufferer is ever mindful of the agony of the time when he made common cause with us, and bore instead of us our sin and sorrow. Therefore we may ask our fellow-sufferer to remember us with somewhat more of confidence than Joseph may have felt when he asked his fellow-sufferer to remember him. For have we not his own gracious words, —"Can a woman forget her sucking child, that she should not have compassion on the son of her womb? yea, they may forget, yet will I not forget thee. Behold, I have graven thee upon the palms of my hands; thy walls are continually before me" (Is. xlix. 15, 16).

II. The case of the chief baker stands out in sad contrast to that of his companion in tribulation (ver. 16-19). He had not been so ready to place his trust in Joseph, and to own him as entitled to speak for God. Rather, as we may too probably gather from the whole scope of the narrative, he had continued incredulous, perhaps contemptuous. When Joseph spoke so simply,—" Do not interpretations belong to God? tell me the dreams I pray you,"—he may have been inclined to rail at him, saying: If thou be such a favourite of heaven, save thyself. Wouldst thou be where thou art, if God were so with thee as to warrant thine assumption of being his mouthpiece? So this unbeliever may have derided Joseph's claim at first. But now his comrade's good fortune, as he perhaps accounts it, tempts and encourages him to try his chance. He may have the luck to get as favourable a response from the oracle; and, at all events, it can do no harm to make the experiment. He, too, will now tell his dream, and abide the issue.

Alas! it is only ominous of evil. The servant of the Lord can speak of nothing but judgment. And if the doomed man should still affect to be sceptical, and set coming wrath at defiance, three short days are enough to dispel his miserable delusion, and prove Joseph a true prophet, alike of death and of deliverance. "It came to pass the third day, which was Pharaoh's birthday, that he made a feast unto all his servants : and he lifted up the head of the chief butler and of the chief baker among his servants. And he restored the chief butler to his butlership again ; and he gave the cup into Pharaoh's hand ; but he hanged the chief baker, as Joseph had interpreted to them" (ver.20-22).

1. Thus "one is taken and another left." For that, in the first place, is a lesson to be learned from this prison-scene. It is as it was in the days of Noah ; and as it shall be also in the days of the Son of Man : "I tell you, in that night there shall be two men in one bed ; the one shall be taken and the other shall be left. Two women shall be grinding together ; the one shall be taken, and the other left. Two men shall be in the field ; the one shall be taken, and the other left" (Luke xvii. 34-36). Even so it seems good in God's sight. Any two of us may be together in the same prison or in the same palace, —in the same trial or in the same triumph,—in the same sorrow or in the same joy,—sleeping together in the same bed, —grinding together at the same mill,—working or walking together in the same field ; both apparently alike good,— both destined surely to be alike safe. But how long can we reckon on our companionship lasting? How soon and how suddenly may that saying come true ; "One shall be taken, the other left?" How does it concern every one of us, in the view of that separating and sifting day, to be looking out for himself individually. Whoever I may be with in bed, at the mill, in the field, my being with him then will avail me nothing. Let me give earnest heed myself to the things which belong to my peace, before they be for ever hid from my eyes. And let me remember the Lord's own solemn and emphatic warning : "Whosoever shall seek to save his life

shall lose it ; and whosoever shall lose his life shall preserve it (Luke xvii. 33).

2. If Joseph was " set for the fall " of one and " the rising again" of another, and "for a sign that should be spoken against that the thoughts "—if not of many yet of some— " hearts should be revealed" (Luke ii. 34, 35),—behold a greater than Joseph is here. Jesus is still set forth before our eyes, cruci- fied between two malefactors. His cross draws the line sharply between them. Both alike are sinners, breakers of the law. Both alike are guilty, justly condemned. Both alike are utterly helpless in their condemnation. But that central cross discriminates between them ! It sets them, near as they are, at infinite distance apart !

On one side is the man of broken spirit, of contrite heart, accepting the punishment of his sin, consenting to lose his life that he may preserve it,—to have no life of his own, that he may owe all his life to Christ. On the other side is he who still seeks to save his life,—who even in the jaws of inevitable death will not give in,—who will not renounce his own poor conceit of innocence, goodness, and security, and agree to accept life in Christ, as the free gift of God.

On which of these sides art thou my brother ? To which of these two crosses, on the right and on the left of Christ's cross, art thou willing to be nailed ? Wilt thou be crucified with Christ,—trusting in him, praying to him, looking to him, believing his sure word, " To-day shalt thou be with me in paradise ?" Or wilt thou be crucified without Christ,—near him, but yet without him,—setting him at naught, and thyself alone braving the terror of the Lord, of which his crucifixion is so sure and sad a presage and pledge ?

3. If Joseph said to the man whose sentence of release he had pronounced, Think of me—and if he had some good ground for thinking that his friend ought to think of him, and would think of him—how much more may he who is greater than Joseph, and who procures for us—not by the

interpretation of a dream merely but by what costs him something more than that—a sentence of release from doom and
restoration to favour infinitely more valuable than the butler
got—how much more may he, I say, prefer such a request to
us—Remember me. Surely it is a sad thing if our hearts
have not a better memory for Jesus than this man had for
Joseph. And yet what need of constant watchfulness and
prayer that such ingratitude may not be ours! And what
reason to bless God have we in the fact, that so many means
and appliances are provided for helping us always to remember
him—his blessed word ever in our hands ; his gracious gospel
preached to us ; the holy sacrament of communion ; his Spirit
taking of what is his and showing it to us.

4. If it had been Joseph who had been asked to remember
his fellow-sufferer, that asking would not have been in vain.
Jesus at all events will not suffer any one of us to say to him
in vain, " Lord, remember me, now that thou art come to thy
kingdom!" "We have not an high priest who cannot be
touched with the feeling of our infirmities."

When we appeal to him, by his remembrance of all his
own sufferings to remember us in our sufferings, the appeal
touches his heart. Remember, Lord, thy loving-kindnesses.
Call to mind all thy dealings with the sick, the sorrowful, the
poor, in the days of thy flesh. Call to mind all thine own
trials and afflictions manifold. Remember us, Lord ; and
show in thy remembrance of us that thou art " the same
yesterday, to-day, and for ever."

55

THE END OF HUMILIATION AND BEGINNING OF EXALTATION

Genesis 41:1-37

" THEN spake the chief butler unto Pharaoh, saying, I do remember my faults this day " (ver. 9). It was the day of Pharaoh's two dreams (ver. 1-8). The chief butler's remembrance of his faults that day was seasonable and providential. One would say also that his previous forgetfulness was seasonable and providential too. If his memory had been prompter and his gratitude warmer he might have spoken too soon. The story of the prison dreams, with their opposite interpretations, if he had told it immediately upon his escape from punishment and restoration to favour, would probably have been laughed to scorn by Pharaoh and his courtiers, or listened to with indifference, as an idle fancy that had beguiled the weary hours of captivity. It is otherwise received when, at the right time, it comes naturally out.

The king is greatly alarmed ; and the alarm is evidently from the Lord. " His spirit is troubled ;" and the trouble visits him in a tangible shape ; it takes the form of a well-defined dream. And there is a reduplication of the dream, for the sake of emphasis. It was in this way that the king's mind could be most directly and most deeply impressed. For he is, we may suppose, like his servants, susceptible and excitable on the subject of night visions ; apt to give shape and significancy in the morning to the vagaries of fancy haunting him in his nocturnal slumbers. And he has not usually found any difficulty in getting the professed diviners or soothsayers who frequent his court to suggest a plausible interpretation, in accordance with his own known or suspected leanings. For the most part, this game doubtless has been played between him and his wise men very safely—with reference to the trifles of the passing day—its comparatively insignificant incidents and affairs. The monarch might regulate his employment of his hours of business and recreation—he might settle how long he was to sit in council, what causes he was to try, or where he was to hunt, or how he was to beguile his vacant leisure—by what they shrewdly told him was the meaning of " his thoughts upon his bed." But now, through his own favourite and familiar method of attempting to pry into God's secrets, the Spirit of God does actually reveal to him these secrets ; and in a way fitted to move his own spirit to its utmost depths. He seizes upon what the king and all his court and kingdom would acknowledge to be a trustworthy means of divine communication. He takes into his own hands, and works for his own ends, the telegraph then and there supposed to be in use for conveying heaven's messages to earth. He turns it to account for the conveyance of a true telegraphic message. And he does so in such a manner as to authenticate unmistakeably the message, and secure for it prompt belief.

I. The effect produced on Pharaoh's mind is such as to show that his dreams are from the Lord,—that the Spirit of God is dealing with his spirit through their instrumentality. He must have had abundance of various sorts of dreams before ; many of them strange enough. He must often therefore have been bewildered and perplexed, until he got some cunning counsellor to put skilful sense, or skilful nonsense, on the riddle. But he has never been so moved before as now. The dreams are so clear, distinct, and precise,—and the coincidence between them is so marked,—as to stamp upon them a peculiar character. They are unlike the usual tangled web that imagination weaves for the slumbering soul, or the wild chimerical plots that it sometimes, with a sort of strange consistency, works out to a sort of probable issue. The double visitation, the second coming after the first with a definite waking interval between, is quite out of the ordinary course. The king cannot get rid of the idea that something very special is intended ; and in the circumstances, the idea is natural and reasonable. He is not in the position of those who have the written divine word, or even authentic divine tradition, to be their guide to a knowledge of God's will ; he has, as yet, neither inspired prophet nor inspired book to be his teacher. In the case of any who have either of these sure depositories of divine revelation to appeal to, the giving heed to dreamy portents and presages of good or evil is fond dotage. But it is otherwise with this Egyptian prince. He is to be all the better thought of for his lying open to such discoveries and lessons as it may please heaven in any way to send. In the present instance, at all events, it is impossible not to recognise a divine work in him, as well as a divine warning to him, in his dreams, and in the trouble of his spirit which they occasioned. The same Spirit inspires or suggests the dreams, and opens the heart to receive them in the manner in which he would have them to be received.

II. The impression on Pharaoh's mind is deepened by the utter helplessness of his ordinary advisers ; the magicians and all the wise men are at fault. It is not merely that they find this to be a case which so baffles the usual arts of dream-reading that they must simply give it up as an insoluble problem, a riddle that they cannot guess the answer to. I suppose they may have sometimes failed before in this game, and acknowledged their failure ;—or if they always contrived to get up some interpretation, according to some mystic science of divination, or skilful system of hieroglyphics, why did they break down now ? Why not put a bold face on their ignor-

ance, as they must have known very well how to do, and try
to satisfy the king with some plausible cast of fortune-telling ?
They were not in such straits as Nebuchadnezzar's counsellors
were reduced to ; they were not asked to divine both the
dream and the interpretation of it together ; they had the
dreams given them. Were they so poor of invention, such
bunglers in their trade, so bankrupt in ingenuity, as not to be
able among them to get up some oracle in seeming accordance
with the dreams, that might be specious enough to amuse
their master for the passing time,—and safe enough for their
credit, whatever the passing time might in the end bring forth ?
Ah ! they felt that it was not to the passing time merely that
the dreams related ; more than that ; they saw in them something altogether beyond their craft. They neither attempted
to put a meaning on the dreams,— nor to persuade the dreamer
that it was not worth his while to seek a meaning. They were
very much in the predicament of a future Pharaoh's magicians,
when they found that they could not do miracles with their en-
chantments. They were constrained to own the finger of the
Lord. Here is something which, with all our wisdom, we
cannot aspire to touch. Here is wisdom beyond ours ; wisdom
really divine. That there is a divine significancy in these
night visions they cannot deny, though what it is they cannot
say. They are reduced to silence. And their silence increases
Pharaoh's uneasiness ;—he longs for light from above.

III. At this stage, Joseph's name is mentioned to the
king (ver. 9-13). There comes into the royal presence one who
has a fault to confess, a debt of gratitude to discharge, and
good news to tell. Two years have passed since the memorable prison scene, when he and his companion had their opposite
destinations announced to them by Joseph. For two years he
has been basking in the sunshine of royal favour, all unmindful, alas ! of him whom he once hailed as his deliverer, and
who was still, in spite of his pathetic petition, left to languish
unheeded in disgrace and sorrow. The perplexity at court

awakens this forgetful man. His royal master's spirit is troubled, and they who usually minister to his peace are at fault. It is the very occasion for Joseph's interference. And why is not Joseph here? Why have I not introduced him to the king's notice long ago? For anything I can guess, if I had remembered him, Joseph might have had already a place near the king, entitling him to do the same office to him that he so happily did to me. At all events the time has fully come now. In the attitude of a penitent,—not taking credit to himself for what he has to say to the king about Joseph, but only lamenting bitterly that he has not said it long before,—he comes now to bear his late, but yet seasonable, testimony. It is the testimony of a believer,—of one believing in Joseph, and in Joseph's God,—so far at least as to own Joseph as a prophet. It was in the name of God,—it was as one acting on behalf of God, and by the authority and inspiration of God,—that Joseph announced to the chief butler the message that had relieved and refreshed his soul. It is as one who claims, and is competent, to speak for God, that the chief butler now introduces Joseph to the notice of Pharaoh. His frank confession, his simple statement, tells upon the king. Better than eloquence or rhetoric is such speech for Joseph;—the speech of a man repenting of his fault in not " thinking of " his deliverer before, but ready now to testify of him,—to " testify for him before kings."

IV. Upon a hasty summons, and after brief preparation, Joseph is brought into royal presence and stands before Pharaoh (ver. 14-16). And he stands before Pharaoh in the same character in which he conferred in the prison with his fellow-prisoners. He speaks as one having authority—as one having authority to speak peace. Meek he is, and lowly in heart. He gives himself no airs, as those were wont to do who affected, by dint of their superior wisdom, or in virtue of their superior sanctity, to scale heaven's heights and pry into heaven's mysteries. But yet there is no sycophancy or hesi-

tancy about him ;—no look or attitude as of one seeking to
please his great hearer, or as of one drawing his bow at a
venture. He is simply speaking as the Holy Ghost moves
him. He is declaring the counsel of God,—delivering God's
message,—announcing God's will. He is, one might almost
say, by anticipation, acting upon the Lord's injunction ;—
" When they bring you unto the synagogues, and unto magistrates, and powers, take ye no thought how or what thing ye shall
answer, or what ye shall say : for the Holy Ghost shall teach
you in the same hour what ye ought to say " (Luke xii. 11, 12).

V. It would seem to be in the character which he himself
assumes, that Joseph is acknowledged by Pharaoh. The king
apparently believes what Joseph says ;—" It is not in me ; God
shall give Pharaoh an answer of peace." This may be fairly
inferred from his proceeding at once to tell his dreams (ver.
19-24), as well as from the ready acceptance which he gives
to the interpretation of them (ver. 28-32). It is as a witness
for God that Joseph speaks ; and it is God who opens
Pharaoh's heart to receive the things spoken by Joseph in
that capacity. It is idle, and worse than idle, to be seeking
other explanations of this great fact. There were no predis-
posing causes ;—there was no concurrence of favourable circumstances. The dreams could not suggest their own
solution. The stated and accredited functionaries, whose
business it was to solve them, and whose training was all in
that line, adepts as they were in the trade, were struck dumb.
An Israelitish captive, who had been bought and sold for a
slave,—a convict charged but lately with a foul crime,—a
poor, weary prisoner, scarcely out of the dungeon pit,—scarcely
rid of his felon dress,—hastily cleansed and attired that he
may make a decent appearance in the royal presence,—it is
he who is hailed as the revealer of heaven's secrets and the
arbiter of a kingdom's destiny. Upon the bare uncorroborated
testimony of one who had been in jail along with him, on the
warrant of a single instance of successful prognostication,

which might have been held to be a shrewd guess or a lucky hit,—this youth of thirty years, setting aside all the grey-haired sages round the throne, wields "the sword of the Spirit which is the word of God," and by means of it, sways the rod of empire. For Pharaoh is not disobedient, or unbelieving. There is that in Joseph's look and voice which carries in it the unmistakeable impress both of divine truth and of divine authority; and there is that in the plain prophecy he utters which flashes conviction on the heart. The monarch at once gives in. And so, as it would seem, does the whole court. Not a mouth is opened, not a hand is raised, against the motion or proposal of Joseph (ver. 33-36). On the contrary, it is unanimously approved of;—" The thing was good in the eyes of Pharaoh, and in the eyes of all his servants" (ver. 37).

It is no trifling motion, no ordinary proposal. It is not as if it were meant to regulate, by the omen of a dream, a day's diversion or a point of courtly etiquette. It is not even as if some question of a battle or a retreat, of peace or war, were made to turn on what a night vision might be construed to portend. Here the contemplated measures must stretch over a period of twice seven years; and not Egypt only, through all its borders, but the whole surrounding world must be embraced in their wide sweep. What Joseph ventures to suggest, as the corollary or practical application of the exposition of God's will that he has been giving, amounts almost to a universal revolution. And how unhesitatingly does he make the suggestion,—with what a tone and aspect of command; firm, though humble; not even waiting to be asked; but going on, after he has read out God's meaning in the dreams, to deliver in continuation and without pause his whole message,—whether men will hear or whether they will forbear. He is sent to speak for God;—" he speaks as one having authority."

Does he foresee the issue as regards himself? Is he already, in his own mind, anticipating the king's purpose of advancing him to the high office which he recommends to be instituted ? Is it a secret impulse of ambition throbbing in his bosom that prompts the recommendation,—as if he saw now within his grasp the elevation above his brethren that those early dreams of his had prefigured,—those dreams which had wrought him hitherto nothing but much woe ?

I cannot think so. Such an idea was most unlikely to enter into his mind spontaneously ; nor is it at all according to the analogy of the divine procedure in like cases that God should have put it into his mind. Enough of inspiration was communicated to him by the Spirit to serve the purpose of his office as a prophet, but no more. His own future was as dark as ever to himself, however clear he was commissioned to make Egypt's future to Egypt's king.

One can imagine Joseph's doubt as to the reception his bold and free speech is to have. It may irritate and provoke ; or it may move only contempt. The man is a deceiver, or he is mad ;—this whole story about famine eating up plenty is got up to serve a purpose. He is suborned by some parties who have an interest in the trades likely to be affected if his advice is followed ; or he is simply a wild schemer. Let him not be suffered to mix with the king's counsellors. Potiphar's house, or the prison adjoining it, is a fitter place for him. Joseph could not have been surprised if some such murmurs had met his ear, when, after his bold address, he stood silent and calm in that royal and courtly presence. Even if his reading of the dreams should be believed, and the course he indicated should in consequence be followed, were there not hundreds of " discreet and wise men" within call, on any one of whom this vast responsibility might be laid ? Who among the many thousands in Egypt at that moment was less likely, in the eyes of men, to sit at the king's right hand, on the throne of absolute dominion, than the man,—" not yet fifty years old,"—who has just been undergoing a penal sentence of suffering and shame ?

In the case of this, as of another exaltation, is not that saying true?—" The stone which the builders refused is become the head stone of the corner. This is the Lord's doing; it is marvellous in our eyes" (Ps. cxviii. 22, 23). Have we not here a very pregnant and significant type of what Peter proclaimed to the " rulers of the people and elders of Israel," when he said, " Be it known unto you all, and to all the people of Israel, that by the name of Jesus Christ of Nazareth, whom ye crucified, whom God raised from the dead, even by him doth this man stand here before you whole. This is the stone which was set at nought of you builders, which is become the head of the corner. Neither is there salvation in any other: for there is none other name under heaven given among men, whereby we must be saved."

56

EXALTATION—HEADSHIP OVER ALL—FOR THE CHURCH

Genesis 41:37-57

The king sent and loosed him ; even the ruler of the people, and let him go free.   He made him lord of his house, and ruler of all his substance : to bind his princes at his pleasure ; and teach his senators wisdom.—
Psalm 105:20-22

Him hath God exalted with his right hand to be a Prince and a Saviour.
Acts 5:31

The elevation of Joseph in Egypt, if it is to be rightly apprehended in its spiritual aspect and bearings, must be viewed primarily in its relation to the chosen family.   In a sense, he is "head over all things to the church, which is his body." For Israel's sake Joseph is preserved from death, delivered from the lowest depths of suffering and shame, and invested with what was then the highest power on earth,—the rod of the strength of the Egyptian Pharaohs.   The effects of his administration, as prime minister or grand vizier, on Egypt itself and the rest of the world, are comparatively subordinate, and one might say, with reference to the main object of this narrative, incidental.   It may be interesting and important to trace these, so far as the scanty materials within our reach may enable us, with tolerable probability, to do so.   But the chief purpose of this wonderful work of God had respect to the household of Abraham, Isaac, and Jacob,—the household of faith,—to whom were committed the oracles of God, and of whom, as concerning the flesh, Christ was to come. In the light of that purpose, the whole scene is to be contemplated.

I. Pharaoh's sudden resolution, carrying as it seems to have done, the approval and concurrence of all his counsellors and courtiers, is utterly inexplicable, on any other supposition than simply its being the Lord's doing (ver. 37, 38). Daniel's advancement by Darius, Mordecai's advancement by Ahasuerus, wonderful as they are, may be more easily accounted for than this preferment of Joseph. They had, both of them, got a certain position in the eyes of the heathen princes and people with whom they were connected, before they were so signally promoted. But this Joseph, who was he? A Hebrew slave, alleged to have betrayed a kind master's confidence and sought to injure him in the tenderest point;—a poor prisoner, friendless and forsaken,—who has just hastily exchanged his sordid jail costume for a somewhat more decent attire. Is he to be raised over the heads of all the wise and noble of the land, and set on a pinnacle of advancement to which none of them could ever have dreamt of aspiring?

The freaks and whims of oriental despotism are indeed endless, and many strange stories are told about them. But even Arabian imagination, in its wildest and most capricious flights, has given us scarcely anything so romantic as this abrupt transition in the case of Joseph, from the dungeon to the throne—from a criminal's doom to a royal favourite's renown and glory.

And yet it does not read like romance. The whole thing is told so simply,—the account is so naturally given,—the entire narrative is so plain, so homely, so unostentatious, that no mind or heart, open to the fair impression of what is genuine and artless, can fail to see in it and feel in it the stamp of truth. It is not gorgeous and fantastic fiction, but the most simple and unsophisticated telling of a true tale. It is no got-up fable, but a real, old-world, matter-of-fact story; having a life-like air about it not to be mistaken. The king speaks and acts with calm dignity and good sense, and with thorough self-possession. His appeal to his servants is rational and sober. And the entire affair is carried through with such a measure of serious thought as well as prompt decision, as to indicate that not any rash impulse, but a deep and settled conviction, is the source and regulating principle of Pharaoh's purpose and proceedings all throughout.

Surely there is evidence in all this of what is done being done in faith. And it must have been, one would say, considering all the circumstances, faith having a divine origin as well as a divine warrant; faith in God's word, wrought by God's Spirit; like that faith through which, by grace, we are saved,—it must have been " the gift of God " (Eph. ii. 8).

II. The manner of Joseph's investiture with the insignia of office is worthy of notice.

(1.) He is thoroughly acquitted and justified,—declared to be free from all blame, and justly entitled to favour (ver. 39). No doubt Pharaoh's commendation of him turns chiefly on his discernment and intelligence,—on his discretion and wisdom ; but it must be held to cover his whole character. It recognises his standing as righteous and worthy. All stain of the criminality that had been imputed to him is gone. He has suffered enough on that account, and is now free. He in whom the Spirit of God so manifestly is,—he to whom God has showed such things,—may for a time be under a cloud ; bearing a load of guilt not his own. But he cannot be long held in humiliation. The divine insight and foresight, which, even in his humiliation, he manifests, as regards the plans and purposes of God,—especially in their bearing upon others whose safety and welfare may be mixed up with his own destiny,—must soon issue in his being advanced, for their sakes and on their account, if not even by their instrumentality, to the position in which he can do them good. And the first step would seem to be his personal vindication,—his being acknowledged as one in whom no fault is found, and exalted as one of whom it may be said, in a sense, that in him " are hid all the treasures of wisdom and knowledge " (Col. ii. 3).

(2.) He is addressed in terms inviting him to highest pre-eminence (ver. 40.) " Sit thou on my right hand," is virtually the word,—sit beside me and preside over all my realm. His place is still, of course, to be subordinate ; he wields a delegated authority. But save his own seat on the throne, there is nothing which this great king reserves to himself, or exempts from the command that he is giving to the mediatorial prince whom he is setting up. All things in Egypt are put under Joseph ; as it is testified of one greater than Joseph that God " hath put all things under his feet." And the single reservation is, in both instances virtually the same. When the Father says of his son Jesus, all things are put under him, " it is manifest that he is excepted which did put all things under him " (1 Cor. xv. 27). When Pharaoh exalts Joseph to be over all his house, and all his people, he puts in what is in substance the same caveat : " Only in the throne will I be greater than thou."

(3.) He is proclaimed as one before whom all are to bow the knee,—having visible honour put upon him, and even a new name given to him, for this very end, that before him every knee may bow (ver. 41-45). The ring, the vestures of fine linen, the gold chain about his neck, appear conspicu ously as badges of the favour he has, and the power he wields, when he " rides forth prosperously in his majesty." The name which he receives, and which was doubtless pro- claimed before him,—Revealer of secrets, or as some say, Saviour of the world,—announces his merit. It is fitting that before such a chariot, and at such a name, every knee should bow. It is the chariot of grace ;—it is the name of salvation.

(4.) He is to be known as having his home in high places ;—in the high places into which his deep humiliation,

followed by his wondrous elevation, introduces him. He is
to be seen familiarly established and happily domesticated
there ; receiving a noble spouse (ver. 45).

Pharaoh's arrangement of this marriage for his favourite
Prime Minister is according to the common usage of Eastern
courts. It is meant to confirm Joseph's allegiance, and be a
pledge of his fidelity ;—while at the same time it encourages
his loyal zeal, and adds weight to his delegated authority.
On that footing Joseph accepts the proposal. Nor can his
acceptance of it be criticised or judged according to the
ordinary rules applicable to the children of Abraham, which
were undoubtedly meant to tell against all matrimonial
alliances with the heathen. The position of Joseph is manifestly peculiar. If he is to have a home at all, he has no
choice as to whom he may have to share it with him.

It is well, moreover, that Joseph should thus unequivocally assume the princely rank which his espousing, by the
king's command, the daughter of one who was a priest, or a
prince, or both, secured to him. He is in that way manifested as no intruder in the palaces and lordly halls of Egypt,
but worthy and entitled to have his dwelling-place among
them. He is manifested, moreover, as not merely a son of
Israel, but a brother of Egypt ;—fitly, therefore, set forth in
his high estate as appointed to save both Jew and Gentile ;
being now personally allied to both.

Thus inaugurated in his high office, " Joseph went out
over all the land of Egypt" (ver. 45). His humiliation is all
over while he is yet comparatively young—certainly not more
than "thirty years old" (ver. 46). It is cut short,—shall we
say,—in mercy, before his heavy sufferings have exhausted
his frame. And now he is to have length of days in his
exaltation ; honour and majesty are laid upon him ; all
power is given to him (ver. 46). It is given by delegation
doubtless, but it is by absolute delegation. He rules
supreme ; not as one who reports cases and causes to the

king, and is the mere executioner of the king's decree ; but as one who has authority himself. So he goes out from the presence of Pharaoh ; virtually Pharaoh has said, " I have set my king upon my hill," when he says, " Thou shalt be over my house,—according to thy word shall all my people be ruled." And a name is given him above every other name then known in all the world ; the name of Revealer or Saviour. And before him " every knee is to bow." He rides forth gloriously in chariot of state ;—declared now, by no doubtful sign, to be no stranger, but the highest of Egypt's own princely sons ; without whom " not a hand or foot is to be lifted in all the land." So this Joseph now reigns, set far above ordinary " principalities and powers."

III. Joseph is exalted for a special purpose,—and to the accomplishment of that purpose he makes all his power subservient (ver. 47-49). His rule is a rule of far-seeing providence ; he rules, in a sense, as seeing the end from the beginning. Coming evil is anticipated and provided for. The rich and precious abundance of the early years of his reign is not suffered to be lost or wasted. It is stored for future use,—when in a season of want and destitution it may be available, if not for the full relief, at least for the partial alleviation of the distress. The government is upon the shoulders of one who will lay up, as in a storehouse, the fruits of the large outpouring of heaven's blessing that is to characterise the beginning of the dispensation over which he has to preside and watch,—so that in the worst of times that may be at hand, some food may still be forthcoming. Granaries are filled for evil days.

IV. Before these evil days come, two names of good omen have become " household words" to all who watch the signs of the times, and the ways of him who, having been exalted to be a prince and a saviour, is himself a sign, and does nothing without a meaning (ver. 50-52). The glad father welcomes the children whom God gives him,—in whom he sees the

pledges of toil and travail over and fruitfulness to come,—
of labour and sorrow now to be forgotten and a prosperous
issue of it all before him. He sees his seed and is satisfied.
And what satisfies him may satisfy all who can sympathise
with him. Whatever may be coming on the land and on the
world; however the heavens may be as brass, and the earth
as iron, and the river of Egypt may be dry, and there may be
a great cry for bread, and much perishing for lack of it; still
he is at the helm, he is at the head of all,—who, in the full
knowledge of all that may be impending, can yet give forth
cheerful tokens for the upholding of men's hearts; naming
one son Manasseh, or "miserable toil forgotten;" and the other
Ephraim, or " God makes fruitful."

V. And now the evil days are near; " The seven years of
dearth began to come, according as Joseph had said : and the
dearth was in all lands" (ver. 53, 54). It is a growing distress.
At first, while dearth is in all the surrounding countries, Egypt
is an exception ; " there is bread in Egypt." Soon, however,
Egypt also suffers (ver. 55). " All the land of Egypt is
famished ; " and there is a universal cry for bread. The
famine is over all the face of the earth. " It waxes sore even
in the land of Egypt," in spite of the opening of all the storehouses ; it is sore in all lands (ver. 57). One only comfort
there is,—one only hope for Egypt and all lands. Joseph is
exalted ; Joseph is in authority. The residue of whatever
supply may be available is with him. He has in his hands
the keys. He has received all power to amass around himself,
and dispense at his pleasure, the whole staple and staff of life.
Pharaoh sends all suitors and suppliants to him, " Go unto
Joseph ; what he saith to you, do" (ver. 55). Joseph opens all
the storehouses and sells to the Egyptians (ver. 56). " All
countries come into Egypt to Joseph for to buy corn" (ver. 57).
A perishing world hangs on this great fact, that Joseph reigns.

Thus far, Joseph's rise from obscure and unjust oppression

to the highest place which any one could hold by delegation in the world of that day, is a personal triumph to himself and a public benefit to Egypt and to the nations generally. The exact and full bearing of his promotion on Israel, as the church and people of God, is to be unfolded immediately. But at this stage, we see him simply as one receiving the due acknowledgment and reward of his thoroughly tried righteousness, and receiving it, not for his own gratification, but for the general good. Personally, he is now fully vindicated and righted, while the meaning of his previous shame and sorrow is made plain. He is himself, in a sense, "made perfect through suffering." He has undergone a discipline of obedience and patience, such as admirably prepares his gracious spirit for the high office which he is to fill, and the momentous functions he is to discharge. It may not perhaps be easy to trace a very close connection, either of merit or of natural consequence, between the precise nature of his sufferings in his humiliation and the kind of recompense awarded to him in his elevation. It may not be safe to give the reins too freely to fancy, as it might be tempted to run wild in the domain of typical analogies. But surely there is a meaning in the circumstance of Joseph's lowly and afflicted experience having in it something of the nature of vicariousness,—inasmuch as no sin of his own brought it upon him,—and inasmuch also as he suffered for the fault of others, and suffered, to some extent, for the benefit of others. And at all events, in the high estate to which he is now promoted,—very much through that lowly and afflicted experience as the cause or the occasion,—this feature is conspicuously seen. It is not for himself that he receives honour and reigns supreme. He acts for others ; he benefits the world. He uses his power for the relieving of want and woe,—for the dispensing of that bread by which man ordinarily lives. Worthily and fitly does he represent him who, being raised up on high, receives gifts for men ;—in whom it pleases the Father that all fulness should dwell ;—and out of whose fulness all may receive.

57

CONVICTION OF SIN—YOUR SIN SHALL FIND YOU OUT

Genesis 42:1-24

Him hath God exalted with his right hand to be a Prince and a Saviour,
for to give repentance to Israel, and forgiveness of sins. Acts 5:31

JOSEPH in his elevation, like Jesus in his exaltation, is in the
first instance a light to lighten the Gentiles. He has been
rejected by the house of Israel. The gifts which, when he is
raised on high, he has to dispense, come first therefore upon
the Gentiles. But it soon appears that he is to be the glory
also of God's people Israel. He is come to the kingdom for
this end, that Israel may be saved.

The chosen family in Canaan, visited by the famine, are in
sore straits, "looking," as Jacob plaintively expresses it, looking helplessly "one upon another." They hear of corn in
Egypt, and of embassies going thither from all the surrounding
countries to obtain, if possible, a share. For themselves, they
may have tried to put off the evil day, and to husband their
resources ; affecting a self-sufficient independence, while their
neighbours have been fain to bend the knee to this new ruler
in Egypt, who holds, as it would seem, the destinies of the
world in his power. But it will not do. These proud sons of
Jacob must give in at last, and, like others, bow as suppliants
before this prince, in whose hands alone fulness dwells. They
are in want,—themselves and their little ones like to perish.
Their father's voice, too often unheeded in their prosperity, is
now heard in their distress : " Behold I have heard that there

is corn in Egypt : get you down thither, and buy for us from thence ; that we may live, and not die " (ver. 1, 2). They prepare, accordingly, to set out for Egypt.

All of them ? All the eleven ? No ! Twenty years have not sufficed to efface from the old man's memory the heavy loss he sustained when he had to weep for Joseph. Never, perhaps, has his mind been altogether reconciled to the story which the brothers told. Some suspicion of foul play on their part having had something to do with Joseph's strange disappearance continues to haunt him painfully. At all events he will not risk Benjamin in their company ;—Joseph's young brother, the sole remaining pledge of poor Rachel's love, Jacob will keep at home ;—so " Joseph's ten brethren went down to buy corn in Egypt. But Benjamin, Joseph's brother, Jacob sent not with his brethren ; for he said, Lest peradventure mischief befall him " (ver. 3, 4).

Along with many similar cavalcades or caravans, the men of Israel, with their attendants, reach Egypt, and have an audience of the governor: "Joseph's brethren came, and bowed down themselves before him with their faces to the earth. And Joseph saw his brethren, and he knew them, but made himself strange unto them, and spake roughly unto them " (ver. 5-7).

Now here let us once for all fix it in our minds that Joseph had a part to play,—and he must needs play it out, and play it out correctly and consistently. He has to enact and sustain the character of an Egyptian nobleman or prince—the Egyptian king's prime minister or vizier. It is idle and frivolous to be raising minute questions, and discussing captious criticisms, about some petty details of his conduct and demeanour in that character ;—as about his using the current off-hand formula of asseveration (ver. 16) ;—or about his giving himself, on a subsequent occasion (xliv. 15), in a half-serious, half-light sort of way, the air and manner of an Eastern sage or soothsayer,— familiar with magic arts. Once admit that Joseph has for a

little while to keep up his disguise, to personate Pharaoh's
viceroy, without letting his home-yearnings betray him—and
all the rest follows as a matter of course. If the personification
is to be probable and complete, he must of necessity speak
and act "according to the card," or trick. The only point of
difficulty really is the question that may be raised as to the
propriety of his thus acting a part at all.

It will scarcely do to maintain the abstract and absolute
unlawfulness of such a procedure,—to say that it is positively
and in all circumstances wrong. Jesus himself on one occasion,
in his interview with the Syrophenician woman, assumed the
lordly port of a pharisee,—and doubtless looked the pharisee
thoroughly well, when he used the pharisee's characteristic and
contemptuous language about giving the children's meat to
"dogs." And again, when on the resurrection morn, he was
walking with the disciples, and they stopped in the village, he
"made as if he would have gone farther." So when Joseph
made himself strange to his brethren, at first,—and continued
thereafter for a considerable time, and during several interviews, to make himself strange,—it is not necessarily involved
in his doing so, that his temporary concealment, or stratagem,
if you will,—was unjustifiable. It may have been so,—it may
have been a mistake,—a fault,—a sin. If it was a measure
adopted merely at his own hand, it was probably all that ;—
in which case, we must be content with explaining how Joseph
might have reasons of his own for acting as he did. For,
without altogether vindicating him, we might hold him partly
excused by his remembrance of former injury, and by the
necessity, as he might suppose, of observing great precaution
now, and testing his brethren rather sharply. And we might
on that theory trace the manner in which the Lord overruled
Joseph's scarcely warrantable policy for good to all the parties
concerned.

I cannot, however, I confess, bring myself to believe that
Joseph was left to himself in this matter ; I feel persuaded

that we must regard him as all along acting by inspiration. He surely has some intimation of the mind and will óf God to guide him. He has been honoured already, more than once, as a prophet of the Lord. He has plainly spoken and acted by inspiration as a prophet, first, in his dealings with his fellow-prisoners, and thereafter in his delivery of his message to Pharaoh, and his assumption, at Pharaoh's call, of the high post to which, on the faith of his message being authentic, he is raised. Surely now, at this crisis of his exercise of authority—when the very exigency for which he has come to his all but kingly power has arrived,—in the matter of his treatment of the family for whose preservation he is where he is,— Joseph is not left to his own unaided discretion. He is a prophet still as well as a prince. He has divine warrant for what he does.

Something of that sort, I think, may be intended to be intimated, when it is said (ver. 9), that he " remembered the dreams which he dreamed." It was the Lord that brought them to his remembrance, and Joseph, I am persuaded, recognised the Lord in this. At once he perceives that this affair of his brethren coming to him is of the Lord. It is not a common occurrence ; it is not mere casual coincidence. The Lord is here,—in this place and in this business ; and therefore the Lord must regulate the whole, and fix the time and manner of discovery. If he had been left to himself, Joseph would not have hesitated a moment ; his is not a cold or crafty temperament ; he is no manœuvrer ; he would have had all over within the first few minutes. But the Lord restrains him. He is, I cannot doubt, consciously in the Lord's hand,— doing violence to his own nature to serve the Lord's purposes. And much of the interest and pathos of these scenes will be found to lie in the strong working of that nature under the control and guidance of the Lord.

1. Do we not see the inward struggle in the very first

reception of his brothers by Joseph ? (ver. 7). Not only did he "make himself strange" to them; in order that he might do so more effectually, "he spake roughly unto them;" asking vehemently the abrupt and almost rude question: "Whence came ye ?" Surely that was not his way of receiving strangers generally when they came from other countries to buy corn; his ordinary manner could not be so uncourteous. In the king's place, he was himself "every inch a king;" filling the seat of power, and wielding its sceptre with graceful dignity and condescension. But when he saw his brethren he knew them; his heart yearned towards them, and the early home, and the fond father, of whom they put him in mind. It costs him an effort to keep silence. But something seals his lips; the time is not yet come. He must keep down therefore the rising tide of feeling. And so,—as is not uncommon in such a case,—he hides, under a gruff exterior, the deep inward movement of his heart.

2. As the interview proceeds, the struggle in Joseph's bosom grows more intense (ver. 8, 9). The simple reply of his brothers to his question, "Whence come ye ?"—"From the land of Canaan to buy food" (ver. 7), is a touching appeal to him. From any little company of strangers visiting Egypt at that terrible crisis, such a plain answer must have had a certain pathetic power. Whence come ye ? From our fatherland to buy food! As uttered by the sons of Israel, it causes a sad picture of family distress to rise before Joseph's view. He remembers the old dreams of his childhood that had caused so much heartburning, and produced, as it seemed, so much wickedness and misery. Fain would he explain to them even now, as he did explain to them afterwards, how these dreams were receiving a fulfilment equally for the good of all, and how they need not therefore any longer occasion jealousy or estrangement. Fain would he point to God's overruling providence as superseding all past misunderstandings, and opening the way for them all, as brethren, to dwell together in unity. But

there must be reserve still for a little. Natural affection must be held, as it were, in abeyance, and its working must be violently repressed. Is it to overcome, as by a sort of reaction, this growing home-feeling which threatens to unman him, that Joseph, as Egypt's governor, puts on an air of still increasing severity? He has a part to play; he must brave it out. And so he does, with vehemence enough, when he so abruptly accuses them:—"Ye are spies; to see the nakedness of the land ye are come" (ver. 9).

3. Their next explanation and remonstrance, so meek and humble, must have still farther moved Joseph's bowels of relenting pity; "Nay, my lord, but to buy food are thy servants come. We are all one man's sons; we are true men, thy servants are no spies" (ver. 10, 11). How are these brethren changed! Where now is all their proud contempt and bitter wrath: "Behold this dreamer cometh, away with him?" How crest-fallen are they! Even the charge of being spies elicits not a spark of the old fire of passion; nor have they the heart to meet it with any strong or emphatic indignation. Their disclaimer is sufficiently dejected,—for they are poor and needy. Is it a gratification to Joseph to see them brought so low? Nay, it cuts him to the heart. That these men, the men who used to envy him, and to lord it so cruelly over him, are now so abased at his feet—prostrate before the brother they would have slain—it is a sight he can scarcely stand! And then, when in answer to his still more violent demeanour, assumed to cover his still growing weakness; "Nay, but to see the nakedness of the land ye are come" (ver. 12,— they enter with such simplicity into that sad family story of which he himself formed so great a part; "Thy servants are twelve brethren, the sons of one man in the land of Canaan; and, behold, the youngest is this day with our father, and one is not" (ver. 13)—one can imagine the force which Joseph puts upon himself when, as if giving way to a transport of blind suspicious fury that will listen to neither reasoning nor remon-

strance,—in the truest style of oriental and despotic passion,—
he breaks out into the language of unmeasured reproach and
threatening (ver. 14-16).

4. Such a storm of wordy rage was quite in character,—
especially when followed, as it was, by a corresponding deed,
—the actual consignment of these unoffending men to prison
(ver. 17). Strange as the scene would seem to us, if we could
fancy it enacted by a judge, or any one in authority among us,
it would excite little surprise among the counsellors and
courtiers of Egypt. All the less, because Joseph was a stranger
from another country : and they might therefore give him
credit for knowing more than they could know about what
sort of people were likely to come from the region to which
he had himself belonged. He therefore might detect signs
of false dealing not apparent to others in these ten weary
travellers who professed to have come on so harmless an errand,
and to tell so plaintive a story. He might be aware of circumstances connected with the foreign parts whence they had
journeyed, fitted to cause just apprehension of some underhand
design, however plausible their tale. And then, short as their
sojourn had been in Egypt, for a day or two only, while they
waited for an audience of the vizier, the brothers had probably
kept themselves apart. They had not accommodated themselves to the Egyptian usages, either social or religious ;
having evidently strange ways and a strange worship of their
own. To hear the new prime minister, who, as they recol-
lected, was himself a native of the land of Canaan (ver. 7),—
or the land of the Hebrews (xl. 15 ; xli. 12),—denouncing
these, his seeming fellow-countrymen, as false spies, would
probably be rather welcome than otherwise to the lords of
Egypt. And the spectacle was an edifying one of this Hebrew
prime minister, showing so forcibly how the zeal of his master's
house had eaten him up ;—how concern for Pharaoh's safety
and the security of his kingdom, had so completely got the
better of all other considerations as actually to make him for-

get the proper limits of magisterial decorum, and lose his temper upon the very throne itself, in his eagerness to detect and denounce this Hebrew or Canaanite treachery, lurking under the mask of a pitiful cry for bread.

5. Joseph's policy is successful,—his acting is perfect. The terms he proposes to these suspected spies, are such as befit the furious mood which it suits him to affect. Let one of your number fetch that youngest brother you speak of so pathetically,—and thus verify, at least in part, your not very probable account of yourselves. For it needs verification. If the state of the household you belong to is such as you describe it, why should that old father of yours have risked so many of you on this embassy? Or if he was willing to risk so many, why not one more? And what is this about another being amissing—another of this suspicious round. dozen of sons? Let us have proof, at all events, that you are telling the truth about the twelfth, if you cannot account for the eleventh. Let a messenger go and bring him. Send one of your number on that errand and let the other nine stay here in prison and await his return; the governor will be responsible for their safe custody; and the term of their confinement need not be long.

But grievously as these men were abased, they were not brought quite so low as to be willing at once to acquiesce in so cruel an arrangement as this; for so it must have appeared to them, whatever Joseph might mean by it. They felt, for themselves, how oppressive and unjust it was. They felt, for their father, what a blow it must be to him. They might well therefore hesitate, and rather suffer themselves to be all inprisoned together than agree to the seeming tyrant's intolerable terms. So they lie in ward three days.

6. On the third day Joseph sees them again (ver. 18), and resumes his intercourse with them. Is it another public audience that is meant here, or a private visit paid to them in prison? Are they brought again before the governor for

another hearing, and for the final decision of their cause? Or does the governor, in a less official capacity, condescend to have a conference with them in their confinement? This last is the more probable view, though the point is not very clear —nor indeed very material. Joseph cannot bear to have his brothers left long to languish in the suspense and gloom of the dreary captivity to which he has himself consigned them. He must have further dealing with them. And it is quite in accordance with Eastern manners, that he should seek to have such farther dealing with them, in a more easy and familiar way than the etiquette of state formality allowed. He has a modified proposal to submit to them; and, in submitting it, he has an avowal to make on his own part, which must have not a little surprised them. " This do and live; for I fear God" (ver. 18); I am of the same faith with you. Though governor in Egypt, I am no worshipper of Egypt's idols; I know and acknowledge the true God, as I see that you also do. And therefore I relax my otherwise inex- orable conditions in your favour. I am almost inclined to believe that, after all, you may be true men; and I am disposed to treat you accordingly. I cannot indeed altogether dispense with proof; I must, in consistency, require of you the evidence I have already publicly committed myself to ask—the bring- ing of your youngest brother hither. But let it be done in the easiest manner (ver. 19, 20). The distress at your home need not be unrelieved; the father's anxiety need not be pro- longed or aggravated. I must still insist on one of you remaining as a hostage;—but the rest may go and carry corn for the famine of your house.

Joseph is all but betrayed. He fears God as they do; and for the common fear they have, he and they, of the true God, he relents in his harsh treatment of them. He speaks to them with comparative kindness. Fain would he embrace them, and kneel with them, as in the olden time, when they all used to join together in the unbroken family circle, as their father led the worship of the one living and true God, in the midst of abounding idolatry. "I fear God" as ye do, and cannot suffer you to perish : "Ye shall not die." He is on the point of breaking down and discovering himself. If he would keep up his assumed state and air of authority, he has need to retire apart, and be alone.

7. As he stands aside, his brethren are left in strange bewilderment and dismay. They have agreed generally to the governor's modified proposition ; for that would seem to be implied in its being said, "and they did so" (ver. 20). But they have to fix among themselves who shall be the one to remain bound. The governor withdraws, and lets them deliberate and decide at their discretion. It is a cruel question of debate. Evil as they have shown themselves in too many respects to be, these men are still brothers ; and in the extremity in which they now are, their brotherly affection is stirred to its utmost depths. A terrible decimation is demanded of them ; one of the ten must run the risk of almost hopeless imprisonment, if not even of a worse fate, in the hands of this arbitrary Egyptian ruler. Which of them is to volunteer ? Or shall they cast lots ? Or commit the issue to the blind hazard of the dice ? They gaze on one another. Blank consternation is upon every countenance. Who dare make a proposal ? Who dare suggest a name ? It is a time for conscience to work. The scourges which their vices have made for them begin, at that dark hour, to lash and sting them. Individually and separately, they have black sins enough to play the part of scorpions. Reuben has his foul outrage on his father's bed ; Judah has his wretched incest ; Simeon and Levi have their horrid revenge on Shechem ;— each of the ten has his own several offence rising like a ghost, to shake his nerves in this stern trial. But there is one spectre common to them all,—one deed of darkness to which they all are privy, and of which none else has knowledge : "They said one to another, We are verily guilty concerning our brother,

in that we saw the anguish of his soul, when he besought us, and we would not hear; therefore is this distress come upon us" (ver. 21).

As with one accord, they recall the scene at Dothan. Strange and startling coincidence! Their innocent young brother, the good and tender child, struggling in their hands, uttering his feeble, plaintive, wailing cry for mercy,—calling on the father who so loved him,—alas! how far off in his utmost need,—lifting his clasped hands and streaming eyes to them in vain;—the whole villany they yet, in spite of all that, had the heart to perpetrate, is fresh before them. Their common sorrow recalls their common sin. It is a righteous judgment that has come upon them for their fratricidal guilt. This man's pitilessness to us requites our pitilessness to our brother. The ruler now will not hear us, as we would not hear the boy then. God,—the God whom this extraordinary man says he fears as well as we,—God is just. He has raised him up, and given him power over us, to avenge the cause of Joseph.

Is it, can it be, that some strange dreamy resemblance between this dark-browed Egyptian vizier and the fair face of that little child, has been haunting these men, as he has been talking with them? Is it nature's mysterious spell working in them a sort of half-recognition of the brother whom they so remorselessly made away with? Is there a dim foreshadowing of what is to be realised fully by-and-by, when they are to see face to face their acknowledged victim, and literally, one would almost say, look on him whom they have pierced? It may be so. At any rate, their sin is terribly finding them out: nor have they a word to say to excuse or comfort one another.

Joseph would fain interfere, if he could, to pour soothing balm into their wounded spirits, as he afterwards delighted to do. But that may not yet be. He is compelled to listen in silence to their keen and bitter self-upbraidings. His time for speaking a word in season to their weary souls,—their time for receiving it aright,—is not yet come. The only one in that gloomy company who ventures to open his mouth, does but add, however unintentionally, vinegar and gall to the smarting wound: "Reuben answered them, saying, Spake I not unto you, saying, Do not sin against the child? and ye would not hear; therefore, behold, also his blood is required" (ver. 22).

I cannot think that Reuben says this in the mere spirit of self-justification. It is not as exulting in his superiority over them,—for he is really sharing their punishment, as by his silence heretofore he has become an accomplice in their crime,—it is not as claiming for himself any peculiar immunity or exemption, but as circumstantially aggravating and enhancing the common guilt,—that Reuben urges home the deliberation with which the deed was done. It was no sudden impulse, he reminds himself and them. We talked the matter over. I remonstrated;—would that I had done so more decidedly! You went on against warning and entreaty to consummate the wickedness. It was a black business for you, for all of us. Therefore is this distress come upon us. His blood is required at our hands.

8. Joseph can hold out no longer; he must cut short this distressing scene. He understands all that they say, as having withdrawn a little aside, he overhears it all. They are not aware of this;—for, as a matter of course, his conversation with them, in order to the keeping up of his character, is carried on through an interpreter (ver. 23). But not a syllable of that sad, conscience-stricken, communing of theirs escapes his ear; not a syllable of it fails to reach his heart. He is compelled to exercise patience, self-denial, and self-restraint. It is a sort of self-crucifixion for him to be obliged to stand by and witness such anguish. A word from him would assuage it; but that word he may not utter. He must needs be obedient to the unseen influence under which his prophetic soul is acting. It is obedience that costs him, if not " strong crying," yet " tears :" " He turned himself about

from them and wept" (ver. 24). And then, to end the
miserable suspense, and bring this most painful negotiation to
a close ;—since they will not, or cannot, settle among themselves, which of them is to remain as a prisoner and hostage ;
—Joseph, "returning to them again, and communing with
them," summarily cuts the knot himself by another rough act
of authority. Passing by Reuben, whom, in the circumstances,
he could not find it in his heart to punish, he lays his hand on
the next in order of age, Simeon. "Binding him before their
eyes," he bids the rest depart homeward, as best they may, in
safety and in peace (ver. 24).

The liberal provision which Joseph caused his servants to
make for these departing strangers,—the purchase-money of
the corn being returned along with the corn, in every man's
sack (ver. 25, 26) ; the surprise occasioned by the discovery of
this circumstance in one instance on the journey (ver. 27) ;
and the alarm felt, when on their arrival at home it was
found to be the same with all (ver. 35) ;—these particulars,—
as well as Jacob's bitter grief on hearing of the governor's
detention of Simeon and demand for Benjamin (ver. 36) ;—
may properly fall to be considered, so far as it is necessary to
dwell on them, in connection with the second visit of the
patriarchs to Egypt.

Meanwhile, this first visit is instructive. It furnishes a
lesson, or more than one, as to the special providence of God,
and the working of conscience in men. In particular, it
exhibits Joseph in his exaltation, set for the trial of men's
hearts,—to prove and humble as well as to relieve and save.
For it is not by a sovereign and summary exercise of authority
or power,—that he is to effect the purpose for which he is
raised on high, and to deliver and bless his brethren. It is
through a process of conviction that he is to bring to them
salvation. He is as one who hides himself until he has
broken the hard heart, and wrought in them something of

that "godly sorrow which worketh repentance unto salvation, not to be repented of" (2 Cor. vii. 10).

In this respect he fitly represents a greater than himself, one raised to a higher glory, for a wider purpose of grace. Jesus is "exalted, a prince and a Saviour, to give repentance unto Israel, and the remission of sins;"—not the remission of sins only—but repentance and the remission of sins together. Joseph could have no difficulty about giving his brothers remission of sins; he has forgiven them long ago in his heart, and right gladly would he assure them of that at once. But, acting under divine guidance, he must so deal with them as to force upon them a deep and salutary exercise of soul, which in the end is to be blessed for their more complete peace,— their more thorough unity and prosperity,—in the day when the full joy of reconciliation is to be experienced.

I know not, brother, how it may be the purpose of our Joseph, who is Jesus, to deal with thine inquiring and anxious soul; he is sovereign in dispensing his gifts of pardon and peace, assurance and joy. It may be his gracious pleasure that thou shouldest have them now,—or for anything I can tell, not till by-and-by. In either case, thou art called to deep and salutary exercises of penitential sorrow. If instant relief for thy burdened conscience is granted, and he whom thou hast pierced utters at once the words, "Be of good cheer, it is I, thy sins be forgiven thee;"—with what a flood of tears shouldest thou be graciously mourning for these very forgiven sins! And if it should be otherwise with thee,—if it should seem as if this assured forgiveness were long of coming, and the prince, the Saviour, were long of showing himself,—surely thou canst not pretend that thou hast any right to complain. Thou canst no more take it amiss than Joseph's brothers could, that thou shouldest have bitter days and nights to spend in thinking over all thy heinous guilt. Only make conscience of thinking over it with broken spirit and contrite heart;— not murmuring, not rebelling, not even feeling it to be hard, but accepting the punishment of thy sins ;—and hold on, not despairing, but hoping against hope,—waiting on the Lord. For in the end it will be no mattter of regret to thee that thou hast been led to lay the foundation of thy faith very deep. The joy of morning will be all the sweeter for the weeping that has endured for a night. Let us therefore exhort one another to penitence and patience, in the spirit of the prophet's call : " Come, and let us return unto the Lord : for he hath torn, and he will heal us ; he hath smitten, and he will bind us up. After two days will he revive us ; in the third day he will raise us up, and we shall live in his sight. Then shall we know, if we follow on to know the Lord : his going forth is prepared as the morning : and he shall come unto us as the rain, as the latter and former rain unto the earth " (Hosea vi. 1-3).

58

THE TRIAL AND TRIUMPH OF FAITH

Genesis 42:25-43:14

Why sayest thou, O Jacob, and speakest, O Israel, My way is hid
from the Lord, and my judgment is passed over from my God?—
Isaiah 40:27

He giveth power to the faint : and to them that have no might he increaseth strength. Isaiah 40:29

THE issue of the first visit of Israel's sons to Egypt is of a
doubtful complexion. They get the corn they need ; but they
leave one of their number in prison. And the condition on
which alone they can hope to have him released, is one which
it cannot but be difficult, if not impossible, to persuade their
father to fulfil. In three successive pictures, as it were, we
trace the onward progress of the action, from this point where
all seems dark.

I. The homeward journey of these stricken men might
well be sad and dreary. The strange conduct of Joseph, in
his personated character of Egyptian ruler, must have been
very perplexing ; it must have seemed to them the more so,
the more they thought and talked of it,—and what else could
they think or talk of by the way ? They could scarcely look
upon it as an ordinary instance of official severity and caprice,
even according to the usages of tyranny in that olden time.
There is something inexplicable about this naturalised Canaanite in Egypt ; this man who came to Egypt as a slave,
like what Joseph must have been after they had sold him ; a
slave " stolen away," according to his own account, to the chief

butler, "out of the land of the Hebrews;" who now, in so re-markable a manner, has got promotion to the right hand of Pharaoh, and wields all his power. For they must have heard some rumours of his antecedents while they were so near him; and therefore they are the more perplexed by his treatment of them. The extraordinary curiosity and interest which he manifests about their family concerns, even in the midst of his seeming vehemence and passion, cannot but strike their minds. The fact of his pitiless treatment of them, so vividly recalling their pitiless treatment of Joseph, must still farther impress them. The man is harsh. But yet there is a certain tender pathos in his harshness to which they cannot be insensible. There is a kind of fascination about him, even when he calls them spies;—something that keeps them submissive, and gives him an influence over them, even when he appears to be casting them off. He is of a relenting mood also; he does not insist on his first cruel proposition; he is content to retain a single hostage. He honourably pledges his faith, not only for the safe custody, but for the good treatment of this one brother, till the others come again; and he gives liberal and hospitable instructions as to their departure in peace and plenty: "Then Joseph commanded to fill their sacks with corn, and to restore every man's money into his sack, and to give them provision for the way" (ver. 25).

These instructions, indeed, and the effects of them, are only partially known to the travellers at starting. The restoration of their money is managed secretly. But "the provision for the way" they could not but be aware of; and it must have appeared to them to be a special instance of God's providence over them, that after undergoing such humiliation and alarm, they should be thus handsomely dismissed and forwarded on their homeward journey.

Soon, however, a startling circumstance agitates their minds by the way. "As one of them opened his sack to give his ass provender in the inn, he espied his money: for, behold, it was in his sack's mouth. And he said unto his brethren, My money is restored ; and, lo, it is even in my sack : and their heart failed them, and they were afraid, saying one to another, What is this that God hath done unto us?" (ver. 26-28).

They are greatly at a loss. What can this mean ? It can scarcely be accident or chance. Is it then a device to entrap and ensnare them ? Are they already pursued by emissaries of the Egyptian lord, commissioned to arrest them, and bring them back on a pretended charge of fraud or theft ? That can scarcely be,—for if he had intended to lay hold of them, why should he not rather have kept them, as he at first proposed, on the charge of their being spies? The thing is unaccountable. But be the explanation what it may, these men feel that it is the Lord who is dealing with them in so singular a manner. It is still their sin that is finding them out. All this dark and strange turn of affairs is the Lord's visitation, moving them to repentance. And whatever gleams of light and hope break in upon them, through the variable mood of this mysterious governor,—so incongruously compounded of fury and of tenderness,—that too is of the Lord. It is the Lord who is causing them to " sing of mercy and of judgment," in the exercise of that long-suffering of his which is to them salvation.

II. The scene on their return home is deeply affecting.

First, they simply narrate to their father Jacob all that had passed in Egypt (29-34). This time there is no concealment or disguise ; no story invented to explain the loss of Simeon, and cover over the demand for Benjamin. The deceit once practised on their venerable parent has borne such bitter fruit, and their consciences, in the crisis of their own danger, have been so exercised about it, that they have no heart to try the same sort of policy again. Thus far, these men are now " Israelites indeed, in whom is no guile." Then, the wonder and alarm of the discovery of every man's money in his sack's mouth, they share in all simplicity with Jacob (ver. 35).

Again, they may well ask, what can this mean? It surely is
not the Egyptian ruler's ordinary way of dealing with all
strangers coming to buy food in Egypt. And it clearly appears now that it is not a stratagem to procure their detention.
What then? Is it intended, by this act of liberality, to lay
them under an additional obligation or necessity to return,
and carry with them Benjamin? Is it to put them more upon
their honour, so that they cannot help revisiting Egypt to have
this mysterious matter cleared up? They are afraid;—their
father as well as they. The mystery only heightens the old
man's distress, in the view of the whole untoward transaction.

For it is the representation of Jacob's deep dejection
that chiefly fills the eye and the heart in this picture of family
grief. How affecting is his first burst of complaint and expostulation! "Me have ye bereaved of my children: Joseph
is not, and Simeon is not, and ye will take Benjamin away:
all these things are against me" (ver. 36). You have lost me
two sons already. Will you insist on my losing a third? Did
you really give in to that cruel man's cruel terms, and not only
consent to let him keep Simeon from me, but promise that he
should have Benjamin, my Rachel's Benjamin, also? Would
nothing content that ravenous Egyptian vulture but that he
must make a prey of two more of my brood of loved sons,
over and above that one of whose fatal loss you so simply, yet
so touchingly, told him? And could you bring yourselves to
acquiesce? Then am I forlorn indeed! Who, or what, is
favourable or propitious to me? "All these things are against
me."

It is a sad and bitter cry. Sinful, no doubt, it is, or tends
to be, at least if the feeling is persisted in and indulged. But
the utterance of sorrow, as nature prompts, is not to be restrained; it is not forbidden by the Lord, but rather encouraged. Jacob soon gives evidence enough of his mind and
heart being schooled into an attitude of meek submission; and
the schooling may have been none the worse for his giving

vent freely at first to the irrepressible anguish of his soul. At all events, he carries our pity and sympathy in his distrust of his sons, and his disposition to lay the blame of this miserable state of things on them. We enter into his feelings when, looking back to their unbrotherly treatment of Joseph, even as he knew it—and he did not know the worst—and considering all their conduct since—he gives himself up to a sense of utter desolation. Will you leave me nothing? Will you take from me all? It is too much! "All these things are against me!" Even his settled obstinacy of purpose, as he sets himself against what his sons would have him to do, we are scarcely inclined very seriously to blame.

Reuben is undoubtedly in earnest in the pledge which he is willing to give of his confidence that no harm will in the end come to Benjamin; "Slay my two sons, if I bring him not to thee; deliver him into my hand, and I will bring him to thee again" (ver. 37). Doubtless he would be as anxious to keep Benjamin safe as he was to keep Joseph safe. And he has evidently good hope concerning the issue of this affair—having shrewdly observed, we may suppose, something of that relenting softness in the Egyptian ruler's nature that cropped out in the midst of his rough and rugged manner—and being persuaded that compliance with his whim of having Benjamin sent as one of them, would conciliate his favour and remove his suspicions, whether real or feigned. Hence probably his readiness to offer such a guarantee as the placing of his own sons in his father's hand. His language, perhaps, is not to be understood quite literally; he could scarcely suppose that even if he failed to bring back Benjamin, his father would actually take him at his word, and put the two youths assigned as hostages to death. But it is a strong and anxious way of expressing, on the one hand, his solicitude to carry out what the ruler in Egypt had required, and on the other hand, his conviction that it was quite safe to do so—that the ruler would be found true to his part of the engagement—that

Simeon would be restored, food in plenty secured, and Benjamin brought home again unharmed.

Jacob, however, is not persuaded or convinced by his eldest son's confident importunity. He knows nothing of Reuben's former care for the preservation of Joseph ; it cannot therefore be expected that he should now be more willing to commit Benjamin to him than to the others. At anyrate, the old man is firm in his determination not to run any risk of losing Joseph's only brother,—Rachel's only child. I could not stand it, he plaintively exclaims. Urge me no more. My mind is made up. " My son shall not go down with you ; for his brother is dead, and he is left alone : if mischief befall him by the way in which ye go, then shall ye bring down my gray hairs with sorrow to the grave " (ver. 38).

III. But Jacob undergoes a change of mind (xliii. 1-14).

At first sight it might seem to be a change wrought under the pressure of mere physical necessity. As long as the supply of food brought from Egypt lasts, things remain on the footing of Jacob's expressed determination not to part with his youngest son. There is silence on the subject in the household ; for it is needless to prolong the painful and irritating discussion. There may even be hope that it may never be needful to revive it. Before their stock in hand is exhausted, plenty may have returned to the land of Canaan ; and when Egypt's lordly potentate ceases to have the immense power which his command of Egypt's full granaries gives him over a starving world, he may become less tyrannical and more placable, and may be got to consent on easier terms to Simeon's release. But it is otherwise ordered by the Lord. The famine continues to become more severe rather than more mild. The corn brought out of Egypt is eaten up. The patriarch-father himself, as responsible for the household's subsistence, is the first to turn his thoughts to the land of plenty, and the storehouses on the banks of the Nile : " Go again, buy us a little food " (ver. 1, 2).

It is for the sons now to object, and to remind Jacob of

the governor's solemn protest: "Ye shall not see my face, except your brother be with you" (ver. 3-5). They have reason on their side. They know, as their father cannot fully know, how the case actually stands. They cannot but insist upon it, as the condition of their complying with their father's command to return to Egypt, that they shall be allowed to carry Benjamin with them. How otherwise can they face the incensed and passionate viceroy, if they so flagrantly break faith with him, and so balk his fierce humour, as to ask an audience of him without that younger brother of theirs, whom he had set his heart on seeing, and whose presence with them he had so vehemently declared to be the only proof he would accept of their being not spies, but true men?

Such considerations they urge upon their father, not, as it would seem, undutifully or unfeelingly. On the contrary, they are evidently affected by the old man's burst of sorrowful passion: "Wherefore dealt ye so ill with me, as to tell the man whether ye had yet a brother?" (ver. 6). There is a deep pathos in the simplicity of this question; and scarcely less in the earnestness of their reply;—"The man asked us straitly of our state, and of our kindred, saying, Is your father yet alive? have ye another brother? and we told him according to the tenor of these words: could we certainly know that he would say, Bring your brother down?" (ver. 7.)

We could not help it, is their apology; that strange man pressed us so closely that there was no resisting him. And how could we anticipate that he would make so cruel a use of the information,—the sad family tale,—which, under the rack of an accusation of treachery, he remorselessly extracted from our lips!

The subdued tone of this defence, and explanation on the part of his sons, may have gone far to overcome their father's scruples. He must have seen now that they were in real earnest, and that they were acting under the pressure of stern necessity. At first, when immediately on their return home, they made the proposal, Jacob may have been slow to admit this. He may have been apt to suspect some sinister design, —or at least to hope that in the long run his sons would depart from so grievous a condition, and admit that a second embassy for food might be undertaken without regard to it. Now, however, when in such straits as the household are reduced to, these fathers of families persist in their averment that they dare not go to Egypt without Benjamin,—and when they give so simple, full, and touching a detail of the way in which it all came about,—the old man is not only satisfied as to the truthfulness of his sons, but made to see also that the Lord's hand is in the matter.

Judah's eager pleading, therefore, is now more a word in season than Reuben's somewhat premature offer of security had been, " Send the lad with me, and we will arise and go ; that we may live, and not die, both we, and thou, and also our little ones. I will be surety for him ; of my hand shalt thou require him : if I bring him not unto thee, and set him before thee, then let me bear the blame for ever: For except we had lingered, surely now we had returned this second time " (ver. 8-10).

The patriarch recovers his calm trust in God, his dignified composure. He resumes once again the firm and manly attitude which one who has known the Lord as his covenant-God ought always to maintain in adversity. There is no more any querulous complaining, any universal despondency,—" all these things are against me !" With a feeling of glad relief we see him erect and strong ;—taking his proper place at the head of this whole affair ;—issuing in unfaltering terms his directions as to the conduct of the enterprise.

" Their father Israel"—Yes! he is Israel once more—"their father Israel said unto them, If it must be so now, do this ; take of the best fruits of the land in your vessels, and carry down the man a present ; and the money that was brought again in the mouth of your sacks, carry it again in your hand :

peradventure it was an oversight " (ver. 11, 12). He speaks as became him, with his own due authority. He cheerfully yields up his Benjamin ; " Take also your brother, and arise, go again unto the man " (ver. 13). And he concludes his address with the words of pious benediction and prayer ;—words of comfortable hope for them ;—and for himself, blessed words of absolutely unreserved and unconditional resignation ; " God Almighty give you mercy before the man, that he may send away your other brother, and Benjamin. If I be bereaved of my children, I am bereaved " (ver. 14).

I scarcely know if any position in Jacob's eventful experience is more noble, in a spiritual point of view, than that which is here described. The closing declaration, " If I be bereaved of my children, I am bereaved," is, in the view of all the circumstances, an instance of acquiescence in the will of God, all but unparalleled. Jacob is now in extreme old age, and he is about to be left alone, so far as the companionship of his sons is concerned. When, long ago, the ten brothers went from home to feed their flocks, Joseph was the comfort of his father's heart,—Benjamin being but a child. In his love to the ten, Jacob sends Joseph to Shechem,—and Joseph goes on to Dothan,—and there disappears. Jacob has still Benjamin, as well as the ten, to comfort him in his being bereaved of Joseph. When the ten are first constrained to go to Egypt for food, Jacob has still Benjamin left to comfort him. But now, he is to be literally left alone ; Benjamin goes with the rest. And however it may be necessary to put a good face on the mission, and send the brothers off with a hopeful blessing, it is for the father a terrible venture. Already Simeon is the tenant of an Egyptian prison. This new embassy, in which all the rest join, may end in their all sharing Simeon's fate,—if not even in a worse catastrophe than that. Jacob consents to the surrender. Leave him Benjamin, and you leave him something to look to, and lean on, after the flesh. When he gives up Benjamin, what remains? It is all, henceforth, with Jacob, an exercise of mere and simple faith,—"enduring as seeing him who is invisible."

Let any one imagine the state of Jacob after he has thus sent all his sons away. It is the very triumph of that faith which is "the substance of things hoped for, the evidence of things not seen." Weeks or months must elapse before any tidings can reach him of the good or ill success of this expedition. The vessel that carries such a venture in its bosom may not be heard of till his grey hairs, through weary watching, have become greyer still. His fond eye, dimmed with the bitter tears of age, sees them—scarcely sees them—leaving him perhaps for ever on this earth. He may look on them, he may look on Benjamin, no more on this side of the grave. He has no express promise that he shall. What probable presumption is there that he shall? It is indeed a dark and doubtful prospect. But, by God's grace, the very extremity of the emergency rouses the old believer to a new venture of faith. He has trusted God before; he will trust him still. "I will trust and not be afraid," is his language; "Though he slay me, yet will I trust him."

And this is the man whom but yesterday we saw thoroughly unmanned, and indulging almost in a childish burst of passionate upbraiding against his God, as well as against his sons— "All these things are against me?" He is like one sunk in the mingled imbecility and obstinacy of helpless dotage. Where is his manly reason? Where his religious resignation—his shrewd sense—his strong faith? What a change now!

Jacob is himself; he is Israel! The pilgrim of half a century is on his feet again, with staff in hand, and eye fixed once more on "the city which hath foundations, whose builder and maker is God." This is not his rest; his tent in Canaan is not his home; its dear fellowships are not his portion. All things are not against him, though "all these things,"—"the things that are seen,"—may seem to be so. They, however, are but "temporal." "The things which are not seen are eternal ;" and they are not against him. "The earthly house of his tabernacle" may be "dissolved," before his sons come back, before Benjamin can be with him again. But he has "a building of God, an house not made with hands, eternal in the heavens."

Thus, a second time, "when he is weak, then is he strong ;" —strong in faith, seeing an unseen Lord, leaning on an unseen powerful arm, looking up into an unseen loving face, looking out for an unseen glorious home. Strong in such faith, he can attend to what is urgent in the occasion on hand, going into even its minute business details. He can order his household gravely but cheerfully, in a crisis that makes the hearts of the other inmates fail. He can bid what may be a final farewell to these stalwart and goodly young men, who, in spite of all their faults, are his sons still. He can take what may be his last look of the Benoni,—the Benjamin,—his dying Rachel left him. And calmly committing himself and his way to the God who blessed him at Bethel, and led him to Syria, and brought him back to Canaan,—the God who has guided and guarded him all his life hitherto,—the God of whom he can say, "I know in whom I have believed,"—he will walk on for the rest of his earthly sojourn,—not wearily, not grudgingly,—but rejoicingly, hopefully,—not weeping always, as if all things were against him,—but praising God who makes all things work together for his good. He will walk, and work, and suffer, and wait, as "a stranger and pilgrim on the earth, declaring plainly that he seeks a better country, even a heavenly."

59

THE DISCOVERY—MAN'S EXTREMITY GOD'S OPPORTUNITY

Genesis 43:15-45:3

They shall look upon me whom they have pierced.   Zechariah 12:10
They were afraid; but he said unto them, It is I; be not afraid.—
  John 6:19,20

" Joseph made haste " (xliii. 30) ; that may be said to be the
explanation of Joseph's whole conduct on the occasion of his
brethren's second visit to Egypt.   He was, if we may judge
from the outset of the narrative, nervous, agitated, restless :
his manner abrupt, his movements quick, his whole demeanour
like that of a man, as we say, in a flutter, or in a flurry,—in a
state of excitement which he can scarcely control.   He is all on
edge, for the crisis is come.   He has to save appearances, and
play his part as a rough-speaking Egyptian vizier, for a little
longer.   But it is with far more difficulty than before that he
does so now.   There is a hurried fitfulness about his way of
dealing with the case that almost betrays him too soon.   He
has enough to do to change his position, as it were, every
moment, that he may keep his countenance, and not break
down.   All throughout, I think, this indication of an inward
struggle is to be traced ; and it gives intense interest, if I
mistake not, to the successive parts of the scene.

I. There is an audience at the public levee : " The men
stood before Joseph " (xliii. 15).   The first sight of his returning brethren is almost more than he can stand ; he makes

haste to cut short the interview. The appearance of Benjamin is evidently too much for him (ver. 16); it is his presence that overpowers him, and makes him fain to turn from his brethren without venturing to open his lips to them. He speaks hastily to the ruler of his house,—barely summoning courage to give these Hebrew strangers in charge to him, that he may carry them from the place of public audience to his own private residence in the palace, and prepare for their sitting at meat with him at noon. Allowing no time for explanations, he is glad thus hastily to dismiss them, even rudely as it might seem, from his presence, lest on the very seat of authority, his self-possession should give way.

For the dismissal is very summary,—and is felt by the brethren to be so: "The men were afraid" (ver. 17). No wonder, one would say, that the men were afraid. They apprehended evil from their being brought into Joseph's house. The governor must have some private and personal cause of offence, about which he wishes to reckon with them more closely, than he could do in an open levee. They at once conjecture what it is; it must be about "the money that was returned in their sacks:" it must be "that he may seek occasion against us, and take us for bondmen, and our asses" (ver. 18). They shrink from entering the house, until they have entreated their conductor to hear their explanation, ending with the protestation:—"We cannot tell who put our money in our sacks" (ver. 19-22). The ruler of Joseph's house takes pains kindly to reassure them; "He said, Peace be to you, fear not; your God, and the God of your father, hath given you treasure in your sacks; I had your money. And he brought Simeon out unto them" (ver. 23). His manner of reassuring them is very remarkable; he uses the language, not of respect only, but even of sympathy. If he does not himself fear the true God, he reverences those who do. He is Joseph's confidential servant,—near his person,—high in his esteem. His master has not disguised or dissembled his reli-

gion ; the man has seen and noted his avoiding all participation in Egyptian idolatry, and his devout consistent worship
of one Supreme Being He has gathered that these strangers
are of the same sort of faith with his master ; and that this
probably is the explanation of their having been so liberally
treated formerly, as well as of their being about to be so
hospitably entertained now.   They come from the same part
of the world to which the ruler traces his origin, and own the
same God as he does.   So the man accounts to himself for
what has taken place,—and so he comforts them.   It is your
God, your hereditary God, who has done this ; therefore have
peace and fear not.   See, here is your brother Simeon, whom
you left a prisoner and hostage, safe and well.   There is no
treachery or harsh treatment intended ; Simeon's restoration
to you is surely a sufficient pledge of the governor's good
faith.   Thus they are set at ease.   So " the man brought the
men into Joseph's house, and gave them water, and they
washed their feet, and he gave their asses provender. And they
made ready the present against Joseph came at noon : for
they heard that they should eat bread there " (ver. 24, 25).

II. The scene at the banquet in the governor's house, it is
almost an offence to touch, in the way either of criticism or of
comment.   Joseph's demeanour is still hurried and agitated ;
—he is more than ever put to it to keep up his incognito and
suppress his vehement emotion, by the assumption of an abrupt
and hasty manner.

The reception, as it were, in the withdrawing-room, opens
in the usual style of oriental courtesy.   The strangers, introduced as guests, offer their presents in the customary form,
and make the prescribed obeisance (ver. 26).   The great man,
acting the part of a princely host or entertainer, is gracious
and condescending in his polite enquiries (ver. 27).   And, as
it would seem, he receives with that air of civil and courtly
satisfaction which it becomes him to show, their grateful and
deferential reply, and their repeated prostration of themselves

(ver. 28). So far the conversation proceeds decorously and with dignity. It may be noticed, however, that the governor has his eyes cast down, and keeps them fixed on the ground. He does not look his invited guests in the face. Is it contempt? or indifference? or mere absence of mind? Or is it that he fears he may break down and betray himself?—But now he looks up. His eager gaze is fastened again, as in the former brief interview, on Benjamin,—"his mother's son," as the narrative with touching simplicity remarks. He cannot stand it. Scarcely has he contrived to ask, with seeming unconcern, the obvious question that might be expected of him in the circumstances, when his self command gives way;—and fairly unmanned, with a broken benediction hastily muttered over the lad's head, he rushes out to vent his full heart alone! It is a touch of nature,—such as throughout all time, and all the world over, makes men kin. " He lifted up his eyes, and saw his brother Benjamin, his mother's son, and said, Is this your younger brother, of whom ye spake unto me? And he said, God be gracious unto thee, my son. And Joseph made haste: for his bowels did yearn upon his brother: and he sought where to weep; and he entered into his chamber, and wept there " (ver. 29, 30).

How, after all, he got through the trying ordeal of the feast, we may, according to our several temperaments, conjecture. He "makes haste." That is his only safety. Without pause or interruption he hurries on the ceremonial. All, indeed, is ordered in due form, and according to strict etiquette. There is no breach of decorum, no cause of offence to any. The governor has so completely recovered his composure that, " refraining himself," he can attend even to the minute points and punctilios of the entertainment. He takes his place, and gives his orders, as if nothing had occurred to disconcert him (ver. 31). All traces of recent tears are wiped away. He leaves his chamber outwardly serene and calm,—and gives directions for the meal to be served. He takes care that the proper distinction is kept up between himself and his guests, as well as between the Egyptian courtiers and these Hebrew strangers ; separate tables being prepared, in deference to a prejudice of which it would be irrelevant here to inquire the cause (ver. 32). Nay, he carries his careful discrimination still farther. With an exactness that strikes them with strange surprise, he arranges the eleven according to seniority, —so well does he remember them, individually as well as collectively (ver. 33). And paying very special attention and a very marked compliment to them all, he gratifies his feelings by singling out, in a way that might not awaken suspicion, the youngest and most interesting of their number, and loading him, probably according to the custom of the court, with peculiar tokens of his kindness : " He took and sent messes unto them from before him : but Benjamin's mess was five times so much as any of theirs. And they drank, and were merry with him" (ver. 34). Thus, as we may suppose, he hurries over the banquet ; allowing himself no time to think or feel,—promoting the general hilarity,—and carrying off his own intensity of suppressed emotion under an air of busy and, as it might seem, even officious hospitality.

III. The ingenious device which Joseph adopted for securing Benjamin alone,—on the evening of the day on which he entertained his brethren, and in the view of their departure homeward early next morning,—is in keeping with his assumed character of an Egyptian vizier. It is such a trick as one might imagine to be keenly relished by some of those capricious potentates of whose whims we read in oriental fable. Why Joseph should have chosen to resort to an expedient of that sort, unless it were simply that he meant to play out his part well and consistently to the last, it is really idle to ask. Perhaps it was a hasty thought. He is not quite prepared to discover himself ; and yet he can scarcely bear to let them all, —or in particular, to let Benjamin away. It will not do to repeat the old stratagem of affecting still to believe them spies, demanding still more specific proof of their being true men, and keeping one of them in security till they bring the proof demanded. He must try a new stroke of policy. And this device of the pretended divining cup may answer as well as any. It will not awaken suspicion or surprise among his ordinary Egyptian attendants ; it is the kind of clever child's-play with which they are familiar.

The steward of Joseph's house hears with all gravity the order given, and prepares to obey it (ver. 1, 2). With equal gravity, when the men have departed next morning, he hears and obeys the order to pursue them and recover the cup (ver. 3-5). He shrewdly guesses his master's design,—and sets himself coolly to carry it out.

The men are suddenly arrested in their journey (ver. 6). They hear with consternation this new charge of theft, and with solemn emphasis disclaim it (ver. 7). They appeal to the proof of honesty they have given in bringing back the money they had found in the mouth of their sacks, on the occasion of their former visit (ver. 8). And they challenge investigation, with all the confidence of conscious innocency. If there be a thief among us, you may punish, not only him, but all of us, —for we vouch for one another ; " With whomsoever of thy servants the cup be found, both let him die, and we also will be my lord's bondmen" (ver. 9). With the utmost mildness and moderation, as it would appear to them, their captor accepts, but with a just modification, their challenge. It is enough that the guilty one of your number should himself suffer, not death, but bondage,—while all the rest of you go free (ver. 10). So the search proceeds,—the imperturbable steward calmly superintending it, as if he knew nothing of what was coming. Deliberately taking the eldest first, and, one after another, exhausting all who are scatheless, he comes at last to the seeming culprit ; " The cup was found in Benjamin's sack" (ver. 11, 12).

Briefly, but how pathetically, is the effect of this exposure told! The brothers are startled and stunned. What can all this mean? What new and overwhelming evidence is this of their old sin finding them out? Is it a reality that has befallen them, or a horrid dream that haunts them? It cannot be that Benjamin, their best and fairest, has committed such a crime,—that he has requited the singular favour the strange governor showed him by such ingratitude,—that he has stained his young hands with sudden baseness. There is some dark mystery about the matter; God is dealing with them terribly in his wrath. And now, what is to be done? Is Benjamin to be surrendered, and are they to go? That, very likely, is what Joseph really wants. His heart, when he is alone after the banquet, yearns for Benjamin;—somehow, anyhow, let the others be off as they may, he must have " his mother's son." And the scheme he hits upon may serve his purpose to detach Benjamin from the rest, and restore him to his embrace. He may even now be preparing a glad surprise for the affrighted youth who, when he is brought back alone, is to find in him, instead of an unjust and angry tyrant, a loving brother, and powerful patron and friend. If so, he is to be so far disappointed. The brothers will not consent to part company with the accused ; whatever danger there may be, or whatever disgrace, they will share it with him. They are changed from what they were when they could so cruelly, and without a cause, sell their father's favourite child. Not even when there seems to be a cause, will they give up their father's last comfort now ; " They rent their clothes, and laded every man his ass, and returned to the city" (ver. 13).

IV. Thus the whole company return together: " And Judah and his brethren,"—Judah taking the lead now, for he had taken the lead in persuading Jacob to part with Benjamin, and had come under the most solemn obligations for his safety,— " Judah and his brethren came to Joseph's house (for he was yet there) ; and they fell before him to the ground " (ver. 14). This return of all his brethren together may have taken Joseph by surprise. It was still early morning. Joseph had not left his home to transact business in his public court; they found him in comparative privacy, in his palace. Their coming back in a body was fitted, perhaps, at first to disconcert, and yet afterwards it served to facilitate his plan. It was more than he had expected or desired. And it seemed to stand in the way of his special design to obtain possession of Benjamin. But at the same time, he could scarcely resent it; for it indicated a more gracious frame of mind than he may have been giving them credit for. And along with their subdued and humble deportment, all throughout, it may have had something to do with the impulse to discover himself, which, as the conversation went on, soon proved too strong for him.

At first, indeed, he keeps up his assumed sternness and gruffness of manner. He speaks as one justly offended by the secret meanness and villany, thus by supernatural or magical means discovered : " What deed is this that ye have done ? Wot ye not that such a man as I can certainly divine" (ver. 15). He makes an attempt, also, to accomplish the object upon which his heart is set,—to separate Benjamin from the rest, and keep him with him while the others may go. This appears as the colloquy proceeds. The reply made to his first angry accusation is not very coherent : " Judah said, What shall we say unto my lord ? what shall we speak ? or how shall we clear ourselves ? God hath found out the iniquity of thy servants. Behold, we are my lord's servants ; both we, and he also with whom the cup is found " (ver. 16). Judah speaks as one in great trepidation ; he is utterly at a loss how to explain what has occurred. But, at all events, he is clear enough in his intimation that they all mean to make common cause with Benjamin. How the cup got into Benjamin's sack, they cannot tell ; for they cannot believe it to be Benjamin's own doing. Be it accident, however, or contrivance, or legerdemain, they take it as a blow struck by the divine hand at all of them together. It is God touching them at the tenderest point,—wounding them all in common through their youngest —Benjamin—whom their father had, with so many misgivings and forebodings, committed to them, and whom it concerned their common honour to carry back to the old man in safety. It is a common calamity, a common judgment. Judah frankly tells this stern lord of Egypt that they so regard it. They accept it at the hand of God as the common punishment of their untold common sin. They had offended together; and they will now also suffer together.

Not so is Joseph's rejoinder, in the character of ruler and judge. He takes high ground in justice and equity. It is Benjamin, "his mother's son," that he longs to have. It is Benjamin that he would fain contrive to keep, under all this affectation of fair and impartial dealing. It is Benjamin, and Benjamin alone that he wants: "God forbid that I should do so; but the man in whose hand the cup is found, he shall be my servant; and as for you, get you up in peace unto your father" (ver. 17).

V. The speech of Judah, however, alters the whole aspect of the case. The simple, natural, resistless eloquence of that most pathetic appeal, breaks down all Joseph's reserve. It may well do so. It is such an outbreak of genuine feeling as a heart like Joseph's cannot withstand. If the idea had really entered into his mind,—and much of the narrative would seem to indicate that it had,—of getting Benjamin alone to be his companion in his splendid exile, and letting the separation otherwise between himself and his father's house in the meantime continue;—if doubts as to how his other brethren might be disposed to regard him, had made him hesitate about the best way of treating them; if such considerations, connected with their former envious and cruel malice,—which might rankle still in their bosoms though all sense of it was long gone from his,—had moved him to make a difference between Benjamin and them;—Judah's appeal was fitted to work a thorough change. For it is indeed a noble pleading. The speaker rises to the occasion ;—for the occasion makes the speaker. It is the very soul of truest oratory. And it is directed, perhaps unconsciously on the orator's part, to the very point of breaking down Joseph's partial purpose on behalf of Benjamin.

Joseph may mean it for a kindness. Very soon, if Benjamin is anyhow kept and the rest are suffered to go, he will relieve his young brother's anxiety, and make him a sharer in all his own prosperity. It will be his fond delight to advance Benjamin to Pharaoh's favour and Egypt's highest honour. But if any such romantic notion has been floating in Joseph's brain, the speech of Judah is the very thing to recall him to sober thought. It sets before him, in vivid picture, the actual realities of the case, as the brother, in his overwhelming agony of spirit, simply tells an unvarnished tale of truth.

First, he adjures the governor, in most melting strains, to give him a favourable hearing: " O my lord, let thy servant, I pray thee, speak a word in my lord's ears ; and let not thine anger burn against thy servant ; for thou art even as Pharaoh" (ver. 18). It is a courtly opening; but it is quite artless and sincere ; as much so as the opening of Paul's noble appeal to King Agrippa. The speaker is in earnest ; in the earnestness almost of despair. Next, he reminds the governor of the way in which he had wrung from them the information about their domestic circumstances, of which he is now making so cruel a use (ver. 19-23). He paints now, in a few graphic strokes, the scene between them and their father, when the old man's consent to risk Benjamin was obtained, at the cost almost of a broken heart (ver. 24-29). Unwittingly he sends a shaft into Joseph's bosom, as he represents his father bewailing his beloved Rachel and her two sons,—one already lost, and the other about to be torn away. The old man, says Judah, assured us, ah! how pathetically,—and his trembling, weeping agitation confirmed the assurance,—that the loss of Benjamin, after the loss of Joseph, was more than he could survive. How then, he asks, can I face my father if I go

home without Benjamin? " Now therefore, when I come to
thy servant my father, and the lad be not with us (seeing
that his life is bound up in the lad's life); it shall come to
pass, when he seeth that the lad is not with us, that he will
die: and thy servants shall bring down the gray hairs of thy
servant our father with sorrow to the grave" (ver. 30, 31).
I made myself, he continues, answerable to my father for the
lad's safe return; let me, therefore, instead of him, be the
victim of thy displeasure (ver. 32, 33). Take me, and let the
lad go. I dare not, I cannot, face the fatal despair which his
absence must cause ;—" For how shall I go up to my father,
and the lad be not with me? lest peradventure I see the evil
that shall come on my father" (ver. 34).

The whole pleading most thrillingly touches the right
chord in Joseph's soul. Instead of Egypt's splendour, to be
shared with Benjamin when he has entrapped him, as it were,
by guile,—there rises before his eyes the image of a forlorn
and desolate old man, whose fond caresses are yet fresh in his
remembrance. Judah's affecting words, accompanied, one
cannot doubt, with tears, in which they all share, awaken
home feelings that cannot be suppressed. The aspect of
severity can be maintained no longer. It is time for Joseph
to relent. " Then Joseph could not refrain himself before all
them that stood by him ; and he cried, Cause every man to go
out from me. And there stood no man with him while Joseph
made himself known unto his brethren. And he wept aloud :
and the Egyptians and the house of Pharaoh heard. And
Joseph said unto his brethren, I am Joseph : does my father
yet live ?" (ver. 1-3).

Over the scene of the discovery a veil of reserve is cast ;
Joseph is alone with his brethren. No strangers witness his
emotion ; but the loud burst of his weeping is overheard
without. His brethren cannot speak for trouble and terror ;
but he invites them to draw near, and addresses to them
words of peace ; " Be not grieved nor angry with yourselves

that ye sold me hither : for God did send me before you to preserve life " (ver. 3-5). It is as in the day when that prophecy shall be fulfilled, " I will pour upon the house of David, and upon the inhabitants of Jerusalem, the spirit of grace and of supplications : and they shall look upon me whom they have pierced, and they shall mourn for him" (Zech. xii. 10). Blessed are they who so mourn, for they shall be comforted.

Two observations on this scene may be allowed.

I. The precise moment of Joseph's making himself known to his brethren,—whether we regard it as chosen by himself, or as chosen for him by God through the working of his natural feelings,—is highly significant. Certainly, it looks as if it was a sudden thought,—an abrupt change of mind ;—as if up to this time Joseph had really been intending to keep Benjamin, ostensibly for a slave, and to send the rest sorrowing and despairing away,—but now, moved by Judah's pathetic pleading, found himself unable to persist in his purpose any longer. If so, it is a circumstance surely very suggestive. Jesus, I suppose, put on an air of stern and frowning severity, when he made as if he would spurn away from him, like a dog, the woman of Canaan,—and he kept up that aspect till the instant of his being constrained by the woman's importunity to say, " O woman, great is thy faith." What a sudden change, and how seasonable ! Instantly that face beams with its wonted halo of love,—that eye is dim with its wonted tear of pity,— that mouth utters its wonted words,—such as never man spake but this man ! There, it was great faith that seemingly wrote the change,—here, it is great need. Nay rather, there and here alike, it is great need ;—great need, prompting great earnestness and urgency—great boldness and perseverance. It was great need that furnished the woman with that keen and witty logic of hers ;—" Truth, Lord, but the dogs eat of the crumbs of the children's table." It was great need that gave Judah that matchless, persuasive eloquence, which otherwise his tongue never would have known. It is great need that touches Joseph's heart. It is thy great need that touches thy Joseph's heart, O poor sinner, O fainting soul? Thy sin is terribly finding thee out; and all is very dark! The very Lord of grace and glory, on whom thy fate hangs, keeps an ominous silence;—or is about to deal out to thee a rigid measure of inexorable justice. Still cleave to him, O thou guilty one, with guilt of deepest dye on thy conscience,—cleave to him, O thou of little faith, sinking in a stormy sea. Cry to him; plead with him; wrestle with him! Refuse to let him go until he bless thee.

Lo! he smiles,—he weeps. That dark brow unbends. Those withdrawn arms are stretched out. Thou art in his embrace. He cannot refrain himself. He makes himself known to thee,—to thee, the chief of sinners—to whom he rejoices affectionately to say,—I am Jesus, thy Saviour, thy friend, thy brother.

II. The manner of this disclosure is as significant as the time of it. All is unmingled tenderness and love. Not a word of upbraiding,—not a look of reproach,—not a sigh of regret or complaint. All is peace. If their old sin,—then freshly, oh! how freshly and poignantly remembered by them, —is mentioned by him at all, it is only that he may assure them of its being thoroughly forgiven. He would even seem almost to excuse it, or to excuse them,—showing how their conduct wrought out the gracious saving purpose of God. At all events, he will have them to think of that gracious saving purpose now, as giving them a pledge of there being mercy enough with God for the very worst of them, and for the very worst deed that any of them has done.

So the apostles preached Christ to his betrayers and murderers,—telling them that the blood which they so cruelly shed, and which they so madly imprecated upon their own heads, was flowing as a fountain to cleanse them from all sin,—the sin even of crucifying the Lord of glory. So Christ discovers himself to you, O ye men of broken spirits and contrite hearts, when the Holy Spirit is showing you how you have been piercing him. " I am Jesus whom thou persecutest ;" " Saul ! Saul ! why persecutest thou me ?"—that is the utmost of his reproof. Or rather, it is his affectionate, most touching, altogether irresistible expostulation.

Could the brothers withstand that appeal,—I am Joseph your brother whom ye sold into Egypt ? Could Saul withstand that appeal,—I am Jesus whom thou persecutest ? Canst thou withstand the appeal, when he whom thou hast been piercing, wounding, grieving afresh, till this very hour, speaks to thee as he never spoke to thee before—or speaks to thee as he has often spoken to thee before,—but with new power, as now at last thou feelest in thy inmost soul,—" I, even I, am he that blotteth out thy transgressions for mine own sake, and will not remember thy sins."

60

A TRUE BROTHER—A GENEROUS KING—A GLAD FATHER

Genesis 45:1-28

A new commandment I give unto you, that ye love one another ; as I
have loved you, that ye also love one another.   John 13:34
Kings shall be thy nursing fathers. Isaiah 49:23
A wise son maketh a glad father. Proverbs 10:1

JOSEPH, Pharaoh, Jacob, stand out conspicuous in this chapter,
—Joseph's brotherly and filial love (ver. 4-15),—Pharaoh's
grateful and generous hospitality (ver. 16-20),—Jacob's piety
(ver. 21-28).

I. The address of Joseph to his brethren, is singular for
its rare mixture of authority and tenderness.   There is in it the
calm and conscious air of the prince and prophet, tempered
with all a son's reverence, and all a brother's fond familiarity.
It is worthy of Joseph,—of his simple character, and of his
exalted rank (ver. 4-15).

The first outburst of irrepressible feeling being over, Joseph
sets himself to encourage his troubled and terrified brethren,—
too troubled and too terrified to be able to answer his plain
question, " Doth my father yet live" (ver. 3).   He kindly bids
them draw near—" Come near to me, I pray you."   And as
they come near, he repeats his intimation, " I am Joseph,"—
adding to it these two particulars,—" your brother, whom ye
sold into Egypt."   In doing so, he means to speak comfort
and peace to them.   It is not by way of reproach that he reminds

them of the past ; but rather to press home upon them the
assurance that he is still their brother.   Neither his present
elevation, nor the deep shame and suffering which preceded it,
has separated him from them.   In spite of all that might
seem to have put a wide gulph between him and them, he is
not estranged from them.   All throughout, in the hands of the
Ishmaelites, in Potiphar's house, in the cruel disgrace and pain
of his unjust imprisonment, he has never ceased to feel himself
to be their brother, notwithstanding their unbrotherly treatment of him.   Seated on the throne of sovereign power, he is
not too elevated to call them brethren still : " I am Joseph
your brother."   And if now he recalls the sad scene of their
last parting in Canaan,—" whom ye sold into Egypt"—it is
not that he may upbraid them with what they then did, but
that he may show how it has been all ordered and overruled
for good (ver. 5-8).   It brought about what God designed ;
" God did send me hither."   And it is for you that I am here ;
—" to preserve you a posterity and save your lives by a great
deliverance."   And not for you only, but for the Gentile world
also, for " he hath made me a father to Pharaoh," to benefit
" all the land of Egypt."   This is not your doing, but God's.

Thus reassured, Joseph's brethren are prepared to await
his orders.   It cannot surprise them to find that his first concern is about his father.   Once and again has Joseph, even
when keeping himself unknown, inquired about the old man's
life and health, with an earnestness and particularity that might
seem to them unaccountable on the part of a mere stranger,
and one so high in rank at a foreign court.   Now the mystery
is solved.   That Joseph should be thus thoughtful about the
fond parent whose favourite child he had been, is only natural.
But surely, in the circumstances, it must have cut these men
to the heart to think of the long estrangement of which they
had been the cause !   Could they listen unmoved to their
brother's eager and impetuous urgency ?   " Haste ye " (ver. 9) ;
—and again : " ye shall haste " (ver. 13).   It is all hot haste,

to relieve the aged Patriarch's anxiety, and cheer his long darkened soul with tidings of great joy,—to tell him of his long lost son's greatness and glory,—and above all, to bring him to that son's embrace, and place him in peace and plenty under his fostering care ; " Haste ye, and go up to my father, and say unto him, Thus saith thy son Joseph, God hath made me lord of all Egypt : come down unto me, tarry not." " I will nourish thee." " And behold your eyes see, and the eyes of my brother Benjamin, that it is my mouth that speaketh unto you. And ye shall tell my father of all my glory in Egypt, and of all that ye have seen ; and ye shall haste and bring down my father hither" (ver. 9-13).

Surely this is a message which it may well cost these men tears of penitential sorrow to receive, as it must cost them tears of shame to deliver it. Such love as Jacob's for his son, and Joseph's for his father, it has not hitherto entered into their minds to conceive. And it is such love that they have been so deeply and cruelly wounding. It is a new measure they now get, by which to estimate their crime. It is somewhat of the nature of that insight which, through the Spirit's teaching, the smitten soul gets into the mutual love of the Father and the Son ; an insight that gives hitherto unimagined significancy to the dread transaction between them which guilt made necessary, and into the exceeding sinfulness of sin as causing that state of things between the Father and the Son, of which the cry upon the cross is the expression—" My God, my God, why hast thou forsaken me ! "—making it needful for the son to become " an outcast from his God," and needful for the Father to say, " Awake, O sword, against my Shepherd ! " —and all in love, O my soul, to thee !

And then, what a message for these men to deliver ! To look their injured father in the face and tell him of the long lie by which they have made his old age miserable ; to recant the mean and cruel falsehood ; to confess all their dark deed of villany ; thus to disclose and undo the past—what a humiliation! They had need to be furnished with a gospel of the best sort,—glad tidings of great joy,—to overcome their abashed embarrassment in speaking to Joseph's father concerning Joseph.

Joseph himself seems to feel this. And, accordingly, he is at great pains to encourage them. Again and again he resumes the task. He would have them to turn their eyes away from themselves to him,—from their own sin and shame, to his glorious saving power. You see me, he cries; " your eyes see." It is no delusion; I am not a spirit, or a ghost; I am your own brother, raised up by God to this height of princely dignity on very purpose to be your saviour. " Your eyes see, and the eyes of my brother Benjamin." He believes me; why should not 'you? True, you may feel that you have wronged me, and sinned against me, as Benjamin never did; you have that to answer for with which his conscience is not burdened. But what of that? I make no distinction now between him and you. I do not place you at a disadvantage. " Your eyes see," as well as "the eyes of my brother Benjamin, that it is my mouth that speaketh unto you" (ver. 12); —not to him only,—but to you as well,—and speaketh to you peace. It is I who speak to you,—not now through an interpreter, as if I could address you only in a strange tongue;—but plainly,—face to face,—mouth to mouth. And I speak to you, not to upbraid you with the past, but to send you on what, in spite of all the past, should be a pleasant errand now. Return home, to your own house, and tell what great things God has wrought. Be not disconcerted or dismayed. Let your faltering tongue, overcoming all your natural misgivings, give forth its errand: " Ye shall tell my father of all my glory in Egypt, and of all that ye have seen; and ye shall haste and bring down my father hither" (ver. 13). This grateful office rendered to him will obliterate the dark memory of every old offence. If the new insight you have

got into my father's love for me, and mine for him, aggravates your distress when you think of the breach you have
caused,—let it console you to be partakers of the joy that
there is in our meeting, father and son, now that all that pain
is over.

But not even yet is Joseph satisfied that he has done
enough. Still fresh tokens of his heart's love are lavished on
Benjamin and on them all,—kisses and tears: "He fell
upon his brother Benjamin's neck, and wept; and Benjamin
wept upon his neck. Moreover he kissed all his brethren,
and wept upon them" (ver. 14, 15). Nor will he leave
off kissing them all and weeping with them, pouring out
his soul in a flood of sympathy, until he has fairly vanquished all their fear, and brought them to converse freely,
boldly, familiarly: "after that, his brethren talked with him"
(ver. 15).

Ah! truly, Joseph is the model of what a brother ought
to be, "a brother born for adversity!" He is the sort of
brother you need in your deep grief, ye sin-sick, sin-laden,
sorrow-laden children—the fitting type of the brother you
have in the well-beloved Son of the Father! He is never
weary of speaking peace to you,—assuring you that he
remembers not any wrong of yours against him; that the
blood which your sin shed cleanseth that sin away; that he
whom you crucified is at God's right hand, mighty to save!
How is he ever striving, by his word and Spirit, to reveal
himself to you, and to get you to see him! How does he
raise you from the dust and set you on a rock that you may
sound his praise! How does he plead with you and expostulate
with you, that you may lay aside all your doubts and hesitancy,
and believe him when he talks with you, and bids you go on
your way to the Father rejoicing! How does he kiss you
and weep with you,—loading you with tenderest caresses,—
refusing to be content until you, his brethren, take heart, and
summon courage,—to "talk with him."

" To talk with him ! " Yes ! For that is what he wants —what alone can prove that all at last is right between him and you—that there is no more dislike, or jealousy, or suspicion, or servile dread—that you do indeed now know him, and trust him, and love him, as a brother. He would not merely talk affectionately with you—he would have you to talk confidingly and confidentially with him. That is what alone could satisfy Joseph. It is what alone will satisfy your Joseph, your Jesus. Receive then his kindly advances. Believe his gracious words. Let him show himself to you, and embrace you and sympathise with you. " And after that," as " his brethren," " talk with him." Frankly, unreservedly, in the confidence of brotherly familiarity, talk with him ; of his Father and your Father, of the house with many mansions, of the coming joy of the re-united family's home-meeting there ; or of his past experience in his humiliation ; or of your own present experience in your sin and sorrow ; or of his kingdom ; or of your own grief ; or of duty ; or of trial ; or of death ; or of his church ; or of your own household and friends. Only talk with him, ye brethren of his, of all, of anything, that may interest him and you. He refuses to let you go until you " talk with him."

II. On this occasion, the conduct of Pharaoh is princely and truly noble. It is in keeping with all that we read of this illustrious monarch—surely no ordinary specimen of the race of oriental kings, as we are apt to conceive of them. The grace and generosity of his cordial congratulation is at once a pleasing proof of the high place which Joseph's wise fidelity has won for him in his royal master's esteem, and a refreshing instance of the king's own goodness of heart—his kindly nature—his grateful appreciation of true and honest service ; " And the fame thereof was heard in Pharaoh's house, saying, Joseph's brethren are come : and it pleased Pharaoh well, and his servants " (ver. 16).

The discovery of his vizier's lineage and family connections

might have been distasteful to a sovereign of narrow mind.
The melting scene of kissing and tears might have awakened,
in the stern bosom of a tyrant, no other emotion than contempt for such womanish weakness.   The liberty which Joseph
took in disposing, as it would seem, upon his own authority,
of Egypt's territory, and alienating what he chose of it to a
strange tribe, might have been resented as the insolence of
upstart greatness.   But it is not so.   Pharaoh is above all such
petty jealousies;—he delights in the story which he hears;—its
romance excites him and its pathos touches him.   He has
thorough sympathy with his favourite, who has served him so
well, in this new and strange turn of fortune, as well as in all
the varied experience that has gone before and prepared the way
for it.   And he carries the whole court along with him in his
sympathy.   Joseph's proposed arrangements for his father's
and his family's accommodation are approved of warmly, and
promptly seconded (ver. 17-20).   The king in fact cannot do
enough to testify his regard for Joseph.   Not only is there to
be a goodly portion of Egypt's best awaiting the acceptance of
Jacob and his house, when they come from Canaan ; it is
the monarch's pride and pleasure to undertake the whole
charge of the removal.   And all expedition must be used.
Whatever conveyances are needed for the little ones and the
wives, Egypt is to supply them, that no time may be lost in
preparing to start from Canaan.   Nor is the packing of the
household goods to be suffered to cause delay.   There is no
need to care for the stuff.   Let it be abandoned and left
behind, rather than that there should be any tarrying.   Why
be burdened with such impediments ?   Let the old man, and
all who live with him, come quickly.   Let them come themselves, and make a bonfire of their furniture and property, or
a legacy to their neighbours.   Why should they be troubled
about these things, when " the good of all the land of Egypt is
theirs, and they may eat the fat of it ?"   So impatient is this

right-hearted, large-hearted prince to carry out the hospitable thoughts on which he is intent.

It must have been with deeply gratified feelings that Joseph came forth from his interview with so kind a master, and proceeded to give his final instructions to his departing brethren. Such confidence as is reposed in him, such sympathy as is shown with him, such royal bountifulness, may well repay years of suffering and toil. Frankly he acknowledges and accepts Pharaoh's liberality, and faithfully he executes his commands. His brethren are now thoroughly furnished and equipped with all necessaries for their journey and return (ver. 21-23). Thereafter, with one parting word of admonition, Joseph dismisses them in peace ; " So he sent his brethren away, and they departed : and he said unto them, See that ye fall not out by the way " (ver. 24).

Is there a quaint dash of humour in this significant hint : " See that ye fall not out by the way ? "—a touch of sly, sarcastic, good-natured irony ? Nay, it is no time,—and Joseph has no heart,—for that. There is a graver, deeper, better, meaning in what he says. These brethren of his have been getting a new lesson in the school of love,—in the divine faculty of holy charity. They have just come to the knowledge of a kind and degree of love, of which they had no conception before. For in truth love like Joseph's to his father and his brethren is a new thing to them. The very idea of it is new. Hence they are so slow to take it in, to understand it,—to believe that it can be real. But they have been got to see it and to feel it. They have now some insight into Joseph's open heart. He has given them such discoveries of what is in it that they can stand out incredulous no lon er. Love so tender and so true ; so prodigal of self ; so min ul of all but self ; so self-sacrificing and self-forgetting ; so meek, so merciful, so mild, so melting ; love that can so forgive, and pity, and embrace, and weep ; love that will take no denial and suffer no repulse, but will have the loved ones, almost in their own despite, in its embrace; Joseph's love; the love of Joseph's heart; has found entrance into their long frozen hearts, and opened the warm fountains of tears and gladness there. Forgiven much, they love much. Joseph they love as they never thought to have loved a living being before; and they love one another as they never loved one another before. But it is a new affection. They are novices and raw recruits in this discipline of charity. The old nature in them may still be apt to get the better of the new creation. They may well therefore be grateful for that deep, love-thrilling, voice of admonition, "See that ye fall not out by the way."

"A new commandment," says the Lord, "I give unto you, That ye love one another; as I have loved you, that ye also love one another" (John xiii. 34). Like Joseph's brethren, if you have been moved to believe in Jesus, you have been taking a new lesson in the way of loving. You have become acquainted with a style and manner of love far transcending even Joseph's. The love of Jesus! Who can know it? But something of it you know. Experimentally you know it. For have you not bathed his feet with your tears, and wiped them with the hairs of your head? Have you not heard his voice, "Neither do I condemn thee"? Have you not looked to him lifted up on the cross, laying down his life for you?

Yes. It is a new commandment,—to love as he loves. And its observance among yourselves, and towards all men, is with you the growth of a new nature. Take therefore always in good part every warning against the risk of this new-born grace of love or charity giving way, under the irksome annoyances of the road you have to travel, and the infirmities of the brethren with whom you have to travel it. See that ye "walk in love, as Christ also loved you, and gave himself for you an offering and a sacrifice to God for a sweet smelling savour" (Eph. v. 2). "See that ye fall not out by the way."

III. The arrival of the brethren at their father's house in Canaan, closes this touching scene—"They went up out of

Egypt, and came into the land of Canaan unto Jacob their father, and told him, saying, Joseph is yet alive, and he is governor over all the land of Egypt" (ver. 25, 26).

The patriarch's reception of their news is simply told;— "Jacob's heart fainted, for he believed them not" (ver. 26). He believed them not. Is it for very joy—as it is said of the assembled disciples, when they saw the risen Lord, and his pierced hands and feet, that they yet believed not for joy? Or is it that he cannot trust their truthfulness? And yet the fact that they are all there,—Simeon and Benjamin and all of them,—may attest what they tell. However they may have deceived him before, can he fail to see evidence in their whole manner now that they are giving him a true report? Nay, it is enough to say that under this new excess of emotion the old man's heart fainted. For a time he could not take the tidings in; they quite overwhelmed and overmastered him. And no marvel. He has to undo the past of years. He has to turn back the whole tide and current of his feelings, from the dismal day when he accepted as a fact Joseph's death, and began to make up his mind to a stern and sad submission. For the rest of acquiescence in a fixed and certain doom, is now to be suddenly exchanged for the restless agitation of reviving hope. At once everything is unsettled again and in suspense. The very idea of its being possible that Joseph may be yet alive, is more than the old man's shattered nerves can stand; "His heart fainted."

But he rallies, and can listen to their detailed account of the whole wondrous providence they have to report; "And they told him all the words of Joseph, which he had said unto them" (ver. 27). Gradually his mind is strengthened to take it all in. Piecemeal, as it were, or bit by bit, the reality of the strange transactions of which he hears becomes more and more palpable. The actual sight of the conveyances provided for carrying him and his house bodily to Egypt, helps him to realise as true what looks so like a tale or a dream (ver. 27),

It is no imagination, no vision, no deception ; the visible, tangible, sensible, evidences of the fact are there before his eyes. The spirit of the aged and tried believer revives. He can still believe,—and find that " all things are possible to him that believeth." He is still Israel,—nay, now again he is more than ever Israel,—strong to prevail with God. " Israel said, It is enough ; Joseph my son is yet alive : I will go and see him before I die " (ver. 28). It is as Israel that he says this. It is as Israel that he rises to the emergency,—and shakes off the fainting helplessness of unbelief. " His spirit " revives to the obedience of faith, " It is enough ;"—and to the joy of faith, " Joseph my son is yet alive ;"—and to the walk of faith, " I will go and see him before I die."

Thus the patriarch again approves himself to be worthy of the name of Israel. For I cannot but think that there is a meaning in the use of this name, at this crisis. There is a remarkable change here from Jacob to Israel. " Jacob's heart fainted" at first ; but " Israel said, It is enough." As Jacob, the patriarch has been weak,—apt to say, as he refuses to be comforted, " I will go down into the grave unto my son mourning,"—or " all these things are against me,"—or " me ye have bereaved," or "ye shall bring down my gray hairs with sorrow into the grave." Occasionally he has been roused to an exercise of his wonted strength of faith,—as when, after much hesitation, " Israel their father " consented to risk Benjamin with his brothers into Egypt. He has doubtless been disciplining himself into submission to the sovereign hand of God, learning to be still and know that he is God,—to be dumb, not opening his mouth, for God hath done it. But he has been despondent still,—fearful of evil,—slow to take in the fulness of the blessing of the gospel of peace,—ready to imagine, even when he hears good news, that it may be too good news to be true. Now however he is Israel once more. He will doubt no longer. Is anything too hard for the Lord ? Has he not, even in the Lord's wrestling with

him, overcome ?   Is not this the answer to many a prayer for
light on the dark dealings of the Lord with him ?   Is it not
an answer infinitely beyond what he could ask or think ?
" At evening time" there is to be "light" indeed! (Zech.
xiv. 7).   " They told him all the words of Joseph ; and when
he saw the waggons which Joseph had sent to carry him,
the spirit of Jacob their father revived ; and Israel said, It is
enough ; Joseph my son is yet alive : I will go and see him
before I die" (ver. 27, 28).

61

FAITH QUITTING CANAAN FOR EGYPT—CANAAN LEFT FOR JUDGMENT

Genesis 46:1-27

Israel also came into Egypt; and Jacob sojourned in the land of Ham.—
Psalm 105:23

Thou knewest not the time of thy visitation. Luke 19:44

EGYPT is now to be for a long period, measured by centuries, the home or refuge of God's chosen Israel, in order that, in the fulness of time, a signal historical event may become a significant Messianic prophecy. To Moses, the Lord said: "Thou shalt say unto Pharaoh, thus saith the Lord, Israel is my son, even my first-born; and I say unto thee, Let my son go that he may serve me" (Exod. iv. 22, 23). By the mouth of Hosea, the Lord says: "When Israel was a child, then I loved him, and called my son out of Egypt" (Hosea xi. 1). And the inspired Evangelist interprets and applies the symbolic prediction. Mary's husband "arose, took the young child and his mother by night, and departed into Egypt; and was there until the death of Herod, that it might be fulfilled which was spoken of the Lord by the prophet, saying, Out of Egypt have I called my son" (Matt. ii. 14, 15). To lay a foundation for this divine oracle, involving as it does a great general principle of the divine administration,—that salvation comes through suffering, liberty through service, life through death,—the descent of the holy family into Egypt is ordained.

Jacob yields to the solicitation of Joseph, and the invitation of Pharaoh. He makes up his mind to leave Canaan; and that, not for a short personal visit merely to his son in Egypt, but for a protracted sojourn of his whole household there. They are to be established and domesticated for long generations on the banks of the Nile. In all this Jacob exercises faith. It is by faith that he goes down, with all his children, into Egypt. It is by faith that he takes the step which is to prove so critical, not for himself only, but for the people and nation of which he is the head; by faith having for its object, not merely a human message or testimony, however cheering and consoling, but a divine warrant.

This is made palpable by the transaction between him and his covenant-God which marks his departure from the land of promise, and his committal of himself and his house to a strange country (ver. 1-4). The scene of the transaction is fitly chosen; it is Beersheba,—on the confines of the sacred territory. There Abraham made a covenant by oath with his neighbour Abimelech, the Philistine King of Gerar;—planting a grove, and calling upon the name of Jehovah the everlasting God (xxi. 22, 23). He was dwelling at Beersheba when the great trial of his faith took place, in the matter of the command to sacrifice Isaac (xxii.) At Beersheba, in the days of Isaac, the transaction with the king of Gerar, whence its name was derived, was in a remarkable manner repeated (xxvi.) It was for the most part Isaac's home, where he was residing when he blessed Jacob and Esau (xxviii.) It was afterwards a border city, marking one of the limits of the land of Israel (Judges xx. 1). Jacob probably lived near it, and had occasion to pass through it on his way to Egypt.

He pauses there. The place reminds him of his father Isaac, and of his father's habitual fear and worship of God. If he has been moved to undertake the journey on Joseph's invitation and at the entreaty of his other sons, relying on Pharaoh's royal honour,—and as yet with too little consultation and prayer for ascertaining the will and seeking the countenance of the Lord,—he feels his need of this at Beer-sheba. He cannot pass a spot hallowed by so many pious memories, and so full of the associations of his father's house ; he cannot quit the last corner of the holy land of promise on which his foot is to stand ; he cannot bid a final farewell to Canaan, the country promised to his race ;—at his age, it must be a final farewell ;—without a solemn renewal of his covenant with the Lord,—without waiting for a renewal of the covenant on the part of the Lord himself. Therefore " he offered sacrifices unto the God of his father Isaac. And God spake unto Israel in the visions of the night, and said, Jacob, Jacob. And he said, Here am I " (ver. 1, 2).

The burden of the divine communication is, " Fear not to go down into Egypt " (ver. 3). For there was cause of fear in Jacob's circumstances ;—there might well be fear in Jacob's heart. It was a hazardous movement on which he was venturing. To flit and change his place of residence at all, at so great an age, is of itself a trial. Leave me to repose, the much vexed and weary patriarch might have said ; let Joseph come to visit me, and bring such tokens of his filial love as he may choose. But why must I unsettle all my ways of life, lift my feet from the very side of the quiet ancestral grave in which I long to rest, and undertake toil and travel from which my tottering frame shrinks, to become in my last days a stranger among strangers of a strange and foreign tongue ? Then, is it safe to reckon on security in that strange land ? Joseph's affection may be sure, but his life is precarious. His heart towards me may be trusted, but is the king's heart towards him to be equally relied on ? A sudden caprice in the monarch's breast, or a sudden revolution in his realms, or an invading foe, or a change of dynasty, or any one of many possible, nay probable, contingencies, may change Joseph's seat near the throne to his old bed in prison, as abruptly as the prison was exchanged for the throne. And where then is Israel ? It can be no cause of wonder to find Jacob at Beersheba beginning to be afraid.

The first eagerness of his desire to go to Joseph, the first excitement of the good news from a far country on the strength of which he has been persuaded to go,—may well be giving place to certain anxieties and ominous alarms, as he now more calmly considers the risks and dangers of his undertaking.

Especially he might be apt to fear, as he called to mind the dark prophecy with which he must have been familiar, which held suspended over his house the doom of a long and bitter subjection to a foreign foe. He could not but have fresh in his memory and before his eye, at Beersheba, the scene of that memorable night when the Lord appeared to Abraham and justified him as a believer (xv). Jacob is probably on the very spot where Abraham then lay. In spirit, as he recalls the past, and is in Abraham's place ;—in the midst, as his fancy puts it, of the materials of Abraham's sacrifice ;—that ominous voice of woe,—"thy seed shall be a stranger,"—"shall serve,"— "shall be afflicted four hundred years,"—is sounding in his ears. Is the time come ? Is he, under the impulse of natural affection sorely tried, and now at last longing to be gratified, bringing on the fulfilment of that terrible oracle ? Ah ! he may well tremble, and shrink,—and hesitate on the brink,— and almost resolve to turn back.

But the Lord says, "Fear not." (1.) Fear not, for "I am God, the God of thy father." I am God the Almighty, having all power ; and I am thy father's God, pledged in covenant to make all things work together for good to his seed and thine. (2.) Fear not, for "I will there make of thee a great nation ;" not here, but there ; in Egypt. Thy going down into Egypt does not frustrate, it fulfils my purpose. It may be a trial, and the beginning of trials ; but it is an indispensable preliminary to the triumph. (3.) Fear not, for "I will go down with thee unto Egypt." "I will not leave thee nor forsake thee." Whatever ill may there await thee or thy seed, "I will not leave you comfortless ; I will come unto you." (4.) Fear not, for if I send thee and go with thee, "I will also surely bring thee up again." In thy posterity, in the great nation I am to make of thee, I will bring thee up again. And even thyself personally I will bring up. Thy bones shall not rest in Egypt; they shall be laid here, in Canaan. And in the resurrection thou shalt inherit the land. (5.) Fear not, finally, though the years of thy pilgrimage are to close in death, far off from the holy land. For, as I said to Abraham on that awful night, "Thou shalt go to thy fathers in peace,"—so say I to thee,—Thou shalt fall asleep in peace, in the arms of thy beloved,—"Joseph shall put his hand upon thine eyes" (ver. 3, 4). "Fear not," therefore, "thou worm Jacob" (Is. xli. 14).

Reassured by so gracious and seasonable a vision—now strong in faith as the Israel of God—the patriarch pursues his journey (ver. 5-7). Nothing occurs by the way deserving notice—no incident or adventure of any interest. "All his seed brought he with him into Egypt."

Thus the descent into Egypt is accomplished. It is a critical era in the history of the chosen race. And it is therefore only natural that occasion should at this stage be taken for a sort of census, that may bring out its exact state, as regards the gross number of which it is composed, and the several tribes into which it is to be distributed.

The list or catalogue given of Israel's family (ver. 8-27) has occasioned considerable difficulty. In the first place, the number seventy (ver. 27), while it agrees with that given in other parts of the Hebrew Pentateuch (Exod. 1-5; Deut. 10-22), differs from that given by Stephen, in his defence before the Sanhedrim (Acts vii. 14). He makes it seventy-five, according to the Greek Translation of the Old Testament then in common use. The names also are somewhat perplexing. A minute examination of them, and a comparison of this list with two other enumerations of the original heads of the Jewish community, apparently somewhat parallel or cognate to this one (Num. xxvi.; 1 Chron. ii.-viii.), suggest questions of identity not easily solved. And the mention of two females, and only two, Dinah (ver. 15) and Serah (ver. 17), is embarrassing. Great labour and research have been expended by learned men on the clearing up of these perplexing points of detail—and much ingenuity has been exercised—not altogether with a satisfactory result. This should not be either a surprise or a stumbling-block to any candid mind ; and that, as I think, for two sufficient reasons.*

1. It is very obvious that in a book like the Bible, composed and compiled at sundry times and in diverse manners, and containing varied and minute chronologies and genealogies, there must be many things that would be better understood, and could be more easily explained long ago, at the time, than they can be now ; just as we believe, from its prophetic character, that there may be some of these very things that will come to be more clear, in themselves and in their use, as the end of all draws near. Meanwhile we need not be greatly troubled if we have to confess that not a few knotty questions of the sort indicated defy satisfactory solution.

---

* For more particular satisfaction, the following additional remarks may be useful. (1.) Nowhere is there a greater likelihood of errors having crept into the sacred text, through careless or ignorant copying of manuscripts, than in lists of proper names and such like—and nowhere is it less easy to discover or correct the errors by sound criticism. (2.) The principles upon which these genealogical trees or tables were constructed among the Israelites, can be only very imperfectly known or conjectured. For generations before the writing of the books of Moses, they must have been traditionally preserved by being handed down in the chosen family—perhaps embodied in current song or poetry—some of them even committed, in a rude fragmentary way, to public or domestic registers, or records of some sort. They were probably not meant to be exhaustive, or to comprehend all the individuals concerned. A selection was apparently made of heads, or chiefs, or leading persons—and so made, for the most part, as, for the sake of easy memory, to give a round number rather than a fractional or broken one. (3.) Here, for instance, in particular, it is not conceivable

2. We must allow to men writing under the inspiration of the Spirit the same liberty of using current popular phraseology, and stating matters of notoriety in the customary way, that we would concede to any honest author in the like circumstances. Such an author does not scruple to give the round numbers, and broad, brief summaries, artificially framed as helps to memory, or as making a neat scheme or system in the story or the genealogy,—when these are the familiar modes of reckoning among his readers, and when, as they stand, they sufficiently answer the purpose he has in view. If he were not to do so, if he were not to be thus far accommodating to prevalent usage, if he were to affect a minute, martinet, and punctilious accuracy, even down to trifling details of that sort;—altering when there was no real occasion for it, and as if for mere alteration's sake, commonly received versions of familiar records and traditions;—not only would he be justly chargeable with a certain prudish pedantry, but he would fatally damage his chance of acceptance and usefulness among the people. The liberty which any honest writer would exercise in such particulars, ought not to be denied to one writing by inspiration. The Spirit, superintending what

that there were only two women in Israel deserving of mention upon the occasion of the settlement in Egypt. We read (ver. 5-7) of Jacob's daughters, and the wives and daughters of his sons; and again of Jacob's sons' wives (ver. 27), as being over and above the seventy. The presumption is that as for the most part heads of future houses in Israel are here singled out, so there may have been others at the time equally conspicuous of whom no mention is made. (4.) Probably the number seventy or seventy-five—for evidently it was not held to be material which of the two was preferred—was technical and artificial, if we may so speak—not intended to be an exact historical enumeration, but a kind of convenient, shorthand summary—representing clearly enough to the successive generations of Israelites the state of the household at the time of the settlement in Egypt —and capable of easy application to the more complete and regular arrangement of the tribes, whether on their coming out of Egypt, or in the wilderness, or in Canaan.

is written, and making himself responsible for every word of it, is not bound to make the author whom he inspires more of a pedant in point of accuracy than you or I would choose to be, in alluding to old histories, quoting old books, and using old registers and recollections.

The essential element in the narrative here is, that a mere handful of men and women was all Israel,—as it went down into Egypt. Very slowly hitherto had the chosen race increased. Abraham, after he was told that his seed was to out-number the stars and the sand, had to wait for years before his one chosen child of promise came. Sixty years after, Jacob was born ; and another interval of at least eighty years elapsed before he became a father. For nearly two centuries the promise to Abraham hung by a single, often a doubtful, thread. Even now, after another half century,—when the period of his seed's bondage in a strange land, of which Abraham had been warned, is about to begin to run,—it is a single family that migrates from Canaan to Egypt,—as much so as when Abraham, in the character of a patriarchal chief, led and ruled his household at the first. There is scarcely yet the incipient form or outward aspect of a tribe. The idea of a great nation is still in the clouds.

Did any such idea occur to Pharaoh, when he sanctioned and enforced so warmly his prime minister Joseph's invitation? Was it a permanent settlement of Joseph's kinsmen in his dominions that he had in view ? Did he contemplate their growing into a distinct people, preserving their nationality, and becoming formidable for their numbers ? Or did he mean that their sojourn in his realm should be short,—limited to the duration of the famine which occasioned it ? Or, if he wished them to stay longer, did he anticipate their getting merged and lost in the general mass of Egypt's teeming population ? Who can tell ? In all likelihood Pharaoh had no fixed purpose or expectation about the matter at all. Joseph was a favourite, and he was glad to show kindness to Joseph's father and brethren. Joseph, while conforming to Egyptian usages in things civil, has retained his own peculiar religious notions and practices; his father and his brethren may very likely do the same. The king does not care much about the matter; he does not look far before him. He little dreams of what fruit the tiny seed now planted in his land is to bear; he knows not he is unconsciously fulfilling the divine decree.

Has Jacob,. or have his sons, or any one of them,—Joseph for instance,—any clearer insight? Or are they all led like the blind by a way that they know not? Joseph probably has as yet no suspicion that he is bringing the family down to Egypt for such a destiny as awaits them; he simply desires to have them with him to share the sunshine of royal favour. His heart is in Canaan, which he believes to be the heritage of his house. In his care at the first about their dwelling apart,—not less than in his care at last about his own bones, —we see evidence of his faith in the promise made to Abraham. But in bringing his father's family into Egypt he little reckons on the long interval that is to elapse before Canaan is again reached. And his brethren, in this whole affair, seem to have walked all along by sense rather than by faith.

But Jacob was a believer in regard to it. He had in view the fulfilment in Egypt of that prophecy of mingled weal and woe which Abraham received;—about his seed growing into a great nation; and about their doing so under oppression calling ultimately for the signal vengeance of the Most High against their oppressors. It needed a strong faith to sustain aged Israel in taking a step thus pregnant with so much evil. He does not take it in ignorance; his eyes are open to all its issues. But he is cheered by the assurance of a glorious, joyous, return home at last,—and by the hope, meanwhile, of having Joseph to close his eyes in peace.

And now Canaan has no longer within its borders the leaven of God's chosen seed, but is left to its old inhabitants, until their iniquities shall be full. Not a foot of the soil beyond a sepulchre, the sepulchre which Abraham bought from the sons of Heth ;—for the well which he got by treaty with Abimelech at Beersheba, and the parcel of ground which Jacob bought, were both of them uncertain possessions at this time, and need not be taken into account ;—save a sepulchre, then, not an inch of the territory belonged to the departing family. All connection with the land is broken off. Once only, at the burial of Jacob, is there any revisiting of its borders. And thereafter it is all as if never foot of a God-fearing man, or a God-fearing family, had trod its soil.

What traces, what memories, what influences have the Israel of God bequeathed, now that the time of their sojourn is for the present over? Alas! how much is there to humble and sadden them, if they will but pause and think, as they cast their last look on the plains and on the people they are leaving behind them! Crimes and sins of heinous dye,— instances of unbelief in God and conformity to an ungodly world,—unbrotherly dissensions,—unneighbourly revenges,— scandals, stumbling-blocks, which their evil lusts and passions have put in the way of those whom a consistent walk, and holy example, and pure and warm charity, might have won ;— such recollections may well overwhelm them with bitter shame and sorrow, as they bid a final adieu to the scenes of their long sojourn in the land of their pilgrimage. Some recollections of piety and love will doubtless linger, when they are gone, among the people who have been the witnesses of their walk. But ah! how dimly has their light been shining! How uncertain a sound has their trumpet been giving! It would have been good for them, during the years of their witness-bearing for God among ungodly men, had they been anticipating the day when that witness-bearing must cease, and had they asked themselves beforehand how then, at its close, they would be able to stand the retrospect!

Surely, for every church, for every believer, there is a lesson here. I must soon quit the place that now knows me, and quit it for ever. What savour, of death unto death, or of life unto life, will my occupancy of it leave when it is over, when I am gone,—and the place that now knows me knows me no more?

62

ISRAEL'S WELCOME IN EGYPT—TO BE KEPT THERE TILL THE TIME COMES

Genesis 46:28-47:10

The Lord shall be known in Egypt. Isaiah 19:20

Taking together the end of one chapter and the beginning of another, we have an incident complete in itself, and of great significancy, as regards the purpose of God in the development of his church's history. The chosen seed, like " a corn of wheat," is to " fall into the ground and die," in order that after many days it may " bring forth much fruit" (John xii. 24). The long underground concealment of the Egyptian sojourn and captivity, preparatory to the great resurrection of the nation at the time of the Exodus, is now about to begin. And the manner of its commencement is to be clearly marked. It is to be no obscure and stealthy midnight movement, but an honourable transaction, signalised in high places,—as was the burial of Jesus, when Joseph of Arimathea got Pilate's consent to pay all respect, along with Nicodemus, to the body of the crucified. Thus Jacob is received, on his arrival in Egypt, with all honour, first, by his son Joseph (xlvi. 28-34), and next by the king (xlvii. 1-10).

Joseph's reception of his father and brethren is both affectionate and politic. There is in it the warm, gushing affection of a loving son and brother ; but there is in it also the sagacious policy of a prince and ruler, who has to manage the affair on hand, as one of government and diplomacy, with a sound and wise discretion. Jacob makes his entry, as it would seem, with some measure of state. Either by way of precaution, or to show that he comes as an independent patriarchal chief, he abstains from going at once direct to his son. He is to make it manifest from the first, before the eyes of all the Egyptians, that while he comes on Joseph's invitation, he does not come to occupy a subordinate position ;—as if he and his household were to be mere hangers on, as it were, in Joseph's palace, to swell the number of his attendants, and be simply pensioners at his table. That is not Joseph's own desire or design. He wishes his father to take his proper place, as the acknowledged and honoured head of a distinct patriarchal community. Accordingly a suitable residence has been prepared and set apart for him in Goshen,—and thither Jacob turns aside (ver. 28).

From thence, in due form, he sends Judah as an ambassador to announce his arrival to Joseph (ver. 28). There is evidently something of the nature of courtly ceremony here,—as there is also in Joseph's stately manner of approach to Jacob ; he " made ready his chariot, and went up to meet Israel his father to Goshen, and presented himself unto him " (ver. 29). It may have been to keep up appearances before the Egyptians that this was thus arranged ; if so, it was probably a wise policy.

All policy, however, is forgotten when son and father meet : " He fell on his neck, and wept on his neck a good while" (ver. 29). It is all nature now ; and it is nature, as is nature's wont, with much matter in little bulk ;—a whole scene compressed into a few words,—and these the simplest.

To enlarge here would be presumptuous.

No weeping like that of Joseph, lasting " a good while," —if we take in all the circumstances ; the early fondness, the long, long separation, the wondrous re-union ;—no such weeping anytime or anywhere else, except when " Jesus wept !"

And only once again is the resistless pathos of Jacob's plaintive word of acquiescence paralleled ;—" Now let me die, since I have seen thy face, because thou art yet alive !"—once and once only,—in the " Nunc Dimittis ;" " Lord, now lettest thou thy servant depart in peace, according to thy word ; for mine eyes have seen thy salvation."

But Joseph is a ruler, as well as a son and brother ; in the capacity of ruler he must make due provision for the emergency that has occurred. Nor is that so easy as might at first appear. If it were only the hospitable entertainment of his kindred that he had to look to, it would be no difficult task to provide for that. He stands so well with the king, and has such absolute command over all the resources of the kingdom, that he can at once secure for his kinsmen all honourable accommodation in the house and court of Pharaoh. But that is not enough for him ; it is not what he wants. He is willing that his father's family should cast in their lot with him in Egypt. But the dizzy height of his own preferment does not blind his eyes to the necessity of placing them, if it be possible, on a footing which they may maintain, independently of his own precarious favour with the king, or the king's successors. Nor is he insensible, we may well suppose, to the satisfaction of being himself discovered to be one of a family for whom he can claim an independent standing. He would have those whom he is introducing to a share in his exaltation established, as a peculiar people, in the possession of a territory of their own. Hence his care beforehand as to the manner of their introduction to Pharaoh. He proposes to take advantage of their business being that of shepherds, to secure for them the separate habitation in the fertile region of Goshen which it is his aim that they shall have. He will even make his own use—for their good—of the ill repute in which their occupation is held : "for every shepherd is an abomination unto the Egyptians " (ver. 33, 34).

What special reason there was for this antipathy is not

said. It may have been the recollection of some recent invasion of a shepherd tribe from the desert. Or it may have been the result of Egypt's high civilisation, causing settled trades or manufactures to be of chief repute, and casting discredit on the old modes of life which roving hordes, with no property but their flocks and herds, were accustomed to pursue. Be that as it may, it is a shrewd device of policy on the part of Joseph,—if it be not rather the inspiration of divine wisdom,—to make the very lowliness of the calling of his brethren the means at once of their security and of their isolation. It is not by claiming for them a high public rank, and pushing them forward as entitled to honourable consideration for their relationship to him, that he wins for them the place which he deems it best and safest for them to occupy. No. It is rather in the position of the outcast of the world,—the despised and rejected of Egypt's busy merchants and proud fastidious fashionables, —that he sees fit to place them. He would rather have them to be an abomination than a delight to the Egyptians. Egypt's frown is better for them than Egypt's flattery and fellowship.

It is the same now. The world's hatred is safer for the friends of Jesus than the world's smiles. "Blessed are ye, when men shall hate you, and when they shall separate you from their company, and shall reproach you, and cast out your name as evil, for the Son of man's sake" (Luke vi. 22).

Joseph's introduction or presentation of his kindred to Pharaoh is evidently an affair of some little delicacy. He manages it with his usual tact; or rather with that mixture of sagacious policy and strong feeling which seems to have been natural to his character. We have seen how he has prepared his brethren, "his father's house," beforehand, and primed them, as it were, for the royal audience awaiting them. He has come to an understanding with them as to what he is to say about them in introducing them to the king, and what they, when introduced, are to say to the king about themselves.

And now he goes about the business, as arranged, with a certain elaborate observance of form that agrees well with ancient oriental manners. There is also, however, on the part of Joseph an evident design to maintain the independent standing and dignity of his father's house, and to give to their settlement in Egypt the prestige of a sort of royal recognition of their independence.

I. Joseph enters the royal presence alone, and makes his report to Pharaoh (ver. 1). He tells the king of the arrival of his father and brethren, and also that he has taken it upon himself to settle them at Goshen. It is a fertile district, fitted for pasture rather than for agriculture. It is on the frontiers of Egypt, towards the Arabian wilds, where roving nomadic tribes of shepherds are accustomed to pitch their tents and feed their flocks. It has been conjectured that it was a district from which some invading Arab host had only very recently been expelled, and which, though reclaimed and recovered by the Egyptian monarch, as a part of his dominions, was not yet occupied, and was not likely to be speedily or fully occupied, by Egypt's native population. For the highly civilised Egyptians, who had made great progress in arts as well as arms, preferred for the most part a more central position and more settled employments. They were growers of wheat and all sorts of grain. They were skilled in linen and other manufactures. They carried on a considerable trade. Hence they naturally shrunk from the neighbourhood of the constantly migrating hordes, who lived by pasturage and by plunder,—whose wealth was in flocks and herds, as their home was in camps, and their joy in war. A locality like Goshen, on the very borders of the land, and scarcely regained out of the grasp of these alert and almost ubiquitous enemies, ever on the watch for fresh mischief, might be apt to lie waste for want of Egyptian settlers ; and in its ambiguous state of half conquest and half occupancy, might be a source of weakness rather than of strength to the Egyptian commonwealth. In such a condi-

tion of affairs, it might be a good stroke of policy to have it
inhabited by a young and enterprising family of shepherds,
disposed to detach themselves from the princes of Palestine
and the wild chiefs of Arabia, and to cast in their lot, for whatever reason of necessity or choice, with the fame and the fortunes of Egypt. So we may suppose Joseph to have reasoned,
when, on his own responsibility, he took the step which he
now reports to Pharaoh. Evidently he felt that it was a step
which needed some explanation. And he has prepared the
explanation, which he first states himself, and then expects his
brethren, according to the instructions he has given them, to
confirm. He dwells, as he has taught them to dwell, on the
fact of their being shepherds. That being their trade, where
could he put them, with their flocks and herds, more properly
than in the region which lay waiting, as it were, for such a
race to possess it? It is the very thing needed to strengthen
Egypt's outworks, and keep wild rovers at bay. " Behold they
are in the land of Goshen."

Two remarks here suggest themselves,—the first applicable
to Joseph's part in this arrangement; the second applicable to
the overruling hand of God which may be seen in it.

First, as to Joseph,—is it not noticeable that he does not
push the fortunes of his family at court? Who else in his
place would have failed to do so? The ball is at his foot; the
kingdom's resources are at his disposal. His relatives could
not be refused preferment if he asked it for them. Offices in
his own household, and in the king's, await their acceptance, if
Joseph will but give the word. Provincial appointments, all
over the country and its dependencies, may be theirs. Unbounded wealth and honour may come to all of them, if Joseph
chooses to use his opportunity on their behalf. And why does
he not? Why banish them to distant obscurity in Goshen?
Is it that he distrusts them, and thinks that they might not
do him credit if he promoted them? Nay, he has had them
at his table. He is not ashamed to own them as brethren,

and set them before the king. Judah's rare eloquence and Benjamin's simple beauty would have made themselves felt any day in Egypt's highest circles. What then is it that weighs with Joseph in his preferring the humble sphere of Goshen for his family, rather than the riches of Egypt? What can it be but faith—the same faith which moves him, for himself and his sons, to make common cause with them?

For it seems all but certain, from the narrative,—and it is exceedingly remarkable,—that from the moment of his bringing down his father and brethren from Canaan, Joseph took the place, as far as possible, and acted the part, not of the vizier and prime minister of Pharaoh, but of a child of Israel. We read, indeed, of his completing the operation which the famine had suggested, and effecting a great change in the tenure of property all over Egypt. He remained at his post till his work was done. But beyond all question, his heart was in Goshen; he was an Israelite indeed. It was not to Pharaoh but to Jacob that he looked for an inheritance to his two boys. He sits loose to Pharaoh's palace; all his hope is in Goshen's tents. Surely this is faith. He thus declares himself to be " a stranger and sojourner on the earth," and to be " looking for a city." The promised Saviour,—the seed of the woman bruising the serpent's head, and so becoming the source of blessing to all the nations of the earth,—the divine favour and the heavenly rest,—these are all precious to him ; and they are all bound up with Israel. Therefore he will be himself one of Israel's sons. And for Israel he will choose a place where " the people may dwell alone." He will not hazard the risk of their participation in Egypt's glory. It is better and safer for them, as God's chosen people, to be humble shepherds feeding their flocks in Goshen.

Secondly, in the whole of this matter, the over-ruling providence of the Lord is conspicuous. He brings Israel into Egypt at the right time, and with the right place prepared for their habitation. Goshen is made vacant for their reception, and Pharaoh finds it to be for his and for Egypt's good to have Israel located there. It is not man's planning—it is the Lord's doing. He causes a wild roving shepherd tribe to overrun, so as to depopulate and lay waste, an outlying portion of Egypt's realm. Again he causes them to retire before Egypt's mustering hosts. Then Joseph is sold; the famine comes; Joseph is promoted; his brethren come down for food; and discovery takes place. Thus Israel is brought into Egypt; and in Egypt Goshen is ready for Israel. Time, place, and circumstances, all are fitting into one another. And it is altogether the doing of the Lord.

II. Having himself prepared the way, by reporting to Pharaoh what he has done, Joseph now solicits and obtains for a select number of his brethren an audience of the king (ver. 2). This also is an affair of state, like the formal reception of an embassy. Joseph would not have his people to appear before Pharaoh as a miscellaneous crowd of suppliants, or a company of needy adventurers. They approach the throne by a deputation; the " five men " act as representatives of an orderly community, prepared to negotiate a treaty with Egypt and Egypt's monarch. They have to ask a favour, no doubt: but they do not ask it after the manner of abject mendicants. Their whole bearing is erect and dignified. In answer to the king's inquiry, " What is your occupation?" there is a frank avowal of their hereditary character and calling: " Thy servants are shepherds, both we and also our fathers " (ver. 3); and they have no hesitation in following up their avowal with a proposal that might almost, in their circumstances, seem presumptuous. They certainly state their case with great coolness, and prefer their petition, respectfully enough it is true, but with not a little confidence; " Now therefore, we pray thee, let thy servants dwell in the land of Goshen " (ver. 4).

Thus these brethren of Joseph claim at Pharaoh's hands the humble portion of the good things of Egypt that they need. And Joseph has power and influence enough to secure that their claim shall be allowed. For it is to Joseph that they are indebted. It is he who obtains for them the boon ; it is with him that Pharaoh deals ; " Pharaoh spake unto Joseph, saying, Thy father and thy brethren are come unto thee : the land of Egypt is before thee ; in the best of the land make thy father and brethren to dwell ; in the land of Goshen let them dwell " (ver. 5, 6). The land of Egypt is before thee ; the best of it may be chosen. If Goshen is preferred, by all means let it be Goshen. That may not be in some respects the best. The overflowing Nile may cause some other parts of Egypt to teem with more luxuriant harvests. But it may be the best for them. At all events it is heartily at their service.

The gift is princely, and the manner of giving is princely ; there is in it an air of courtesy and liberality worthy of a king ; of one who was then the highest of earth's kings. He gives simply and freely. And, by a refinement of kind graciousness, as if to lessen the burden of the obligation, he adds the suggestion that their services may be turned to account. The benefit is not all on one side ; there is an honourable way of requiting Pharaoh's goodness ; " If thou knowest any men of activity among them, then make them rulers over my cattle " (ver. 6).

III. The personal interview between the king and Jacob is one more of the scenes in this most affecting history on which few would choose or venture to expatiate (ver. 7-10). The simple pathos of the narrative is only marred by anything like lengthened comment or exposition.

The meeting begins and ends with benediction. When " Joseph brought in his father Jacob and set him before Pharaoh," " Jacob blessed Pharaoh." When " he went out from before Pharaoh," " Jacob blessed Pharaoh" (ver. 7, 10).

" Without all contradiction, the less is blessed of the better" (Heb. vii. 7) ; that is the construction divinely placed on Melchizedek's blessing Abraham. May not the same construction be placed on Jacob's blessing Pharaoh?

Pharaoh's intermediate question indeed, coming in between the two benedictions, may seem to savour of an assumption of superiority (ver. 8). He plays the king,—does he not?—according to the customary kingly fashion of condescension, when he asks " How old art thou?" And yet it was a natural enough question, and it might be put in all simplicity. Jacob's countenance and gait betokened extreme old age. Sin and sorrow, anxiety and care, had left their deep traces on a face furrowed by many a tear; his frame tottered under the load of griefs as well as years. But he had the calm look of faith,—his dim eye caught a beam of heavenly light,—and there was authority in his voice,—when " he blessed Pharaoh!" His reply to Pharaoh's kind inquiry is very touching; it must have deepened the impression made by his grey hairs and venerable mien. It is a reply which, familiar as it is from long-past reading and recollection, one cannot recall to memory, even now, without a thrilling sense of reality; as the scene represents itself almost visibly before the mind's eye.

There is Pharaoh,—at first, as I suppose, seated in state on the throne,—prepared, first by Joseph's explanation, then by the audience granted to the five brethren, for the formal reception of Jacob, the head and chief of the family. What sort of approach to him, on the patriarch's side, the monarch may have anticipated, who can tell? He did not probably look for prostration, or anything like abject and servile obeisance. But was he prepared,—was even Joseph prepared,—for the majesty,—it must have been something majestic,—of Jacob's act? Lifting up his hands, at the full height of his stature, without one preliminary word of salutation or gesture of compliment to the king, the old man pours out his soul in prayer;—asking God's best blessing on the royal head;—and in God's name, pronouncing the customary blessing of Abraham's house and seed!

We have no more trace in history of this Pharaoh; he passes from the stage with Jacob's blessing on him. May we not say that he passes from it with the blessing upon him of Jacob's God? He has had a strange experience, for the king of a heathen land. He has had not a little personal knowledge of the true God, Jehovah, the God of Israel. Visions by night have awakened him to seriousness. A godly youth, discovered in prison by his godliness, has brought God, as the revealer of secrets, and the ruler of events, very near to him. The chosen seed, the Israel of God, have come to be entrusted to his keeping. And now the last we see of him is when he talks with Jacob, and receives his blessing.

If he intended to receive the patriarch, as chief of the new tribe he is inviting to a settlement in his dominions, formally and in state, as from the throne,—the patriarch's first appearance, as he entered the royal presence, must have changed his purpose. The tables, as it were, are turned. Jacob,—with heart full of grateful feeling as all the king's kindness rushes fresh upon him,—and conscious of his power, as Israel, to prevail as a prince with God in invoking a worthy recompense, —" Jacob blesses Pharaoh." Shall we say that the king feels himself to be blessed,—the less by the better,—a monarch of earth by a servant of the monarch of heaven? He quits the throne accordingly and accepts the patriarch's benediction. It is the benediction of an old man. How old, he asks? The answer moves him all the more: "And Jacob said unto Pharaoh, The days of the years of my pilgrimage are an hundred and thirty years: few and evil have the days of the years of my life been, and have not attained unto the days of the years of the life of my fathers, in the days of their pilgrimage. And Jacob blessed Pharaoh, and went out from before Pharaoh." It is the benediction of a much tried and much exercised old man. He invites and welcomes its repetition; for he has heard from Joseph something of Israel's God, and Israel's hope. Let us leave him, humbling himself to receive twice over the blessing of the aged saint. Let us gratefully own God's grace in his dealings, first and last, with this right royal king of Egypt.

And from all these particulars connected with the settlement of the chosen family in the land in which they were to " dree a weary weird," to work out a sad period of bondage, let us learn such lessons as these :—1. How the Lord makes place and time suitable for any crisis which he has appointed to happen, in the history of his people collectively, and of every one of them apart. If Egypt must be your destiny, he will find for you a Goshen,—and have it ready for you at the very hour you need it. 2. How Jesus may be trusted by you to claim for you at the hands of the world, and its princes, and its people, whatever may be for your good. He will see to it that you have whatever Goshen you require at the hands of any Pharaoh,—and you may humbly accept it without undue humiliation or shame. 3. How he who has the hearts of all men in his hands can dispose whatever Pharaoh you come in contact with to be at peace with you and do you good. And 4. How he can make your contact with any and every Pharaoh conducive to his good as well as yours,—if in faith you realise your power, the power of your prayer, with God,—and if on every occasion of your being introduced to such a one, when he asks you any simple question about yourself, you make it the occasion of your calling down from heaven a blessing upon him.

63

JOSEPH'S EGYPTIAN POLICY—ISRAEL'S QUIET REST

Genesis 47:11-28

To teach his senators wisdom.   Psalm 105:22
My people shall dwell in a peaceable habitation.   Isaiah 32:18

Two topics occur in this passage for consideration, the policy of Joseph as ruler in Egypt,—and the position of Israel as settled in Egypt. Of these, the former is to be regarded as quite subordinate to the latter.

I. The Egyptian policy of Joseph is very briefly noticed; and in the most incidental way; some fourteen verses comprise the whole. Evidently it is not a full account of the transaction that is given; and evidently also, it is an account of it simply in an Israelitish point of view. It is not narrated as a part of the universal history of the world,—nor even as a part of the history of Egypt. The change, or revolution, is only so far described as to explain the position of the Israelites in Egypt, and account for their future treatment there. It is, accordingly, imbedded, as it were, in the continuous narrative of their Egyptian experience; so that it comes in, as it were, incidentally. We might quite well omit it all (ver. 13-26), and read the story of Israel without that intervening break.

Joseph, after obtaining the sanction of Pharaoh, proceeded to carry out his plan and settle the chosen family, as a peculiar people, in a territory which they could call their own. And having so placed them, he nourished them; not as if they were mere mendicants receiving alms,—but in an orderly manner, and with a full recognition of their separate standing, as a tribe or patriarchal community, welcomed as such, in a friendly manner, by Egypt and its prince (ver. 11, 12). With this account of the beginning of their settlement, the account of their progress fitly joins in (ver. 27). The intermediate narrative is quite parenthetical. The account of Joseph's conduct, as ruler in Egypt, is an altogether irrelevant, not to say impertinent, interruption, unless we hold that it is brought in with a view to its bearing on the fortunes of Israel.

But looking at it in itself, what are the facts of the case ? For there would seem to have been from of old, and to be still, not a little misapprehension in many quarters in regard to this matter. The facts are few and simple. At the beginning of the years of famine, Joseph sold the grain, stored up during the seven years of plenty, for money (ver. 14). It is not insinuated that he acted the part of an extortioner, but only that he did, in point of fact, obtain possession of the money, and hand it over to Pharaoh. The grain market followed the natural course of trade. Joseph had corn,—the people had money ; but Joseph's corn outlasted the people's money. Then when " money failed," Joseph took cattle (ver. 15-17). How long the money lasted is not said ; but the cattle lasted, as payment for corn, only for a year. The next year, probably the last, or last but one, of the famine, the people had nothing to give for corn but their lands and their persons (ver. 18, 19). Joseph took their land (ver. 20) ; and as to their persons, he enforced a general removal from the country into towns (ver. 21). The priests alone were exempted (ver. 22) ; it would seem that their land had been already surrendered to the crown, and that they had become pensioners dependent on the king. The ordinary population ceased to be landowners, and came under a system which implied their being, as a general rule, settled in cities, rather than living a rural life. They were still, however, to have an interest in the soil. The cultivation of it, after it became the king's, was offered to them on easy terms (ver. 23-26). Leases might be had, for anything we know, for any number of years; or there might be no need of leases. The annual rent to be paid by the people for liberty to till the ground was fixed. It was to be always and everywhere a fifth part of the produce. Four parts of it were absolutely their own.

These are the plain facts here recorded,—without comment or explanation. They surely afford far too scanty materials for determining whether Joseph, at this crisis, acted a wise and patriotic part for Egypt, or made himself the tool of a tyrant, for the establishment of an arbitrary throne. We would need to know more of the constitution and laws of Egypt, both before and after Joseph's administration, than either old history records, or new researches among the tombs and pyramids have as yet discovered,—before we could be in a position to pronounce a dogmatic opinion on the subject. Certainly, it is only a most perverse ingenuity that can extract out of the few bare and simple statements in this brief passage, evidence to convict Joseph of a cunning Machiavellian plot to lay Egypt and its inhabitants prostrate at Pharaoh's feet. On the contrary, for anything that here appears, his manner of turning to account the years of increasing famine, may have been as much for the people's benefit as for that of the prince. He was the king's loyal servant; but he was also the saviour, in a temporal sense, of the king's subjects. He certainly took measures for abolishing all feudal tenures of property that were independent of the king. But that may have been no harm. He struck at the root, perhaps, of the heritable jurisdiction of petty princes and landlords, accustomed, as we may conjecture, to wield the power even of capital punishment over their vassals. He ordained that all occupiers and cultivators of estates should hold them directly of the crown. But he fixed a uniform and easy condition. And if his measures tended to foster a busy town population, rather than one over-crowded and enslaved in the country,—considering Egypt's place and opportunities as a manufacturing and trading country, —that can scarcely be held to have been a wicked act of power. Certainly, there is no trace of Egypt's having become less prosperous or less influential in consequence of Joseph's rule. The opposite rather is the fair inference.

But it is chiefly important to observe the bearing of Joseph's Egyptian policy upon the condition and prospects of Israel. It put an end to a state of things that might admit of rival clans and their chiefs acting on their own account, so as to thwart the supreme government. It concentrated au-thority in one royal head. And so it made it easier for the Pharaoh who was Joseph's friend to secure the peaceful settle-ment of the family in Goshen; while it also made it easier, long afterwards, for the Pharaoh who "knew not Joseph," to enslave and oppress the nation into which the family was then fast growing. That is probably the reason, and the only reason, why the matter is noticed at all in this history, how-ever briefly and parenthetically. It is simply to explain how the introduction into the country of a new race or a new nationality,—which at an earlier date, and under a different order of things, might have occasioned heart-burnings and dissensions, and even kindled the flames of civil war,—could be quietly accomplished by the mere will and word of the king who now, thanks to Joseph's sagacity, was reigning as a king indeed; wielding a sovereign sceptre—and not merely holding an uneasy and uncertain balance among a set of turbulent lords of the soil, ready to make him their sport or their victim, to fawn on him and set him at defiance by turns. And it is also to show how, in the very conjuncture of circumstances which brought Israel into Egypt, and prepared Egypt for Israel, he who sees the end from the beginning was so ordering and overruling events, as to bring out of an arrangement which seemed all to wear a smiling and favourable aspect towards his people, that very discipline of long and dreary bondage which was to fulfil his own previously announced purpose, and pave the way for their terrible and glorious deliverance at the last.

II. And now the people of Israel are at rest,—in a settled habitation,—dwelling in peace and safety,—with none to make them afraid (ver. 27, 28). They have their own houses and possessions undisturbed,—their own institutions and usages,— their own family order,—their own patriarchal rule,—their own religious services—worshipping God every man under his own vine and his own fig-tree.

It is a goodly and pleasant scene to look upon. All the past is forgotten ; its trials and temptations, its sins and sorrows,—its dark passages of deceit and envy, of malice, lust, and blood,—its cruel separations,—its anxious suspense,—its trembling hope,—its whole tragic interest of pity and terror. All is over. The intricate plot is for the present unravelled, —the strange wild romance is ended. And now there is a pause ; all is quiet. There, in Goshen, tranquillity reigns— unruffled calm,—complete repose. The old man's vexed soul is to taste, before he quits this earthly scene, a serene peace hitherto but little known. Before the few and evil days of his pilgrimage close, he is to " see his children's children, and peace upon Israel" (Ps. cxxviii). No details are given, no particulars specified ; for quiet times furnish few materials for history. So these uneventful years swiftly pass, until "the time draws nigh that Israel must die."

64

THE DYING SAINT'S CARE FOR THE BODY AS WELL AS THE SOUL

Genesis 47:29-31

The hope and resurrection of the dead—The hope of Israel.   Acts 23:6 and Acts 28:20

" JACOB lived in the land of Egypt seventeen years " (ver. 28). They were, we may venture to believe, years of tranquillity and quiet domestic joy.   Though in a strange land, he might say, with the contented Shunammite, " I dwell among my own people " (2 Kings iv. 13).   He had his sons around him, now at last living together as brethren in unity ; having learned of Joseph to love as they had been loved.

It was a short time, not only in itself, but even as compared with the patriarch's entire life.   For " so,"—taking these seventeen years into account,—" the whole age of Jacob was an hundred forty and seven years " (ver. 18).   It was not much more than a tenth of his allotted earthly span, that Jacob was permitted thus to spend in Goshen's retired haven of calm, after more than a century of exposure to the fitful storms and breezes of an uneasy voyage.   We might almost wish that he had got a longer interval of preparatory repose before he was called to pass from earth's tumult to heaven's final rest.   But that is not the mind of God.   The allowance of even these seventeen years, between his tossing on the sea and his safe arrival in port, is a signal instance of the Lord's kind consideration.   But this is not his rest ; here he has no continuing city; the hour of his departure comes at last. " The time drew near that Israel must die " (ver. 29).

It is a time that is drawing near to every happy home, to every loving household; the fondest home-circle must be thus invaded, the most loving home-fellowship must be thus broken up. A few short years of holy and peaceful sojourning together may be granted to you. But the years are numbered, —and the time draws near when one of you must die.

How solemn is the parting-knell! It has a voice to every house, every home, every band of brothers, every circle of companions. What are you about together? How are you living together? Are you encouraging one another in sin; forgetting God, and following pleasure? Are you striving with another, envying one another, injuring one another? The time draws near when one of you must die! Are you, on the contrary, walking together in the good way of the Lord, —seeking the Lord together,—working together for the Lord, —communing much together, oh! how lovingly, in the Lord! Still the time draws near when one of you must die!

Have you in the midst of you a venerable patriarch, a brother, or a father, much beloved in the Lord,—a parent, a counsellor, a friend, a pastor, who is to you as a sort of head, —whose words of wisdom should be your guide,—whose ever ready arm is your stay,—whose ever ready smile or tear of sympathy is your consolation? Ah! if at any time you are tempted, on the one hand, to make too much of him,—to reckon on him as your help for years to come,—to lean on him, it may be, instead of looking to God,—to idolise him,— or count him a necessity of your well-being;—or if at any time you are tempted, on the other hand, to make too little of him, to put away his counsels and warnings till a more convenient season;—may it not be good in either case to be realising the solemn fact,—that the time draws near when your Israel must die.

For Israel himself, the drawing near of the time when he

must die, implies work to be done,—directions to be given,—
preparations to be made. He must " set his house in order,
since he is to die and not live" (Is. xxxviii. 1). He must
settle his family affairs, and arrange about his funeral.

This last is his first concern; he gives commandment
about the disposal of his body. The future of his soul
occasions to him no anxiety; on that head he has nothing to
fear, or to ask. He is ready to depart in peace,—his eyes
having seen the salvation of God. This is no case of a deathbed repentance—no hasty and desperate attempt, after years
of wilful neglect of God's grace, to pacify the alarm of
conscience at the last hour. Jacob has long walked with God.
His infirmities and faults may have been many,—his circumstances have been very trying. But his long experience of the
divine forbearance and kindness, and the recent outburst of
light at his " evening time," must have drawn closer the cords
of love that bound him to the God of his fathers, as his own
God. He can calmly, therefore, resign his spirit into the Lord's
keeping. It is about his body and its burial that he is
solicitous : and his solicitude is very great. It leads to his
having very close dealing with Joseph on the subject, and to
his exacting from Joseph a very solemn pledge. Using the
same significant form that Abraham did, when he adjured his
old servant and made him take an oath in the matter of a
spouse to be found for Isaac,—he causes Joseph to swear with
the same deep emphasis in the matter of a grave to be provided for himself : "Put, I pray thee, thy hand under my thigh,
and deal kindly and truly with me : bury me not, I pray thee,
in Egypt: but I will lie with my fathers ; and thou shalt
carry me out of Egypt, and bury me in their burying-place.
And he said, I will do as thou hast said. And he said, Swear
unto me. And he sware unto him. And Israel bowed himself upon the bed's head " (ver. 29-31).

The old man is now content. His soul is to be with God,
his body is to rest in Canaan.

What does all this mean? Why this extreme concern as to where his body is to lie? Is it mere natural feeling,—the fond imagination of a sort of pleasure in being laid near kindred dust,—sharing the narrow bed and the long home of loved ones lost and mourned? It may be so in part. Something of that ineradicable instinct of human nature would seem to be indicated, when the dying patriarch afterwards repeats the same request : " Bury me with my fathers in the cave that is in the field of Ephron. There they buried Abraham and Sarah his wife ; there they buried Isaac and Rebekah his wife ; and there I buried Leah " (xlix. 29-31). There is a touch of tenderness in this last remembrance,—" there I buried Leah,"—that cannot but affect the heart.

Partly, then, it may have been natural feeling that moved Jacob ;—and partly also wise policy and true patriotism. That the remains of the last of their patriarchal chiefs should be carried up by his people, and with much state deposited in the family vault, was an arrangement well fitted to prevent their settling down in Egypt as their final home. It tended to keep alive their sense of their high calling as the destined heirs of Canaan.

But there must have been something more than mere natural feeling and wise patriotism in this extreme urgency of Jacob. These and the like motives might incline him to give a hint, to indicate a wish, to leave behind him an order. But the deep solemnity of the oath evidently betokens something far more serious ;—more spiritual ;—more intimately connected with his own personal religious experience, and his hope for eternity.

" I believe in the resurrection of the body,"—that is the only true and full interpretation of this remarkable procedure of the departing patriarch. " I know that my Redeemer liveth, and that he shall stand at the latter day upon the earth. And though after my skin worms destroy this body, yet in my flesh shall I see God." That was Job's creed ; and it was

Jacob's. Job, trusting in a living Redeemer, looked hopefully through the loathsomeness of the tomb to a bright resurrection morning. So also did Jacob. He too knew that he had a Redeemer who liveth,—that he had for his Redeemer the Living One. He therefore looked through death to life,— through his dying in the body to his living again in the body. He believed assuredly that the promises made to him living in the body must be fulfilled to him living again in the body, —since they were the promises of him " who is the God, not of the dead, but of the living." Therefore his body must rise again, that in his risen body he may receive the promised inheritance. That promised inheritance is identified with the land within whose borders he desires his body to be laid. His being buried there is his taking infeftment in it with the very body in which, when it is raised in glory, he is to receive the promised " recompense of reward."

In this assurance Jacob was willing to close his pilgrimage, as not only a stranger and sojourner in Canaan, but an exile in Egypt. He was willing to have the promise postponed to the future life, and to await, for its fulfilment, the resurrection of the body. And in token of this assurance, and of this willingness, he issues instructions, under the solemn sanction of a deep oath, respecting his body's burial in the land of promise.

Is not his faith mine ? And his hope ? When the time draws near that I must die,—believing, I may commit my soul to God. And my body too. I need not, it is true, be so anxious as Jacob was about the place or manner of my body's interment. I have not the same occasion. I am not called to teach the same prophetic lesson. I may sit very loose to the question where my lifeless frame is to lie,—in ocean's deep bed,—or on earth's wildest waste. But it is not because I hold the body cheap. No. It is because I know that he to whom it is still united will see to its safe keeping, wherever it may rest,—and will restore it to me soon, invested with his own glory,—and will bestow upon me, when it is restored to me, the promised everlasting inheritance in " the new heavens and the new earth, wherein dwelleth righteousness."

65

THE BLESSING ON JOSEPH'S CHILDREN—JACOB'S DYING FAITH

Genesis 48:1-22

By faith Jacob, when he was a dying, blessed both the sons of Joseph ; and worshipped, leaning upon the top of his staff. Hebrews 11:21

THIS scene, or transaction, is partly natural and partly supernatural; or rather it is both throughout. It is faith prevailing against sense, and triumphing over it. But the triumph appears in its being an affair of sense, or of nature, which grace turns into an affair of faith. Grace reigns in it by faith ; and it does so all the more conspicuously because there is in it so much of nature.

Besides the usual symptoms of age and approaching death, Jacob has a special warning in an attack of illness. He is sick; and the sickness is the occasion of a second parting interview, as it were, between him and Joseph (ver. 1). Possibly the former interview may have been supposed on both sides to be the last. Warned by marks and signs of growing weakness, that the time draws near that he must die, Israel has sent for Joseph, and has concluded with him a solemn covenant as to the disposal of his body after his decease. Evidently that was a matter to be arranged, at least in the first instance, with Joseph ; he alone had the power to carry out the plan on which Jacob's heart was set. The interposition of Joseph's influence and authority was needed,—and Jacob takes a pledge from him that it shall not be wanting.

So that solemn conference closes,—and the old man's heart is at rest.   Joseph withdraws,—perhaps scarcely expecting to see his father again.

But Jacob lives on.   He has not fulfilled all his task ; he has not done all his death-bed work.   For himself, he has made full provision ; his soul is to be with God, and his body is to rest in Canaan.   But he must be mindful of others—of his family, viewed as God's church—and in the first instance, of Joseph, their saviour and his.   And this must be specially, and in a marked way, the doing of the Lord.   Accordingly the Lord sends sickness upon Jacob ; and the rumour of the sickness brings Joseph.   It is not as it was on that former occasion ; Jacob does not " call his son Joseph."   There is a providential cause.   Jacob falls sick, and Joseph of his own accord comes to see him.

He comes on the impulse of natural affection.   He will visit his old and failing father once more ; and he will take with him his two sons, that their grandfather may give them a part-ing blessing.   It is all natural, and simply natural.   Faith, no doubt, moved Jacob, on that first occasion of his becoming sensible of his approaching dissolution, to call his son Joseph, and give him directions as to his funeral.   But here, at the outset, there is no sending in faith, or coming in faith ; but only what might seem a becoming expression of the love which Joseph felt for his dying parent, and the esteem in which he held him, and would have his sons to hold him.

Very soon, however, faith begins to manifest itself, and to give a turn to the interview far transcending the range of sense or of nature : " Israel strengthened himself, and sat upon the bed " (ver. 2).   For the use of the name " Israel " is here, as I think it is always, or almost always, significant.   It is not merely an occasional substitute for the name " Jacob," with a view to variety.   It seems to mark the transition, in the patri-arch's experience or frame of mind, from natural weakness to strong faith.   " Jacob " is a worm—" thou worm Jacob " (Is.

xli. 14). "Israel" is a prince, having power with God and prevailing—able to sustain the wrestling of the Angel—and to overcome (Hosea xii. 3, 4).

Thus it is "Israel" (xlvii. 27) who takes up his abode in Egypt, in Goshen ; for it is no little strength of faith that reconciles him to what his doing so implies. It is "Jacob" (ver. 28) who lives in the land of Egypt seventeen years ;— "Jacob" makes out the few and evil days of the years of his life till they are an hundred forty and seven—a bent and feeble old man. But when they draw near their close (ver. 29), it is "Israel" who is to die. And upon Joseph's swearing to carry him out of Egypt and bury him in Canaan—it is no "Jacob" —no—it is "Israel" who, in the firm and full faith of the resurrection and the inheritance, "bows himself on the bed's head" (ver. 31).

So it is here. It is "Jacob"—sick and prostrate—who is told, "Behold thy son Joseph cometh unto thee." But it is "Israel" who instantly thereupon "strengthens himself and sits upon his bed." Yes! It is "Israel"—though at first it is as "Jacob" that he speaks in welcoming his son : "And Jacob said unto Joseph" (ver. 3).

His speech is all of faith and by faith. The visit of Joseph and his two sons cannot but be soothing and gratifying to his natural affection ; but that is not what breathes in the old man's words. He is divinely moved within to accept the incident as a divine hint from above. It is not as giving vent to his own feelings that he speaks—but as having a commission to execute, which God has put into his mind, and for which God makes him see and feel that the opportunity has now providentially come.

I. At once and abruptly he begins a recital of the Lord's dealings with him from the beginning. And it is fitly said that it is "Jacob" who does so. The whole of his first speech (ver. 3-7) is specially appropriate to "Jacob." It begins with a devout acknowledgment of his obligation to grace ; he recalls

the appearance of God Almighty to him at Bethel (ver. 3, 4).
Twice did God appear to him there—first, on his flight into
Padan-aram, and again after his return to Canaan. The two
appearances were intimately connected, and might almost be
regarded as one ; the second being the complement or accomplishment of the first. Both were times of quickening and
revival. The first may have wrought his conversion. Flying
from the wrath of his injured brother, and laden with the guilt
of sin against God, he received a gracious visit and was moved
to make a solemn vow. That scene must have been fresh in
his memory at this time. But it is probably the last of the
two appearances that he has chiefly in view. Then he was re-
awakened to a full apprehension of his high calling as the heir
of the promise. And it is that character that he here takes ;
in that character, he transacts with Joseph. Thou comest to
see thy poor sick father Jacob ; and thou bringest thy sons
with thee, to gladden his dim eyes and sinking heart. Thou
meanest to speak comfortably to him. All well. Thy filial
love is owned and rewarded. Thy father, as the Jacob to
whom God Almighty appeared at Luz, and gave the promise
of Canaan for an everlasting possession for him and his seed
after him, has somewhat to say to thee. It is good news (ver.
5, 6). Thou art a prince in Egypt. Thou art married to one
of Egypt's daughters ; and naturalised as one of Egypt's sons.
It might seem as if thy house were to be established among
Egypt's noblest families. But no. Thy portion is still with
the seed of Abraham. And it is a double portion ; I adopt as
mine thy two first-born sons. Each of them is to have a
standing as my son in the sacred household. It may be God's
will that thou shouldst found a family in Egypt ; if so, it must
be in thine other children. These two whom thou hast brought
to me I claim and adopt as mine.*

* Did Jacob intend thus to transfer to Joseph the right of primogeniture ? It may be so. For we read elsewhere concerning Reuben, the first-
born of Israel, that for his sin " his birthright was given unto the sons of

It warms the old man's heart to be made, in his last days, the channel of conveying to his son Joseph so emphatic a token of the divine favour as his being represented, in two lines, in the chosen household. It brings back tender memories and reawakens buried love (ver. 7). Hence his reference to Rachel ; an irrelevant reference, but all the more touching on that account. It is Rachel's child who stands beside his bed ; to Rachel's child it is his last joy on earth to communicate the divine decree. It is Rachel's child whom he is permitted thus to crown with double honour.

II. But it is the religious faith, rather than the natural affection, indicated in this transaction, that is chiefly to be noticed. At first, apparently, Jacob's dim eyes had not recognised his two grandchildren separately. But now they are brought forward with formal courtesy, and some sort of ceremony, to receive Jacob's embrace and blessing. The old man kisses and embraces them ; and then simply expresses his gratification and gratitude : "I had not thought to see thy face ; and lo, God hath showed me also thy seed" (ver. 8-11). Then comes the solemn patriarchal, or rather prophetic act. With his hands upon their heads the aged seer announces the will of the Lord. "Israel stretched out his right hand, and laid it upon Ephraim's head, who was the younger, and his

Joseph the son of Israel : and the genealogy is not to be reckoned after the birthright. For Judah prevailed above his brethren, and of him came the chief ruler ; but the birthright was Joseph's" (1 Chron. v. 1, 2). This is confessedly an obscure intimation. It may mean that—Reuben, Simeon, and Levi being set aside for special offences—Judah came to stand in the position of pre-eminence. Or it may mean that, while Reuben, in some sense, retained his first place in the reckoning of the genealogy—the birthright was virtually shared between Joseph, who received a double portion in his sons, and Judah, to whom the sovereignty was assigned. At all events, the statement is remarkable : "The birthright was Joseph's." And it seems to point to this transaction—Jacob's conferring a double portion on Joseph, in the persons of his two sons—as the first formal intimation of the divine purpose to that effect.

left upon Manasseh's head, guiding his hands wittingly ; for Manasseh was the first-born" (ver. 12-14).

This strange act receives a twofold explanation.

1. Generally, as applicable to both of Joseph's sons alike, the divine purpose is declared. " He blessed Joseph, and said, God, before whom my fathers Abraham and Isaac did walk, the God which fed me all my life long unto this day, the Angel which redeemed me from all evil, bless the lads ; and let my name be named on them, and the name of my fathers Abraham and Isaac ; and let them grow into a multitude in the midst of the earth" (ver. 15, 16). It is "Israel" who thus speaks ; and what he says is primarily a benediction upon Joseph. It is he who is thus signally owned and honoured in his sons. And the benediction runs in the name of God in a somewhat peculiar way ; as " the Angel which redeemed him from all evil." It is a remarkable form of expression. It can scarcely be restricted to time, or to deliverance from temporal evil. It may include that ; but it surely goes beyond it. The God of Abraham, Isaac, and Israel, is here spoken of as redeeming from all evil, comprehensively,—from all the evil of the fall. He is the destined seed of the woman, bruising the head of the serpent, and setting his victims free. So Israel hails, in the God before whom Abraham and Isaac had walked,—in the God who had fed him all his life long unto this day,—the great Mediator, the Angel of Jehovah who is himself Jehovah, the redresser of all the ills to which flesh is heir. It is the Messianic blessing, in its widest range, that Israel invokes upon the lads. He would have them to be made partakers of the hope which they all,—Abraham, Isaac, and himself,—had, when they walked as strangers on the earth, and died in faith, resting on the promised Saviour.

2. " Israel " distinguishes the lads in thus blessing them. Joseph has noticed the misplacing of his sons (ver. 13, 14) ; but he has not ventured to interfere until his father's lips are closed. Now, however, he will have the mistake rectified :

" Not so, my father : for this is the first-born ; put thy right hand upon his head " (ver. 17, 18). But it is no mistake ; his father knows what he is about; and what he has done he has done deliberately (ver. 19). " Israel " is acting in this matter for God ; announcing, not a wish of his own, or a determination of his own will, but an oracle of God. And one proof of its being so is the sovereignty which it asserts and vindicates as belonging to God. It is a sovereignty which it is his prerogative to exercise, without giving account to any. And it is his pleasure to exercise it,—especially in the sacred family, and in connection with the covenant-promise of redemption by the Angel, of which that family is the depository,—in a way that reverses human notions, and makes it plain that all is of God. " For the purpose of God, according to election, must stand, not of works, but of him that calleth." " It is not of him that willeth, nor of him that runneth, but of God that showeth mercy." So it had ever been in God's dealings with the patriarchs in time past ; so it was to be still. So it was, and is, in the time of the complete fulfilment of the promise,— when the Angel of the Covenant actually accomplishes the redemption from all evil of which Jacob speaks. The law, or rule, under whose operation the economy of grace ordinarily proceeds, is always the same,—humbling to human wisdom, glorifying to the divine sovereignty. The last are often first, and the first last. " He came unto his own, and his own received him not. But as many as received him, to them gave he power to become the sons of God, even to them that believe on his name : which were born, not of blood, nor of the will of the flesh, nor of the will of man, but of God" (John i. 11-13).

But the blessing, though with a distinction thus made, in the exercise of sovereignty, between the lads,—as if to show that it is the blessing of the same God who gave the oracle, " The elder shall serve the younger,"—is still comprehensive enough to embrace both. And as embracing both, it is so rich and full, that nothing beyond it can be imagined as desirable for any one : "He blessed them that day, saying, In thee shall Israel bless, saying, God make thee as Ephraim and as Manasseh" (ver. 20).

That surely must be a blessing, inclusive of "the promise which godliness has, both of the life that now is, and of the life that is to come" (1 Tim. iv. 8). No other blessing could dying "Israel" hold to be a model blessing for his seed,—for all time to come.

III. And now the patriarch closes the affecting interview with one more declaration of his faith : "Behold I die, but God shall be with you, and bring you again unto the land of your fathers" (ver. 21). As to himself, he dies in sure and certain hope of the resurrection and of an inheritance beyond the grave. For Joseph, and for all his family whom he leaves behind, he gives his dying confirmation to the assurance that the earthly inheritance is certain to the family of Abraham at last. And in testimony of his faith to that effect, he leaves a final and very peculiar bequest to Joseph : " Moreover, I have given to thee one portion above thy brethren, which I took out of the hand of the Amorite with my sword and with my bow" (ver. 22).

It is a bequest of special significancy. It is like the transaction into which Jeremiah entered, on the eve of the captivity at Babylon, when under divine guidance he negotiated with his uncle for the redemption and purchase of the field in Anathoth (Jerem. xxxii). That act of the prophet was designed emphatically to attest his full and firm faith in the promise of God, that the people would be delivered out of their Babylonian bondage, and would resume possession of the land of their fathers. So confident is Jeremiah of the fulfilment of that promise, that when all the country is in the enemy's hand, and Jerusalem itself is about to fall, he completes the purchase of the alienated property of his house,—and causes the title-deeds to be duly delivered for safe custody to a competent witness, —with the same calm assurance with which such a matter might have been adjusted in the palmiest days of Solomon's reign. That must have been a striking and affecting spectacle to the poor Jews about to be carried off to weep beside the river of Babylon.

So now, at Jacob's deathbed,—and long after, when the memory of that deathbed, traditionally preserved in song or story, shed a ray of dim light on the darkness of the Egyptian oppression,—this act of the patriarch, disposing of property in Canaan in favour of his beloved son, as unhesitatingly as if he were the actual owner of the whole country, must have served to keep alive the steadfast belief in which Jacob died, that "God would bring them again unto the land of their fathers."

In this view of the bequest, the precise locality of the "portion" bequeathed,—and the precise manner in which Jacob acquired it,—need not occasion much inquiry. It may have been the identical spot which he purchased at Sychem, and which he may have been forced afterwards to vindicate by arms, against some unjust attempt to dispute his title. But be that as it may, the portion was now, and for ages would con- tinue to be, out of the reach of himself and his seed. He fore- sees the long sojourn in Egypt already begun ; he knows that the chosen seed are not to see Canaan for centuries. And knowing that, he leaves the portion as a legacy to Joseph ;— the faith in which he leaves it being a better legacy by far.

Thus, "by faith Jacob, when he was a dying, blessed both the sons of Joseph ; and worshipped, leaning upon the top of his staff" (Heb. xi. 21). The blessing which he pronounced on his grandsons was an act of worship as well as an exercise of faith ; it was a believing acknowledgment of the Redeeming Angel, in whose name it ran. There may have gone along with it worship more express and formal. But the material point is that the worship, whether virtual or explicit, was pilgrim- worship. Jacob "worshipped upon the top of his staff." It may have been for support to his feeble frame that he did so ; his worshipping upon the top of his staff may be thus sufficiently accounted for. In leaning on it, however, he must have been reminded, by the very sense of his frailty that made him lean on it, that he was a pilgrim on the earth, and that his pilgrimage was very near its close. It is as one going on a journey that he worships, when he blesses the sons of Joseph. Staff in hand, he worships and blesses,—as, long afterwards, his descendants were commanded to do when they kept the Passover (Exod. xii. 11). He is going hence. His worship and his blessing have respect to a hereafter,—to the resurrection state in which he himself, and Joseph's sons, and all his true seed, are to receive the everlasting inheritance.

And what shall we say of Joseph's faith in all this strange procedure? What is he doing here? He is giving up his two sons to Jacob. He is consenting virtually to their being disinherited, as regards their position and prospects in Egypt. He is casting in their lot with the family now on the very brink of servitude. What a sacrifice for himself and them!

It does not appear that Joseph left, through any other son, a name to be ranked among the nobles of the Egyptian court; there is no trace of his having founded a family. No explanation can be given of that fact, especially in the view of his bringing his sons to be blessed by Jacob,—except that he did all by faith. It was with him as with Moses. "By faith Moses, when he was come to years, refused to be called the son of Pharaoh's daughter; choosing rather to suffer affliction with the people of God, than to enjoy the pleasures of sin for a season; esteeming the reproach of Christ greater riches than the treasures in Egypt: for he had respect unto the recompence of the reward" (Heb. xi. 24-26). Joseph made the same choice; and he made it in the exercise of the same faith.

66

JACOB'S DYING PROPHECY—JUDAH'S EXALTED LOT— SHILOH COMING

Genesis 49:1-12

My beloved is white and ruddy, the chiefest among ten thousand. The
Song of Solomon 5:10

He brought me to the banqueting-house, and his banner over me was love.
The Song of Solomon 2:4

THERE is a solemn assembly in the patriarch's dying chamber,
—around his dying bed : " Jacob called unto his sons, and
said, Gather yourselves together" (ver. 1). " Gather yourselves together," is his summons,—all of you,—not one cut off.
This is Jacob's privilege, above what his grandfather and his
father had. They had to submit to a pruning process,—
painfully losing natural branches,—that the promise might be
seen to be of grace, and of the election of grace. Abraham
had to give up Ishmael, born after the flesh,—and to consent
to his seed being called in Isaac, the son by promise. Isaac
had to let Esau go, and confirm the covenant in Jacob. But
in Jacob the family is one ; the heads of the chosen race are
complete. Expansion, not contraction, is henceforth to be the
rule. The stream is to be widened, and not narrowed any
more. All his sons are " gathered" round Jacob. They are
to learn what is to befall them in after time (ver. 1) ; they are
to listen to a far-reaching prophecy. It is no " Lochiel's
warning" of " coming events casting their shadows before,"—
no dreamy oracle of gifted, second-sight diviner,—that they are

to hear. Nor is it the utterance of such almost preternatural sagacity of insight and foresight as has sometimes been supposed to be the dying privilege of peculiarly saintly men. The patriarch speaks under the inspiration of the Omniscient Spirit. He has really before him what is to befall his sons, in their offspring, " in the last days."

These last days are the Messianic times. Jacob's eye of faith and hope is fixed upon the advent of the promised Saviour when he sees and sketches the nearer or remoter fortunes of his descendants. On that back-ground the different destinies of the tribes of Israel stand out in bold relief to his inspired view.

" Hear," he cries, with voice divinely strengthened and divinely moved, to pour out in a rapt divine song what he saw in rapt divine vision,—" gather yourselves together, and hear, ye sons of Jacob ; and hearken unto Israel your father" (ver. 2). Hear, ye sons of " Jacob." Ye are Jacob's sons,—sons of " the worm Jacob,"—in yourselves worms, as he is,—weak, unworthy, vile. But your father is not " Jacob" merely ; he is " Israel" also ; and it is " unto Israel your father" that you are to " hearken." You are called as " sons of Jacob." You are called to hearken to " your father Israel." So this wonderful divine prophecy, or prophetic poem, is introduced.

The minute exposition of it I do not mean to undertake ; a very cursory survey is all that I can attempt.

Two things may be noticed at the outset. First, It is partly retrospective as well as prospective. It proceeds upon a review of the past, as well as upon fore-knowledge of the future. Jacob reads off the fortunes of his sons, in their respective races, under the light of what they had shown themselves to be. This does not detract from the prophetic character of the poem ; for its predictions are not such mere conjectures as observation might suggest. But an important principle in the divine administration is thus brought out. It is that of transmitted character ;—and, within certain limits, transmitted destiny too. What his sons were, and what they did, must tell powerfully, for weal or for woe, on what the tribes that spring from them are to enjoy or suffer. Secondly, The chief interest of the prophecy centres in two of its utterances,—that about Judah, and that about Joseph. It may thus be divided into two parts, in the first of which Judah is conspicuous and pre-eminent,—in the second Joseph. And he, it is to be kept in mind, is represented chiefly by his younger son Ephraim.

Judah, then, on the one hand, and Joseph, cr Ephriam, on the other,—are the leading and prominent figures in this prophetic picture. And all the subsequent history shows that the tribes bearing these names played the principal part in the working out of the destiny of the chosen nation ;—Judah in the south, Ephraim in the north ;—Judah faithful to David's line, Ephraim the head of the revolted provinces. So also, all through the prophecies, Judah and Ephraim are the well-known names of the two kingdoms.* Judah and Ephraim,—which is Joseph,—are representative or leading tribes along the whole line of the eventful history of the Jewish people. And therefore they fitly occupy the prominent places in the two parts of Jacob's dying oracle respectively. Judah stands pre-eminent among the first four sons of Jacob (ver. 3-12) ; Joseph, again, ranks as chief among the remaining eight (ver. 13-27).

Keeping these preliminary remarks in view, I now briefly sketch the patriarch's successive oracles concerning the tribes of Israel.

I. Reuben comes first (ver. 3, 4). He should have been strong ; he proved himself to be " unstable as water." The contrast is emphatic and affecting, as it brings out what the old man would have had his eldest son to be, and what he turned out to be. My might,—the prime of my strength,—all that I had of excellency, in respect of dignity or power,—all might

*Isaiah 7:17; 11:13; Ezekiel 37:15-17; Hosea *passim*.

have been his. But he lost it all by his instability; he wanted self-control. Impatient and impetuous, he was like an unruly stream, soon spending its force, and then becoming languid. He had manifested this temperament in the commission of a horrible crime. It was great wickedness; but it was great weakness too. His father fastens on the weakness of it; the entire want of self-command which it too plainly showed. And he foresees that, if this is to be the character of his tribe, it must mar all prospect of high fame or fortune.

Did it not really do so when, upon the first success of Moses, after the long wandering in the wilderness, Reuben grasped at the earliest chance of repose and self-indulgence,— and sought a settlement on the east of the Jordan, in the first country conquered, before Canaan proper was reached?

But besides his natural vice of instability, transmitted as a hereditary taint to his tribe, we must recognise here also, as affecting them as well as him, the judgment of God upon his sin. The guilt he had contracted lost him his birthright, as the inspired historian testifies (1 Chron. v. 1, 2). He was still indeed to retain his place, in the reckoning of the genealogy, as the first-born: but the rights and privileges of primogeniture were to pass from him.

II. Simeon and Levi, as next in order, have a joint oracle given forth concerning them (ver. 5-7). Their father speaks very plainly. He denounces unsparingly their sin, in the matter of their sister Dinah. Their vile treachery and bloody cruelty had troubled him at the time; and now, on his deathbed, he looks back upon it with unabated, or rather with enhanced, horror. He solemnly anathematises their fierce anger and cruel wrath; in fact, their share in their father's last blessing is very like a curse. He does not indeed altogether cast them out. They are still to be reckoned among his sons,—and the tribes springing from them are to be numbered among the people. But it is to be in a way marking them out as the objects of retributive judgment. They are to

be " in Jacob,"—" in Israel ;" but they are to be " divided
in Jacob, and scattered in Israel." It is a hard sentence.
All the rest are to have quiet settlements in the land ; they
alone are to be, as it would seem, without fixed habitations.
That is their doom ; the doom apparently of both alike.
But, as it turns out, there is a difference. And it is a difference illustrating both the goodness and the severity of God.
In Simeon's case there is severity ; the sentence takes effect
without mitigation. His tribe was from the first very small,
feeble, and insignificant. However respectable in point of
numbers at the Exodus (Num. i. 23), it seems to have lost
position and influence during the years of sojourn in the
wilderness ; for when the tribes had their several portions
assigned to them after the victories of Joshua, the children of
Simeon had their inheritance within that of the children of
Judah (Josh. xix. 9 ; Judges i. 3, 17). It was otherwise
with Levi. The sentence was indeed executed even more
literally upon his posterity than upon that of Simeon. But
it was turned from a curse into a blessing. It was over-ruled
for their highest good. They had no separate inheritance of
their own among their brethren. But they had the Lord
himself for their inheritance (Deut. x. 9). " Divided in Jacob
and scattered in Israel " they were. But it was in the
character of the chosen priests and ministers of the Lord.

III. Reuben, Simeon, and Levi being disposed of and set
aside, Judah comes upon the field of the patriarch's vision.
He has listened with trembling awe to the stern denunciation
of the crimes of his elder brothers. He too has sins upon his
conscience that may well shake his nerves. His sons have
been born in uncleanness,—and he has had a hand in selling
Joseph into Egypt, though it might be said that it was to save
his life. But no such ban lies upon him as lay upon the
three that went before. We may gather from his noble
speech before Joseph, that his filial and fraternal love was
pure and strong. He is one who can understand his father ;

and feel for him and with him more than the rest could do. And at all events, the purpose of God according to the election of grace must stand. It is in Judah that the seed of Abraham is to be called. In him the dying Israel " sees the day of Christ afar off and is glad." His song is now a song of triumphant jubilation and joy.

Judah is to verify in his history the significant name which he got in his birth (ver. 8). When his mother Leah bare him, she said, " Now will I praise the Lord," therefore she called his name Judah. His name is Praise. Others as well as his mother are to call his name Praise ; his brethren are to praise him (ver. 8) ; he is to be pre-eminent among them by their own consent. For the victories he is to win over his enemies and theirs, his father's children are to yield him allegiance and loyal service (ver. 8). He is to be lion-like in his power and prowess (ver. 9). As the king of the forest, he is to master his prey ;—as the young lion, springing upon it ; —as the old lion, couching and terrible when roused. He is to be invincible in war. And above all, he is to be a legitimate prince, a lawful ruler, and he is to continue to be so until another rise, one springing from him,—in whom at last his high and blessed destiny is to be fulfilled—" until Shiloh come " (ver. 10).

Who is this Shiloh ? And what does his name import ? The aged seer beholds him, and hails him. Far on in the stream of time,—along the royal line of the son whose name is Praise, he catches sight of another son, whose name is Peace !

Judah, thou art Praise ! Thou art to be a conqueror. Thou art to have a lion's strength. Thou art to reign and decree justice. I see before me all thy glorious lot. But in thee, through thee, behind thee, I see another,—one greater than thou art. Lo ! he comes. He who is Peace,—" our peace,"—comes. And as I see him coming, what a scene bursts upon my ravished sight, my straining eyes !

1. What a " gathering together in one of all things in

him!" (Ephes. i. 10). "Unto him shall the gathering of the people be" (ver. 10). Nations are flowing to him,—multitudes of all tongues and kindreds. Well they may. For he is giving peace,—he is speaking peace;—peace from heaven;—peace on earth. Shiloh comes; all wars cease; all the nations are one in him.

2. And with what plenty of all richest and choicest blessings do I see him loaded!—"Binding his foal unto the vine, and his ass's colt unto the choice vine; he washed his garments in wine, and his clothes in the blood of grapes" (ver. 11). He comes—a prince,—"thy king," O Israel,—"meek, riding on an ass, and on a colt the foal of an ass." He comes to travel no more, but to tarry. It is in the midst of a most fruitful vineyard; he binds his humble steed to one of its noblest trees. "This is my rest,—here will I stay." The wine is flowing copiously; the red blood of the grapes is so abundant that he washes his garments in it. The nations gathering round him partake of all this fulness. They drink the wine with him in the kingdom.

3. And then how fair is this glorious peacemaker, this bountiful and blessed prince, as I see him coming!—"His eyes shall be red with wine, and his teeth white with milk" (ver. 12). Shiloh comes;—"fairer than the sons of men" (Ps. xlv. 2). "My beloved is white and ruddy, the chiefest among ten thousand. His mouth is most sweet; yea, he is altogether lovely" (Song v. 10, 16). What brightness in his eye!—what milk-white beauty in his teeth! My soul is ravished with his loveliness and his love. O let Shiloh come. Come, thou who art all my salvation and all my desire; yea, come quickly.

I need not stay to show how the history of the tribe of Judah corresponded, in all its leading outlines, to the prophetic sketch of it given so long before by Jacob. Very early Judah began to have a certain acknowledged pre-eminence among the tribes of Israel. The first place in the march, in the battle, in the encampment, would seem to have been assigned from the very beginning to Judah. In the land of promise Judah soon began to acquire a position and influence which none of the rest of the tribes could challenge. In David and his victories; in Solomon and his glory; in the unbroken line of their descendants; in the preserving of the royal family through the captivity of Babylon and all subsequent changes,—in humble circumstances, indeed, but still distinguishable as inheriting a right to reign which none but they could claim;—in all this we clearly trace the fulfilment of the oracle;—the exaltation of Judah fully consummated,— and perpetuated also till the appointed era arrived.

But I must offer a word of explanation as to the view which I have ventured to give of the closing portion of the oracle concerning him. I assume, as all but universally admitted, that the Messiah is the party indicated by the name Shiloh. Usually, however, the reference to him is restricted to the few words in the tenth verse "until Shiloh come, and unto him shall the gathering of the people be." The eleventh and twelfth verses are applied to Judah; and are understood as describing the luxuriant fertility of the portion that the tribe of Judah had in Canaan,—its overflowing fulness of fruit and fruitfulness.

Now this application of these verses is open to some remarks. First, it is by no means clear that Judah's portion deserved to be so glowingly depicted; the language is too rich for that. Then, secondly, there is great awkwardness in the introduction of this abrupt reference to the Messiah as merely, and so briefly, parenthetical. But, thirdly, there is no incongruity at all, if we take what is said by Jacob, after his mention of Shiloh, as being all said of that illustrious personage. Israel sees Judah first, and then Shiloh; he no more sees Judah at all, but only Shiloh; he has done with Judah; Shiloh is all in all. And finally, the description that follows is in entire harmony with the Messianic prophecies of later days. Nay more, I cannot but discern in this old Messianic oracle the germs of some of the Messianic characteristics which later prophecies have acknowledged and developed. Thus, in the "foal and ass's colt," may we not have the rudimentary idea of what was afterwards expanded by Zechariah into the prophecy which was literally fulfilled in our Lord's triumphant entry into Jerusalem (Zech. ix. 9). It was no mere arbitrary sign that was thus given beforehand by the prophet. It was the index of a meek and lowly mind, such as becomes Shiloh —the Prince of Peace. Though he is the lion of the tribe of Judah, he does not multiply horses, as the kings that affected oriental pomp used to do, against the express commandment of the law. He rides, like the old Judges, on an ass, and a colt, the foal of an ass; in humble guise; willing to be as the poorest of the people. Then again, is not the image of wine, the blood of the grape, a very common emblem of the spiritual refreshment which the Messiah has to bestow? The idea of its abundance, even to the washing of his garments in it, is in thorough keeping with subsequent prophetic symbols. And once more, may we not see in the picture of beauty briefly drawn at the close of all—"His eyes shall be red with wine, and his teeth white with milk" (ver. 12).—what might be the suggestive source of not a little of the language used in the Song, to bring out the rapturous admiration in which the Bridegroom King is held by his loving spouse?

Taken thus, the sublime utterance of Israel is consistent with itself, and worthy of its occasion and its object. He does full justice to Judah. He invests him with all the natural attributes of strength, and all the conventional insignia of rank and power. He salutes him as raised to the highest pinnacle of earthly glory. But exactly then, and at that point, Judah disappears from his range of vision; and he does not come upon it again. It is all filled with the surpassing glory of one far greater than Judah; coming with peace, as well as praise, for his name;—coming to "gather into one all things in himself;"—coming triumphant, but meek and lowly in his triumph;—coming to shed abroad from himself all abundance of wine;—coming to be "glorified in his saints and admired in all them that believe."

How much, or how little, the patriarch knew of a previous coming of that illustrious one,—to obey, and suffer, and die,— we cannot tell. He knew at least that "without shedding of blood there is no remission," and that "through much tribulation lies the entrance into the kingdom of heaven." We who live now, under the partial realisation of Jacob's great vision, know all that better than he could do. We know "Christ and him crucified." We know Jesus, who was once crucified, as now exalted at the right hand of God. But do we fix our eye as steadfastly as Jacob did on what is our hope now;—the fuller realisation of this vision at the glorious appearing of the Lord from heaven? Do the words—"till Shiloh come"—cause our hearts to thrill as they did the heart of dying Jacob? Do we enter into the mind of him who, ages afterwards, as he closed the volume of the Revelation, exclaimed, "Even so come, Lord Jesus"?

67

WAITING FOR THE SALVATION OF THE LORD— SEEING THE SALVATION OF THE LORD

Genesis 49:18

I have waited for thy salvation, O Lord.

THIS is a remarkable ejaculation in the circumstances. What can it mean? Is it a part of the oracle about Dan, at the close of which it comes in? Is it Dan who is to be understood as using these words? Does Jacob put them into the mouth of that tribe as expressive of their future character? Or is it the old man speaking for himself—breaking out, in the midst of what he feels to be his somewhat weary work, into a pathetic appeal to God for rest?

Whatever may be its import, I cannot but take it to be the utterance of his own emotion; the irrepressible sighing of his own heart. Perhaps it indicates some little disappointment. The picture of the prospective fortunes of his house which the Spirit is setting before him is not all bright. On the contrary, it has in it too many features of resemblance to what he has already met with in his actual family history. The future is to be too like the past; what his sons have been their several posterities are to be. Reuben, Simeon, Levi, have passed in review before his divinely opened eyes, with little to give him comfortable hope. In Judah, indeed, he has seen a glorious sight—Shiloh coming and gathering to him all nations—the king, meek, and riding upon an ass—setting up a kingdom of peace and plenty—resting and giving rest amid overflowing abundance of wine of the choicest grapes—himself all fair—" the chiefest among ten thousand, and altogether lovely." But the very glimpse he has thus got of Messiah's royal beauty causes a kind of reaction. It is brief and evanescent, like a flash of light across the dark and lowering sky. He has instantly to change his hand and check his pride. The strain has risen for a moment to heaven's holy harmony of joy and glory; it comes down again at once to earth's broken music. The burden may not be quite so heavy as before. Elements of material prosperity are in the busy scenes which its glowing language depicts. There is Zebulun along the sea-coast, almost rivalling great Zidon in its commerce (ver. 13). Issachar also is seen stretching his lazy length in his rich inland valleys, unambitious of distinction in policy or war—content with the alternate animal rest and servile toil of a rude life of rural safety and abundance (ver. 14, 15). And Dan rises conspicuous—giving rulers and judges to all Israel —having the wisdom of the serpent, at least, if not the harmlessness of the dove, to help him forward (ver. 16, 17). So far, there is a somewhat better outlook for them than for the first three. But it is not quite such as to satisfy the patriarch. His spirit, wrought up to its highest pitch by what he has seen of Shiloh in Judah, feels, as it were, a shock, a jar. Is this all he is to get of insight into the grace and glory of him whose day he sees afar off with such gladness of heart? Must he have his mind again filled with images of mere terrestrial significancy? This is not quite what he thinks he might have anticipated; it is not exactly what he would have desired. " I have waited for thy salvation, O Lord."

What it was that Jacob waited for may be made matter of doubtful disputation. Any signal deliverance wrought by God may be called, in Scripture language, " his salvation." The miracle of the Red Sea is so called (Exod. xiv. 13); and so also is the victory granted to the good king Jehoshaphat, upon his prayer and fasting, without his army striking a blow

(2 Chron. xx. 17). In these and similar instances the meaning is fixed by the connection in which the expression stands. But it occurs very often, indeed for the most part, with nothing to restrict or qualify it—especially in the Psalms, and in some chapters of Isaiah. "My salvation," says the Lord to the church. And the church, or the believer, answers, "Thy salvation, O Lord."

When thus used absolutely, without any particular event being specified, it may denote simply the Lord's saving power and grace generally; and thus understood, it includes much that is fitted to awaken interest and call forth desire. That God saves,—and how God saves,—are the two parts of it;—both of them, if we look at them in the right light, not a little wonderful. In the first place, that God saves at all,—that he can save, being such as he is, and men being such as they are, is not quite so much a matter of course as we are apt to fancy. For, let us remember, it is such salvation as can be called his, emphatically his,—that is now in question;—such salvation as may be fitly and worthily ascribed to him. And therefore, secondly, the manner of it is all-important,—how he saves. An insight into that is indispensable.

"Thy salvation, O Lord,"—thy manner of saving! How it is possible for thee to save at all,—upon what principles, after what fashion, thou art minded to save,—what may make it possible for thee to save, if I may so say, safely,—without derogating from thine infinite perfections,—without prejudice to thyself, O Lord, and to the glorious majesty of thy throne and law,—that to me is a marvel! It is a mystery,—the knowledge of it is too wonderful for me. "It is high, I cannot attain unto it."

Thou hast indeed been a saviour to me, O Lord! Thou hast been so on many an occasion, in many a danger, in many a trying hour. Thou hast been continually "delivering my soul from death, mine eyes from tears, and my feet from falling" (Ps. cxvi. 8).

Surely thy dealings with me personally prove that thou savest,—that it is thy delight, thy very nature, to save. And they teach something also as to the manner of thy salvation; —how much there is in it of long-suffering patience, generous forbearance, tender pity;—how much there is in it also of utterly undeserved and gratuitous loving-kindness;—how much of wisdom and kind consideration;—how much of what is fitted to touch the conscience and win the heart.

Still there is darkness. That thy salvation should be of such a sort in my case,—that thou shouldst have so saved, so often, such an one as I am,—is to my mind only an aggravation of the darkness.

Nor is the darkness dispelled when I look away from my own personal history to other instances of thy power to save. These have been very terrible in many of their accompaniments,—so terrible, that in spite of all that I have tasted of thy saving goodness, I may well doubt if I am really saved after all,—I who have so abused thy goodness that even it may all the more condemn me. I cannot but ask if the deluge of wrath must not at last be my portion, rather than the ark of safety,—the fire of Sodom's judgment, rather than the little city Zoar.

Nay, even the sacrificial rite which I have been accustomed to observe,—the plunging of the knife into the innocent victim slain in my stead,—can only very partially chase the gloom away. The awful truth it proclaims, that "without shedding of blood there is no remission," does but suggest the anxious question,—Can this blood suffice?

Ah! it might well be with deep and poignant grief that the dying Israel, feeling himself to be still,—to be at that dread moment more than ever,—the poor, weak, sinful worm, Jacob,—uttered this plaintive voice, in the midst of his prophesying,—"I have waited for thy salvation, O Lord."

He had thought he was now at last to obtain full satisfaction. He would gladly have laid an arrest on the bright and beauteous form that flitted past him, as he saw for a moment the coming Shiloh. Fain would he have sought leave to gaze on him a little longer ;—if by any means he might see in him any sign of a better ransom than "the blood of bulls or of goats" could ever furnish. But the vision vanishes swiftly and sadly from his view. The great problem of reconciling the final welfare of the guilty with interests of even higher moment in the righteous government of the Most High, —the question of questions,—"How can man be just with God ?"—How can God himself be "a just God and a Saviour?" —is scarcely at all more clearly solved than it was before. It is still as one who has not yet attained that he has to say ; "I have waited for thy salvation, O Lord."

May not something of the same spirit be traced in other Old Testament references,—especially in the Psalms and in Isaiah,—to the salvation of the Lord ; and in the attitude of the church, or of the believer, towards that salvation ?

Thus in the thirty-fifth Psalm, we have such supplications as these : "Plead my cause, O Lord, with them that strive against me ;—Say unto my soul, I am thy salvation." "My soul shall be joyful in the Lord, it shall rejoice in his salvation" (ver. 1, 3, 9). Here there is waiting for the salvation of the Lord,—waiting in confident expectation. It is waiting under a cloud. It is waiting under the cloud occasioned by the triumph of the ungodly, in their persecution of the righteous ;—"For without cause have they hid for me their net in a pit, which without cause they have digged for my soul" (ver. 7). The problem, the question, is still virtually the same. How is the riddle of God's providence to be read ?

I cannot be at rest while I see violence and wrong prevailing,—and the meek ready to perish. But I know that the Lord reigneth in righteousness. There must be a time, not only of righteous deliverance for his poor and oppressed ones, but of righteous reckoning with their oppressors. I confidently anticipate such a time. Therefore I say that "my soul shall be joyful in the Lord;"—"it shall rejoice in thy salvation,"—for which "I have waited, O Lord." It is no malignant joy in human misery; it is the joy of seeing God's character vindicated, and his rule upheld, by his own righteous method of deliverance being at last realised and fulfilled.

Then, again, the fiftieth Psalm closes emphatically thus:—"Whoso offereth praise glorifieth me: and to him that ordereth his conversation aright will I show the salvation of God" (ver. 23). That is God's own promise. He will show to the upright the divine salvation,—the only sort of salvation that is worthy of himself. Let us remember the argument of that fiftieth Psalm. After a tender expostulation with those who are really his own among the people, for not trusting, loving, and praying to him enough,—and a terrible denunciation of those who are merely hypocrites and self-deceivers,—who take God's covenant in their mouth and yet conform to the world and its wicked ways,—the Lord finds the source, at once of the weak unsteadfastness of the godly, and of the reckless presumption of the worldly, in the "silence" which in his providence he is now "keeping," and the too common and natural misinterpretation and abuse of that silence on the part of both sorts or classes of men. It is the silence of forbearance, and of the delay of judgment, which encourages the profane and is apt to perplex the pious. But both will soon have light enough on the only way of salvation that is consistent with righteousness. "These things hast thou done, and I kept silence,—thou thoughtest I was altogether such an one as thyself,—but I will reprove thee, and set them in order before thine eyes." There is to be a speaking out, on the part of him who is now "keeping silence." And it is in connection with that prospect that it is said;—"To him that ordereth his conversation aright, will I show the salvation of God." I will show him the salvation that alone can be of God;—the salvation that is righteous as well as gracious. Therefore such a one may confidently and humbly reply,—"I wait,"—I have waited, and will still wait,—"for thy salvation, O Lord."

But it is in the 119th Psalm pre-eminently that this great thought of the Lord's salvation is made matter of devout meditation and prayer. " Quicken me in thy righteousness. Let thy mercies come also unto me, O Lord ; even thy salvation, according to thy word " (ver. 40, 41). " Let my heart be sound in thy precepts, that I be not ashamed; my soul fainteth for thy salvation ; but I hope in thy word " (ver. 80, 81). " Mine eyes fail for thy salvation, and for the word of thy righteousness " (ver. 123). " Lord, I have hoped for thy salvation, and done thy commandments " (ver. 166). " I have longed for thy salvation, O Lord, and thy law is my delight " (ver. 174).

Surely all this is indeed " waiting for the salvation of the Lord !" And it. is the waiting of one who is thoroughly on the side and in the interests of God ; of his " righteousness," his " precepts," his " word ;" " the word of his righteousness," his " commandments," his " law."

In every instance in which he speaks of the salvation of the Lord, the Psalmist speaks of it in connection with a prior and paramount recognition of the Lord's own character and claims. (1.) " Let thy salvation come to me ;" (2.) " my soul fainteth for thy salvation ;" (3.) " mine eyes fail for thy salvation ;" (4.) " I have hoped for thy salvation ;" (5.) " I have longed for thy salvation ;" these are strong, earnest, and emphatic breathings of devout desire. But as to the first, the salvation must come " according to thy word ;" as to the second, " my heart must be sound in thy precepts ;" as to the third, thy salvation must be identical with " the word of thy righteousness ;" while the fourth and fifth stand connected with the devout profession :—" I have done thy commandments,"—" Thy law is my delight."

No salvation could content me that is not in harmony with these high and holy principles ;—these deep convictions of my soul. No salvation could approve itself as thine that did not meet this inexorable condition.

But the Psalmist feels that in none of the salvations with which he is familiar, whether personal, or domestic, or national, is it met adequately and sufficiently. Much there is in all of them to manifest both the goodness and the severity of God; for there are always tokens of his displeasure against sin, in the midst of all his loving-kindness to the sinner. But in none of them can either retributive justice or saving mercy be seen to be complete, and to have its perfect work. Both the righteousness and the grace halt, and fail of their full accomplishment. The onlooker is still staggered by the seeming impunity of evil; only a partial and doubtful victory being secured on the side of good. If he is of one mind with the Psalmist,—if he is of one mind with the Psalmist's Lord,—he waits for what, as being more thoroughly according to his law, may more worthily be called " his salvation."

In a remarkable series of prophecies in Isaiah (xlvi.-lvi.), the Lord speaks of " his salvation." And he speaks of it as no longer to be waited for, at least not much longer, but as now at hand and within reach. " I bring near my righteousness; it shall not be far off, and my salvation shall not tarry; and I will place salvation in Zion for Israel my glory" (Is. xlvi. 13). "My righteousness is near; my salvation is gone forth, and mine arms shall judge the people; the isles shall wait upon me, and on mine arm shall they trust" (Is. li. 5). " Thus saith the Lord, Keep ye my judgment, and do justice; for my salvation is near to come, and my righteousness to be revealed" (Is. lvi. 1).

This salvation of the Lord is brought near in the train of righteousness—his own righteousness. What righteousness that is, the description of the Messiah which stands in the very heart of this glorious evangelical prophecy, indicates beyond all possibility of doubt.

For, in the fifty-third chapter, not only is the fact of the

Lord's salvation being near confirmed, but the manner of it also is declared ;—and in so far as that can be done before-hand, it is declared clearly and fully. The righteousness of God :—a righteousness that is in every view his,—provided by him, wrought out by him, accepted by him, applied by him ; a righteousness infinitely worthy of him, and therefore worthy of being called his ;—commensurate with his own perfect righteousness of nature ;—corresponding perfectly to the right-eousness of his government and law ;—a righteousness having in it both precious blood to expiate deadly guilt and sinless obedience to win eternal life ;—such a righteousness, in the holy person and atoning work of him whom the prophet describes as " wounded for our transgressions,"—goes before, and opens up the way for, the Lord's salvation ;—a salvation as worthy of him, and of being called his, as is the righteousness which is its pioneer ;—such a salvation as the Psalmist had before his eyes ;—such a salvation as Jacob would fain have seen, when he said ; " I have waited for thy salvation, O Lord."

Need I trace this thought running through the Old Testa-ment, any farther ? Let me simply bring it down to Gospel times.

The aged Simeon here sufficiently shows the way. He was one who could say with Jacob ; " I have waited for thy salvation, O Lord." But he had not to say it exactly as Jacob had to say it. The patriarch must be content to depart with the language, so far, of ungratified curiosity, or rather, of unsatisfied desire, on his lips—" I have waited." Not so this " just and devout" man. He " waited for the consolation of Israel,"—the salvation of the Lord. But he was not to have to say, even at the last, " I have waited ;" that was not to be his dying ejaculation. For " it was revealed unto him by the Holy Ghost that he should not see death before he had seen the Lord's Christ." And accordingly in the temple he took up the child Jesus in his arms and blessed God and said ; " Lord, now lettest thou thy servant depart in peace, according to thy word: for mine eyes have seen thy salvation." He saw the Lord's anointed Saviour, and the Lord's way of saving Jew and Gentile by him. He saw the tribulation through which, in righteousness, the salvation was to be accomplished. He saw the sharp sword that was to pierce alike the Saviour and the saved. He saw the light and glory for which the sharp sword was to open up the way (Luke ii. 25-35).

Simeon's attitude, rather than Jacob's, may be said to be ours. And yet may not the two be combined? May we not enter all the more into Jacob's "waiting," the more we enter into Simeon's "seeing?" We should be able to say, with a fulness of meaning which even Simeon could not grasp, that our eyes have seen the salvation of the Lord. Not the infant Jesus in the temple has been disclosed to us,—but besides, the man Christ Jesus,—in his life, and death, and resurrection; teaching, doing good, obeying and suffering. Christ crucified, Christ glorified, it is ours to see; to see in the light of inspired apostolic revelation; to see with eye opened and purged by the same Spirit who inspired that revelation. Truly, we see the salvation of the Lord as Simeon could scarcely be said to see it!

What then? Is there to be no more waiting for it? Nay, if we see it as Simeon could scarcely see it, we will say with more intensity than Jacob could say: "I have waited, —I wait,—for thy salvation, O Lord." For this surely is a case in which it must hold true "that increase of appetite grows by what it feeds on." The more we see of the salvation, the more we wait for something more of it still to be seen. In fact, there can be no real waiting without some seeing. Jacob must have been able, in some measure, to enter into Simeon's grateful acknowledgment,—"Mine eyes have seen thy salvation;" else he never would have felt his own longing,—"I have waited for thy salvation, O Lord." And Simeon, when he found what had been revealed to him fulfilled, and could say, "Mine eyes have seen thy salvation,"

did not cease to wait,—nay rather he waited all the more,—
" for thy salvation, O Lord."

For the salvation of the Lord ;—what it is ; of what sort,
and in what way effected ; how the Lord saves, and all that is
implied in his saving ;—is as immense and inexhaustible as is
his own infinite fulness,—the " fulness of the Godhead" that
" dwells bodily in Christ." Therefore, for deeper insight into
it and for larger enjoyment of it, there must always be waiting,—waiting evermore. Even in eternity there is waiting
for it. The dying saint,—the dying sinner scarcely daring to
own the name of saint, weary and way-worn, conscious of little
in himself but ignorance, infirmity, and unbelief, yet still holding on,—may be apt almost to complain—" I have waited for
thy salvation, O Lord ;" and alas ! I seem to have been
waiting all but in vain ! What of its light and joy is mine ?
What of its sensible comfort ? What of its full assurance ?
What of its beatific vision ? its rapture ? its triumph ? What
of the outburst—" I know, I see, I mount, I fly ?" Depressed
and doubting, or at the best, " faint yet pursuing,"—he asks,
Is this then, after all, the salvation that I have been waiting
for, O Lord ? Is this indeed thy salvation ? Nay it is not.
It is not, at least, the whole of it. Be thankful for the
earnest of it, which is " waiting for it." Thou hast been
waiting for it ; and thou mayst have to wait for it still.
Waiting for it is thy security now ; waiting for it will be thine
eternal joy in heaven.

Let no one therefore ever say, dying or living, in any other
spirit than that in which Jacob said it—" I have waited for
thy salvation, O Lord." For, with whatever sense of the
vanity of earthly things, and the unsatisfactory nature of even
the best earthly prospects, for himself and his, he said it,—of
one thing we may be sure, he did not say it in the spirit of
unbelief. On the contrary, if I am right in my impression of
what he meant, he was moved to say it by the very sight his
faith had just got of Shiloh coming. He had hoped to have

seen more of him; for in him he saw the salvation for which he had waited. But let him have seen ever so much more of him, he must still have gone away from earth unsatisfied. And let him have seen ever so little, he is in a position, as he goes away, to say with Simeon, "Mine eyes have seen thy salvation."

How is this salvation to be waited for? What is implied in waiting for it? Let one or two texts give the answer.

1. "Surely his salvation is nigh them that fear him" (Ps. lxxxv. 9). Do we "fear him?" Do we deprecate the Lord's wrath, as that Psalm does?—"Cause thine anger against us to cease;" "Wilt thou be angry with us for ever?" "Wilt thou draw out thine anger to all generations?" Are we as much in earnest as the Psalmist is about God's favour toward us, and our revival toward him? "Thou hast been favourable;" "Thou hast forgiven;" "Wilt thou not revive us again, that thy people may rejoice in thee?" Do we thus wait for his salvation? —"Show us thy mercy, O Lord, and grant us thy salvation." Do we moreover wait in the attitude of obedient faith,—"I will hear what God the Lord will speak;" and of believing hope, —"for he will speak peace to his people, and to his saints;" and of thorough separation from evil and an evil world,— "let them not turn again to folly"? Then, surely, his salvation is nigh to us, as "to them that fear him." All the more it is so, if we make what follows your own special and personal prayer; "That glory may dwell in our land, mercy and truth meeting together, righteousness and peace kissing each other."

2. For, as another Psalm puts it (xcvi. 2), if like Simeon, we see—and like Jacob, we wait for—the Lord's salvation; let us "sing unto the Lord, and bless his name, and show forth his salvation from day to day."

Yes! let us show forth his salvation; let us tell all men that he saves, and how he saves; let us make known the way of saving grace. The more we do so the more shall we have of insight and experience—of hope and expectation—with regard to it. Both Simeon and Jacob tried that method; let us try it also. The more we try it, the more shall we have cause to say with Simeon, "Mine eyes have seen thy salvation;"— and with Jacob, "I have waited for thy salvation, O Lord."

3. The actual result or issue, present or prospective, of this "showing of the Lord's salvation," is a great help to us in our own experience, as "seeing it," and yet "waiting for it." The Psalmist celebrates, in anticipation, a glorious time, "O sing unto the Lord a new song; for he hath done marvellous things: his right hand and his holy arm, hath gotten him the victory. The Lord hath made known his salvation; his righteousness hath he openly showed in the sight of the heathen. He hath remembered his mercy and his truth toward the house of Israel: all the ends of the earth have seen the salvation of our God" (Ps. xcviii. 1-3). So also does the prophet. "The Lord hath made bare his holy arm in the eyes of all the nations; and all the ends of the earth shall see the salvation of our God" (Is. lii. 10). Who can doubt that when these days come, there will be a "seeing of the Lord's salvation," with Simeon; and a "waiting for it," with Jacob, greatly beyond what there is of either now? And yet, might there not be even now more than there is of insight and sympathy—of experience and hope—as regards this salvation of the Lord? Let there be realised, on a small scale, under our immediate cognisance, what we believe is to be realised universally, under the eyes of all intelligences at last—a fresh original exhibition of the power of saving truth over the consciences and affections of men. Let us throw ourselves, heart and soul, into the midst of any saving work of the Lord —personally at home or by sympathy abroad. Let us lay ourselves alongside of any one soul into whose mouth the Lord has put the new song, and enter into the marvellous things which the Lord hath done for that soul. Our seeing the Lord's salvation for ourselves—our waiting for it—will thus become, more and more, seeing and waiting indeed.

4. Let the saying in Lamentations (iii. 26) be kept in mind : " It is good for a man both to hope, and quietly to wait for the salvation of God." Let no man object to a waiting posture,—even though it should continue to be a waiting posture to the end ;—even though he should feel as if it is all waiting, and only waiting, that he has to acknowledge as his experience ;—" I have waited for thy salvation, O Lord." For this waiting posture is very becoming and very blessed. It is good to wait ;—not to wait in indolence, or idleness, or indifference ;—not to wait with the sluggard's folded hands, or the fatalist's dark, stern, moody apathy of soul ; but to wait intelligently ;—with desire and hope ;—to wait, because we know something of the blessedness of what we wait for :—to wait in patience, because what we have already tasted of what we wait for is so rich a boon, and so thoroughly undeserved, that we may well be content to wait, ever so long, for ever so little more of it.

As regards the Lord's first coming, and its immediate fruit, there should be on our part, as on Simeon's, the actual, present seeing of the salvation of the Lord. The righteousness in the train of which it comes is not to be waited for. That is near ; Christ is near, " Jehovah our righteousness." " Moses describeth the righteousness which is of the law, That the man which doeth those things shall live by them. But the righteousness which is of faith speaketh on this wise, Say not in thine heart, Who shall ascend into heaven ? (that is, to bring Christ down from above) or, Who shall descend into the deep ? (that is, to bring up Christ again from the dead). But what saith it ? The word is nigh thee, even in thy mouth, and in thy heart : that is, the word of faith which we preach ; that if thou shalt confess with thy mouth the Lord Jesus, and shalt believe in thine heart that God hath raised him from the dead, thou shalt be saved. For with the heart man believeth unto righteousness ; and with the mouth confession is made unto salvation. For the scripture saith, Whosoever believeth on him shall not be ashamed" (Rom. x. 5-11).

Not waiting therefore,—but looking, seeing, embracing,— is our duty and privilege, when Christ is set forth as come, already come,—crucified, already crucified,—risen, already risen;—"delivered for our offences, and raised again for our justification."

But he cometh again. "Unto them that look for him shall he appear the second time, without sin, unto salvation" (Heb. ix. 28). And looking for him now is waiting for him, with "loins girt and lamps burning." It is watching also, as not knowing at what hour the Master may come ; but yet "knowing the time, that now it is high time to awake out of sleep, for now is our salvation nearer than when we believed" (Rom. xiii. 11).

68

CLOSE OF JACOB'S DYING PROPHECY—THE BLESSING ON JOSEPH

Genesis 49:19-32

Now I am come to make thee understand what shall befall thy people in the latter days : for yet the vision is for many days.   Daniel 10:14

Let the blessing come upon the head of Joseph, and upon the top of the head of him that was separated from his brethren.   Deut. 33:16

Of the twelve tribes, as represented by his twelve sons, in this last oracular vaticination of "Jacob who is Israel," three are connected, as it would seem, with Judah—namely, Reuben, Simeon, and Levi,—the other seven belong more properly to Joseph.

These last are called in order.   Zebulun, Issachar, and Dan come first.   At Dan, the patriarch pauses for a moment. Under the somewhat disappointing impression of a descent from the glorious vision of the Messiah, vouchsafed to him in connection with Judah, he utters the ejaculation, " I have waited for thy salvation, O Lord ;" and then he resumes his task.   The remaining members of his household pass in review before him,—Gad, Asher, Naphtali, Joseph, and Benjamin.   With the exception of Joseph, they are all very summarily disposed of.

The utterances regarding them indeed are so brief and enigmatical as to defy, at this distance of time, anything like a really discriminating application of them, or a trustworthy historical verification of them. They doubtless suggested marks and badges, of which a college of heralds might have made good use in emblazoning the escutcheons and banners of the tribes. Gad is represented as a multitudinous host, with signs in its ranks both of defeat and of victory,—but ending in victory; "Gad, a troop shall overcome him; but he shall overcome at the last" (ver. 19). Asher is a giver, or receiver, of rich and princely banquets; "Out of Asher his bread shall be fat, and he shall yield royal dainties" (ver. 20). Naphtali is an animal of speed and beauty running at large, and uttering pleasant voices; "Naphtali is a hind let loose: he giveth goodly words" (ver. 21). And Benjamin is an animal sly and predatory, prowling secretly in the dark for victims; "Benjamin shall ravin as a wolf: in the morning he shall devour the prey, and at night he shall divide the spoil" (ver. 27).

These are all significant enough delineations; they may have served as watchwords among the tribes when their fortunes came to be developed. And it is not difficult to trace points of correspondence between the curt hints thus addressed to his sons, and the actual circumstances of their families to such an extent as sufficiently to vindicate the inspiration of the dying patriarch. At the same time, it must not be forgotten that these hints are very curt, and that much modesty and forbearance ought to be exhibited by any who would interpret them particularly;—still more by any who would take exception to them as incapable of explanation. They may well be left in some obscurity,—at least for the present, —for we cannot say what light the future may yet shed on these early archives.

Even the oracle about Joseph is to be cautiously handled. It is fuller than the rest. The old man's heart is in it. It is like the swan's fabled strain in dying. He pours it out with a richness and copiousness of expression, altogether unlike the summary conciseness with which he dispatches the others (ver. 22-26).

First, growth and fertility,—exuberant growth, luxuriant fertility,—are ascribed to this "rod out of the stem" of Israel, —this "branch growing out of his roots." The parent tree gives off in him a shoot that becomes itself prolific of goodly offshoots of its own; "Joseph is a fruitful bough, even a fruitful bough by a well; whose branches run over the wall" (ver. 22).

Again, secondly, he appears as an archer. He is beset for a time by other archers, vexing and wounding him in their envy. But his weapon is unhurt, and his strength is unimpaired. One mightier than himself shields him from harm, and nerves him for endurance and triumph; "The archers have sorely grieved him, and shot at him, and hated him: but his bow abode in strength, and the arms of his hands were made strong by the hands of the mighty God of Jacob; (from thence is the shepherd, the stone of Israel:) even by the God of thy father, who shall help thee; and by the Almighty, who shall bless thee" (ver. 23-25).

Then, thirdly, the varied abundance of the good things provided for him is indicated; He "shall bless thee with blessings of heaven above, blessings of the deep that lieth under, blessings of the breasts, and of the womb" (ver. 25).

And finally, in the fourth place, as if he would exhaust his whole soul in one last loving embrace of his favourite son, —the son so worthy of his favour,—the dying patriarch intimates that, signal as were the blessings he had himself got heaped upon his head by his pious and believing forefathers, he would have them surpassed and excelled by the blessings he invokes on Joseph,—as much as the great, old, far-off hills, that are ever the same, surpass and excel in grandeur the little fields of ever-changing tint, on which the passing seasons, year by year, leave their evanescent hues;—"The blessings of thy father have prevailed above the blessings of my progenitors unto the utmost bound of the everlasting hills: they shall be on the head of Joseph" (ver. 26).

Such is to be Joseph's happy portion;—a portion in

respect of which he is to be as much distinguished from the other sons of Israel in prosperity, as he was in trial ;—for all these blessings are " on the crown of the head of him that was separate from his brethren " (ver. 26).

There is, it must be owned, a good deal of vagueness in all this benediction,—at least to our apprehension now. Considered as a prophecy, it is general rather than specific,—indefinite rather than precise ;—furnishing few, if any, points of minute identification between its foreshadowings and the subsequent history. Nor is much additional light thrown upon it by what looks almost like an explanation or amplification of it, in the dying speech of Moses (Deut. xxxiii. 13-17).

It is unquestionable that in after time Joseph, as represented principally by the tribe of Ephraim,—for the division of Manasseh into two parts necessarily weakened the influence of his tribe,—held a most conspicuous place in Israel's territory, and played a most conspicuous part in Israel's history. All that Jacob said of him was fulfilled in large measure, before the sad revolt of the tribes among which he took the lead from the throne of the house of David, and the temple-worship of the Lord in Jerusalem. A cloud has since come over the destinies of Joseph's house ;—whether or not ever again to be raised, it may be left to time to show.

One clause in the benediction is peculiar,—the parenthetical clause; "From thence is the shepherd, the stone of Israel" (ver. 24). These are divine Messianic titles,—appropriated in subsequent Scripture to the Jehovah of the chosen people's worship, —the Angel-Jehovah of their believing hope. Is this the origin of that use of them ? Is Joseph honoured as one acting instead of God towards his brethren,—and as, in that respect, the type and herald of him who comes to save ? Is it meant to be intimated that this is the crown and consummation of the warfare and work, the office and ministry, for which " his bow abode in strength, and the arms of his hands were made strong by the hands of the mighty God of Jacob,"—that in virtue of it, he is "the shepherd, the stone of Israel;"—having been raised up to prefigure him who is the true Shepherd, feeding his flock and giving his life for the sheep,—and who is also the stone, the rock, on which the church is built,—the sure foundation laid in Zion?

Thus the dying patriarch reads off the histories of his descendants. Thus he divides the several families that are afterwards to constitute the commonwealth of Israel; "All these are the twelve tribes of Israel: and this is it that their father spake unto them, and blessed them; every one according to his blessing he blessed them" (ver. 28).

Having discharged this last office, his mind returns to his own situation and his own prospects. He reiterates his earnest and anxious entreaty as to the disposal of his body;—"And he charged them, and said unto them, I am to be gathered unto my people: bury me with my fathers" (ver. 29). He is particular,—after the garrulous manner of old age shall I say?— nay rather, for it is the true explanation, in the intensity of his believing hope; he is minutely particular in pointing out the identical spot where he wishes his remains to be laid;—"In the cave that is in the field of Ephron the Hittite, in the cave that is in the field of Machpelah, which is before Mamre, in the land of Canaan, which Abraham bought with the field of Ephron the Hittite for a possession of a burying-place" (ver. 29-30). He indicates the reason of his anxiety, and the longing desire which he has to serve himself heir, in his burial, to his father and grandfather. They, with their wives, reposed in that tomb in which he has already laid his Leah. He would fain lie there himself;—"There they buried Abraham and Sarah his wife; there they buried Isaac and Rebekah his wife; and there I buried Leah" (ver. 31). And, as if to obviate all objections, and vindicate, with his dying breath, his unquestionable right to the place of sepulture in which he so solemnly adjures his sons to lay him, he adverts to the original acquisition of the property by Abraham, for the burial of Sarah ; —thus justifying his grandsire's far-seeing prophetic wisdom in refusing to take it as a gift, and insisting on having it by purchase ;—" The purchase of the field and of the cave that is therein was from the children of Heth" (ver. 32).

So ends this closing interview of Jacob with his sons. They have for themselves his last solemn warnings and blessings, —and his last orders as to his own remains.

69

THE DEATH OF JACOB—HIS CHARACTER AND
HISTORY

Genesis 49:33-50:1

Mark the perfect man, and behold the upright : for the end of that man is
peace.   Psalm 37:37

Fear not, thou worm Jacob.   Isaiah 41:14

Hear ye this, O house of Jacob, which are called by the name of Israel.—
Isaiah 48:1

THE strangely chequered course of Jacob's earthly history is
run.   His end is peace; and according to God's promise
(xlvi. 4), Joseph closes his eyes;—" When Jacob had made an
end of commanding his sons, he gathered up his feet into the
bed, and yielded up the ghost, and was gathered unto his
people.   And Joseph fell upon his father's face, and wept upon
him, and kissed him" (xlix. 33 ; l. 1).

The manner of his death is simply told.   First, he com-
poses himself to rest, and as it were, to sleep; he calmly
assumes the attitude of repose.   He has done with life ;—its
business is all ended.   When "the time drew near that Israel
must die" (xlvii. 29), he at once proceeded, with wonderful self-
possession, to set his house in order,—to give directions, "by
faith," concerning his burial,—to bless, "by faith," the two sons
of Joseph,—to pronounce, " by faith," the inspired oracles that
told what was to befall his children in the latter days,—and
to charge them once more solemnly with the obligation to lay
his body in the grave of his fathers Abraham and Isaac,—in
the land which his seed were to receive for an inheritance.

And now, his deathbed work being over, he lies down exhausted, quietly to await the summons to his long home. It comes. He resigns his spirit to him who gave it; he commends his soul to God. And he has gone home,—gone to be one of the kindred multitude that have gone before.

It might be unsafe to make much of these expressions in themselves—" he yielded up the ghost, and was gathered unto his people,"—or to put on them a very strict literal interpretation. They are expressions used generally to denote death, in almost any circumstances. One cannot help imagining, however, that as used originally in early times, and with reference to their verbal derivation and significancy, they may have meant more than they were understood afterwards to mean, when they became the hackneyed familiarities of common speech. They certainly seem to indicate two ideas of death, not unlikely to occur to primitive thought ;—the one, that of a sort of acquiescence or contented surrender ;—the other, that of being involved in a sweeping and comprehensive cast of the fatal net, which draws into a common receptacle or reservoir the successive swarms of the human race. The one is a kind of voluntary parting with life ; the other is being swallowed up in the mysterious, unseen realm which collects in its capacious bosom, one after another, the busy generations that, one after another, people this changing world. Be that, however, as it may, there can be no doubt that these words denote a calm and peaceful close of the patriarch's troubled career.

It had indeed been a troubled career. From first to last it was a sore, sad struggle of the flesh against the spirit, and the spirit against the flesh. Let us recall some of its stages.

I. There was misunderstanding from the beginning—misunderstanding and unbelief. The oracle which accompanied his birth should have ensured order and peace ; it turned out, on the contrary, to be the occasion of confusion and strife. It was no secret in the household. The two brothers, while yet boys, or lads, evidently knew all about it, and made it a ground of quarrel and bone of contention. The parents were divided in regard to it. The mother and her favourite younger son were in favour of what it foretold; the father and his first-born, on the other hand, would rather stand out for the natural right of primogeniture, and set the oracle at defiance, or let it fulfil itself as it best could. Hence the unseemly and un-brotherly scene of the birthright sold for a mess of pottage;—Jacob seizing his opportunity—Esau despising his privilege. Hence the still more melancholy scene of the wretched struggle for the blessing;—the father trying to go against the Lord's decree—the mother seeking to accomplish it by fraud. It was the oracle that set them all at variance, through their un-belief. They all sinned and were sinned against;—with what proportions of wrong sustained and guilt contracted, it is vain to inquire.

But certainly, of all the household, Jacob was in the worst and most difficult position. Had the oracle been believed and obeyed, he might have taken the place assigned to him, with such wise and loving counsel, on the part of father and mother alike, as would have prevented all family heartburnings, and united parents and children together in looking to the promised Seed and Saviour, with a view to whom it was that the younger son was chosen. His being thus chosen, with this view, would not then have stirred in him either pride, or envy, or deceit. But he found himself an occasion of strife. He sought to end it by a sort of compromise with his brother—for the transaction of the mess of pottage seems, on his part, to have been of the nature of a compromise—the symbol of his surrendering the temporal inheritance for the spiritualities of the birthright. But the miserable jealousy of favouritism grows. And between the one parent bent on what must frustrate the oracle, and the other devising carnal means for its accomplish-ment, Jacob, not yet himself strong in faith, falls a ready vic-tim to the policy which, instead of trusting God with the bringing to pass of his own purposes in his own time and way, will insist on taking what is altogether God's matter into its own control, and planning and acting at its own hand on God's behalf.

II. A brighter scene opens at Bethel. It is a critical time. He is now wholly in the Lord's hands ; not in the hands of a misjudging father, on the one side, or of a weak, fond, erring mother, on the other. Forsaken, virtually, by father and mother, " the Lord takes him up " (Ps. xxvii. 10).

On that night, as his head leans on his pillow of stone, he is alone with God. He is very near heaven—heaven is very near him. It is open to him. God from heaven, God in heaven, deals with him. A covenant is ratified—a personal covenant. The two parties mutually give themselves to one another. Jacob is now a new man ; old things are passed away—all things are become new. So he begins his lonely pilgrimage in Syria.

For it is to be to him spiritually a lonely pilgrimage, in which, with much in his outward lot to harass and distract him, he may have enough of difficulty in walking with him whose covenant he has embraced. He falls into very worldly society, and becomes familiar with worldly ways. The kindness he meets with among his mother's kindred is sadly marred by covetousness and cruel craft. He is hurt and wounded in his tenderest and purest affections. His domestic comfort is blighted in the very bud. He is entangled by human guile in a breach of the holy and honourable law of marriage ordained by God—and one breach leads on to more. A happy household, a godly seed, can scarcely be looked for. What prosperity he meets with is embittered by the unscrupulous artifices against which he has continually to guard. At home, in his family—abroad, in his business—it is an uneasy life he has to lead. Certainly there is not much in it that is congenial to the spirit of the solemn and significant transaction at Bethel. He is in danger of adopting heathen customs, and has begun to adopt them, like his descendants long afterwards who " were mingled among the heathen, and learned their works." It is well for him that his rest in Padan-aram is rudely broken.

III. But it is not change of scene only that will arrest a tendency to backsliding, or heal backsliding begun, and restore the soul. Jacob is recalled from the land of his exile, and is to sojourn again in the land where God personally met him, and dealt graciously with him. But he is not to re-enter it without a fresh awakening. A new personal meeting, a new gracious dealing, on the part of the Lord, awaits him ere he re-crosses, now become two bands, the Jordan which he passed over before with his staff. He fears the opposition of Esau. He has to encounter the opposition of Jehovah. The Lord, to whom he has cried for help against his brother's dreaded vengeance, himself stands against him as his adversary,—as one who has a controversy with him. A night of wrestling ensues. Jacob's faith is quickened greatly. In the strength of the Lord, he sustains till day-break the wrestling of the Lord with him. He will not be driven back, or give up, or give in. " Behind a frowning providence he sees a smiling face." In the man wrestling with him, he recognises his covenant God and Saviour. Therefore, "when he is weak then is he strong." Even when the Lord is contending with him, he will " endure, as seeing him who is invisible,"—seeing in the seeming enemy, the unseen friend. Even when the Lord breaks his very bones,—or touches them so that they are out of joint,—he will hold on in faith. And when his great antagonist seems to cease his wrestling, and makes as if he would leave him to complain, " all my bones are out of joint,"—he will not let him go until he blesses him, and gives him cause to say that " the very bones which he has broken now rejoice." The mysterious wrestler will not indeed have his name revealed,—that name which the Incarnation at last disclosed (Mat. i. 21). But Jacob gets his blessing.

So, as a prince, by his strength he has power with God. Seeing God face to face, and having his life preserved, he becomes Israel. The worm Jacob becomes a prince, having power over the Angel and prevailing. And so, having that way of faith which pleases the Lord, he finds God making his enemies to be at peace with him (Prov. xvi. 7), and causing him to dwell safely in the land.

IV. Still, Jacob's revival is not complete. The Lord needs yet again to visit him, for he is tempted to take his ease.

Forgetful apparently of his old vow at Bethel,—pledging him to return thither after his wandering, and there consecrate anew himself and his possessions to the Lord,—he lingers on the confines, where he first finds rest. He worships God, indeed, and erects an altar; but it is without thoroughly purging his house and household of all idolatry, and all heathen wickedness. He is apt to settle on his lees. The reins of domestic discipline also are relaxed. Intercourse with the surrounding world is too freely allowed; and there is a tolerated conformity to its ways;—the swift and sad result being first a daughter's dishonour, and then the cruel and cowardly revenge inflicted by her brothers. Another divine interposition is needed,—another decided step. God must remind Jacob, of what surely he should not have needed to be reminded of, —his old Bethel experiences and Bethel pledges. Roused seasonably from apathy and spiritual sloth, he at last "makes haste and delays not to keep God's commandment." He makes thorough work of the purifying of his house,—"enduring in it no evil thing." All cherished remnants of idolatrous and heathen worship are cast out. He carries his household, thus purged, to Bethel. He fulfils his vow. And though sad breaches in his family mark the occasion,—the death of Rebekah's nurse, before the renewal of the covenant at Bethel, and the death of Rachel afterwards, in giving birth to her youngest son,—it is not in his case as it was in the case of the rebuilder of Jericho (1 Kings xvi. 34). These are not judgments but chastisements. Jacob shows his sense of their being so, when, parting with his beloved, he takes her Benoni to be his Benjamin.

V. It is when thus awakened, chastened, and comforted, that Jacob receives, upon his father Isaac's death, the patriarchate, or patriarchal headship. His brother Esau having been led, as it would seem, of his own accord, though of course under special providential guidance, to migrate, with his whole establishment, already growing into tribes or dukedoms, into the wide regions ever since occupied by his posterity,—Jacob quietly succeeds his father, and takes his place as the representative and chief of the chosen race. Together the two brothers, friends at last, bury their father Isaac. And it is graciously so ordered that when Jacob comes, in terms of the oracle to serve himself heir, he does so, on the one hand, with no objection or opposition on the part of his brother Esau, but on the contrary, as it would seem, with his acquiescence, if not even with his consent; and he does so, on the other hand, in connection with such fresh and recent dealings of the Lord with him, both by his word and by his providence, as are evidently blessed by the Spirit for his personal quickening and revival. It is with mingled feelings that after all his trials he now takes the place of Abraham and of Isaac.

VI. In that capacity he has still sharp discipline to endure. Not to speak of the sins of Reuben and Judah, he has to pass through the whole trial connected with Joseph.

Here too, as in former instances, the root of much, if not all, of the evil is to be found in unbelief;—in an unbelieving disregard of the mind and purpose of God, sufficiently revealed, and in sufficient time. If the manifestly inspired dreams with which the young lad was twice visited had been duly observed and turned to account,—if pains had been taken to make them the ground of patient expectation on the part of all the family, instead of their being allowed to become the occasion of jealousy and suspicion,—how much domestic sin and sorrow might have been avoided! But his father rebuked him, and his brethren envied him. And though his father's rebuke might be slight and passing, since he was, and was deservedly, a favourite child, his brethren's envy remained and rankled. Instead of faith leaving it to God to bring to pass his own end by his own means, there is the sin of unbelief which we have so often had occasion to point out. Man's fond folly and fierce passion must come in. God is not acknowledged; his salvation is not waited for. Hence misery at home;—and abroad, cruel " plotting against the righteous." The dreamer is still, in spite of his dreams, the favoured, if not petted child,—and his brothers must somehow get rid of him. Thus long years of grief are brought upon Jacob. His patriarchal reign is, alas! no reign of righteousness, and peace, and joy. He has to mourn for Joseph as lost,—lost by a horrid fate,—torn, as he is made to think, by savage beasts. And with all their anxiety to comfort him, his remaining sons, conscious of hypocrisy and the cruellest lie men ever told,—can only very partially succeed. Wild also, and lawless, they too often are in their own lives. Benjamin, his Rachel's Benjamin, —the last pledge of her dying love,—is almost the only earthly consolation of his fast declining years. But now comes the famine,—and even Benjamin must go. Yet once more Jacob is to be thoroughly bereaved. A strange, inscrutable, stern necessity, shuts him up, and hedges in his way. There is no outlet,—no escape ; any where; any how. He must part with all ; yes! all ; to please an Egyptian tyrant,—to satisfy his jealousy and gratify his caprice ;—or else he and his must starve. The nest is bare! The last and dearest fledgling is rudely torn away, to glut the insatiate maw of the all-devouring monster that the Nile seems to have brought forth. What remains for Jacob but to sit alone and weep ;—going down in disconsolate sorrow to the grave?

VII. At last there begins to dawn upon him some glimpse of light—some insight into the meaning of what has been so dark in the divine providence towards him.

But even here, what the light, as it dawns, reveals, is not all bright and clear. In the tidings that Joseph is alive in Egypt, and has prepared in Egypt a home for his father and all his house,—in the importunate message which Joseph sends, in his own name, and the king's,—in the waggons, and carriages, and provisions, all ready at his door for the journey,—Jacob's slowly opening mind begins to recognise a hint, or solemn intimation, that the time has come for the fulfilment of the Lord's prediction to Abraham ; " Know of a surety that thy seed shall be a stranger in a land that is not theirs, and shall serve them ; and they shall afflict them four hundred years ; and also that nation, whom they shall serve, will I judge : and afterward shall they come out with great substance" (xv. 13, 14).

It is not simply a visit he is about to pay. It is not even merely a temporary sojourn of a few years he is to make, till the calamity of the famine is overpast. Jacob's eyes are opened to the truth. The summons from Egypt is the signal of a far more serious and ominous crisis. It rings in his ears as a very solemn curfew-knell,—ushering in a long, long night of weariness and woe. This is worse than the flight to Padan-aram. That was personal to himself, and on the face of it only temporary. This is the uprooting out of the chosen land of the entire family tree ;— and long ages are to pass before " the vine brought out of Egypt" is to be planted in it again. It is not merely that he is now too old himself to cherish the hope of a return. That is not the case. Like Moses, whose " eye " in his old age " was not dim, nor his natural strength abated," Jacob is so hale and hearty that there is nothing to hinder his paying Joseph even a long visit in Egypt, and yet cherishing good and warrantable expectation of coming back to die in Canaan. Nor need the fact of his taking all his well-nigh starving household with him to a temporary asylum in a country where there is plenty, occasion much concern. But Jacob sees more clearly the real meaning of the movement ; he does not shut his eyes to its ultimate as well as its immediate bearings. It is—he knows that it is—the beginning of the predicted captivity of his race. And knowing this, he acquiesces in faith,—his faith being strengthened by one more visit paid to him by the Lord. It might seem hard that it should fall to him, in his old age, and after all his trials,—when he would fain lie down and die where his fathers Abraham and Isaac had died before him,—to lead, as it were, this forlorn hope,—to be the conductor of his people, not out of bondage, but into the worst extremity of bondage. Jacob, however, makes no remonstrance, and utters no complaint. Gratefully accepting the Lord's promise for himself and his seed, he goes down into Egypt to end his days there.

And now this Jacob is dead. " After life's fitful fever he sleeps well,"—commending his soul to God, and his body to be buried in Canaan's hallowed soil, in hope of the resurrection-day. His character and experience remain on record for our learning.

His character may not be great perhaps as men count greatness ; not exalted ; not noble ; not fit for high achievements ; but weak, rather, if you will, and inclined to the arts of weakness ; not always amiable, any more than admirable ; apt to suffer by contrast with some of the finer natural qualities which such a man as his brother Esau occasionally exhibits. Yet surely, on the whole, it is a character worthy of study, and not without attractions. At anyrate, it is all before us ; the worst and the best. We see what materials grace and faith had to work with. And we see what, in the actual result, grace and faith made of these materials. We see grace making a weak man strong ; for surely to the last he was strong in faith. It made " the worm Jacob " " the prince Israel." Let us " follow his faith ;" considering the end of his conversation—" Jesus Christ, the same yesterday, to-day, and for ever " (Heb. xiii. 8).

His varied, chequered, troubled experience,—is it not full of instruction and comfort to the spiritually exercised soul ? It is almost,—next to David's,—the most so of any left on record in the Old Testament. There is scarcely a mood of mind into which sin or sorrow can cast a believer that may not find a type, or parallel, or example, in Jacob. Weakness in himself, as well as weakness caused by his suffering wrong at the hands of others,—and these others familiar friends as well as foes,—foes of his own household,—Jacob certainly exhibits. Much of his history is written for our warning ; in much of it he is a beacon rather than a pattern. But much also is written for our encouragement and guidance. In running the race set before us, "faint yet pursuing," amid many cares and fears, many faults and infirmities, we may learn not a little from Jacob, while we seek to walk as strangers and pilgrims on the earth,—"waiting for thy salvation, O Lord."

70

THE BURIAL OF JACOB—THE LAST SCENE IN CANAAN

Genesis 50:1-13

So Jacob went down into Egypt, and died, he, and our fathers ; and were carried over into Sychem, and laid in the sepulchre that Abraham bought for a sum of money of the sons of Emmor, the father of Sychem. Acts 7:15,16

THE burial of Jacob was an affair of state. It was a public ceremony conducted with national pomp. This must surely have been Pharaoh's doing. Jacob himself never could have dreamed of it ; and it does not seem to have entered into the mind of Joseph to solicit or expect it. He assumes indeed at once, as a matter of right, or a matter of course, the position of head of the family ;—and it is evidently conceded to him, without dispute or hesitation, by his brethren. He takes the charge and oversight of the whole business, and adopts measures for carrying his father's last wishes into effect, and having his body carried to Canaan. But he does so, evidently, not in the character of a prince of Egypt, the vizier or prime minister of the king, but in the character of Israel's son,— now, on Israel's decease, the acknowledged patriarchal chief of the tribe or clan.

And this, probably, is the simple explanation of a circumstance for which many frivolous and conjectural reasons have been imagined,—his communicating with Pharaoh on this occasion, not himself personally, but by a message sent through third parties (ver. 4). He has, for the time, withdrawn from the court; and is in deep seclusion, either in his own apartments, or more probably, in the bosom of his father's house. He had already made it manifest enough, that in the height of his Egyptian glory and prosperity, he was so far from being ashamed of his connection with a wandering horde of shepherds from Canaan, that he counted that connection to be even more desirable, more to be coveted and prized, than the monarch's favour and all its fruit. He had not, indeed, exactly the same alternative before him which long afterwards tried and proved the faith of Moses. He had not literally to choose between "the reproach of Christ and the treasures of Egypt,"—between "suffering affliction with the people of God, and enjoying the pleasures of sin for a season." But he gave unequivocal evidence of the same faith that Moses exercised, when he sought so earnestly his dying father's blessing for himself and his sons. He thus deliberately preferred, for himself and for them, to share the fortunes of Abraham's seed, through the long years of predicted bondage that he knew were soon to come, as preliminary to the possession of the promised land,—rather than to stand aloof, as he might have done, and be content with patronising the settlers in Goshen, without compromising or risking his rank and position in the palace and in the kingdom of Egypt.

Plainly, during Jacob's lifetime, Joseph counted it better to be Jacob's son than to be the nearest to Pharaoh's throne. And now that Jacob is dead, his feeling and his faith are unchanged.

He has closed his father's eyes,—and given vent to a burst of uncontrollable grief;—"Joseph fell upon his father's face, and wept upon him, and kissed him" (ver. 1). He looks back from that aged deathbed, through the vista of more than half-a-century of troubled life, and recalls the days when, as a child, he got that "coat of many colours,"—the last gift of fond fatherly love, before it was so rudely rent and so cruelly crushed. He proceeds to execute the task that now remains. Though shut up in the retirement of mourning, whether at Goshen or in his own palace,—keeping his chamber in privacy,—he has his attendants at his call. He issues orders for the embalming of his father's body, in the usual way, and by the usual function-aries, so as to make it fit for the long journey in prospect;—" Joseph commanded his servants the physicians to embalm his father: and the physicians embalmed Israel " (ver. 2). Forty days thus pass away;—so much time being required to com-plete the process of embalming, in due form;—" Forty days were fulfilled for Jacob; for so are fulfilled the days of those which are embalmed " (ver. 3). Joseph, meanwhile, continues mourning in private. And the Egyptians of his household,—whether through hired officials or under the impulse of their own natural sympathy does not appear,—mourn more openly in public;—" The Egyptians mourned for Jacob threescore and ten days " (ver. 3).

These seventy days of mourning being past, and all now being ready, Joseph prepares to start on his melancholy jour-ney towards Canaan.

Being Pharaoh's servant, he has to obtain Pharaoh's leave; " When the days of his mourning were past, Joseph spake unto the house of Pharaoh, saying, If now I have found grace in your eyes, speak I pray you, in the ears of Pharaoh " (ver. 4). He does not go to ask it himself. This is not certainly, —it could not be,—from any distrust of the king. Perhaps the etiquette of court excluded from the royal presence one whose appearance in the attire of first mourning might cast a gloom over the royal household. Perhaps he felt that he could scarcely venture to face his master and friend, who had shown such kindness to himself and his lost father, without the risk of being too much overcome. Or perhaps he deemed it more becoming, when he was acting, not as Pharaoh's favourite minister, but as the head and representative of an-other race, to approach the king thus humbly, through the officers of the household ;—the customary channel for conveying addresses and petitions to the throne.

Be this as it may, what Joseph asks his Egyptian friends to say on his behalf to his beloved and loving sovereign, is very simple and touching ; " My father made me swear, saying, Lo, I die ; in my grave which I have digged for me in the land of Canaan, there shalt thou bury me. Now therefore let me go up, I pray thee, and bury my father, and I will come again" (ver. 5). They are simply to tell how Jacob laid Joseph under a vow,—and that in a manner more than ordinarily solemn and affecting. My father was old before he left Canaan,—older in sorrow than in years ; he reckoned his grave to be already dug there. It had been opened for his grandfather and his father,—and for their wives,—and for his own. In his eyes it stood ever open for himself. He spoke of it to me with his latest breath as "the grave which I digged for me in the land of Canaan." I took an oath to bury him there. I ask permission to go up and fulfil my oath. And I promise instantly to return.

Such brief leave of absence, for such a sacred duty, Joseph asks his friends to solicit on his behalf.

There is no hint of his desiring a pompous funeral ; he has no thought of anything of the sort. His one wish is simply to do his father's bidding. It is Pharaoh himself, evidently, who makes a national affair of what might otherwise have been nothing more than a family arrangement.

The king grants his favourite minister's request after a kingly fashion ;—" Pharaoh said, Go up and bury thy father, according as he made thee swear" (ver. 6). The father of the man who has laid him and his kingdom under such obligations,—carrying them so well through the crisis of such a famine, and making it the occasion of consolidating the empire and confirming its supremacy among the nations,—is not to be buried as a common man. Joseph is by all means to accomplish his promise, and carry the loved remains to Canaan.

But he is to do so in a manner worthy of the great prince whose favour he has won, to whom he is a second self. It is to be, not merely a Hebrew, but an Egyptian ceremonial : " Joseph went up to bury his father : and with him went up all the servants of Pharaoh, the elders of his house, and all the elders of the land of Egypt, and all the house of Joseph, and his brethren, and his father's house : only their little ones, and their flocks, and their herds, they left in the land of Goshen. And there went up with him both chariots and horsemen : and it was a very great company " (ver. 7, 8, 9).

Goshen is deserted of all but " the little ones, and flocks, and herds." Even the old men and the women, as it would seem,—with the exception probably of a remnant to look after the little ones, and flocks, and herds,—are eager to swell the train. All Joseph's house, and his brethren's houses, and the whole house of his father, are on the march. And along with them, there are the chief men of Pharaoh's household and the flower of Egypt's chivalry ; the elders or princes of the king's court, as well as those of the whole land ; with chariots and horsemen in abundance.

It was a goodly cavalcade,—a " very great company." It was Pharaoh's way of signalising the man whom he delighted to honour. And it was a tribute of regard, that would probably more exalt Joseph in the eyes of all Egypt,—and that would certainly, as we may well believe, come more home to Joseph's own heart—than his first investiture with the fine linen and the gold chain when he was proclaimed ruler over all the land. It must have been to Joseph almost as if his royal master had, with his own hands, carried his father's head to the grave. The Egyptians saw how Pharaoh loved Joseph ; and they fully sympathised with both.

The procession thus formed moved towards Canaan. They did not, as it would seem, proceed by the most direct and shortest route. They went circuitously ; following, it is believed, very much the line of march which the Israelites took, when they left Egypt four hundred years after,—to wander forty years in the wilderness, and to be at last brought into the promised land.

So " they came to the thrashing-floor of Atad" (ver. 10). That spot where the funeral cavalcade halted, was, as is commonly supposed, on the east side of the Jordan;—"beyond Jordan " (ver. 10), looking from Egypt. This of itself would indicate a round-about journey ;—rendered necessary, perhaps, or expedient, by the risk of collision with the roving and unfriendly tribes of the desert. At any rate, at Atad they call a halt, and the company is there for a time to be divided. The Egyptians are to remain stationary there, while Jacob's sons go on to complete the sad work which they have on hand in Canaan.

But before they separate, there is an entire week spent by the whole host together in a great and very sore lamentation. The mourning, according to old eastern usage, is loud and clamorous. And it is universal. Not the Hebrews alone give way to their emotions; their Egyptian companions also join in the vociferous wailing. In fact, it would seem as if they played the first part, and took the lead. It was their parting burst of grief as they suffered the Hebrews to go on alone from the thrashing-floor of Atad to the burial-place in Canaan. The onlookers remarked that it was an Egyptian mourning. And they commemorated it as such ;—" When the inhabitants of the land, the Canaanites, saw the mourning in the floor of Atad, they said, This is a grievous mourning to the Egyptians : wherefore the name of it was called Abel-mizraim," —the mourning of the Egyptians,—"which is beyond Jordan" (ver. 11).

The Egyptian convoy having thus halted on the confines or borders of Canaan ;—either because their having come thus far was deemed a sufficient token of respect, or perhaps because their farther advance might have been misconstrued

as a hostile demonstration ;—the family of Jacob proceed, by
themselves, across the Jordan into the land of Canaan proper,
and accomplish their purpose peaceably, without difficulty or
disturbance : " His sons did unto him according as he commanded them : for his sons carried him into the land of
Canaan, and buried him in the cave of the field of Machpelah,
which Abraham bought with the field for a possession of a
burying-place of Ephron the Hittite, before Mamre" (ver. 12,
13). Then, leaving the buried body of the patriarch in the
cave of the field of Machpelah, they slowly and sadly retrace
their steps ;—" Joseph returned into Egypt, he and his
brethren, and all that went up with him to bury his father,
after he had buried his father " (ver. 14.)

It is their last look at the inheritance promised to their
fathers. They themselves are to return to it no more ; and
ages of oppression are to roll on before their children see it.
Joseph in particular must have had feelings peculiar to himself
on the occasion. He had not been in Canaan since he was a
lad. What boyish memories must the sight of its once familiar
haunts awaken ! And now he may not linger to refresh old
recollections and explore new charms. He has to do with
nothing in it save his father's opened grave. It is a glimpse
even more transient and unsatisfying than Moses got from
Pisgah, that Joseph gets at Machpelah. He is to walk by
faith and not by sight. In faith he turns away from the home
of his ancestors,—the destined home of his posterity,—of
which, in circumstances so solemn, he has caught, as it were,
a passing view. And with his brothers, and their train, he
sets his face again towards Egypt.

It is almost like a second selling to the Midianites,—a
second going down to captivity. It is as if he were a second
time exchanging Canaan's bright promise for Egypt's dark and
bitter slavery !

But, strong in faith, he is prepared for present duty. He
must keep his word to Pharaoh. Egypt is the place where

God would have him to be. So he sets out, with the family of which he is now the head, to take what may befall him or them in that foreign land of banishment and bondage.

How far, or in what way, this incident of Jacob's funeral may have affected the relations between the Egyptians and the Canaanites, it is altogether vain and idle to speculate. Conjectures may be formed as to the effect, in after-times, of what the Canaanites witnessed at the thrashing-floor of Atad, and of the way in which they thought it worth while to preserve the memory of it. It is just possible that they may have conceived the idea of the Egyptians having some purpose of helping the Israelites, at a future convenient season, to obtain possession of the territory in which they took such formal infeftment by the burial within its borders of their great father Jacob. The rumour of the prophecy about Abraham's seed may, at an earlier period, have aroused their suspicion and alarm,—and it may have been some relief to them to see Jacob and his whole house migrating into Egypt. But now, after the lapse of a few years, these strange worshippers of a God unknown to them are back again among them,—and upon an errand that quietly assumes a right of property in their territory, and not obscurely points to that right being held to cover something more than a privilege of burial,—some wider inheritance than a grave. And they come with the backing of all Egypt's pomp and power. No doubt Egypt may pretend that it is a simple compliment to him who has been Egypt's saviour and benefactor,—thus to honour his father's funeral with such a public national demonstration. But such grievous mourning among the Egyptians as Abel-mizraim has witnessed is scarcely quite natural in the circumstances,—and, before now, a reconnoitring expedition, with ultimately hostile intent, has been covered by an ingenious stratagem of this sort. There may be some covered wile under this very loud wailing.

So the Canaanites may have reasoned. And their reasoning in this way may have led, by-and-by, to a reaction among the Egyptians. As the memory of Joseph and his services became faint, and a different dynasty of Pharaohs occupied the throne, and the Israelites multiplied and became formidable for their numbers, it might become the policy of Egypt to allay the apprehensions of the neighbouring nationalities by reversing the course adopted at Jacob's burial, and resorting to measures of repression and severity. If the Canaanites still retained the jealousy of which the scene at Abel-mizraim may have sowed the seeds, and indicated fear lest the same partiality for Joseph, which led to such a display of Egyptian sympathy towards him at his father's death, might prompt a still more formidable display of sympathy towards his race in their assertion of their claim to Canaan,—what more likely to prevent misunderstanding and preserve peace, than Egypt's beginning to treat Israel precisely as we learn that it did, when " a new king arose over Egypt who knew not Joseph," and " the people of the children of Israel increased abundantly, and waxed exceeding mighty ?" (Exod. i. 7, 8). We may find here one, at least, of many causes that may have contributed to that result.

Be this, however, as it may,—and it is no more than a conjecture, however plausible or probable,—the state-funeral of Jacob, with all Egyptian as well as Hebrew honours, marks the culminating point of Israel's favour and prosperity in the land that was to witness their long bondage. After that signal mark of distinction, the chosen family begin, as it would seem, to fall out of public view ;—to become isolated and detached ;—gradually ceasing to attract notice ;—left very much to themselves, to tend their flocks and occupy the terri-tory assigned to them,—and to increase and multiply till they grow into a people numerous and strong and compact enough for invading and possessing Canaan. This in fact is to be their safety. They are to be let alone. Not until a much later period is the vast Hebrew population in and around Goshen to force itself, as a matter of surprise, on the attention of the Egyptian rulers, and to awaken jealousy and alarm. Meanwhile they are, in a sense, hidden by the Lord in a secure place, until the time comes for his displaying the power of his outstretched arm in signal judgment on their oppressors, and a glorious deliverance wrought out for them.

71

JOSEPH AND HIS BRETHREN—THE FULL ASSURANCE
OF RECONCILIATION

Genesis 50:14-21

And now, brethren, I wot that through ignorance ye did it, as did also
your rulers. But those things, which God before had shewed by the
mouth of all his prophets, that Christ should suffer, he hath so fulfilled. Repent ye therefore, and be converted, that your sins may be
blotted out, when the times of refreshing shall come from the presence
of the Lord. Acts 3:17-19

THE funeral obsequies in Canaan being over, the entire cavalcade return to Egypt: "Joseph returned into Egypt, he and
his brethren, and all that went up with him to bury his father,
after he had buried his father" (ver. 14); and it might seem
that things would now fall, as a matter of course, into the usual
quiet routine. Surely by this time there should be a complete
understanding among all the parties in the agitating scenes
that have been enacted, as to the footing on which they are to
be towards one another. Joseph has finished his good work
of settling his father's household in "quiet habitations;" and
they have nothing to do but peaceably pursue their ordinary
occupations, grateful to Joseph and Pharaoh,—above all, grateful to God. But this assured state of things is not to be
immediately realised. There is to be still farther explanation,
—a still more express and formal adjustment, as it were, of all
outstanding claims and liabilities. The covenant of peace is

to be again renewed, and ratified even more solemnly and affectionately than before.

Once more, therefore, let us look at Joseph and his brethren, as they are seen confronted with one another, after their father's death has left them to themselves.

The brothers are agitated by a fear not unnatural. Conscience again makes cowards of them. In spite of all the kindness they have experienced at Joseph's hand, they have the idea that he may have been dissembling his purpose of retaliation, and under the mask of smiles, really all the while only " nursing his wrath to keep it warm." Like Esau in his rage against his brother, they think perhaps that Joseph may have been restrained by the awe in which he held their father, and so may have postponed his revenge till after his decease : " When Joseph's brethren saw that their father was dead, they said, Joseph will peradventure hate us, and will certainly requite us all the evil which we did unto him " (ver. 15).

To avert this danger, they have recourse to two expedients. They first send a message to Joseph, professing to embody a commandment of Jacob : " Thy father did command before he died, saying, So shall ye say unto Joseph, Forgive, I pray thee now, the trespass of thy brethren, and their sin ; for they did unto thee evil ; and now, we pray thee, forgive the trespass of the servants of the God of thy father " (ver. 16, 17). And then they follow up the message with a personal appeal : they " went and fell down before his face ; and they said, Behold, we be thy servants" (ver. 18).

It has been supposed that the commandment which they put into the mouth of their father after his death may have been a fabrication of their own to serve their purpose ; but one scarcely likes to imagine that it was so. It is at least as probable that they may have mentioned to Jacob, while he was yet alive, the apprehension which they entertained. And to soothe and satisfy them,—though he could not deem it necessary so far as Joseph was concerned,—he may have authorised them to make some such use of his name as they did make. In fact, it may have been his way of intimating his own full and thorough forgiveness of their sin. And at all events it could do no harm to endorse, as it were, with his paternal sanction, what he knew to be his beloved son's brotherly feeling towards these conscience-stricken men.

The message, with its mention of his father's mind and will, touches Joseph's heart to the quick. His brethren also, who seem to have followed close at the heels of their messenger, spoke doubtless to the same effect. "And Joseph wept when they spake unto him" (ver. 17).

Was it for their fancying such an interposition of their father's authority to be necessary in order to pacify him that Joseph wept? Or was it because he could not but be moved by such an instance of his father's common love to all his children? It may have been a mixture of both emotions. Why this distrust of me, as if in so solemn a manner, and by an authority so sacred, I must be commanded to forgive?—I who, as your own hearts might have told you, had forgiven you long before? But be it so. My father's command makes my forgiveness of you all the sweeter to me, as well as all the surer to you. Gladly, in his name, as well as from myself, do I forgive you now anew. It is his act now as well as mine. Let my warm gushing tears attest at once my deep reverence for him, and my tender love to you. Is not that the meaning of these gracious drops? Is it any wonder, in the circumstances, that "Joseph wept when they spake unto him?"

The submissive language of these men, following upon their citation of their father's command, is striking and significant at this late stage of the history. It carries us back to those early dreams which gave so much offence. The very parties who took umbrage then, now bear witness, in their own demeanour, to the literal fulfilment of the augury which the dreams contained. In spite of all the unbelief and opposition of men, the counsel of the Lord stands sure. The lesson, as to the special and particular providence of God, which this whole divine drama of Joseph's life is fitted and designed to teach, is now at last complete ; the end explains and vindicates the beginning. The complicated plot unravels and exhausts itself ; and there is simplicity at the close. It is seen that " the Lord reigneth."

So Joseph himself reads the divine lesson, and explains the divine plot, if one may so call it,—using dramatic language in reference to so dramatic a series of incidents. That he does so is implied in his reply to the somewhat abject prostration of his brethren :—" Fear not ; for am I in the place of God ? But as for you, ye thought evil against me ; but God meant it unto good, to bring to pass, as it is this day, to save much people alive " (ver. 19, 20). He might have been gratified by their homage. It might have pleased him to see them thus compelled to own the superiority on his part which his dreams foretold,—and the very idea of which they so murderously resented,—if he had regarded the matter in a selfish light, or from a selfish point of view. But it is not himself that he considers at all ; he forgets self. It is the Lord's hand that he sees in the whole wondrous history. It is the Lord's sovereignty, wisdom, and grace, that he recognises, and would have his brethren to recognise throughout it all. Think not of me ; look not to me. Who am I, that you should bow so humbly to me ? Am I in the place of God, that I should take it upon me to judge you ? What, after all, have you done to me ? You meant evil ; but God has over-ruled it for good. It is not with me that you have to deal ; nor am I to deal with you. Let us, all of us, cease from taking so narrow a view, and one so merely human. Do not make me your judge ; do not prostrate yourselves before me, as if I had any right or inclination to punish or revenge. I do not count you to have injured me. You were but the instruments in God's hands of accomplishing his purpose, which for you and me alike has turned out to be so gracious. Let us together own his providence in all that has fallen out. Surely to you his long-suffering is and must be salvation,—his goodness may well indeed move you to repentance. And for me, seeing that all you did to me has turned out so well,—so well for you, as well as for me, and so well for him that is gone,—let me acknowledge in it all, not your hand, but the Lord's. If I am to be now, as your homage implies, your chief and head,—by your own consent and choice, as well as by the Lord's design and doing,—let my patriarchal reign and headship over you be one of mutual confidence and love on both sides. Let all the past, your sin and my suffering, be swallowed up in our common owning of God's wondrous working in his ways toward the children of men. He does all things well. He has made me, through your treatment of me, the means of saving much people alive; it is the Lord's doing, let it be marvellous in our eyes. So Joseph reassures his brethren; " Now therefore fear ye not: I will nourish you, and your little ones. And he comforted them, and spake kindly unto them " (ver. 21).

It is a noble instance of forgiveness,—a signal exhibition of the spirit of faith and love,—the very " meekness and gentleness of Christ." But does it not point to something higher? Is not a greater than Joseph here? Have we not here Christ himself, of whom Joseph in all this is so fitting a type?

See then now Jesus,—the true Joseph,—our Joseph. He too suffered at the hands of his brethren. They all conspired against him ;—you, brother, and I, among the rest. We nailed him to the accursed tree. We caused his blood to flow, and the cry of agony to be wrung from his lips,—" My God, my God, why hast thou forsaken me?"

Is " the Spirit of grace and of supplications poured out upon us " now? Are we " looking on him whom we have pierced, and mourning as one mourneth for an only son?" Do we feel as if such wrong as we have done to him, in distrusting, persecuting, crucifying him, never could be overlooked?—as if he must needs, in spite of all his patience and all his pity, resent at last our unworthy treatment of him? He addresses us almost in the very words of Joseph,—" Fear not; for am I in the place of God?" Have I come to judge and condemn? Nay! It is mine to save. And does he not add, as did his apostles, when preaching to his actual betrayers and murderers, —Lay not too much to heart what you have done to me; however you meant it, has it not turned out for good? So God intended it,—to bring to pass, through your means, the saving of much people, the saving of you this day. Me ye have not really injured. Lo! The cross on which you lifted me up has become a throne—a throne on which I am exalted, to be a Prince and a Saviour. It is my Father's doing; my Father's will. You could " do nothing against me, except it were given to you from above" (John xix. 11). " The prince of this world," though he " cometh to me, hath nothing in me " (John xiv. 30). It is neither your purpose, nor his, that is fulfilled in me. But " I love the Father, and as he has given me commandment, so I do " (John xiv. 31).

Yes! You may remind me, as his brethren reminded Joseph, of my Father's commandment. I had his commandment to die for you. I have his commandment to save you, —to pardon and to bless. " All that the Father giveth me shall come to me: and him that cometh unto me I will in no wise cast out. For I came down from heaven, not to do my own will, but the will of him that sent me. And this is the Father's will which hath sent me, that of all which he hath given me, I should lose nothing, but should raise it up at the last day. And this is the will of him that sent me, that every one which seeth the Son, and believeth on him, may have everlasting life: and I will raise him up at the last day" (John vi. 37-40).

It might have seemed something very like an insult or an impertinence, on the part of Joseph's brethren, to bring to bear upon him, as if he needed it, the pressure of parental authority;—" Thy father did command : "—not our father, they say, gratifying us,—but thy father constraining thee. And yet, after all, can we wonder ? The more they knew of Joseph, since they had come to live on friendly terms with him,—the more they saw of his beautiful character,—the more they experienced of his bountiful generosity,—the more must their former grudge against him, and the horrid deed of treachery and cruelty which it prompted, have appeared in their eyes utterly inexcusable and unpardonable. Every day's new insight into Joseph's heart, as they looked on him whom they had pierced, must have pierced their hearts with new and fresh poignancy of grief and fear. Is it surprising that their consciences misgave them ? Is it surprising that they should have felt Joseph's kindness to them to be too much to last,— the assurance of his perfect and unchanging forgiveness to be too good news to be true ? Need we wonder that they should have tried to enlist their father on their side,—and get him to enforce, by a dying charge to Joseph, that loving and beloved son's own purpose of mercy, if it should begin to falter ? So Joseph may have felt. He is not, therefore, offended. He willingly accepts his father's commandment, as even a better reason for forgiving his brethren than his own spontaneous inclination.

Is not this the very mind of Jesus? Is not this the security which he gives to us? Is he not ever anxious to assure us that what he does for us and to us, is all done in obedience to his Father's commandment ? Nor does he wait till we quote that commandment of his Father to him ; he testifies of it to us. He is beforehand with us. He himself interposes this great guarantee,—this sure warrant of faith. It is not my doing, he seems to say of that salvation which he works out for us. My laying down my life for you,—my forgiving your sins on the earth,—my receiving you when you come to me,—my raising you up at the last day ;—all that is not really my doing. No. Not my doing: " I came not to do my own will, but the will of him that sent me." It is his will; it is his commandment; for you and me alike. It is he who commands you to look to me, and believe in me. It is he who commands me not to cast you out in any wise, but to receive you, and give you everlasting life, and raise you up at the last day. Yes! it is my Father's commandment; and "as he giveth me commandment so I do." For I love the Father; I and the Father are one. Therefore you are safe in casting yourselves into my arms; safe as the sheep of my pasture. " My sheep hear my voice, and I know them, and they follow me: and I give unto them eternal life; and they shall never perish, neither shall any man pluck them out of my hand. My Father, which gave them me, is greater than all; and no man is able to pluck them out of my Father's hand. I and my Father are one " (John x. 27-30).

72

FAITH AND HOPE IN DEATH—LOOKING FROM EGYPT TO CANAAN

Genesis 50:22-26

By faith Joseph, when he died, made mention of the departing of the children of Israel; and gave commandment concerning his bones.— Hebrews 11:22

THIS is entirely a Hebrew ending of the life of Joseph. Not a trace of his Egyptian connection is in it; nothing of what pertains to his position as Pharaoh's favourite minister, and ruler over all the land of Egypt.

How is it so ? Has he forfeited or lost the king's regard ? Has he experienced the vicissitudes of royal caprice and courtly life ? Is he in disgrace ? or in compulsory retirement ? —the victim of conspiracy or of jealousy—awakened, perhaps, by his open leanings towards Canaan and the prospects of his family there ? Nothing of the sort appears. The brief notice, in the Book of Exodus, of the change of Egyptian policy which led to Israel's oppression, surely implies the reverse; that Joseph's influence continued unabated, not only while he lived, but even long afterwards ; " There arose up a new king over Egypt, which knew not Joseph " (Exod. i. 8). It is not probable that the king's friendly disposition towards Joseph, which had been shown so conspicuously at the funeral of his father Jacob, suffered any diminution during the fifty years of his own surviving lifetime. All the more remarkable is the fact that the record of these years, and of their close, has so much of a Hebrew, and so little, or rather absolutely nothing, of an Egyptian character and complexion.

The observation, indeed, as has been already seen, may be extended more widely. From the moment of the Hebrew family coming on the stage, the Egyptian element in the drama becomes subordinate, and occupies the background. It appears, indeed—and now and then appears prominently enough—as for instance in the princely arrangements made first for Jacob's removal to Egypt, and then for his burial in Canaan. Still it is in a Hebrew point of view, that these instances of the Egyptian monarch's munificent kindness are recorded. And it remains true that, so far as Joseph in particular is concerned, his Egyptian rank, state, and power, are made little account of in the narrative, after his relations to his own family are resumed.

Now why is it so? It is not enough to allege the merely natural partiality of a Hebrew historian, smitten with the spirit of national prejudice or pride—counting Egypt comparatively nothing, and the interests of the house of Israel all in all. For that very spirit would rather naturally have led such a historian to give a studied, and even exaggerated, elaboration of all that might tend to keep up the idea of Joseph's Egyptian glory—as shedding its halo on the people, few in number and of doubtful respectability as to profession or occupation, who claimed the benefit of his name. The more he could tell of Joseph's greatness in Egypt, and his great influence with Egypt's king, after the settlement of the Israelites in Goshen, the more would he think that he advanced the renown of his race. The singular abstinence, in the inspired record, from all such glorying—and its simple merging of Joseph, the Egyptian Vizier, in Joseph, as first the son of Jacob and then his heir—must be felt by every competent judge to be a strong internal proof or presumption of its inspiration. This is certainly not the manner of men.

It is not thus that even an honest Hebrew annalist, left to himself, would have delineated the close of Joseph's career.

Between his father's death and his own, upwards of half-a-century intervened ; and the whole period is passed over in all but entire silence. Not a hint is given of the way in which these years were spent. All that we learn is that the two elements or conditions of prosperity, usually held of much account among men—and especially among the Israelites—and reckoned to be the reward or acknowledgment of righteousness, were found realised in the case of Joseph. Length of days was his—and the privilege of seeing his race perpetuated: " Joseph dwelt in Egypt, he, and his father's house : and Joseph lived an hundred and ten years. And Joseph saw Ephraim's children of the third generation ; the children also of Machir the son of Manasseh were brought up upon Joseph's knees " (ver. 22, 23). He lived long ; and his great-grand-children were fondled on his knee and trained under his eye. " He saw his children's children ; and," so far as appears, " peace upon Israel " (Ps. cxxviii. 6). The gathering clouds did not obscure his setting sun. His end was peace.

He died, believing. For " by faith Joseph, when he died, made mention of the departing of the children of Israel ; and gave commandment concerning his bones " (Heb. xi. 22). So the apostle testifies concerning his dying charge, in which he " took an oath of the children of Israel, saying, God will surely visit you, and ye shall carry up my bones from hence " (ver. 25).

But it may be asked, why did he not follow his father's example, in the order he gave as to his remains? He exercised and manifested the same faith that Jacob did when he " gave commandment concerning his bones ;" but he did not give the same commandment ; he did not ask to be at once buried in Canaan. He was content that his bones should be in Egypt for ages yet to come. He made no arrangement for such a funeral for himself as he had given his father. Why so? Why should he not have left the same request to his children, that his father left to him? It was not surely because he had not the power; his influence had not so far declined as that supposition would imply. The reigning Pharaoh would not have made any objection to that being done for Joseph which had been allowed in the case of Jacob. There may, indeed, have been some change of circumstances. The relations between the Egyptians and the Canaanites may have been somewhat altered; and it is easy to imagine grounds of policy or expediency on which it might not be right or wise for Joseph to contemplate a repetition, in his own case, of the significant scene which had marked the burial of Jacob. But it seems more probable that the difference between his dying request and that of his father, in regard to this matter, has a deeper meaning, in a spiritual point of view.

1. It is very obvious that Joseph's commandment concerning his bones had far more distinct and pointed reference to the future than Jacob's had. In fact, Jacob's dying requests (xlvii. 28-31; xlix. 29-32) have no explicit reference to the future at all. He dwells only on the past. We know indeed that his faith did embrace the future. He went down to Egypt (xlvi. 3, 4), upon the guarantee of a promise that he was to become a great nation there, and was to be brought up again to Canaan. And in both of the passages in which he intimates his wish as to his burial,—in the benediction of Joseph's sons and in the prophetic pictures of the twelve tribes,—he gives abundant evidence of his believing grasp of things to come. Still it is remarkable that in what he says about the disposal of his remains, there is no particular allusion to the future. He dwells upon the past, with all its hereditary associations and its incidents of domestic tenderness.

This was natural and right. He had but recently left Canaan,—and he was an old man when he left it. What he longs and cares for is, that his dust should mingle with kind-

red dust, in the grave in which his nearest and dearest relatives have been laid.

In Joseph's commandment concerning his bones, on the
other hand, the past is not mentioned ; it is the future alone
that he contemplates. And this also is natural and right.

Jacob belongs to the generations that have lived and died
in Canaan ; he is associated with Abraham and Isaac. Joseph
again is the fountain-head of the generations that are to spring
up in Egypt ; he is identified with the house of Israel as it is
to be perpetuated in Egypt, down to the exodus in the time
of Moses.

The two different commandments given by Jacob and by
Joseph respectively, are thus seen to be appropriate. That of
Joseph, however, would seem to indicate the stronger and
higher faith. And accordingly it is Joseph's commandment,
and not Jacob's, that the apostle, in writing to the Hebrews,
signalises. He does full justice, it is true, to Jacob's blessing
of both the sons of Joseph (Heb. xi. 21). But in the matter
of " the commandment he gave concerning his bones" (Heb.
xi. 22), Joseph stands out as a more conspicuous example of
faith than Jacob. Mere natural affection, and the touching
memory of the olden time, may, to a large extent, explain what
Jacob said on the subject. Joseph, on the other hand, has his
eye exclusively fixed on what is " hoped for" and " unseen."

The orders issued, the directions given, correspond with
these two different states of mind.

Take my body back to Canaan,—away at once from Egypt ;
let it rest beside the bodies of my fathers and my wife. Let
my lot be with them,—in the land which you, my posterity,
are to inherit,—but still rather as one of them, than as one of
you. Such is the meaning of Jacob's injunction.

Joseph, on the other hand, prefers rather to cast in his lot,
so far as the disposal of his corporeal frame is concerned, with
the present and coming races of Israel in Egypt.

Keep me among you,—my unburied bones,—my embalmed body. I desire not to be separated from you. Even after death, I would, as far as possible, be one of you. I have no doubt of your return to Canaan; and my dying wish is to return, so far as my bones can represent me, along with you. I do not choose that any part of me should reach Canaan before you ; for I do not choose that even my decease should separate me from you. My father belonged to our ancestry, and sought to be with them in his grave ; I belong to you and your seed. I am content to "bide my time ;" to wait for the consummation of my desire concerning my body,—which is, after all, identical with my father's—until what I believe, as he believed it, is realised and fulfilled ;—for " God will surely visit you, and ye shall carry up my bones from hence" (ver. 25).

2. The possession of Joseph's bones,—the custody of them under so solemn a charge,—must have been a signal benefit to the Israelites in Egypt ;—more so than the possession of Jacob's bones would have been. The two arrangements, fitted into one another,—the last being the complement of the first ; —and taken together, they completed the lesson which the Israelites, in their peculiar circumstances, needed to learn.

To have laid up the body of Jacob,—swathed and embalmed,—in the form of a mummy, according to Egyptian usage,—to be kept for some thirty or forty generations,—as an heirloom in their tribes,—would have been palpably unnatural and unsuitable. Such a mode of dealing with the Hebrew patriarch's remains,—he being a mere stranger in Egypt,—but yesterday come down into the land,—while all his ties were elsewhere,—would have been incongruous. His burial in Canaan is, in every view, more becoming and more in harmony with his history.

It is otherwise with Joseph,—himself almost a naturalised Egyptian,—and as an Israelite, associated far more with Israel in Egypt, than with Israel in Canaan.

And then, the difference of the times and circumstances is to be noted.

When Jacob died, Israel was in the first full flush of favour and prosperity in Egypt ; the world in Egypt was smiling on them. They were feeding their flocks in the best pastures, and basking in the sunshine of royal patronage. They needed to be reminded that Egypt, though the land of plenty, was not their rest,—that Canaan was their home.

When Joseph died, a change was near at hand. Already, there may have been ominous signs of approaching trouble. The prophetic warning which Abraham got was about to be accomplished. They needed to be reconciled to Egypt as the house of bondage, by the assurance of a joyous return to Canaan at last.

Both of these needs are suitably met by the dying commandments of Jacob and of Joseph respectively, " concerning their bones."

Jacob virtually says :—You are now in the enjoyment of all worldly ease and plenty. The famine is past,—and with the famine, other sore miseries besides. You have abundance of the good things of this life,—and the evil consequences of former sins and errors are put right. Egypt, which is your world, is now a sort of paradise to you. But forget not Canaan. You are merely strangers and sojourners here ; your real citizenship is elsewhere. The world in Egypt is all smiles ; but let not its smiles ensnare or enslave you. Set not your hearts upon it. Love it not, nor the things of it. As you carry your dead father up to Canaan, let what you are doing teach you to keep Canaan ever in view. Egypt has its pleasures,—alas! too often sinful ; but the promises are all bound up with Canaan. There, where you lay me, beside Abraham and Isaac, let your hope always be centred. Let the habit of your life be fashioned, not after Egypt's license, but after Canaan's holy covenant.

Joseph again, in an altered state of things, may be held to say :—Egypt, which is the world to you, is about to become a house of bondage,—a furnace of affliction. Its smiles are to give place to frowns,—its joys to bitter grief. There is to be little more of bright sunshine in this world for you, but only ever-deepening gloom. But courage ! Be of good cheer. Be not dismayed. The darkness will not last for ever. This weary Egypt, this region of cloud and storm,—of oppression, trouble, and woe,—is not to be your dwelling-place always. Canaan is erelong to open to you its blessed gates. I am sure of it ; so sure of it am I, that I specially ask you not to do for me what I did for Jacob.

I am as intensely bent as he was on having Canaan as my final rest ; I intend that my bones shall lie there with his. But I would not prevent or anticipate you. I leave my bones with you, to be carried up to Canaan, only when you go up to Canaan yourselves. Keep them. And as often as you look at the coffin in which they are put, let your faith and hope become as bright as mine now is. Be assured, as I am assured, that the tribulations of Egypt are to end in the peace and joy of Canaan.

How far Joseph's purpose may have been accomplished,— how far the preservation of his body, in a state of constant preparation for being carried up out of Egypt to Canaan, may have contributed to keep up, among the Israelites, during the years of their affliction, the memory of the Abrahamic cove- nant and the expectation of the promised deliverance,—it is impossible to say. The history here is almost a complete blank, an utter void. Beyond the briefest possible notices, we have no account of the rise and progress of the Egyptian persecution of the Israelites. And we have no account whatever of the religious state of the Israelites during the persecution. But we know that when the time of the Exodus came, the commandment of Joseph concerning his bones was freshly remembered and faithfully obeyed (Exod. xiii. 19 ; Josh. xxiv. 32). And we can scarcely doubt that the sacred deposit had the effect of keeping alive, at least among the more thoughtful and spiritually enlightened of the people, that trust in the God of their fathers, and in his promises, which enabled, as we may well believe, others besides the parents of Moses, to brave the wrath of the king, and hold fast the hope of a Saviour. Certainly, Joseph's dying act had a strong tendency to effect such a result. As a manifestation of his own faith, it was fitted to confirm the faith of the people in his assurance, " God will surely visit you."

" So Joseph died, being an hundred and ten years old ; and they embalmed him, and he was put in a coffin in Egypt" (ver. 26). And so ends the history or biography, which far above all others, save only one, rivets the mind and ravishes the heart.

The two stand out alone,—the life of Joseph and the life of Jesus,—parallel at least in many important aspects, if not intended to stand in a closer relation to one another.

The parallelism is of itself suggestive. To one living before the coming of Christ, if he was at all spiritually minded, it was fitted to suggest thoughts connected with the Saviour yet to come. Taken in connection with the rite of sacrifice, and other evidently anticipative usages and ordinances, it could scarcely fail to afford some insight into the necessary conditions which the Saviour must fulfil, as well as also into the manner of his fulfilment of them. To us now, under the guidance of the same Spirit who inspired the two great biographies, their parallelism may furnish the means of a not unprofitable comparison between the two deliverers and their respective deliverances.

I. The character of Joseph fits him pre-eminently for being a type of Christ. The two qualities most conspicuous in Joseph, apart from his personal innocence and blamelessness, are on the one hand, his meekness and gentleness, and on the other hand, his commanding and authoritative wisdom and benevolence. His personal purity, his spotless and stainless integrity,—the result conspicuously in him of renewing grace, tried and tested by temptation,—made him a fitting pattern of him who was " holy, harmless, undefiled, and separate from sinners." And then, when we add to that, first, his unresisting and uncomplaining endurance of wrong,—and secondly, his capacity of rule and government,—we have the very features or attributes of personal worth or excellency,—in kind though not of course in degree,—that constitute the beauty and the strength of "the man Christ Jesus;"—the suffering and reigning Jesus.

II. The personal history of Joseph is eminently typical, both in the deep humiliation to which he was subjected, and in the glory which followed. He suffers, not for any sins of his own, but through the sins of those to whom he would do good. He bears, in a sense, the blame and the doom which others had deserved. Strict and proper substitution, indeed, there is not, and could not be, in his case. Of that peculiar characteristic of the sufferings of Christ the only exact type is to be found in the animal sacrifices of the old economy,—the slain lamb,—the blood of bulls and of goats ; and even that is imperfect, as representing him, who "through the eternal Spirit offered himself without spot to God." But short of that, in the load of sorrow and shame which Joseph in his innocency and tried holiness had to bear, weighing him down to the very gates of death,—in the cup which he had to drink, and which he took, not as at the hands of men only, but immediately from the hand of God,—the cup filled to overflowing with the pressed fruit of other men's sins,—we have what assimilates in no ordinary degree Joseph—betrayed, sold, condemned, and as good as dead in his hopeless dungeon, —to Jesus, amid the circumstances of his life-long grief, and his last agony. And then the bright side of the picture, in Joseph's case as in that of Jesus, is his elevation to the right hand of the great king; his investiture with full authority and command over all the king's resources in all his realms ; his receiving power over all that he may give life to many; his being exalted a Prince and a Saviour.

III. The actual salvation wrought is of a typical sort. It is so in itself; for it is the giving of life;—" to save much people alive." It is deliverance from death,—certain and inevitable death. It is " the filling of the hungry with good things, while the rich are sent empty away." And then, as to the manner of it,—the extent to which it reaches, and the way in which its blessings are diffused,—is not Joseph, like Jesus, " a light to lighten the Gentiles, and the glory of God's people Israel?" He is " a light to lighten the Gentiles." For at first " he came unto his own, and his own received him not." His brethren, the sons of Israel, to whom he carried a message of peace from home, cast him out. It was in Gentile Egypt that the first light of his saving power and glory shone. But " God's people Israel" were soon embraced in the shining of it.

Is it not so in the dispensation of the gospel salvation? Will it not be seen to be so, more and more, as the end draws near? Now are the times of the Gentiles. Now is Jesus the light of the Gentiles. But the Lord hath not cast off Israel. " Blindness" indeed " in part is happened to Israel, until the fulness of the Gentiles be come in." But in the end, " all Israel shall be saved: as it is written, There shall come out of Zion the Deliverer, and shall turn away ungodliness from Jacob. For this is my covenant unto them, when I shall take away their sins" (Rom. xi. 25-27).

IV. The death of Joseph,—or rather " the commandment which he gave concerning his bones,"—may also be regarded as in some sense typical. It has something like a counterpart in the confidence with which the Messiah speaks of his own resurrection in that Messianic Psalm : " Therefore my heart is glad, and my glory rejoiceth; my flesh also shall rest in hope. For thou wilt not leave my soul in hell; neither wilt thou suffer thine Holy One to see corruption. Thou wilt show me the path of life: in thy presence is fulness of joy ; at thy right hand there are pleasures for evermore" (Ps. xvi. 9-11).

In a higher sense, and with a deeper meaning than Joseph could reach,—Jesus, when he spoke of his death, pointed to the inheritance which his risen saints are to share with him, their risen Saviour.

But, laying its typical meaning aside, let us once more think of Joseph's dying charge, as distinguished from that of Jacob,—or rather let us take them both together. They had their separate voices to utter,—their separate lessons to teach.

Dying Jacob would carry his children's minds and hearts away from Egypt's pomps and pleasures, its vanities and prosperities, to the quiet rest of Canaan, where his bones are laid.

Dying Joseph would reconcile his brethren to the toil and woe of Egypt's long bondage, by the animating consideration that they still have him, in a sense, among them,—his body committed to their charge,—in the full assurance of its being carried by them to Canaan, when they go thither in triumph at last.

May it not be said of us, if we believe in Jesus, that in the death of every saint who falls asleep before our eyes, we have the two views, the two lessons, combined ?

A father in Israel, or a brother beloved, dies. We say of him that he departs. He departs to be with Christ, which is far better. He is gone to Canaan. He passes into heaven. And as he passes away from us, " he being dead, yet speaketh."

What is he saying to us ? Cleave not to Egypt. Be not drawn by the world's smiles to love the world. I leave you, perhaps, prosperous and happy ; but I ask you to go with me, in spirit, as I enter the promised land. Let there be, as it were, a funeral service there, in which you join. Nay, rather, come with me and see how blessed is my entrance into Canaan's rest. And ever after feel that Canaan is your rest too. Egypt is not your home. Be its Goshen pastures ever so pleasant, and ever so plentiful, love them not. Be often, in spirit, returning with me to Canaan.

Again, what else is he saying to us? Weary not in Egypt. Be not impatient. Earth may be to you a house of bondage, all sad and dreary. But my bones are with you in it. My body, still united to Christ, rests in its grave among you. I am sure of its being brought to Canaan ere long. It is but a little while. All earth's groans are past. The dead are raised,—the living changed. All are with the Lord. " I would not have you to be ignorant, brethren, concerning them which are asleep, that ye sorrow not, even as others which have no hope. For if we believe that Jesus died and rose again, even so them also which sleep in Jesus will God bring with him. For this we say unto you by the word of the Lord, that we which are alive and remain unto the coming of the Lord, shall not prevent them which are asleep. For the Lord himself shall descend from heaven with a shout, with the voice of the archangel, and with the trump of God : and the dead in Christ shall rise first : Then we which are alive and remain shall be caught up together with them in the clouds, to meet the Lord in the air : and so shall we ever be with the Lord. Wherefore comfort one another with these words " (1 Thess. iv. 13-18).

APPENDIX

1. OBSERVATIONS ON THE STRUCTURE OF THE BOOK OF GENESIS AS A WHOLE

I PUT into the form of a postscript what some may think might perhaps be more properly placed as a preface or introduction ; and I do so because it gives some general, and sufficiently desultory views that have been suggested to me in a review of the entire book, rather than an explanation of the method of my exposition of it. These views, in short, partake more of the nature and character of afterthought than of the nature and character of forethought.

I. Moses, as it seems to me, has fared very much as Homer has fared, at the hands of minute critics. In particular, the Book of Genesis has undergone the same sort of treatment as the Iliad. Both have been disintegrated, and torn into shreds and fragments ; parcelled out among a motley and miscellaneous crowd of unknown documents and imaginary authors ; and resolved into a mere medley of traditionary hymns or songs, strung together,—if not at random, by some fortuitous concourse of atoms ;—by some marvel or miracle giving undesigned concinnity and completeness to the whole.

For that is the phenomenon which is to be accounted for in both cases alike. And in both cases alike it is the answer to the objection urged against the historical tradition of a single authorship.

The force of the answer lies in its being an appeal from word-catching and hair-splitting analysis, to the broad, general impression which a large-minded and large-hearted earnest reader cannot fail to receive. No one who throws his own soul into the Iliad, if he is at all capable of doing so, can have the slightest doubt as to its being a single soul with whom he has communion. He desiderates and demands a Homer ; not a lot of song-writers but a solitary seer ; a " *vates sacer ;*" a genius creating unity because it is itself one. I believe it to be the same with Genesis. I think it has the stamp and impress of an undivided authorship. There is a completeness about it,—an epic roundness, with beginning, middle, and end, —and with a marvellous adaptation and subordination of seeming episodes to the onward march of the plot,—that I confess I would rather question the unity of the Ænead, on the score of such interludes as that of Nisus and Euryales,— or the unity of Hamlet, on the score of the grave-digging scene,—than I would deny to this Book of Genesis the unity of a sole and single authorship—not to speak of a sole and single divine inspiration.

II. Having this conviction, I am not much troubled with questions raised as to the pre-existing materials of which the author may have made use, or the subsequent emendations, interpolations, and alterations, which the book may have undergone from age to age, until its final revision was adjusted, perhaps in the time of Ezra, when the canon of the Old Testament Scriptures is supposed by many to have been finally fixed.

I have no faith, I confess, in the imaginary library of such a visionary as Ewald. I do not suppose that scholars will allow him, with impunity, to " call" books, like " spirits, from the vasty deep ;"—as if he could recover the burnt Sybilline leaves, and read them off to us as clearly as Tarquin, if he had chosen, might have heard them read.

At the same time, in maintaining the unity of Genesis and

of its authorship, it is important to explain that this is quite consistent with there being many traces in the book, both of earlier documents or traditions, and of later editings and revisions. In fact, from the very nature of the case, it must be so. When the book was written, there must have been a literature of some sort—lyrical, legendary, monumental—of which the writer could not fail to take advantage. And it is absurd to suppose that the learned men who had to deal with the book, —imperfectly preserved from age to age till the canon was complete, would deny themselves the liberty,—especially if they were under divine inspiration,—of making such corrections and explanations as, in the circumstances, the lapse of time required.

III. But I must add that, while fully admitting these obvious considerations,—and indeed relying on them as accounting for, if they do not explain, not a few textual difficulties,—I cannot see my way to concur in the theory that distinct documents, such as may be separately and systematically characterised, are to be found recognisable in this book.

I am unable, for instance, to see the necessity for assuming the two annalists, the " Jehovist" and the " Elohist,"—into whose double thread our critical friends are so fond of resolving the Mosaic cord. I very much doubt the possibility of a clear and consistent " redding of the marches" between the two, if it is to be carried out all through ; and I think there is " a more excellent way" of meeting the difficulty.

I have adverted to this in my exposition of the first two chapters of Genesis, and elsewhere in these volumes ; borrowing light from the Lord's statement to Moses, " And I appeared unto Abraham, unto Isaac, and unto Jacob, by the name of God Almighty, but by my name Jehovah was I not known to them " (Exodus vi. 3).

That statement, I apprehend, can scarcely be taken literally to mean that the name—" Jehovah "—by which the Supreme Being announced himself to Moses and the Israelites in Egypt had never been in use before among the patriarchs.

It rather points, as I think, to the difference of signification between the two names ;—the one, Eloim, denoting sovereignty and power, the other, Jehovah, suggesting the idea of faithfulness or unchangeableness (Mal. iii. 6) ;—and to the suitableness of the two names to the two eras in question respectively. In former patriarchal times, God appears chiefly in the character of one choosing or electing those who are to be the objects of his favour, giving them " exceeding great and precious promises," and ratifying and confirming with them a most gracious covenant. With such a transaction on his part, the assertion of absolute sovereignty and almighty power is in harmony and in keeping. Now, on the other hand, when he is about to come forward and interpose for the purpose of fulfilling these old assurances, and with that view, wishes to secure the confidence of the new generation in whose experience and with whose co-operation the work is to be done, —the appeal to the immutability of his nature, as proving or implying " the immutability of his counsel" (Heb. vi. 17), is relevant and appropriate. Formerly he spoke as the omnipotent ruler over all, whose hand none can stay, to whom none can say what doest thou! Now he speaks as the I AM, " the same yesterday, to-day, and for ever."

Considering the importance attached in these days and among that people to the import and bearing of names, I prefer some such explanation of this passage in Exodus to one which would make it the assertion of a mere historical fact as to the dates of the two names being in use ;—and a fact too, which, if it is to be understood strictly according to the letter, must be regarded as of doubtful probability. And I am persuaded that in the passages in Genesis in which either name occurs, a reason can for the most part be found for its being employed rather than the other, founded on the nature of the subject treated of, or the view which the writer desires to give of the events or incidents he may be recording, without its being necessary to postulate distinct fragments with distinct authorships.

I believe, as I have attempted to show, that we have a parallel and illustrative instance in the manner of using the two names, Jacob and Israel; the one denoting natural weakness, tending to guile, the other divine strength apprehended by prevailing faith. On many occasions, as it would seem, the selection of the one name rather than the other is determined by the attitude in which the patriarch is presented, or the act in which he is engaged. I would not indeed press this principle of interpretation too far, either in the case of the two patriarchal designations, or in the case of the two divine titles; and I repeat that I am not troubled by the hypothesis of advantage having been taken by Moses of materials previously current in the form of traditionary narratives or songs. Surely, however, it is being wise above what is written, to pretend so confidently as some do, to disentangle the Elohist and the Jehovist elements in the narrative. It turns the mind away from higher and more spiritual considerations which the appropriateness of the name used to the theme on hand might suggest; and it breaks the continuity of a history which, I venture again to say, presents in its onward movement, from first to last, a specimen of epic oneness unparalleled in literature; its very digressions and apparent interruptions admitting of satisfactory and probable explanation.*

IV. There are some other points relative to the mode of interpreting such a book as Genesis, upon which questions might be raised and explanations given; and there are several principles of exposition, to which reference is incidentally made in these pages, and which might admit of fuller illustration and vindication. One, for example, is the extent to which we may avail ourselves of the undoubted fact of an oral revelation having preceded the written word, as affecting the manner in which that word would probably be composed, and the kind of evidence it might be expected to afford of the leading truths of religion. Another is the amount of acquaintance with the

---

*See, for instance, my remarks on Chapter 38

doctrines of the Gospel which may be presumed in the early world, as rather alluded to and taken for granted, than communicated for the first time, in God's successive discoveries of himself to the fathers. Then a third question might turn upon the value of incidental quotations from the Old Testament in the New, as warranting the application of hints thus given considerably beyond the particular passages quoted, as well as upon the legitimate use of resemblances, parallelisms, and analogies, occurring in the comparison of incidents and predictions, under different and far distant dispensations. While a fourth, and very interesting problem, might be to fix the limit between a sound and safe discretion and a fanciful license, in filling up the brief sketches and outlines of the inspired record, and drawing inferences from them ;—presuming upon a certain spiritual tact, or taste, or apprehension, a feeling of probability, a sense of concinnity, or congruity, which, even apart from such precise and palpable evidence as can be critically or logically stated, will often give to a rightly constituted and rightly exercised understanding, a prompt and full assurance of the mind of the Spirit.

But I do not feel myself called upon, even if I were competent, to discuss such matters critically and abstractly : I think it enough to indicate, that in preparing these papers, I have had them in my view. How far I have succeeded in practically applying the rules and methods indicated within due bounds, it is not for me to judge. In one particular, perhaps, I may be censured for going too far, although not, as I am of opinion, justly. I refer to the amount of knowledge on the fundamental articles of revealed religion, and especially on the remedial plan of the Gospel, which I have assumed to have existed among men before the written word came into being. That written word, as it seems to me, takes for granted such knowledge to a considerable extent, and proceeds upon the faith of it—supplementing it and correcting it often by allusions and hints, rather than formally teaching or communicating it, as if for the first time. I refer to such heads of doctrine as the being and attributes of God; the unity of the divine nature, with perhaps some intimation of the plurality of persons in that unity; the guilt or condemnation of sin; the manner of its remission through a propitiatory sacrifice; the calling and conversion of sinners; the promised Saviour; the resurrection and final judgment; the eternal state. I do not of course mean that the knowledge on these subjects which the written word might assume, and to which it might appeal, was at all so full and accurate as what revelation gives; and in revelation itself I trace a growing clearness of development. I admit also that, depending on oral tradition alone for its transmission from age to age, the knowledge must have deteriorated in its character, and become corrupt and imperfect, when the written word began its teaching, as compared with what it was at first, as given by God originally. All that I contend for is, that we may fairly regard the written word as in such particulars reviving and ratifying the primeval creed, not yet wholly lost, and may interpret therefore upon the principle of its assuming and appealing to a measure of intelligence in those to whom it was given, that would enable them, under the guidance of the Spirit, to understand its suggestions and intimations better, and draw the right inferential conclusions better, than we sometimes give them credit for.

2*

For the unbelieving husband is sanctified by the wife, and the unbelieving
wife is sanctified by the husband : else were your children unclean ;
but now are they holy.—For what knowest thou, O wife, whether
thou shalt save thy husband ? or how knowest thou, O man, whether
thou shalt save thy wife ?" 1 Corinthians 7:14,16

In these two verses the apostle gives the *rationalè* or explanation of the practical rules he is laying down relative to the
case of a married person becoming a believer, while the
partner in the marriage-state remains unconverted. In substance the apostle decides that the marriage-tie is not dissolved by the conversion of either party to the faith of the
gospel.

An apparent exception is made in the intermediate verse,—
or rather a caution is added,—to the effect that what he says
of a believing husband or wife who might think it a duty to
separate from an unbeliever, does not apply when it is the
unbelieving party that refuses to remain connected with the
believing. That is altogether a different matter. If the
unconverted husband will not live with the converted wife,
but insists on leaving her, on account of her conversion, let
him go ; and so, also, let the unbelieving wife go, if she will
not continue to be the wife of her believing husband. In every
such instance, where the movement is on the part of the unbelieving or unconverted spouse, the believing or converted one incurs
no responsibility, and is in fact utterly helpless. He is not,

therefore, to distress or vex himself. The marriage-tie is not, in such circumstances, to become a bondage; nor is the peace of the church to be broken by questions and litigations of such a nature. For, let it be noted, the exceptional case could only arise in countries in which the law or custom tolerated, if it did not sanction, this pretence for dissolving marriage; and in which, therefore, a heathen husband forsaking his wife, on the express ground of her being a convert to Christianity, or a heathen wife forsaking her husband on that ground, would be protected or patronised. The exception, accordingly, does not weaken the ordinary and general rule that the conversion of either party does not break the marriage-tie. And above all, it does not touch the obligation laid upon the converted party to continue true and faithful to that tie, if the other party is willing. The direction on that point is plain and unequivocal, without reserve or qualification; "If any brother hath a wife that believeth not, and she be pleased to dwell with him, let him not put her away. And the woman which hath an husband that believeth not, and if he be pleased to dwell with her, let her not leave him" (ver. 12, 13).

This direction is in the first place introduced by Paul (10, 11), as a corollary or inference from the broad general statute respecting marriage and divorce, laid down by the Lord personally;—"It hath been said, whosoever shall put away his wife, let him give her a writing of divorcement: but I say unto you, that whosoever shall put away his wife, saving for the cause of fornication, causeth her to commit adultery: and whosoever shall marry her that is divorced committeth adultery" (Matt. v. 31, 32). What the apostle goes on secondly to ordain (12, 13), as to a believer continuing to live with an unbeliever, is his commentary upon the text, as it stands in the legal code of the great Lawgiver himself. There is really nothing here to raise any question as to differences and degrees of authority or inspiration in the

Bible; nothing even postponing the word written by an apostle to the word spoken by Christ himself, in the flesh; as if it were of less weight and value, or were less truly and literally the oracle of God. All that Paul intends is to distinguish the text in the law of marriage, from the commentary; the text as settled by the Lord himself personally, from the commentary or application dictated by the Holy Ghost to the apostles.

The general law of marriage and divorce, says Paul to the Corinthians, is expressly determined and declared, once for all, by the divine founder of our religion; and that law, in the precise letter of it, sufficiently disposes of one of the points raised among you; namely, how far it is right generally to hold the marriage-tie broken on considerations of religion. This was enough to expose and put down the error of those who affected to think that the gospel of Christ made them too pure and spiritual to continue still in the married state;—an error springing out of the spurious and fictitious refining upon the gospel style and standard of holiness to which the eastern philosophy gave rise.

But another point might be mooted, which the mere text of the law, as laid down by the Lord personally, might not be supposed to meet; namely, the special point, as to the case of one of the parties becoming Christian and the other remaining heathen. This point might occasion difficulty; particularly among the Jewish members of the church; when they thought of the stern denunciation of such mixed marriages by their lawgiver; and the stern and unrelenting measures taken to dissolve them by the reformers of their polity, Ezra and Nehemiah (Exod. xxxiv. 16; Deut. vii. 3; Ezra ix. and x.; Neh. xiii. 23). Paul, therefore, proceeds to deal with that point;—not doubtfully, as if uncertain of his inspiration and authority;—but plainly and peremptorily. He takes up the text of the law, as laid down by the Lord, and unhesitatingly adds his comment or explanation. He gives his interpretation of it, or his finding under it, to the effect of ordering the believing husband or wife to remain even with an unbelieving partner. Such, as he determines it, is the fair import and legitimate force of the law spoken by the Lord himself ;—so far virtually superseding or reversing the Mosaic rule, enforced by Ezra and Nehemiah—a rule evidently rendered necessary by the peculiar position of the Jewish nation ; and not therefore always or universally applicable and binding.

Now, in the two verses before us (14 and 16), the apostle brings out the theory or principle upon which this practical rule of conduct is to be vindicated or explained. He assigns for it a twofold reason ; a reason somewhat formal, and if we may so speak, relative or relational, connected with the standing which a Christian household has before God ; and another reason more real, practical, and moral, bearing upon the opportunities of doing good which the household economy presents. For we may conceive of a really conscientious member of the Corinthian church,—particularly if he were a Jewish convert,—bringing forward a double objection against the apostle's rule. You desire me to continue joined in the marriage yoke with one who is still an unbeliever ; not even in name and by profession a follower of Jesus. But I have two serious difficulties and scruples of conscience about doing so. In the first place, may not my standing in relation to God be thereby affected ? And in the second place, may not my personal character run the risk of being contaminated, tainted, and corrupted ? My position or standing as a believer in the sight of God is one of holiness ;—in the sense of his having separated me, and set me apart for himself, so that I am in a new and peculiar covenant-relation to him ;—called and consecrated to be his. May not that position be compromised if I remain a member of a heathen or unchristian family, which, as such, is in the relation of an unclean or common thing to God ? Again, by God's grace I have obtained the gift of saving faith—and I seek to live by faith, and walk by faith, with God, in the world ? Is there no danger of my being drawn away and enticed, if, in so near a fellowship as that of marriage, I still associate with an unconverted person ? May I not be tempted to apostatise or become a backslider ? May I not thus fall away from my steadfastness ?

No, says the apostle. Your two difficulties are, indeed, such as might naturally occur to you : your scruples are not idle and vain. But they may be met.

Thus, as to the first, mark the grace and condescension of God. Such is the favour you find, as a believer, in his sight, and such his benignant complacency in you, that he consents to see your family in you, and not you in your family ; to give your family the benefit of your relation of nearness and friendship to himself, instead of your having the loss and damage of their relation of estrangement ; to view the household as partaking in your consecration to be the Lord's, rather than you as partaking in their unblessed standing before him ; to account them, in this sense, holy for your sake, and not you common or unclean for theirs. On this head, therefore, you need have no anxiety.

And again, as to the other point, your reasonable and commendable fear lest your faith should be undermined and corrupted by such association with an unbeliever ; consider that, by the grace of God, in answer to your prayers, the result may be the very reverse. Your tender and holy walk ;—rendered all the more tender and holy by the very apprehension you feel lest the spirituality of your views, and the heavenliness of your aims, should suffer from the sphere in which you are forced to move ;—your faithful testimony—your consistent conduct — your affectionate assiduities — your discreet utterance of a word in season—your patience, gentleness, and love ;—may be the means, in the hand of the Spirit, of converting to God the very party whose influence you dread as likely to draw your own soul away from him ; " For what

knowest thou, O wife, whether thou shalt save thy husband ?
or how knowest thou, O man, whether thou shalt save thy
wife ?" (ver. 16). Or, as the apostle Peter has it—" Likewise, ye wives, be in subjection to your own husbands ; that,
if any obey not the word, they also may without the word be
won by the conversation of the wives ; while they behold your
chaste conversation coupled with fear—(1 Peter iii. 1, 2).

Thus the apostle disposes of the two scruples which a
believer might feel, as to complying with the rule he has
announced ; and establishes that rule, by laying down two
principles, deeply seated in the domestic constitution, as it is
ordained by God to be the central element alike of society and
of the church. It is to the first of these principles that I propose now to call attention.

The principle upon which God proceeds in dealing with a
household as represented by a believing head, whether it be the
husband or the wife, has its origin, of course, in his own sove
reign appointment. It is of his mere good pleasure that he
adopts a method of this kind in counting up the families of
men ;—reckoning as his own, and as in an important sense
holy unto himself, every family that has even one of its heads
in a position to commend it in believing prayer to him. We
do not, therefore, require to bring arguments of natural reason
in support of an arrangement which confessedly rests exclusively on the divine will, and could only be discovered and
ascertained by a divine revelation of that will. At the same
time, it may be satisfactory to observe—1. That there is no
valid presumption against it on any grounds of natural reason
and the common sense of mankind ; 2. That it is according to
the analogy of the divine procedure in the whole government
of this world ; and 3. That it is of great practical value to us,
and altogether worthy of God.

1. The holiness here ascribed to the family of a believing
parent has been often called *federal* or *covenant* holiness ; and

the expression provokes contempt in certain quarters. "The phrase 'federally holy' is unintelligible, and conveys no idea." Such is the brief oracular utterance of a popular American writer (Barnes), whose notes on the different books of the Bible, however valuable for the literary, historical, geographical, and antiquarian information they contain, are far from being safe guides either doctrinally or spiritually; and whose shallow criticisms would but ill supplant the sound and masculine theology of the older commentators. "The phrase," he says flippantly, "the phrase 'federally holy' is unintelligible, and conveys no idea." The remark is the result of ignorance. If, indeed, holiness here means personal purity and likeness to God,—piety, godliness, moral goodness;—if it expresses a quality or attribute of personal character;—then, undoubtedly, to speak of any one being "federally holy"—holy in respect of a covenant standing or relation,—while not personally a sanctified believer,—would be not merely unintelligible, but wicked,—not merely absurd, but profane. But it is notorious, every scholar knows, that that is not the meaning of the words "sanctify" and "holy" in this passage. The objectors themselves do not and cannot put that meaning on these words; and they know that it is not the meaning which sound divines and competent critics attach to them. In fact, the original term here rendered "holy,"—with the verb from it, to "sanctify," or "make holy,"—rarely, if ever, does, either in the Old Testament* or in the New, denote personal character. It does not necessarily imply any inward goodness or good quality at all. It is commonly used simply as a term of outward rela-

---

* I mean, of course, the corresponding word in Hebrew to the Greek word here. For there are two words in Hebrew, and two corresponding words in Greek, both translated holy in one English version; but never confounded in the original languages. The one refers to personal character, inferring piety and love; the other denotes consecration or setting apart for a sacred use, and is applied to things as well as persons. It is the latter that, with its cognate verb, is employed here.

tionship; denoting the use, destination, office, or official character of a person or thing;—having reference to the light in which God may be pleased to regard any one,—the treatment which God may bestow upon him,—the footing on which God may place him;—and not to what he really and personally is.

Thus viewed, the idea is surely simple enough. Take two familiar illustrations :—

(1.) I have occasion to deal with some one among you in a matter that brings us into the closest terms of mutual friendship and partnership with one another. Strictly speaking, it is entirely and exclusively a personal matter between you and me as individuals. But when the negotiation is completed, the compact sealed, and the league between us personally fairly established, somewhat of the effect or influence of the transaction reaches beyond you, as an individual, to those connected with you. Your family and your friends, though they may be far from being on the same terms with me individually as you yourself are,—nay, though they may continue strangers or even enemies,—are yet, somehow, different, as to my esteem of them, from what they were before;—and partly, at least, share in the interest with which I consider you.

(2.) When Joseph presented his aged father and his brethren to Pharaoh, the king did not treat them as common persons, —far less did he regard them as unclean, although Hebrew shepherds were apt to be an abomination to Egyptians. In themselves Jacob and his sons were nothing to Pharaoh. They had no claim upon his notice ; and there was no reason why they should find any especial favour in his sight. But, as belonging to Joseph, whom he so warmly esteemed, and so eagerly delighted to honour,—they became at once the objects of the king's liveliest sympathy;—and were admitted by him to a standing to which they could never otherwise have attained.

Is there anything unreasonable in such a mode of procedure ? Or can any cause be shown why God may not formally and systematically adopt it, in his dealings with the families of those whom he counts his own?

2. On the contrary, the analogy of providence and grace creates a probability on the other side. I do not now refer to the two great economies, or covenants,—that of works, and that of redemption or salvation,—in the one of which God deals with the whole family of mankind as represented by the first Adam, while in the other, he constitutes the second Adam, the Lord from heaven, the representative and surety of all the elect. The principle of both of these dispensations alike, under which paradise is forfeited and is regained,—man is lost and is found,—affords a presumption in favour of the arrangement now in question. But apart from that, it clearly appears to be a principle of the divine plan of government generally,—that individuals grouped together in organised bodies or communities should have a sort of reflex or imputed character in the sight of God,—borrowed from the character or profession of their natural or their constituted federal heads. Thus God had a special favour for all who were related to Abraham, even after the lapse of ages, and in a remote line of descent; not regarding them as standing in the same position with the general mass of men, but reckoning himself to have peculiar claims upon them,—and them also to have peculiar claims on him,—in respect of the place Abraham held in his esteem (2 Chron. xx. 7; Ps. cv. 6, 9, 42; Is. li. 2). No doubt the seed of Abraham, spiritually understood, is Christ, and believers viewed as one with Christ (Gal. iii. 16). But the literal offspring of Abraham were, and are, clearly accounted by God to be peculiarly his own, for Abraham's sake. And the very circumstance of Christ and his Church being represented so emphatically as Abraham's seed, proves the principle for which we are contending. It shows a desire in the divine mind to place even the bestowal of his saving grace and saving gifts upon the footing of the family relationship and the kindness which he bears to the family-head.

The same remarks will apply to the light in which God viewed those who could claim kindred with Jacob, as well as those of the house and lineage of David (Jer. xxxiii. 26). And subordinate instances might be quoted, such as that perhaps of the Rechabites (Jer. xxxv.); where the whole spirit of the incident is lost, if we do not consider it as an example of a family covenant, connected with a family blessing. Jonadab the son of Rechab acted plainly as the head of a house. As such he was owned by God, and all his house in him. And the special praise of his posterity is that they recognised and realised that fact.

Let it be observed here, in the first place, that we speak merely of the general principle of the divine procedure, and not of its particular application. The general principle is that when God chooses any one, and admits him into a relation of friendship with himself, he delights to extend to others connected with the chosen one, and does extend to them, merely because they are so connected, a certain participation in the benefit. Whether it may be temporal or spiritual blessings that are more immediately involved, is not at present material, and does not effect the analogy. It is enough to have shown, that when God admits the head of a household, or race, into a relation of holiness, or devotedness, or consecration to himself, —it is his method, his way, his rule, to extend that relation beyond the individual, so as to comprehend those belonging to him, and in some distinct sense, naturally, or by appointment, represented by him. Again, secondly, let it be noted that the principle is not made void by the fact that in spite of all this, those who are thus graciously treated and accounted virtually holy, never actually become in their own persons holy. It is the worse for them : their guilt is aggravated, and the severity of their doom enhanced. But their unbelief does not make void the faithfulness of God, or prove that he did not admit them into a relation of covenant-nearness to himself, for their father's sake ;—a relation carrying with it precious advantages and opportunities,—signal means and pledges of grace;—and involving, in proportion, all the heavier responsibilities.

If it be asked what we can bring forward out of the New Testament as favouring this view of the analogy of God's dealing with men? — I simply point to the numerous instances in the early church of the conversion and baptism of whole households, along with their respective heads (such as John iv. 53 ; Acts xvi. 34, xviii. 8 ; 1 Cor. i. 16),—together with the allusions in the messages at the end of the epistles to household churches (Rom. xvi.) I raise no question here directly as to the administration of ordinances. But I own it does appear to me impossible to explain these intimations of entire families becoming Christian all at once, and households becoming in a sense Christian churches, — without having recourse to the principle,—that the heads, one or both, often acted in name of the family ; and that, in so doing, they were accepted and approved ; and the family, in them, was accounted no more common or unclean, but holy. And let it be remembered that these are not exceptional cases. They are the ordinary and current sort of specimens, left on record, of the way in which Christianity at first grew and established itself.

On the whole, I can see nothing contrary to the analogy of God's ways on earth, in the arrangement according to which, for the sake of a believing parent or head, he regards the whole household as brought into a peculiar relation of federal holiness to himself ;—taken out of the common class, or category, of ungodly families in the world ;—and invested, at least in some sense and to some effects, with a sacred character in his eyes.

3. I say to some effects. For it is not a mere nominal or ideal character of holiness that is ascribed to the family of a believing head ; but one that is at least in some sense, and to some effects, real. No doubt it is a sort of virtual or representative holiness that the household are described, in this text,

as possessing, and not a personal holiness : for it is assumed that the husband or wife referred to is still an unbeliever ; and probably the children too. But the distinction here recognised between holy and unclean is not on that account either unmeaning or unimportant.

To come to the point at once ; the essential question in the whole discussion is substantially this,—Does the covenant of grace, as administered on earth, embrace any but actual believers ? Have any others an interest in it ? Are any others within its pale ?

I speak of the covenant as administered upon earth. For of course, as regards the counsels of heaven, it comprehends, not merely all who at any given moment are actually believers, but all the elect who ever have believed, or ever are to believe, to the end of time ; and it excludes all else. But as regards its administration on earth, by the word and Spirit of God, and by ordinances and fellowship,—it is certainly, in one view, less comprehensive, for it takes in only a portion of those who are to be saved. May it not, in another view, be more comprehensive, taking in others besides the actually saved ? It is true, none such can be comprehended in it, so as to have a saving interest in its benefits. In that sense, none but the elect can be embraced in it. But does it follow that there can be no sense in which others may be within it ? May not God impose covenant-obligations on others besides believers ?—obligations superadding to all the other grounds on which unbelief is a sin, the peculiar and heavy aggravation of its being a breach of covenant ? May he not, indeed, make this very arrangement, when realised in the case of the elect themselves, one of the means of conversion, and one of the motives of faith ? May He not give covenant privileges, promises, and pledges, to others besides believers,—such as, upon covenant-principles, afford facilities and encouragements to believe ? May He not accept a covenant-profession of penitence and faith,—so far at least as to take it, if we may so speak, in good part,—make it the occasion of suspending his judgments, in the exercise of his forbearance,—and even perhaps turn it into the commencement of a gracious and saving work in the soul? In all these respects,—in respect of covenant-obligations imposed,—covenant-privileges, promises, and pledges bestowed,—and covenant-professions owned,—God may surely admit others besides believers to an interest in his covenant as administered on earth, and recognise them as standing in a covenant relation to himself.

Is it asked what we mean by the word covenant, as used in this connection? In reply, let us bear in mind that the covenant of grace is not a voluntary compact or agreement between God and us, implying or requiring the consent of parties. It may be so between God and his eternal Son, or in the councils of the Godhead, Father, Son, and Holy Ghost. But in its relation to us, it is simply the solemn act of God, binding himself to us, and binding us to himself. Doubtless, in order to our having a saving interest in it, consent, concurrence, acquiescence, or in one word, obedience, is indispensable. But it does not follow that this is necessary in order to our having any interest at all, of any sort, in it. God himself, at his own hand, as it were, and by his own mere act or arrangement, may give us an interest in it, and regard us and deal with us as having an interest in it ;—a real interest too, as we may ere long find,—to our profit or to our cost ; — to our profit, if, owning our covenant relation, and feeling it, we lament our guilt, and cry for mercy, with a full and vivid apprehension of the extent of our responsibilities, and the faithfulness of God's pledges ; to our cost, if—imagining ourselves to be at liberty to consult our own discretion, apart from divinely imposed and divinely sealed and sanctioned vows—we trifle with the overtures of the blessed Gospel ;—dealing with them as if we were free to dispose of them as we think fit ;—until we come to " count the blood of the covenant wherewith we were sanctified an unholy being, and do despite to the Spirit of all grace."

I have done little, or rather nothing more than attempt a statement of the point at issue. To argue it out is more than it would be fitting in this place to undertake. There are two questions, however, which, before passing on to the application of the subject, I may briefly suggest.

I. Has the covenant of grace ever been administered on earth without such a margin as we plead for? Has the church of God ever existed in the world otherwise than as. the kernel of a nut? Has God ever constituted a society of real believers, really and savingly in covenant with himself, otherwise than as they might be contained within a wider body;—which also he condescends to acknowledge, as in a certain covenant relation to himself? Assuredly, before the coming of Christ, nothing of the sort appeared among men. It is on all hands confessed that during all the period intervening between the fall and the Christian era the true people of God, the really saved, were hidden and almost lost, in the far larger and miscellaneous community, in which alone, however, and as a part of it, they had any place and standing. In other words, they actually were what the general mass to which they belonged should have been ;—were accounted, and were bound to be. In point of real attainment, they were what the society and all its members were in point of obligation, privilege, and profession. This was the state of matters when the church in covenant with God was to be found in the Jewish nation ; co-extensive with that nation in one view ;—but alas ! far more restricted in another.

Is there any proof, or even presumption, that all this is changed under the New Testament form of the dispensation ? The covenant is the same ; its obligations, pledges, and professions are in substance the same. True, the Jewish nation as such is no longer the shell or husk containing the kernel. But as of old, in Mesopotamia, the work began with the call of Abraham,—went on to the recognition of his household in him,—and issued in the setting apart of the nation springing out of his loins ;—so, in gospel times, individuals again were called ;—but not merely as individuals. Their families were consecrated in them, and along with them. And not families only, but communities, churches, and nations also, are recognised as capable of sustaining a high and holy relation to God ;—exactly as the church and nation of Israel did of old. In fact, no one can read the Acts and the Apostolic Epistles without perceiving that from the very first societies were formed, capable of being collectively addressed as in a covenant relation of holiness to the Lord ;—while yet only a portion were personally believers, or personally holy. We conclude, therefore, that the church has never existed upon earth otherwise than as a centre or nucleus of real holiness, found within the circumference of a body virtually or federally holy.

II. Our second question is, Can the covenant of grace be administered otherwise on the earth ?—at least so long as the earth shall continue to be a scene of trial and probation ? God, if we may so speak, by a wide cast of the net, brings men,— not as individuals merely, but in families and communities,— into a certain covenant relation to himself ; in respect of which they are brought under the responsibilities, and partake of the influences, of the kingdom of Heaven. For the ordinary means of grace, let it be remembered, and the common operations of the Spirit, are covenant-blessings, enjoyed upon the footing of a covenant-obligation to improve them. Thus God engages and binds men, in families and communities, as well as individually, to the acceptance of his offered mercy, through the obedience of the faith ; and calls them, in the way of gospel ordinances, to seek and to secure the great salvation. He puts them to the proof; he places them under training, discipline, and trial; that they may be tested as to what manner of spirit they are of; that the thoughts of many hearts may be revealed. To some extent this is done by the mere preaching of the gospel, for the first time, among any people, and the call to individual sinners to repent. But as Christianity takes root, and new generations rise up under the light of the gospel, it would seem to be essential to the great experiment which God is carrying on,—that he should deal with families and communities of men as such ;—reckoning them, by a gracious and liberal construction of what is professed on their behalf, to be within the range of his holy covenant ;—viewing them as represented in their believing head ;—and on that ground, treating them as already his,—as separate and holy unto himself,—and so treating them, as such, that they may become really what he wishes them to be ;—or if not, may be the more absolutely without excuse. It is as if a king should say of a family, or city, whose heads and representatives are loyal, I accept your family,—your people,—in you. So far, I take their loyalty for granted,—that in you, on your account, and for your sake, I will treat them as if they already were, or would immediately become, themselves loyal. Virtually they shall be loyal, in my esteem of them ; as such they shall be admitted to much of my confidence, and many—nay, if they will, all,—of the benefits of my reign. And as such, moreover, they shall be ultimately accountable to me. I give them thus a fair opening and start. I place them in the most advantageous position for being faithful and happy subjects. I put them upon honour. I pledge myself to them, and I pledge them to myself. And if, after all, they turn out rebellious,— theirs is not the guilt of ordinary rebellion, but guilt aggravated, on their part, by the breach of my covenant with them.

The principle I have been endeavouring to explain is one

of deep significancy and wide application ;—affecting, as it does, not only the whole character and constitution of the Church, as visible here below ;—but the warrant and nature of all domestic, social, and national religion. If that principle, or something equivalent to it, be not admitted, there may be individual believers associating, more or less formally, with one another ; but there can scarcely be such an idea as that of a Christian community, a Christian family, or a Christian nation. I cannot, however, dwell upon these larger views. I close with two brief practical remarks.

1. Am I the believing head of a family, or one of its heads ? Let me see in what position, through the gracious condescension of God, my faith places the household. It takes it out of the class of common households, and brings it into an interesting and affecting relation to the Lord. He is pleased to look upon it as in me, and for my sake, invested with a certain character of holiness in his sight. Surely this consideration should not only reconcile me to the continued obligation of all my family ties and duties ; it should do more. It should give me great freedom, encouragement, and enlargement, in pleading with God on behalf of all my household, and pleading with them on God's behalf. And it should fill me with a very profound apprehension of the enhanced responsibility lying upon them all ;—the more especially since, according to God's sovereign ordinance, that enhanced responsibility is entailed on them through me.

How very solemn and awful, in this view of it, is the relation of the holy believing head of a family to all the members of it ! Do I believe that, not merely myself, but my household with me, are in a covenant relation to God ;—in so far, at least, as covenant obligations, privileges, and professions are concerned ? Have I avowed and acted on that belief, by applying for baptism, the initial seal of the covenant, for my children ? How holy, then, should they be in my esteem !

how sacred! With what reverence should I treat them!—
with what scrupulous and trembling care to keep them from
all pollution; with what watchful anxiety to have them
washed and sanctified and justified, in the name of the Lord
Jesus, and by the Spirit of our God! Strange that such a
doctrine as this should be represented in any quarter as having
a tendency to relax parental diligence, and minister to carnal
security and sloth!

2. Are you the members of a family that is blessed in
having a believing head? Are you the children of Christian
parents? As such, have you been acknowledged by the Church
on earth, and sealed by God himself, in the sacrament of
baptism? Consider, how solemnly you are pledged and engaged to be the Lord's! But you may say that you are not
bound by a transaction to which you did not give your consent.
It is unreasonable, as well as unscriptural, to say so.

You are bound in many ways, and to many duties, without
your own consent. As children, you are bound to your parents;
—as citizens, to your country;—without your previous concurrence asked or obtained. God binds you, and he has a right to
bind you. And so, in like manner, he binds you as members
of a Christian family. Solemnly, and in covenant, he binds
you to himself. Does this offend you? Consider, on the
other hand, that he also, and in like manner, graciously binds
himself to you. If you are under covenant obligations, you
have also covenant promises and privileges and pledges.

Ah, my young friends! your birth in a Christian land;
your baptism in a Christian church; your pure and happy
home in the bosom of a Christian family,—with a godly father
to teach you, and a godly mother to watch over you,—and
both together to pray for you and to pray with you;—these
things are, none of them, either accidental or insignificant.
They bespeak a gracious purpose—they have all a gracious
meaning. True, they will not of themselves avail to save you.

But they do much to put you in the way of salvation. And who can tell how terribly they will aggravate your inexcusable guilt and your inevitable condemnation,—if, under all the sacred influences, and all the sacred pledges, involved in your connection with a Christian land, a Christian church, a Christian family, you continue still unsanctified and unsaved !